Street by Stree[t]

C000148940

BIRMINGHAM
WOLVERHAMPTON
DUDLEY, SOLIHULL, STOURBRIDGE,
WALSALL, WEST BROMWICH
Aldridge, Brownhills, Codsall, Coleshill, Dorridge, Halesowen, Knowle, Pelsall, Sutton Coldfield, Wombourne

3rd edition November 2007
© Automobile Association Developments Limited 2007

Original edition printed May 2001

 This product includes map data licensed from Ordnance Survey® with the permission of the Controller of Her Majesty's Stationery Office. © Crown copyright 2007. All rights reserved. Licence number 100021153.

The copyright in all PAF is owned by Royal Mail Group plc.

Published by AA Publishing (a trading name of Automobile Association Developments Limited, whose registered office is Fanum House, Basing View, Basingstoke, Hampshire RG21 4EA. Registered number 1878835).

Produced by the Mapping Services Department of The Automobile Association. (A03490)

A CIP Catalogue record for this book is available from the British Library.

Printed by Oriental Press in Dubai

The contents of this atlas are believed to be correct at the time of the latest revision. However, the publishers cannot be held responsible or liable for any loss or damage occasioned to any person acting or refraining from action as a result of any use or reliance on any material in this atlas, nor for any errors, omissions or changes in such material. This does not affect your statutory rights. The publishers would welcome information to correct any errors or omissions and to keep this atlas up to date. Please write to Publishing, The Automobile Association, Fanum House (FH12), Basing View, Basingstoke, Hampshire, RG21 4EA. E-mail: streetbystreet@theaa.com

Ref: ML33y

Key to map pages	ii–iii
Key to map symbols	iv–1
Enlarged map pages	2–7
Main map pages	8–199
Index – towns & villages	200
Index – streets	201–243
Index – featured places	243–252
Acknowledgements	252

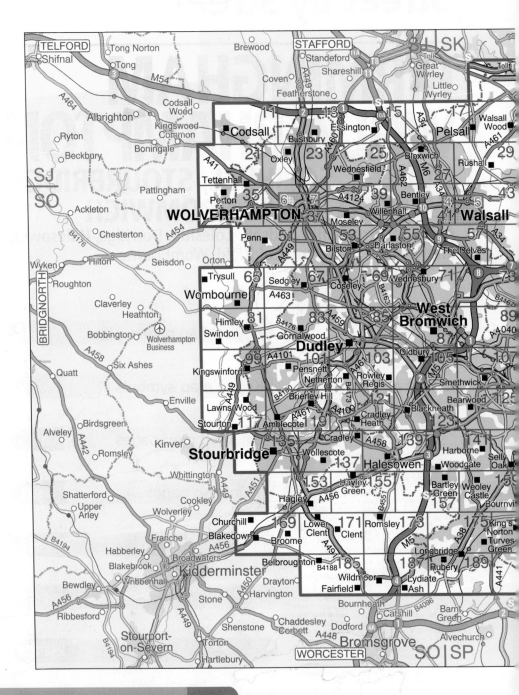

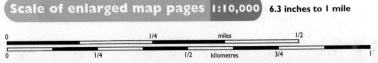

Scale of enlarged map pages 1:10,000 6.3 inches to 1 mile

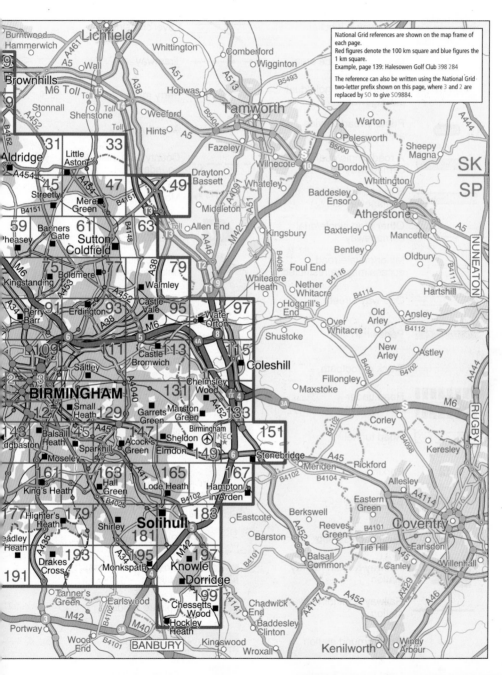

National Grid references are shown on the map frame of each page.
Red figures denote the 100 km square and blue figures the 1 km square.
Example, page 139: Halesowen Golf Club 398 284

The reference can also be written using the National Grid two-letter prefix shown on this page, where 3 and 2 are replaced by SO to give SO9884.

4.2 inches to 1 mile

Scale of main map pages   **1:15,000**

| 0 | 1/4 | miles | 1/2 | 3/4 | 1 |

| 0 | 1/4 | 1/2 | kilometres | 3/4 | 1 | 1 1/4 | 1 1/2 |

Junction 9	Motorway & junction	LC	Level crossing
Services	Motorway service area		Tramway
	Primary road single/dual carriageway		Ferry route
Services	Primary road service area		Airport runway
	A road single/dual carriageway		County, administrative boundary
	B road single/dual carriageway		Mounds
	Other road single/dual carriageway	17	Page continuation 1:15,000
	Minor/private road, access may be restricted	3	Page continuation to enlarged scale 1:10,000
	One-way street		River/canal, lake, pier
	Pedestrian area		Aqueduct, lock, weir
	Track or footpath	465 ▲ Winter Hill	Peak (with height in metres)
	Road under construction		Beach
	Road tunnel		Woodland
P	Parking		Park
P+	Park & Ride		Cemetery
	Bus/coach station		Built-up area
	Railway & main railway station		Industrial/business building
	Railway & minor railway station		Leisure building
⊖	Underground station		Retail building
⊖	Light railway & station		Other building
+++++++++	Preserved private railway	IKEA	IKEA store

⊓⊔⊓⊔⊓⊔	City wall	♜	Castle
A&E	Hospital with 24-hour A&E department	🏛	Historic house or building
PO	Post Office	Wakehurst Place (NT)	National Trust property
📖	Public library	Ⓜ	Museum or art gallery
i	Tourist Information Centre	🏃	Roman antiquity
i	Seasonal Tourist Information Centre	⚱	Ancient site, battlefield or monument
⛽ ⛽	Petrol station, 24 hour Major suppliers only	🏭	Industrial interest
✝	Church/chapel	❁	Garden
🚻	Public toilets	◉	Garden Centre Garden Centre Association Member
♿	Toilet with disabled facilities	🌷	Garden Centre Wyevale Garden Centre
PH	Public house AA recommended	🌲	Arboretum
🍴	Restaurant AA inspected	🛒	Farm or animal centre
Madeira Hotel	Hotel AA inspected	🦌	Zoological or wildlife collection
🎭	Theatre or performing arts centre	🦜	Bird collection
🎥	Cinema	🦆	Nature reserve
⚑	Golf course	🐟	Aquarium
▲	Camping AA inspected	V	Visitor or heritage centre
🚐	Caravan site AA inspected	♈	Country park
▲🚐	Camping & caravan site AA inspected	◠	Cave
🎡	Theme park	🪟	Windmill
🏰	Abbey, cathedral or priory	🛢	Distillery, brewery or vineyard

BIRMINGHAM

I grid square represents 250 metres

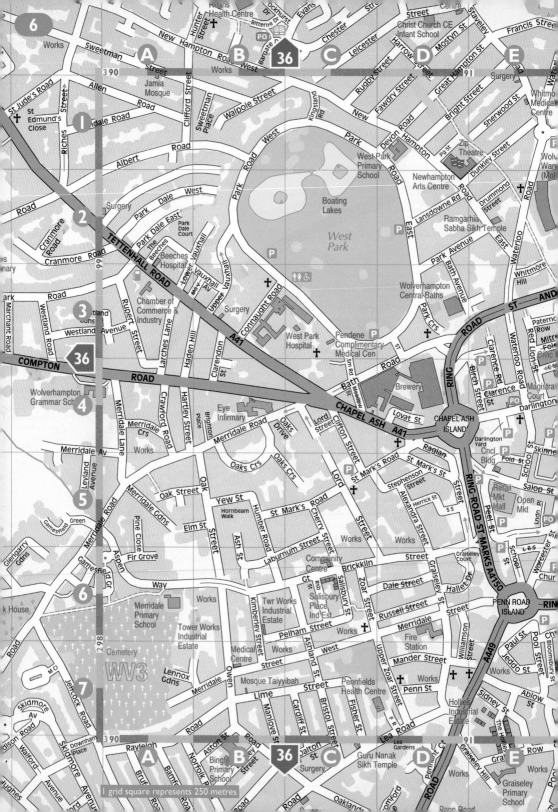

8

Industrial Est

Conduit Road

Red Lion Crs

Braemar Road

Red Lion Av

Red Lion Lane

Knights Court

Betty's Lane

Works

Cy Brk Rd

Rolling Mi Rd

B4154

402

A

Norton Canes Business Park

Premier Travel Inn

Norton Canes Service Area

Norton Canes Greyhound Track

B

Chasewater

Brownhills Road

03

C

D

Brownhills West Station

Chase Watersports Centre

Beacon Way

M6 TOLL

Cannock Chase Extension Canal

Water Light Railway

07

Albutts Road

Mayfields Drive

Blithfield Road

Cherwell Drive

Pear Tree Lane

Hednesford Rd

Poole Crescent

Beacon Way

PO

2

Watling Street Business Park

WATLING STREET A5

Little Norton

Tyne Cl

Cherwell

Tamar Cl

Shannon Drive

Kennet Close

Severn Road

Medway Rd

Wilkin Road

Waterside Way

Lawnoaks Cl

WATLING

Brownhills West JMI School

A452

CHESTER

Lane

3

Lime La

LIME LANE

06

Wyrley Common

B4154

Beacon Way

Coppice Lane

4

Engine Lane

West Coppice Road

Coppice Side

Coppice Side Industrial Estate

5

305

402

Staffordshire County Walsall

Collier Close

Apex Road

PELSALL ROAD

Coppice Crescent

Croft Crescent

North

03

Beacon Way

A4124

Pelsall Road

Clifton Av

Bullows Road

Honeysuckle Close

Larksp

Clayhan

A

B

18

C

A4124 ROAD

D

Cornflower

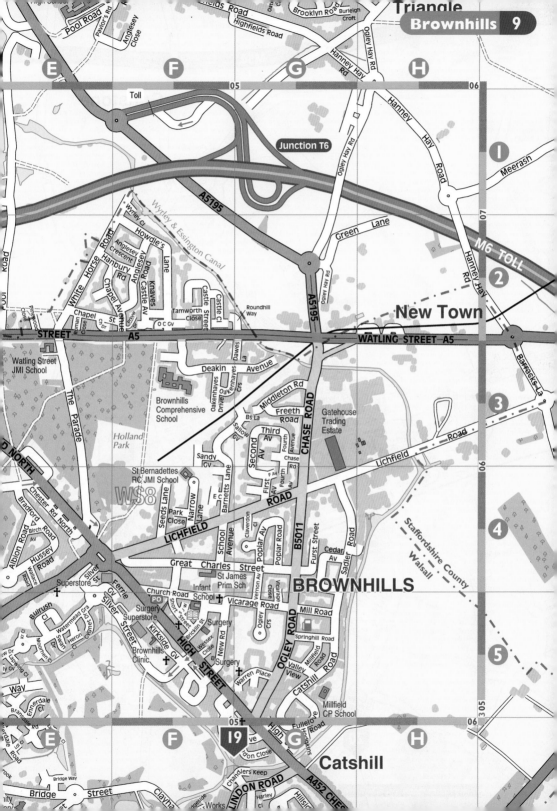

E   F   G   H

93

Featherstone

Thistletown Dr
Bellflower Cl
Campion Dr
Dunin Ct
Turnstone Dr
Plover Cl
Wecca Cl
Brook House La
Whitgreave Primary School
North Crs
F

Penderell Cl
Brookhouse
Huddlestone
S Crs
Surgery
South Crs
94B
PO

East Rd
Whilmot Close
White Houses La

Junction 1

I

Brookhouse

M54

Hilton Cross Business Park

A460

Moseley Old Hall (NT)

Moseley Old Hall La

CANNOCK   ROAD

Hilton Cross

Hilton Main Industrial Estate

2

04

Kirkfields
Lane
Heaton Cl
Rudyard Cl
Elton Cl
Blackbrook Wy
Ainsworth Rd
Bridgem
Gatcombe Cl
Abbeyfield
Abbeyfield Rd
Abbeyfield
Moseley Rd
Moseley Road

Blackbrook Way

Northycote Lane

Monarch's Way

3

Surgery
Cromwell Rd
Wychall Dr
Bettany Gd
Cavalier Circ
Westering Pkwy
Webley
Hayes
Brentm
Legs Lane

Monarch's Way

14
Monarch's Way

A460

Crispsbrooke Road
Cromwell Rd
Egerton Road
Pendrill Road
Pendrill Road
Legs Lane
Northycote Farm

Monarch's Way

4

Northcote Secondary School
Alton
Giffard Road
Wentworth Road
Bushbury Lane
Underhill Lane

Westcroft

303

Bushbury

Cemetery

Northwood Park
Rushall Road
Broadway
Hellier Rd
Collingwood Rd
Bushbury Health Centre
PO
Smirra Gdns
Hilton Gdns
Collingwood Primary School

Underhill Lane
Underhill Drive
Waterhead Drive
Highfield Av
Wildtree
Greenacres Av
Westcroft Special School & Sports College
Old Hampton Lane

5

CANNOCK   ROAD

Wd Hys

93

94

E   23   F   G   24   H

Bushbury Baths
Bushbury Hill J&I School
Moreton Community School
Tennyson Road
Keats
Larkin Close
Newman Road
Westcroft Av
Addison
Berrybrook Pri

Hayes Road

Grassy La

Wood Hayes

Elston Hall Lane
Sandy
Linley Drive

Oaken

Middle Lane
Manor Fold
Hollybush Lane
Lansd...
Stafford Lane
Pine Walk
Poplars
Farway Gdns
Wayside Acres

385
86

A   **B**   **C**   **10**   **D**

A41
Shop
Stafford Lane
Oaken Lane
Hawth... Lane
Beec...

I

02

Greenhills
Heathfields

Wergs Hall Road

2

Wrottesley Hall

HOLYHEAD ROAD

Heath House

Heath House

Monarch's Way

3

01

Park Road

A41

Wrottesley Road

Westcroft Road

Wergs

4

Cranmoor

Monarch's Way

Cranmoor Lodge Farm

Wrottesley Park Road

5

300

The Parkway

Bowen Cooke...
Fowler Ct
Dean Ct
Stephenson Dr
Webb
Collet...
Edward Rd
Mere Oak Rd
Cocton Dr
Mercia
The Parkway
Idonia Road
Harale...
Drive

Turnberry Gv
Hawkstone Ct
St Andrews Drive
Hoylake
Moor Pk
Glenea gles
Troon Ct
Shackleton Dr
Franklyn Gr
Shawbury
Gaydon
Ans...
Egewin...
Offa's D...
Dr...
Manston Dr
Athelstan Gv
Penda Gv
Levington Close

385
86

A   **B**   **34**   **C**   **D**

Portrait
Wytham Ct
Formby...
dale
Clovelly
Drive
The Parkw...
Andrews Dr
darwin
...ot Gv
Lakes Medical Cen
Perton First Sch
Perton Clinc
Milton Ct
Coleridge Drive
Church Rd
Stanley
Browning Grove
Wrds...
Auden Ct
Epsom
Sandown First School
Sandown Dr
Gainsborou...
Spenser Av

Perton

PO

Elgin Ct
Meon

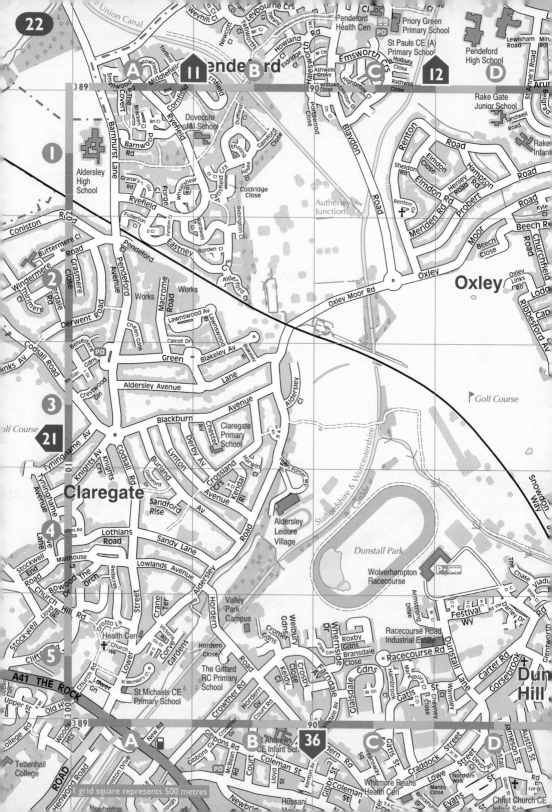

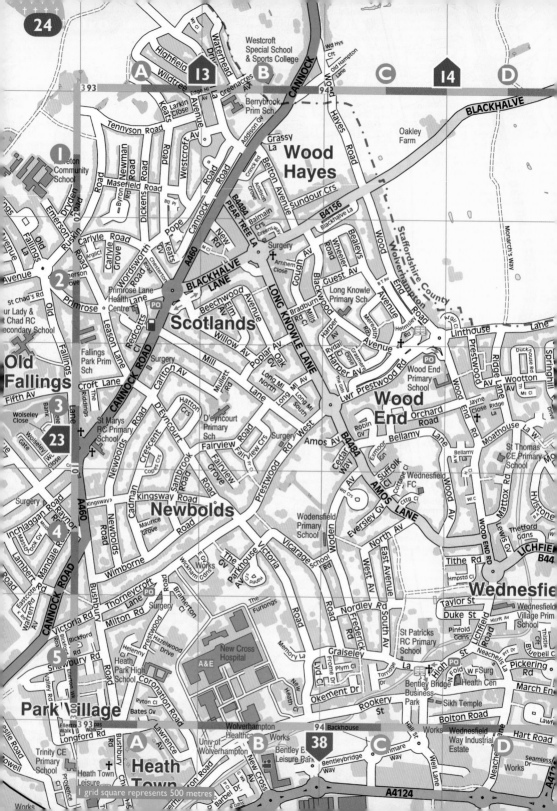

Westcroft Special School & Sports College

Highfield Drive

393

Wildtree Avenue

Waterhead Drive

Edge Hl

Greenacres

Old Hampton Lane

Wd Hys Cft

BLACKHALVE

CANNOCK

Wood Hayes Road

Berrybrook Prim Sch

Grassy La

Hayes Road

Oakley Farm

Wood Hayes

Monarch's Way

I Treton Community School

Newman Road

Tennyson Road

Keats Road

Larkin Close

Westcroft Av

Cannock Road

Addison Gv

Belton Avenue

Cnnck Rd

Sundour Crs

B4156

Masefield Road

Byron Road

Dickens Road

Dryden Road

Ruskin Road

Pope

Keats

Btl Pl

Cannock Road

Balmain Crs

Greens Way

Blackhalve La

2 Emerson Grove

Carlyle Road

Carlyle Grove

Wordsworth

A460

Chesterton Road

PEAR TREE LA

BA484

New Road

M Cl

Surgery

Arnhem Close

Good AV

Blackwood Road

Wheeler Road

Bealeys AV

Guest Av

Staffordshire County Wolverhampton

St Chad's Rd

Primrose

ur Lady & : Chad RC :econdary School

Primrose Lane Health Lane Centre

PO

BLACKHALVE LANE

Scotlands

Beechwood

Elm Av

Willow Av

Poplar Av

Oak

LONG KNOWLE LANE

Bradburn Rd

Mills

Harper AV

Rydal

Grasmere

Meredith

Helmsley

Long Knowle Primary Sch

Avenue

Wolverhampton Road

Linthouse Lane

Prestwood

Ridge Lane

Duck House Rd

Springhill

Wootton AV

Ms Cl

Old Fallings

Fifth Av

Fallings Park Prim Sch

Leason Lane

Redcotts Cl

Croft Lane

CANNOCK ROAD

The Riddings

Carlton Av

Surgery

Mill

Mullett Rd

Long Ml North

Long Ml South

Ml AV

Lwr Prestwood Rd

Harper Av

PO

Wood End Primary School

Wood End

Orchard Road

Wood End Rd

Jayne Close

Ridge La

St Thomas CE Primary School

Wolseley Close

3

23

St Marys RC Primary School

D'eyncourt Crescent

Cadman

Newbolds

Copes Crs

D'eyncourt Primary Sch

Fairview Rd

Fall View Av

Surgery West

Surgery Rd

Amos AV

Robin Gv

BA484

Exmoor Gdn

Bellamy

Cedar Way

Suffolk Cl

Cottage Cl

Bellamy Lane

H Cl

Wc Cl

Wolseley Wc Close

Inchlaggan Road

Raynor Road

Mossdb Rock Cft

A460

Newbolds Road

Wimborne

Maurice Grove

Kingsway

Kingsway Road

Newbolds

Fairview Grove

Prestwood Road

Sambrook

Wodensfield Primary School

Amos AV

Wednesfield FC

Cttg Cl

Eversley Gv

Wodem Rd

North Av

AMOS LANE

Wood End Rd

Moathouse La

Wc Cl

Thetford Gdns

Mattox Rd

Lews Gv

Hystone

LICHFIELD B44

Surgery

4

Lambert Rd

Eastcrote Rd

Warrend Rd

Mandale R

Cannock Road

The Parkhouse Gv

Works Gdns

Victoria Road

Vicarage Road

North Av

East Avenue

Nordley Rd

Frederick Rd

South Av

West Av

Tithe Rd

Wood End Rd

Taylor St

Duke St

Lichfield

Hicrft Av

Pinfold Gdns

Wednesfield Village Prim School

Thistle

Neachells La

Prt Cl

Bluebell Cl

Pickering Rd

March Ln

Hart Road

5

Shrewbury Road

Bickford Rd

Victoria Rd

Thorneycroft Lane

Milton Rd

Helenny Cl

Heath Park High School

Bramerton Cl

Prestwood Drive

Hazelwood Drive

Surgery

PO

New Cross Hospital

A&E

Coronation Road

Ryton Cl

Bates Gv

The Furlongs

Memory La

Graiseley

Frome Rd

Lloyd Rd

Plym Cl

Torndne Dr

Okement Dr

New Heath Cl

Rookery St

St Patricks RC Primary School

Bentley Bridge Business Park

La

High St

PO

Lichfield

W F Surg

Health Cen

Sikh Temple

Bolton Road

Neachells La

Wednesfield Way Industrial Estate

Lawfi

Seamless Dr

Works

Park Village

Valley Rd

Longford Rd

Ellerton Walk

3 93 pas

Lawrence Av

Wolverhampton Healthca

Univ of Wolverhampton

94 Backhouse

Works

Bentley B Leisure Park

Bentleybridge Way

Chmare Way

Hall St

Works

Hart Road

Trinity CE Primary School

Heath Town Leisure

Heath Town

Barbel Dr

A4124

1 grid square represents 500 metres

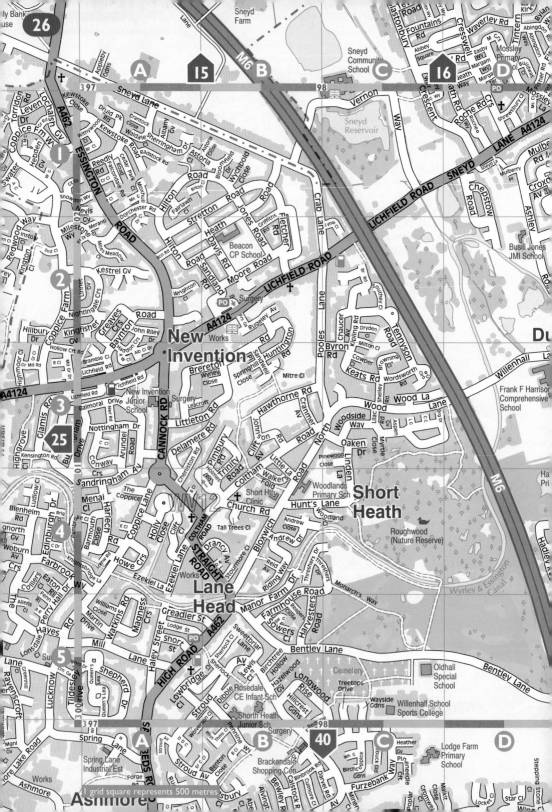

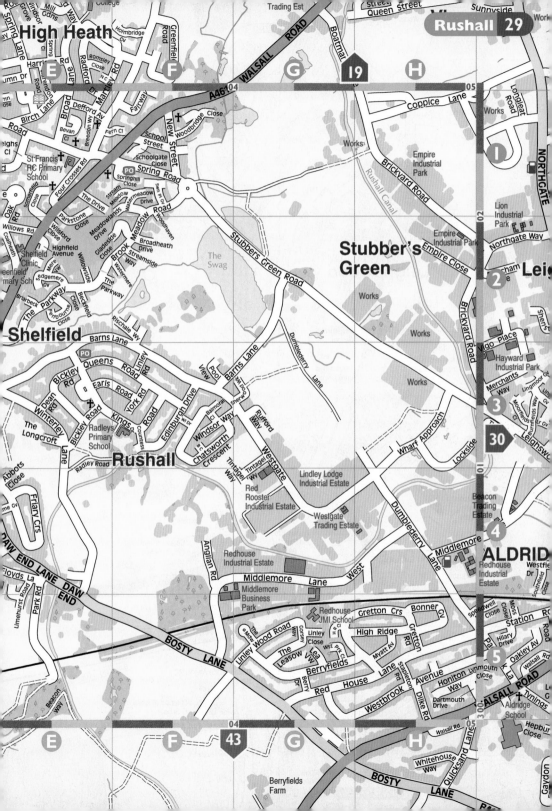

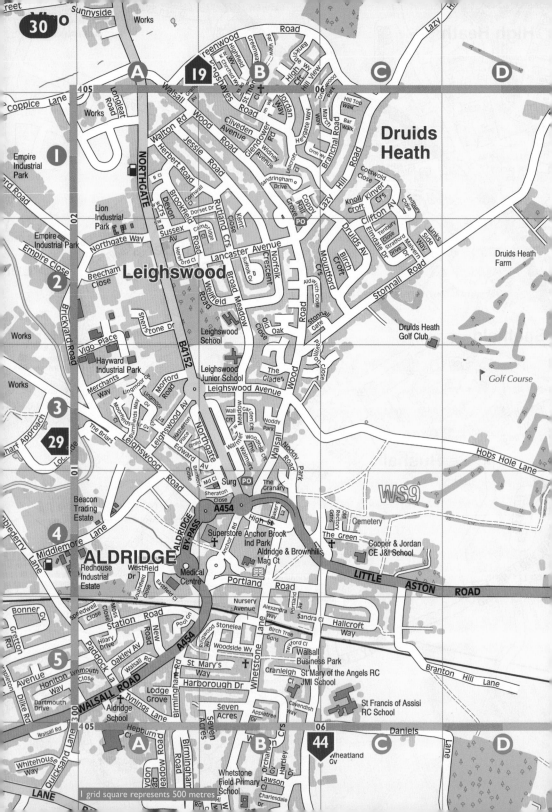

Druids Heath

Leighswood

ALDRIDGE

Druids Heath Farm

Golf Course

Hobs Hole Lane

WS9

E F 12 G H 13

Little Hay

Shenstone
Woodend

Green
Barn

**Little
Hay**

Green Barns Lane

Little Hay Lane

Green Barns Lane

Alder Farm

Camp Farm

Woodland Ct

Smarts Avenue

BIRMINGHAM RD

A5127

Little Hay Lane

Watford — Gap — Road

Common Road

Staffordshire County

Birmingham

Camp Road

Hillwood

Hill

Wood

Road

Hill Wood

E Keating Dunton F 12 47 G H 13

Haycroft
Drive

Gdns St Cl WC

Dunton
Close

Hill Beech Ws Mr

Hathaway Road

Hill Cl

wney Dr

Close

Woodside
Farm

I 2 02 3 01 4 5 3 00

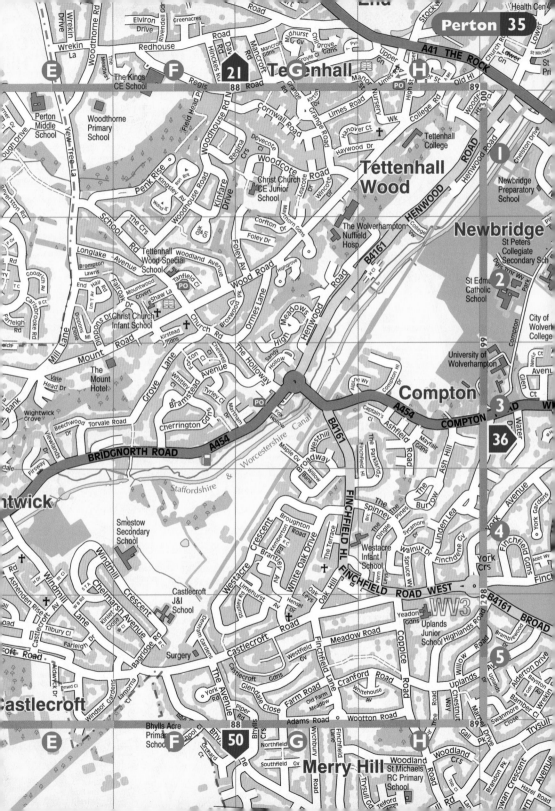

I grid square represents 500 metres

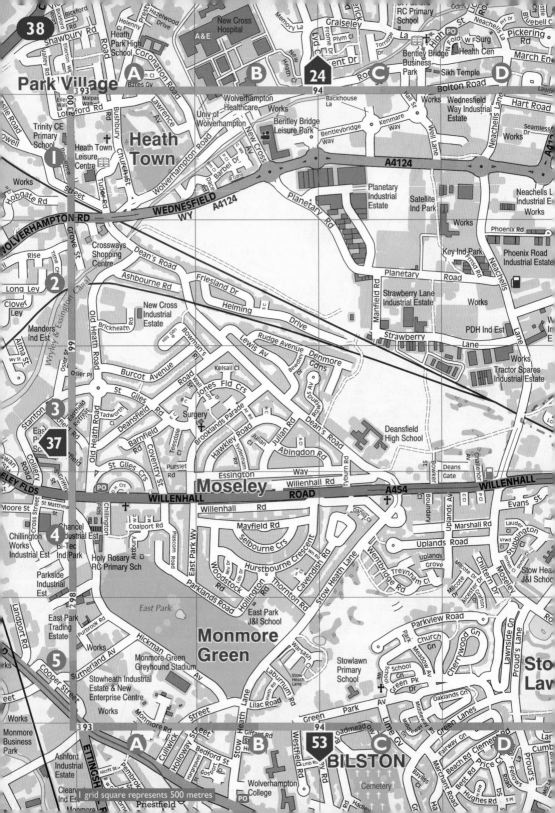

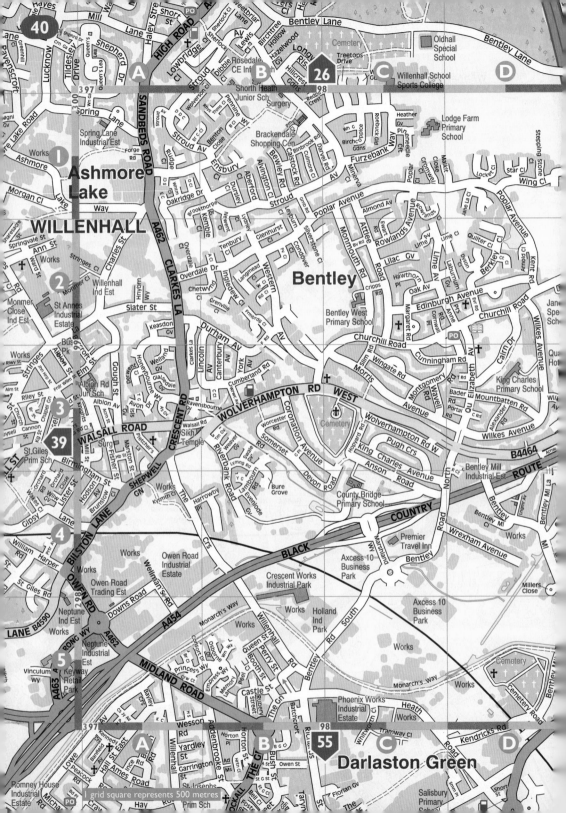

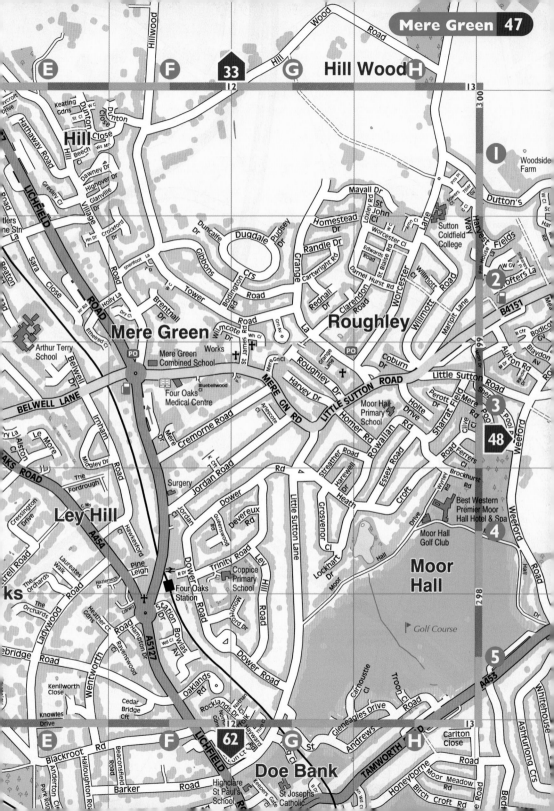

E
F
G
H

CRANEBROOK HILL

16
17
300

lead

CARROWAY HEAD HILL

A453

Shirral Drive

Shirral Drive

I

Shirrall Hall
Farm

Trickley
Coppice

Staffordshire County
Warwickshire County

2
...er House
Farm

99

Coppice Lane

3

Wood
Farm

4

New Park
Wood

298

Langley Brook

5

LONDON ROAD

A38

**Littleworth
End**

...ill Road

16
17

E
F
G
H

M6 Toll

Langley Mill
Farm

LONDON

Hill
Farm

50

Castlecroft Road

Castlecroft

A

B

35

C

D

Surgery

The

York Rd

Windsor Gardens

Lamoma

School Cl

Bhylls Lane

Bagridge Rd

Castlecroft Gdns

Castlecroft

Westfield Gv

Finchfield Lane

Cranford Road

Whitehouse Av

Meadow

School Hi

ppice

Willow

Uplands

Chestnut Way

Gall

Fir Tree Road

Woodland

Crs

Bhylls Acre
Primary
School

Adams Road

Wootton Road

Wychbury Road

Finchfield Lane

Telford Gdns

Trysull Gdns

Old Farm
Meadow

Northfield Gv

Southfield Gv

Merry Hill

St Michaels
RC Primary
School

Woodland

Attwell

Trysull Rd

1

Bellencroft Gardens

Langley Road

PO

Coalway Road

Hilary Dn

Grendon Gdr

Pinfold Grove

Chadwick

Leasowes Drive

Maternity
Welfare
Clinic

2

Langl
Farm

Drive Fields

Fareham Crescent

Hamble Road

Warstones Gdns

Rindleford Av

Warstones

North Green

East Gn

Kingslow Av

Highgate Av

Drive

WV4

Swancote Drive

Kinver Drive

Beckbury

West Gn

Arley Gv

Wolverley Av

Reedhar

Oakley Rd

Oakle Gv

Buckley Rd

Lower
Penn

3

Dirtyfoot Lane

Highfields
School

Westcroft
Farm

Boundary Way

Warstones

Stourton Dr

South Green

Ludstone Av

Claverley Drive

Tenbury Gdns

Reedham Gv

Drive

Springdale
J&I School

Warstones Crs

Tenbury

4

Springhill Lane

East Croft Road

Enville Road

Spring
Hill

Fairview Road

Warstones Road

Wynchcombe Av

Hollybush Lane

Rutland Av

Lytto

Hilston Av

Springhill Grove

Foxhills Rd

Springhill Avenue

Bryan Av

Orton Gv

Braden Av

Anita Myatt
Health Cen

A449

Cemetery

5

Orton Lane

Showell Lane

Springhill Park

Wynn
Crs

Norton Cl

Larkswood Dr

Springhill

Springhill Lane

Foxlands Dr

Chandler Dr

Holden Rd

Buttons Farm Road

Foxlands Avenue

Orton

Stourbridge
Road

Bearnett Dr

Lloyd Drive

A

B

65

C

D

I grid square represents 500 metres

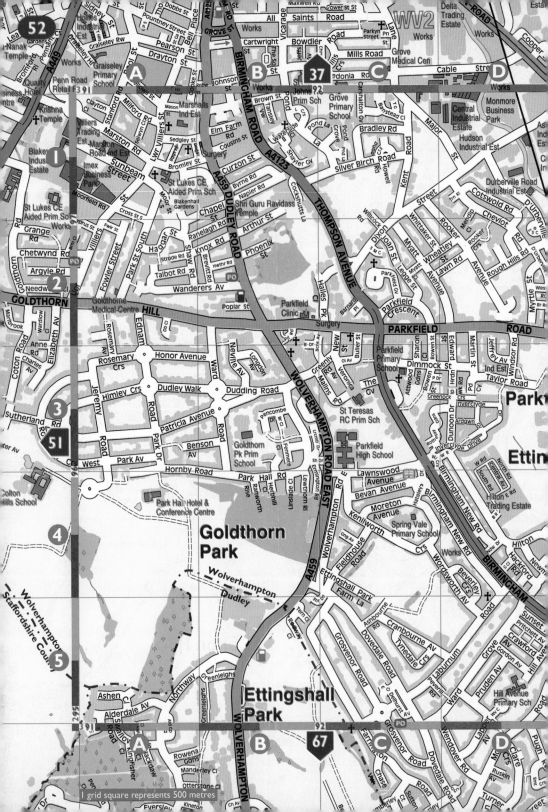

I grid square represents 500 metres

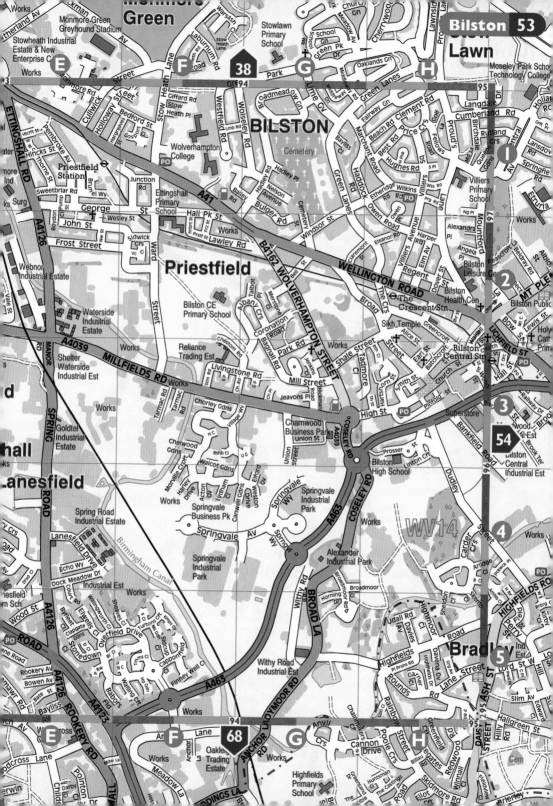

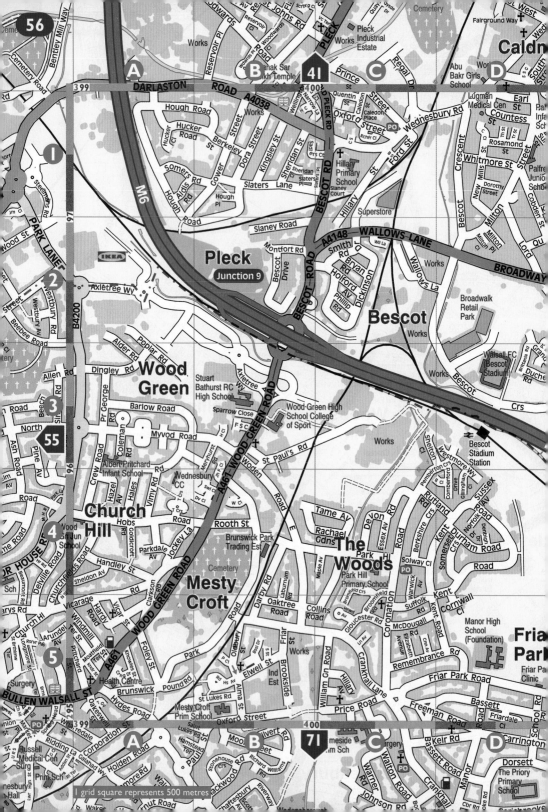

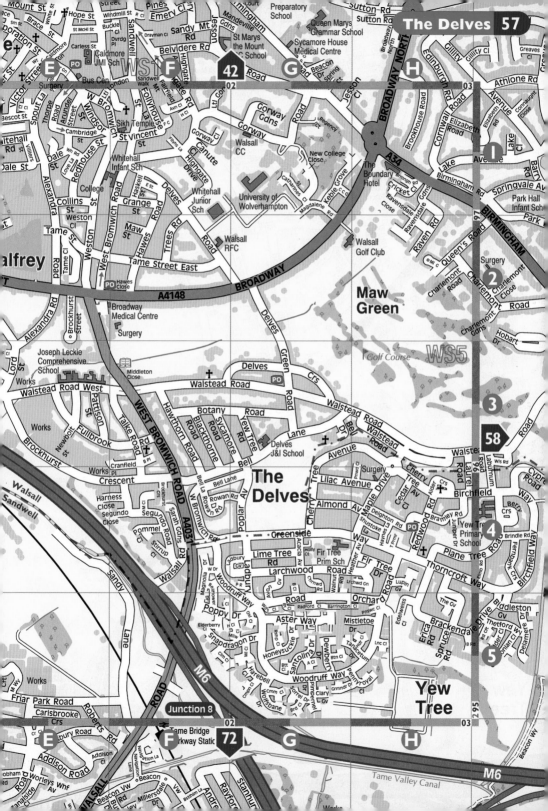

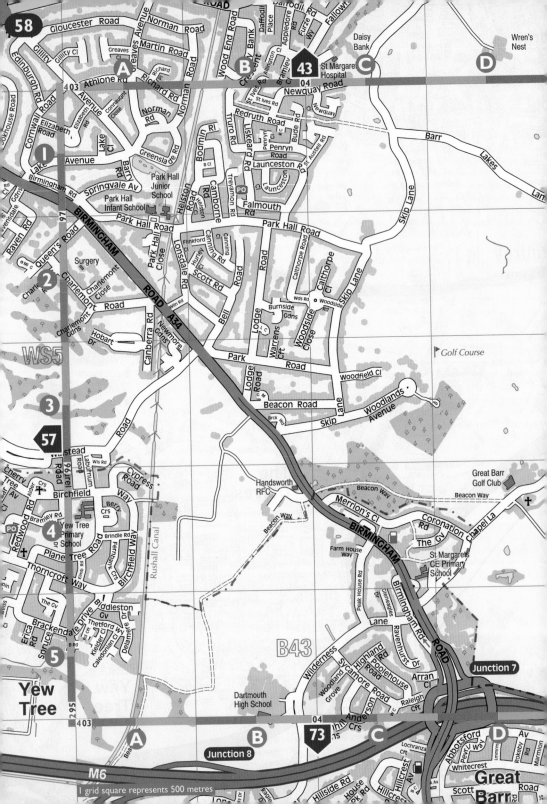

E F 44 G H

Crook L

Oakwood

Alder Wy

Ashwood Gr

Lilac Rd

Laurel Dr

Maxholm Road

Aldridge Road

I

5

06

07

Bodens Lane

Pinfold Lane

Crook Lane

Barr Beacon

Beacon Farm

BEACON ROAD

Beacon Way

Bridle Lane

2

Crook House

Crook Lane

Pinfold Lane

Doe Bank Lane

Doe Bank Wood

Doe Ba

3

Chapel Lane

Old Hall

Old Hall La

B4154

The Barr Beacon School

Meadow View JMI School

Hogarth Av

Frampton Way

Brooking Close

Lorimer

Stanfield Rd

Beecheld Wy

60

Goodwill

Clausen

Gv

Wimperis Way

Yeames Close

Rippingille Rd

Pheasey Park Farm Primary School

Pomeroy

Horsley Rd

P Cl

Romney

Cookesley

Sthr Cl

Brent Wy

Vw

Sargeant Close

Stanhope Way

A4041 ROAD

Aviemore Crs

Kinross Crs

Dunbar

Nevison

Raymout Gv

Roxburgh Gv

Beacon Rd

Morland Road

Raeburn Road

Gainsborough Crescent

Crs

Queslett Road

Sundridge Rd

Sheen

Sundridge Rd

Brockhurst

Gv

Pheasey

Crail Gv

Berwick Gv

Park

Waverley Av

Garnet Av

Comsey Rd

Selvey Av

Stonehurst Road

BEACON RD

Beacon Road

Collingwood Dr

Linton Rd

Leighton Cl

Tyndale Av

Hillingford Av

Chantrey

Eastdale

Farmer

Crome Rd

Collingwood Dr

Surgery

RC

Surgery

Lambeth Rd

Copthor

Drive

Handsworth

Farm Road

Pinley Gv

Kelway Av

Ivanhoe Rd

Foxwood Av

B4154

Moreton Av

Ques

Hillingford Av

Cartermede

Queslett Crescent

QUESLETT ROAD A4041

Queslett Road

Calver

Churchbridge

Kings Business Park

David Lloyd Birmingham

Privet Cl

Century Industrial Estate

5

E F 74 G H

06

07

Whitecrest Primary School

M6

Horns Crs

Selstore

Ringinglow Road

Ashgrove Road

Brackenfield

Works

Select Avenue

Winster Grove Industrial Cen

Winster Gv

Winster Grove Industrial Estate

Shady Lane

Aldri

East Rd

Fairbour

Thornclift

Ambl

PO

E F 46 G H

Sutton Park

Upper Nut Hurst

Blackroot Pool

I

2

Keeper's Pool

Rowton's Well

Holly Hurst

3

62

Wyn Leisu Cent

4

Wyndley Pool

Wy Sw Ba

Wyndle

Monmouth

Rushbrooke Dr

Durley Dr

Lowe Dr

Drive

Alcester Dr

Golf Course

Powell's Pool

Stonehouse Rd

Monmouth

Drive

5

Elwell Rd

Roxburgh Rd

Jevons

Markham Road

Avery Road

Alcester Dr

Grendon Drive

Halton Road

Denholm

Boldmere Golf Club

Corbridge Road

Stonehouse Road

Braemar

Road

Dunchurch Cres

Milcote Dr

Road

Warwick Rd

B73

Carnwath Rd

Molly Rd

A452

CHESTER ROAD NORTH

ROAD NORTH

F 76 G H

Falstone Rd

Dalkeith Rd

Melrose Avenue

Mather Av

JOCKEY

A453

St Nicholas RC JMI School

Superstore

New

Stirling

Wakefield

Parkwood Dr

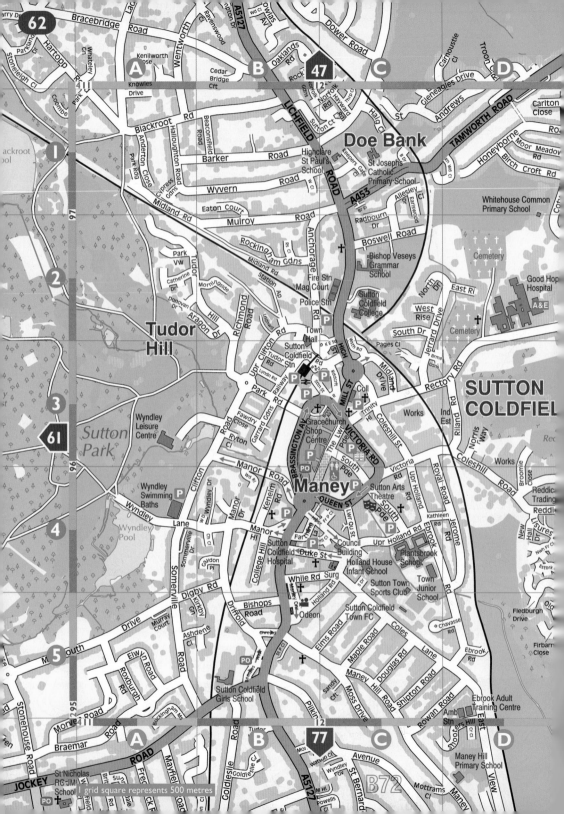

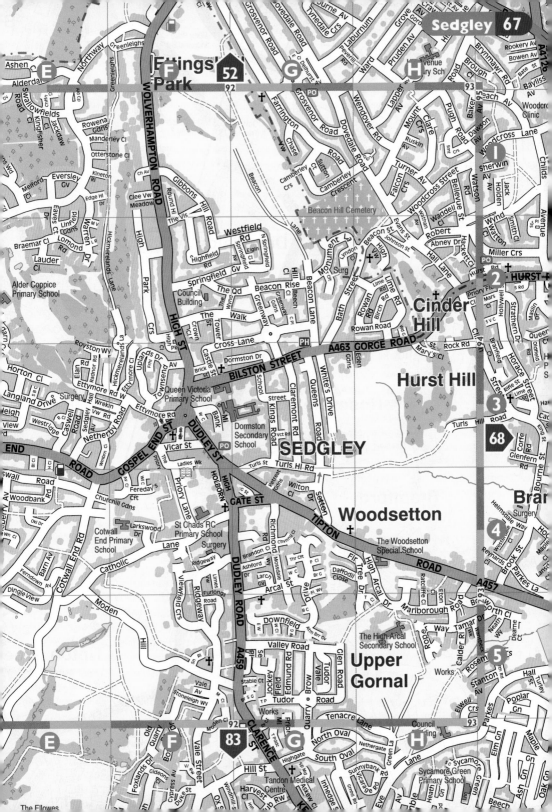

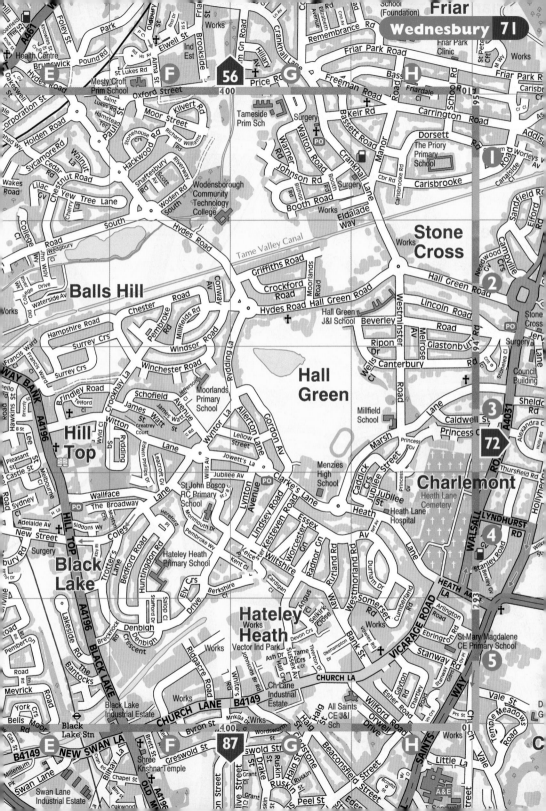

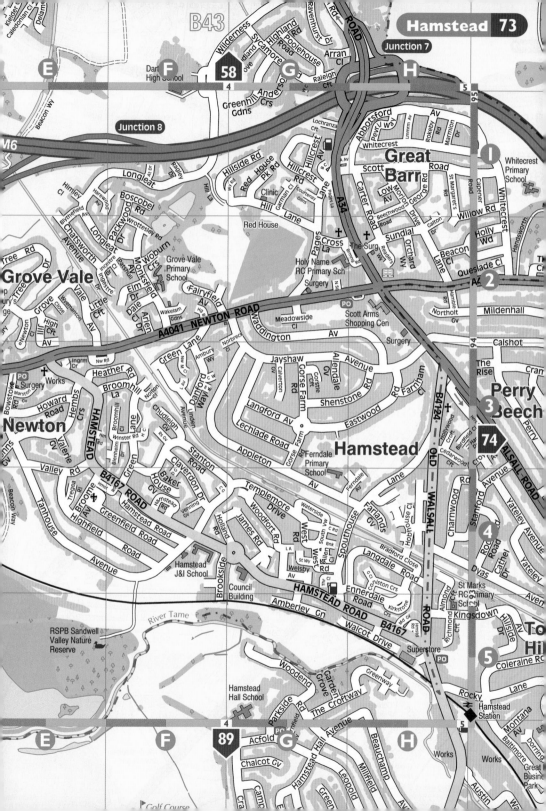

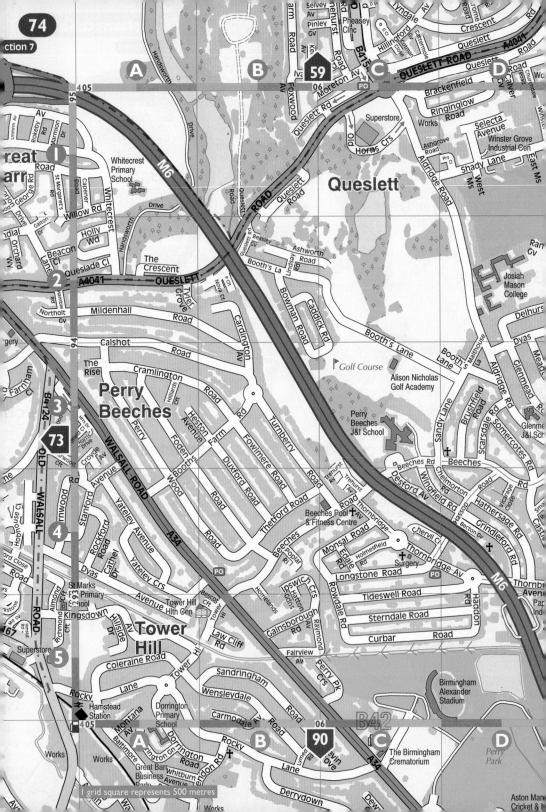

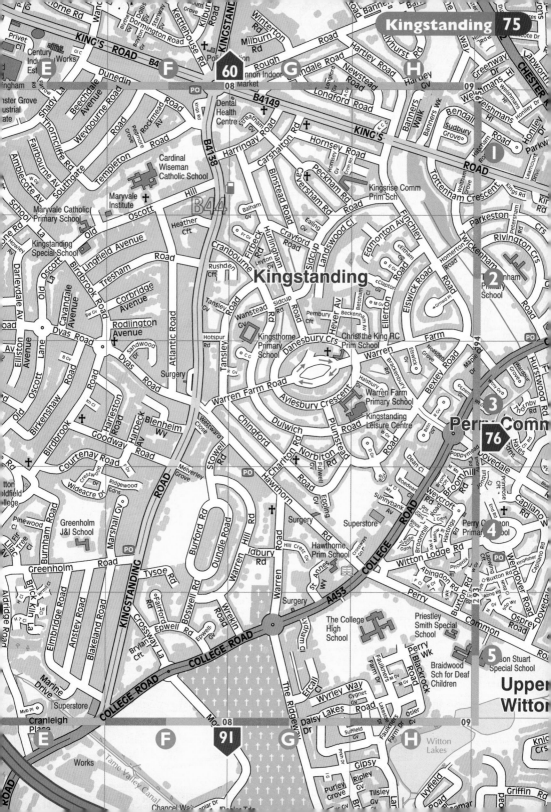

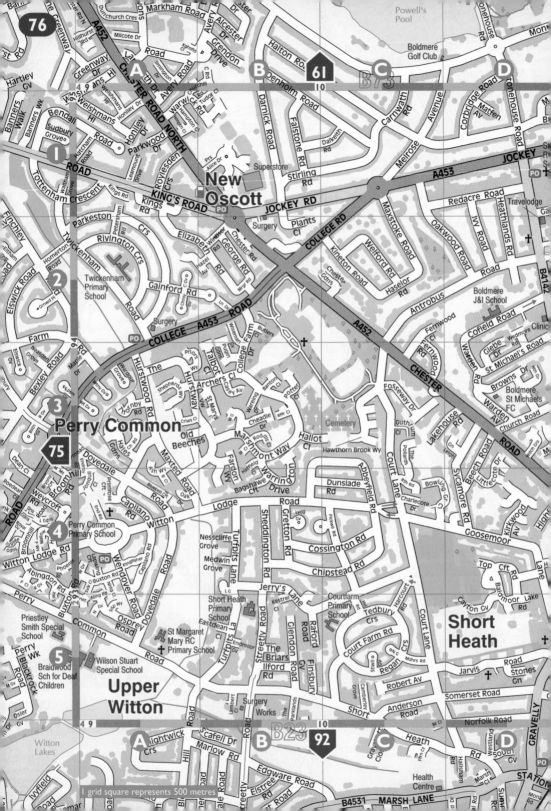

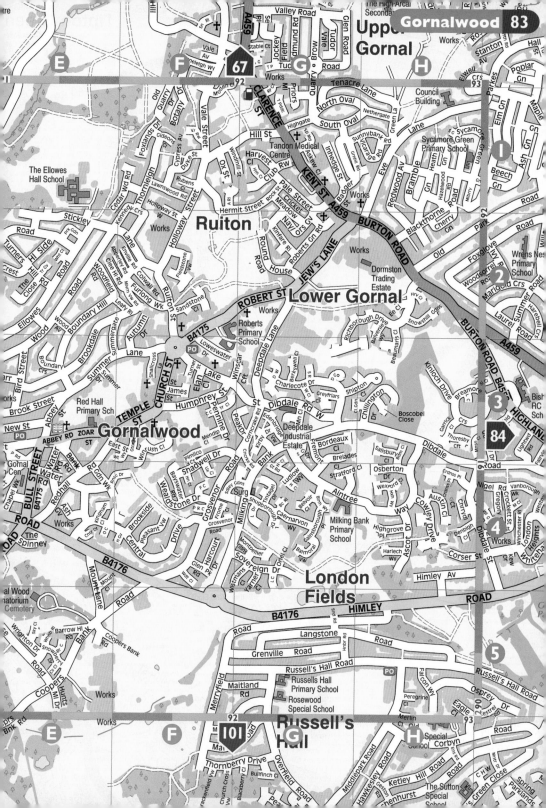

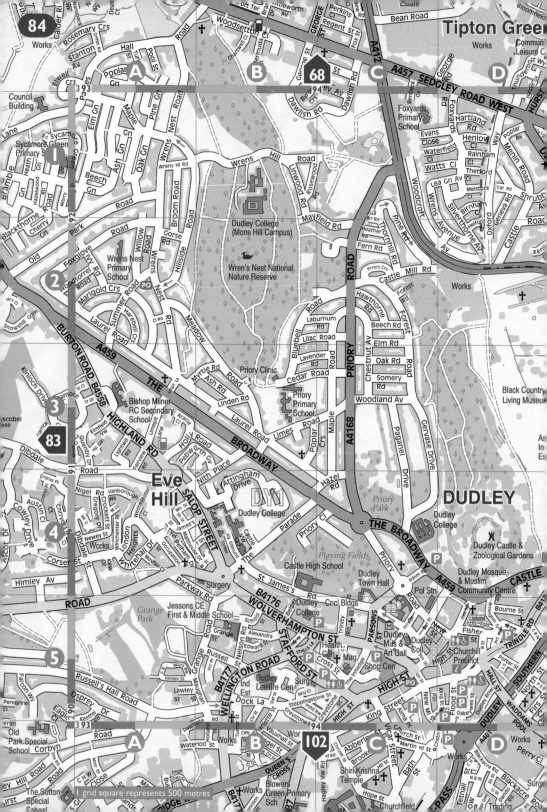

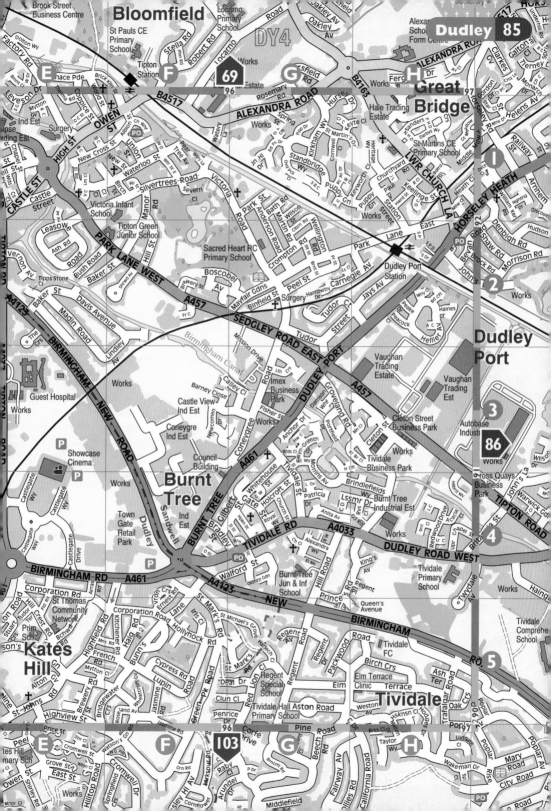

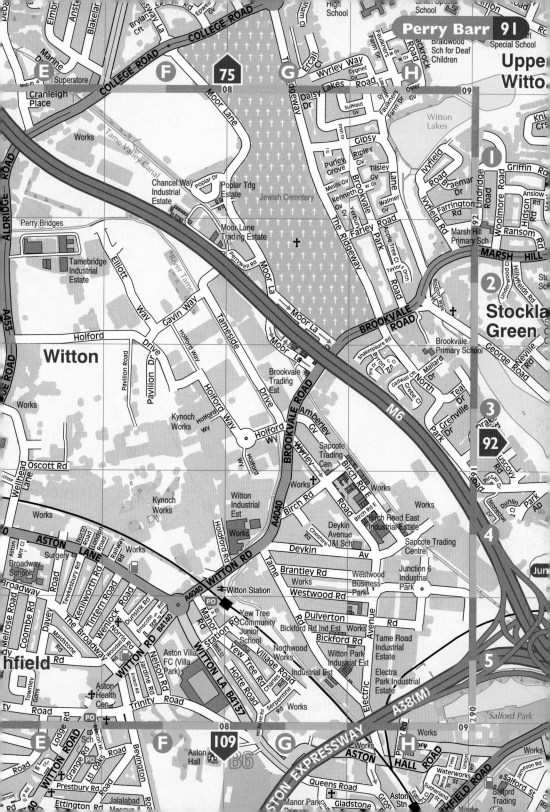

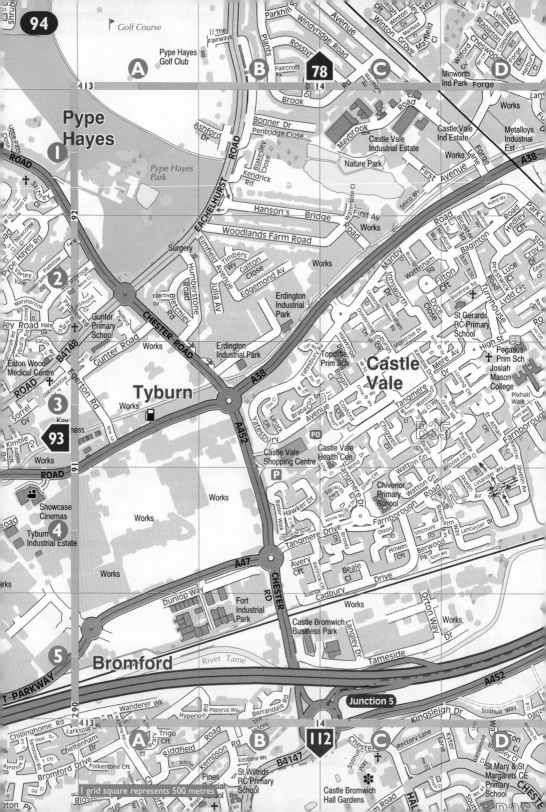

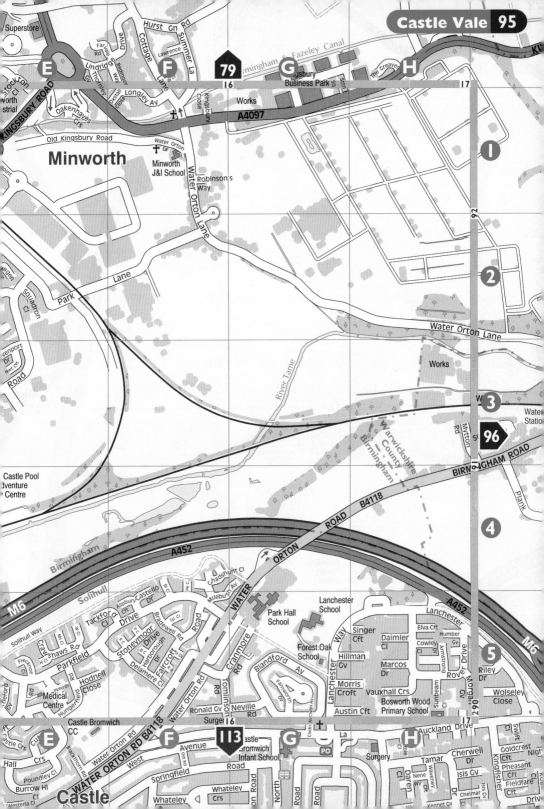

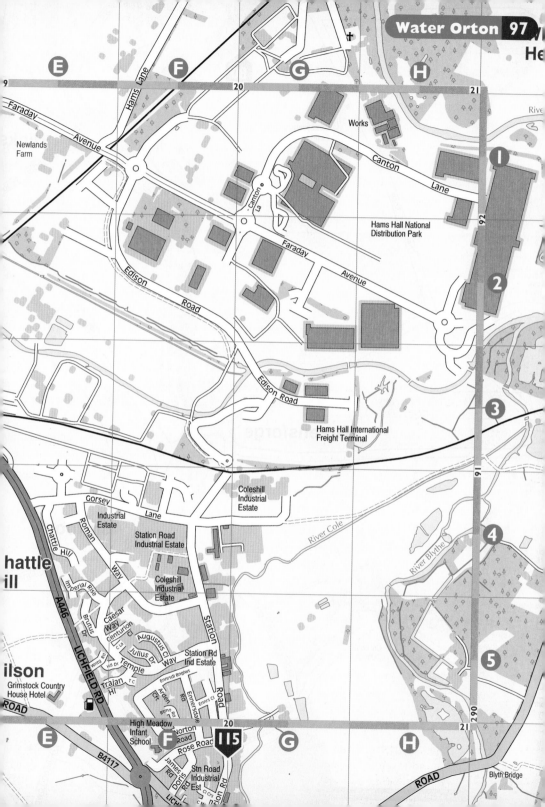

E   F   G   H

9

20

21

Hams Lane

River

†

Faraday

Avenue

Newlands
Farm

Works

Canton
Lane

I

Canton
La

Hams Hall National
Distribution Park

92

Edison

Road

Faraday

Avenue

2

Edison Road

3

Hams Hall International
Freight Terminal

91

Gorsey

Lane

Coleshill
Industrial
Estate

Industrial
Estate

Station Road
Industrial Estate

River Cole

River Blythe

4

hattle
ill

Chattle Hill

A446

Roman

Way

Imperial Rise

Coleshill
Industrial
Estate

Station

Caesar
Way

Brutus
Dr

Centurion
Cl

Augustus Cl

Cl.Ca

Julius Dr

Temple

Wmtg
Rd

Hd Dr

T C

Station Rd
Ind Estate

Ennrsdt Bnglws

5

290

ilson

Grimstock Country
House Hotel

LICHFIELD RD

Trajan
HI

Ardeley
Cft

Bttmn

Ennersdale

Ennrs Cl

ROAD

ROAD

Blyth Bridge

E   F   G   H

20

21

B4117

High Meadow
Infant School

Norton
Road

Rose Road

I15

Station Rd

James
Rd

Doris
Rd

Stn Road
Industrial
Rd Est

Cl Cfs

LICH

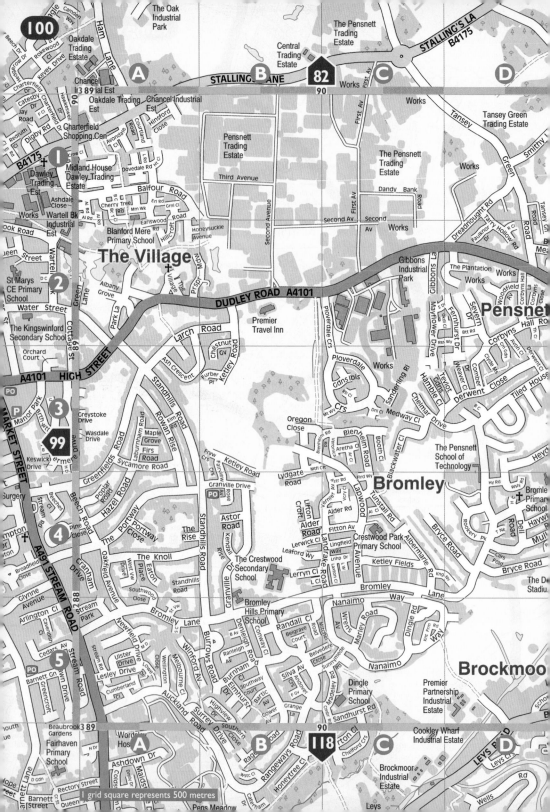

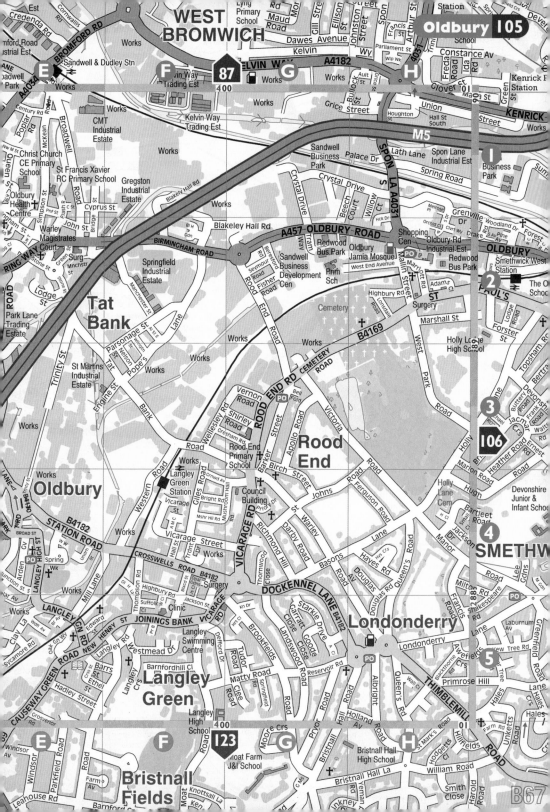

A38(M)

Copley Hi

A38(M)

Minstead Road

TYBURN RD—A38

92

Hawkesyard

St. Downside Ro

Dominic's Road

Ansell Rd

Stoneyhurst Road

Abbotts Rd

Bracel

Road

Rd

Ryl

A Salford Park   **B** Works   10 Works   **C** Walker Dr Works Way Works **D**

Standard Way

Thompson Dr

Hanover Drive

409

90

Works

Priory Rd

Priory Rd

HALL ROAD

Waterworks

Hills

Sutherland Rd

Plume Street

Union

LICHFIELD ROAD

Holborn Hill

Janeson Rd

Premier St

Works

Wharton St Industrial Estate

Wharton St

Works

M6

Walker Dr

Walker Dr

Jarvis

Jarvis

Jarvis

Way

I

Thimble Mi

Stn

Salford St

Salford Trading Est

Crompton Rd

B4137

CUCKOO RD

Argyle Street

Wharton St

Vue

Star City

Nechells

Watson Rd

Gravelly Ind Park

Council Building

2

Long Acre Trading Estate

Thimble MI La

Long Acre Trading Estate

Eliot St

Cook St

Long Acre

Chattaway St

Addison Rd

Nechells Rd

St Clements CE Primary School

Mosque & Teaching Centre

Malvern HI Rd

Butlin St

Old Stables Walk

PO

Brockley Pl

Stanley Rd

P Pl

Mount St

Nechells Primary School

Mount Street Business Park

Dunton Trading Estate

Needham St

HEARTLANDS PKWY

Watson Road

P

Washwood Heath Gas Works

Works

HEARTLANDS

Cem

Railway Ter

Aston Church Rd

Trevor St

Stuart St

Mn Wy

C

Trevor St

Trevor Street Industrial Est

Works

Saltley Business Park

Cumbria Wy

Aston Church Rd

Works

Washwood Heath

Leigh JI (NC) School

Warren

Salim Mosque

Works

Common Lane

Council Building

3

Works

Marton

Centre Industrial Estate

Ocky La

Police Stn

109

St Clements Rd

Thornberry Walk

Cattells Gv

Centre Link Industrial Estate

Mount Street Business Cen

Mount St

Dorset Rd

Pennine Way

Dorset Rd

Arley

Med Cen

Bennetts Rd

Sandway Gdns

Chartist Rd

WASHWOOD

BA516

Leigh Road

WASHWOOD

Lime Tree Rd

Glenpark Road

Haycroft

Swan CI

Crmn Rd

Ward Park

Road

Wdct Dr

B7

B4132

Bloomsbury St

Fowler St

Lingard

Cato St N

Nechells Pl

HEARTLANDS PARKWAY

Carlton Business Cen

Saltley Trading Est

Al Huda Mosque Girls School

Clayton Rd

Cate St

WASHWOOD HEATH RD

Hutton Rd

Exton Wy

Berry Rd

Easby Wy

Wright Road

Salisbury Rd

Nigel Rd

Wavell Rd

Wright Way

HIGHFIELD ROAD

Highfield Primary Sch

Glenpark Road

Harts Surgery

Nansen Road

Nansen J&I School

4

SALTLEY RD

SALTLEY VIADUCT HIGH ST

Mainstream Forty Seven Ind Park

Alderflat Pl

Cranby St

Crawford St

Dorset Rd

Pln Wy

B4145

PO

Havelock Rd

St Saviours CE Primary Sch

Alum Rock Road

Phillimore Rd

Ralph Road

Herrick Road

Teall Rd

Saltley Health Cen

Council Building

Surgery

Cremore Av

Park View School

Hazelbeach Rd

Clipston Rd

Farndon Rd

Foxton Road

Melvina Rd

Cato St

Devon

Mainstream Way

Duddeston

Mainstream Ind Park

Network Park Ind Est

Cornwall Industrial Estate

George Arthur Rd

Jersey Rd

Ashley Gdns

Reginald Road

Saviour's Rd

Edmund Road

Ellesmere Road

BOWYER ROAD

Hartopp Rd

Alumrock Medical Centre

Gowan Road

Works

PO

Shaw Hill Primary Sch

Jackson Rd

Maitland Rd

Alum

5

Vauxhall Trading Est

Read Bu Park

Alma Crs

Duddeston

Inkerman St

Adderley Trading Estate

Duddeston Mill Trading Est

ASH ROAD

The Gv

Hams Rd

ADDERLEY ROAD

Arden Rd

Mosque

Hall

College Rd

Raymond Rd

Saltley

Nechells Green

Works

409

Adderley Industrial Est

Adderley

A   Saltley Industrial Cen   **B**   ARDEN RD   **128**   10   **C**   Rosar Primary School   Parkfield Prim Sch   **D**

Alexander Way

Bell Dr

Road

Couchman Road

Parkfield Rd

Hancock Rd

Alderson Rd

Ludlow Rd

Woodlands

Adderley Primary Sch

Bordesley Green Trading Est

College Rd

Bridge Rd

Anthony Rd

Whitacre Road

Geranium Gv

Lupin Gv

Bordesley

Adderley Park Station

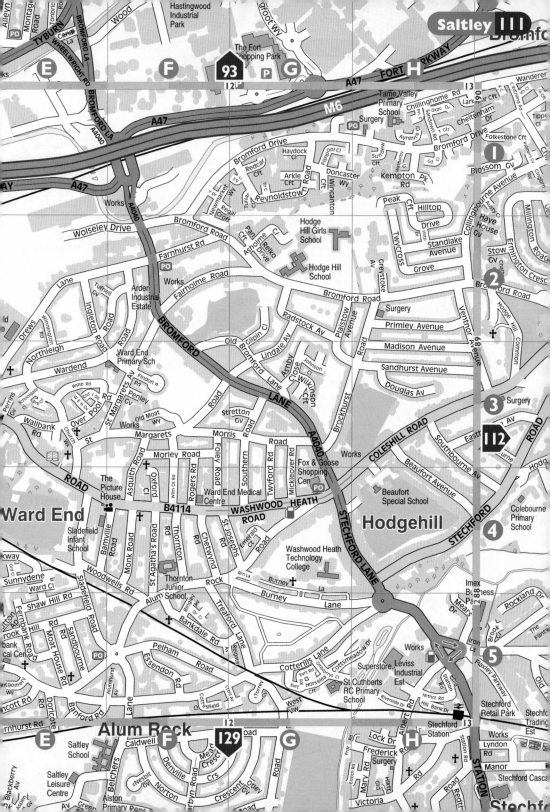

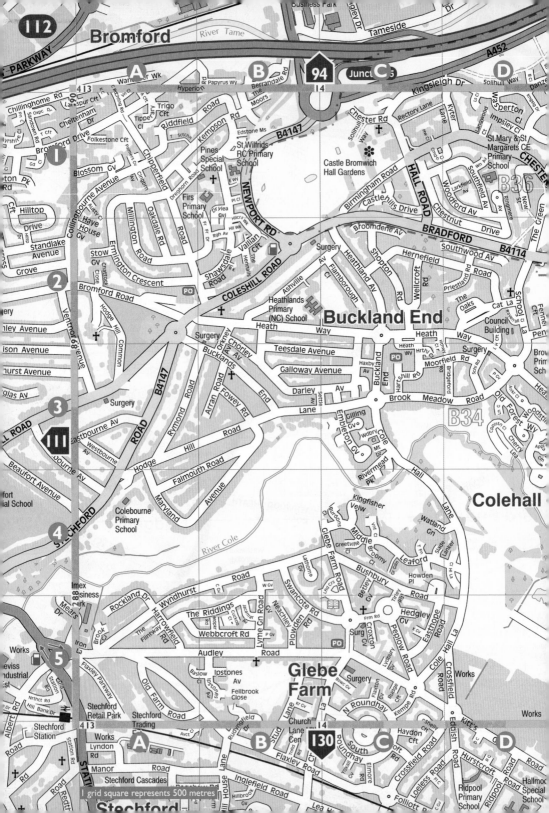

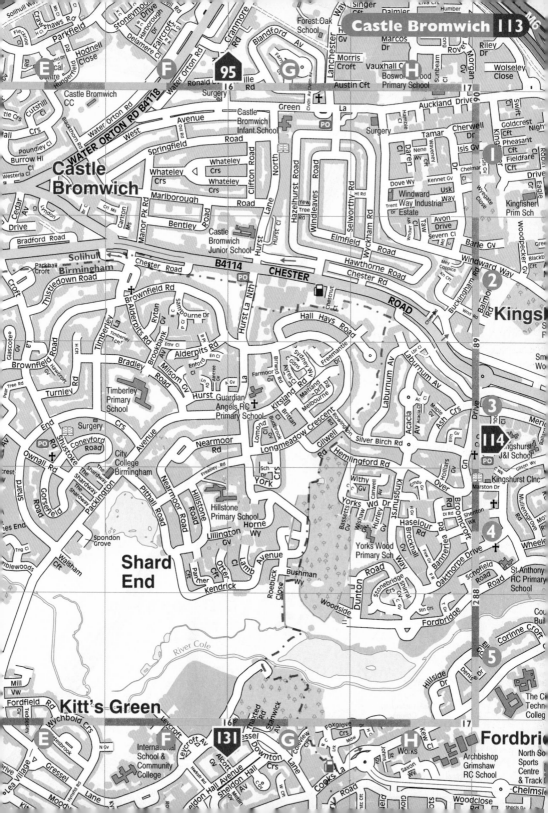

1 grid square represents 500 metres

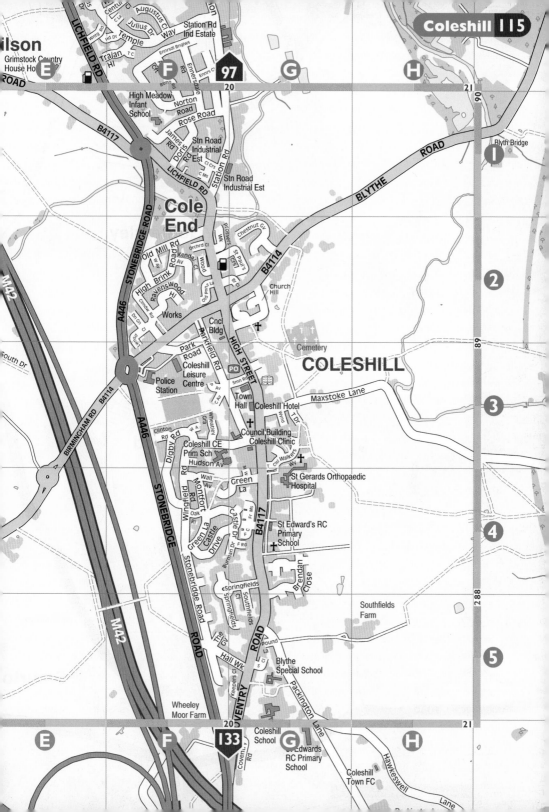

ilson

Grimstock Country
House Ho

E

F

97

20

G

H

21

90

Blyth Bridge

1

GRIMSTOCK ROAD

LICHFIELD RD

B4117

Station Rd
Ind Estate

High Meadow
Infant
School

Norton
Road

Rose Road

James
Rd

Doris

Stn Road
Industrial
Est

Station Rd

Stn Road
Industrial Est

Augustus Cl

Julius Dr

Temple
Way

Trajan
Hl

Centurn

Cl

BLYTHE ROAD

**Cole
End**

STONEBRIDGE ROAD

A446

LICHFIELD RD

Old Mill Rd

High Brink Road

Ravenswood

Hl

Works

Prossers
Wk

Orchd Cl

Kenda
Av

Wood

Chestnut Cv

St Paul's

B4114

Church
Hill

2

89

Cncl
Bldg

Park
Road

Parkfield Rd

Coleshill
Leisure
Centre

Police
Station

HIGH STREET

PO

Smn Rd

Cemetery

COLESHILL

Maxstoke Lane

3

B4114

BIRMINGHAM RD

A446

Town
Hall

Coleshill Hotel

T Dr

Clinton
Rd

Digby Rd

Wheatley
Gra

Coleshill CE
Prim Sch

Hudson Av

Council Building
Coleshill Clinic

Cncl Walkers

St Gerards Orthopaedic
Hospital

4

88

M42

STONEBRIDGE

Wall
Av

Montfort
Rd

Highfield

Oak
Rd

Green La
Castle
Drive

Green
La

Burman Dr

Castle Dr

B4117

Fr Ms

Fr Rd

St Edward's RC
Primary
School

Springfields

Springfields

Southfields

Brendan
Close

Southfields
Farm

5

The Cv

Hall Wk

Keepers Cl

ROAD

COVENTRY ROAD

pound

Blythe
Special School

Packington Lane

Wheeley
Moor Farm

E

F

133

20

Coventry Rd

Coleshill
School

G

Edwards
RC Primary
School

Coleshill
Town FC

H

21

Hawkeswell
Lane

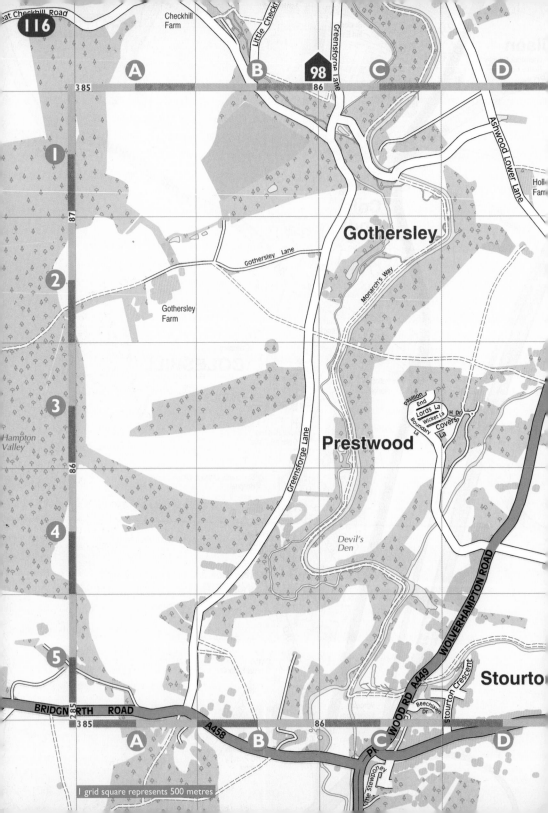

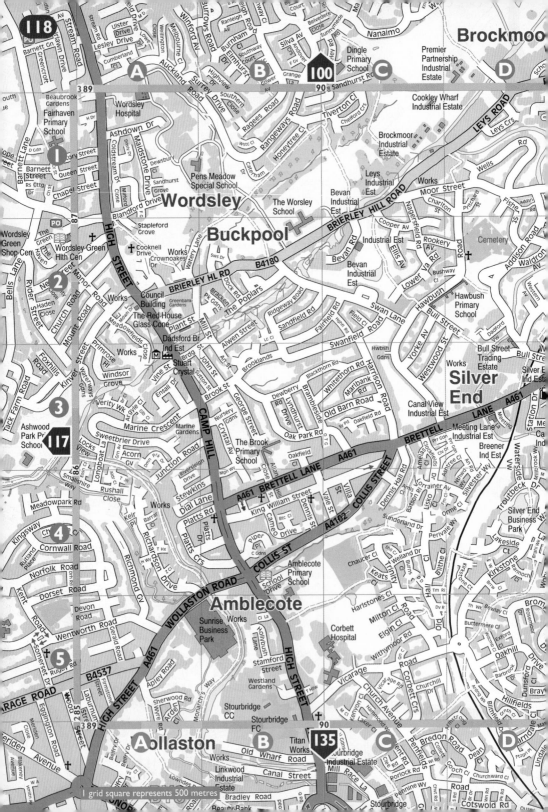

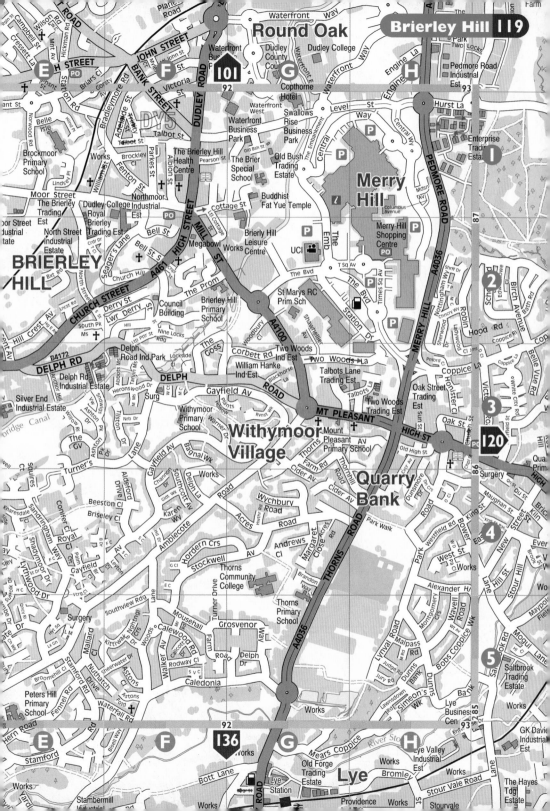

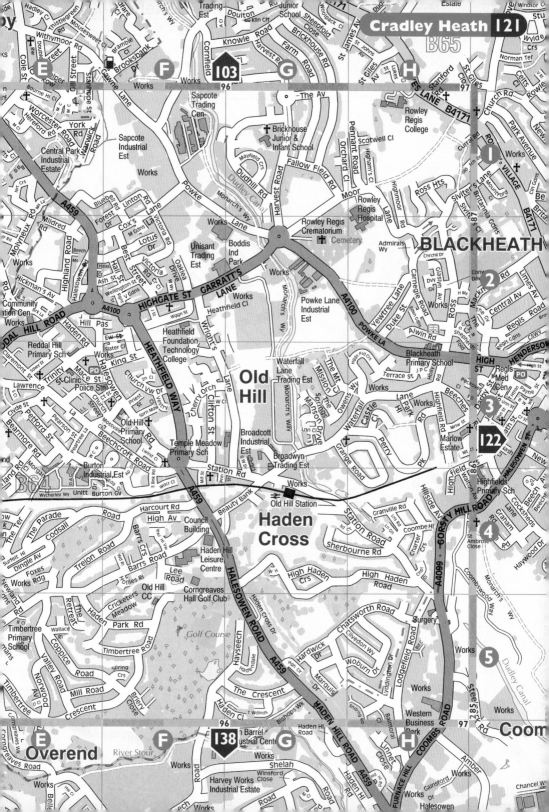

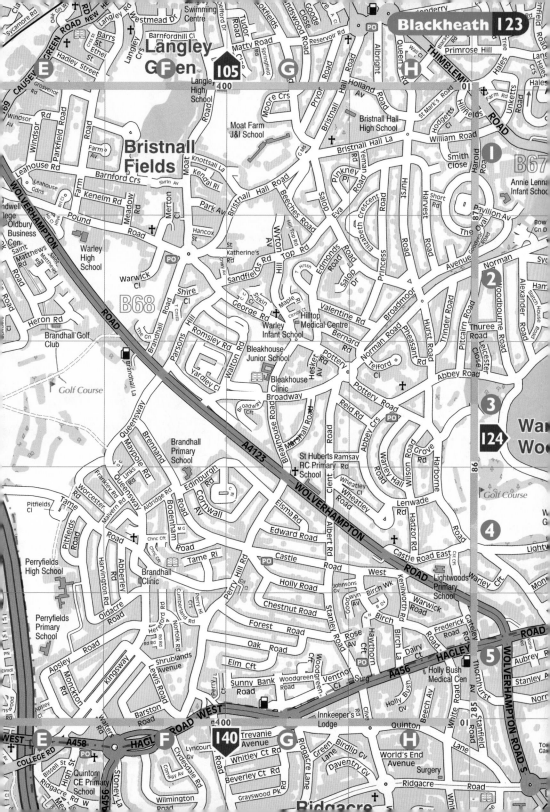

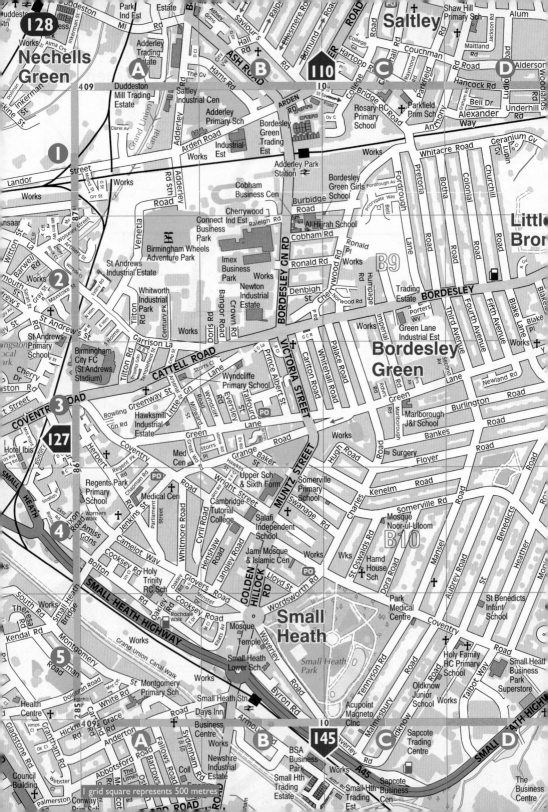

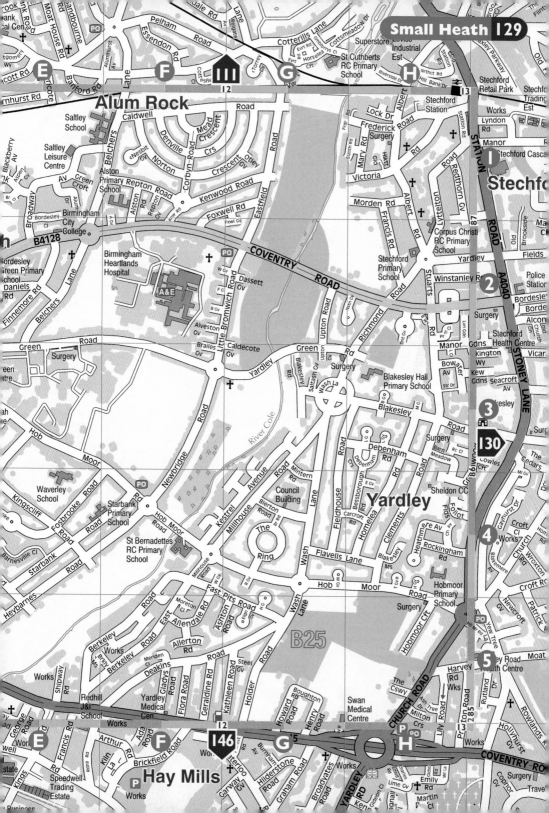

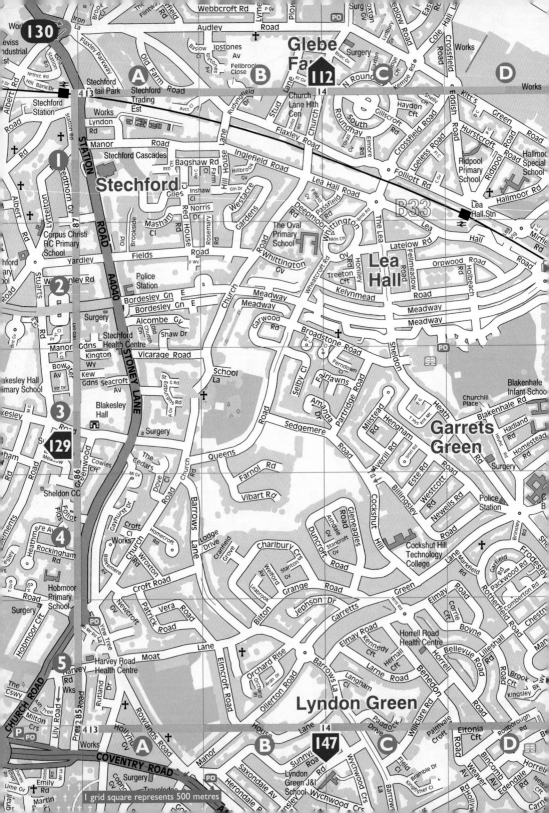

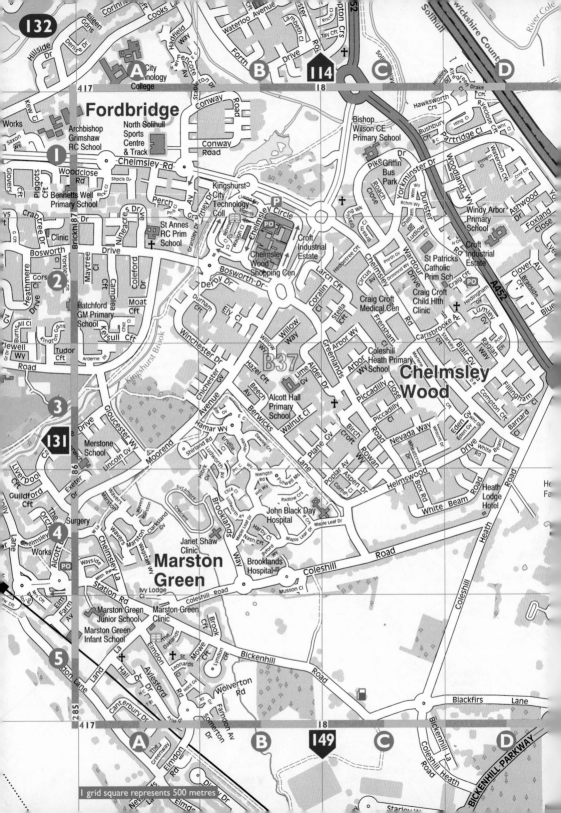

E F G H

Wheeley Moor Farm

Blythe Special School

Coleshill School

St Edwards RC Primary School

Coleshill Town FC

Packington Lane Farm

Hawkeswell Farm

Hawk La

I

2

Pool Farm

M6

M6

Junction 4

Junction 7/7a

Coleshill

Heath

M6

Road

M42

A446

Coleshill Pool

Stonebridge

Packington Lane

Bannerley Pool

3

4

King's Court

Crescent

CHESTER ROAD

Trident Court

Parkway

Bishop's Court

A452

Birmingham Business Park

Knights Court

M42

Solihull Pkwy

Solihull Parkway

ROAD

5

Blackfirs

Lane

Premier Travel Inn

Garden Centre

A4

A452

E F G H

Little

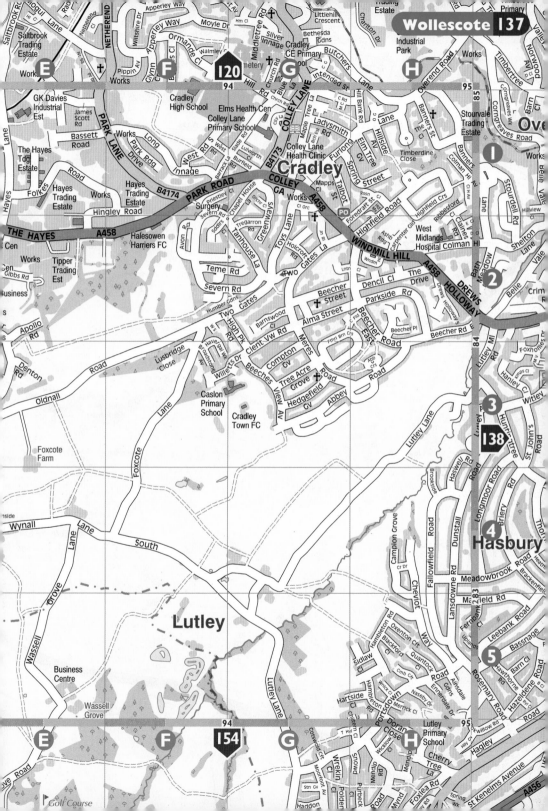

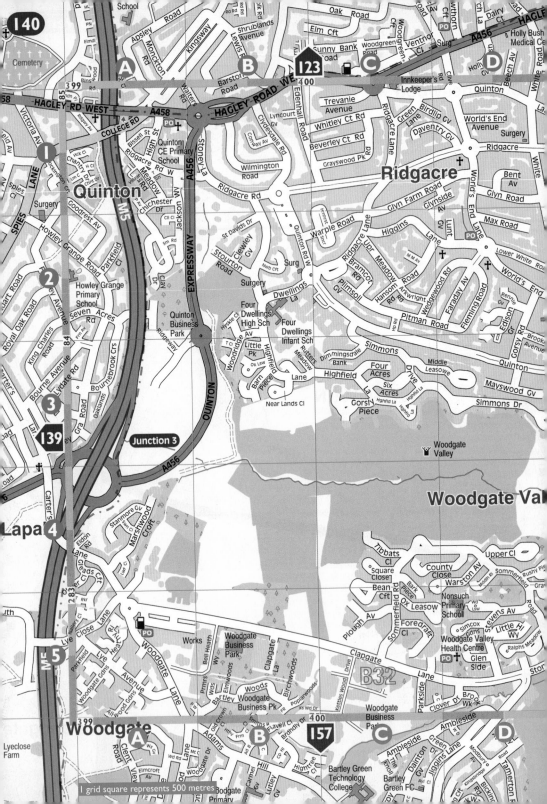

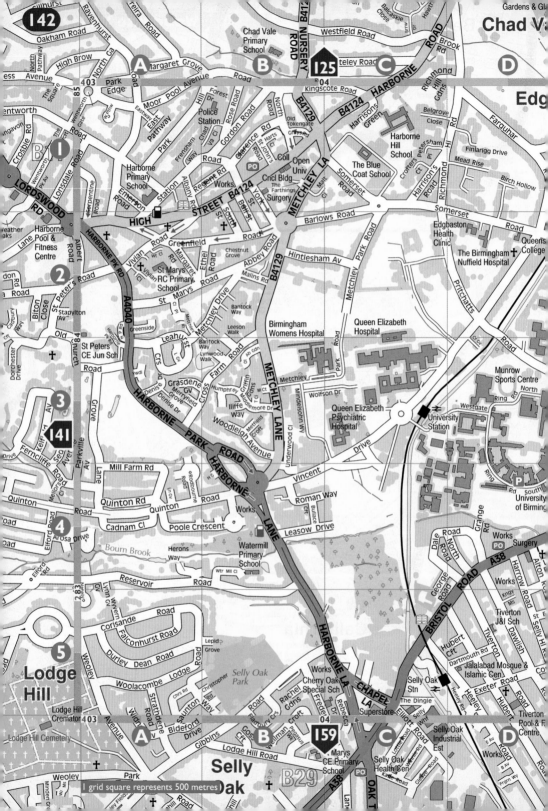

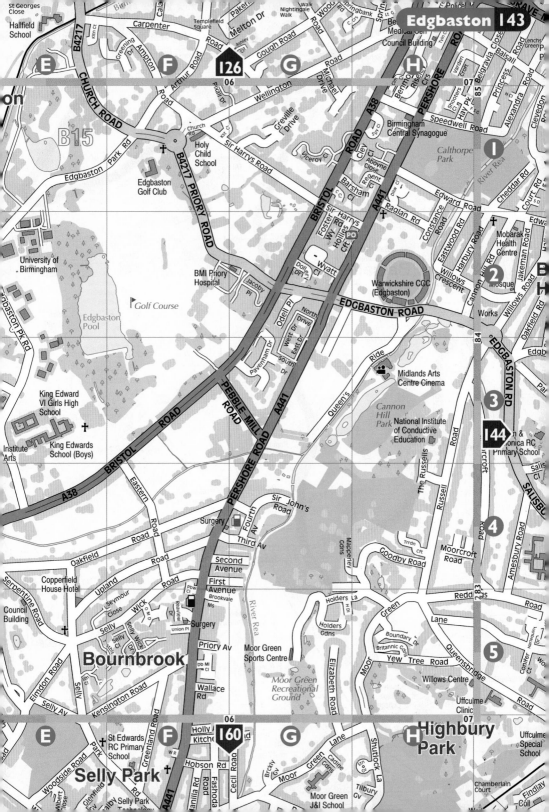

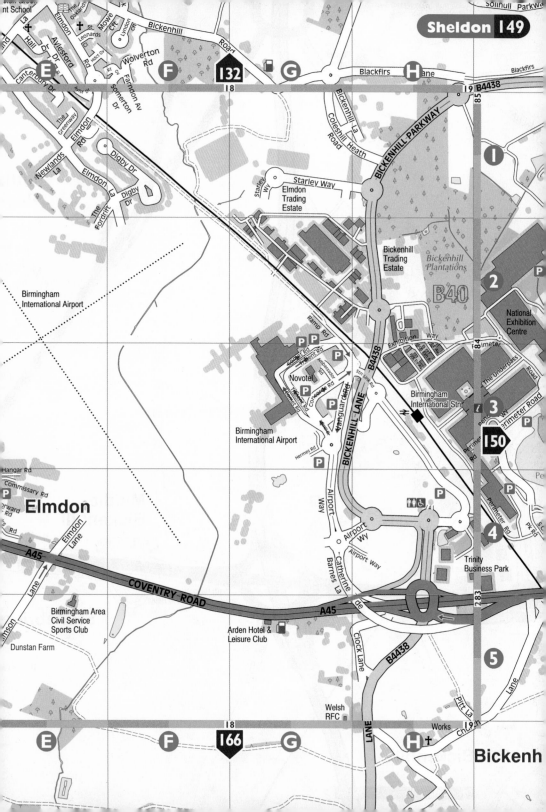

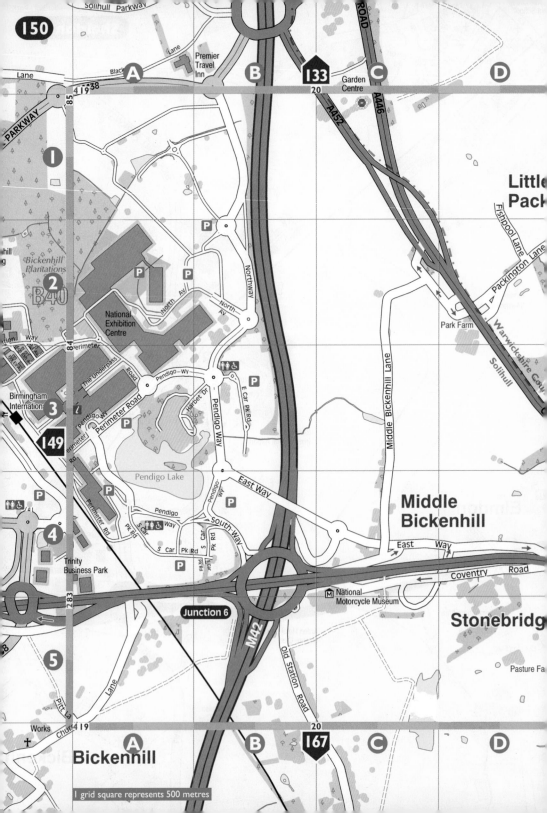

150

PARKWAY

Solihull Parkway

Lane

Black   Lane

A   41938

Premier Travel Inn

B

133
20

ROAD

Garden Centre

A452

A446

C

D

Little
Pack

Fishpool Lane

Packington Lane

1

Bickenhill Plantations

hill
g

2
B40

North Av

North Av

National Exhibition Centre

Northway

North Av

Warwickshire Gou

Solihull

Park Farm

Middle Bickenhill Lane

Way

Perimeter

Perimeter

Road

The Underpass

Pendigo-Wy

Harbet Dr

E Car Pk Rd

3
Birmingham International

149

Pendigo Wy

Perimeter Road

Pendigo Wy

Perimeter Rd

Pendigo Lake

Pendigo Way

East Way

Middle Bickenhill

4

Pendigo-Wy

Trinity Business Park

Perimeter Rd

Pendigo Way

Pk Rd

S Car

S Car Pk Rd

South-Way

S Car Pk Rd

East   Way

Coventry   Road

National Motorcycle Museum

5

Junction 6

M42

Old Station Road

Stonebridge

Pasture Fa

Pitt La

Lane

Church

419

Works

A   20

Bickenhill

B

167

C

D

1 grid square represents 500 metres

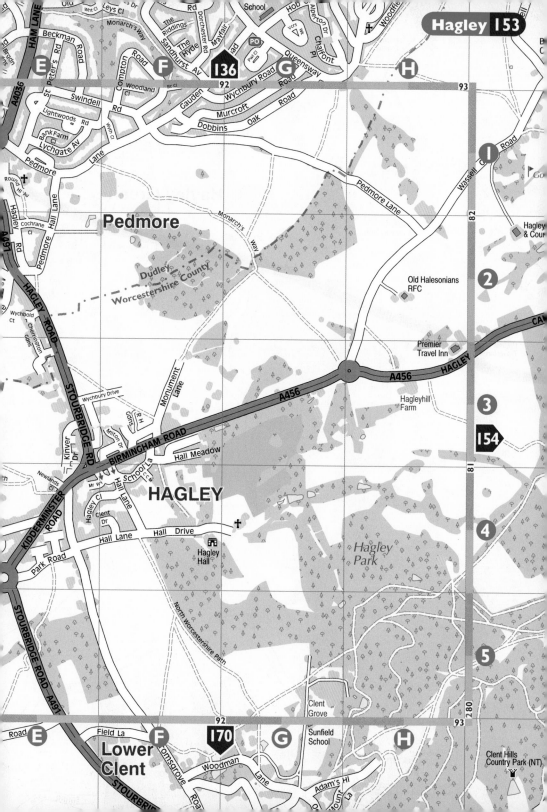

154

A — Business Centre

B

137

C — Lutley Lane

D — Sidlaw Cl · Hartside · Hamleton Rd · Blackford Cl · Quantock Cl · Road · Emerdale · Way

Wassell Grove

393 · 94

I — Wassell Grove Road

Golf Course

82

2 — Old Hales RFC · Hagley Golf & Country Club

Cotswold Cft · Moorfoot Av · T Hyt Cl · Chiltern Cl · Wickow Cl · Snowd · Wrekin Cl · Polden Cl · Purbeck · Haddon Cft · Mendip Cft · Stn Gv · Mendip · Road · Long Mynd · Doran Close · Lutley Primary School · Cherry Tree La · Foxlea Rd · Hagley Rd · Mendip Rd

Hayley Green

Birley Gv · The Lawley

HAGLEY ROAD

A456 · Hagley Green Hospital · Hagtt Dr · Waugh Dr

CAUSEWAY

Hayley Pk Road · Causey Farm Road · Abbot Rd · Knlstw gns

3 — Premier Travel Inn · Hagley · Hagleyhill Farm

Hagley Wood

153

81

Spring Farm

4

Hagley Wood Lane

Uffmoor Lane

Chapel Lane · Chapel Farm

5

The Four Stones

Worcestershire Path

Ivy Lane · St

280

393 · 94

A — Clent Hills Country Park (NT)

B

171

C · Worcestershire Prth

D · Ho

Spring Lane

I grid square represents 500 metres

138

156

172

Hunnington

B62

Uffmoor Wood

Tack Farm

Goodrest Farm

Hollies Farm

Horsepool Farm

Fox Farm

Bromsgrove Rd

B4551

BROMSGROVE ROAD

B4551

MANOR WAY

A456

A456

Uffmoor Lane

Quarry La

HAGLEY

Belbroughton Rd

Blakedown Rd

Broadway

Hasbury CE Primary School

Churchill Rd

Foxhunt Rd

Hasbury

Ashfield Gv

Barn Cl

Huntlands Rd

Uffmoor Est

Kelms Avenue

Hazelbeech Road

Bassn...

Hawthorne Rd

Kenswick Dr

Wythall Rd

Waxla

Red Hl

The Cl

St Kenelm's Rd

Yew Tree Pl

Kenelm St

Kenelm Road

The Alders

The Hedgerows

Waverley Crs

Eastleigh Dr

PO

St Kenelms CE First School

Fox Farm Road

Hillcrest Road

Park Lane

E F G H

I

2

3

4

5

96 97

95

82

81

80

E F G H

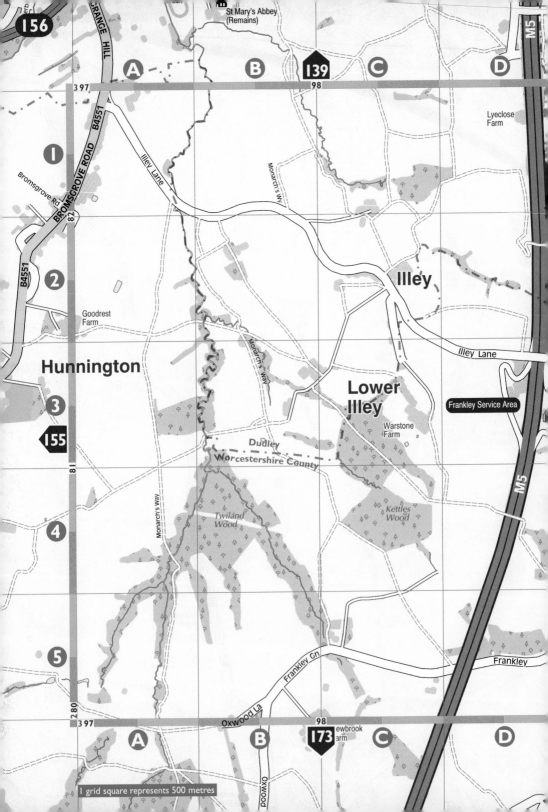

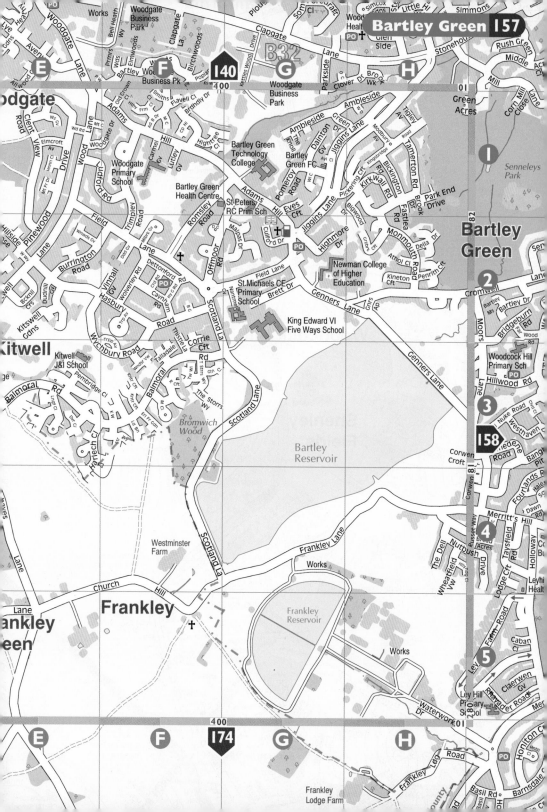

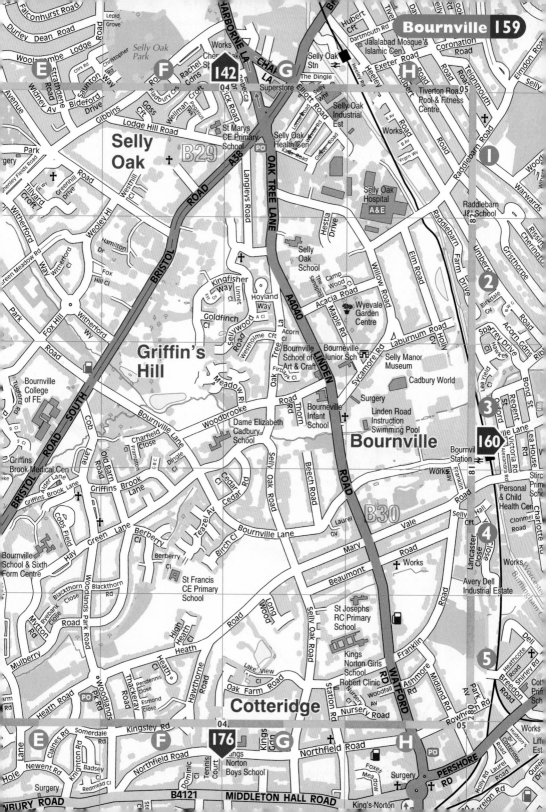

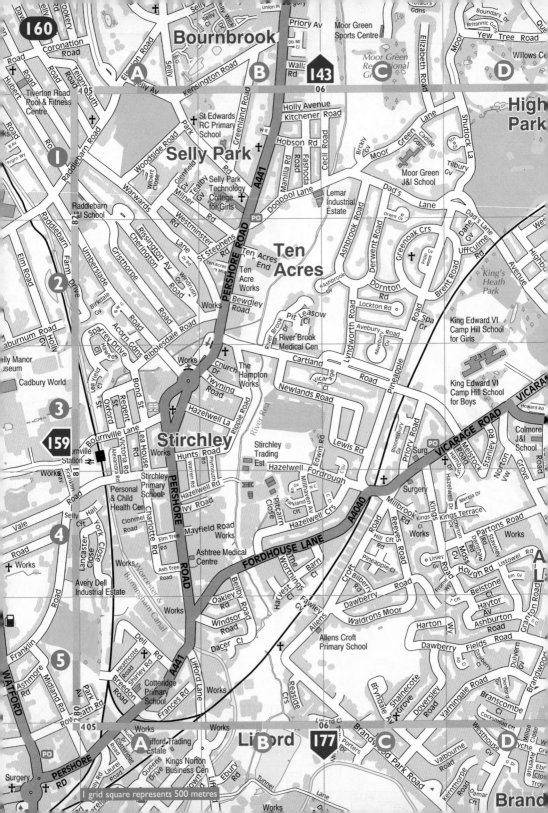

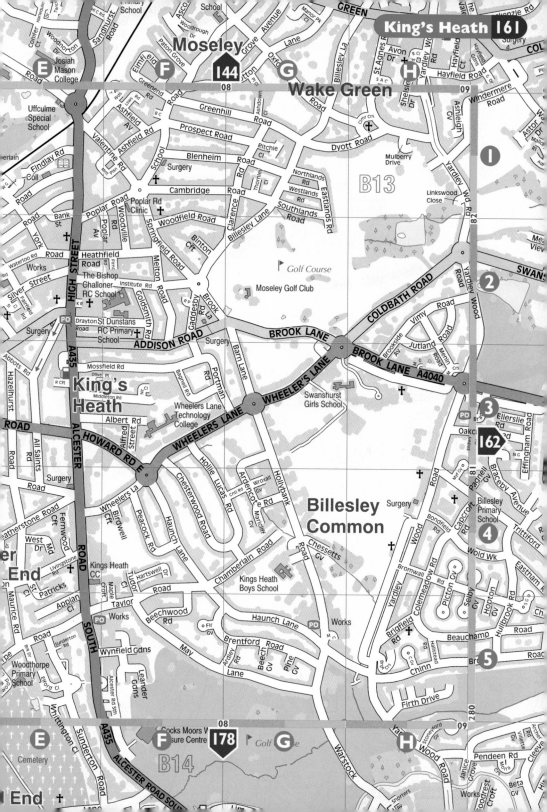

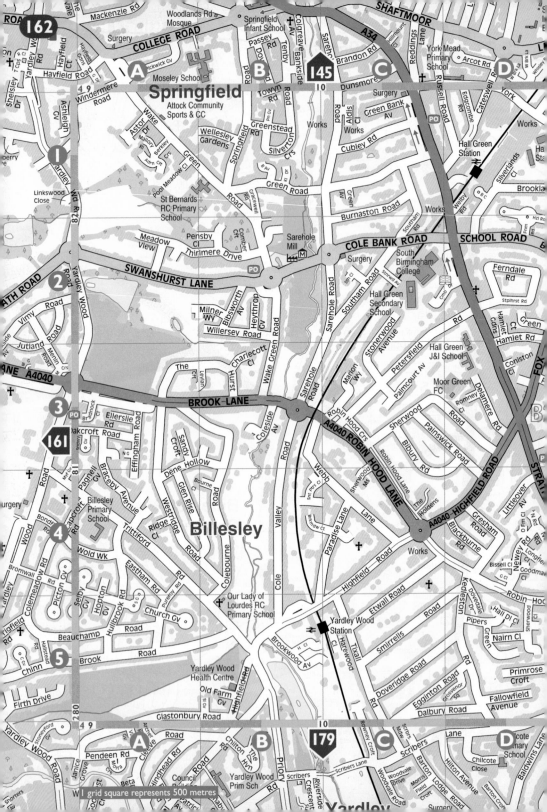

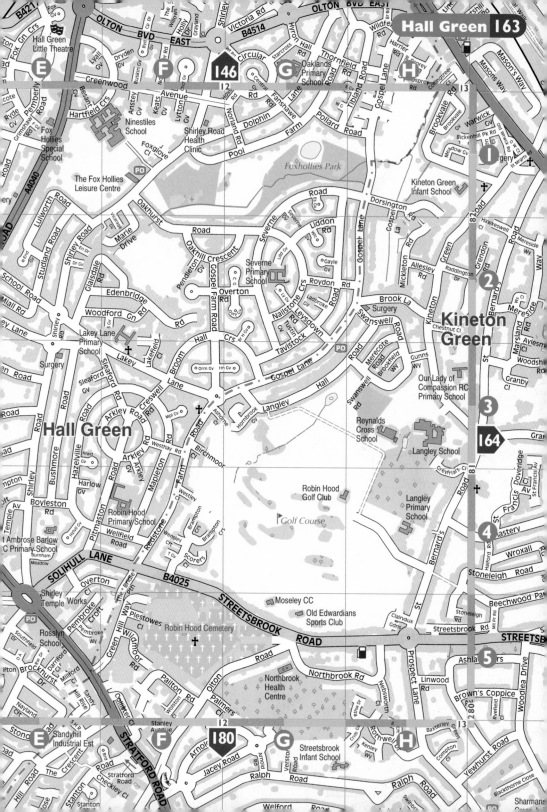

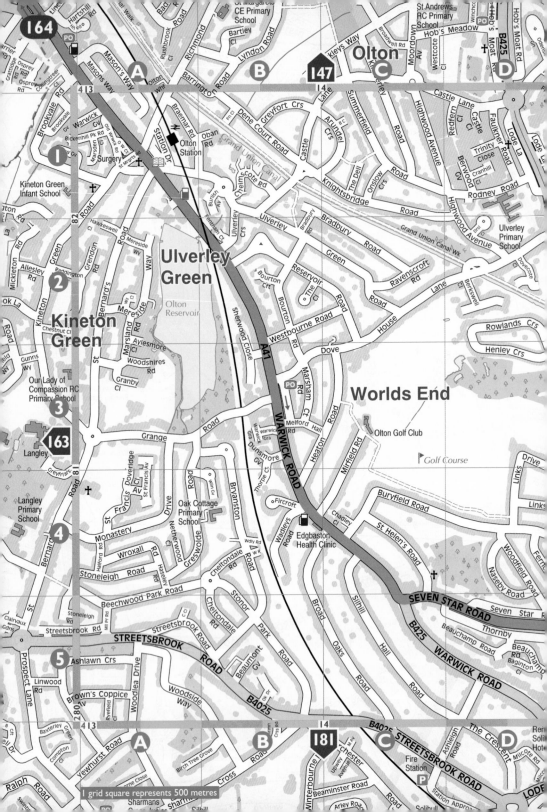

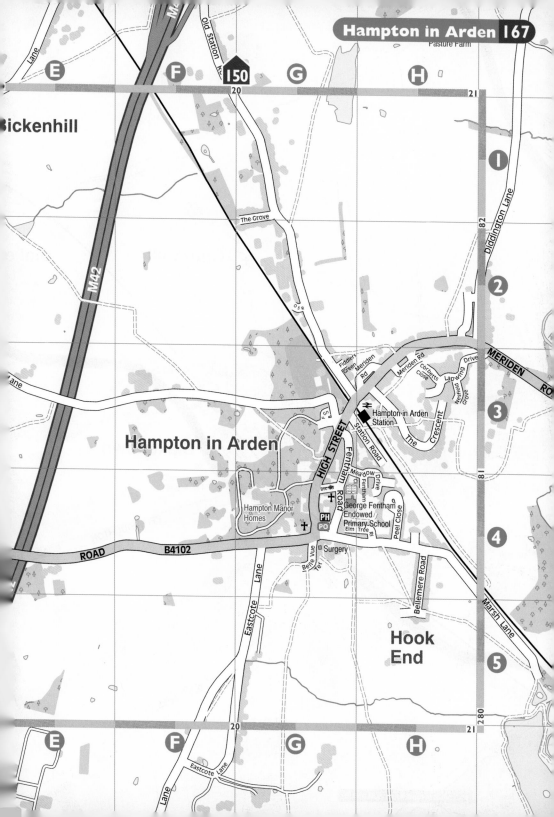

Pasture Farm

E   F   150   G   H

20   21

Bickenhill

I

Diddington Lane

82

The Grove

2

O S R

MERIDEN RO

Fiddlers Green

Meriden Rd

Meriden Rd

Corbetts Close

Lapwing Drive

Nesfield Grove

3

81

M42

Hampton in Arden Station

The Crescent

Hampton in Arden

HIGH STREET

Fentham Road

Station Road

Meadow Drive

Fentham Close

4

Hampton Manor Homes

George Fentham Endowed Primary School

Elm Tree Rd

Peel Close

PH

PO

ROAD   B4102

Eastcote Lane

Belle Vue Ter

Surgery

Bellemere Road

Marsh Lane

Hook End

5

E   F   20   G   H

21

280

Eastcote Lane

Lane

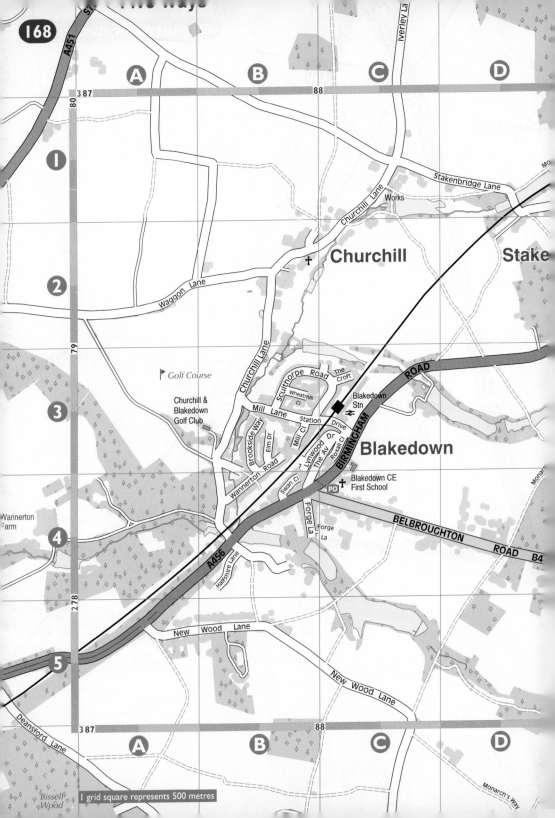

A451

S

The Ways

3 87

80

88

A   B   C   D

1

2

3

4

5

79

278

3 87

88

A   B   C   D

Stakenbridge Lane

Churchill Lane

Works

✝ **Churchill**

Stake

Golf Course

Churchill Lane

Churchill &
Blakedown
Golf Club

Sculthorpe Road

The Croft

Wheatmill Cl

ROAD

Blakedown
Stn

Mill   Lane

Station

Brookside Way

Elm Dr

Mill Cl

Lynwood

The Av

Roxall Cl

Drive

BIRMINGHAM

Blakedown

Wannerton Road

Swan Cl

PO ✝ Blakedown CE
First School

Wannerton
Farm

A456

Halfshire Lane

Forge La

Forge
La

BELBROUGHTON   ROAD   B4

Monarch

New   Wood   Lane

New   Wood   Lane

Deansford   Lane

Monarch's Way

Bissell
Wood

1 grid square represents 500 metres

Iverley La

Mo

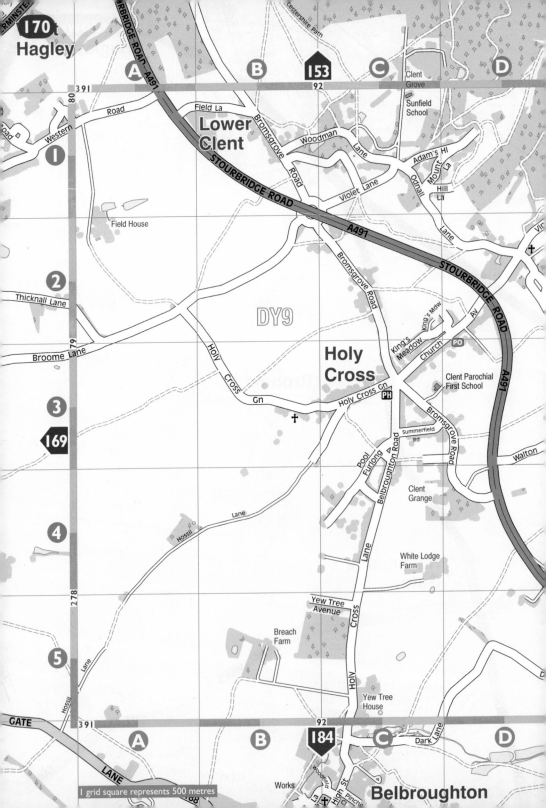

E **F** **154** 94 **G** Ivy La. **H** 95 80

Clent Hills
Country Park (NT)

North Worcestershire pth

Spring Lane

Whitehall
Farm

Clatterbach La

Rumbow Lane

Holt Lane

Fieldh

I

Clent

Walton Rd

Highfield
Lane

Walton Pool

Walton
House

Moor Hall Dr

Moorhall
Farm

Moor Hall Drive

**Rumbow
Cottages**

2

79

Daleswood
Farm

3

172 wood

Great
Farley
Wood

4

Shut Mill Lane

278

Munches Lane

Gorse
Farm

Gorse Green Lane

Sling
Common

**Bell
Heath**

Woodfield Lane

5

Newtown

A491

STOURBRIDGE ROAD

Clents Lane

E

F **Bell
End** **185** 94 **G** **H** 95

Stourbridge Rd

Heath End Road

Chapel

LANE

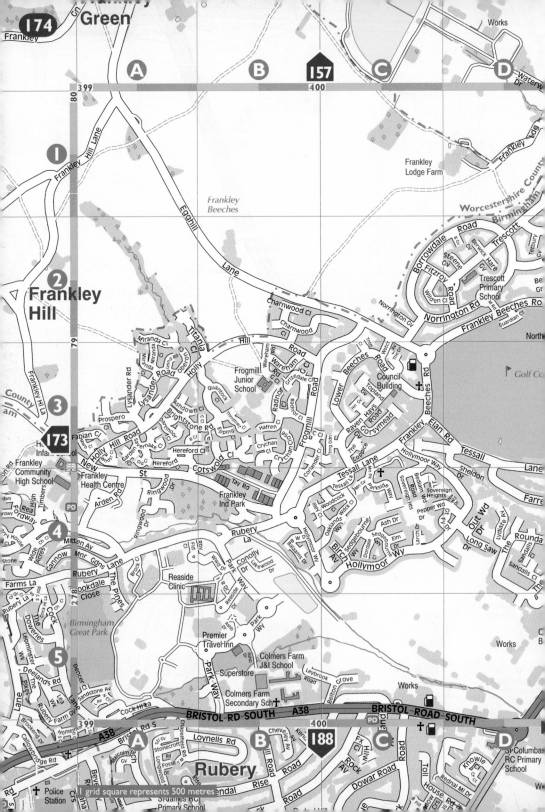

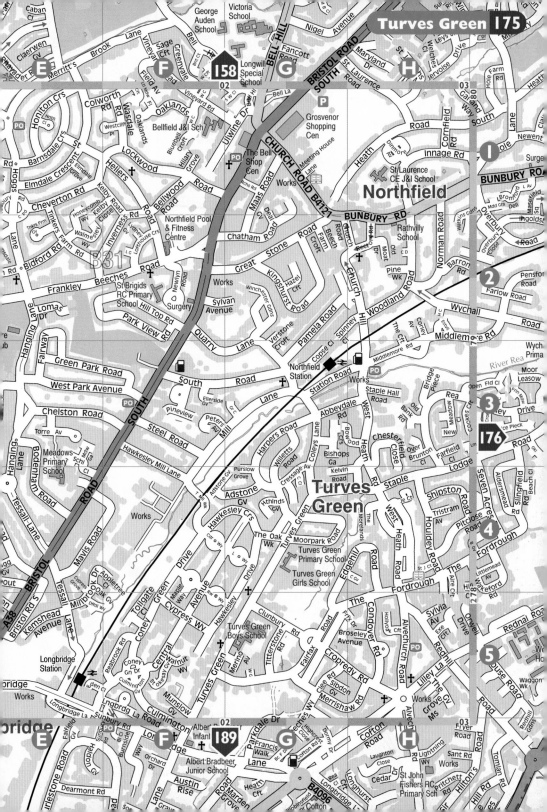

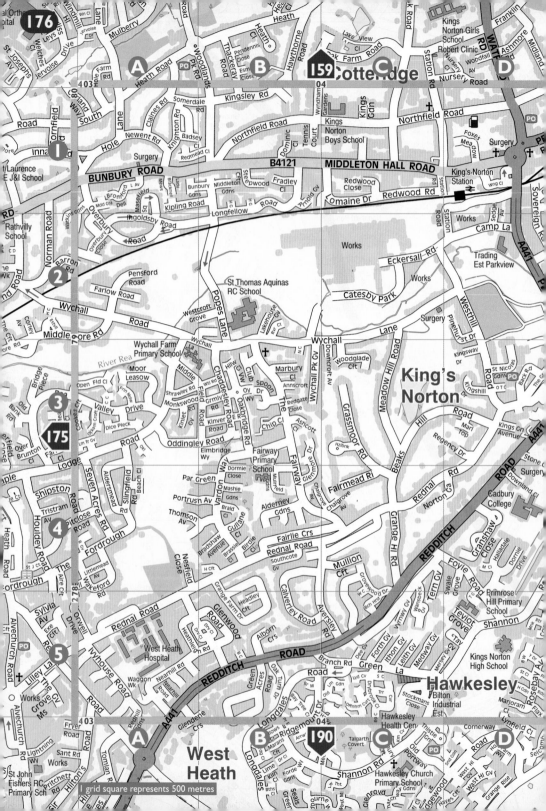

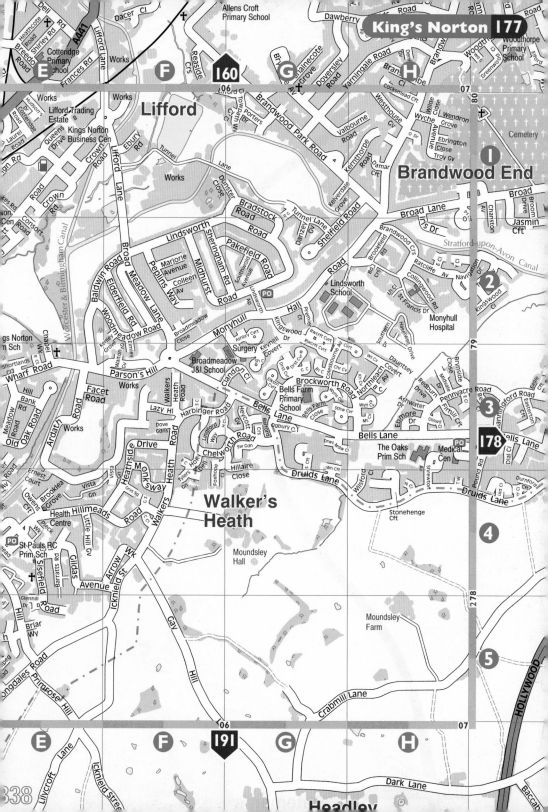

E F **162** G H

I

2

PO

180

3

4

5

E F **193** G H

Yardley Wood

Yardley Wood
Health Centre

Old Farm Gv

Yardley Wood
Prim Sch

Council
Building

Glastonbury Road

Chilcote
Primary
School

Chilcote
Close

Scribers Lane

Scribers Lane

Woodvale
Drive

Woodvale Road

Barton Lodge Road

Hilton Avenue

Baldwins
Lane

Baldwins Lane

Sanddate

Stonor

Road

Blythsford Rd

Sandy Hill

Skelcher Road

Glascote Close

Hasluck
Junior

Newborough
Road

Newborough
Road

Works

PO

Warstock

Ravenshill

Riley
Road

Riversdale
Road

Daimler
Road

Bach MI
Dr

Slade Lane

Priory
Road

Barbara Road

Gracemere Crescent

Acheson
Road

Watwood
Road

Deirene
Road

Geoffrey Road

Berkeley
Road

Stroud

Road

Hasluck
Chnstn Av

Middleton Road

Surgery

Burman
Infant
School

Hazel
Oak
School

Burman Road

Sansome Road

Baldwins
Lane

Surgery

Coton
Grove

Windmill
Road

Colebrook

Hasluck's Green

Nethercote Gardens

Atherstone Rd

Colebrook

Limbrick

Hasluck's Green Road

Wiseacre
Croft

Solihull Lodge

Peterbrook
Primary
School

Mill Lodge
Primary
School

High
Street

Hexton Cl

Myton Dr

Oxhill Road

Hargrave
Road

Mountford

Peterbrook

Peterbrook

Road

Aqueduct
Road

Cole

Green Lane

Shirley
Station

Neville

Road

Binton Road

Undridge
Road

Kingshurst

Loxley
Road

Hawkesbury
Rd

Neville

Road

Bills
Lane

Bills
Lane

Peterbrook

Berry
Mound

Warwickshire County

Solihull

Wake Green
FC

Drawbridge Rd

Littlemead Road

Haslucks Green Road

Snowford

**Major's
Green**

Rolan
Drive

Three
Corner
Close

Nursery
Gdns

Rushleigh Rd

Folds
Rd

Langcomb

Binley

Road

Amington Dr

Whitlock's End
Farm

North Worcestershire Path

Heath Lane

Haslucks Green Road

Whitlock's

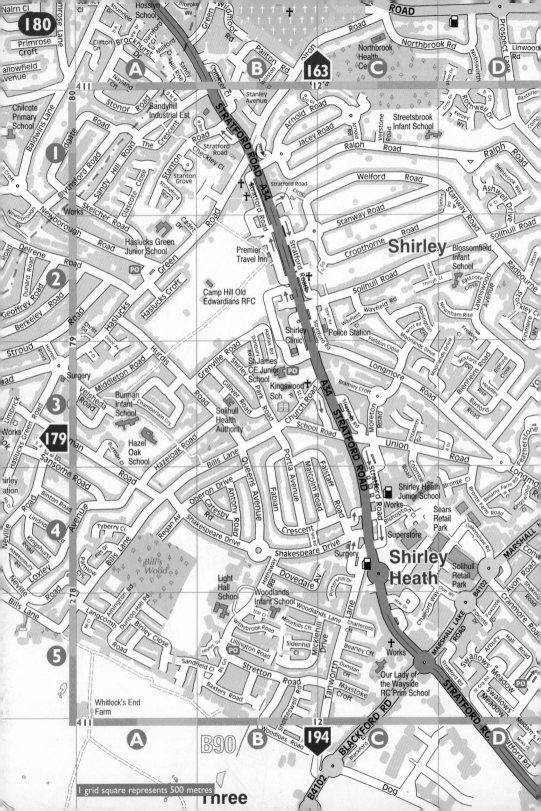

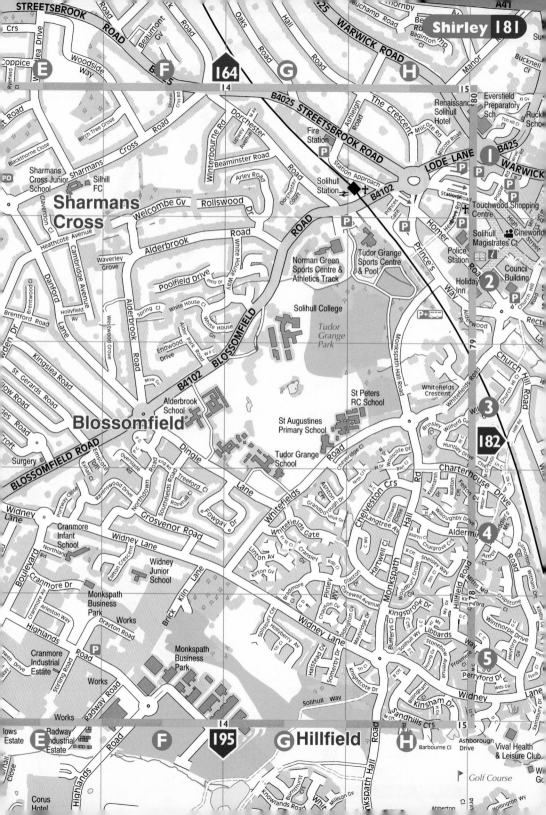

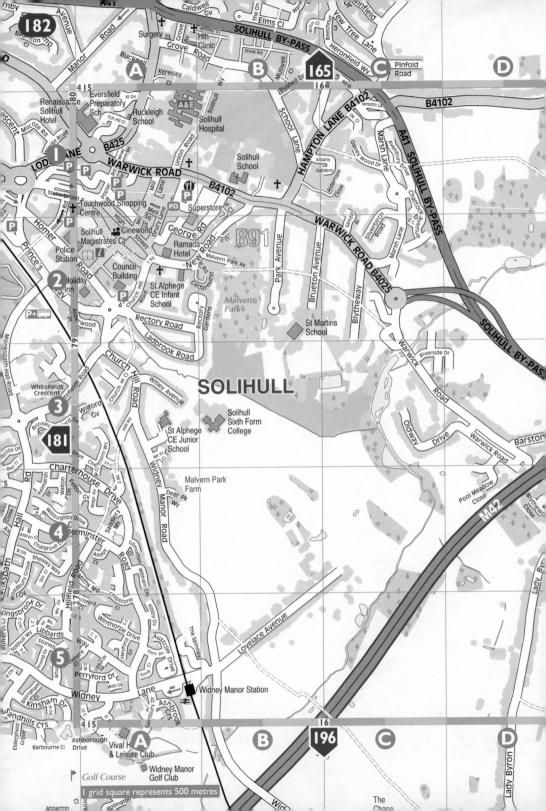

184

A B **170** C D

GATE **391** 92

Hossil Lane

I

LANE

B4188

Brookfield

Drayton RD

77

QUEENS HL

Nash La

Works

Woodfield

High St Ch

High St

Forge

PO

Pinchers

Belbroughton

Woodgate Way

Dark Lane

Yew House

HIGH ST

DRAYTON

Church Hill

RD

Church Rd

W orc

B4188

HARTLE

Hartl

The Glebe

Surgery

Belbroughton CE
First School

Drayton Villa
Farm

2

Drayton Road

Weybridge
Works

Bradford

3

Drayton
House

76

Bradford
Lane

Bradford
House

rayton

4

Hurst
Farm

Waystone
Lane

Hockley Brook Lane

5

Dordale Road

Hockley Brook Lane

Woodlands
Farm

275

391 92

**Broom
Hill**

Dordale Road

A B C D

Hockle

1 grid square represents 500 metres

Bournes

Sling Common

Gorse Farm

Gorse Green Lane

E **F** **171** **G** **H** Newtown

94

Bell Heath

STOURBRIDGE ROAD

Galtons Lane

Bell End

Stourbridge Rd

LANE

Bell Hall

Heath End Road

Chapel Lane

I

Madeley Road

Bonfire Hill

95

Mad Heat

Castle Bourne

Lane

A491

Lower Madeley Farm

2

Mearse Lane

Hagley Hill Farm

Mearse Farm

STOURBRIDGE ROAD

3

186 A491

76

Fairfield Court

Stourbridge Cl

4

Swan Lane

Fairfield

Fairfield Villa FC

Pepperwood Cl

Lane

Fairfield First School

5

B4091

PO

Wood Lane

275

94 95

E **F** **G** **H**

Monarch's Way

Pepper

Orchard Vis

Bournheath

STOURBRIDGE RO

Road

Yew Tree Lane

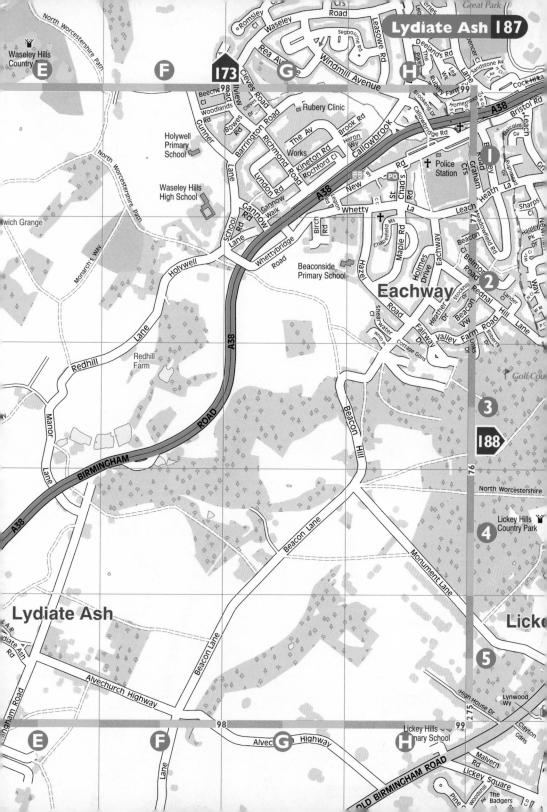

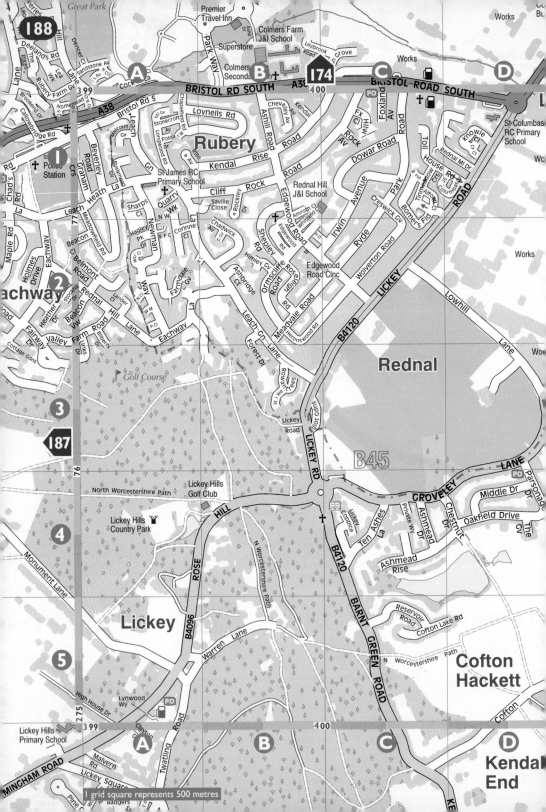

Cofton Common

Cofton Richards Farm

Upper Bittell Reservoir

Hopwoo

Grovely Farm

Longbridge Station

Albert Bradbeer Infant School

Albert Bradbeer Junior School

Cofton Medical Cen

Cofton Primary School

St John Fishers RC Primary Sch

The Westmead Hotel

North Worcestershire Path

175

190

GROVELEY LANE

LONGBRIDGE LANE

BIRMINGHAM ROAD

REDDITCH ROAD

A441

E F **177** G H

B38

Longdales Road

Primrose Hill

Lilycroft Lane

Ickfield Street

Works

Grimpits Lane

Headley Heath Lane

Hill Lane

Middle Lane

Crabmill Lane

Dark Lane

Baccabox

HOLLYWOOD

I

77

Headley Heath

† Glenfield House

Packhorse Lane

2

Ickfield Street

Bell Green Lane

Middle Lane

HOLLYWOOD

3

192

7b Oliver

Woodrush RFC

Clewshaw Lane

4

Worce

Forhill

Clewshaw Lane

PH

Lea End Lane

Forhill Ash

North Worcestershire Path

Brockhill Lane

Blackgreves Farm

5

W Gr

E F G H

Ickfield Street

Golf Course

275

Severn Way

von Dr

Ct

Church View

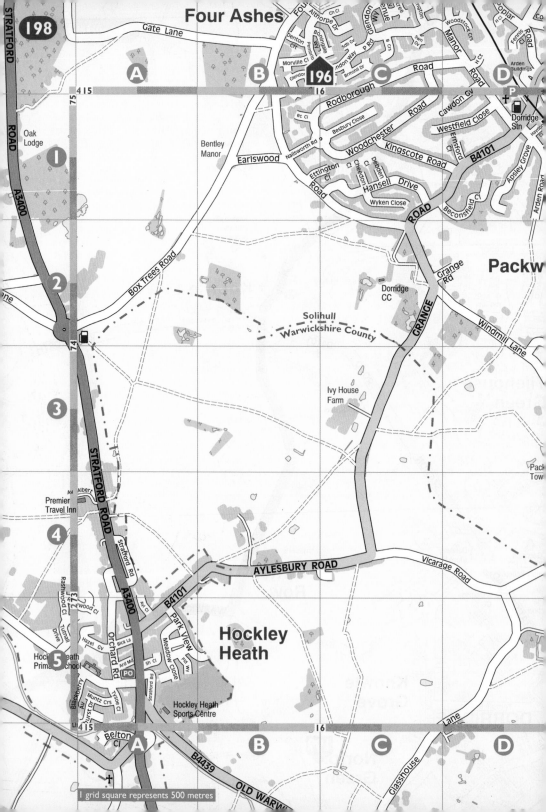

Knowle Grove

197 B9**G** Lane

E **DORRIDGE**

F

H Inkeeper's Lodge

Warwick Road

Grand Union Canal

I

Knowle Wood Road

Foxbury Dr

Woodcote Dr

Norton Green

Norton Green

Paddock Drive

Dorridge Road

Gladstone Road Walcot Green

Clyde Road

Blue Lake Road

Darley Green Road

The Ards

Arden Drive

Gullet

Parkfield

Heronbrook House

Bakers Lane

Poplar Farm

2

74

Cha Ane

3

Grand Union Canal Walk

Pool Lane

Darley Green

Packwood Road

Chessetts Wood Road

Surgery

Chessetts Wood

Valley Lane

4

273

Packwood

Chapel Lane

Valley Farm

Cheswood Grange

5

18

19

E

F

G

H

Packwood Lane

Packwood House (NT)

Chessetts Wood Road

Priory

Acock's Green ... 146 A4
Alcester Lane's End ... 160 D4
Aldridge ... 30 A4
Alum Rock ... 129 E1
Amblecote ... 118 B5
Ashmore Lake ... 39 H1
Ashmore Park ... 25 F1
Ashwood ... 98 C4
Aston ... 109 F3
Bacon's End ... 114 C5
Balls Hill ... 71 E2
Balsall Heath ... 144 A2
Banners Gate ... 60 C4
Baptist End ... 102 C3
Barr Common ... 44 C2
Bartley Green ... 157 H2
Bateman's Green ... 192 B1
Bearwood ... 124 C2
Beech Lanes ... 124 A5
Belbroughton ... 184 C5
Bell End ... 185 F1
Belle Vale ... 138 B2
Bell Heath ... 171 H5
Bentley ... 40 E2
Bentley Heath ... 196 C3
Bescot ... 56 C2
Bickenhill ... 166 D1
Bilbrook ... 11 E3
Billesley ... 162 A4
Billesley Common ... 161 G3
Bilston ... 63 C1
Birch End ... 72 A4
Birches Green ... 93 E3
Birchfield ... 90 D5
Birchills ... 41 H2
Birmingham ... 2 C7
Blackheath ... 121 H2
Black Lake ... 71 E4
Blakedown ... 168 C3
Blakeley ... 81 F1
Blakenall Heath ... 51 H1
Blakenhall ... 51 H1
Bloomfield ... 69 F5
Blossomfield ... 181 E3
Bloxwich ... 27 E1
Boldmere ... 77 E2
Bordesley ... 127 G2
Bordesley Green ... 128 C3
Bournbrook ... 143 E5
Bourne Vale ... 44 C2
Bournville ... 159 H5
Bowling Green ... 120 D1
Brades Village ... 86 B5
Bradley ... 53 H5
Bradmore ... 36 A5
Bramford ... 68 A4
Brandwood End ... 177 H1
The Bratch ... 64 D3
Brierley Hill ... 119 E2
Bristnall Fields ... 123 F1
Brockmoor ... 100 D5
Bromford ... 94 A5
Bromley ... 100 C4
Broome ... 169 G3
Broom Hill ... 184 B5
Brownhills ... 9 G4
Brown's Green ... 89 H2
Buckland End ... 112 C2
Buckpool ... 118 B2
Burnt Tree ... 85 F4
Bushbury ... 13 F4
Caldmore ... 4 B7
California ... 141 F5
Carroway Head ... 48 D1
Castle Bromwich ... 113 E1
Castlecroft ... 35 C5
Castle Vale ... 94 C3
Catherine-de-Barnes ... 166 A5
Catshill ... 19 C1
Causeway Green ... 122 D1
Chad Valley ... 125 H5
Chapman's Hill ... 172 D4
Charlemont ... 71 H4
Chattle Hill ... 97 E4
Chelmsley Wood ... 132 C3
Chessetts Wood ... 199 H3
Cheswick Green ... 195 E4
The Chuckery ... 15 C5
Churchfield ... 88 A1
Church Hill ... 56 A4
Churchill ... 168 C2
Cinder Hill ... 67 H2
Claregate ... 21 H4
Clayhanger ... 18 D1
Clent ... 171 E2
Coal Pool ... 28 B5
Codsall ... 10 B3
Cofton Common ... 189 F2
Cofton Hackett ... 188 D5
Cole End ... 115 F1
Colehall ... 112 D4
Coleshill ... 115 G3
Colton Hills ... 51 G5
Compton ... 35 H3
Coombeswood ... 139 E1
Copt Heath ... 183 E4
Coseley ... 68 C2

Cotteridge ... 159 G5
Coven Heath ... 12 C1
Cradley ... 137 G1
Cradley Heath ... 120 C4
Dam Mill ... 21 F1
Darby End ... 102 D5
Darby's Hill ... 103 H2
Darlaston ... 54 D1
Darlaston Green ... 55 G1
Darley Green ... 199 E3
Daw End ... 28 D5
Dayhouse Bank ... 172 D3
Deepfields ... 68 B2
The Delves ... 57 G4
Dickens Heath ... 194 A3
Digbeth ... 3 J6
Doe Bank ... 62 C1
Dorridge ... 197 E5
Drakes Cross ... 192 C2
Druids Heath ... 30 C1
Dudley ... 84 D4
Dudley Port ... 86 A2
Dudley's Fields ... 26 D2
Dudley Wood ... 120 C2
Dunstall Hill ... 22 D5
Eachway ... 187 H2
Edgbaston ... 142 D1
Elmdon ... 149 E4
Elmdon Heath ... 165 G3
Erdington ... 93 E3
Essington ... 14 D4
Ettingshall ... 52 D3
Ettingshall Park ... 52 B5
Eve Hill ... 84 A4
Fairfield ... 185 G5
Falcon Lodge ... 63 H2
Fallings Heath ... 55 G3
Fishley ... 17 E3
Fordbridge ... 132 A1
Fordhouses ... 12 A5
Forhill ... 191 E4
Four Ashes ... 196 A5
Four Oaks ... 46 C2
Four Oaks Park ... 46 D5
Frankley ... 157 F5
Frankley ... 175 H5
Frankley Green ... 175 F5
Frankley Hill ... 173 H2
Friar Park ... 56 D5
Garrets Green ... 130 C3
Gib Heath ... 108 A2
Giggetty ... 80 C1
Gilbertstone ... 147 F1
Gilson ... 97 E5
Glebe Farm ... 112 B5
Golds Green ... 70 C3
Goldthorn Park ... 52 B4
Gornalwood ... 83 E3
Goscote ... 28 B2
Gospel End Village ... 66 B3
Gothersley ... 116 C2
Gravelly Hill ... 92 D4
Great Barr ... 73 H1
Great Bridge ... 69 H5
Greensforge ... 98 B3
Griffins Hill ... 159 F3
Grimes Hill ... 192 D4
Grove Vale ... 73 E2
Gunstone ... 10 C1
Guns Village ... 87 E2
The Gutter ... 186 A1
Hackman's Gate ... 169 F4
Haden Cross ... 121 G4
Hagley ... 153 F4
Halesowen ... 139 E3
Hall Green ... 71 G3
Hall Green ... 163 E3
Hampton in Arden ... 167 F3
Hamstead ... 73 G3
Handsworth ... 89 F4
Handsworth Wood ... 90 B3
Harborne ... 141 G1
Harden ... 28 B3
Hardwick ... 45 F3
Hartle ... 184 D2
Hart's Hill ... 101 G4
Harvills Hawthorn ... 70 B4
Hasbury ... 138 A4
Hasluck's Green ... 179 G3
Hateley Heath ... 71 G5
Hawkesley ... 176 C5
Hawne ... 138 C2
Hayley Green ... 154 C1
Hay Mills ... 146 B1
Headley Heath ... 191 G1
Heath End ... 28 B1
Heath Town ... 38 A1
Highbridge ... 18 A1
Highbury Park ... 160 D1
Highgate ... 127 F4
High Heath ... 18 C5
High Heath ... 48 D5
Highter's Heath ... 178 D3
Hill ... 47 E1
Hillfield ... 195 G1
Hill Hook ... 32 C4
Hill Top ... 71 E3

Hill Wood ... 33 G5
Himley ... 81 F3
Hinksford ... 98 D1
Hockley Heath ... 198 B5
Hodgehill ... 111 H4
Holly Bank ... 19 H4
Hollywood ... 178 D5
Holy Cross ... 170 C3
Hook End ... 167 H5
Hopwood ... 190 A5
Horseley Heath ... 86 A1
Hunnington ... 155 H3
Hurst Green ... 122 D4
Hurst Hill ... 67 H3
Illey ... 156 C2
Kates Hill ... 85 E5
Kineton Green ... 163 H2
King's Heath ... 161 E3
King's Hill ... 55 H5
Kingshurst ... 114 A2
King's Norton ... 176 C3
Kingstanding ... 75 G2
Kingswinford ... 99 F3
Kitt's Green ... 113 E5
Kitwell ... 157 E3
Knowle ... 197 G2
Knowle Grove ... 197 F5
The Knowle ... 103 G4
Ladywood ... 126 A2
Lambert's End ... 87 E3
Lane Green ... 11 E4
Lane Head ... 26 A4
Lanesfield ... 53 E4
Langley ... 104 D4
Langley Green ... 105 F5
Lapal ... 139 H4
Lawns Wood ... 117 F1
Lea End ... 190 D5
Lea Hall ... 130 C2
Leamore ... 27 E4
Lee Bank ... 126 C4
Leighswood ... 30 A2
Ley Hill ... 47 E4
Lickey ... 188 A5
Lifford ... 177 F1
Little Aston ... 32 A5
Little Bloxwich ... 17 F4
Little Bromwich ... 128 D2
Little Hay ... 33 G1
Little Norton ... 8 B2
Little Packington ... 149 H4
Littleworth End ... 49 E5
Lode Heath ... 165 E4
Lodge Hill ... 141 H5
Londonderry ... 105 G5
London Fields ... 83 G4
Longbridge ... 188 D1
Lower Bradley ... 54 B4
Lower Clent ... 170 B1
Lower Gornal ... 83 G2
Lower Illey ... 156 C3
Low Hill ... 25 F3
Lozells ... 108 C2
The Lunt ... 54 C1
Lutley ... 137 F5
Lydiate Ash ... 187 E5
Lye ... 117 G4
Lyndon Green ... 130 B5
Madeley Heath ... 186 A1
Major's Green ... 179 F5
Maney ... 62 B4
Marston Green ... 132 A4
Maw Green ... 56 B1
Mayer's Green ... 88 A3
Mere Green ... 47 F2
Merridale ... 36 A5
Merry Hill ... 50 C1
Merry Hill ... 119 H1
Mesty Croft ... 56 A4
Middle Bickenhill ... 150 C4
Mill Green ... 31 C5
MilWorth ... 95 E1
Monkspath ... 195 G5
Monmore Green ... 38 B5
Moor Hall ... 47 H4
Moseley ... 38 B4
Moseley ... 144 B5
Moxley ... 54 D4
Mushroom Green ... 120 B3
Nechells ... 110 B1
Nechells Green ... 109 H5
Netherton ... 102 B4
Newbolds ... 24 C2
Newbridge ... 35 H2
New Invention ... 26 A2
New Oscott ... 76 B1
Newton ... 73 E3
New Town ... 9 H2
New Town ... 86 B2
Newtown ... 16 C2
Newtown ... 108 C4
Northfield ... 175 H1
Norton ... 135 E5
Norton Green ... 199 F1
Oakham ... 103 F2
Ocker Hill ... 70 A2
Oldbury ... 105 E4

Old Fallings ... 23 H3
Old Hill ... 121 G3
Old Perton ... 34 A2
Old Swinford ... 135 G4
Olton ... 147 G5
Orton Hill ... 65 E1
Ounsdale ... 64 D5
Overend ... 138 A1
Over Green ... 79 H2
Oxbarn ... 51 E1
Oxley ... 22 D2
Packwood ... 199 E4
Packwood Gullet ... 198 D2
Palfrey ... 56 D2
Palmers Cross ... 21 F2
Parkfield ... 52 D3
Park Village ... 23 H5
Pedmore ... 153 F2
Pelsall ... 18 B4
Pelsall Wood ... 8 D5
Pendeford ... 11 C5
Penn ... 51 E2
Pennsett ... 100 D2
Perry Barr ... 90 B1
Perry Beeches ... 74 A3
Perry Common ... 75 H5
Perton ... 34 C1
Pheasey ... 59 G4
Pleck ... 56 B2
Portobello ... 39 E3
Portway ... 104 A3
Prestwood ... 116 C3
Priestfield ... 53 F2
Primrose Hill ... 102 D5
Princes End ... 69 G2
Pype Hayes ... 93 H1
Quarry Bank ... 119 H4
Queslett ... 74 C1
Quinton ... 140 A1
Reddicap Heath ... 63 G4
Rednal ... 188 C3
Ridgacre ... 140 C1
Romsley ... 172 C1
Romsley Hill ... 172 C3
Rood End ... 105 G3
Roseville ... 68 A3
Rotten Row ... 197 G4
Rotton Park ... 107 G5
Roughley ... 47 G2
Round Oak ... 101 G5
Round's Green ... 104 C5
Rowley Regis ... 103 H4
Rubery ... 188 A1
Ruiton ... 83 F2
Rumbow Cottages ... 171 H2
Rumbush ... 193 G5
Rushall ... 29 E3
Russell's Hall ... 101 G1
Saltley ... 110 C5
Sandwell ... 106 C3
Scotlands ... 24 C2
Sedgley ... 67 G2
Selly Oak ... 159 F1
Selly Park ... 160 A1
Shard End ... 113 F4
Sharmans Cross ... 181 E1
Sheldon ... 147 H2
Shelfield ... 29 E2
Shenley Fields ... 158 A3
Shenstone Woodend ... 33 E1
Shire Oak ... 19 F2
Shire Oak Hill ... 19 H2
Shirley ... 180 C2
Shirley Heath ... 180 C4
Short Cross ... 138 C3
Short Heath ... 26 C4
Short Heath ... 76 D5
Silver End ... 118 D5
Silver Street ... 192 A3
Small Heath ... 128 B5
Smestow ... 80 A2
Smethwick ... 106 A4
Soho ... 107 E5
Solihull ... 182 A3
Solihull Lodge ... 179 E3
South Yardley ... 146 D1
Sparkbrook ... 127 H5
Sparkhill ... 145 E4
Springfield ... 7 K1
Springfield ... 103 F4
Springfield ... 162 A1
Springhill ... 15 H2
Spring Hill ... 50 C4
Stakenbridge ... 168 D2
Stambermill ... 136 A2
Stechford ... 130 A1
Stirchley ... 160 A3
Stockfield ... 146 C3
Stockland Green ... 92 A2
Stockwell End ... 22 D2
Stonebridge ... 150 D5
Stone Cross ... 71 H2
Stourbridge ... 134 D5
Stourton ... 116 D5
Stow Lawn ... 38 D5
The Straits ... 82 D1
Streetly ... 45 H4

Stubber's Green ... 29
Summer Hill ... 69
Sutton Coldfield ... 62
Swan Village ... 69
Swindon ... 80
Tansley Hill ... 103
Tat Bank ... 105
Ten Acres ... 160
Tettenhall ... 21
Tettenhall Wood ... 35
Thimble End ... 78
Three Maypoles ... 194
Tidbury Green ... 193
Tile Cross ... 131
Tilehouse Green ... 197
Tipton ... 69
Tipton Green ... 68
Tividale ... 85
Toll End ... 69
Trueman's Heath ... 193
Trysull ... 64
Tudor Hill ... 62
Turves Green ... 175
Tyburn ... 94
Tyseley ... 146
Ulverley Green ... 164
Upper Gornal ... 67
Upper Witton ... 76
Vauxhall ... 127
Vigo ... 19
The Village ... 100
Wake Green ... 161
Walker's Heath ... 177
Wallbrook ... 68
Wall Heath ... 99
Wallington Heath ... 16
Walmley ... 77
Walmley Ash ... 78
Walsall ... 5
Walsall Wood ... 18
Walton Pool ... 171
Ward End ... 111
Warley Woods ... 124
Warstock ... 179
Washwood Heath ... 110
Water Orton ... 96
Watford Gap ... 32
Wednesbury ... 70
Wednesbury Oak ... 69
Wednesfield ... 38
Weoley Castle ... 158
Wergs ... 20
West Bromwich ... 87
Westcroft ... 13
West Hagley ... 152
West Heath ... 190
Whitehouse Gate ... 104
Whitehouse Common ... 63
Whitlock's End ... 193
Wightwick ... 34
Wildmoor ... 186
Willenhall ... 38
Winson Green ... 107
Withymoor Village ... 119
Witton ... 91
Wollaston ... 133
Wollescote ... 136
Wolverhampton ... 7
Wombourne ... 64
Woodcock Hill ... 158
Woodgate ... 156
Woodgate Valley ... 140
Wood Green ... 56
Wood Hayes ... 24
Woods Bank ... 55
Woodsetton ... 67
Woodside ... 101
The Woods ... 56
Wordsley ... 118
Worlds End ... 164
Wylde Green ... 77
Yardley ... 129
Yardley Wood ... 162
Yew Tree ... 57

USING THE STREET INDEX

Street names are listed alphabetically. Each street name is followed by its postal town or area locality, the Postcode District, the page number, and the reference to the square in which the name is found.

Standard index entries are shown as follows:

Abberley Cl *HALE* B63 .... **138** B5

Street names and selected addresses not shown on the map due to scale restrictions are shown in the index with an asterisk:

Aaron Manby Ct *TPTN/OCK* DY4 *..**69** F3

ENERAL ABBREVIATIONS

C ACCESS
/ ALLEY
APPROACH
ARCADE
S ASSOCIATION
AVENUE
H BEACH
DS BUILDINGS
D BEND
K BANK
BRIDGE
K BROOK
M BOTTOM
S BUSINESS
D BOULEVARD
BYPASS
TH CATHEDRAL
M CEMETERY
N CENTRE
T CROFT
CHURCH
A CHASE
YD CHURCHYARD
R CIRCLE
RC CIRCUS
CLOSE
FS CLIFFS
P CAMP
R CORNER
COUNTY
LL COLLEGE
M COMMON
MM COMMISSION
N CONVENT
T COTTAGE
TS COTTAGES
CAPE
S COPSE
CREEK
EM CREMATORIUM
S CRESCENT
VY CAUSEWAY
COURT
RL CENTRAL
S COURTS
CTYD COURTYARD
CUTT CUTTINGS
CV COVE
CYN CANYON
DEPT DEPARTMENT
DL DALE
DM DAM
DR DRIVE
DRO DROVE
DRY DRIVEWAY
DWGS DWELLINGS
E EAST
EMB EMBANKMENT
EMBY EMBASSY
ESP ESPLANADE
EST ESTATE
EX EXCHANGE
EXPY EXPRESSWAY
EXT EXTENSION
F/O FLYOVER
FC FOOTBALL CLUB
FK FORK
FLD FIELD
FLDS FIELDS
FLS FALLS
FM FARM
FT FORT
FTS FLATS
FWY FREEWAY
FY FERRY
GA GATE
GAL GALLERY
GDN GARDEN
GDNS GARDENS
GLD GLADE
GLN GLEN
GN GREEN
GND GROUND
GRA GRANGE
GRG GARAGE
GT GREAT
GTWY GATEWAY
GV GROVE
HGR HIGHER
HL HILL
HLS HILLS
HO HOUSE
HOL HOLLOW
HOSP HOSPITAL
HRB HARBOUR
HTH HEATH
HTS HEIGHTS
HVN HAVEN
HWY HIGHWAY
IMP IMPERIAL
IN INLET
IND EST INDUSTRIAL ESTATE
INF INFIRMARY
INFO INFORMATION
INT INTERCHANGE
IS ISLAND
JCT JUNCTION
JTY JETTY
KG KING
KNL KNOLL
L LAKE
LA LANE
LDG LODGE
LGT LIGHT
LK LOCK
LKS LAKES
LNDG LANDING
LTL LITTLE
LWR LOWER
MAG MAGISTRATE
MAN MANSIONS
MD MEAD
MDW MEADOWS
MEM MEMORIAL
MI MILL
MKT MARKET
MKTS MARKETS
ML MALL
MNR MANOR
MS MEWS
MSN MISSION
MT MOUNT
MTN MOUNTAIN
MTS MOUNTAINS
MUS MUSEUM
MWY MOTORWAY
N NORTH
NE NORTH EAST
NW NORTH WEST
O/P OVERPASS
OFF OFFICE
ORCH ORCHARD
OV OVAL
PAL PALACE
PAS PASSAGE
PAV PAVILION
PDE PARADE
PH PUBLIC HOUSE
PK PARK
PKWY PARKWAY
PL PLACE
PLN PLAIN
PLNS PLAINS
PLZ PLAZA
POL POLICE STATION
PR PRINCE
PREC PRECINCT
PREP PREPARATORY
PRIM PRIMARY
PROM PROMENADE
PRS PRINCESS
PRT PORT
PT POINT
PTH PATH
PZ PIAZZA
QD QUADRANT
QU QUEEN
QY QUAY
R RIVER
RBT ROUNDABOUT
RD ROAD
RDG RIDGE
REP REPUBLIC
RES RESERVOIR
RFC RUGBY FOOTBALL CLUB
RI RISE
RP RAMP
RW ROW
S SOUTH
SCH SCHOOL
SE SOUTH EAST
SER SERVICE AREA
SH SHORE
SHOP SHOPPING
SKWY SKYWAY
SMT SUMMIT
SOC SOCIETY
SP SPUR
SPR SPRING
SQ SQUARE
ST STREET
STN STATION
STR STREAM
STRD STRAND
SW SOUTH WEST
TDG TRADING
TER TERRACE
THWY THROUGHWAY
TNL TUNNEL
TOLL TOLLWAY
TPK TURNPIKE
TR TRACK
TRL TRAIL
TWR TOWER
U/P UNDERPASS
UNI UNIVERSITY
UPR UPPER
V VALE
VA VALLEY
VIAD VIADUCT
VIL VILLA
VIS VISTA
VLG VILLAGE
VLS VILLAS
VW VIEW
W WEST
WD WOOD
WHF WHARF
WK WALK
WKS WALKS
WLS WELLS
WY WAY
YD YARD
YHA YOUTH HOSTEL

OSTCODE TOWNS AND AREA ABBREVIATIONS

GN Acock's Green
DR Aldridge
E/KHTH/YWD Alcester Lane's End/King's Heath/Yardley Wood
E Alvechurch
/WIT Aston/Witton
MR/CCFT Bradmore/Castlecroft
D/HDSWWD Birchfield/Handsworth Wood
AMNEC Birmingham N.E.C.
TH/HG Balsall Heath/Highgate
S/COS Bilston/Coseley
DE/SHDE Buckland End/Shard End
IL/PFLD Blakenhall/Priestfield
HTH/ROWR Blackheath/Rowley Regis
X/PEL Bloxwich/Pelsall
TWD Burntwood
RD Bordesley
RVE Bromsgrove east
RVW Bromsgrove west
YHL Brierley Hill
VNH Brownhills
LLE Bournville
CBHAM Central Birmingham
CBHAMNE Central Birmingham northeast
CBHAMNW Central Birmingham northwest
CBHAMW Central Birmingham west
CBROM Castle Bromwich
CDSL Codsall
CDYHTH Cradley Heath
CHWD/FDBR/MGN Chelmsley Wood/Fordbridge/Marston Green
CNCK/NC Cannock/Norton Canes
COVEN Coven
CSCFLD/WYGN Central Sutton Coldfield/Wylde Green
CSHL/WTROR Coleshill/Water Orton
CVALE Castle Vale
DARL/WED Darlaston/Wednesbury
DIG/EDG Digbeth/Edgbaston
DOR/KN Dorridge/Knowle
DSYBK/YTR Daisy Bank/Yew Tree
DUDN Dudley north
DUDS Dudley south
DUNHL/THL/PER Dunstall Hill/Tettenhall/Perton
EDG Edgbaston
ERDE/BCHGN Erdington east/Birches Green
ERDW/GRVHL Erdington west/Gravelly Hill
ETTPK/GDPK/PENN Ettingshall Park/Goldthorn Park/Penn
FOAKS/STRLY Four Oaks/Streetly
GTB/HAM Great Barr/Hamstead
GTWY Great Wyrley
HAG/WOL Hagley/Wollescote
HALE Halesowen
HDSW Handsworth
HHTH/SAND Hateley Heath/Sandwell
HIA/OLT Hampton in Arden/Olton
HLGN/YWD Hall Green/Yardley Wood
HLYWD Hollywood
HOCK/TIA Hockley Heath/Tanworth-in-Arden
HRBN Harborne
HWK/WKHTH Hawkesley/Walker's Heath
KGSTG Kingstanding
KGSWFD Kingswinford
KIDD Kidderminster
KINVER Kinver
LDYWD/EDGR Ladywood/Edgbaston Reservoir
LGLYGN/QTN Langley Green/Quinton
LGN/SDN/BHAMAIR Lyndon Green/Sheldon/Birmingham Airport
LICHS Lichfield south
LOZ/NWT Lozells/Newtown
MGN/WHC Mere Green/Whitehouse Common
MOS/BIL Moseley/Billesley
NFLD/LBR Northfield/Longbridge
OLDBY Oldbury
PBAR/PBCH Perry Bar/Perry Beeches
POL/KGSB/FAZ Polesworth/Kingsbury/Fazeley
RBRY Rubery
RCOVN/BALC/EX Rural Coventry north/Balsall Common/Exhall
RIDG/WDGT Ridgacre/Woodgate
RMSLY Romsley
RUSH/SHEL Rushall/Shelfield
SCFLD/BOLD Sutton Coldfield/Boldmere
SEDG Sedgley
SHHTH Short Heath
SHLY Shirley
SLYOAK Selly Oak
SMHTH Small Heath
SMTHWK Smethwick
SMTHWKW Smethwick west
SOLH Solihull
SPARK Sparkhill/Sparkbrook
STETCH Stetchford
STRBR Stourbridge
TPTN/OCK Tipton/Ocker Hill
VAUX/NECH Vauxhall/Nechells
WALM/CURD Walmley/Curdworth
WASH/WDE Washwood Heath/Ward End
WBROM West Bromwich
WLNHL Willenhall
WMBN Wombourne
WNSFLD Wednesfield
WOLV Wolverhampton
WOLVN Wolverhampton north
WSL Walsall
WSLW Walsall west
WSNGN Winson Green
YDLY Yardley

Index - streets

A

on Manby Ct
TPTN/OCK DY4 * 69 F3
oerley Cl HALE B63 138 B5
oerley Rd
LGLYGN/QTN B68 123 F4
SEDG DY3 83 E2
oerley St DUDS DY2 102 C1
SMTHWK B66 107 F4
oerton Cl HALE B63 139 E4
oerton Gv SHLY B90 195 H1
oess Gv YDLY B25 130 A3
oey Cl HHTH/SAND B71 87 G1
oey Crs HALE B63 137 H3
LGLYGN/QTN B68 123 H3
oeydale Rd NFLD/LBR B31 175 G3
oey Dr BLOX/PEL WS3 18 A2
oeyfield Rd
ERDW/GRVHL B23 76 C3
WOLVN WV10 13 E3
oey Rd DUDS DY2 102 D3
ERDW/GRVHL B23 92 B4
HALE B63 137 G3
HRBN B17 142 B2
EDG DY3 83 E3
MTHWKW B67 123 H3
ey Sq BLOX/PEL WS3 16 A5
ey St SEDG DY3 83 E3
WSNGN B18 108 A4
ey St North WSNGN B18 108 A4
ot Rd HALE B63 154 C2
ots Cl DOR/KN B93 197 E1
RUSH/SHEL WS4 29 E4
otsford Av GTB/HAM B43 73 H1
otsford Dr DUDN DY1 101 G2
tsford Rd SPARK B11 145 E1
ots Ms BRLYHL DY5 119 F3
Abbots Rd
ALE/KHTH/YWD B14 161 E3
Abbots Wy BDMR/CCFT WV3 36 A4
WSNGN B18 108 B3
Abbotts Pl BLOX/PEL WS3 27 H1
Abbotts Rd ERDE/BCHGN B24 92 D5
Abbotts St BLOX/PEL WS3 17 F5
Abdon Av SLYOAK B29 158 D3
Aberdeen St WSNGN B18 107 G5
Aberford Cl SHHTH WV12 40 B1
Abigails Cl
LGN/SDN/BHAMAIR B26 130 D5
Abingdon Cl WOLV WV1 38 B3
Abingdon Rd BLOX/PEL WS3 16 B5
DUDS DY2 120 D1
ERDW/GRVHL B23 75 H4
WOLV WV1 38 B3
Abingdon Wy BLOX/PEL WS3 16 B5
CVALE B35 94 C3
Ablewell St WSL WS1 5 F4
Ablow St BKHL/PFLD WV2 6 E7
Abney Dr BILS/COS WV14 67 H2
Aboyne Cl DIG/EDG B5 143 H1
Ab Rw CBHAMNE B4 3 K3
Acacia Av
CHWD/FDBR/MGN B37 113 H3
DSYBK/YTR WS5 57 G4
Acacia Cl
CHWD/FDBR/MGN B37 113 H3
DUDN DY1 84 A3
OLDBY B69 85 H4
Acacia Crs CDSL WV8 10 D4
Acacia Dr BILS/COS WV14 68 A4
Acacia Rd BVILLE B30 159 G2
Accord Ms DARL/WED WS10 55 F1
Acfold Rd BFLD/HDSWWD B20 89 G1
Acheson Rd HLGN/YWD B28 179 H2
Ackleton Gdns
BDMR/CCFT WV3 51 F1
Ackleton Gv SLYOAK B29 158 B2
Acorn Cl ACGN B27 146 B2
BVILLE B30 159 G2
WBROM B70 87 F4
Acorn Gdns SLYOAK B29 160 A2
Acorn Gv CBHAMW B1 2 A4
CDSL WV8 10 A5
STRBR DY8 118 A3
Acorn Rd RMSLY B62 122 A4
WNSFLD WV11 25 G1
Acorn St WLNHL WV13 40 A3
Acre Ri SHHTH WV12 25 H5
Acres Rd BRLYHL DY5 119 G4
Acton Dr SEDG DY3 82 D3
Acton Gv BILS/COS WV14 53 F4
KGSTG B44 75 G1
Adams Brook Dr
RIDG/WDGT B32 157 F1
Adams Cl SMTHWK B66 105 H2
TPTN/OCK DY4 69 F2
Adam's Hl HAG/WOL DY9 170 C1
RIDG/WDGT B32 157 G1
Adams Rd BDMR/CCFT WV3 50 C1
BRWNH WS8 19 G2
Adams St VAUX/NECH B7 3 K1
WBROM B70 87 E3
WSLW WS2 4 B2
Ada Rd SMTHWK B66 124 D1
YDLY B25 146 B1
Ada Wrighton Cl SHHTH WV12 26 A3
Addenbrooke Dr
SCFLD/BOLD B73 77 F1
Addenbrooke Rd
SMTHWKW B67 124 B1
Addenbrooke St
BLOX/PEL WS3 27 G3
DARL/WED WS10 40 B5
Addenbrook Wy
TPTN/OCK DY4 70 B3
Adderley Gdns
WASH/WDE B8 110 B5
Adderley Park Cl
WASH/WDE B8 * 110 C5
Adderley Rd WASH/WDE B8 128 A1
Adderley Rd South
WASH/WDE B8 128 A1
Adderley St BORD B9 127 G3
Addington Wy OLDBY B69 86 B3
Addison Cl DARL/WED WS10 72 A1
Addison Cft SEDG DY3 82 C1
Addison Gv WNSFLD WV11 24 B1
Addison Pl BILS/COS WV14 54 B1
CSHL/WTROR B46 96 B3
Addison Rd
ALE/KHTH/YWD B14 161 F3
BDMR/CCFT WV3 36 B5
BRLYHL DY5 118 D2
DARL/WED WS10 72 A1
VAUX/NECH B7 110 A1
Addison St DARL/WED WS10 70 D1
Addison Ter DARL/WED WS10 * 70 D1
Adelaide Av WBROM B70 71 E4
Adelaide St BHTH/HG B12 127 F4
BRLYHL DY5 119 F1
Adelaide Wk BKHL/PFLD WV2 7 J7
Adey Rd WNSFLD WV11 25 F2
Adkins La SMTHWKW B67 124 B3
Admington Rd STETCH B33 131 E4
Admiral Pl MOS/BIL B13 144 B3
Admirals Wy
BLKHTH/ROWR B65 121 H2
Adrian Cft MOS/BIL B13 162 A1
Adria Rd SPARK B11 144 D3
Adshead Rd DUDS DY2 102 C2
Adstone Gv NFLD/LBR B31 175 G4
Advent Gdns WBROM B70 * 87 F3
Adwalton Rd
DUNHL/THL/PER WV6 34 D2
Agenoria Dr STRBR DY8 135 F2
Ainsdale Cl STRBR DY8 135 F5
Ainsdale Gdns HALE B63 137 H5
Ainsworth Rd WOLVN WV10 13 E3
Aintree Gv BKDE/SHDE B34 113 F3
Aintree Rd WOLVN WV10 12 D3
Aintree Wy DUDN DY1 83 G4
Aire Cft NFLD/LBR B31 175 H4
Airfield Dr ALDR WS9 43 G2
Airport Wy HIA/OLT B92 149 G4
Akrill Cl WBROM B70 * 87 F1
The Akrill Cottage Homes
WBROM B70 * 87 F1
Alamein Rd WLNHL WV13 39 E4
Albany Crs BILS/COS WV14 53 G2
Albany Gdns SOLH B91 182 B1
Albany Gv KGSWFD DY6 100 A2
WNSFLD WV11 26 A1
Albany Rd HRBN B17 142 A1
Albemarle Rd STRBR DY8 135 F5
Albermarle Rd KGSWFD DY6 100 C4
Albert Av BHTH/HG B12 144 C1
Albert Clarke Dr SHHTH WV12 26 A3
Albert Cl CDSL WV8 10 A3
Albert Dr HALE B63 138 B5
SEDG DY3 80 C4
Albert Rd ALE/KHTH/YWD B14 161 F3
AST/WIT B6 109 E2
DUNHL/THL/PER WV6 6 A1
ERDW/GRVHL B23 92 B3
HALE B63 138 B5
HDSW B21 89 G5
HRBN B17 141 H2
LGLYGN/QTN B68 123 G4
STETCH B33 129 H1
Albert St BRLYHL DY5 101 F2
DARL/WED WS10 70 C1
DIG/EDG B5 3 J4
HAG/WOL DY9 136 C2
KGSWFD DY6 99 F1
OLDBY B69 105 E1
STRBR DY8 135 F2
TPTN/OCK DY4 69 F3

WBROM B70 87 G5
WSLW WS2 4 E2
Albert St East OLDBY B69 105 F2
Albion Av WLNHL WV13 40 A3
Albion Field Dr
HHTH/SAND B71 87 H2
Albion Industrial Est
WBROM B70 86 D4
Albion Rd BRWNH WS8 9 E4
HDSW B21 89 F5
HHTH/SAND B71 106 C1
SPARK B11 145 F2
WBROM B70 86 D4
Albion St BILS/COS WV14 54 A2
BRLYHL DY5 119 F1
CBHAMW B1 2 B3
KGSWFD DY6 99 F1
OLDBY B69 86 C5
TPTN/OCK DY4 85 F1
WLNHL WV13 39 H3
WOLV WV1 7 H4
Alborn Crs HWK/WKHTH B38 176 B5
Albrighton Rd HALE B63 138 A4
Albright Rd LGLYGN/QTN B68 105 H5
Albury Wk SPARK B11 127 G5
Albutts Rd CNCK/NC WS11 8 B1
Alcester Dr SCFLD/BOLD B73 61 F5
WLNHL WV13 38 D5
Alcester Rd HLYWD B47 192 B4
MOS/BIL B13 144 B4
Alcester Rd South
ALE/KHTH/YWD B14 178 B4
Alcester St BHTH/HG B12 127 F4
Alcombe Gv STETCH B33 130 A2
Alcott Cl DOR/KN B93 198 D1
Alcott Gv STETCH B33 131 F1
Alcott La
CHWD/FDBR/MGN B37 131 H4
The Alcove BLOX/PEL WS3 17 F5
Aldbourne Wy
HWK/WKHTH B38 190 B1
Aldbury Rd
ALE/KHTH/YWD B14 178 C3
Aldeburgh Cl BLOX/PEL WS3 16 C4
Aldeford Dr BRLYHL DY5 119 F4
Alderbrook Cl SEDG DY3 66 D2
Alderbrook Rd SOLH B91 181 F2
Alder Cl HLYWD B47 192 D2
WALM/CURD B76 78 A4
Alder Coppice SEDG DY3 52 A5
Alder Crs DSYBK/YTR WS5 57 H4
Alder Dl BDMR/CCFT WV3 36 A4
Alderdale Av SEDG DY3 52 A5
Alderdale Crs HIA/OLT B92 165 G3
Alder Dr
CHWD/FDBR/MGN B37 132 B3
Alderflat Pl VAUX/NECH B7 110 A4
Alderford Cl CDSL WV8 22 B2
Alder Gv RMSLY B62 139 G1
Alderham Cl SOLH B91 182 C1
Alderhithe Gv
FOAKS/STRLY B74 45 H2
Alder La BVILLE B30 159 E4
Alderlea Cl STRBR DY8 135 G5
Alderley Crs BLOX/PEL WS3 28 A5
Alderminster Rd SOLH B91 181 H4
Aldermore Dr MGN/WHC B75 * 63 F2
Alderney Gdns
HWK/WKHTH B38 176 B4
Alder Park Rd SOLH B91 181 F3
Alderpits Rd BKDE/SHDE B34 113 F3
Alder Rd DARL/WED WS10 56 A2
KGSWFD DY6 100 C4
MOS/BIL B13 144 C3
Aldersea Dr AST/WIT B6 109 F2
Aldershaw Rd
LGN/SDN/BHAMAIR B26 147 E2
Aldershaws SHLY B90 194 A3
Aldersley Av
DUNHL/THL/PER WV6 22 A3
Aldersley Cl
DUNHL/THL/PER WV6 22 B3
Aldersley Rd
DUNHL/THL/PER WV6 22 B5
Aldersmead Rd NFLD/LBR B31 176 A4
Alderson Rd WASH/WDE B8 110 D5
The Alders RMSLY B62 172 B1
Alderton Cl SOLH B91 181 H4
Alderton Dr BDMR/CCFT WV3 36 A5
Alder Wy FOAKS/STRLY B74 45 E5
Alderwood Pl SOLH B91 181 H2
Alderwood Ri SEDG DY3 83 F1
Aldgate Dr BRLYHL DY5 119 E5
Aldgate Gv LOZ/NWT B19 108 D4
Aldis Cl HLGN/YWD B28 162 C1
WSLW WS2 * 56 A1
Aldis Rd WSLW WS2 56 A1
Aldridge By-Pass ALDR WS9 30 A4
Aldridge Cl LGLYGN/QTN B68 105 G5
STRBR DY8 118 A4
Aldridge Rd ALDR WS9 31 G5
FOAKS/STRLY B74 44 D5
KGSTG B44 74 C1
LGLYGN/QTN B68 123 F4
RUSH/SHEL WS4 42 D2
Aldridge St DARL/WED WS10 55 F1
Aldwych Cl ALDR WS9 30 B2
Aldwyck Dr BDMR/CCFT WV3 35 E5
Alexander Gdns
PBAR/PBCH B42 90 D3
Alexander Hl BRLYHL DY5 119 H4
Alexander Rd ACGN B27 146 B3
CDSL WV8 11 E4
SMTHWKW B67 124 A2
WSLW WS2 40 D3
Alexander Ter
SMTHWKW B67 * 106 B3
Alexander Wy WASH/WDE B8 128 D1
Alexandra Av HDSW B21 107 F2
Alexandra Crs HHTH/SAND B71 72 A3
Alexandra Pl BILS/COS WV14 53 H2
Alexandra Rd BVILLE B30 160 A3
DARL/WED WS10 55 G2
DIG/EDG B5 144 A1
ETTPK/GDPK/PENN WV4 51 G3
HALE B63 138 B4
HDSW B21 107 F2
TPTN/OCK DY4 85 G1
WSL WS1 57 E3
Alexandra St BDMR/CCFT WV3 6 D5
DUDN DY1 84 B5
Alexandra Wy ALDR WS9 30 B5
OLDBY B69 85 G4
Alford Cl RBRY B45 188 C1
Alfreda Av HLYWD B47 178 B5
Alfred Rd HDSW B21 107 G1
SPARK B11 144 D2
Alfred St ALE/KHTH/YWD B14 161 F3
AST/WIT B6 109 H1
BHTH/HG B12 144 D2
BLOX/PEL WS3 27 F1
DARL/WED WS10 55 E3
SMTHWK B66 106 D2
WBROM B70 87 H2
Algernon Rd
LDYWD/EDGR B16 107 F5
Alice St BILS/COS WV14 53 H2
Alison Cl TPTN/OCK DY4 69 G1
Alison Dr STRBR DY8 135 E5
Alison Rd RMSLY B62 139 G4
Allan Cl STRBR DY8 118 B3
Allbut St CDYHTH B64 120 D3
Allcock St BORD B9 127 G3
TPTN/OCK DY4 70 A3
Allcroft Rd SPARK B11 145 H5
Allenby Cl KGSWFD DY6 100 C4
Allen Cl GTB/HAM B43 73 G4
Allendale Gv GTB/HAM B43 73 G3
Allendale Rd WALM/CURD B76 78 A3
YDLY B25 129 F5
Allen Dr DARL/WED WS10 55 E2
WBROM B70 88 B5
Allen Rd DARL/WED WS10 55 H3
TPTN/OCK DY4 69 F2
Allens Av WSNGN B18 * 107 H3
Allens Cl SHHTH WV12 25 H5
Allens Croft Rd
ALE/KHTH/YWD B14 160 B5
Allens Farm Rd NFLD/LBR B31 174 D2
Allens La BLOX/PEL WS3 17 H5
Allens Rd WSNGN B18 107 H3
Allen St WBROM B70 87 F3
Allerdale Rd BRWNH WS8 19 E1
Allerton La HHTH/SAND B71 71 G3
Allerton Rd YDLY B25 129 F5
Allesley Cl FOAKS/STRLY B74 62 C1
Allesley Rd HIA/OLT B92 163 H2
Allesley St AST/WIT B6 109 E4
Alleston Rd WOLVN WV10 23 F1
Alleyne Gv ERDE/BCHGN B24 93 E4
Alleyne Rd ERDE/BCHGN B24 93 E5
The Alley SEDG DY3 82 D3
Allingham Gv GTB/HAM B43 59 H4
Allington Cl DSYBK/YTR WS5 43 F5
Allison St DIG/EDG B5 3 J6
Allman Rd ERDE/BCHGN B24 93 F2
Allmyn Dr FOAKS/STRLY B74 60 C2
All Saints Dr FOAKS/STRLY B74 46 D3
All Saints Rd
ALE/KHTH/YWD B14 161 E3
BKHL/PFLD WV2 7 J7
DARL/WED WS10 55 G2
WSNGN B18 108 B4
All Saints' St WSNGN B18 108 A4
All Saints Wy HHTH/SAND B71 87 H1
Allsops Cl BLKHTH/ROWR B65 103 F5
Allwell Dr ALE/KHTH/YWD B14 178 B3
Allwood Gdns
RIDG/WDGT B32 140 A5
Alma Av TPTN/OCK DY4 69 G4
Alma Crs VAUX/NECH B7 109 H5
Alma Pl DUDS DY2 84 C5
Alma St DARL/WED WS10 55 E2
HALE B63 137 G2
LOZ/NWT B19 109 E3
SMTHWK B66 107 E3
WLNHL WV13 39 H3
WOLVN WV10 23 E3
WSLW WS2 41 H1
Alma Wy LOZ/NWT B19 108 D2
Almond Av DSYBK/YTR WS5 57 G4
WSLW WS2 40 C1
Almond Cl BLOX/PEL WS3 17 H5
SLYOAK B29 158 C4
Almond Cft PBAR/PBCH B42 73 H5
Almond Gv
DUNHL/THL/PER WV6 37 E1
Almond Rd KGSWFD DY6 100 A1
Alnwick Rd BLOX/PEL WS3 16 C3
Alperton Dr HAG/WOL DY9 136 C5
Alpha Cl BHTH/HG B12 144 A1
Alpine Dr DUDS DY2 102 B5
Alpine Wy BDMR/CCFT WV3 35 G3
Alport Cft BORD B9 127 H2
Alston Cl FOAKS/STRLY B74 47 E3
SOLH B91 165 F4
Alston Gv BORD B9 129 F1
Alston Rd BORD B9 129 F1
OLDBY B69 104 C2
SOLH B91 165 F4
Alston St LDYWD/EDGR B16 125 H2
Althorpe Dr DOR/KN B93 196 B5
Alton Av SHHTH WV12 25 H5
Alton Cl WOLVN WV10 13 E4
Alton Cottages
ETTPK/GDPK/PENN WV4 * 66 B2
Alton Gv DUDS DY2 85 E5
HHTH/SAND B71 72 A4
Alton Rd SLYOAK B29 142 D4
Alum Dr BORD B9 129 E1
Alumhurst Av WASH/WDE B8 111 F5
Alum Rock Rd WASH/WDE B8 110 D4
Alumwell Cl WSLW WS2 * 41 F4
Alum Well Rd WSLW WS2 41 F4
Alvaston Cl BLOX/PEL WS3 17 E4
Alvechurch Hwy BRGRVE B60 187 E5
Alvechurch Rd HALE B63 138 B5
NFLD/LBR B31 189 H1
Alverley Cl KGSWFD DY6 99 F1
Alverstoke Cl COVEN WV9 11 H5
Alveston Gv BORD B9 129 F2
DOR/KN B93 197 F1
Alveston Rd HLYWD B47 192 C1
Alvin Cl RMSLY B62 122 D4
Alvington Cl SHHTH WV12 40 B1
Alwen St STRBR DY8 118 B3
Alwin Rd BLKHTH/ROWR B65 121 H2
Alwold Rd SLYOAK B29 141 G5
Amanda Av
ETTPK/GDPK/PENN WV4 51 F4
Amanda Dr LGN/SDN/BHAMAIR B26
130 B3
Ambassador Rd LGN/SDN/BHAMAIR
B26 149 G3
Amber Dr OLDBY B69 * 105 E4
Ambergate Cl BLOX/PEL WS3 17 E4
Ambergate Dr KGSWFD DY6 99 G1
Amberley Gn GTB/HAM B43 73 G5
Amberley Gv AST/WIT B6 91 G3
Amberley Rd HIA/OLT B92 147 F4
Amberley Wy FOAKS/STRLY B74 45 E4
Amber Wy RMSLY B62 138 D1
Amberwood Cl WSLW WS2 40 B2
Amblecote Av KGSTG B44 75 E1
Amblecote Rd BRLYHL DY5 119 F4
Ambleside RIDG/WDGT B32 157 G1
Ambleside Cl BILS/COS WV14 54 A4
Ambleside Dr BRLYHL DY5 119 E4
Ambleside Gv SHHTH WV12 25 H1
Ambleside Wy KGSWFD DY6 99 H3
Ambrose Cl WLNHL WV13 39 E3
Ambrose Crs KGSWFD DY6 99 H1
Ambury Wy GTB/HAM B43 73 F3
Amelas Cl BRLYHL DY5 118 C4
Amersham Cl RIDG/WDGT B32 141 E2
Amesbury Rd MOS/BIL B13 144 A4
Ames Rd DARL/WED WS10 55 E1
Amherst Av
BFLD/HDSWWD B20 90 A3
Amington Cl MGN/WHC B75 47 H2
Amington Rd SHLY B90 180 A5
YDLY B25 146 B1
Amiss Gdns SMHTH B10 128 A4
Amity Cl SMTHWK B66 * 106 D4
Amos Av WNSFLD WV11 24 B3
Amos La WNSFLD WV11 24 C4
Amos Rd HAG/WOL DY9 136 D5
Amphlett Cft TPTN/OCK DY4 85 H2
Amphletts Cl DUDS DY2 121 E1
Ampleforth Dr WLNHL WV13 39 H5
Ampton Rd EDG B15 126 B5
Amroth Cl RBRY B45 188 B1
Amwell Gv
ALE/KHTH/YWD B14 178 B2
Anchorage Rd
ERDW/GRVHL B23 92 B3
FOAKS/STRLY B74 62 B2
Anchor Cl LDYWD/EDGR B16 125 G3
Anchor Crs WSNGN B18 107 H4
Anchor Dr TPTN/OCK DY4 85 G3
Anchor Hl BRLYHL DY5 119 E3
Anchor La BILS/COS WV14 68 B1
SOLH B91 165 F4
Anchor Rd ALDR WS9 30 B4
BILS/COS WV14 68 C1
Andersleigh Dr BILS/COS WV14 68 A3
Anderson Crs GTB/HAM B43 75 G1
Anderson Rd ERDW/GRVHL B23 76 C5
SMTHWK B66 124 C3
TPTN/OCK DY4 85 G1
Anderton Cl FOAKS/STRLY B74 62 A1
Anderton Park Rd
MOS/BIL B13 144 C4
Anderton Rd SPARK B11 145 E1
Anderton St CBHAMW B1 2 A4
Andover Crs KGSWFD DY6 100 B5
Andover St DIG/EDG B5 3 K5
Andrew Cl SHHTH WV12 26 B4
Andrew Dr SHHTH WV12 26 B4
Andrew Gdns HDSW B21 89 G5
Andrew Rd HALE B63 138 C4
HHTH/SAND B71 72 B1
TPTN/OCK DY4 69 G2
Andrews Cl BRLYHL DY5 119 G4
Andrews Rd ALDR WS9 19 H3
Anerley Gv KGSTG B44 60 B4
Anerley Rd KGSTG B44 60 B4
Angela Av BLKHTH/ROWR B65 104 B5
Angela Pl BILS/COS WV14 53 H2
Angelica Cl DSYBK/YTR WS5 57 G5
Angelina St BHTH/HG B12 127 F5
Angel Pas STRBR DY8 135 G2
Angel St DUDN DY1 102 B1
Anglesey Av CBROM B36 114 B3
Anglesey Crs BRWNH WS8 9 F2
Anglesey Rd BRWNH WS8 9 F2
Anglesey St LOZ/NWT B19 108 C2
Anglian Rd ALDR WS9 29 F4
Angus Cl HHTH/SAND B71 71 G5
Anita Av TPTN/OCK DY4 85 G4
Anita Cft ERDW/GRVHL B23 92 C4
Ankadine Rd STRBR DY8 135 H1
Ankerdine Ct HALE B63 138 C4
Ankermoor Cl
BKDE/SHDE B34 112 D3
Annan Av WOLVN WV10 23 G3
Ann Ct
LGN/SDN/BHAMAIR B26 148 B3
Anne Cl WBROM B70 86 C3
Anne Gv TPTN/OCK DY4 69 H2
Anne Rd BRLYHL DY5 120 A3
ETTPK/GDPK/PENN WV4 51 H3
SMTHWK B66 107 E2
Ann Rd HLYWD B47 192 C5
Annscroft HWK/WKHTH B38 176 B3
Ann St WLNHL WV13 39 H2
Ansbro Cl WSNGN B18 107 H4
Ansculf Rd BRLYHL DY5 118 D3
Ansell Rd ERDE/BCHGN B24 92 D5
SPARK B11 145 E1
Anslow Gdns WNSFLD WV11 25 F1
Anslow Rd ERDW/GRVHL B23 92 A1
Anson Cl DUNHL/THL/PER WV6 20 C5
Anson Gv ACGN B27 146 D5
Anson Rd WBROM B70 70 C4
WSLW WS2 40 C3
Anstey Cft
CHWD/FDBR/MGN B37 * 114 A5
Anstey Gv ACGN B27 163 F1
Anstey Rd KGSTG B44 75 E5
Anston Wy WNSFLD WV11 24 D3
Anstruther Rd EDG B15 125 G5
Anthony Rd WASH/WDE B8 128 C1
Anton Dr WALM/CURD B76 78 C5
Antony Rd SHLY B90 180 B4
Antringham Gdns EDG B15 125 F4
Antrobus Rd HDSW B21 89 G5
SCFLD/BOLD B73 76 C2
Anvil Crs BILS/COS WV14 68 C1
Anvil Dr OLDBY B69 104 C3
Apex Rd BRWNH WS8 8 C5
Apley Rd STRBR DY8 118 A5
Apollo Cft ERDE/BCHGN B24 93 H3
Apollo Rd HAG/WOL DY9 137 E2
LGLYGN/QTN B68 105 G3
Apollo Wy BFLD/HDSWWD B20 90 C5
Apperley Wy HALE B63 120 B5
Appian Cl ALE/KHTH/YWD B14 161 E5
Appian Wy SHLY B90 194 D4
Appleby Cl ALE/KHTH/YWD B14 160 D5
Appleby Gdns WNSFLD WV11 15 G5
Appleby Gv SHLY B90 195 H2
Applecross FOAKS/STRLY B74 46 D4
Appledore Rd DSYBK/YTR WS5 43 F5
Appledorne Gdns
BKDE/SHDE B34 112 D3
Applesham Cl SPARK B11 145 F1
Appleton Av GTB/HAM B43 73 G3
STRBR DY8 135 G5
Appleton Cl BVILLE B30 159 G2
Appleton Crs
ETTPK/GDPK/PENN WV4 51 G3
Apple Tree Cl ERDW/GRVHL B23 91 H2
Appletree Cl NFLD/LBR B31 175 E4
SOLH B91 166 B5
Appletree Gv ALDR WS9 30 B5
DUNHL/THL/PER WV6 23 E5
Applewood Gv CDYHTH B64 121 F4
April Cft MOS/BIL B13 144 D5
Apse Cl WMBN WV5 64 D4
Apsley Cl LGLYGN/QTN B68 123 E5
Apsley Gv DOR/KN B93 198 D1
ERDE/BCHGN B24 93 E4
Apsley Rd LGLYGN/QTN B68 123 E5
Aqueduct Rd SHLY B90 179 G3
Aragon Dr SCFLD/BOLD B73 62 A2
Arboretum Rd WSL WS1 5 G2
Arbor Ga ALDR WS9 19 H3
Arbor Wy
CHWD/FDBR/MGN B37 132 C3
Arbury Dr STRBR DY8 117 H1
Arbury Hall Rd SHLY B90 180 D5
Arcal St SEDG DY3 67 G4
Archer Cl DARL/WED WS10 55 G5
LGLYGN/QTN B68 * 105 F5
Archer Ct HAG/WOL DY9 136 C5
Archer Gdns CDYHTH B64 120 C3
Archer Rd
ALE/KHTH/YWD B14 179 E1
BLOX/PEL WS3 28 A4
Archers Cl ERDW/GRVHL B23 76 A3
Archer Wy BLKHTH/ROWR B65 122 B3
The Arches SMHTH B10 * 127 H4
Arch Hill St DUDS DY2 102 C4
Archibald Rd LOZ/NWT B19 108 C1
Arcot Rd HLGN/YWD B28 145 H5
Ardath Rd HWK/WKHTH B38 177 E3
Ardav Rd WBROM B70 70 D3
Arden Buildings DOR/KN B93 196 D5
Arden Cl STRBR DY8 135 E1
Ardencote Rd MOS/BIL B13 161 G4
Arden Ct HIA/OLT B92 * 167 G3
Arden Cft CSHL/WTROR B46 97 F5
HIA/OLT B92 148 A3
Arden Dr DOR/KN B93 198 D1
LGN/SDN/BHAMAIR B26 130 B5
MGN/WHC B75 63 H3
SCFLD/BOLD B73 77 F3
Arden Gv LDYWD/EDGR B16 126 A3
OLDBY B69 105 E4
Ardenleigh Wy
ERDE/BCHGN B24 93 E4
Arden Meads HOCK/TIA B94 198 A5
Arden Oak Rd
LGN/SDN/BHAMAIR B26 148 B2
Arden Pl BILS/COS WV14 54 D4
Arden Rd ACGN B27 146 B3
AST/WIT B6 108 D1
DOR/KN B93 198 D1
HLYWD B47 192 C2
RBRY B45 174 A4
SMTHWKW B67 106 C5
WASH/WDE B8 128 B1
Arden Vale Rd DOR/KN B93 197 F1
Arderne Dr
CHWD/FDBR/MGN B37 132 A3
Ardgowan Gv
ETTPK/GDPK/PENN WV4 52 D3
Ardingley Wk BRLYHL DY5 118 D5
Ardley Cl DUDS DY2 102 D1
Ardley Rd ALE/KHTH/YWD B14 161 G5
Aretha Cl KGSWFD DY6 100 C3
Argil Cl WOLVN WV10 24 A2
Argus Cl WALM/CURD B76 63 F5
Argyle Cl RUSH/SHEL WS4 5 K1
STRBR DY8 118 A3
Argyle Rd BKHL/PFLD WV2 51 H2
RUSH/SHEL WS4 5 K1
Argyle St VAUX/NECH B7 110 A1
Arkle Cft BLKHTH/ROWR B65 103 F3
CBROM B36 111 G1
Arkley Gv HLGN/YWD B28 163 F3
Arkley Rd HLGN/YWD B28 163 F3
Arkwright Rd RIDG/WDGT B32 140 C2
WSLW WS2 27 F5
Arlen Dr GTB/HAM B43 73 F2
Arlescote Cl MGN/WHC B75 47 G2
Arlescote Rd HIA/OLT B92 148 A5
Arleston Wy SHLY B90 181 E5
Arley Cl OLDBY B69 104 B4
Arley Dr STRBR DY8 135 E4
Arley Gv
ETTPK/GDPK/PENN WV4 50 D3
Arley Rd SLYOAK B29 142 D4
SOLH B91 181 G1
WASH/WDE B8 110 B3
Arley Vls WSNGN B18 * 107 F5
Arlidge Cl BILS/COS WV14 53 H4
Arlington Cl KGSWFD DY6 99 H5
Arlington Ct STRBR DY8 135 H3
Arlington Gdns STRBR DY8 * 135 H3
Arlington Gv
ALE/KHTH/YWD B14 178 D3
Arlington Rd
ALE/KHTH/YWD B14 178 D2
HHTH/SAND B71 71 H5
Armada Cl ERDW/GRVHL B23 92 B5
Armoury Rd SPARK B11 145 G1
Armside Cl BLOX/PEL WS3 18 B3
Armstead Rd COVEN WV9 12 A4
Armstrong Cl STRBR DY8 135
Armstrong Dr CBROM B36 95
DUNHL/THL/PER WV6 22
WSLW WS2 41
Armstrong Wy WLNHL WV13 39
Arnhem Cl WNSFLD WV11 24
Arnhem Rd WLNHL WV13 39
Arnhem Wy TPTN/OCK DY4 86
Arnold Cl WSLW WS2 40
Arnold Gv BVILLE B30 176
SHLY B90 180
Arnold Rd SHLY B90 180
Arnwood Cl WSLW WS2 40
Arosa Dr HRBN B17 141
Arps Rd CDSL WV8 10
Arran Cl GTB/HAM B43 58
Arran Rd BKDE/SHDE B34 112
Arran Wy CBROM B36 114
Arras Rd DUDN DY1 85
Arrow Cl DOR/KN B93 197
Arrowfield Gn
HWK/WKHTH B38 190
Arrow Rd BLOX/PEL WS3 28
Arrow Wk HWK/WKHTH B38 177
Arsenal St BORD B9 128
Arter St BHTH/HG B12 144
Arthur Gunby Cl
MGN/WHC B75 * 63
Arthur Harris Cl SMTHWK B66 124
Arthur Pl CBHAMW B1 2
Arthur Rd EDG B15 143
ERDE/BCHGN B24 93
HDSW B21 107
TPTN/OCK DY4 69
YDLY B25 146
Arthur St BILS/COS WV14 * 53
BKHL/PFLD WV2 52
SMHTH B10 127
WBROM B70 87
Artillery St BORD B9 127
Arton Cft ERDE/BCHGN B24 92
Arundel Av DARL/WED WS10 55
Arundel Crs HIA/OLT B92 164
Arundel Dr OLDBY B69 103
Arundel Gv
DUNHL/THL/PER WV6 35
Arundel Pl SPARK B11 144
Arundel Rd
ALE/KHTH/YWD B14 178
SHHTH WV12 26
STRBR DY8 117
WOLVN WV10 12
Arundel St WSL WS1 57
Arun Wy WALM/CURD B76 78
Asbury Rd DARL/WED WS10 72
Ascot Cl LDYWD/EDGR B16 125
OLDBY B69 104
Ascot Dr DUDN DY1 83
ETTPK/GDPK/PENN WV4 5
Ascote La SHLY B90 194
Ascot Gdns STRBR DY8 117
Ascot Rd MOS/BIL B13 144
Ash Av BHTH/HG B12 144
Ashborough Dr SOLH B91 195
Ashbourne Gv AST/WIT B6 * 109
Ashbourne Rdg HALE B63 137
Ashbourne Rd BLOX/PEL WS3 17
ETTPK/GDPK/PENN WV4 52
LDYWD/EDGR B16 125
WOLV WV1 38
Ashbourne Wy SHLY B90 180
Ashbridge Ct RBRY B45 188
Ashbrook Crs SOLH B91 182
Ashbrook Dr RBRY B45 174
Ashbrook Gv BVILLE B30 160
Ashbrook Rd BVILLE B30 160
Ashburn Gv WLNHL WV13 40
Ashburton Rd
ALE/KHTH/YWD B14 160
Ashbury Covert BVILLE B30 177
Ashby Cl WASH/WDE B8 11
Ashby Ct SOLH B91 182
Ash Cl CDSL WV8 10
Ashcombe Av
BFLD/HDSWWD B20 89
Ashcombe Gdns
ERDE/BCHGN B24 93
Ashcott Cl HWK/WKHTH B38 176
Ash Crs
CHWD/FDBR/MGN B37 113
KGSWFD DY6 100
Ashcroft SMTHWK B66 * 107
TPTN/OCK DY4 * 85
Ashcroft Gv
BFLD/HDSWWD B20 90
Ashdale Cl KGSWFD DY6 99
Ashdale Dr
ALE/KHTH/YWD B14 178
Ashdale Gv
LGN/SDN/BHAMAIR B26 130
Ashdene Cl SCFLD/BOLD B73 62
Ashdene Gdns STRBR DY8 117
Ashdown Cl MOS/BIL B13 161
RBRY B45 174
Ashdown Dr STRBR DY8 118
Ash Dr HHTH/SAND B71 71
NFLD/LBR B31 174
Ashen Cl SEDG DY3 52
Ashenden Ri BDMR/CCFT WV3 35
Ashenhurst Rd DUDN DY1 101
Ashes Rd OLDBY B69 104
Ashfern Dr WALM/CURD B76 78
Ashfield Av
ALE/KHTH/YWD B14 161
Ashfield Cl BLOX/PEL WS3 42
Ashfield Crs DUDS DY2 120
HAG/WOL DY9 136
Ashfield Gv HALE B63 138
WOLVN WV10 12
Ashfield Rd
ALE/KHTH/YWD B14 161
BDMR/CCFT WV3 35
BILS/COS WV14 54
WOLVN WV10 11
Ashford Cl ERDE/BCHGN B24 9
Ashford Dr SEDG DY3 6
WALM/CURD B76 9
Ashfurlong Crs MGN/WHC B75 6
Ash Gn DUDN DY1 8
Ash Gv BORD B9 * 12

HAC/WOL DY9 ....136 B4
SEDG DY3 * 83 E4
hgrove Rd KGSTG B44 ....74 C1
h rd BDMR/CCFT WV3 ....35 H4
hill Rd RBRY B45 ....188 B1
shland St BDMR/CCFT WV3 ....6 C6
hlawn Crs SOLH B91 ....163 H5
shleigh Dr
 BFLD/HDSWWD B20 ....90 B4
shleigh Gv MOX/BIL B13 ....161 H1
shleigh Rd OLDBY B69 ....104 A1
 SOLH B91 ....181 H1
shley Cl EDG B15 ....85 C5
 KGSWFD DY6 ....99 C5
 STRBR DY8 ....134 D5
shley Gdns CDSL WV8 ....10 B3
 WASH/WDE B8 ....110 B5
shley Mt
 DUNHL/THL/PER WV6 ....21 H5
shley Rd BLOX/PEL WS3 ....26 D1
 ERDW/GRVHL B23 ....92 C3
 ETTPK/GDPK/PENN WV4 ....51 E5
 SMTHWK B66 ....107 E5
shley St BILS/COS WV14 ....56 A2
 BLKHTH/ROWR B65 ....122 A3
shley Ter SLYOAK B29 * 159 C1
shmead Dr RBRY B45 ....188 C4
shmead Gv ERDE/BCHGN B24 ....93 E4
shmead Rd WBROM B70 ....70 D4
shmore Av WNSFLD WV11 ....25 C1
shmore Lake Rd SHHTH WV12 ....39 H1
shmore Lake Wy
 SHHTH WV12 ....39 H1
shmore Rd BVILLE B30 ....159 H5
hold Farm Rd
 ERDE/BCHGN B24 ....93 G4
holme Cl CBROM B36 ....111 G2
horme Cl HLGN/YWD D28 ....163 F3
h rd DARL/WED WS10 ....55 H3
 DUDN DY1 ....84 B3
 TPTN/OCK DY4 ....85 E2
 WASH/WDE B8 ....110 B5
hstead Cd WALM/CURD B76 ....78 D5
h St BDMR/CCFT WV3 ....6 B5
 BILS/COS WV14 ....54 A5
 BLOX/PEL WS3 ....27 H1
 CDYHTH B64 ....121 E2
ited Cinc CBHAMNE B4 ....5 H5
hton Cft OLDBY B69 ....85 H5
hton Park Dr BRLYHL DY5 ....119 H5
hton Cft LDYWD/EDCR B16 ....126 A2
hton Rd YDLY B25 ....129 F5
htree Cl BRLYHL DY5 ....118 C4
htree Gv BILS/COS WV14 ....54 D5
htree Rd BLOX/PEL WS3 ....18 A4
htree Rd BVILLE B30 ....160 A4
htree Rd OLDBY B69 ....104 B1
hurst Rd WALM/CURD B76 ....78 D5
hville Av BKDE/SHDE B34 ....112 B2
hville Dr HALE B63 ....138 C2
hwater Dr
 ALE/KHTH/YWD B14 ....177 H1
h Wy ERDW/GRVHL B23 ....76 A3
 SPARK B11 ....144 D2
hwell Dr SHLY B90 ....180 D1
hwells Gv COVEN WV9 ....11 H5
hwin Rd HDSW B21 ....107 H2
hwood Av STRBR DY8 ....117 C2
hwood Cl FOAKS/STRLY B74 ....45 E5
 OLDBY B69 ....104 D5
hwood Dr
 CHWD/FDBR/MGN B37 ....132 D1
hwood Gv
 ETTPK/GDPK/PENN WV4 ....51 G3
hwood Lower La
 KINVER DY7 ....98 C4
hworth Rd PBAR/PBCH B42 ....74 B2
kew Bridge Rd SEDG DY3 * 82 D3
kew Cl SEDG DY3 ....83 G1
sbury Cft CBROM B36 ....95 F5
sbury Cl ACGN B27 ....146 B5
sen Dr
 CHWD/FDBR/MGN B37 ....132 D1
sen Gdns
 BFLD/HDSWWD B20 ....90 B5
sen Gv BORD B9 ....129 E1
shHLYWD B47 ....192 D3
 SHHTH WV12 ....26 C3
sen Wy BDMR/CCFT WV3 ....6 A6
quith Dr OLDBY B69 ....85 F5
quith Rd WASH/WDE B8 ....111 F4
bury Cl BLOX/PEL WS3 ....16 C3
 WOLV WV1 ....38 A4
te Hi COVEN WV9 ....12 A4
tley Av DSYBK/YTR WS5 ....57 G5
tley Rd HDSW B21 ....89 F5
ley Cl TPTN/OCK DY4 ....70 B5
ley Rd HDSW B21 ....89 F5
on Brook Cn AST/WIT B6 * 109 E3
on Brook St AST/WIT B6 ....109 E3
on Brook St East
 AST/WIT B6 ....109 F4
on Bury EDC B15 ....125 G4
on Church Rd
 /VAUX/NECH B7 ....110 A2
on Cl BILS/COS WV14 ....54 C4
on Hall Rd AST/WIT B6 ....109 G1
on La BFLD/HDSWWD B20 ....91 E4
on Manor Cl
 BFLD/HDSWWD B20 ....91 G4
on Rd OLDBY B69 ....85 G5
 /VAUX/NECH B7 * 3 J1
 WLNHL WV13 ....39 G3
on North Rd AST/WIT B6 ....109 F3
ns Cl BRLYHL DY5 ....119 F5
ns Fold BRLYHL DY5 ....119 F5
on St BDMR/CCFT WV3 ....36 C5
 BHAMNE B4 ....3 J2
PTN/OCK DY4 ....70 A5
on Dr MOS/BIL B13 ....162 A1
dcia Cl SHHTH WV12 ....26 B1

Astor Rd FOAKS/STRLY B74 ....45 G4
 KGSWFD DY6 ....100 B4
Athelney Ct BLOX/PEL WS3 * 18 A4
Athelstan Gv
 DUNHL/THL/PER WV6 ....20 C5
Atherstone Cl SHLY B90 ....179 G3
Atherstone Rd WOLV WV1 ....38 A3
Athlone Rd DSYBK/YTR WS5 ....43 E5
Athol Cl RIDG/WDGT B32 ....157 H2
Athole St BHTH/HG B12 ....127 G5
Atlantic Rd KGSTG B44 ....75 F3
Atlantic Wy DARL/WED WS10 ....70 C2
Atlas Cft WOLV WV10 ....23 H3
Atlas Est AST/WIT B6 * 91 C4
Atlas Gv WBROM B70 ....86 D3
Attenborough Cl
 LOZ/NWT B19 ....108 D4
Attingham Dr DUDN DY1 ....84 B4
Attleboro La
 GTB/HAM B43 ....73 F1
Attlee Cl OLDBY B69 ....86 B4
Attlee Crs BILS/COS WV14 ....69 E1
Attlee Rd WSLW WS2 ....40 C2
Attwell Pk BDMR/CCFT WV3 ....37 C5
Attwell Rd TPTN/OCK DY4 ....69 F2
Attwood Cl WASH/WDE B8 ....111 E5
Attwood Gdns
 ETTPK/GDPK/PENN WV4 ....52 C3
Attwood St HAG/WOL DY9 ....138 B2
 HALE B63 ....138 D2
Aubrey Rd RIDG/WDGT B32 ....124 A5
 SMTHB10 ....106 A5
Auchinleck Sq EDG B15 * 126 B5
Auckland Dr CBROM B36 ....113 H1
Auckland Rd KGSWFD DY6 ....100 A5
 SMTHWKW B66 ....106 B5
 SPARK B11 ....127 C5
Auden Ct DUNHL/THL/PER WV6 ....34 D1
Augusta Rd ACGN B27 ....146 C2
Augusta Rd East MOS/BIL B13 ....144 B5
Augusta St HOCK/TIA B94 * 2 C1
Augustine Gv FOAKS/STRLY B74 ....32 D5
 WSNGN B18 ....107 H5
Augustus Cl CSHL/WTROR B46 ....97 F5
Augustus Ct EDG B15 ....125 H4
Augustus Rd EDG B15 ....125 C4
Augustus St WSLW WS2 ....4 C4
Aulton Rd MGN/WHC B75 ....32 A5
Ault St WBROM B70 ....87 E4
Austcliff Dr SOLH B91 ....182 A5
Austen Pl EDG B15 ....126 B4
Austin Cl ACGN B27 ....146 D5
 DUDN DY1 ....83 H4
Austin Cft CBROM B36 ....95 C5
Austin Ri NFLD/LBR B31 ....189 F1
Austin Rd HDSW B21 ....89 F5
Austin St DUNHL/THL/PER WV6 ....36 D1
Austrey Cl BRFD/HDSWWD B20 ....90 A1
Austrey Cl DOR/KN B93 ....197 E2
Austrey Gv SLYOAK B29 * 158 C2
Austrey Rd KGSWFD DY6 ....100 C4
Austy Cl CBROM B36 ....112 A1
Autherley Jct COVEN WV9 * 22 C1
Autumn Berry Gv SEDG DY3 ....82 A4
Autumn Cl RUSH/SHEL WS4 ....18 C5
Autumn Dr RUSH/SHEL WS4 ....18 C5
 SEDG DY3 ....83 F3
Autumn Gv LOZ/NWT B19 ....108 C5
Avalon Cl ERDE/BCHGN B24 ....93 F2
Avebury Gv BVILLE B30 ....160 C3
Avebury Rd BVILLE B30 ....160 C2
Ave Maria Cl CDYHTH B64 ....121 E3
Avenue Cl DOR/KN B93 ....182 C1
Avenue Albert HOCK/TIA B94 ....198 A4
Avenue Cl DOR/KN B93 ....182 C1
 VAUX/NECH B7 ....109 G4
Avenue Rd
 ALE/KHTH/YWD B14 ....160 D2
 AST/WIT B6 ....109 G3
 BDMR/CCFT WV3 ....36 A3
 BILS/COS WV14 ....68 C3
 BLKHTH/ROWR B65 ....122 B3
 DARL/WED WS10 ....55 F2
 DOR/KN B93 ....197 E3
 DUDN DY1 ....101 C3
 ERDW/GRVHL B23 ....92 D2
 HDSW B21 ....89 F4
The Avenue ACGN B27 ....146 D4
 BDMR/CCFT WV3 ....35 H5
 BLKHTH/ROWR B65 ....121 C5
 DARL/WED WS10 ....55 H2
 ETTPK/GDPK/PENN WV4 ....51 E4
 KIDD DY10 ....168 B5
 RBRY B45 ....187 C1
 WALM/CURD B76 ....78 B1
Averill Rd
 LGN/SDN/BHAMAIR B26 ....130 C4
Avern Cl TPTN/OCK DY4 ....69 H5
Aversley Rd HWK/WKHTH B38 ....176 B5
Avery Cft CVALE B35 ....94 B4
Avery Dell BVILLE B30 * 160 B5
Avery Dr ACGN B27 ....146 C3
Avery Myers Cl
 LGLYGN/QTN B68 ....105 F4
Aviemore Crs GTB/HAM B43 ....59 F4
Avington Cl SEDG DY3 ....82 A5
Avion Cl WSL WS1 ....57 F1
Avocet Cl STETCH B33 ....130 A1
Avon Cl BRLYHL DY5 ....100 D2
 DUNHL/THL/PER WV6 ....34 D2
Avon Crs BLOX/PEL WS3 ....28 C1
Avondale Cl KGSWFD DY6 ....100 A1
Avondale Rd
 DUNHL/THL/PER WV6 ....36 B2
 SPARK B11 ....145 F3
Avon Dr CBROM B36 ....113 H2
 MOS/BIL B13 ....144 D5
 WLNHL WV13 ....40 A3
Avon Gv DSYBK/YTR WS5 ....57 G5
Avon Ms STRBR DY8 * 117 C2
Avon Rd BLOX/PEL WS3 ....28 A1
 HALE B63 ....137 F2
 SHLY B90 ....180 D5
 STRBR DY8 ....135 F4
Avon St SPARK B11 ....145 E2

Avro Wy CVALE B35 ....94 D3
Awbridge Br WMBN WV5 ....94 D3
Awbridge Rd DUDN DY1 ....120 C1
Awefields Crs SMTHWKW B67 ....105 H5
Awlmakers Gv BLOX/PEL WS3 ....27 G5
Axletree Wy DARL/WED WS10 ....56 B3
Ayala Cft CBROM B36 ....112 A1
Aylesbury Cl HOCK/TIA B94 ....198 A5
Aylesbury Crs KGSTG B44 ....75 G5
Aylesbury Rd HOCK/TIA B94 ....198 B4
Aylesford Cl SEDG DY3 ....66 D1
Aylesford Dr
 CHWD/FDBR/MGN B37 ....132 A5
Aylesford Rd HDSW B21 ....89 F5
Aylesmore Cl HIA/OLT B92 ....164 A2
 RIDG/WDGT B32 ....157 G1
Ayre Rd ERDE/BCHGN B24 ....93 F2
Ayres Cl BKDE/SHDE B34 ....113 G3
Ayrshire Cl CBROM B36 ....111 H1
Ayrton Cl DUNHL/THL/PER WV6 ....35 E1
Azalea Cl DUDN DY1 ....10 D4
Azalea Gv BORD B9 ....128 D2
Aziz Isaac Cl
 LGLYGN/QTN B68 * 105 G3

B

Babington Rd HDSW B21 ....107 H3
Bablake Cft HIA/OLT B92 ....164 C1
Babors Fld BILS/COS WV14 ....53 E5
Babworth Cl COVEN WV9 ....11 F5
Baccabox La HLYWD B47 ....192 A1
Bacchus Rd WSNGN B18 ....107 H3
Bache Rd WBROM B70 ....87 G5
Bach Mill Dr HLGN/YWD D28 ....179 F2
Backhouse La WNSFLD WV11 ....38 C1
Back La ALDR WS9 ....31 E1
 LICHS WS14 ....32 B1
 SHLY B90 ....194 A3
Back Rd HWK/WKHTH B38 ....176 D3
Baddesley Rd HIA/OLT B92 ....147 E5
Bader Rd BDMR/CCFT WV3 ....35 H4
 WSLW WS2 ....40 D3
Bader Wk CVALE B35 ....94 B4
Badger Cl SHLY B90 ....194 D4
Badger Dr WOLV WV10 ....37 F1
Badgers Bank Rd
 FOAKS/STRLY B74 ....32 D5
Badgers Cl BLOX/PEL WS3 ....18 A2
Badgers Crft RMSLY B62 ....121 H5
Badger St HAG/WOL DY9 ....136 A4
 SEDG DY3 ....85 C1
Badminton Cl DUDN DY1 ....83 H3
Badon Covert
 ALE/KHTH/YWD B14 ....177 H5
Badsey Cl NFLD/LBR B31 ....176 A1
Badsey Rd OLDBY B69 ....104 B4
Baggeridge Cl SEDG DY3 ....66 C5
Baginton Cl SOLH B91 ....164 D5
Baginton Rd CVALE B35 ....94 B3
Bagley St STRBR DY8 ....135 E1
Bagnall Cl YDLY B25 ....146 D1
Bagnall Rd BILS/COS WV14 ....53 G2
Bagnall Rd BILS/COS WV14 ....27 G3
Bagnall St BLOX/PEL WS3 * 28 A4
Bagnall St MOS/BIL B13 ....161 F3
Bagnall Wk BRLYHL DY5 ....119 F3
Bagot St CBHAMNE B4 ....3 H1
Bagridge Cl BDMR/CCFT WV3 ....35 F5
Bagridge Rd BDMR/CCFT WV3 ....35 F5
Bagshawe Cft
 ERDW/GRVHL B23 ....76 B4
Bagshaw Rd STETCH B33 ....130 A1
Bailey Rd BILS/COS WV14 ....53 F1
Bailey St WBROM B70 ....87 F3
 WOLV WV10 ....7 J3
Baker Av BILS/COS WV14 ....67 H1
Baker House La GTB/HAM B43 ....73 F4
Baker Rd BILS/COS WV14 ....54 A5
Bakers Gdns CDSL WV8 ....10 A3
Baker's La ALDR WS9 ....30 D1
 DOR/KN B93 ....199 G2
 FOAKS/STRLY B74 ....60 B3
Baker St HDSW B21 ....107 H1
 SMHTH B10 ....128 B5
 SPARK B11 ....145 E3
 TPTN/OCK DY4 ....85 E2
 WBROM B70 ....87 F3
Bakers Wy SEDG DY3 ....80 C4
Bakewell Cl BLOX/PEL WS3 ....17 E4
Balaams Cl NFLD/LBR B31 ....174 B4
Balaams Wood Dr
 NFLD/LBR B31 ....174 B4
Balaclava Rd
 ALE/KHTH/YWD B14 ....161 E2
Balcaskie Cl EDG B15 ....125 C5
Balden Rd RIDG/WDGT B32 ....124 A5
Baldmoor Lake Rd
 ERDW/GRVHL B23 ....76 D4
Bald's La HAG/WOL DY9 ....136 D2
Baldwin Cl OLDBY B69 ....86 A4
Baldwin Rd BVILLE B30 ....177 E2
Baldwins La HLGN/YWD B28 ....179 H1
Baldwin St BILS/COS WV14 ....54 B4
 SMTHWK B66 ....106 D3
Baldwin Wy SEDG DY3 ....80 C4
Balfour Crs
 DUNHL/THL/PER WV6 ....36 B1
Balfour Dr OLDBY B69 ....86 B4
Balfour Rd KGSWFD DY6 ....100 A1
Balfour St BHTH/HG B12 ....144 A1
Balham Gv KGSTG B44 ....75 H5
Balking Cl BILS/COS WV14 ....53 F5
Ballarat Wk STRBR DY8 ....135 F2
Ballard Crs DUDS DY2 ....102 D4
Ballard Rd DUDS DY2 ....102 D4
Ballard Wk
 CHWD/FDBR/MGN B37 ....114 A3
Ball Flds TPTN/OCK DY4 ....86 A1
Ball La WOLN WV10 ....12 C1
Ballot St SMTHWK B66 ....106 D4
Balls Hi WSL WS1 ....5 G3
Balls St WSL WS1 ....5 G3

Balmain Crs WNSFLD WV11 ....24 B2
Balmoral Cl RMSLY B62 ....121 H5
 RUSH/SHEL WS4 ....29 H3
Balmoral Dr BRWNH WV5 ....25 H3
 SHHTH WV12 ....25 H3
Balmoral Rd CBROM B36 ....114 A2
 ERDW/GRVHL B23 ....92 D1
 ETTPK/GDPK/PENN WV4 ....52 D1
 FOAKS/STRLY B74 ....32 D5
 RIDG/WDGT B32 ....157 C2
 STRBR DY8 ....117 G2
Balmoral Vw DUDN DY1 ....83 G4
Balmoral Wy
 BLKHTH/ROWR B65 ....104 B5
 WSLW WS2 ....41 H3
Balsall Heath Rd DIG/EDG B5 ....127 E5
Baltimore Rd PBAR/PBCH B42 ....90 A1
Balvenie Wy DUDN DY1 ....83 H3
Bamber Cl BDMR/CCFT WV3 ....36 A5
Bamford Cl BLOX/PEL WS3 ....17 E4
Bamford Rd BDMR/CCFT WV3 ....36 C5
 BLOX/PEL WS3 ....17 E4
Bampfylde Pl PBAR/PBCH B42 * 74 C4
Bamville Rd WASH/WDE B8 ....111 E4
Banbery Dr WMBN WV5 ....80 D2
Banbrook Cl HIA/OLT B92 ....165 F2
Banbury Cl SEDG DY3 ....67 G5
Banbury Cft
 CHWD/FDBR/MGN B37 ....131 H2
Banbury St DIG/EDG B5 ....3 J5
Bancroft Cl BILS/COS WV14 ....68 B4
Bandywood Rd KGSTG B44 ....60 A4
Banfield Av DARL/WED WS10 ....55 E1
Banfield Rd DARL/WED WS10 ....55 E1
Bangham Pit Rd
 NFLD/LBR B31 ....158 A3
Bangor Rd BORD B9 ....128 D2
Bangor Vls DARL/WED WS10 * 55 H2
Bankdale Rd WASH/WDE B8 ....111 G5
Bankes Rd SMHTH B10 ....128 C5
Bank Farm Cl HAG/WOL DY9 ....153 E1
Bankfield Rd BILS/COS WV14 ....53 H5
 TPTN/OCK DY4 ....70 A3
Bank Rd DUDS DY2 ....102 D3
 SEDG DY3 ....83 E3
Banklands Rd DUDS DY2 ....103 C4
Bank Rd DUDS DY2 ....102 D3
 MOS/BIL B13 ....145 F5
 WMBN WV5 ....80 D4
Bankside FOAKS/STRLY B74 ....60 B1
Bankside Wy ALDR WS9 ....19 H5
Banks St WLNHL WV13 ....39 C3
Bank St ALE/KHTH/YWD B14 ....161 E2
 BILS/COS WV14 ....68 C3
 BRLYHL DY5 ....101 F5
 DUDS DY2 ....102 B1
 HAG/WOL DY9 ....136 D2
 HHTH/SAND DY1 ....71 G5
 WOLN WV10 ....23 G5
 WSL WS1 ....5 G4
Bankwell St BRLYHL DY5 ....101 F5
Bannerlea Rd
 CHWD/FDBR/MGN B37 ....113 H4
Bannerley Rd STETCH B33 ....131 F3
Banners Ct SCFLD/BOLD B73 * 60 D5
Banners Gate Rd
 SCFLD/BOLD B73 ....60 D5
Banners Gv ERDW/GRVHL B23 ....77 E5
Banners La HALE B63 ....137 F1
Banners St HALE B63 ....137 H1
Banners Wk KGSTG B44 ....75 H1
Bannister Rd DARL/WED WS10 ....70 B1
Bannister St CSTCH B33 * 121 E2
Banstead Cl BKHL/PFLD WV2 ....52 C1
Bantock Av BDMR/CCFT WV3 ....35 E2
Bantock Gdns
 BDMR/CCFT WV3 ....36 A4
The Bantocks WBROM B70 ....71 E5
Bantock Wy HRBN B17 ....142 B2
Bantry Cl LGN/SDN/BHAMAIR B26 ....148 A3
Baptist End Rd DUDS DY2 ....102 B2
Barbara Rd HLGN/YWD D28 ....179 G2
Barbel Dr WOLV WV10 ....25 E3
Barberry Cft BILS/COS WV14 ....54 A4
Barbers La ALDR WS9 ....30 A2
Barbourne Cl SOLH B91 ....195 H1
Barbrook Dr BRLYHL DY5 ....118 C5
Barchester Rd DOR/KN B93 ....197 E4
 SLYOAK B29 ....158 C1
Barclay Rd SMTHWKW B67 ....124 A1
Barcroft WLNHL WV13 * 39 H2
Bardenholme Gdns
 HAG/WOL DY9 ....136 B4
Bardfield Cl PBAR/PBCH B42 ....73 H3
Bardon Dr SHLY B90 ....180 D3
Bard St SPARK B11 ....145 E2
Bardwell Cl CDSL WV8 ....22 B2
Barford Cl DARL/WED WS10 ....40 A5
 WALM/CURD B76 ....63 F4
Barford Crs HWK/WKHTH B38 ....177 C3
Barford Rd DHLY B90 ....108 B5
 WSNGN B18 ....107 G5
Barford St DIG/EDG B5 ....127 F3
Bargate Dr
 DUNHL/THL/PER WV6 ....36 C1
Bargery Rd WNSFLD WV11 ....25 C1
Barham Cl SHLY B90 ....195 G3
Barker Rd FOAKS/STRLY B74 ....62 B1
Barker St LGLYGN/QTN B68 ....105 F5
 LOZ/NWT B19 ....108 B2
Bark Piece RIDG/WDGT B32 ....157 G2
Barlands Cft BKDE/SHDE B34 ....112 D3
Barle Gv CBROM B36 ....113 H1
Barley La ALDR WS9 ....45 E3
Barley Cft
 DUNHL/THL/PER WV6 ....34 B2
Barleyfield Ri KGSWFD DY6 ....99 E1
Barleyfield Rw WSL WS1 ....4 E4
Barlow Cl LGLYGN/QTN B68 ....123 E1
 RBRY B45 ....173 G3
Barlow Dr WBROM B70 ....88 B5
Barlow Rd DARL/WED WS10 ....55 E1
Barlows Rd EDG B15 ....142 B2
Barmouth Cl SHHTH WV12 ....26 A4
Barnabas Rd ERDW/GRVHL B23 ....92 D1

Barnaby Sq WOLV WV10 ....13 F3
Barnard Cl
 CHWD/FDBR/MGN B37 ....132 D3
Barnard Rd BKHL/PFLD WV2 ....52 C2
Barnard Rd MGN/WHC B75 ....63 F1
 WNSFLD WV11 ....25 E1
Barn Av SEDG DY3 ....67 E4
Barnbrook Rd DOR/KN B93 ....197 E1
Barn Cl BVILLE B30 ....160 B4
 HAG/WOL DY9 ....136 A3
 HALE B63 ....138 A5
Barn Cft RIDG/WDGT B32 ....158 A1
Barncroft Rd OLDBY B69 ....103 C1
Barncroft St WBROM B70 ....71 E5
Barnes Cl STETCH B33 ....131 G2
Barnes Hi SLYOAK B29 ....141 F5
Barnes Meadow Pl
 BILS/COS WV14 ....68 B3
Barnesville Cl SMHTH B10 ....129 E4
Barnet Rd ERDW/GRVHL B23 ....92 B1
Barnett Cl BILS/COS WV14 ....53 H4
 KGSWFD DY6 ....99 H5
Barnett Gn STRBR DY8 ....99 H5
Barnett La FOAKS/STRLY B74 ....99 H4
 STRBR DY8 ....117 H1
Barnett Rd WLNHL WV13 ....39 E4
Barnetts La BRWNH WV8 ....9 G3
Barnett St STRBR DY8 ....117 H1
 TPTN/OCK DY4 ....85 G4
Barney Cl TPTN/OCK DY4 ....85 F4
Barn Farm Cl BILS/COS WV14 ....54 C1
Barnfield Dr HIA/OLT B92 ....165 H2
Barnfield Gv
 BFLD/HDSWWD B20 ....89 G1
Barnfield Rd RMSLY B62 ....122 B5
 TPTN/OCK DY4 ....69 E4
 WOLV WV1 ....38 A3
Barnford Cl SMTHWK B66 ....128 A3
Barnford Crs LGLYGN/QTN B68 ....123 E1
Barnfordhill Cl
 LGLYGN/QTN B68 ....105 F5
Barnhurst La CDSL WV8 ....11 F4
Barn La HDSW B21 ....107 G2
 MOS/BIL B13 ....147 E3
Barn Meadow YDLY B25 ....129 H3
Barnmoor Ri SOLH B91 ....165 E3
Barn Owl Dr BLOX/PEL WS3 ....17 H5
Barnpark Covert
 ALE/KHTH/YWD B14 ....177 G5
Barn Piece RIDG/WDGT B32 ....140 B3
Barnsbury Av
 CSCFLD/WYGN B72 ....77 G5
Barns Cft FOAKS/STRLY B74 ....31 F3
Barnsdale Crs NFLD/LBR B31 ....175 E1
Barns La ALDR WS9 ....29 F3
Barnsley Rd HRBN B17 ....124 C4
Barnstaple Rd SMTHWK B66 ....106 D4
Barnt Green Rd RBRY B45 ....188 C5
Barnwood Rd CDSL WV8 ....22 A1
 RIDG/WDGT B32 ....141 F3
Barons Cl HRBN B17 ....123 G4
Barrack La HALE B63 ....137 F1
Barrack Cl AST/WIT B6 ....92 B4
Barracks La BLOX/PEL WS3 ....28 A2
Barracks Cl BLOX/PEL WS3 ....27 H2
Barrack St VAUX/NECH B7 ....109 G5
 WBROM B70 ....87 E3
Barra Cft CVALE B35 ....94 D2
Barrar Cl STRBR DY8 ....118 A4
Barratts Cft BRLYHL DY5 ....83 E5
Barratts Rd HWK/WKHTH B38 ....177 E4
Barr Common Cl ALDR WS9 ....30 A3
Barr Common Rd ALDR WS9 ....44 B2
Barrett St LDYWD/EDCR B16 ....107 E3
Barrhill Cl GTB/HAM B43 ....73 C1
Barrington Cl DSYBK/YTR WS5 ....57 G5
 WOLN WV10 ....11 H5
Barrington Rd HIA/OLT B92 ....147 E5
 RBRY B45 ....187 C1
Barron Cl NFLD/LBR B31 ....175 H2
Barron Rd NFLD/LBR B31 ....19 F3
Barrow Hill Rd BRLYHL DY5 ....83 E5
Barrows La
 LGN/SDN/BHAMAIR B26 ....147 G2
Barrows Rd SPARK B11 ....145 E1
Barrs Crs CDYHTH B64 ....121 E5
Barrs Rd CDYHTH B64 ....121 F4
Barrs St LGLYGN/QTN B68 ....105 E5
Barr St LOZ/NWT B19 ....108 C4
Barry Rd DSYBK/YTR WS5 ....58 A1
Barsham Cl DIG/EDG B5 ....143 G1
Barsham Dr BRLYHL DY5 ....119 E4
Barston La SOLH B91 ....182 D3
Barston Rd LGLYGN/QTN B68 ....140 B1
Bartholomew Rw DIG/EDG B5 ....3 J4
Bartholomew St DIG/EDG B5 ....3 J4
Bartic Av KGSWFD DY6 ....100 B5
Bartleet Rd SMTHWKW B67 ....105 H4
Bartlett Cl TPTN/OCK DY4 ....69 H2
Bartley Cl HIA/OLT B92 ....147 E1
Bartley Dr NFLD/LBR B31 ....158 A2
Bartley Ms NFLD/LBR B31 ....158 A2
Bartley Woods
 RIDG/WDGT B32 ....140 B3
Barton Dr DOR/KN B93 ....199 H1
Barton La KGSWFD DY6 ....99 G1
Barton Lodge Rd
 HLGN/YWD B28 ....179 G1
Barton Rd
 ETTPK/GDPK/PENN WV4 ....52 D4
Bartons Bank AST/WIT B6 ....109 E2
Barton St WBROM B70 ....87 G4
Bar Wk ALDR WS9 ....30 C1
Barwell Cl DOR/KN B93 ....196 C4
Barwell Rd BORD B9 ....128 A1
Barwick St CBHAMNW B3 ....3 F4
Basalt Cl WSLW WS2 ....41 E1
Basil Gv NFLD/LBR B31 ....175 E1
Basil Rd NFLD/LBR B31 ....175 E1
Baslow Cl BLOX/PEL WS3 ....16 D4
 STETCH B33 ....112 A5

Baslow Rd BLOX/PEL WS3......16 E4
Basons La LGLYGN/QTN B68....105 C4
Bassano Rd
  BLKHTH/ROWR B65............122 A3
Bassenthwaite Ct KGSWFD DY6..99 H3
Bassett Cl
  ETTPK/GDPK/PENN WV4......50 C2
  SHHTH WV12........................40 B1
  WALM/CURD B76..................63 E4
Bassett Cft SMHTH B10.........127 H4
Bassett Gv DARL/WED WS10.....71 C1
  HALE B63...........................137 E1
Bassetts Gv
  CHWD/FDBR/MGN B37........113 C4
Bassett St WSLW WS2.............41 G3
Bassnage Rd HALE B63.........138 A5
Batchcroft BILS/COS WV14......53 H3
  DARL/WED WS10..................40 B5
Batchelor Cl STRBR DY8........118 B4
Bateman Dr SCFLD/BOLD B73....77 F2
Bateman Rd
  CSHL/WTROR B46.................97 F5
Batemans La HLYWD B47.......192 A3
Bates Cl WALM/CURD B76.........78 C4
Bates Gv WNSFLD WV11..........24 A5
Bate St
  ETTPK/GDPK/PENN WV4......53 E5
  WSLW WS1............................4 D1
Bath Av WOLV WV1..................6 D2
Bathearston Cl
  HWK/WKHTH B38...............190 B1
Bath Meadow HALE B63........138 A2
Bath Pas DIG/EDG B5..............3 G7
Bath Rd BDMR/CCFT WV3........6 C4
  BRLYHL DY5.......................120 A2
  STRBR DY8........................135 F1
  TPTN/OCK DY4......................85 G1
  WSL WS1...............................4 E7
Bath Rw EDG B15.................126 C3
  OLDBY B69.........................104 B1
Bath St BILS/COS WV14.........54 A3
  CBHAMNE B4..........................3 G2
  DUDS DY2...........................102 C1
  SEDG DY3.............................67 G2
  WLNH WV13..........................39 H4
  WOLV WV1 *............................7 J5
  WSL WS1................................4 E5
Bath Wk BTHTH/HG B12........144 A2
Batmans Hill Rd
  BILS/COS WV14.....................69 E1
Batson Ri STRBR DY8...........118 C4
Battenhall Rd HRBN B17.......141 G2
Battery Wy SPARK B11..........145 G3
Battlefield HI WMBN WV5........65 F4
Battlefield La WMBN WV5........65 F5
Bavaro Gdns BRLYHL DY5......120 A2
Baverstock Rd
  ALE/KHTH/YWD B14...........178 B3
Baxterley Gn SOLH B91........180 D1
  WALM/CURD B76..................78 B2
Baxter Rd BRLYHL DY5.........119 E2
Baxters Gn SHLY B90............180 B5
Baxters Rd SHLY B90............180 B5
Bay Av BILS/COS WV14............54 B4
Bayer St BILS/COS WV14..........68 C3
Bayford Av
  LGN/SDN/BHAMAIR B26.....148 A3
  NFLD/LBR B31....................189 E2
Bayley Crs DARL/WED WS10....40 A5
Bayleys La TPTN/OCK DY4........70 A4
Baylie St STRBR DY8............135 F3
Baylis Av WNSFLD WV11.........25 F2
Bayliss Av
  ETTPK/GDPK/PENN WV4......68 A1
Bayliss Cl BILS/COS WV14........53 C1
  NFLD/LBR B31....................158 D5
Baynton Rd SHHTH WV12........29 E2
Bayston Av BDMR/CCFT WV3....36 A5
Bayston Rd
  ALE/KHTH/YWD B14...........178 A1
Bayswater Rd
  BFLD/HDSWWD B20..............90 D5
  SEDG DY3.............................83 F4
Baytree Cl BLOX/PEL WS3......16 C3
Bay Tree Cl HWK/WKHTH B38..176 B5
Baytree Rd BLOX/PEL WS3......16 C4
Baywell Cl SHLY B90.............195 G1
Beach Av BILS/COS WV14........68 A1
Beach Brook Cl SPARK B11....144 D2
Beachburn Wy
  BFLD/HDSWWD B20..............90 A3
Beach Dr NFLD/LBR B31.......176 A4
Beachcroft Rd KGSWFD DY6....99 G1
Beach Dr HALE B63..............138 C2
Beach Rd BILS/COS WV14.......53 H1
  SPARK B11..........................144 D2
Beach St HALE B63..............138 C2
Beachwood Av KGSWFD DY6....81 C5
Beacon Cl GTB/HAM B43........73 H2
  RBRY B45...........................187 H2
  SMTHWK B66.......................106 C2
Beacon Dr WSL WS1...............51 F1
Beacon Hi ALDR WS9.............44 C4
  AST/WIT B6.........................109 E1
  RBRY B45...........................187 G5
Beacon La BRGRVE B60.........187 F5
  SEDG DY3.............................67 C2
Beacon Ri ALDR WS9.............44 B2
  HAG/WOL DY9.....................136 B3
  SEDG DY3.............................67 C2
Beacon Rd ALDR WS9.............59 F1
  DSYBK/YTR WS5...................58 B3
  KGSTG B44...........................60 D4
  SCFLD/BOLD B73.................77 E3
  SHHTH WV12........................26 A2
Beaconsfield Av
  ETTPK/GDPK/PENN WV4......52 B3
Beaconsfield Ct WSL WS1........5 K6
Beaconsfield Crs
  BHTH/HG B12 *..................144 A2
Beaconsfield Dr
  ETTPK/GDPK/PENN WV4......52 B3
Beaconsfield Rd
  BHTH/HG B12.....................144 A3
  FOAKS/STRLY B74.................62 B1
Beaconsfield St
  HHTH/SAND WS4...................87 H1
Beacon St BILS/COS WV14......67 H2
  WSL WS1................................5 J5
Beacon Vw RBRY B45...........187 H2

Beacon View Dr
  FOAKS/STRLY B74.................60 B2
Beacon View Rd
  HHTH/SAND B71.....................72 B1
Beacon Wy ALDR WS9............19 C4
  RUSH/SHEL WS4....................42 D1
Beakes Rd SMTHWK B67......124 B1
Beaks Farm Gdns
  LDYWD/EDGR B16..............125 F2
Beaks Hill Rd
  HWK/WKHTH B38...............176 C4
Beak St CBHAMW B1................3 F6
Beale Cl CVALE B35................94 C4
Beales St AST/WIT B6..........109 H1
Beale St STRBR DY8.............135 F2
Bealeys Av WNSFLD WV11......24 C2
Bealeys La BLOX/PEL WS3.....16 C5
Beamans Cl HIA/OLT B92.......147 G3
Beanfield Rd SOLH B91........181 F1
Bean Cft RIDG/WDGT B32....140 C5
Bean Rd DUDS DY2...............102 D1
  TPTN/OCK DY4......................68 C5
Beardmore Rd
  CSCFLD/WYGN B72................77 G3
Bearing Dr WNSFLD WV11......39 E1
Bearley Cft SHLY B90...........180 C5
Bearmore Rd CDYHTH B64....121 E3
Bearnett Dr
  ETTPK/GDPK/PENN WV4......65 C1
Bearnett La WMBN WV5.........65 F2
Bearwood Rd SMTHWK B66...124 C2
Beasley Gv GTB/HAM B43......74 B2
Beaton Cl WLNHL WV13.........39 E3
Beaton Rd FOAKS/STRLY B74..47 E2
Beatrice St BLOX/PEL WS3.....27 C4
Beatrice Wk OLDBY B69.........85 C4
Beauchamp Av
  BFLD/HDSWWD B20..............89 H1
Beauchamp Cl
  CHWD/FDBR/MGN B37.......132 B2
  WALM/CURD B76..................78 D4
Beauchamp Rd MOS/BIL B13..161 H5
  SOLH B91............................164 D5
Beaudesert Cl HLYWD B47....192 C2
Beaudesert Rd
  BFLD/HDSWWD B20..............108 B1
  HLYWD B47..........................192 C2
Beaufort Av BKDE/SHDE B34..111 H5
Beaufort Rd
  LDYWD/EDGR B16..............125 H3
Beaufort Wy ALDR WS9..........44 B1
Beaulieu Av KGSWFD DY6.....100 B5
Beaumaris Cl DUDN DY1.........83 H3
Beaumont Cl TPTN/OCK DY4...69 E5
Beaumont Dr BRLYHL DY5....118 D5
  HRBN B17...........................141 H3
Beaumont Gdns WSNGN B18..107 H3
Beaumont Gv SOLH B91.......164 B5
Beaumont Rd BVILLE B30......159 G4
  DARL/WED WS10...................55 H4
  RMSLY B62.........................122 C4
Beausale Dr DOR/KN B93......197 F1
Beauty Bank CDYHTH B64....121 F4
Beauty Bank Crs STRBR DY8..135 E1
Beaver Cl WNSFLD WV11........25 F5
Bebington Cl CDSL WV8..........22 B1
Beccles Dr WLNHL WV13.........39 F5
Beckbury Av
  ETTPK/GDPK/PENN WV4......50 C3
Beckbury Rd SLYOAK B29.....158 C1
Beck Cl SMTHWK B66...........106 C5
Beckenham Av KGSTG B44......75 G2
Beckensall Cl DUDN DY1.........83 D4
Becket Cl FOAKS/STRLY B74....32 D4
Beckett St BILS/COS WV14.....54 A2
Beckfield Cl
  ALE/KHTH/YWD B14...........178 A3
  RUSH/SHEL WS4....................29 E2
Beckford Cft DOR/KN B93 *...196 D5
Beckman Rd HAG/WOL DY9...136 A5
Beckminster Rd BDMR/CCFT WV3*51 F1
Beconsfield Cl DOR/KN B93...198 D1
Becton Gv PBAR/PBCH B42....74 D4
Bedcote Pl STRBR DY8..........135 H2
Beddoes Rd FOAKS/STRLY B74..86 B1
Beddow Av BILS/COS WV14.....68 C4
Beddoes Rd BLOX/PEL WS3....28 A5
Bedford Dr MGN/WHC B75.....63 E1
Bedford Rd BHTH/HG B12....127 G4
  HHTH/SAND B71.....................71 F4
  MGN/WHC B75......................63 E1
Bedford St TPTN/OCK DY4......85 H1
  WOLV WV1.............................7 G5
Bedford Ter LOZ/NWT B19 *..108 D1
Bedlam Wood Rd
  NFLD/LBR B31....................174 C4
Bedworth Cft TPTN/OCK DY4...85 H2
Bedworth Gv BORD B9...........129 F2
Beebee Rd DARL/WED WS10....55 H2
Beecham Cl ALDR WS9...........30 A2
Beech Av BHTH/HG B12.........144 A1
  CHWD/FDBR/MGN B37.......132 B3
  RIDG/WDGT B32..................140 D1
  RMSLY B62.........................122 A4
Beech Cl MGN/WHC B75.........47 E1
  SEDG DY3.............................67 G2
  WOLVN WV10........................22 D2
Beech Ct SMTHWK B66.........105 C2
  WSL WS1................................5 H6
Beech Crs DARL/WED WS10....55 H3
  TPTN/OCK DY4......................70 A3
Beechcroft Crs
  FOAKS/STRLY B74.................44 D4
Beechcroft Dr HALE B63.......137 C5
Beechcroft Ct WSL WS1 *........5 K6
Beechcroft Rd CBROM B36....112 D1
  CDYHTH B64.......................121 E3
Beechdale Av KGSTG B44.......75 E1
Beechdale Rd BLOX/PEL WS3..26 D2
Beech Dene Cv
  ERDW/GRVHL B23.................92 C1
Beecher Pi HALE B63............137 H2
Beecher Rd East HALE B63...137 H2
Beecher St HALE B63............137 C2
Beeches Av ACGN B27...........146 C3
Beeches Cl KGSWFD DY6........99 H4
Beeches Dr ERDE/BCHGN B24..93 G2

Beeches Farm Dr
  NFLD/LBR B31....................189 G1
Beeches Ms HAG/WOL DY9....169 E1
Beeches Pl BLOX/PEL WS3......27 H3
Beeches Rd
  BLKHTH/ROWR B65.............121 H3
  BLOX/PEL WS3....................27 H4
  LGLYGN/QTN B68................125 G1
  PBAR/PBCH B42....................74 B4
  WBROM B70...........................88 A4
  WOLV WV1.............................6 A2
The Beeches EDG B15..........126 C4
  WBROM B70...........................88 A4
  WOLV WV1 *............................6 A2
Beeches View Av HALE B63...137 G3
Beeches Wk SCFLD/BOLD B73..62 B5
Beeches Wy NFLD/LBR B31....189 G1
Beechey Cl CTB/HAM B43.......59 H5
Beech Farm Cft NFLD/LBR B31..175 C2
Beechfield Cl RMSLY B62......122 A4
Beechfield Gv BILS/COS WV14..68 B4
Beechfield Rd SMTHWK B66...106 B5
  SPARK B11..........................144 D1
Beech Gdns CDSL WV8............10 B5
Beech Ga FOAKS/STRLY B74....31 H5
Beechglade
  BFLD/HDSWWD B20..............89 H2
Beech Gn DUDN DY1..............84 A1
Beech Gv ALE/KHTH/YWD B14..161 G5
Beech Hill Rd
  CSCFLD/WYGN B72................77 G4
Beech Hurst HWK/WKHTH B38..176 C5
Beechlawn Dr KINVER DY7....116 C5
Beech Ms CDYHTH B64........121 E2
Beechmore Rd
  LGN/SDN/BHAMAIR B26.....147 F2
Beechmount Dr
  ERDW/GRVHL B23.................77 E5
Beechnut Cl SOLH B91.........165 F5
Beechnut La SOLH B91.........165 G5
Beech Rd BVILLE B30............159 C3
  DARL/WED WS10...................55 H3
  DUDN DY1.............................84 C2
  ERDW/GRVHL B23.................76 D4
  HLYWD B47..........................192 D2
  KGSWFD DY6.........................99 H4
  OLDBY B69.........................103 C1
  STRBR DY8........................135 E4
  WLNHL WV13........................39 E3
  WOLVN WV10........................22 D2
Beech Tree Av WNSFLD WV11..24 C2
Beech Tree Cl KGSWFD DY6...100 A2
Beech Tree Rd ALDR WS9.......19 F5
Beech Wk HWK/WKHTH B38...176 D5
Beech Wy SMTHWK B66.......106 C4
Beechwood Av WNSFLD WV11..24 B2
Beechwood Cl BLOX/PEL WS3..16 D4
  SHLY B90............................194 D4
Beechwood Ct
  DUNHL/THL/PER WV6 *........35 G2
Beechwood Cft
  FOAKS/STRLY B74.................32 B5
Beechwood Dr
  DUNHL/THL/PER WV6............35 E3
Beechwood Park Rd
  SOLH B91............................164 A5
Beechwood Rd
  ALE/KHTH/YWD B14...........161 F5
  DUDS DY2...........................85 G5
  GTB/HAM B43........................73 H2
  HHTH/SAND B71.....................72 C4
  SMTHWK B66.......................124 A4
  WBROM B70...........................88 A5
Bee La WOLVN WV10..............12 D4
Beeston Cl AST/WIT B6........109 C2
  BRLYHL DY5.......................119 E4
Beeton Rd WSNGN B18.........107 C3
Beet St BLKHTH/ROWR B65...122 A3
Beever Rd TPTN/OCK DY4......70 B4
Beggars Bush La WMBN WV5...81 F1
Beighton Cl FOAKS/STRLY B74..32 D4
Beilby Rd BVILLE B30...........160 B4
Beilbroughton Rd
  HAG/WOL DY9.....................170 C4
  HALE B63...........................138 B5
  KIDD DY10.........................168 C4
Beilchers La BORD B9...........129 F1
Beldray Pk BILS/COS WV14 *...54 A2
Beldray Rd BILS/COS WV14.....54 A2
Belfry Cl BLOX/PEL WS3.........16 C4
Belfry Dr STRBR DY8...........135 E1
The Belfry
  DUNHL/THL/PER WV6............34 B1
Belgrade Rd WOLVN WV10......12 B5
Belgrave Cl KGSWFD DY6.....100 D5
Belgrave Int DIG/EDG B5.......126 D5
Belgrave Middleway
  DIG/EDG B5........................127 E5
Belgrave Rd BHTH/HG B12....144 B1
  RMSLY B62.........................122 B4
Belgrave Ter HDSW B21........108 A2
Belgravia Cl DIG/EDG B5.......127 E5
Belgravia Ct DIG/EDG B15 *...142 C1
Belinda Cl WLNHL WV13.........39 F2
Bellamy Cl SHLY B90............180 D4
Bellamy Farm Rd SHLY B90...180 D4
Bellamy La WNSFLD WV11......24 D3
Bell Barn Rd DIG/EDG B5......126 D4
Bell Cl BORD B9....................128 C1
  CBROM B36.........................114 B3
  DARL/WED WS10...................55 F1
Bellcroft LDYWD/EDGR B16.....2 A6
Bell Dr DSYBK/YTR WS5.........57 G5
  WASH/WDE B8.....................128 D1
Bellefield Av WSNGN B18......107 C5
Bellefield Rd WSNGN B18.....107 C5
Bellemere Rd HIA/OLT B92....167 H5
Bellencroft Gdns
  BDMR/CCFT WV3...................50 B1
Bell End BLKHTH/ROWR B65..122 A1
Belle V HALE B63.................138 A2
Bellevue DIG/EDG B5............138 C3
Belle Vue STRBR DY8...........117 C2
Bellevue Av
  LDYWD/EDGR B16 *.............107 F5
Belle Vue Dr RMSLY B62......139 G1
Belle Vue Gdns
  BLKHTH/ROWR B65 *...........122 A1

Belle Vue Rd BRLYHL DY5.....120 A3
Bellevue Rd BILS/COS WV14...67 H1
  LGN/SDN/BHAMAIR B26.....130 C5
Bellevue St BILS/COS WV14.....67 H1
Belle Vue Ter HIA/OLT B92....167 G4
Belle Wk MOS/BIL B13..........144 D5
Bellfarm Ms CDYHTH B64 *...121 F2
Bellflower Dr DSYBK/YTR WS5..57 F5
Bell Fold LGLYGN/QTN B68...105 G3
Bell Green La
  HWK/WKHTH B38...............191 H3
Bell Heather Rd BRWNH WS8...18 D1
Bell Heath Wy
  RIDG/WDGT B32..................140 B5
Bell HI NFLD/LBR B31...........175 C1
Bell Holloway NFLD/LBR B31...158 B5
Bellington Cft SHLY B90.......195 C2
Bellis St LDYWD/EDGR B16...125 G3
Bell La BLOX/PEL WS3...........27 F1
  DSYBK/YTR WS5...................57 C4
  NFLD/LBR B31....................175 C1
  STETCH B33........................131 C3
Bellman Cl DARL/WED WS10...55 F1
Bell Meadow HAG/WOL DY9..152 D3
Bell Pl BRKL/PFLD WV2 *........57 E5
Bell Rd DSYBK/YTR WS5.........58 B2
  DUDS DY2...........................102 C4
  WMBN WV5...........................64 B2
Bells Farm Cl
  ALE/KHTH/YWD B14...........177 C3
  STRBR DY8........................117 H3
Bells Moor Rd WBROM B70......71 E5
Bell St BILS/COS WV14............68 C1
  BRLYHL DY5.......................119 F2
  DARL/WED WS10...................55 F1
  TPTN/OCK DY4......................85 E1
  WBROM B70...........................87 H4
  WOLV WV1.............................7 F5
Bell St South BRLYHL DY5.....119 F2
Bell Vue Rd
  BLKHTH/ROWR B65.............122 A2
Bellwood Rd NFLD/LBR B31...175 F1
Belmont Cl ALDR WS9............30 A3
  TPTN/OCK DY4......................69 F5
Belmont Covert
  NFLD/LBR B31....................158 D4
Belmont Crs NFLD/LBR B31...158 D4
Belmont Gdns BILS/COS WV14..54 C4
Belmont Pas BORD B9..........127 G2
Belmont Rd BRLYHL DY5......101 F3
  ETTPK/GDPK/PENN WV4......51 G3
  HAC/WOL DY9.....................136 C3
  HDSW B21...........................107 F1
  RBRY B45...........................187 H2
  SMTHWK B66.......................124 C2
Belmont Rd East HDSW B21...107 F1
Belmont Rw DIG/EDG B5.........3 K3
Belmont St BILS/COS WV14.....54 C4
Belper DUDS DY2 *.................67 H3
Belper Rd BILS/COS WV14.......54 C4
Belper Rw DUDS DY2............103 E5
Belstone Cl
  ALE/KHTH/YWD B14...........160 D5
Belton Av WNSFLD WV11.........24 B1
Belton Gv RBRY B45.............174 C5
Belvedere Av
  ETTPK/GDPK/PENN WV4......51 H3
Belvedere Cl KGSWFD DY6...100 B5
Belvedere Gdns
  DUNHL/THL/PER WV6............21 G3
Belvedere Rd
  ERDE/BCHGN B24.................93 E4
Belvide Gdns CDSL WV8..........10 B5
Belvidere Gdns SPARK B11....144 D3
Belvidere Rd WSL WS1.............5 F7
Belvoir Cl DUDN DY1..............83 G4
Belwell Dr FOAKS/STRLY B74..47 E3
Belwell La FOAKS/STRLY B74..47 E3
Bembridge Cl SHHTH WV12....25 H2
Bembridge Rd STETCH B33...130 C2
Benacre Dr DIG/EDG B5............3 K5
Benbeck Gv TPTN/OCK DY4.....84 C1
Bendall Rd KGSTG B44............75 H1
Benedon Rd
  LGN/SDN/BHAMAIR B26.....130 C5
Benmore Av DIG/EDG B5.......143 H1
Bennett Av DUDN DY1............68 B5
Bennett Rd FOAKS/STRLY B74..46 B2
Bennett's Hi CBHAMNW B3 *....3 E5
Bennetts Rd WASH/WDE B8...110 B3
Ben Nevis Wy STRBR DY8.....135 C1
Benson Av
  ETTPK/GDPK/PENN WV4......52 A3
Benson Cl
  DUNHL/THL/PER WV6............20 C5
Benson Rd
  ALE/KHTH/YWD B14...........178 D4
  WSNGN B18........................107 H3
Bent Av RIDG/WDGT B32......140 D1
Bentham Ct NFLD/LBR B31...158 B5
Bentley Bridge Pk
  WNSFLD WV11 *....................38 B1
Bentleybridge Wy
  WNSFLD WV11......................38 C1
Bentley Dr CDSL WV8.............10 B5
  WSLW WS2............................41 F5
Bentley La SHHTH WV12.........26 B5
  WSLW WS2............................41 E1
Bentley Mill Cl WSLW WS2......40 D4
Bentley Mill La WSLW WS2.....40 C4
Bentley Mill Wy WSLW WS2....40 D5
Bentley New Dr WSLW WS2....41 F2
Bentley Pl WSLW WS2............41 G3
Bentley Rd CBROM B36........113 F2
Bentley Rd North WSLW WS2..40 C4
Bentley Rd South
  DARL/WED WS10...................40 B5
Bentmead Gv
  DUNHL/THL/PER WV6............
Benton Av SPARK B11...........145 E1
Benton Cl SHHTH WV12.........40 B1

Benton Crs BLOX/PEL WS3......17
Benton Rd SPARK B11...........145
Bentons Mill Cft
  VAUX/NECH B7.....................110
Ben St BRLYHL DY5..............101
Ben Willetts Wk
  BLKHTH/ROWR B65.............122
Beoley Cl SCFLD/WYGN B72....77
Beoley Gv RBRY B45............188
Berberry Cl BVILLE B30..........158
Beresford Crs WBROM B70......87
Beresford Dr SCFLD/BOLD B73..77
Beresford Rd BLOX/PEL WS3...28
  OLDBY B69.........................105
Bericote Cft ACGN B27.........146
Berkeley Cl
  DUNHL/THL/PER WV6.............
Berkeley Cl East.....................40
Berkeley Dr KGSWFD DY6.......99
Berkeley Ms YDLY B25..........129
Berkeley Rd WSLW WS2..........
Berkeley Rd East YDLY B25....129
Berkeley St WSLW WS2...........
Berkley Crs MOS/BIL B13......161
Berkley St CBHAMW B1............
Berkshire Cl HHTH/SAND B71...71
Berkshire Crs DARL/WED WS10..71
The Berkshire BLOX/PEL WS3 *..16
Berkswell Cl DUDN DY1...........83
  FOAKS/STRLY B74.................46
Bermuda Cl DUDN DY1............68
Bernard Pl WSNGN B18 *......107
Bernard Rd HRBN B17..........124
  LGLYGN/QTN B68................123
  TPTN/OCK DY4......................69
Bernard St HHTH/SAND B71....87
  WSL WS1..............................
Berners St LOZ/NWT B19......108
Bernhard Dr HDSW B21.........107
Bernwall Cl STRBR DY8.........135
Berrandale Rd CBROM B36......94
Berrington Dr BILS/COS WV14..68
Berrington Wk DIG/EDG B5....127
Berrow Dr EDG B15..............125
Berrowside Rd
  BKDE/SHDE B34..................113
Berry Av DARL/WED WS10.......55
Berrybush Gdns SEDG DY3.....67
Berry Cl LOZ/NWT B19.........108
Berry Crs DSYBK/YTR WS5......58
Berry Dr ALDR WS9................29
  SMTHWK B66........................
Berryfield Rd
  LGN/SDN/BHAMAIR B26.....148
Berryfields Rd ALDR WS9.......29
Berryfields Rd
  WALM/CURD B76..................63
Berry Hall La SOLH B91........183
Berrymound Vw HLYWD B47...193
Berry Rd DUDN DY1................68
  WASH/WDE B8......................
Berry St WOLV WV1.................
  WSNGN B18..........................
Bertha Rd SPARK B11...........145
Bertram Cl TPTN/OCK DY4......70
Bertram Rd BORD B9...........128
  SMTHWK B67.......................
Berwick Gv GTB/HAM B43......59
  NFLD/LBR B31....................187
Berwicks La
  CHWD/FDBR/MGN B37.......132
Berwood Farm Rd
  ERDE/BCHGN B24..................77
Berwood Gdns
  ERDE/BCHGN B24..................77
Berwood La ERDE/BCHGN B24..94
Berwood Pk CVALE B35...........
Berwood Rd
  CSCFLD/WYGN B72................77
Besant Gv ACGN B27............146
Besbury Cl DOR/KN B93........198
Bescot Crs WSL WS1...............
Bescot Cft PBAR/PBCH B42......
Bescot Dr WSLW WS2..............
Bescot Rd WSLW WS2.............
Bescot St WSL WS1..................
Besford Gv NFLD/LBR B31....174
  SHLY B90............................195
Bessborough Rd YDLY B25....129
Best Rd BILS/COS WV14..........54
Best St CDYHTH B64............121
Best Wk CDYHTH B64............123
Beswick Gv STETCH B33.......112
Beta Gv ALE/KHTH/YWD B14..179
Bethesda Gdns HALE B63......120
Betjeman Pl WOLVN WV10.......22
Betley Gv STETCH B33............
Betony Cl DSYBK/YTR WS5......57
Betsham Cl KGSTG B44..........75
Bettany Gld WOLVN WV10.......13
Betteridge Dr WALM/CURD B76..63
Bett Rd BFLD/HDSWWD B20...90
Bevan Av
  ETTPK/GDPK/PENN WV4......52
Bevan Cl BILS/COS WV14........54
  RUSH/SHEL WS4....................29
Bevan Rd BRLYHL DY5..........118
  TPTN/OCK DY4......................85
Bevan Wy SMTHWK B66........106
Beverley Cl CSCFLD/WYGN B72..77
Beverley Court Rd
  RIDG/WDGT B32..................
Beverley Crs
  ETTPK/GDPK/PENN WV4......52
Beverley Cft ERDW/GRVHL B23..92
Beverley Dr KGSWFD DY6.......81
Beverley Gv
  LGN/SDN/BHAMAIR B26.....147
Beverley Rd HHTH/SAND B71...71
  RBRY B45...........................188

Bewdley Av BHTH/HG B12 ....144 C1
Bewdley Dr WNSWD WV4 * 38 B3
Bewdley Rd BVILLE B30 ....160 B2
Bewdley Rd WS WSNGN B18 * 107 F5
Bewley Cl BRLYHL DY5 ....118 C5
Bewlys Av BFLD/HDSWWD B20 ....89 C2
Bexhill Gv EDG B15 ....126 C3
Bexley Gv HHTH/SAND B71 ....72 A4
Bexley Rd KGSTG B44 ....75 H3
Bhylls Crs BDMR/CCFT WV3 ....50 C1
Bhylls La BDMR/CCFT WV3 ....50 B1
Bibbey's Gn WOLVN WV10 ....13 F3
Bibsworth Av MOS/BIL B13 ....162 B2
Bibury Rd HLGN/YWD B28 ....162 C3
Bicester Sq CVALE B35 ....94 D2
Bickenhill La
  CHWD/FDBR/MGN B37 ....132 C5
  HIA/OLT B92 ....166 C4
Bickenhill Park Rd
  HIA/OLT B92 ....163 H1
Bickenhill Pkwy
  CHWD/FDBR/MGN B37 ....149 H1
Bickford Rd AST/WIT B6 ....91 C5
  WOLVN WV10 ....11 H3
Bickington Rd FOAKS/STRLY B74 ....32 C5
SPARK B11 * 144 D2
Bickley Gv
  LGN/SDN/BHAMAIR B26 ....147 H2
Bickley Rd BILS/COS WV14 ....54 C2
  RUSH/SHEL WS4 ....29 E3
Bickton Cl
  ALE/KHTH/YWD B14 ....178 A3
Biddings La BILS/COS WV14 ....68 B1
Biddlestone Pl
  DARL/WED WS10 ....54 D1
Biddleston Gv DSYBK/YTR WS5 ....58 A5
Bideford Dr SLYOAK B29 ....159 E1
Bideford Rd SMTHWK B66 ....106 D4
Bidford Cl SHLY B90 ....180 D3
Bidford Rd NFLD/LBR B31 ....175 E2
Bierton Rd YDLY B25 ....129 C4
Biggin Cl CVALE B35 ....94 C3
  DUNHL/THL/PER WV6 ....20 C5
The Big Peg WSNGN B18 * 2 C2
Bigwood Dr MGN/WHC B75 ....63 G2
  RIDG/WDGT B32 ....157 G1
Bilberry Crs WALM/CURD B76 ....63 E5
Bilberry Dr RBRY B45 ....188 A2
Bilberry Rd
  ALE/KHTH/YWD B14 ....160 C4
Bilboe Rd BILS/COS WV14 ....54 B5
Bilbrook Ct CDSL WV8 ....10 C4
Bilbrook Gv CDSL WV8 ....10 C4
  SLYOAK B29 ....141 F5
Bilbrook Rd CDSL WV8 ....10 C3
Bilhay La WBROM B70 ....87 E1
Bilhay St WBROM B70 ....87 F1
Billau Rd BILS/COS WV14 ....68 C1
Billesley La MOS/BIL B13 ....161 G2
Billingham Cl SOLH B91 ....181 H5
Billingsley Rd
  LGN/SDN/BHAMAIR B26 ....130 C4
Bills La SHLY B90 ....179 H5
Billsmore Gn HIA/OLT B92 ....165 E3
Bills St DARL/WED WS10 ....55 C2
Billy Buns La WMBN WV5 ....65 E5
Billy Wright Cl
  ETTPK/GDPK/PENN WV4 ....50 D2
Bilport La DARL/WED WS10 ....72 D1
Bilston La WLNHL WV13 ....39 H5
Bilston Rd DARL/WED WS10 ....55 F2
  DARL/WED WS10 ....69 H1
  TPTN/OCK DY4 ....54 C1
  WLNHL WV13 ....54 C1
Bilston St DARL/WED WS10 ....55 F2
  SEDG DY3 ....67 E3
  WLNHL WV13 ....39 G4
Bilston Street Island WOLV WV1 ....7 H5
Bilton Grange Rd
  LGN/SDN/BHAMAIR B26 ....130 B1
Bincomb Av
  LGN/SDN/BHAMAIR B26 ....147 H1
Binfield St TPTN/OCK DY4 ....85 C2
Bingley Av WASH/WDE B8 ....111 F5
Bingley St WV BDMR/CCFT WV3 ....36 C5
Binley Cl SHLY B90 ....180 A5
  YDLY B25 ....146 D1
Binstead Rd KGSTG B44 ....75 C1
Binswood Rd RMSLY B62 ....123 G5
Binton Cft MOS/BIL B13 ....161 F2
Binton Rd SHLY B90 ....179 H4
Birbeck Pl BRLYHL DY5 ....100 D3
Birchall St BHTH/HG B12 ....127 F3
Birch Av BRLYHL DY5 ....9 E4
  BRWNH WS8 ....9 E4
  NFLD/LBR B31 ....174 C4
Birch Cl BVILLE B30 ....159 F4
  WALM/CURD B76 ....78 B1
Birchcoppice Gdns
  SHHTH WV12 ....40 C1
Birch Crs ALDR WS9 ....85 H5
  CHWD/FDBR/MGN B37 ....132 C5
  ERDE/BCHGN B24 ....93 C3
Birchcroft SMTHWK B66 ....107 E4
Birch Croft Rd MGN/WHC B75 ....62 D1
Birchdale BILS/COS WV14 ....53 H1
Birchdale Av ERDW/GRVHL B23 ....92 C3
Birchdale Rd ERDE/BCHGN B23 ....92 B1
Birch Dr FOAKS/STRLY B74 ....32 B5
  MGN/WHC B75 ....63 F1
  RMSLY B62 ....122 A1
  STRBR DY8 ....135 E1
Birches Barn Av
  BDMR/CCFT WV3 ....51 F1
Birches Barn Rd
  BDMR/CCFT WV3 ....36 B5
Birches Cl MOS/BIL B13 ....161 F1
Birches Green Rd
  ERDE/BCHGN B24 ....93 F4

Birches Park Rd CDSL WV8 ....10 C5
Birches Ri WLNHL WV13 ....39 F4
Birches Rd CDSL WV8 ....10 D5
Birchfield Av
  DUNHL/THL/PER WV6 ....21 F4
Birchfield Cl HALE B63 ....138 A5
Birchfield Crs HAG/WOL DY9 ....136 D4
Birchfield Gdns AST/WIT B6 * 108 D1
Birchfield La OLDBY B69 ....104 C5
Birchfield Rd
  BFLD/HDSWWD B20 ....90 D5
  HAG/WOL DY9 ....136 D4
  LOZ/NWT B19 ....108 D1
Birchfields Rd WNSFLD WV11 ....25 C5
Birchfield Wy DSYBK/YTR WS5 ....57 H5
Birchgate HAG/WOL DY9 ....136 D3
Birchglade BDMR/CCFT WV3 ....35 H4
Birch Gv LGLYGN/QTN B68 ....123 H5
Birch Hill Av WMBN WV5 ....80 C1
Birch Hollow EDG B15 ....143 G2
Birch Pll PI WMBN WV5 ....80 D1
Birchills St WSLW WS2 ....4 A2
Birch La ALDR WS9 ....30 D1
  LGLYGN/QTN B68 ....123 H5
  RUSH/SHEL WS4 ....29 E1
Birchley Park Av OLDBY B69 ....104 C3
Birchley Ri HIA/OLT B92 ....145 H2
Birchmoor Cl HLGN/YWD B28 ....163 F3
Birchover Rd WSLW WS2 ....41 E1
Birch Rd AST/WIT B6 ....91 G4
  LGLYGN/QTN B68 ....123 H5
  RBRY B45 ....187 G2
  SEDG DY3 ....67 H2
  WNSFLD WV11 ....25 F1
Birch Rd East AST/WIT B6 ....91 H4
  LGLYGN/QTN B68 ....105 G5
  TPTN/OCK DY4 ....85 E1
  WOLV WV1 ....6 E4
Birch Ter DUDS DY2 ....102 C5
Birch Tree Gdns ALDR WS9 ....30 D5
Birchtree Gdns BRLYHL DY5 ....120 A3
Birch Tree Gv SOLH B91 ....181 E1
Birchtree Rd ERDE/BCHGN B24 ....93 H2
Birchtrees Cft
  LGN/SDN/BHAMAIR B26 ....146 D2
Birchtrees Dr STECH B33 ....131 F1
Birch Wk LGLYGN/QTN B68 ....123 H5
Birchwood Cl WNSFLD WV11 ....15 E4
Birchwood Crs BHTH/HG B12 ....144 D2
Birchwood Rd BHTH/HG B12 ....144 D2
  ETTPK/GDPK/PENN WV4 ....51 C3
Birchwoods RIDG/WDGT B32 ....140 B5
Birchy Cl SHLY B90 ....193 H2
Birchy Leasowes La SHLY B90 ....193 G3
Bird Rd DARL/WED WS10 ....55 H5
Bird End HHTH/SAND S71 ....75 E3
Birdie Cl HWK/WKHTH B38 ....176 B4
Birdip Gv RIDG/WDGT B32 ....140 C1
Birds Meadow BRLYHL DY5 ....100 D2
Bird St SEDG DY3 ....66 A3
Birdwell Cft MOS/BIL B13 ....161 F4
Birkdale Av SLYOAK B29 ....159 H1
Birkdale Cl STRBR DY8 ....152 B1
  WOLV WV1 ....38 A3
Birkdale Dr OLDBY B69 ....105 C2
Birkdale Gv SLYOAK B29 ....160 A2
Birkdale Rd BLOX/PEL WS3 ....16 C4
Birkenshaw Rd KGSTG B44 ....75 E3
Birley Gv HALE B63 ....154 C2
Birmingham New Rd
  DUDN DY1 ....85 C2
  ETTPK/GDPK/PENN WV4 ....52 D4
Birmingham Rd ALDR WS9 ....44 A1
  BKHL/PFLD WV2 ....37 F5
  BLKHTH/ROWR B65 ....122 A2
  BRGRVW B61 ....199 C5
  CBROM B36 ....112 C1
  CHWD/FDBR/MGN B37 ....114 C4
  CSCFLD/WYGN B72 ....77 F3
  DSYBK/YTR WS5 ....57 H1
  DUDN DY1 ....85 C4
  HAG/WOL DY9 ....153 F4
  HALE B63 ....138 D4
  KIDD DY10 ....168 C3
  LICHS WS14 ....33 E3
  OLDBY B69 ....105 F2
  RCOVN/BALC/EX CV7 ....151 F4
  WBROM B70 ....88 A5
  WSL WS1 ....5 H7
Birmingham St
  DARL/WED WS10 ....55 F2
  DUDS DY2 ....84 D5
  HALE B63 ....138 D4
  OLDBY B69 ....105 E1
  STRBR DY8 ....135 H2
  WLNHL WV13 ....39 H4
  WSL WS1 ....5 F5
Birnham Cl TPTN/OCK DY4 ....84 D1
Bisbrook Cft SOLH B91 ....165 F4
Bisley Gv BRLYHL DY5 ....136 B1
Bishbury Cl EDG B15 ....125 C4
Bishop Asbury Crs
  GTB/HAM B43 ....72 D3
Bishop Cl RBRY B45 ....173 G4
Bishop Cl DARL/WED WS10 ....71 G1
Bishops Cl DUDS DY2 ....103 E1
  SMTHWK B66 ....107 E5
Bishop's Ct
  CHWD/FDBR/MGN B37 ....133 E4
Bishops Ga NFLD/LBR B31 ....175 G3
Bishopsgate St EDG B15 ....2 B7
Bishops Meadow
  MGN/WHC B75 ....47 E5
Bishops Rd SCFLD/BOLD B73 ....62 B5
Bishops Wk CDYHTH B64 ....138 C1
Bishops Wy FOAKS/STRLY B74 ....32 C5
Bishopton Cl SHLY B90 ....180 C4
Bishopton Rd SMTHWK B66 ....124 B3
Bishton Gv DUDS DY2 ....102 D5
Bissel Dr DARL/WED WS10 ....56 B5
Bissell Cl HLGN/YWD B28 ....162 D4
Bissell St BHTH/HG B12 ....127 E4
  RIDG/WDGT B32 ....140 A1
Bissel St BILS/COS WV14 ....54 B3
Biton Cl HRBN B17 ....141 H2
Bittell Cl NFLD/LBR B31 ....189 F1

WOLVN WV10 ....13 E3
Bitterne Dr DUNHL/THL/PER WV636C1
Blackacre Rd DUDS DY2 ....102 D1
Blackberry Cl DUDN DY1 ....101 H2
Blackberry Cl DUDN DY1 ....101 C1
Blackberry La ALDR WS9 ....19 H5
  BLKHTH/ROWR B65 ....103 F4
  FOAKS/STRLY B74 ....46 C1
  HALE B63 ....138 C5
Blackbird Cft CBROM B36 ....114 A2
Blackbrook Cl DUDS DY2 ....120 A1
Blackbrook Rd DUDS DY2 ....102 A4
Blackbrook Wy WOLVN WV10 ....13 E3
Blackburn Av
  DUNHL/THL/PER WV6 ....22 A3
Blackburne Rd
  HLGN/YWD B28 ....162 D4
Blackbushe Cl HRBN B17 ....124 B5
Blackcat Cl
  CHWD/FDBR/MGN B37 ....132 A1
Black Country New Rd
  DARL/WED WS10 ....54 C2
Black Country Route
  BILS/COS WV14 ....54 B2
Blackdown Cl RBRY B45 ....174 A3
Blackdown Rd DOR/KN B93 ....197 F2
Blackfirs La BHAMNEC B40 ....133 E5
  CHWD/FDBR/MGN B37 ....132 D5
Blackford Cl HALE B63 ....137 C3
Blackford Rd SHLY B90 ....194 C1
  SPARK B11 ....145 E3
Blackhalve La WNSFLD WV11 ....24 B2
Blackham Dr SCFLD/BOLD B73 ....77 G4
Blackham Rd WNSFLD WV11 ....25 F2
Blacks Haynes Rd SLYOAK B29 ....158 C3
Black Horse Cl
  DARL/WED WS10 ....55 F5
Blackhorse La BRLYHL DY5 ....119 C3
Blackmoor Cft STECH B33 ....131 F2
Blackrock Rd
  ERDW/GRVHL B23 ....92 B1
Blackroot Rd FOAKS/STRLY B74 ....62 A1
Blacksmith Cl RIDG/WDGT B32 ....140 B4
Blacksmiths La HOCK/TIA B94 ....198 A5
Blacksmith Wy WBROM B70 ....87 G4
Blackthorn Cl DUDS DY2 ....102 A5
Blackthorne Cl SOLH B91 ....181 E1
Blackthorne Rd
  DSYBK/YTR WS5 ....57 F3
  DUDN DY1 ....83 H2
  SMTHWKW B67 ....105 H5
Blackthorn Rd BVILLE B30 ....159 E4
  CBROM B36 ....113 E1
  STRBR DY8 ....118 B3
Blackwater Cl KGSWFD DY6 ....100 C4
Blackwell Rd
  CSCFLD/WYGN B72 ....77 H2
Blackwood Av WNSFLD WV11 ....24 B2
Blackwood Dr
  FOAKS/STRLY B74 ....45 E5
Blades Rd WBROM B70 ....86 B2
Blaenwern Dr HALE B63 ....120 B5
Blagdon Rd HALE B63 ....138 C1
Blair Gv
  CHWD/FDBR/MGN B37 ....133 D3
Blakedon Rd DARL/WED WS10 ....55 C5
Blakedown Rd HALE B63 ....138 B5
Blake Hall Cl BRLYHL DY5 ....118 D5
Blakeland Rd KGSTG B44 ....75 E5
Blakeland St BORD B9 ....128 D2
Blake La BORD B9 ....128 D2
Blakeley Av
  DUNHL/THL/PER WV6 ....22 B3
Blakeley Hall Gdns OLDBY B69 ....105 F2
Blakeley Hall Rd OLDBY B69 ....105 F2
Blakeley Heath Dr WMBN WV5 ....81 E1
Blakeley Ri
  DUNHL/THL/PER WV6 ....22 B3
Blakeley Wood Rd
  TPTN/OCK DY4 ....70 A3
Blakely Hall Rd OLDBY B69 ....105 F1
Blakemere Av YDLY B25 ....130 A4
Blakemore Cl RIDG/WDGT B32 ....141 F4
Blakemore Dr MGN/WHC B75 ....63 F2
Blakemore Rd ALDR WS9 ....19 H4
  WBROM B70 ....87 G4
Blakenall Cl BLOX/PEL WS3 ....27 H1
Blakenall Heath BLOX/PEL WS3 ....27 H2
Blakenall La BLOX/PEL WS3 ....27 H2
Blakenall Rw BLOX/PEL WS3 ....27 H2
Blakeney Av HRBN B17 ....124 C5
  STRBR DY8 ....134 D1
Blakeney Cl SEDG DY3 ....67 E3
Blakenhale Rd STECH B33 ....130 D5
Blakenhall Gdns
  BKHL/PFLD WV2 ....52 B1
Blake Pl BORD B9 ....129 E1
Blakesley Cl WALM/CURD B76 ....94 B1
Blakesley Ms YDLY B25 ....129 H4
Blakesley Rd STECH B33 ....129 G3
Blakesley Wy STECH B33 ....129 H2
Blake St FOAKS/STRLY B74 ....32 C4
Blakewood Cl
  BKDE/SHDE B34 ....113 E4
Blandford Av CBROM B36 ....95 C5
Blandford Dr STRBR DY8 ....118 A2
Blandford Rd RIDG/WDGT B32 ....141 F4
Blanefield CDSL WV8 ....22 A1
Blay Av WSLW WS2 ....41 C5
Blaydon Av MGN/WHC B75 ....48 A3
Blaydon Rd COVEN WV9 ....22 C1
Blaythorn Av HIA/OLT B92 ....147 G4
Blaze Hill Rd KGSWFD DY6 ....99 F1
Blaze Pk KGSWFD DY6 ....99 F1
Bleak Hill Rd ERDW/GRVHL B23 ....92 A1
Bleakhouse Rd
  LGLYGN/QTN B68 ....123 C3
Bleak St SMTHWKW B67 ....106 B3
Blenheim Cl RUSH/SHEL WS4 ....29 F3
Blenheim Dr GTB/HAM B43 ....73 E5
Blenheim Rd KGSWFD DY6 ....100 C3
  MOS/BIL B13 ....161 F1
  SHHTH WV12 ....25 H4
  SHLY B90 ....180 D3

Blenheim Wy CVALE B35 ....94 C4
  DUDN DY1 ....83 C4
  KGSTG B44 ....75 F3
Bletchley Rd ERDE/BCHGN B24 ....94 A2
Blewitt Cl CBROM B36 ....95 H4
Blewitt St BRLYHL DY5 ....101 E3
Blithe Cl STRBR DY8 ....118 C4
Blithfield Dr BRLYHL DY5 ....118 C5
Blithfield Gv ERDE/BCHGN B24 ....93 C1
Blithfield Rd BRWNH WS8 ....8 C2
Blockall DARL/WED WS10 ....55 F1
Bloomfield Cl WMBN WV5 ....64 B5
Bloomfield Dr SHHTH WV12 ....26 B5
Bloomfield Pk TPTN/OCK DY4 ....68 D5
Bloomfield Rd MOS/BIL B13 ....144 C4
  TPTN/OCK DY4 ....68 D4
Bloomfield St North HALE B63 ....138 B2
Bloomfield St West HALE B63 ....138 B3
Bloomfield Ter TPTN/OCK DY4 ....68 D5
Bloomsbury Gv
  ALE/KHTH/YWD B14 ....160 C3
Bloomsbury St BKHL/PFLD WV2 ....6 E6
  VAUX/NECH B7 ....109 H4
Bloomsbury Wk
  VAUX/NECH B7 * 109 H4
Bloor Mill Cl WNSWD WV13 * 39 F4
Blossom Av SLYOAK B29 ....142 D5
Blossomfield Cl
  KGSWFD DY6 ....100 A1
Blossomfield Rd SOLH B91 ....181 F3
Blossom Hl ERDE/BCHGN B24 ....93 C2
Blossom Rd ERDE/BCHGN B24 ....93 C2
Blossomville Wy ACGN B27 ....146 B3
Blowers Green Crs DUDS DY2 ....102 B2
Blowers Green Rd DUDS DY2 ....102 B2
Bloxcidge St LGLYGN/QTN B68 ....105 F4
Bloxwich La WSLW WS2 ....41 E2
Bloxwich Rd WSLW WS2 ....27 H4
Bloxwich Rd North
  WLNHL WV13 ....39 G2
Blucher St CBHAMW B1 ....2 E7
Blue Ball La HALE B63 ....137 G1
Bluebell Crs ERDW/GRVHL B23 ....76 A4
Bluebell Crs WNSFLD WV11 ....24 D5
Bluebell Cft ERDW/GRVHL B23 ....76 A4
  NFLD/LBR B31 ....175 F3
Bluebell Dr
  CHWD/FDBR/MGN B37 ....132 D2
  CDYHTH B64 ....121 E1
Bluebell La STRBR DY8 ....118 B3
Bluebellwood Cl
  FOAKS/STRLY B74 ....46 D4
  MGN/WHC B75 ....47 F3
  WALM/CURD B76 ....63 C5
Blue Cedar Dr
  FOAKS/STRLY B74 ....60 B1
Blue Cedars STRBR DY8 ....134 C1
Blue Lake Rd DOR/KN B93 ....199 F1
Blue La East WSLW WS2 ....4 D1
Blue La West WSLW WS2 ....4 B2
Blue Rock Pl OLDBY B69 ....104 A3
Bluestone Wy SOLH B91 ....182 A4
Blundell Rd SPARK B11 ....145 F2
Blythefield Av GTB/HAM B43 ....73 E2
Blythe Gdns CDSL WV8 ....10 B3
Blythe Gv KGSTG B44 ....60 B5
Blythe Rd CSHL/WTROR B46 ....115 H1
Blytheway SOLH B91 ....182 A3
Blythewood Cl SOLH B91 ....182 B4
Blythsford Rd HLGN/YWD B28 ....179 H1
Blythswood Rd SPARK B11 ....146 A3
Blyton Cl LDYWD/EDGR B16 ....107 H5
Board School Gdns SEDG DY3 ....67 G5
Boar Hound Cl WSNGN B18 * 108 A5
Boatman's La ALDR WS9 ....19 E5
Bobbington Wy DUDS DY2 ....102 D4
Bob's Coppice Wk BRLYHL DY5 ....119 H5
Bodenham Rd
  LGLYGN/QTN B68 ....123 F4
  NFLD/LBR B31 ....175 E3
Boden Rd HLGN/YWD B28 ....163 E3
Bodens La ALDR WS9 ....46 B2
Bodicote Gv MGN/WHC B75 ....48 A2
Bodington Rd MGN/WHC B75 ....47 F2
Bodmin Cl WLNHL WV12 ....26 B5
Bodmin Gv VAUX/NECH B7 ....109 H4
Bodmin Ri DSYBK/YTR WS5 ....58 B1
Bodmin Rd DUDS DY2 ....120 C2
Bognop Rd WNSFLD WV11 ....14 B3
Boldmere Cl SCFLD/BOLD B73 ....77 E4
Boldmere Dr SCFLD/BOLD B73 ....77 E3
Boldmere Gdns
  SCFLD/BOLD B73 * 61 H5
Boldmere Ga
  SCFLD/BOLD B73 * 61 H5
Boldmere Rd SCFLD/BOLD B73 ....76 D2
Boldmere Ter SLYOAK B29 * 159 C1
Boleyn Rd RBRY B45 ....173 F3
Bolney Rd RIDG/WDGT B32 ....141 E2
Bolton Rd SMTH B10 ....128 A4
  WNSFLD WV11 ....24 C5
Bolton St BORD B9 ....127 H2
Bolton Wy BLOX/PEL WS3 ....16 A4
Bomers Fld RBRY B45 ....188 C5
Bond Dr CVALE B35 ....94 C4
Bondfield Rd MOS/BIL B13 ....161 H4
Bond Sq WSNGN B18 ....108 A5
Bond St BILS/COS WV14 ....68 A3
  BKHL/PFLD WV2 ....7 F6
  BLKHTH/ROWR B65 ....122 C1
  BVILLE B30 ....160 A1
  LOZ/NWT B19 ....108 C3
  WBROM B70 ....87 C4

Bonville Gdns WOLVN WV10 ....13 E3
Booth Cl BLOX/PEL WS3 ....27 H2
  KGSWFD DY6 ....100 C5
Booths Farm Rd
  PBAR/PBCH B42 ....74 A4
Booth's La PBAR/PBCH B42 ....74 B2
Booth St BLOX/PEL WS3 ....27 C2
  HDSW B21 ....90 B5
  HDSW B21 ....107 E2
Bordeaux Cl DUDN DY1 ....83 C3
Borden Cl CDSL WV8 ....22 B2
Bordesley Circ SMTHH B10 ....127 H5
Bordesley Cl BORD B9 ....129 E2
Bordesley Gn East
  STECH B33 ....130 A2
Bordesley Green Rd BORD B9 ....128 D2
Bordesley Park Rd
  SMTHH B10 ....127 H3
Bordesley St DIG/EDG B5 ....3 J5
Borneo St RUSH/SHEL WS4 ....42 B1
Borough Crs OLDBY B69 ....104 C3
  STRBR DY8 ....135 E2
Borrowdale Cl BRLYHL DY5 ....118 D4
Borrowdale Gv NFLD/LBR B31 ....174 D2
Borrowdale Rd NFLD/LBR B31 ....174 C2
Borrow St WLNHL WV13 ....39 G2
Borwick Av WBROM B70 ....87 E3
Boscobel Av TPTN/OCK DY4 ....85 G2
Boscobel Cl DUDN DY1 ....83 H5
Boscobel Crs WOLV WV1 ....37 E1
Boscobel Rd GTB/HAM B43 ....73 F1
  SHLY B90 ....194 D3
  WSL WS1 ....5 K6
Boscombe Av SPARK B11 ....145 F4
Boscombe Rd SPARK B11 ....145 C5
Boss Dr DUDS DY2 ....102 C2
Bossgate Cl WMBN WV5 ....81 E1
Boston Gv KGSTG B44 ....75 H5
Bosty La ALDR WS9 ....29 E2
Boswell Cl TPTN/OCK DY4 ....70 A2
Boswell Rd BILS/COS WV14 ....54 B1
  FOAKS/STRLY B74 ....62 C2
  KGSTG B44 ....75 F5
Bosworth Cl DSYBK/YTR WS5 ....67 H5
Bosworth Dr
  CHWD/FDBR/MGN B37 ....131 H2
Bosworth Rd
  LGN/SDN/BHAMAIR B26 ....147 E3
Botany Dr DSYBK/YTR WS5 ....57 F3
Botany Rd DSYBK/YTR WS5 ....57 F3
  LDYWD/EDGR B16 * 126 A2
Botha Rd BORD B9 ....128 D2
Botteley Rd WBROM B70 ....71 E5
Bottenham La SEDG DY3 ....80 C5
Botteslow St SLYOAK B29 ....141 G5
Botteville Rd ACGN B27 ....146 C5
Bott La HAG/WOL DY9 ....136 B1
  WSL WS1 ....5 G4
Boughton Rd YDLY B25 ....129 C5
Boulevard BRLYHL DY5 ....119 C2
  SCFLD/BOLD B73 ....77 F3
Boultbee Rd
  CSCFLD/WYGN B72 ....77 G4
Boulton Middleway
  WSNGN B18 ....108 B4
Boulton Retreat HDSW B21 * 107 G1
Boulton Rd HDSW B21 ....107 G2
  SOLH B91 ....165 E3
  SMTHWK B66 ....106 D5
Boulton Sq WBROM B70 ....87 H5
Boulton Wk ERDW/GRVHL B23 ....91 H2
Boundary Av
  BLKHTH/ROWR B65 ....122 C2
Boundary Cl WLNHL WV13 ....38 C4
Boundary Crs SEDG DY3 ....83 E3
Boundary Dr MOS/BIL B13 ....143 H5
Boundary HI SEDG DY3 ....83 E2
Boundary La KINVER DY7 ....116 C3
  SHLY B90 ....194 A2
Boundary Pl HDSW B21 ....89 H5
Boundary Rd ALDR WS9 ....19 F4
  SHLY B90 ....193 C2
  ERDW/GRVHL B23 ....92 C2
  WSL WS1 ....5 J5
Boundary Wy
  DUNHL/THL/PER WV6 ....34 D3
  ETTPK/GDPK/PENN WV4 ....50 C2
Bourlay Cl RBRY B45 ....173 C5
Bournbrook Cl DUDS DY2 ....102 C4
Bourne Av RMSLY B62 ....139 H3
  TPTN/OCK DY4 ....70 A5
Bournebrook Cl DUDS DY2 ....102 C4
Bournebrook Crs RMSLY B62 ....140 A3
Bourne Cl MOS/BIL B13 ....162 A4
  SOLH B91 ....165 G4
Bournedale Cl PBAR/PBCH B42 ....73 H3
Bourne Dr RIDG/WDGT B32 ....102 A3
Bourne Hill Cl DUDS DY2 ....103 E5
Bourne Rd AST/WIT B6 ....109 H2
Bournes Cl HALE B63 ....138 B4
Bournes Crs HALE B63 ....138 A3
Bournes HI HALE B63 ....138 A3
Bourne St DUDS DY2 ....84 D5
  SEDG DY3 ....68 A4
Bourne V ALDR WS9 ....44 D2
Bourne Way Gdns SLYOAK B29 ....160 A2
Bournevale Rd RUSH/SHEL WS4 ....29 G3
Bournville La BVILLE B30 ....159 G4
Bourton Cl DSYBK/YTR WS5 ....57 C5
Bourton Cft HIA/OLT B92 ....164 B2
Bovey Cft WALM/CURD B76 ....78 C4
Bowater Av STECH B33 ....129 H3
Bowater St WBROM B70 ....87 G3
Bowbrook Av SHLY B90 ....195 C5
Bowcroft Gv ERDE/BCHGN B24 ....77 C5
Bowden Rd SMTHWKW B67 ....106 A3
Bowdler Rd BKHL/PFLD WV2 ....37 F5
Bowen Av
  ETTPK/GDPK/PENN WV4 ....53 E5
Bowen-Cooke Av
  DUNHL/THL/PER WV6 ....20 C4
Bowen St
  ETTPK/GDPK/PENN WV4 ....52 C3
Bower La BRLYHL DY5 ....119 H4
Bowercourt Cl SOLH B91 ....181 H4
Bowes Rd RBRY B45 ....187 G1
Bowker St WLNHL WV13 ....38 C3

Bowlas Av FOAKS/STRLY B74 ...... 47 F5
Bowling Green Cl
 DARL/WED WS10 ....55 F1
 ERDW/GRVHL B23 ....76 C4
Bowling Green Dr
 SMTHWKW B67 ....124 A2
Bowling Green La
 BFLD/HDSWWD B20 ....108 A1
Bowling Green Rd DUDS DY2 ...20 D1
 SMHTH B10 ....128 A3
 STRBR DY8 ....135 E2
Bowman Rd PBAR/PBCH B42...74 B2
Bowman's Ri WOLV WV1 ....38 A3
Bowood Dr
 DUNHL/THL/PER WV6............21 H5
Bowood End WALM/CURD B76...62 D5
Bowshot Cl CBROM B36 ....95 F5
Bowstoke Rd GTB/HAM B43...73 E3
Bow St BILS/COS WV14 ....144 C4
 CBHAMW B1 ....126 D3
 WLNHL WV13............39 C4
Bowyer Rd WASH/WDE B8 ......110 C5
Bowyer St BORD B9 ....127 C3
Boxhill Cl AST/WIT B6............137 G2
Box Rd CHWD/FDBR/MGN B37...132 C4
Box St WSL WS1 ....5 C5
Box Trees Rd HOCK/TIA B94...198 A2
Boyd Gv ACGN B27 ....146 B5
Boyton Cl BKHL/PFLD WV2......53 E2
Boylestone Rd HLGN/YWD B28...163 E4
Boyne Rd
 LGN/SDN/BHAMAIR B26 ......130 D5
Boyton Gv KGSTG B44............60 B5
Brabazon Gv CVALE B35 ....94 B3
Brabham Crs FOAKS/STRLY B74...60 B2
Bracadale Av ERDE/BCHGN B24...93 E2
Bracebridge Rd
 ERDE/BCHGN B24 ....92 D5
 FOAKS/STRLY B74 ....47 G5
Bracebridge St AST/WIT B6...109 E3
Braceley Av MOS/BIL B13 ......162 A3
Brace St WSL 4 D7
Brackenbury Rd KGSTG B44...75 H3
Bracken Cl CDSL WV8............22 A1
Bracken Cft
 CHWD/FDBR/MGN B37 ......132 C1
Brackendale Dr
 DSYBK/YTR WS5 ....57 H5
Brackendale Wy
 HAC/WOL DY9 ....136 B3
Bracken Dr MGN/WHC B75 ......63 G3
Brackenfield Rd HALE B63 ......138 A4
 KGSTG B44 ....74 C1
Brackenfield Vw DUDN DY1...101 F1
Bracken Park Gdns
 STRBR DY8 ....118 B2
Bracken Rd ERDE/BCHGN B24...93 G4
Bracken Wy FOAKS/STRLY B74...45 F5
 HWK/WKHTH B38 ....190 B1
Bracken Wd DSYBK/YTR WS5...58 B3
Brackenwood Dr
 WNSFLD WV11 ....25 F5
Brackley Av
 BFLD/HDSWWD B20 ....90 C5
Brackleys Wy HIA/OLT B92......147 F5
Bradburne Wy VAUX/NECH B7...109 G4
Bradbury Cl BRWNH WS8 ......9 H2
Bradbury Rd HIA/OLT B92......164 B2
Braden Rd
 ETTPK/GDPK/PENN WV4......50 D4
Brades Cl HALE B63 ....120 B5
Brades Rd OLDBY B69............104 B1
Bradewell Rd CBROM B36......95 F5
Bradfield Rd PBAR/PBCH B42...74 D4
Bradford Cl GTB/HAM B43 ......73 H4
Bradford La HAG/WOL DY9 ...184 B3
 WSL WS1 ....4 D5
Bradford Rd BKDE/SHDE B34...112 C2
 BRWNH WS8 ....9 E4
 CBROM B36 ....113 E2
 DUDS DY2 ....101 H3
Bradford St DIG/EDG B5............3 H7
 WSL WS1 ....4 D5
Bradgate Cl SHHTH WV12 ......26 A4
Bradgate Dr FOAKS/STRLY B74...32 C5
Bradley La BILS/COS WV14 ......54 B5
Bradleymore Rd BRLYHL DY5...119 E1
Bradley Rd BKDE/SHDE B34...113 F3
 BKHL/PFLD WV2 ....52 C1
 STRBR DY8 ....135 E2
Bradley's Cl CDYHTH B64......121 E5
Bradley La BILS/COS WV14...69 E3
Bradley St BILS/COS WV14 ......54 A4
 BRLYHL DY5 ....100 D2
 SEDG DY3 ....85 F4
Bradmore Cl SOLH B91 ....181 G5
Bradmore Rd BDMR/CCFT WV3...36 B5
Bradnock Cl MOS/BIL B13......162 A3
Bradshaw Av DARL/WED WS10...54 D5
 HWK/WKHTH B38 ....176 B4
Bradshaw Cl EDG B15............126 C4
 TPTN/OCK DY4 ....85 G3
Bradshawe Cl
 HLGN/YWD B28............179 F2
Bradshaw St WOLV WV1 *............7 H4
Bradstock Rd BVILLE B30 ......177 G1
Bradwell Cft MGN/WHC B75...48 A2
Braemar Av SLYOAK B29 ......158 C2
Braemar Cl SEDG DY3 ....67 E2
 SHHTH WV12 ....25 G4
Braemar Dr ERDW/GRVHL B23...91 H1
Braemar Rd HIA/OLT B92......164 A1
 SCFLD/BOLD B73 ....76 D1
Braeside Cft
 CHWD/FDBR/MGN B37......132 D2
Braeside Wy BLOX/PEL WS3...17 H4
Bragg Rd BFLD/HDSWWD B20...90 C4
Braggs Farm La SHLY B90 ......194 A4
Braid Cl HWK/WKHTH B38 ......176 B4
Brailes Cl HIA/OLT B92............165 H1
Brailes Dr WALM/CURD B76 ......63 F5
Brailes Gv BORD B9 ....129 F3
Brailsford Cl WNSFLD WV11 ......25 E2
Brailsford Dr SMTHWK B66 ......106 C4
Braithwaite Dr KGSWFD DY6...99 H3
Braithwaite Rd SPARK B11 ......127 H5

Brake La STRBR DY8............152 A4
Bramah Wy TPTN/OCK DY4......70 A5
Bramber Dr WMBN WV5 ......64 D5
Bramber Wy STRBR DY8 ......135 F5
Bramble Cl AST/WIT B6............109 E2
 BRWNH WS8 ....19 E2
 CDYHTH B64 ....103 F5
 CSHL/WTROR B46 ....115 G2
 NFLD/LBR B31 ....158 B5
 SHHTH WV12 ....26 A3
Bramble Dell BORD B9 ....129 E1
Bramble Dr
 LGN/SDN/BHAMAIR B26 ......147 G1
Bramble Gn DUDN DY1 ....83 H1
Brambleside STRBR DY8 ......118 B3
The Brambles HAG/WOL DY9...136 B4
 WALM/CURD B76 ....78 C4
Bramblewood Dr
 BDMR/CCFT WV3 ....36 A5
Bramblewoods
 BKDE/SHDE B34 ....113 G4
Brambling Wk EDG B15 ......126 C5
Bramcote Dr SOLH B91 ......165 E2
Bramcote Ri FOAKS/STRLY B74...62 C1
Bramcote Rd BKDE/WDGT B32...140 C2
Bramerton Cl WNSFLD WV11...24 A5
Bramford Dr DUDN DY1 ....83 H1
Bramley Cl DSYBK/YTR WS5...43 F5
 GTB/HAM B43 ....59 H5
Bramley Cft SHLY B90 ....180 C3
Bramley Dr
 BFLD/HDSWWD B20 ....90 B3
 HLYWD B47 ....192 D2
Bramley Mews Ct ACGN B27...146 C3
Bramley Rd ACGN B27 ....146 C2
 DSYBK/YTR WS5 ....57 H4
Brampton Av HLGN/YWD B28...163 E4
Brampton Crs SHLY B90............180 D1
Bramshall Dr DOR/KN B93......196 C5
Bramshaw Cl
 ALE/KHTH/YWD B14 ....178 B3
Bramstead Av
 DUNHL/THL/PER WV6............35 F3
Branchal Rd ALDR WS9 ....30 C1
Branch Rd HWK/WKHTH B38...176 B5
Brandhall La LGLYGN/QTN B68...123 F5
Brandhall Rd
 LGLYGN/QTN B68............123 F5
Brandon Cl ALDR WS9 ....45 F2
 SEDG DY3 ....67 G4
 WBROM B70 ....87 F3
Brandon Gv NFLD/LBR B31......189 F1
Brandon Pk BDMR/CCFT WV3...51 E1
Brandon Pl BKDE/SHDE B34...113 F2
Brandon Rd HLGN/YWD B28...163 E3
 RMSLY B62 ....122 C3
 SOLH B91 ....165 E3
Brandon Wy BRLYHL DY5......119 E1
 WBROM B70 ....87 E4
Brandwood Crs BVILLE B30......177 H2
Brandwood Gv
 ALE/KHTH/YWD B14 ....160 D5
Brandwood Park Rd
 ALE/KHTH/YWD B14 ....177 G1
Brandwood Rd
 ALE/KHTH/YWD B14 ....160 D5
Branfield Cl BILS/COS WV14...68 A2
Branksome Av HDSW B21......107 H1
Branscombe Cl
 ALE/KHTH/YWD B14 ....160 D5
Bransdale Cl
 DUNHL/THL/PER WV6............22 C5
Bransdale Rd BRWNH WS8 ......9 E5
Bransford Ri SOLH B91 ....166 B5
Brantford Rd YDLY B25 ......129 G4
Branthill Cft SOLH B91 ......181 H4
Brantley Av BDMR/CCFT WV3...35 G4
Brantley Rd AST/WIT B6 ......91 G4
Branton Hill La ALDR WS9 ......30 C5
Brasshouse La SMTHWK B66...106 B3
Brassie Cl HWK/WKHTH B38...176 B4
Brassington Av
 SCFLD/WYGN B72 ....62 C3
Bratch Cl DUDS DY2 ....120 C1
Bratch Common Rd
 WMBN WV5 ....64 C4
Bratch Hollow WMBN WV5......65 E3
Bratch La WMBN WV5 ....64 D5
Bratch Pk WMBN WV5 ....64 C3
Bratt St WBROM B70............87 H1
Braunston Cl WALM/CURD B76...78 C1
Brayford Av BRLYHL DY5......118 D5
Braymoor Rd STETCH B33......131 G3
Brays Rd
 LGN/SDN/BHAMAIR B26......147 H1
Bray St WLNHL WV13............39 H1
Bream Cl
 CHWD/FDBR/MGN B37......132 C2
 WOLV WV10 ....38 B1
Breamore Cl DUDN DY1 ......83 H3
Brean Av
 LGN/SDN/BHAMAIR B26......147 E2
Brearley Cl LOZ/NWT B19......108 D4
Brearley St HDSW B21 ....107 F1
 LOZ/NWT B19 ....108 D4
Brecknock Rd WBROM B70 ......71 E5
Brecon Dr STRBR DY8 ....135 H1
Brecon Rd
 BFLD/HDSWWD B20 ....108 B1
Bredon Av HAG/WOL DY9 ......136 C4
Bredon Cl HALE B63 ....138 C4
Bredon Cft WSNGN B18............108 A4
Bredon Rd OLDBY B69 ....104 B4
 STRBR DY8 ....135 G1
Breech Cl FOAKS/STRLY B74...60 A1
Breedon Rd BVILLE B30 ......160 A5
Breedon Ter WSNGN B18 *......108 A4
Breedon Wy RUSH/SHEL WS4...29 E1
Breen Rydding Dr
 BILS/COS WV14 ....68 B2
Brelades Cl DUDN DY1 ......83 G3
Brendan Cl CSHL/WTROR B46...115 G4
Brennand Rd
 LGLYGN/QTN B68 ....123 F3
Brentford Rd
 ALE/KHTH/YWD B14 ....161 F5
 SHLY B90 ....180 C3
Brentmill Cl WOLV WV10............13 F5
Brentnall Dr MGN/WHC B75...47 F2

Brenton Rd
 ETTPK/GDPK/PENN WV4......51 F4
Brent Rd BVILLE B30 ....160 C2
Brentwood Cl SOLH B91......181 E2
Brentwood Gv KGSTG B44......99 F2
Brenwood Cl KGSWFD DY6......99 F3
Brereton Cl DUDS DY2 ....85 E5
Brereton Rd SHHTH WV12......26 A3
Bretby Cl DOR/KN B93 ......196 D5
Bretby Gv ERDW/GRVHL B23...77 E5
Bretshall Cl SHLY B90 ....195 F5
Brett Dr RIDG/WDGT B32......157 G2
Brettell La STRBR DY8 ......118 B4
Brettell St DUDS DY2 ....102 B2
Bretton Gdns WOLV WV10 ......23 H4
Bretton Rd ACGN B27 ....146 D5
Brett St HHTH/SAND B71 ......87 F1
Brevitt Rd BKHL/PFLD WV2......52 B2
Brewers Dr BLOX/PEL WS3 ......28 C1
Brewer St WSLW WS2............42 A1
Brewery St AST/WIT B6 ....109 E4
 DUDS DY2 ....85 E5
 HDSW B21 ....107 F1
 SMTHWKW B67 ....106 B3
Brewins Wy BRLYHL DY5......101 H5
Breydon Gv WLNHL WV13......39 F5
Brian Rd SMTHWKW B67......106 A3
Briar Av FOAKS/STRLY B74......45 G4
Briarbeck RUSH/SHEL WS4......29 E2
Briar Cl ERDE/BCHGN B24......93 E2
Briarfield Rd SPARK B11 ......146 A4
Briars Cl BRLYHL DY5 ....101 E5
The Briars ALDR WS9 ....30 A3
 ERDW/GRVHL B23 ....76 B5
 HAG/WOL DY9 ....137 E5
Briar Wy HWK/WKHTH B38......177 E5
Briar Wood Cl BKHL/PFLD WV2...53 E1
Briarwood Cl SHLY B90 ......194 D4
 WOLV WV10 ....25 E4
Brickbridge La WMBN WV5 ......80 C1
Brickfield Rd YDLY B25............146 B1
Brickheath Rd WOLV WV1......38 A2
Brickhill Dr
 CHWD/FDBR/MGN B37......132 A2
Brickhouse La South
 TPTN/OCK DY4 ....70 B5
Brickhouse Rd
 BLKHTH/ROWR B65 ....103 G5
Brick Kiln La HLYWD B47......192 B4
 KGSTG B44 ....59 E5
 SEDG DY3 ....82 C5
 SHLY B90 ....181 F5
Brick Kiln St BRLYHL DY5......101 G4
 TPTN/OCK DY4 ....69 E5
Brickkiln St WOLV WV13......39 F4
Brick St SEDG DY3 ....82 D4
Brickyard Rd ALDR WS9 ....29 H2
Briddsland Rd STETCH B33......131 G2
Bridge Av TPTN/OCK DY4......70 A4
Bridge Cl BILS/COS WV14......53 G4
Bridge Cl MOS/BIL B13............144 D4
Bridge Cft BHTH/HG B12......144 A1
Bridgefoot Rd
 BKDE/SHDE B34 ....112 D5
Bridgelands Wy
 BFLD/HDSWWD B20 ....90 D5
Bridgeman Cft CBROM B36......113 E1
Bridgeman St WSL WS1 ....4 D4
Bridgemary Cl WOLV WV10 ......13 F5
Bridge Meadow Dr
 DOR/KN B93 ....196 D3
Bridgend Cft BRLYHL DY5......100 D3
Bridge Piece NFLD/LBR B31...175 H3
Bridge Rd RUSH/SHEL WS4......28 D1
 TPTN/OCK DY4 ....70 A4
 WASH/WDE B8 ....128 C1
Bridgeside Cl BRWNH WS8 ......19 E1
Bridge St BILS/COS WV14......68 C3
 BRWNH WS8 ....19 E1
 CBHAMW B1 ....2 D7
 DARL/WED WS10 ....70 D1
 HALE B63 ....120 C5
 OLDBY B69 ....105 E2
 STRBR DY8 ....118 A3
 WBROM B70 ....87 F2
 WLNHL WV13 ....39 F4
 WOLV WV10 ....26 C5
 WSL WS1 ....5 G3
Bridge St North SMTHWK B66...106 D3
Bridge St South SMTHWK B66...106 D3
Bridge St West LOZ/NWT B19...108 D3
The Bridge WSL WS1 ....5 G3
Bridge Vw CSHL/WTROR B46 *...115 F2
Bridge Wk ACGN B27 *............146 D4
Bridgewater Av OLDBY B69......105 E5
Bridgewater Crs DUDS DY2...85 E5
Bridgewater Dr BILS/COS WV14...68 C1
 WMBN WV5 ....64 C4
Bridge Wy BRWNH WS8............19 E1
Bridgnorth Av WMBN WV5......80 D2
Bridgnorth Gv SHHTH WV12...25 H4
Bridgnorth Rd
 DUNHL/THL/PER WV6............35 E3
 SEDG DY3 ....80 A1
 STRBR DY8 ....134 C1
Bridgwater Cl ALDR WS9 ......19 F5
Bridle Gv HHTH/SAND B71 ......72 B3
Bridle La ALDR WS9 ....59 H2
 FOAKS/STRLY B74 ....45 G4
Bridle Md HWK/WKHTH B38...176 B5
The Bridle Pth SHLY B90......163 F5
Bridle Rd STRBR DY8 ....134 D1
Bridlewood
 FOAKS/STRLY B74 ....45 F5
Brierley Hill Rd STRBR DY8...118 A2
Brierley La BILS/COS WV14......69 E1
Brier Mill Rd HALE B63 ......139 E4
Briery Cl CDYHTH B64 ....121 F5
Briery Rd HALE B63 ....138 B5
Brigadoon Gdns
 HAG/WOL DY9 ....136 A5
Brigfield Crs MOS/BIL B13......161 H5
Brigfield Rd MOS/BIL B13......161 H5
Brighton Cl WSLW WS2............4 B1
Brighton Pl BDMR/CCFT WV3...36 A6
Brighton Rd BHTH/HG B12......144 B2
Bright St LGLYGN/QTN B68......123 G3
Brightstone Cl WOLV WV10......13 F5
Brightstone Rd RBRY B45......174 B3

Bright St DARL/WED WS10......55 F3
 STRBR DY8 ....134 D2
 WOLV WV1 ....6 D1
Brightwell Crs DOR/KN B93...196 D5
Brimfield Pl DUNHL/THL/PER WV6 *36
 B1
Brindle Cl LGN/SDN/BHAMAIR B26147
 E2
Brindle Rd BILS/COS WV14......54 A4
Brindleside Wy STRBR/YTR WS5...58 A4
Brindley Av WNSFLD WV11......25 C1
Brindley Cl STRBR DY8............118 A3
 WMBN WV5 ....64 B5
Brindley Ct LGLYGN/QTN B68 *...123 F5
 TPTN/OCK DY4 ....85 E1
Brindley Dr CBHAMW B1 ......2 C5
Brindley Pl CBHAMW B1 ......2 B6
Brindley Rd HHTH/SAND B71...71 E3
Brindley Wy SMTHWK B66 *......107 E5
Brineton Gv SLYOAK B29......158 C1
Brineton St WSLW WS2............4 A6
Bringewood Gv
 RIDG/WDGT B32 ....157 F2
Brinklow Cft BKDE/SHDE B34...113 C3
Brinklow Rd SLYOAK B29......141 E5
Brinley Wy KGSWFD DY6 ......99 C3
Brinsford Rd WOLVN WV10......12 C4
Brinsley Cl SOLH B91............181 H3
Brinsley Rd
 LGN/SDN/BHAMAIR B26......130 D4
Brisbane Rd SMTHWKW B67...106 A3
Briseley Cl BRLYHL DY5 ......119 E4
Bristam Cl OLDBY B69 ....104 C3
Bristnall Hall La
 LGLYGN/QTN B68 ....123 G1
Bristnall Hall Rd
 LGLYGN/QTN B68 ....123 G2
Bristol Rd DUDS DY2 ....120 D2
 ERDW/GRVHL B23 ....92 C3
 SLYOAK B29 ....159 F2
Bristol Rd South RBRY B45......188 A1
Bristol St BDMR/CCFT WV3 ......6 C7
 BILS/COS WV14 ....53 H3
 DIG/EDG B5 ....126 D2
Briston Cl BRLYHL DY5 ......119 E4
Britannia Gdns
 BLKHTH/ROWR B65 ....122 A1
Britannia Pk DARL/WED WS10 *...70 B1
 BLKHTH/ROWR B65 ....122 A1
Britannia St OLDBY B69 ....86 A4
Britannic Gdns MOS/BIL B13...143 H5
Britford Cl
 ALE/KHTH/YWD B14 ....178 B2
Brittan Cl BKDE/SHDE B34......113 C3
Brittania Rd WSL WS1 ....56 D3
Britton Dr SCFLD/WYGN B72...77 C3
Britwell Rd SCFLD/BOLD B73...77 E1
Brixfield Wy SHLY B90............194 A3
Brixham Rd LDYWD/EDGBR B16...107 F5
Broad Acres NFLD/LBR B31...158 A2
Broad Cft TPTN/OCK DY4......70 A5
Broadfern Rd DOR/KN B93......183 F5
Broadfield Cl HHTH/SAND B71...72 B3
Broadfields Rd
 ERDW/GRVHL B23 ....77 F4
Broadfield Wk
 LDYWD/EDGBR B16............2 B7
Broadheath Dr
 RUSH/SHEL WS4 ....29 F2
Broadhidley Dr
 RIDG/WDGT B32 ....157 F1
Broadlands WOLVN WV10......12 D2
Broadlands Dr BRLYHL DY5......101 G4
Broad La ALE/KHTH/YWD B14...177 H2
 BDMR/CCFT WV3............36 A5
 BLOX/PEL WS3 ....16 C5
 RUSH/SHEL WS4 ....29 E1
 WNSFLD WV11 ....15 H2
Broad Lane Gdns
 BLOX/PEL WS3 ....16 C5
Broad La North WNSFLD WV11...25 H4
Broad Lanes BILS/COS WV14...53 G4
Broad La South WNSFLD WV11...25 F5
Broad Meadow ALDR WS9......30 B2
Broadmeadow Cl BVILLE B30...177 F2
Broadmeadow Gn
 BILS/COS WV14 ....53 C1
Broad Meadow La BVILLE B30...177 F2
Broadmeadows Rd
 SHHTH WV12 ....26 C2
Broadmoor Av
 LGLYGN/QTN B68 ....123 H2
Broadmoor Cl BILS/COS WV14...53 G4
Broadmoor Rd BILS/COS WV14...53 G4
Broad Oaks WALM/CURD B76...78 C3
Broad Oaks Rd SOLH B91......164 B5
Broadstone Av BLOX/PEL WS3...27 H5
 HALE B63 ....137 F3
Broadstone Cl
 ETTPK/GDPK/PENN WV4......52 B3
Broadstone Rd
 LGN/SDN/BHAMAIR B26......130 B2
Broad St BILS/COS WV14......68 C3
 BRLYHL DY5 ....101 H5
 KGSWFD DY6 ....99 H4
 OLDBY B69 ....105 E4
 WOLV WV1 ....7 G5
Broad Street Jct WOLV WV1 *...7 H3
Broadwaters Av
 DARL/WED WS10 ....55 E4
Broadwaters Rd
 DARL/WED WS10 ....55 E4
Broad Wy RUSH/SHEL WS4......18 C5
Broadway BDMR/CCFT WV3......36 A4
 CDSL WV8 ....10 A4
 LGLYGN/QTN B68 ....123 G3
 SHLY B90 ....180 B1
 WOLVN WV10 ....25 C3
 WSL WS1 ....5 G2
Broadway Av BORD B9 ....129 E2
 HALE B63 ....138 C5
Broadway Cft
 LGLYGN/QTN B68 ....123 G3
 LGN/SDN/BHAMAIR B26......147 G1

Broadway North WSL WS1 ......5 J2
The Broadway
 BFLD/HDSWWD B20 ....90 D4
 DUDN DY1 ....84 A5
 HHTH/SAND B71 ....71 G4
 STRBR DY8 ....134 D5
 WMBN WV5 ....81 E1
Broadway West WSL WS1......56 D2
Broadwell Rd HIA/OLT B92......145 G1
 OLDBY B69 ....105 E1
Broadyates Gv YDLY B25......146 C1
Broadyates Rd YDLY B25......146 C1
Brobury Cft SOLH B91............180 D1
Brock Cl RBRY B45............174 A4
Brockeridge Cl SHHTH WV12...26 A1
Brockhall Gv
 CHWD/FDBR/MGN B37......113 H4
Brockhill La ALVE B48............191 F5
Brockhurst Crs
 DSYBK/YTR WS5 ....57 F4
Brockhurst Dr
 DUNHL/THL/PER WV6............36 C1
 HLGN/YWD B28 ....163 E5
Brockhurst La MGN/WHC B75...50 B3
Brockhurst Pl DSYBK/YTR WS5...57 F3
Brockhurst Rd CBROM B36......111 C3
 MGN/WHC B75 ....50 B3
Brockhurst St WSL WS1......57 E2
Brockley Cl BRLYHL DY5......119 F1
Brockley Gv MOS/BIL B15......162 A1
Brockley Pl VAUX/NECH B7......110 A2
Brockmoor Cl HAG/WOL DY9...136 A5
Brock Rd TPTN/OCK DY4......85 H2
Brockwell Gv KGSTG B44......60 A4
Brockwell Rd KGSTG B44......60 A4
Brockworth Rd
 ALE/KHTH/YWD B14 ....177 G3
Brocton Cl BILS/COS WV14......53 E5
 BLOX/PEL WS3 ....27 E2
Brogden Cl HHTH/SAND B71...72 B3
Bromfield Cl AST/WIT B6......109 E3
Bromfield Crs
 DUNHL/THL/PER WV6............35 F2
Bromford Cl ERDW/GRVHL B23...93 C4
 ERDE/BCHGN B24 ....111 E1
 WBROM B70 ....87 F3
Bromford Hl
 BFLD/HDSWWD B20 ....90 C3
Bromford La ERDE/BCHGN B24...93 G5
 ERDE/BCHGN B24 ....111 E1
 WBROM B70 ....87 E5
Bromford Rd BDMR/CCFT WV3...36 A5
Bromford Crs CBROM B36......111 C2
 CBROM B36 ....112 A2
 DUDS DY2 ....102 A3
 WBROM B70 ....87 E5
Bromley BRLYHL DY5 ....100 D4
Bromley Gdns CDSL WV8......10 C3
Bromley La KGSWFD DY6......99 H5
Bromley Pl
 ETTPK/GDPK/PENN WV4......51 G3
Bromley St BKHL/PFLD WV2......52 B3
 BORD B9 ....127 G3
 HAG/WOL DY9 ....136 D1
Brompton Dr BRLYHL DY5......118 D5
Brompton Lawns
 DUNHL/THL/PER WV6............35 C2
Brompton Pool Rd
 HLGN/YWD B28 ....179 G2
Brompton Rd KGSTG B44......60 A4
Bromsgrove Rd
 HAG/WOL DY9 ....137 E5
 HALE B63 ....139 E4
 RMSLY B62 ....172 C2
Bromsgrove St DIG/EDG B5...126 D3
Bromwall Rd MOS/BIL B13......161 H4
Bromwich Dr MGN/WHC B75...50 B3
Bromwynd Cl BKHL/PFLD WV2...51 H3
Bromyard Av WALM/CURD B76...78 C2
Bromyard Rd SPARK B11......145 G4
Bronte Cl SHLY B90............180 D1
Bronte Rd BKHL/PFLD WV2......52 D2
Bronwen Rd BILS/COS WV14...69 H1
Bronwen Vis
 DARL/WED WS10 *............55 F2
Brookbank Av
 BKDE/SHDE B34 ....113 F4
Brookbank Gdns SEDG DY3......81 G4
Brookbank Rd SEDG DY3......81 G4
Brook Cl ALDR WS9 ....19 G1
 SHLY B90 ....179 H4
 STETCH B33 ....112 A4
Brook Crs HAG/WOL DY9......152 D1
 KGSWFD DY6 ....99 G5
Brook Cft
 CHWD/FDBR/MGN B37......132 B3
 LGN/SDN/BHAMAIR B26......83 E2
Brookdale SEDG DY3............83 E2
Brookdale Dr RBRY B45......173 H1
Brookdale
 ETTPK/GDPK/PENN WV4......52 D2
Brook Dr RIDG/WDGT B32......157 F1
Brookend Dr RBRY B45............187 H1
Brookes Cl LGLYGN/QTN B68...105 E1
Brooke St DUDS DY2 ....102 C1
Brookfield Cl ALDR WS9......30 A1
Brookfield Rd ALDR WS9 ......30 A1
 BVILLE B30 ....177 E1
 CDSL WV8 ....10 C1
 WSNGN B18 ....107 H3
Brookfields Rd
 LGLYGN/QTN B68 ....105 G2
Brookfield Wy HIA/OLT B92...163 H1
 TPTN/OCK DY4 ....85 G3
Brook Gv CDSL WV8............10 D1
Brookhill Cl SHHTH WV12......26 A1
Brook Hill Rd WASH/WDE B8...111 H4
Brook Holloway
 HAG/WOL DY9 ....137 G5
Brookhouse La WOLVN WV10...13 E4
Brook House La WOLVN WV10...13 E4
Brookhouse Rd
 DSYBK/YTR WS5 ....57 F3

ookhus Farm Rd
WALM/CURD B76 78 C3
ooking Cl GTB/HAM B43 59 H4
ookland Gv ALDR WS9 19 F5
ookland Rd ALDR WS9 19 F4
HAG/WOL DY9 152 C5
ooklands STRBR DY8 118 B3
ooklands Cl HLGN/YWD B28 162 D1
ooklands Dr
ALE/KHTH/YWD B14 161 E5
ooklands Gv ALDR WS9 19 F5
ooklands Pde WOLV WV1 38 B3
ooklands Rd
HLGN/YWD B28 162 D1
e Brooklands SEDG DY3 80 C5
ooklands Wy
WD/FDBR/MGN B37 132 B4
ook La ALDR WS9 19 G4
ALE/KHTH/YWD B14 161 F2
CDYHTH B64 121 E2
HIA/OLT B92 163 H2
RIDG/WDGT B32 141 F2
ooklea Gv HWK/WKHTH B38 177 E4
ooklyn Av AST/WIT B6 109 F2
ooklyn Gv BILS/COS WV14 68 D3
KGSWFD DY6 99 F1
ookmans Av
RIDG/WDGT B32 140 D3
ookmeadow Ct
HLGN/YWD B28 162 B4
ook Meadow Rd
BKDE/SHDE B34 112 C3
RUSH/SHEL WS4 29 F2
ook Mdw CDSL WV8 10 D2
ook Rd EDG B15 125 G5
LGLYGN/QTN B68 123 E2
RBRY B45 187 H1
STRBR DY8 135 H4
WLNHL WV13 39 E4
WMBN WV5 64 D5
ooksbank Dr CDYHTH B64 103 F5
ooksby Gv DOR/KN B93 199 E1
ooks Cft CVALE B35 94 C4
ookside DARL/WED WS10 56 B5
GTB/HAM B43 73 F5
NFLD/LBR B31 158 B5
SEDG DY3 83 F4
ookside Av MOS/BIL B13 161 H3
ookside Cl ERDW/GRVHL B23 76 A4
HALE B63 137 H4
WMBN WV5 64 B5
ookside Wy KGSWFD DY6 99 F2
KIDD DY10 168 B3
ooks Rd
CSCFLD/WYGN B72 77 G2
ook St BILS/COS WV14 54 A3
BRLYHL DY5 120 A4
CBHAMNW B3 2 D3
HAG/WOL DY9 136 D2
KGSWFD DY6 81 F5
SEDG DY3 83 E3
SMTHWK B66 106 D3
STRBR DY8 135 E2
TPTN/OCK DY4 69 E5
WBROM B70 87 F2
WSLW WS2 4 B4
ook Ter BILS/COS WV14 54 A3
ookthorpe Dr SHHTH WV12 40 A1
ookvale Gv HIA/OLT B92 163 H1
ookvale Ms SLYOAK B29 143 F5
ookvale Park Rd
ERDW/GRVHL B23 91 H2
ookvale Rd AST/WIT B6 91 G3
HIA/OLT B92 163 H1
ookview SMTHWKW B67 * 124 B1
ook View Cl LOZ/NWT B19 108 C3
ook Wk RIDG/WDGT B32 140 D5
ookwillow Rd HALE B63 137 H5
ookwood Av
HLGN/YWD B28 162 B5
oomcroft Rd
CHWD/FDBR/MGN B37 113 H4
oomdene Av
BKDE/SHDE B34 112 C2
oom Dr ALE/KHTH/YWD B14 178 A1
oome Av GTB/HAM B43 73 E4
oome Cl HALE B63 138 C4
oome Gdns MGN/WHC B75 62 C3
oomehill Cl BRLYHL DY5 119 E5
oome La KIDD DY10 169 E2
oome Rd WOLVN WV10 23 F3
oomfield SMTHWKW B67 106 B4
oomfield Rd
DARL/WED WS10 56 C5
ERDW/GRVHL B23 92 B4
oomfields Cl SOLH B91 165 F5
oomhall Av WNSFLD WV11 24 D4
oom Hall Crs ACGN B27 163 F3
oom Hall Gv ACGN B27 163 G3
oomhill Cl GTB/HAM B43 73 F3
oomhill La GTB/HAM B43 73 E3
oomhill Rd
ERDW/GRVHL B23 75 H4
oomhurst
LDYWD/EDGR B16 125 G4
oomie Cl MGN/WHC B75 62 D4
oom La SHLY B90 194 A2
oomlea Cl FOAKS/STRLY B74 45 E5
oom Rd DSYBK/YTR WS5 57 H5
DUDN DY1 84 A2
oomy Cl BKDE/SHDE B34 112 C4
oseley Av NFLD/LBR B31 175 G5
oseley Brook Cl BORD B9 128 A3
osil Av BFLD/HDSWWD B20 89 G3
ougham St LOZ/NWT B19 108 B2
ough Cl
ETTPK/GDPK/PENN WV4 52 D5
VAUX/NECH B7 109 H3
oughton Ct
DUNHL/THL/PER WV6 35 E2
oughton Crs NFLD/LBR B31 174 D5
oughton Rd
BDMR/CCFT WV3 35 G4
BFLD/HDSWWD B20 108 A1
HAG/WOL DY9 136 B4
ownfield Rd
BKDE/SHDE B34 113 F2
ownhills Rd BRWNH WS8 19 F2
owning Cl SHHTH WV12 26 C3
owning Crs WOLVN WV10 12 C5
Browning Gv
DUNHL/THL/PER WV6 34 C1
Browning Rd SEDG DY3 82 C2
Brownley Rd SHLY B90 195 E1
Brown Lion St TPTN/OCK DY4 69 E4
Brown Rd DARL/WED WS10 55 E1
Brown's Coppice Av SOLH B91 163 H5
Browns Dr SCFLD/BOLD B73 76 D3
Brownsea Cl RBRY B45 173 G4
Brownsea Dr CBHAMW B1 2 E7
Browns Gn BFLD/HDSWWD B20 89 H3
Brownshore La WNSFLD WV11 15 E4
Browns La DOR/KN B93 196 C2
Brownsover Cl CBROM B36 94 D5
Brown St BKHL/PFLD WV2 52 B1
Brownswall Rd SEDG DY3 66 D4
Broxwood Pk
DUNHL/THL/PER WV6 35 F2
Brueton Av SOLH B91 182 B2
Brueton Dr ERDE/BCHGN B24 93 E3
Brueton Rd BILS/COS WV14 54 C1
Bruford Rd BDMR/CCFT WV3 36 C5
Brunel Cl BHTH/HG B12 144 C2
Brunel Ct BILS/COS WV14 69 E3
Brunel Dr TPTN/OCK DY4 69 E2
Brunel Gv
DUNHL/THL/PER WV6 20 C4
Brunel Rd OLDBY B69 104 B3
Brunel St CBHAMW B1 2 E6
Brunel Wk DARL/WED WS10 * 55 H2
Brunel Wy BKHL/PFLD WV2 53 E1
Brunslow Cl WLNHL WV13 40 A4
WOLVN WV10 23 E1
Brunswick Ga STRBR DY8 152 C1
Brunswick Park Rd
DARL/WED WS10 56 A5
Brunswick Rd BHTH/HG B12 144 C2
HDSW B21 89 H5
Brunswick Sq CBHAMW B1 2 B6
Brunswick St CBHAMW B1 2 B6
WSLW WS2 56 C1
Brunswick Ter
DARL/WED WS10 55 H5
Brunton Rd SMHTH B10 128 D5
Brushfield Rd PBAR/PBCH B42 74 B5
Brutus Dr CSHL/WTROR B46 97 E5
Bryan Av
ETTPK/GDPK/PENN WV4 50 D4
Bryan Rd WSLW WS2 56 C2
Bryanston Ct SOLH B91 * 164 B3
Bryanston Rd SOLH B91 164 B4
Bryant St WSNGN B18 107 G4
Bryce Rd BRLYHL DY5 100 D4
Brylan Cft KGSTG B44 75 F5
Bryn Arden Rd
LGN/SDN/BHAMAIR B26 147 E2
Bryndale Av
ALE/KHTH/YWD B14 160 C5
Brynmawr Rd BILS/COS WV14 52 D5
Brynside Cl
ALE/KHTH/YWD B14 177 H3
Bryony Cft ERDW/GRVHL B23 75 H4
Bryony Gdns DARL/WED WS10 55 F1
Bryony Rd SLYOAK B29 158 D3
Buchanan Cl RUSH/SHEL WS4 42 C2
Buchanan Rd RUSH/SHEL WS4 5 J1
Buckbury Cl HAG/WOL DY9 153 F1
Buckbury Cft SHLY B90 195 H2
Buckingham Cl
DARL/WED WS10 56 C4
Buckingham Dr SHHTH WV12 25 H3
Buckingham Gv KGSWFD DY6 99 G2
Buckingham Ms
SCFLD/BOLD B73 77 E1
Buckingham Ri DUDN DY1 83 G4
Buckingham Rd
BLKHTH/ROWR B65 104 B5
CBROM B36 113 H2
ETTPK/GDPK/PENN WV4 51 G4
Buckingham St LOZ/NWT B19 2 E1
Buckland End
BKDE/SHDE B34 112 C3
Bucklands End La
BKDE/SHDE B34 112 B3
Buckle Cl WSL WS1 4 E7
Buckley Rd
ETTPK/GDPK/PENN WV4 50 D3
Buckminster Dr DOR/KN B93 196 C4
Bucknall Crs RIDG/WDGT B32 157 E2
Bucknall Rd WNSFLD WV11 25 G1
Bucknell Cl SOLH B91 165 E5
Buckridge Cl
HWK/WKHTH B38 190 B1
Buckridge La SHLY B90 194 A3
Buckton Cl MGN/WHC B75 48 C5
Budbrook Gv BKDE/SHDE B34 113 G3
Budden Rd BILS/COS WV14 68 D4
Bude Rd DSYBK/YTR WS5 58 B1
Buffery Rd DUDS DY2 102 D2
Bufferys Cl SOLH B91 181 H5
Buildwas Cl BLOX/PEL WS3 16 B5
Bulford Cl
ALE/KHTH/YWD B14 178 B3
Bulger Rd BILS/COS WV14 53 G1
Bullace Cft EDG B15 142 B4
Buller St
ETTPK/GDPK/PENN WV4 52 C3
Bullfields Cl
BLKHTH/ROWR B65 103 F4
Bullfinch Cl DUDN DY1 101 G1
Bullivents Cl DOR/KN B93 196 D3
Bull La BILS/COS WV14 54 D5
WBROM B70 87 E3
WMBN WV5 65 F4
Bullmeadow La WMBN WV5 65 E4
Bullock's Rw WSL WS1 5 F4
Bullock St VAUX/NECH B7 109 G4
WBROM B70 105 H1
Bullows Rd BRWNH WS8 18 C1
Bull Ring HALE B63 138 D4
Bull's La WALM/CURD B76 79 E1
Bull St BRLYHL DY5 118 D3
CBHAM B2 3 G5
DARL/WED WS10 55 G2
DUDN DY1 102 A1
HRBN B17 142 B1
SEDG DY3 83 E4
WBROM B70 87 H4
Bulrush Cl BRWNH WS8 9 E5
Bulwell Cl AST/WIT B6 109 G2
Bumblehole Mdw WMBN WV5 64 D4
Bunbury Gdns BVILLE B30 176 A1
Bunbury Rd NFLD/LBR B31 175 G2
Bundle Hl HALE B63 138 C3
The Bungalows WBROM B70 * 70 D5
Bunkers Hill La BILS/COS WV14 39 E5
Bunn's La DUDS DY2 85 F5
Burbage Cl WOLVN WV10 23 G4
Burbidge Rd BORD B9 128 B1
Burbury St LOZ/NWT B19 108 C3
Burbury St South
LOZ/NWT B19 * 108 C3
Burcot Av WOLV WV1 38 A3
Burcote Rd ERDE/BCHGN B24 93 H3
Burdock Cl DSYBK/YTR WS5 57 G5
Burdock Rd SLYOAK B29 158 C4
Burdons Cl BKDE/SHDE B34 112 C4
Bure Gv WLNHL WV13 40 B4
Burfield Rd HALE B63 137 G1
Burford Cl DSYBK/YTR WS5 57 G4
HIA/OLT B92 147 G4
Burford Rd HLYWD B47 192 B2
KGSTG B44 75 F4
Burgess Cft HIA/OLT B92 165 H3
Burghley Dr HHTH/SAND B71 72 B1
Burghley Wk BRLYHL DY5 118 D4
Burgh Wy WSLW WS2 41 E1
Burhill Wy
CHWD/FDBR/MGN B37 114 B5
Burke Av MOS/BIL B13 162 B1
Burkitt Dr TPTN/OCK DY4 70 A3
Burland Av
DUNHL/THL/PER WV6 22 A3
Burleigh Cl SHHTH WV12 25 H4
Burleigh Rd BDMR/CCFT WV3 51 G1
Burleigh St WSL WS1 5 G5
Burleton Rd STETCH B33 131 G2
Burley Cl SHLY B90 179 H3
Burlington Rd SMHTH B10 128 D3
WBROM B70 87 H5
Burlington St AST/WIT B6 109 E3
Burlish Av HIA/OLT B92 164 B1
Burman Cl SHLY B90 180 A3
Burman Dr CSHL/WTROR B46 115 F4
Burman Rd SHLY B90 179 H3
Burmese Wy
BLKHTH/ROWR B65 103 F3
Burnaston Crs SHLY B90 196 A1
Burnaston Rd HLGN/YWD B28 162 C2
Burnbank Gv
ERDE/BCHGN B24 93 F2
Burn Cl SMTHWK B66 106 C5
Burncross Wy WOLVN WV10 23 H4
Burnell Gdns BDMR/CCFT WV3 36 A5
Burnel Rd SLYOAK B29 141 G5
Burnett Rd FOAKS/STRLY B74 45 H3
Burney La WASH/WDE B8 111 G5
Burnfields Wy ALDR WS9 30 A3
Burnham Av WOLVN WV10 23 E2
YDLY B25 146 C1
Burnham Cl KGSWFD DY6 100 B5
Burnham Meadow
HLGN/YWD B28 163 E4
Burnham Rd KGSTG B44 75 E4
Burnhill Gv SLYOAK B29 158 C2
Burnlea Gv NFLD/LBR B31 176 A4
Burnsall Cl
CHWD/FDBR/MGN B37 131 H2
COVEN WV9 12 A4
Burns Av TPTN/OCK DY4 69 G4
WOLVN WV10 12 D5
Burns Cl STRBR DY8 118 C4
Burns Gv SEDG DY3 82 C3
Burnside Gdns DSYBK/YTR WS5 58 B2
Burnside Wy NFLD/LBR B31 189 F1
Burns Pl DARL/WED WS10 54 C3
Burns Rd DARL/WED WS10 54 C3
Burnthurst Crs SHLY B90 195 G1
Burnt Oak Dr STRBR DY8 135 G2
Burnt Tree TPTN/OCK DY4 85 F4
Burrington Rd
RIDG/WDGT B32 157 E2
Burrowes St WSLW WS2 4 C1
Burrow Hill Cl CBROM B36 113 E1
Burrows Rd KGSWFD DY6 100 B5
Burrows St WSLW WS2 4 B1
The Burrow BDMR/CCFT WV3 35 H4
Burslem Cl BLOX/PEL WS3 16 C3
Bursnips Rd WNSFLD WV11 15 G3
Burton Av RUSH/SHEL WS4 28 D3
Burton Crs WOLVN WV10 7 J2
Burton Farm Rd
RUSH/SHEL WS4 42 D2
Burton Gv CDYHTH B64 121 E4
Burton Rd DUDN DY1 83 H2
WOLVN WV10 7 K1
Burton Wood Dr
BFLD/HDSWWD B20 90 D4
Buryfield Rd SOLH B91 164 C4
Bury Hill Rd OLDBY B69 104 B2
Bush Av SMTHWK B66 107 E4
Bushbury Cft
CHWD/FDBR/MGN B37 132 C1
Bushbury La WOLVN WV10 23 E4
Bushbury Rd STETCH B33 112 C4
WOLVN WV10 38 A1
Bushell Dr SOLH B91 182 B1
Bushey Cl FOAKS/STRLY B74 45 F3
Bushey Fields Rd DUDN DY1 101 G2
Bush Gv BLOX/PEL WS3 18 A5
HDSW B21 89 E5
Bushley Cft SOLH B91 181 H5
Bushman Wy BKDE/SHDE B34 113 G4
Bushmore Rd HLGN/YWD B28 163 E4
Bush Rd DUDS DY2 120 C2
TPTN/OCK DY4 85 E2
Bush St DARL/WED WS10 55 F1
Bushway Cl BRLYHL DY5 118 C2
Bushwood Dr DOR/KN B93 197 E5
Bushwood Rd SLYOAK B29 158 D1
Bustleholme Av
HHTH/SAND B71 72 B2
Bustleholme Crs
HHTH/SAND B71 72 A2
Bustleholme La
HHTH/SAND B71 72 B1
Butchers La HALE B63 120 C5
Butchers Rd HIA/OLT B92 167 G4
Butcroft Gdns
DARL/WED WS10 55 G2
Bute Cl RBRY B45 173 G4
SHHTH WV12 25 H4
Butler Rd HIA/OLT B92 147 F4
Butlers Cl BFLD/HDSWWD B20 90 A3
ERDW/GRVHL B23 76 B2
Butlers La FOAKS/STRLY B74 46 A2
Butlers Prec WSL WS1 4 D3
Butler's Rd BFLD/HDSWWD B20 90 A3
Butler St WBROM B70 87 E2
Butlin St VAUX/NECH B7 110 A2
Buttercup Cl DSYBK/YTR WS5 57 G5
Butterfield Cl
DUNHL/THL/PER WV6 34 B2
Butterfield Rd BRLYHL DY5 100 D2
Buttermere Cl BRLYHL DY5 118 D5
DUNHL/THL/PER WV6 21 H2
Buttermere Ct
DUNHL/THL/PER WV6 34 D1
Buttermere Dr
RIDG/WDGT B32 141 F4
WNSFLD WV11 15 E5
Buttermere Gv SHHTH WV12 25 H1
Butterworth Cl BILS/COS WV14 68 A2
Buttery Rd SMTHWKW B67 106 A3
Buttons Farm Rd
ETTPK/GDPK/PENN WV4 50 D5
Buttress Wy SMTHWK B66 106 C3
Butts Rd
ETTPK/GDPK/PENN WV4 51 F4
RUSH/SHEL WS4 42 B2
Butts St RUSH/SHEL WS4 42 B2
The Butts RUSH/SHEL WS4 42 B2
Buxton Cl BLOX/PEL WS3 17 E4
Buxton Rd BLOX/PEL WS3 17 E4
DUDS DY2 102 A3
ERDW/GRVHL B23 75 H5
SCFLD/BOLD B73 77 E2
Byfield Cl STETCH B33 131 G3
Byfleet Cl
ETTPK/GDPK/PENN WV4 53 E5
Byford Wy
CHWD/FDBR/MGN B37 132 B4
Byland Wy BLOX/PEL WS3 16 B5
Byrchen Moor Gdns
BRLYHL DY5 100 D2
Byrne Rd BKHL/PFLD WV2 52 B1
Byron Av ERDW/GRVHL B23 91 H3
Byron Cl SMHTH B10 * 128 B5
Byron Crs DUDN DY1 84 B1
Byron Cft FOAKS/STRLY B74 32 D4
SEDG DY3 82 C2
Byron Rd SHHTH WV12 26 C3
SMHTH B10 128 B5
WOLVN WV10 24 A1
Byron St BRLYHL DY5 101 F2
HHTH/SAND B71 87 F1
Byways BLOX/PEL WS3 17 E4

C

Caban Cl NFLD/LBR B31 158 A5
Cable Dr WSLW WS2 41 G1
Cable St BKHL/PFLD WV2 53 E1
Cabot Gv DUNHL/THL/PER WV6 34 C1
Cadbury Dr CVALE B35 94 B5
Cadbury Rd MOS/BIL B13 144 D3
Cadbury Wy HRBN B17 141 H2
Caddick Crs HHTH/SAND B71 71 H4
Caddick Rd PBAR/PBCH B42 74 B2
Caddick St BILS/COS WV14 68 A3
Cadet Dr SHLY B90 180 A2
Cadgwith Gdns BILS/COS WV14 69 G1
Cadine Gdns MOS/BIL B13 160 C1
Cadle Rd WOLVN WV10 23 F3
Cadman Crs WOLVN WV10 24 A4
Cadnam Cl HRBN B17 142 A4
WLNHL WV13 39 H5
Caernarvon Cl SHHTH WV12 26 A3
Caernarvon Wy DUDN DY1 83 G4
Caesar Wy CSHL/WTROR B46 97 E5
Cairn Dr WSLW WS2 40 D3
Cairns St WSLW WS2 4 A1
Caister Dr WLNHL WV13 39 F5
Cakemore Rd
BLKHTH/ROWR B65 122 C2
Cala Dr EDG B15 126 B5
Calcot Dr DUNHL/THL/PER WV6 22 A2
Calcutt Wy SHLY B90 194 A2
Caldecote Gv BORD B9 129 G3
Caldeford Av SHLY B90 195 G1
Calder Av WSL WS1 5 H3
Calder Dr WALM/CURD B76 78 C3
Calderfields Cl RUSH/SHEL WS4 42 C2
Calder Gv BFLD/HDSWWD B20 89 H4
Calder Ri DUDN DY1 67 H5
Caldmore Gn WSL WS1 4 E7
Caldmore Rd WSL WS1 4 E5
Caldwell Gv SOLH B91 165 E5
Caldwell Rd BORD B9 129 G1
Caldwell St HHTH/SAND B71 71 H3
Caledonia BRLYHL DY5 119 F5
Caledonian Cl DSYBK/YTR WS5 58 A5
Caledonia Rd BKHL/PFLD WV2 37 G5
Caledonia St BILS/COS WV14 54 A2
Caledon Pl WSLW WS2 56 C1
Caledon St WSLW WS2 56 C1
Calewood Rd BRLYHL DY5 119 F5
California Rd OLDBY B69 103 H1
California Wy RIDG/WDGT B32 141 F4
Callaghan Dr OLDBY B69 86 A3
Callcott Dr BRLYHL DY5 119 F5
Callear Rd DARL/WED WS10 70 B2
Calley Cl TPTN/OCK DY4 85 F3
Callowbridge Rd RBRY B45 187 H1
Callowbrook La RBRY B45 187 H1
Calshot Rd PBAR/PBCH B42 74 A3
Calstock Rd SHHTH WV12 40 B1
Calthorpe Cl DSYBK/YTR WS5 58 C2
Calthorpe Man EDG B15 * 126 B3
Calthorpe Rd
BFLD/HDSWWD B20 90 C4
DSYBK/YTR WS5 58 B2
EDG B15 126 A4
Calver Crs WNSFLD WV11 25 F5
Calver Gv KGSTG B44 59 H5
Calverley Rd
HWK/WKHTH B38 176 B4
Calverton Gv GTB/HAM B43 73 G3
Calves Cft WLNHL WV13 39 G2
Calvin Cl WMBN WV5 80 D1
WOLVN WV10 12 D4
Camberidge Ms
CSHL/WTROR B46 115 F1
Camberley Crs
ETTPK/GDPK/PENN WV4 67 G1
Camberley Dr
ETTPK/GDPK/PENN WV4 51 G4
Camberley Gv
ERDW/GRVHL B23 76 C5
Camberley Ri HHTH/SAND B71 72 B2
Camberley Rd KGSWFD DY6 100 C5
Camborne Cl AST/WIT B6 109 E2
Camborne Rd DSYBK/YTR WS5 58 B1
Cambourne Rd
BLKHTH/ROWR B65 122 A1
Cambrai Dr HLGN/YWD B28 162 C2
Cambria Cl SHLY B90 193 G1
Cambridge Av SCFLD/BOLD B73 77 F3
SOLH B91 181 E2
Cambridge Cl ALDR WS9 30 A2
Cambridge Crs EDG B15 126 D5
Cambridge Dr
CHWD/FDBR/MGN B37 131 H3
Cambridge Rd DUDS DY2 102 A2
MOS/BIL B13 161 F1
SMTHWK B66 106 C2
Cambridge St CBHAMW B1 2 D5
WBROM B70 87 F4
WOLVN WV10 37 F1
WSL WS1 57 E1
Cambridge Wy ACGN B27 146 D3
Camden Cl CBROM B36 112 C1
DSYBK/YTR WS5 * 57 G4
Camden Dr CBHAMW B1 2 B3
Camden St ALDR WS9 19 E3
WSL WS1 4 C7
WSNGN B18 2 A2
Camden Wy KGSWFD DY6 81 H5
Camellia Gdns COVEN WV9 11 H4
Camelot Wy SMHTH B10 128 A4
Cameo Dr STRBR DY8 118 B4
Cameron Rd RUSH/SHEL WS4 5 J1
Camford Gv
ALE/KHTH/YWD B14 178 B2
Cam Gdns BRLYHL DY5 100 D2
Camino Rd RIDG/WDGT B32 141 F4
Camomile Cl DSYBK/YTR WS5 57 G5
Campbell Cl RUSH/SHEL WS4 42 C2
Campbells Gn
LGN/SDN/BHAMAIR B26 147 H2
Campbell St BRLYHL DY5 101 E5
Campden Gn HIA/OLT B92 147 G4
Camp Hl BHTH/HG B12 127 G4
STRBR DY8 118 A3
Camp Hill Circ BHTH/HG B12 127 G4
Camphill La DARL/WED WS10 70 D1
Camp Hill Middleway
BHTH/HG B12 127 G5
Campion Cl DSYBK/YTR WS5 57 G5
ERDE/BCHGN B24 77 G5
WMBN WV5 64 C5
Campion Gv HALE B63 137 H4
Campion Wy SHLY B90 194 A3
Camp La HDSW B21 88 D4
HWK/WKHTH B38 176 D2
Camplea Cft
CHWD/FDBR/MGN B37 132 A2
Camplin Crs
BFLD/HDSWWD B20 89 G1
Camp Rd MGN/WHC B75 33 H4
Camp St BORD B9 128 A3
DARL/WED WS10 70 D1
WOLV WV1 7 F1
Campville Crs HHTH/SAND B71 72 A2
Campville Gv
CHWD/FDBR/MGN B37 113 H4
Camp Wood Cl BVILLE B30 159 G2
Camrose Cft BHTH/HG B12 144 A1
BKDE/SHDE B34 112 D3
Camrose Gdns COVEN WV9 12 A4
Canal La ERDE/BCHGN B24 93 E5
Canal Side BVILLE B30 * 177 E3
DUDS DY2 103 E5
Canalside Cl BLOX/PEL WS3 28 A1
DARL/WED WS10 72 A1
Canal Side Dr
HWK/WKHTH B38 176 D4
Canal St BRLYHL DY5 101 G4
OLDBY B69 104 D2
STRBR DY8 135 F1
Canary Gv LOZ/NWT B19 108 C1
Canberra Gdns
BKDE/SHDE B34 113 G3
Canberra Rd DSYBK/YTR WS5 58 A5
Canberra Wy BHTH/HG B12 * 127 F4
Canford Cl BHTH/HG B12 127 F5
Canford Crs CDSL WV8 10 A4
Canning Cl DSYBK/YTR WS5 58 B2
Canning Gdns WSNGN B18 107 G5
Canning Rd DSYBK/YTR WS5 58 B2
Cannock Rd SHHTH WV12 26 A3
WOLVN WV10 23 H5
Cannon Dr BILS/COS WV14 68 C1
Cannon Hill Gv
BHTH/HG B12 * 144 A2
Cannon Hill Pl BHTH/HG B12 * 144 A2
Cannon Hill Rd BHTH/HG B12 143 H2
Cannon Rd WMBN WV5 65 E5
Cannon St CBHAM B2 3 G5
WLNHL WV13 39 H3
WSLW WS2 42 A1
Cannon St North WSLW WS2 42 A1
Canterbury Av WLNHL WV13 40 B3
Canterbury Cl
BLKHTH/ROWR B65 104 C5
BLOX/PEL WS3 18 A2
ERDW/GRVHL B23 92 B4
HHTH/SAND B71 72 A3
Canterbury Dr
CHWD/FDBR/MGN B37 132 A5
DUNHL/THL/PER WV6 34 B1
Canterbury Rd
BFLD/HDSWWD B20 90 D5
ETTPK/GDPK/PENN WV4 50 D3
HHTH/SAND B71 71 H3
Cantlow Rd MOS/BIL B13 161 G4
Canton La CSHL/WTROR B46 97 H1

Canute Cl WSL WS1............57 F1
Canvey Cl RBRY B45.........173 C4
Canwell Av
  CHWD/FDBR/MGN B37....113 H4
Canwell Gdns BRLYHL DY5....53 F4
Canwell Rd MGN/WHC B75....48 A1
Capcroft Rd MOS/BIL B13....161 H4
Cape Hl SMTHWK B66........106 D5
Capener Rd GTB/HAM B43....74 A1
Capern Gv RIDG/WDGT B32....141 F2
Cape St WBROM B70..........86 C2
  WSNGN B18..............107 F5
Capethorn Rd SMTHWK B66....124 C1
Capilano Rd ERDW/GRVHL B23....76 B3
Capponfield Cl BILS/COS WV14....53 F5
Capstone Av WOLN WV10......22 D2
  WSNGN B18..............108 A5
Captain's Cl BDMR/CCFT WV3....35 H3
Carcroft Rd YDLY B25........129 G4
Cardale St BLKHTH/ROWR B65....122 B2
Carden Cl WBROM B70........86 C2
Carder Crs BILS/COS WV14....53 H4
Carder Dr BRLYHL DY5.......119 E2
Cardiff St BDMR/CCFT WV3....6 C7
Cardigan Cl HHTH/SAND B71....71 G4
Cardigan Dr SHHTH WV12......25 H4
Cardigan St CBHAMNW B4......3 K3
Cardinal Cl HRBN B17........124 C2
Cardington Av PBAR/PBCH B42....74 B2
Cardoness Pl DUDN DY1......83 H4
Careless Gn HAG/WOL DY9....136 D3
Carhampton Rd
  MGN/WHC B75............63 G2
Carillon Gdns
  BLKHTH/ROWR B65........122 A1
Carisbrooke Av
  CHWD/FDBR/MGN B37....132 C2
Carisbrooke Cl
  DARL/WED WS10..........72 A1
Carisbrooke Crs
  DARL/WED WS10..........72 A1
Carisbrooke Gdns
  WOLN WV10..............13 E4
Carisbrooke Rd
  DARL/WED WS10..........71 H1
  DUNHL/THL/PER WV6......35 E2
  HRBN B17...............124 D3
  WOLN WV10..............13 E4
Carless Av HRBN B17........124 D5
Carless St WSL WS1..........4 E7
Carlisle St WSNGN B18......107 G4
Carl St WSLW WS2............27 H5
Carlton Av BILS/COS WV14....54 B1
  FOAKS/STRLY B74........45 F3
  HAG/WOL DY9............136 C4
  HDSW B21...............89 G5
  WNSFLD WV11............24 A3
Carlton Cl DUDN DY1........68 C5
  MGN/WHC B75............62 D1
Carlton Crs FOAKS/STRLY B74....45 G5
Carlton Ms CBROM B36......113 F2
Carlton Rd BDMR/CCFT WV3....51 C1
  BORD B9................128 B3
  SMTHWK B66.............106 C1
Carlyle Gv WOLN WV10.......24 A2
Carlyle Rd BLKHTH/ROWR B65....2 C2
  LDYWD/EDGR B16........125 G3
  LOZ/NWT B19...........108 C1
  WOLN WV10..............23 H2
Carmel Gv RIDG/WDGT B32....141 F2
Carnegie Av PBAR/PBCH B42....74 B5
Carnegie Dr DARL/WED WS10....56 A5
Carnegie Rd
  BLKHTH/ROWR B65........121 H2
Carnford Rd
  LGN/SDN/BHAMAIR B26....147 H1
Carnforth Cl HLGN/YWD DY9....99 F2
Carnoustie Cl BLOX/PEL WS3....16 C4
Carnwath Rd SCFLD/BOLD B75....7 H1
Carol Crs HALE B63.........138 B2
  WNSFLD WV11............25 E4
Carol Gdns STRBR DY8.......118 B4
Caroline Rd MOS/BIL B13....144 B3
Caroline St CBHAMNW B3......2 D2
  DUDS DY2...............85 E5
  WBROM B70..............87 F4
Carpenter Gld HALE B63....137 H2
Carpenter Rd EDG B15......126 B5
Carpenters Ct BHTH/HG B12 *....127 F4
Carpenter's Rd LOZ/NWT B19....108 C2
Carrick Cl BLOX/PEL WS3....18 A2
Carriers Cl WSLW WS2.......40 D4
Carriers Fold WMBN WV5....65 F4
Carrington Rd
  DARL/WED WS10..........71 H1
Carrisbrooke Rd
  DARL/WED WS10..........71 H1
Carroway Head Hl
  MGN/WHC B75............49 E1
Carsbrooke Av
  CBHAMNE B4.............3 H5
Carshalton Gv BKHL/PFLD WV2....37 C5
Carshalton Rd KGSTG B44....75 C1
Cartbridge Crs RUSH/SHEL WS4....28 C5
Cartbridge La RUSH/SHEL WS4....28 C5
Cartbridge La South
  RUSH/SHEL WS4..........28 C5
Carter Rd CDSL WV8.........10 D4
Carter Rd
  DUNHL/THL/PER WV6......22 D5
  GTB/HAM B43............73 H1
Carters Cl CBHAMNE B4......3 H5
Carter's Grn WBROM B70....87 F2
Carters Hurst STETCH B33....130 D3
Carter's La RMSLY B62......139 H4
Cartland Rd BVILLE B30....160 B3
  SPARK B11..............128 A5
The Cartway
  DUNHL/THL/PER WV6......34 B1
Cartwright Gdns OLDBY B69....86 A4
Cartwright Rd MGN/WHC B75....47 G2
Cartwright St BKHL/PFLD WV2....37 H5
Carver Ct TPTN/OCK DY4......69 G2
Carver Gdns STRBR DY8......135 E5
Carver St CBHAMNW B4.......2 A2
Casern Vw SCFLD/BOLD B75....63 G2
Casewell Rd KGSWFD DY6....99 G1
Casey Av ERDW/GRVHL B23....76 B3

Cash Joynson Av
  DARL/WED WS10..........40 A5
Casion Crs STRBR DY8.......134 D3
Caslon Rd HALE B63.........137 C1
Cassandra Cl BRLYHL DY5....83 E5
Cassowary Rd
  BFLD/HDSWWD B20........89 H3
Castello Dr CBROM B36......95 F5
The Castings BILS/COS WV14....68 D1
Castlebridge Rd WNSFLD WV11....25 C3
Castle Cl BRWNH WS8.........9 F2
  CDYHTH B64.............121 H3
  HIA/OLT B92............164 D1
Castle Crs CBROM B36.......113 E1
Castle Cft LGLYGN/QTN B68....123 H4
Castlecroft Av
  BDMR/CCFT WV3..........35 E5
Castlecroft Gdns
  BDMR/CCFT WV3..........35 G5
Castlecroft La
  BDMR/CCFT WV3..........34 D5
Castlecroft Rd
  BDMR/CCFT WV3..........34 D5
  BILS/COS WV14..........54 A4
Castle Dr CSHL/WTROR B46....115 F4
  SHHTH WV12.............25 H5
Castleford Gv SPARK B11 *....145 E3
Castleford Rd SPARK B11....145 E3
Castleford St ALDR WS9......19 C4
Castlegate Dr DUDN DY1......85 E4
Castlegate Wy DUDN DY1 *....85 E4
Castle Grounds DUDN DY1 *....84 D4
Castle Gv STRBR DY8........135 H4
Castle Hts CDYHTH B64 *....121 H4
Castle Hl DUDN DY1.........84 D4
Castlehills Dr CBROM B36....112 C1
Castle La HIA/OLT B92......164 C1
Castle Mill Rd DUDN DY1....84 C2
Castle Rd ALDR WS9.........19 C5
  BVILLE B30.............176 D1
  SLYOAK B29.............158 D1
  TPTN/OCK DY4...........84 D2
Castle Rd East
  LGLYGN/QTN B68.........123 H4
Castle Rd West
  LGLYGN/QTN B68.........123 G4
Castle St BILS/COS WV14....68 C3
  BRWNH WS8..............9 F2
  DARL/WED WS10..........40 B5
  DUDN DY1...............84 D5
  SEDG DY3...............67 F3
  TPTN/OCK DY4...........85 E1
  WBROM B70..............71 E4
  WOLV WV1...............7 G4
Castleton Rd BLOX/PEL WS3....17 E4
  PBAR/PBCH B42..........74 D4
Castletown St DUDS DY2....102 C4
Castle Vw DUDN DY1.........84 D4
Castle View Cl
  DARL/WED WS10..........54 C4
Castle View Rd
  DARL/WED WS10..........54 C4
Caswell Rd SEDG DY3........67 E3
Catalpa Gv FOAKS/STRLY B74....60 A2
Cater Dr WALM/CURD B76....78 B1
Caterham Dr KGSWFD DY6....118 B1
Catesby Dr KGSWFD DY6......99 H1
Catesby Pk HWK/WKNTH B38....176 C2
Catesby Rd SHLY B90.......180 B4
Cateswell Rd HLGN/YWD B28....162 D1
  SPARK B11..............145 H5
Cathcart Rd STRBR DY8......135 E2
Cathedral Cl TPTN/OCK DY4....85 E1
Cathel Dr PBAR/PBCH B42....74 A4
Catherine De Barnes La
  HIA/OLT B92............166 C4
Catherine Dr SCFLD/BOLD B73....62 A2
Catherine Rd BILS/COS WV14....68 A2
Catherines Cl SOLH B91....183 F1
Catherine St AST/WIT B6....109 C2
Catherton Cl TPTN/OCK DY4....70 A1
Catholic La SEDG DY3.......67 E4
Catisfield Crs CDSL WV8....22 B1
Cat & Kittens La WOLN WV10....13 E1
Cat La BKDE/SHDE B34......112 D2
Caton Gv HLGN/YWD B28....163 E3
Cato St North VAUX/NECH B7....110 A4
Catshill Rd BRWNH WS8......9 H1
Cattell Dr WALM/CURD B76....63 H5
Cattell Rd BORD B9.........128 A3
Cattells Gv VAUX/NECH B7....110 A3
Cattermole Gv FOAKS/STRLY B74....45 G3
Cattock Hurst Dr
  SCFLD/WYGN B72.........77 H1
Causeway BLKHTH/ROWR B65....122 A2
Causeway Green Rd
  LGLYGN/QTN B68.........123 E1
Causeway Wy BILS/COS WV14....68 D5
The Causeway YDLY B25......129 H5
Causey Farm Rd HALE B63....154 D2
Cavalier Crs WOLN WV10....13 C5
Cavalier Dr HALE B63.......138 C4
Cavandale Av KGSTG B44....75 E2
Cavell Closet WSLW WS2....4 E3
Cavell Rd DUDS DY2.........85 H5
Cavendish Av
  HWK/WKNTH B38..........177 F4
  KGSWFD DY6.............99 H5
Cavendish Dr HAG/WOL DY9....99 H5
Cavendish Gdns WSLW WS2....41 E1
Cavendish Rd
  LDYWD/EDGR B16........125 F1
  RMSLY B62.............139 H3
  WOLV WV1...............38 B4
  WSLW WS2...............4 A5
Cavendish Wy ALDR WS9......30 B5
Caversham Rd KGSTG B44....75 C2
Cawdon Gv DOR/KN B93......198 C1
Cawdor Crs LDYWD/EDGR B16....125 H3
Caxton Gv KGSTG B44.......76 A2
Caynham Rd RIDG/WDGT B32....157 F2
Cayton Gv ERDW/GRVHL B23....76 D5
Cecil Dr OLDBY B69.........86 B4
Cecil Rd ERDE/BCHGN B24....92 D3
  SLYOAK B29.............160 C1
Cecil St LOZ/NWT B19.......3 G1
  RUSH/SHEL WS4..........42 B2
  STRBR DY8..............135 F2
Cedar Av BILS/COS WV14....68 A4

BRWNH WS8................9 G4
  CBROM B36..............113 E2
Cedar Bridge Cft
  FOAKS/STRLY B74........47 F5
Cedar Cl BVILLE B30.......159 F4
  DSYBK/YTR WS5..........57 H4
  LGLYGN/QTN B68........123 C4
  STRBR DY8..............134 D5
Cedar Dr ERDE/BCHGN B24....93 G1
  FOAKS/STRLY B74........47 F5
  NFLD/LBR B31..........189 H1
Cedar Gv BDMR/CCFT WV3....51 F1
  CDSL WV8...............10 C4
  HAG/WOL DY9............152 C4
Cedarhurst RIDG/WDGT B32....141 G2
  SOLH B91...............182 A2
Cedar Park Rd SHHTH WV12....26 A1
Cedar Rd BVILLE B30.......159 G4
  DARL/WED WS10..........71 E1
  DUDN DY1...............68 A3
  WLNHL WV13.............39 E3
Cedars Av ACGN B27........146 C3
  KGSWFD DY6.............99 H5
  WMBN WV5...............81 E1
The Cedars
  DUNHL/THL/PER WV6 *....36 B2
  YDLY B25...............130 A3
Cedar Wy NFLD/LBR B31......175 F4
  WNSFLD WV11............24 D1
Cedarwood FOAKS/STRLY B74....47 F5
Cedarwood Cft
  PBAR/PBCH B42..........73 H3
Cedar Wood Rd SEDG DY3....83 E2
Celandine Cl KGSWFD DY6....99 G5
Celandine Rd DUDN DY1......84 A2
The Celandines WMBN WV5....64 C5
Celbury Wy GTB/HAM B43....73 F3
Celts Cl BLKHTH/ROWR B65....104 A5
Cemetery La WSNGN B18......108 B4
Cemetery Rd DARL/WED WS10....40 D5
  HAG/WOL DY9............136 B2
  LGLYGN/QTN B68........105 G3
  WLNHL WV13.............39 G2
Cemetery St BILS/COS WV14....54 B4
Cemetery Wy BLOX/PEL WS3....27 F1
Centenary Cl NFLD/LBR B31....175 G4
Centenary Dr HDSW B21......89 H5
Centenary Sq CBHAMNW B1....2 D5
Central Av WOLV WV1........7 F4
  BILS/COS WV14..........54 A1
Central Park Dr WSNGN B18....107 H4
Central Sq ERDW/GRVHL B23 *....93 E2
Central Wy BRLYHL DY5......119 H1
Centre La HALE B63.........138 D4
The Centreway
  ALE/KHTH/YWD B14......179 F1
Centurion Cl CSHL/WTROR B46....97 F5
Century Pk BORD B9........128 A2
Century Rd OLDBY B69......105 E1
Cedmund Crs
  CHWD/FDBR/MGN B37....132 B1
Chaceley Gv
  ERDW/GRVHL B23 *.......76 B4
Chadbury Cft SOLH B91....181 H5
Chadbury Rd HALE B63.......139 E4
Chaddesley Cl OLDBY B69....104 B4
Chaddesley Dr HAG/WOL DY9....152 D1
Chaddesley Rd HALE B63....138 B5
  NFLD/LBR B31..........176 B3
Chadley Cl SOLH B91.......164 D1
Chad Rd DUDN DY1...........68 B4
  EDG B15................125 H4
Chadshunt Cl CBROM B36....95 F4
Chadsmoor Ter
  HHTH/SAND B71.........109 H3
Chadstone Cl SHLY B90....195 H2
Chad Valley Cl HRBN B17....142 B1
Chadwell Gdns CDSL WV8....10 B3
Chadwich La HAG/WOL DY9....186 A2
Chadwick Av RBRY B45......188 B2
Chadwick Cl
  ETTPK/GDPK/PENN WV4....50 C2
  WASH/WDE B8 *..........73 C5
Chadwick Ct MGN/WHC B75....63 F3
Chadworth Av DOR/KN B93....196 C4
Chaffcombe Rd
  LGN/SDN/BHAMAIR B26....148 A1
Chaffinch Cl SEDG DY3......67 E1
Chaffinch Dr CBROM B36....114 B2
Chaffinch Rd HAG/WOL DY9....136 A4
Chainmakers Cl BILS/COS WV14....53 G5
Chain Wk LOZ/NWT B19......108 D2
Chalcot Gv BFLD/HDSWWD B20....89 G1
Chaldon Cl COVEN WV9......12 A5
Chale Gv ALE/KHTH/YWD B14....178 C2
Chalfont Pl HAG/WOL DY9....136 C5
Chalford Rd ERDW/GRVHL B23....76 A3
Chalford Wy SHLY B90......180 C5
Chalgrove Av
  HWK/WKNTH B38..........176 C4
Chalgrove Crs SOLH B91....181 H4
Chalybeate Cl RBRY B45....173 H4
Chamberlain Cl OLDBY B69....86 B4
Chamberlain Crs
  ALE/KHTH/YWD B14......161 E1
  WSNGN B18..............2 C1
Chamberlain Crs SHLY B90....180 A3
Chamberlain Rd MOS/BIL B13....161 F4
Chamberlain's La
  ETTPK/GDPK/PENN WV4....51 E5
Chamberlain Sq CBHAMNW B3....2 E5
Chamberlain Wk
  CSHL/WTROR B46 *.......115 F2
  SMTHWK B66.............106 C3
Chance Cft LGLYGN/QTN B68....123 F4

Chancellor's Cl EDG B15....125 G4
Chancel Wy RMSLY B62......139 E2
Chancery Wy BRLYHL DY5....119 H2
Chandler Dr
  ETTPK/GDPK/PENN WV4....50 D5
Chandlers Cl COVEN WV9....22 C1
  WSNGN B18..............107 H4
Chandlers Keep BRWNH WS8....19 F1
Channon Dr BRLYHL DY5......119 F4
Chanston Av
  ALE/KHTH/YWD B14......178 A1
Chanterelle Gdns
  ETTPK/GDPK/PENN WV4....51 G4
Chantrey Crs BILS/COS WV14....54 B1
  GTB/HAM B43............59 H4
Chantry Av BLOX/PEL WS3....27 G2
Chantry Cl HLYWD B47......192 C1
Chantry Dr RMSLY B62......139 H1
Chantry Heath Crs
  DOR/KN B93............185 F5
Chantry Rd HDSW B21.......107 H1
  KINVER DY7............117 C5
  MOS/BIL B13...........144 A3
Chapel Ash Island
  BDMR/CCFT WV3..........6 C4
Chapel Av WALSALL WS3 *....9 E2
Chapel Cl CDYHTH B64......121 H4
  WMBN WV5...............80 D1
Chapel Dr BRWNH WS8........9 E2
  HLYWD B47..............192 B5
Chapelfield Ms RBRY B45....187 H2
  STRBR DY8..............135 G3
Chapelfield Rd RBRY B45....174 A5
Chapel Fields Rd HIA/OLT B92....147 F5
Chapel Gn WLNHL WV13......39 H5
Chapel House La HALE B63....137 C2
Chapelhouse Rd
  CHWD/FDBR/MGN B37....131 H2
Chapel House St BHTH/HG B12 *....3 K7
Chapel La CDSL WV8.........10 B4
  GTB/HAM B43............58 D4
  HAG/WOL DY9............185 H1
  HOCK/TIA B94..........199 G4
  RMSLY B62.............154 C4
  SEDG DY3...............83 G3
  SLYOAK B29............142 C5
Chapel St BILS/COS WV14....54 B4
  BKHL/PFLD WV2.........52 B1
  BLOX/PEL WS3...........27 H2
  BRLYHL DY5............101 E2
  BRWNH WS8.............9 E3
  CBHAMNE B4.............3 J4
  DARL/WED WS10..........70 D5
  DUDS DY2..............102 D5
  HAG/WOL DY9...........152 C5
  HALE B63..............138 C4
  HDSW B21..............107 F2
  KGSWFD DY6............99 F1
  OLDBY B69.............104 C2
  TPTN/OCK DY4...........85 F1
  WBROM B70.............87 F1
  WMBN WV5..............80 D1
Chapel Vw SMTHWK B66......106 B5
Chapel Wk BVILLE B30......177 E3
  SEDG DY3...............83 E4
Chapelwood Gv
  PBAR/PBCH B42 *........90 D1
Chapman Rd SMHTH B10......128 A4
Chapman's Hl RMSLY B62....172 D5
Chapmans Pas CBHAMW B1 *....2 E7
Chapman St WBROM B70......87 F5
Chapter House WHGSFD B70 *....87 E1
Charfield Cl BVILLE B30....159 F5
Charingworth Rd HIA/OLT B92....148 A5
Charlbury Av
  CHWD/FDBR/MGN B37....131 H2
Charlbury Crs
  LGN/SDN/BHAMAIR B26....130 B4
Charlecote Cft SHLY B90....180 C5
Charlecote Dr DUDN DY1....83 G3
  ERDW/GRVHL B23........76 C4
Charlecote Gdns
  SCFLD/BOLD B73........77 E3
Charlecote Ri WLNHL WV13....39 F4
Charlecott Cl MOS/BIL B13....162 B3
Charlemont Av
  HHTH/SAND B71.........72 B3
Charlemont Cl DSYBK/YTR WS5....58 A2
Charlemont Crs
  HHTH/SAND B71.........72 A3
Charlemont Gdns
  DSYBK/YTR WS5..........57 H2
Charlemont Rd
  DSYBK/YTR WS5..........57 H2
  HHTH/SAND B71.........72 A3
Charles Av AST/WIT B6......91 G5
  BFLD/HDSWWD B20........89 C5
  BRLYHL DY5............120 A3
Charles Crs BLOX/PEL WS3....18 A2
Charles Dr VAUX/NECH B7....109 H3
Charles Edward Rd
  LGN/SDN/BHAMAIR B26....146 D1
Charles Foster St
  DARL/WED WS10..........55 E2
Charles Henry St
  BHTH/HG B12...........127 E4
Charles Holland St
  WLNHL WV13.............39 H3
Charles Rd AST/WIT B6......91 G5
  BLKHTH/ROWR B65.......104 A5
  BLOX/PEL WS3...........18 A2
  HALE B63..............138 B3
  SMHTH B10.............128 C4
  SOLH B91..............181 E3
  STRBR DY8.............135 E3
  TPTN/OCK DY4...........69 G4
Charles St SMTHWK B66......107 E2
  WBROM B70.............86 C1
  WLNHL WV13.............40 A2
  WSLW WS2..............4 A4
Charles Wk
  BLKHTH/ROWR B65........104 A4
Charles Wesley Ct
  BDMR/CCFT WV3 *........51 G1
Charlesworth Av SHLY B90....195 H2
Charleville Rd LOZ/NWT B19....108 B2
Charlotte Cl OLDBY B69....85 G4

Charlotte Gdns SHLY B90....180
Charlotte Rd BILS/COS WV14....160
  DARL/WED WS10..........70
  EDG B15................126
Charlotte St CBHAMNW B3....3
  DUDN DY1..............102
  WSL WS1...............5
Charlton Dr CDYHTH B64....120
Charlton Rd KGSTG B44....75
Charlton St BRLYHL DY5....118
  DUDN DY1...............84
Charminster Av YDLY B25....129
Charnwood Av SEDG DY3....67
Charnwood Cl BILS/COS WV14....54
  BRLYHL DY5............118
  RBRY B45..............188
Charnwood Ct HAG/WOL DY9....136
Charnwood Rd
  DSYBK/YTR WS5..........57
  PBAR/PBCH B42.........73
Charnwood Wy
  ERDE/BCHGN B24........77
The Chase Link BRWNH WS8 *....9
Chasepool Rd SEDG DY3....98
Chase Rd BLOX/PEL WS3....27
  BRWNH WS8.............9
  SEDG DY3..............82
The Chase
  DUNHL/THL/PER WV6......22
  WALM/CURD B76.........77
Chase Vw
  ETTPK/GDPK/PENN WV4....67
Chater Dr WALM/CURD B76....78
Chaters Cl TPTN/OCK DY4....85
Chatham Rd NFLD/LBR B31....175
Chatsworth Av GTB/HAM B43....73
Chatsworth Cl
  CSCFLD/WYGN B72.......77
  SHHTH WV12............194
  SHLY B90..............194
Chatsworth Crs
  RUSH/SHEL WS4..........29
Chatsworth Gdns
  DUNHL/THL/PER WV6......21
Chatsworth Ms STRBR DY8 *....117
Chatsworth Rd RMSLY B62....152
Chattle Hl CSHL/WTROR B46....97
Chattock Av SOLH B91......182
Chattock Cl CBROM B36....112
Chatwell Gv SLYOAK B29....142
Chatwin Pl BILS/COS WV14....54
Chatwin St SMTHWK B66....106
Chatwins Whf TPTN/OCK DY4....85
Chaucer Av SEDG DY3.......82
  SHHTH WV12............26
  TPTN/OCK DY4...........69
Chaucer Cl BILS/COS WV14....68
  ERDW/GRVHL B23........91
  STRBR DY8.............118
Chaucer Crs DUDN DY1......83
Chaucer Gv ACGN B27......163
Chauson Gv SOLH B91......181
Chavasse Rd
  SCFLD/WYGN B72.........62
Chawn Hl HAG/WOL DY9......136
Chawnhill Cl HAG/WOL DY9....136
Chawn Park Dr HAG/WOL DY9....136
Chaynes Gv STETCH B33....131
Cheadle Dr ERDW/GRVHL B23....76
Cheam Gdns
  DUNHL/THL/PER WV6......22
Cheapside BHTH/HG B12....127
  WLNHL WV13.............39
Cheatham St VAUX/NECH B7....110
Checketts St VAUX/NECH B7....4
Checkley Cl SHLY B90......180
Checkley St WALM/CURD B76....78
Cheddar Rd BHTH/HG B12....144
Chedworth Cl SLYOAK B29....158
Cheedon Cl DOR/KN B93....196
Chelford Crs KGSWFD DY6....118
Chells Ce MOS/BIL B13....161
Chelmar Cl CBROM B36......113
Chelmar Dr BRLYHL DY5......99
Chelmarsh Av
  BDMR/CCFT WV3..........35
Chelmorton Rd
  PBAR/PBCH B42.........74
Chelmscote Rd HIA/OLT B92....164
Chelmsley Av
  CSHL/WTROR B46........115
Chelmsley Cir
  CHWD/FDBR/MGN B37....132
Chelmsley Gv STETCH B33....131
Chelmsley La
  CHWD/FDBR/MGN B37....131
Chelsea Cl RIDG/WDGT B32....140
Chelsea Dr FOAKS/STRLY B74....46
Chelsea Wy KGSWFD DY6....99
Chelston Dr
  DUNHL/THL/PER WV6......36
Chelston Rd NFLD/LBR B31....175
Cheltenham Dr CBROM B36....111
  KGSWFD DY6............99
Cheltenham Ms
  FOAKS/STRLY B74........47
Chelthorn Wy SOLH B91....182
Chelveston Crs SOLH B91....181
Chelveston Rd COVEN WV9....11
Chelwood Gdns
  BILS/COS WV14.........53

helworth Rd
HWK/WKHTH B38 177 F3
hem Rd BILS/COS WV14 53 F3
heniston Rd SHHTH WV12 26 A4
hepstow Cl
DUNHL/THL/PER WV6 34 D1
hepstow Gv RBRY B45 188 B2
hepstow Rd BLOX/PEL WS3 26 D1
WOLVN WV10 12 D2
hepstow Vls BHTH/HG B12 * 144 D2
hequerfield Dr
BDMR/CCFT WV3 51 G2
hequers Av WMBN WV5 65 E2
hequer St BDMR/CCFT WV3 51 G2
herhill Covert
ALE/KHTH/YWD B14 177 G3
herington Rd SLYOAK B29 160 A2
heriton Gv
DUNHL/THL/PER WV6 34 C2
herrington Cl NFLD/LBR B31 158 A3
herrington Gdns
DUNHL/THL/PER WV6 35 F3
HAG/WOL DY9 153 E2
herrington Wy SOLH B91 181 H4
herry Crs ERDE/BCHGN B24 92 D3
herrydale Ct DUDN DY1 83 H4
herry Dr BORD B9 127 H3
herry Gn DUDN DY1 83 H2
herry Gv SMTHWK B66 107 E4
STRBR DY8 135 E3
herry Hill Wk DUDN DY1 102 A1
herry La DARL/WED WS10 71 E1
SCFLD/BOLD B73 77 E4
SEDG DY3 81 F3
herry Lea BKDE/SHDE B34 112 D3
herry Orch CDSL WV8 10 B3
CDYHTH B64 121 F3
herry Orchard Av HALE B63 138 B2
herry Orchard Crs HALE B63 138 B2
herry Orchard Rd
BFLD/HDSWWD B20 89 H1
herry Rd TPTN/OCK DY4 69 F4
herry St BDMR/CCFT WV3 6 C5
CBHAM B2 3 G5
HALE B63 138 B2
STRBR DY8 135 E3
herry Tree Av DSYBK/YTR WS5 57 H4
herrytree Ct HAG/WOL DY9 136 C4
herry Tree Cft ACGN B27 146 C2
herry Tree Gdns CDSL WV8 10 D4
herry Tree La CDSL WV8 10 D4
HALE B63 154 D1
herry Tree Rd KGSWFD DY6 100 A1
herry Wk HLYWD B47 192 D3
herrywood Cl BILS/COS WV14 68 C2
herrywood Crs SOLH B91 182 A5
herrywood Gn
BILS/COS WV14 38 D5
herrywood Rd BORD B9 128 B2
FOAKS/STRLY B74 44 D4
herrywood Wy
FOAKS/STRLY B74 46 B1
hervil Cl PBAR/PBCH B42 74 C4
hervil Ri WOLVN WV10 37 H2
herwell Dr BRWNH WS8 8 C2
CBROM B36 113 H1
herwell Gdns AST/WIT B6 * 108 D1
heshire Av SHLY B90 180 A2
heshire Cl STRBR DY8 117 H4
heshire Gv
DUNHL/THL/PER WV6 34 C1
heshire Rd AST/WIT B6 91 G4
SMTHWKW B67 106 C5
WSLW WS2 40 D3
heshunt Pl
ALE/KHTH/YWD B14 * 161 E2
hessetts Gv MOS/BIL B13 161 G4
hessetts Wood Rd
HOCK/TIA B94 199 G3
hester Av
DUNHL/THL/PER WV6 22 B3
hester Cl
CHWD/FDBR/MGN B37 132 A2
WLNHL WV13 40 B3
hesterfield Cl NFLD/LBR B31 175 H3
hesterfield Ct ALDR WS9 * 19 F3
hester Gdns SCFLD/BOLD B73 76 C2
hestergate Cft
ERDE/BCHGN B24 93 H2
hester Pl WSLW WS2 41 F4
hester Ri LGLYGN/QTN B68 123 G4
hester Rd ALDR WS9 45 F2
BRWNH WS8 19 H2
CBROM B36 112 D1
CDYHTH B64 120 C4
CHWD/FDBR/MGN B37 133 E3
DUDS DY2 120 D2
ERDE/BCHGN B24 93 G1
FOAKS/STRLY B74 60 C1
HHTH/SAND B71 71 F2
HIA/OLT B92 150 D3
SCFLD/BOLD B73 76 C3
hester Rd North BRWNH WS8 8 D3
SCFLD/BOLD B73 61 E5
hester St
DUNHL/THL/PER WV6 36 D1
VAUX/NECH B7 109 F4
hesterton Cl SOLH B91 164 A5
hesterton Rd BHTH/HG B12 144 C2
WOLVN WV10 24 A2
hesterwood ALDR WS9 45 E3
HLYWD B47 192 C2
hesterwood Gdns
BFLD/HDSWWD B20 90 D4
hesterwood Rd
MOS/BIL B13 161 F4
hestnut Av DUDN DY1 84 C3
TPTN/OCK DY4 69 F4
hestnut Cl ACGN B27 146 C3
CDSL WV8 10 B5
FOAKS/STRLY B74 45 G3
HIA/OLT B92 163 H2
STRBR DY8 134 C5
hestnut Ct BKDE/SHDE B34 113 G2
hestnut Dr CBROM B36 112 C1
ERDE/BCHGN B24 93 G2
HAG/WOL DY9 169 F1
RBRY B45 188 C4
RUSH/SHEL WS4 28 D2
WMBN WV5 81 E1
Chestnut Gv
CSHL/WTROR B46 115 G2
HRBN B17 142 B2
KGSWFD DY6 100 B3
Chestnut Pl BLOX/PEL WS3 27 H4
Chestnut Rd BLOX/PEL WS3 28 A4
DARL/WED WS10 71 E1
LGLYGN/QTN B68 123 G5
MOS/BIL B13 144 C3
Chestnuts Av
LGN/SDN/BHAMAIR B26 130 D5
Chestnut Wy BDMR/CCFT WV3 35 H5
Chestom Rd
ETTPK/GDPK/PENN WV4 53 F3
Cheston Rd VAUX/NECH B7 109 G3
Cheswell Cl
DUNHL/THL/PER WV6 35 F3
Cheswick Cl WLNHL WV13 39 F5
Cheswick Wy SHLY B90 194 D5
Cheswood Dr WALM/CURD B76 78 D5
Chetland Cft HIA/OLT B92 165 H3
Chettle Rd BILS/COS WV14 54 B5
Chetton Gn WOLVN WV10 12 B4
Chetwood Cl
DUNHL/THL/PER WV6 22 C5
Chetwynd Cl WSLW WS2 40 A2
Chetwynd Rd BKHL/PFLD WV2 51 H2
WASH/WDE B8 111 F4
Cheveley Av RBRY B45 188 B1
Chevening Cl SEDG DY3 67 G4
Cheveridge Cl SOLH B91 181 G4
Cheverton Rd NFLD/LBR B31 175 E2
Cheviot Rd BKHL/PFLD WV2 52 D1
STRBR DY8 135 G1
Cheviot Wy HALE B63 137 H4
Cheylesmore Cl
SCFLD/BOLD B73 62 B4
Cheyne Gdns HLGN/YWD B28 179 G2
Cheyne Wk BRLYHL DY5 119 E5
Cheyney Cl
DUNHL/THL/PER WV6 22 C5
Chichester Av DUDS DY2 102 D4
Chichester Ct
SCFLD/BOLD B73 * 62 B3
Chichester Dr RIDG/WDGT B32 140 A2
Chichester Gv
CHWD/FDBR/MGN B37 132 B3
Chigwell Cl CVALE B35 94 C3
Chilcote Cl HLGN/YWD B28 179 H1
Childs Av BILS/COS WV14 68 A1
Chilgrove Gdns
DUNHL/THL/PER WV6 21 G5
Chilham Dr
CHWD/FDBR/MGN B37 132 C2
Chillinghome Rd CBROM B36 111 H1
Chillington Dr CDSL WV8 10 B3
DUDN DY1 83 H3
Chillington Flds WOLV WV1 38 A4
Chillington Pl BILS/COS WV14 53 G3
Chillington Rd TPTN/OCK DY4 70 A2
Chillington St BKHL/PFLD WV2 37 H5
Chiltern Cl HALE B63 137 G5
SEDG DY3 83 F3
Chiltern Dr WLNHL WV13 38 D4
Chiltern Rd STRBR DY8 135 H1
Chilton Rd
ALE/KHTH/YWD B14 179 F1
Chilwell Cl SOLH B91 181 H4
Chilwell Cft LOZ/NWT B19 109 E3
Chilworth Av WNSFLD WV11 25 F3
Chilworth Cl AST/WIT B6 109 F3
Chimes Cl STETCH B33 131 G3
Chimney Rd TPTN/OCK DY4 70 B4
Chingford Cl STRBR DY8 99 G5
Chingford Rd KGSTG B44 75 G3
Chinley Gv KGSTG B44 76 A2
Chinn Brook Rd MOS/BIL B13 161 H5
Chip Cl HWK/WKHTH B38 176 B3
Chipperfield Rd CBROM B36 112 A1
Chipstead Rd
ERDW/GRVHL B23 76 B4
Chipstone Cl SOLH B91 182 A5
Chirbury Gv NFLD/LBR B31 175 H4
Chirton Gv
ALE/KHTH/YWD B14 160 D4
Chiseldon Cft
ALE/KHTH/YWD B14 178 C2
Chisholm Gv ACGN B27 163 G2
Chiswell Rd WSNGN B18 107 G5
Chivington Cl SHLY B90 195 H2
Chorley Av BKDE/SHDE B34 112 B2
Chorley Gdns BILS/COS WV14 53 F3
Christchurch Cl EDG B15 125 G4
Christ Church Gv WSL WS1 57 G1
Christina Ct HHTH/SAND B71 87 H2
Christine Cl TPTN/OCK DY4 70 A1
Christopher Rd
BKHL/PFLD WV2 37 G5
RMSLY B62 139 G4
SLYOAK B29 142 B5
Chubb St WOLV WV1 7 H3
Chuckery Rd WSL WS1 5 H4
Chudleigh Gv GTB/HAM B43 73 F3
Chudleigh Rd
ERDW/GRVHL B23 92 C2
Church Av
BFLD/HDSWWD B20 * 90 C5
HAG/WOL DY9 170 C3
MOS/BIL B13 * 144 B4
STRBR DY8 118 C5
Churchbridge OLDBY B69 104 D3
Church Cl
CHWD/FDBR/MGN B37 114 A3
HLYWD B47 192 B5
Church Cft HALE B63 138 C3
HRBN B17 141 H3
Church Cross Vw DUDN DY1 101 F1
Churchdale Rd KGSTG B44 59 H5
Church Dr BVILLE B30 160 B3
Churchfield Av TPTN/OCK DY4 69 F3
Churchfield Cl VAUX/NECH B7 110 A3
Churchfield Rd WOLVN WV10 22 D2
Churchfields Rd
DARL/WED WS10 55 H5
Churchfield St DUDS DY2 102 C1
Church Gdns SMTHWKW B67 * 124 C1
Church Gn BFLD/HDSWWD B20 89 H4
BILS/COS WV14 38 C5
Church Gv
BFLD/HDSWWD B20 * 90 B5
MOS/BIL B13 162 A5
Church Hl BRLYHL DY5 119 F2
CDSL WV8 10 B2
CSHL/WTROR B46 115 G2
DARL/WED WS10 55 H5
ETTPK/GDPK/PENN WV4 51 E4
HAG/WOL DY9 184 B2
NFLD/LBR B31 175 G2
RIDG/WDGT B32 157 E5
WSL WS1 5 F4
Church Hill Cl SOLH B91 182 A3
Church Hill Rd
BFLD/HDSWWD B20 90 B5
DUNHL/THL/PER WV6 21 H4
SOLH B91 182 A3
Church Hill St SMTHWKW B67 106 B5
Churchill Cl OLDBY B69 86 A4
Churchill Dr
BLKHTH/ROWR B65 121 H2
STRBR DY8 118 C5
Churchill Gdns SEDG DY3 67 E4
Churchill La KIDD DY10 168 C2
Churchill Pl
LGN/SDN/BHAMAIR B26 130 D3
Churchill Rd BORD B9 128 D2
HALE B63 138 B5
MGN/WHC B75 63 G3
SCFLD/BOLD B73 76 A1
WSLW WS2 40 D2
Church La AST/WIT B6 109 G1
BFLD/HDSWWD B20 89 H4
BKHL/PFLD WV2 6 E6
CDSL WV8 10 B3
HALE B63 138 D3
HHTH/SAND B71 87 F1
HIA/OLT B92 166 D1
STETCH B33 130 B1
WALM/CURD B76 79 H2
Church Moat Wy
BLOX/PEL WS3 27 F2
Churchover Cl
WALM/CURD B76 77 H5
Church Pl BLOX/PEL WS3 27 H2
Church Rd AST/WIT B6 109 G1
BDMR/CCFT WV3 51 E1
BILS/COS WV14 68 D2
BLKHTH/ROWR B65 122 A1
BLOX/PEL WS3 18 A4
BRWNH WS8 9 F5
CDSL WV8 10 B3
DUDS DY2 102 B4
DUNHL/THL/PER WV6 34 C1
EDG B15 143 F1
ERDE/BCHGN B24 93 E2
HAG/WOL DY9 136 C2
HAG/WOL DY9 184 B1
HALE B63 137 G1
LGN/SDN/BHAMAIR B26 148 A2
MOS/BIL B13 144 C4
NFLD/LBR B31 175 G2
PBAR/PBCH B42 90 D1
SCFLD/BOLD B73 76 D3
SEDG DY3 80 C4
SHHTH WV12 26 B4
SHLY B90 180 B3
SMTHWKW B67 106 B5
STETCH B33 130 B2
STRBR DY8 135 H4
WMBN WV5 65 F4
WOLVN WV10 23 E1
YDLY B25 146 D1
Churchside Vw ALDR WS9 19 H5
Church Sq OLDBY B69 105 E2
Church St BILS/COS WV14 53 H3
BKHL/PFLD WV2 6 E6
BLOX/PEL WS3 27 G2
BRLYHL DY5 119 E2
BRWNH WS8 19 E2
CBHAMNW B3 3 F4
CDYHTH B64 121 E3
DARL/WED WS10 54 D4
DUDS DY2 102 C1
HAG/WOL DY9 152 C5
LOZ/NWT B19 108 C2
OLDBY B69 105 E1
RMSLY B62 122 B3
SEDG DY3 83 F3
STRBR DY8 135 G2
TPTN/OCK DY4 85 G4
WBROM B70 87 G3
WLNHL WV13 39 H3
WOLVN WV10 38 A1
WSL WS1 5 F5
Church Ter MGN/WHC B75 * 47 G2
STETCH B33 * 130 A3
Church V BFLD/HDSWWD B20 90 B5
HHTH/SAND B71 71 H5
Church Vw ALDR WS9 19 F4
Church View Cl BLOX/PEL WS3 27 G2
Church View Dr CDYHTH B64 121 F3
Church Vls
BFLD/HDSWWD B20 * 89 G4
Church Wk BDMR/CCFT WV3 51 F1
DUNHL/THL/PER WV6 22 A5
WASH/WDE B8 111 E3
Churchward Cl STRBR DY8 135 H1
Churchward Gv WMBN WV5 65 E3
Church Wy RUSH/SHEL WS4 18 B5
Churchyard Rd TPTN/OCK DY4 85 H1
Churnet Gv
DUNHL/THL/PER WV6 34 D1
Churn Hill Rd ALDR WS9 44 A1
Churns Hill La SEDG DY3 81 F3
Churston Cl BLOX/PEL WS3 16 C4
Cider Av BRLYHL DY5 119 G4
Cinder Bank DUDS DY2 102 C3
Cinder Rd SEDG DY3 82 D4
Cinder Wy DARL/WED WS10 55 G5
Cinquefoil Leasow
TPTN/OCK DY4 70 A5
Circuit Cl WLNHL WV13 39 H2
Circular Rd ACGN B27 163 G1
Circus Av
CHWD/FDBR/MGN B37 132 C2
City Plaza CBHAM B2 * 3 G5
City Rd LDYWD/EDGR B16 125 E2
OLDBY B69 103 H2
City Vw ERDW/GRVHL B23 92 C3
WASH/WDE B8 110 B5
Civic Cl CBHAMW B1 2 C5
Claerwen Gv NFLD/LBR B31 158 A5
Claines Rd HALE B63 137 H2
NFLD/LBR B31 176 A1
Clairvaux Gdns HIA/OLT B92 163 H5
Clandon Cl ALE/KHTH/YWD B14 177 F3
Clanfield Av WNSFLD WV11 25 F2
Clapgate Gdns BILS/COS WV14 53 E5
Clap Gate Gv WMBN WV5 64 C5
Clapgate La RIDG/WDGT B32 140 C5
Clap Gate Rd WMBN WV5 64 C4
Clapton Gv KGSTG B44 75 H2
Clare Av WNSFLD WV11 25 F1
Clare Crs BILS/COS WV14 67 H1
Clare Dr EDG B15 125 H4
Clarel Av WASH/WDE B8 128 A1
Claremont Ms
BDMR/CCFT WV3 51 G1
Claremont Pl WSNGN B18 * 108 A4
Claremont Rd BDMR/CCFT WV3 51 G1
SEDG DY3 67 G3
SMTHWK B66 106 D5
SPARK B11 127 H5
WSNGN B18 108 A3
Claremont St BILS/COS WV14 53 G2
CDYHTH B64 121 E3
Claremont Wy HALE B63 138 C4
Clarence Av HDSW B21 * 107 E1
Clarence Ct LGLYGN/QTN B68 123 G2
Clarence Gdns
FOAKS/STRLY B74 46 D3
Clarence Gv SHLY B90 180 B1
Clarence Rd BILS/COS WV14 54 A1
DUDS DY2 102 D3
ERDW/GRVHL B23 92 B3
FOAKS/STRLY B74 32 C5
HDSW B21 107 E1
HRBN B17 142 B1
MOS/BIL B13 161 G2
SPARK B11 145 E3
WOLV WV1 6 E3
Clarence St SEDG DY3 83 G1
WOLV WV1 6 E4
Clarenden Pl HRBN B17 142 A2
Clarendon Dr TPTN/OCK DY4 70 B3
Clarendon Pl BLOX/PEL WS3 17 H3
RMSLY B62 139 H1
Clarendon Rd
LDYWD/EDGR B16 125 G3
MGN/WHC B75 47 G2
RUSH/SHEL WS4 18 C5
SMTHWKW B67 106 B5
Clarendon St BDMR/CCFT WV3 6 B4
BLOX/PEL WS3 27 F1
Clare Rd BLOX/PEL WS3 28 B4
WOLVN WV10 23 G3
Clarewell Av SOLH B91 181 G4
Clarkes Gv TPTN/OCK DY4 70 A5
Clarke's La HHTH/SAND B71 71 G4
WLNHL WV13 40 A3
Clark Rd BDMR/CCFT WV3 36 B3
Clarksland Gv
CHWD/FDBR/MGN B37 132 A4
Clarks La SHLY B90 194 A2
Clarkson Rd DARL/WED WS10 56 A5
Clark St LDYWD/EDGR B16 125 H2
STRBR DY8 135 E2
Clarry Dr FOAKS/STRLY B74 46 D5
Clary Gv DSYBK/YTR WS5 57 G5
Clatterbach La HAG/WOL DY9 171 E1
Claughton Rd DUDS DY2 84 D5
Claughton Rd North DUDS DY2 84 D5
Clausen Cl GTB/HAM B43 60 A4
Clavedon Cl NFLD/LBR B31 158 A3
Claverdon Cl BRWNH WS8 9 G4
SOLH B91 181 E1
Claverdon Dr FOAKS/STRLY B74 45 H1
GTB/HAM B43 73 F3
Claverdon Gdns ACGN B27 146 B2
Claverley Dr
ETTPK/GDPK/PENN WV4 50 D3
Claybrook St DIG/EDG B5 127 E3
Claycroft Ter DUDN DY1 68 B5
Claydon Gv
ALE/KHTH/YWD B14 178 C2
Claydon Rd KGSWFD DY6 81 G5
Clay Dr RIDG/WDGT B32 140 A2
Clayhanger La BRWNH WS8 18 D1
Clayhanger Rd BRWNH WS8 19 F1
Clay La
LGN/SDN/BHAMAIR B26 147 E3
OLDBY B69 105 E5
Claypit Cl WBROM B70 87 E3
Clay Pit La SHLY B90 194 A3
Claypit La WBROM B70 87 E3
Clayton Cl BKHL/PFLD WV2 52 A1
Clayton Dr CBROM B36 113 E1
Clayton Rd BILS/COS WV14 68 B4
WASH/WDE B8 110 B4
Clear Vw KGSWFD DY6 99 F3
Clearwell Gdns DUDN DY1 83 H3
Clee Hill Dr BDMR/CCFT WV3 34 D4
Clee Hill Rd SEDG DY3 83 E2
Clee Rd DUDN DY1 102 A2
LGLYGN/QTN B68 105 G5
NFLD/LBR B31 175 G5
STRBR DY8 135 G1
Cleeve Dr FOAKS/STRLY B74 32 D4
Cleeve Rd ALE/KHTH/YWD B14 179 E2
BLOX/PEL WS3 16 B4
Cleeve Wy BLOX/PEL WS3 16 B5
Clee View Meadow SEDG DY3 67 F1
Clee View Rd WMBN WV5 80 C1
Clematis Dr COVEN WV9 11 H4
Clement Pl BILS/COS WV14 * 53 H1
Clement Rd BILS/COS WV14 53 H1
RMSLY B62 122 B3
Clements Cl OLDBY B69 104 D5
Clements Rd YDLY B25 129 H4
Clement St CBHAMW B1 2 B4
WSLW WS2 4 B3
Clemson St WLNHL WV13 39 G3
Clent Dr HAG/WOL DY9 153 E4
Clent Hill Dr
BLKHTH/ROWR B65 103 G4
Clent Rd HDSW B21 89 F5
LGLYGN/QTN B68 123 G4
RBRY B45 173 G5
STRBR DY8 135 G1
Clent View Rd HALE B63 137 G3
RIDG/WDGT B32 157 E1
STRBR DY8 134 D5
Clent Vls BHTH/HG B12 * 144 D3
Clent Wy RIDG/WDGT B32 156 D2
Cleobury La HOCK/TIA B94 194 A5
Cleton St TPTN/OCK DY4 85 H3
Clevedon Av CBROM B36 113 G1
Clevedon Rd BHTH/HG B12 144 A1
Cleveland Cl WLNHL WV13 38 D4
WNSFLD WV11 25 F1
Cleveland Pas WOLV WV1 7 F5
Cleveland Rd BKHL/PFLD WV2 7 H6
Cleveland St DUDN DY1 84 B5
STRBR DY8 135 E3
WOLV WV1 7 F5
Cleves Dr RBRY B45 187 G1
Cleves Rd RBRY B45 173 G5
Clewley Dr COVEN WV9 12 A4
Clewley Gv RIDG/WDGT B32 140 B2
Clews Cl WSL WS1 57 E1
Clewshaw La
HWK/WKHTH B38 191 G4
Cley Cl DIG/EDG B5 143 H1
Cliff Dr DARL/WED WS10 70 B3
Cliffe Dr STETCH B33 130 D1
Clifford Rd DOR/KN B93 196 D4
SMTHWKW B67 124 B3
WBROM B70 87 E4
Clifford St DUDN DY1 102 B1
DUNHL/THL/PER WV6 6 A1
LOZ/NWT B19 108 D2
Clifford Wk LOZ/NWT B19 108 D2
Cliff Rock Rd RBRY B45 188 B1
Clift Av SHHTH WV12 26 B3
Clift Cl SHHTH WV12 26 A4
Clifton Av ALDR WS9 30 C2
BRWNH WS8 18 D1
Clifton Cl AST/WIT B6 109 F2
OLDBY B69 104 D5
Clifton Crs SOLH B91 181 F4
Clifton Gdns CDSL WV8 11 E4
Clifton Gn HLGN/YWD B28 163 E5
Clifton La HHTH/SAND B71 72 A3
Clifton Rd AST/WIT B6 109 F2
BHTH/HG B12 144 C2
CBROM B36 113 G1
DUNHL/THL/PER WV6 21 H5
RMSLY B62 122 B4
SCFLD/BOLD B73 62 A4
SMTHWKW B67 106 B5
Clifton St BDMR/CCFT WV3 6 C4
BILS/COS WV14 67 H2
CDYHTH B64 121 F3
STRBR DY8 135 F3
Clifton Ter ERDW/GRVHL B23 * 92 D2
Clinic Dr HAG/WOL DY9 136 C2
Clinton Gv SHLY B90 180 D4
Clinton Rd BILS/COS WV14 54 C1
CSHL/WTROR B46 115 F3
SHLY B90 181 E5
Clinton St WSNGN B18 107 G4
Clipper Vw LDYWD/EDGR B16 125 G3
Clipston Rd WASH/WDE B8 110 D4
Clissold Cl BHTH/HG B12 127 E5
Clissold Pas WSNGN B18 108 A5
Clissold St WSNGN B18 108 A5
Clive Cl MGN/WHC B75 47 H3
Cliveden Av ALDR WS9 30 B1
PBAR/PBCH B42 90 C2
Cliveden Coppice
FOAKS/STRLY B74 46 D4
Clivedon Wy RMSLY B62 121 G5
Cliveland St LOZ/NWT B19 3 G1
Clive Rd RIDG/WDGT B32 123 H5
Clive St HHTH/SAND B71 87 G1
Clockfields Dr BRLYHL DY5 118 C3
Clock La HIA/OLT B92 149 H5
Clockmill Av BLOX/PEL WS3 17 G4
Clockmill Pl BLOX/PEL WS3 17 H4
Clockmill Rd BLOX/PEL WS3 17 G4
Clodeshall Rd WASH/WDE B8 110 C5
Cloister Dr RMSLY B62 139 F4
The Cloisters RUSH/SHEL WS4 5 F1
Clonmel Rd BVILLE B30 160 A4
Clopton Crs
CHWD/FDBR/MGN B37 114 C5
Clopton Rd STETCH B33 131 E4
The Close DARL/WED WS10 55 G5
HALE B63 137 H1
HIA/OLT B92 164 B2
HLYWD B47 192 C3
HRBN B17 124 B5
RMSLY B62 155 G3
SEDG DY3 80 C4
SEDG DY3 83 E2
SLYOAK B29 * 159 F2
Clothier Gdns WLNHL WV13 39 G2
Clothier St WLNHL WV13 39 G2
Cloudbridge Dr HIA/OLT B92 165 H3
Cloudsley Gv HIA/OLT B92 147 F4
Clover Av
CHWD/FDBR/MGN B37 132 D2
Cloverdale
DUNHL/THL/PER WV6 34 B1
Clover Dr RIDG/WDGT B32 140 C5
Clover Hl DSYBK/YTR WS5 43 G5
Clover La KGSWFD DY6 99 E2
Clover Lea Sq WASH/WDE B8 111 E3
Clover Ley WOLVN WV10 37 H2
Clover Piece TPTN/OCK DY4 70 A5
Clover Rd SLYOAK B29 158 C3
Club La WOLVN WV10 12 C1
Club Rw SEDG DY3 83 G1
Club Vw HWK/WKHTH B38 175 G5
Clunbury Cft BKDE/SHDE B34 112 D4
Clunbury Rd NFLD/LBR B31 175 G5
Clun Cl OLDBY B69 85 F5
Clun Rd NFLD/LBR B31 158 B4
Clyde Av RMSLY B62 122 C4
Clyde Ms BRLYHL DY5 100 D3
Clyde Rd DOR/KN B93 199 E1
Clydesdale
LGN/SDN/BHAMAIR B26 147 G2
Clydesdale Rd
RIDG/WDGT B32 140 B1
Clyde St BHTH/HG B12 127 G3
CDYHTH B64 121 E3
Coalbourn La STRBR DY8 118 B5
Coalheath La RUSH/SHEL WS4 29 E2
Coal Pool La BLOX/PEL WS3 28 B5
Coalport Rd WOLV WV1 38 A4

Coalway Av BDMR/CCFT WV3 51 G2
LGN/SDN/BHAMAIR B26 148 A3
Coalway Gdns
BDMR/CCFT WV3 50 D2
Coalway Rd BDMR/CCFT WV3 51 G2
BLOX/PEL WS3 27 E2
ETTPK/GDPK/PENN WV4 50 D2
The Cobbles CSCFLD/WYGN B72 77 G4
Cobble Wk WSNGN B18 * 108 A4
Cobden Cl DARL/WED WS10 55 H2
TPTN/OCK DY4 69 F3
Cobden Gdns BHTH/HG B12 144 A2
Cobden St DARL/WED WS10 55 H2
STRBR DY8 134 D1
WSL WS1 56 D1
Cobham Cl CVALE B35 94 B3
Cobham Court Ms
HAG/WOL DY9 153 F4
Cobham Rd BORD B9 128 B2
DARL/WED WS10 72 A1
HALE B63 138 D3
STRBR DY8 135 G5
Cob La BVILLE B30 159 E3
Cobs Fld BVILLE B30 159 E4
Coburg Cft TPTN/OCK DY4 70 A5
Coburn Dr MGN/WHC B75 47 H3
Cochrane Cl HAG/WOL DY9 153 E2
TPTN/OCK DY4 * 70 A5
Cochrane Rd DUDS DY2 101 H4
Cock Hill La RBRY B45 173 H5
Cocksheds La RMSLY B62 122 A4
Cockshut Hl
LGN/SDN/BHAMAIR B26 130 C4
Cockshutt La BKHL/PFLD WV2 * 52 B1
Cockshutts La BKHL/PFLD WV2 52 B1
Cocksmead Cft
ALE/KHTH/YWD B14 160 D5
Cockthorpe Cl HRBN B17 124 B5
Cocton Cl
DUNHL/THL/PER WV6 20 C5
Codsall Gdns CDSL WV8 10 A3
Codsall Rd CDSL WV8 21 G1
CDYHTH B64 121 E4
Cofield Rd SCFLD/BOLD B73 76 D2
Cofton Ct RBRY B45 188 D1
Cofton Gv NFLD/LBR B31 189 E2
Cofton Lake Rd RBRY B45 188 C5
Cofton Rd NFLD/LBR B31 189 H1
Cokeland Pl CDYHTH B64 120 D4
Colaton Cl WOLVN WV10 37 G1
Colbourne Rd TPTN/OCK DY4 85 G2
Coldbath Rd MOS/BIL B13 161 H2
Coldridge Cl CDSL WV8 22 B1
Coldstream Dr STRBR DY8 118 A1
Coldstream Rd
WALM/CURD B76 78 A3
Cole Bank Rd HLGN/YWD B28 162 C2
Colebourne Rd MOS/BIL B13 162 B4
Colebridge Crs
CSHL/WTROR B46 115 F1
Colebrook Cft SHLY B90 179 H3
Colebrook Rd SHLY B90 179 G3
SPARK B11 145 F2
Cole Ct CHWD/FDBR/MGN B37 132 B2
Coleford Cl STRBR DY8 117 G2
Coleford Dr
CHWD/FDBR/MGN B37 132 A2
Cole Gn SHLY B90 179 G3
Cole Hall La BKDE/SHDE B34 112 D4
Colehurst Cft SHLY B90 195 F2
Coleman Rd DARL/WED WS10 56 A3
Coleman St
DUNHL/THL/PER WV6 36 C1
Colemeadow Rd
CSHL/WTROR B46 115 F2
MOS/BIL B13 161 H5
Colenso Rd LDYWD/EDGR B16 107 E5
Coleraine Rd PBAR/PBCH B42 74 A5
Coleridge Cl BLOX/PEL WS3 * 18 A2
SHHTH WV12 26 C3
Coleridge Dr
DUNHL/THL/PER WV6 34 C1
Coleridge Pas CBHAMNE B4 3 H3
Coleridge Ri SEDG DY3 82 C2
Coleridge Rd GTB/HAM B43 73 G4
Colesbourne Av
ALE/KHTH/YWD B14 177 G3
Colesbourne Rd HIA/OLT B92 147 H4
Coleshill Heath Rd
CHWD/FDBR/MGN B37 149 G1
Coleshill Rd CBROM B36 112 B2
CHWD/FDBR/MGN B37 132 A5
MGN/WHC B75 62 D3
WALM/CURD B76 96 B1
Coleshill St CSCFLD/WYGN B72 62 C3
Coleside Av MOS/BIL B13 162 B3
Coles La CSCFLD/WYGN B72 62 C5
HHTH/SAND B71 71 E4
The Colesleys
CSHL/WTROR B46 115 G3
Cole St DUDS DY2 103 E5
Cole Valley Rd HLGN/YWD B28 162 B4
Coleview Crs STETCH B33 131 G1
Coleville Rd WALM/CURD B76 78 D5
Coleys La NFLD/LBR B31 175 G3
Colgreave Av MOS/BIL B13 145 F5
Colindale Rd KGSTG B44 60 C5
Colleen Av BVILLE B30 177 F2
College Cl DARL/WED WS10 55 H1
College Dr BFLD/HDSWWD B20 89 H4
College Farm Dr
ERDW/GRVHL B23 76 B3
College Ga WASH/WDE B8 110 C5
College Gv
BFLD/HDSWWD B20 * 108 B2
College Hl SCFLD/BOLD B73 62 B4
College Rd
BFLD/HDSWWD B20 89 G4
DUNHL/THL/PER WV6 35 H1
KGSTG B44 91 E1
MOS/BIL B13 145 E5
RMSLY B62 140 A1
STRBR DY8 135 G3
WASH/WDE B8 128 C1
College St WSNGN B18 108 A5
College Vw
DUNHL/THL/PER WV6 35 H2
Collet Rd DUNHL/THL/PER WV6 20 C5
Collets Brook MGN/WHC B75 48 C3
Collett Cl STRBR DY8 135 G1
Colletts Gv
CHWD/FDBR/MGN B37 113 H5
Colley Av WOLVN WV10 23 H2
Colley Ga HALE B63 137 G1
Colley La HALE B63 137 G1
Colley Orch HALE B63 137 G1
Colley St WBROM B70 87 H2
Collier Cl BRWNH WS8 8 C5
Colliers Cl SHHTH WV12 25 H4
Colliers Fold BRLYHL DY5 100 D4
Colliery Dr BLOX/PEL WS3 16 B4
Colliery Rd HHTH/SAND B71 106 C1
WOLV WV1 37 H3
Collindale Ct KGSWFD DY6 81 H5
Collingbourne Av CBROM B36 111 H2
Collingdon Av
LGN/SDN/BHAMAIR B26 148 A1
Collingtree Ct ACGN B27 146 D5
Colling Wk
CHWD/FDBR/MGN B37 114 A4
Collingwood Dr GTB/HAM B43 59 H5
Collingwood Rd BVILLE B30 177 H2
WOLVN WV10 13 E5
Collins Cl RIDG/WDGT B32 140 A2
Collins Rd BRWNH WS8 19 G2
DARL/WED WS10 56 B5
Collins St WBROM B70 86 C3
WSL WS1 57 E1
Collis St STRBR DY8 118 C4
Collister Cl SHLY B90 163 F5
Colly Cft
CHWD/FDBR/MGN B37 113 H4
Collycroft Pl ACGN B27 146 B2
Colman Av WNSFLD WV11 25 F4
Colman Crs LGLYGN/QTN B68 123 G2
Colman Hl HALE B63 137 H2
Colman Hill Av HALE B63 137 H1
Colmore Av
ALE/KHTH/YWD B14 160 D3
Colmore Circ Queensway
CBHAMNW B3 3 G3
Colmore Crs MOS/BIL B13 161 H1
Colmore Dr MGN/WHC B75 63 G3
Colmore Flats LOZ/NWT B19 * 3 F1
Colmore Rd
ALE/KHTH/YWD B14 160 D3
Colmore Rw CBHAMNW B3 3 G4
Coln Cl NFLD/LBR B31 158 B4
Colonial Rd BORD B9 128 D2
Colshaw Rd STRBR DY8 135 E3
Colston Rd ERDE/BCHGN B24 93 F4
Colt Cl FOAKS/STRLY B74 60 A1
Coltham Rd SHHTH WV12 26 B4
Coltishall Cft CVALE B35 94 B4
Coltsfoot Cl WNSFLD WV11 25 E5
Columbia Cl DIG/EDG B5 143 H1
Columbine Cl DSYBK/YTR WS5 57 F5
Columbus Av BRLYHL DY5 119 H1
Colville Cl TPTN/OCK DY4 70 B3
Colville Rd BHTH/HG B12 144 D2
Colwall Rd SEDG DY3 83 F2
Colwall Wk ACGN B27 146 D3
Colworth Rd NFLD/LBR B31 175 E1
Colyns Gv STETCH B33 112 B4
Comber Cft MOS/BIL B13 162 B2
Comber Dr BRLYHL DY5 100 D3
Comberford Ct
DARL/WED WS10 * 56 A5
Comberford Dr
DARL/WED WS10 56 D4
Comberton Rd
LGN/SDN/BHAMAIR B26 130 D5
Combine Cl MGN/WHC B75 47 H1
Comet Rd
LGN/SDN/BHAMAIR B26 149 G3
Commercial Rd WOLV WV1 7 K5
WSLW WS2 27 E3
Commercial St CBHAMW B1 2 D7
Commissary Rd
LGN/SDN/BHAMAIR B26 149 E4
Commonfield Cft
WASH/WDE B8 110 B4
Common La
LGN/SDN/BHAMAIR B26 147 G2
WASH/WDE B8 110 D3
Common Rd WMBN WV5 80 D2
Commonside BLOX/PEL WS3 18 A5
BRLYHL DY5 101 E3
Common Side BRWNH WS8 19 G2
Communication Rw EDG B15 126 C3
Compton Cl SOLH B91 180 D1
Compton Cft
CHWD/FDBR/MGN B37 132 D3
Compton Dr DUDS DY2 103 F1
FOAKS/STRLY B74 60 A1
KGSWFD DY6 99 H4
Compton Gv HALE B63 137 G3
KGSWFD DY6 99 H4
Compton Hill Dr
BDMR/CCFT WV3 35 H3
Compton Pk BDMR/CCFT WV3 36 A3
Compton Rd BDMR/CCFT WV3 36 B3
CDYHTH B64 120 C3
ERDW/GRVHL B23 92 C5
HAG/WOL DY9 153 F1
RMSLY B62 139 H2
Compton Rd West
BDMR/CCFT WV3 35 H3
Comsey Rd GTB/HAM B43 59 F5
Comwall Cl BLOX/PEL WS3 27 G3
Conchar Cl CSCFLD/WYGN B72 77 G2
Conchar Rd CSCFLD/WYGN B72 77 G1
Concorde Dr CVALE B35 94 B4
Concorde Rd
LGN/SDN/BHAMAIR B26 149 G3
Condover Cl WSLW WS2 40 B2
Condover Rd NFLD/LBR B31 175 H5
Coneyford Rd
BKDE/SHDE B34 113 E3
Coney Gn STRBR DY8 135 H2
Coney Green Dr
NFLD/LBR B31 175 F5
Coneygree Rd TPTN/OCK DY4 85 G3
Conifer Cl BRLYHL DY5 119 E4
Conifer Ct MOS/BIL B13 144 A5
Conifer Dr HDSW B21 107 G2
NFLD/LBR B31 175 H2
Conifer Paddock RMSLY B62 122 C4
Conifer Rd FOAKS/STRLY B74 45 E5
Conington Gv HRBN B17 141 G2
Coniston Av HIA/OLT B92 147 F3
Coniston Cl HLGN/YWD B28 162 D3
Coniston Crs GTB/HAM B43 73 H4
Coniston Dr KGSWFD DY6 99 F2
Coniston Rd
DUNHL/THL/PER WV6 21 H2
ERDW/GRVHL B23 92 B1
FOAKS/STRLY B74 45 F2
Connaught Av
DARL/WED WS10 56 C5
Connaught Cl DSYBK/YTR WS5 58 A1
Connaught Dr WMBN WV5 65 E2
Connaught Rd BILS/COS WV14 54 B1
WOLV WV1 6 B3
Connops Wy HAG/WOL DY9 136 C2
Connor Rd HHTH/SAND B71 72 A3
Conolly Dr RBRY B45 174 B4
Conrad Cl BHTH/HG B12 127 G5
Consort Crs BRLYHL DY5 101 E3
Consort Dr DARL/WED WS10 40 A5
Consort Rd BVILLE B30 177 E2
Constable Cl GTB/HAM B43 59 G5
The Constables
LGLYGN/QTN B68 123 F2
Constance Av WBROM B70 87 H5
Constance Rd DIG/EDG B5 143 H2
Constantine La
CSHL/WTROR B46 97 F5
Constantine Wy
BILS/COS WV14 69 G1
Constitution Hl DUDS DY2 102 D1
LOZ/NWT B19 2 E1
Constitution Hl East
DUDS DY2 102 D1
Convent Cl BKHL/PFLD WV2 7 G5
Conway Av HHTH/SAND B71 71 F2
LGLYGN/QTN B68 123 F2
RIDG/WDGT B32 140 B1
Conway Cl DUDN DY1 68 C5
KGSWFD DY6 100 B5
SHLY B90 180 D4
Conway Crs SHHTH WV12 26 A3
Conway Dr
BLKHTH/ROWR B65 122 A2
Conway Gv GTB/HAM B43 73 F4
Conway Rd
CHWD/FDBR/MGN B37 132 B1
DUNHL/THL/PER WV6 34 D2
SHLY B90 180 D4
SPARK B11 145 E1
Conwy Cl WSLW WS2 41 E1
Conybere St BHTH/HG B12 127 F5
Conyworth Cl ACGN B27 146 D3
Cook Av DUDS DY2 102 D2
Cook Cl DOR/KN B93 197 G2
DUNHL/THL/PER WV6 34 C1
Cookes Cft NFLD/LBR B31 176 A3
Cookesley Cl GTB/HAM B43 59 H4
Cooke St BKHL/PFLD WV2 52 A1
Cookley Cl HALE B63 138 B5
Cooknell Dr STRBR DY8 118 A2
Cook Rd BLOX/PEL WS3 17 F5
Cooksey La KGSTG B44 60 B4
Cooksey Rd SMHTH B10 127 H4
Cooks La
CHWD/FDBR/MGN B37 114 B4
Cook St DARL/WED WS10 55 H2
VAUX/NECH B7 110 A2
Coombe Cft COVEN WV9 * 12 A4
Coombe Hl CDYHTH B64 121 H4
Coombe Pk FOAKS/STRLY B74 61 H1
Coombe Rd
BFLD/HDSWWD B20 91 E5
SHLY B90 180 C3
Coombes La NFLD/LBR B31 189 F2
Coombs Rd RMSLY B62 138 D1
Coombswood Wy RMSLY B62 121 H4
Cooper Av BRLYHL DY5 118 C2
Cooper Cl WBROM B70 88 A4
Coopers Bank Rd BRLYHL DY5 101 E1
Coopers La SMTHWK B66 106 C4
Coopers Rd
BFLD/HDSWWD B20 90 A3
Cooper St BKHL/PFLD WV2 37 H5
WBROM B70 87 H3
Copeley Hl ERDW/GRVHL B23 92 A5
Copes Crs WOLVN WV10 24 A4
Cope St BLOX/PEL WS3 27 G4
DARL/WED WS10 55 G2
WSNGN B18 126 A1
Cophall St TPTN/OCK DY4 86 B1
Cophams Cl HIA/OLT B92 148 A5
Coplow Cottages
LDYWD/EDGR B16 * 125 H1
Coplow St LDYWD/EDGR B16 125 H1
Copnor Gv
LGN/SDN/BHAMAIR B26 147 E1
Coppenhall Gv STETCH B33 130 C1
Copperbeach Dr
BHTH/HG B12 144 C2
Copperbeech Cl
RIDG/WDGT B32 141 F2
Copperbeech Dr
BHTH/HG B12 * 144 C2
Copper Beech Dr KGSWFD DY6 81 H5
WMBN WV5 65 F5
Copper Beech Gdns
BFLD/HDSWWD B20 89 H4
Coppice Av HAG/WOL DY9 136 D4
Coppice Cl ERDE/BCHGN B24 92 D3
RBRY B45 187 H1
SEDG DY3 67 E4
SHLY B90 194 C4
SOLH B91 * 164 C3
WNSFLD WV11 25 G1
Coppice Crs BRWNH WS8 8 D5
Coppice Dr ACGN B27 146 B5
Coppice Farm Wy SHHTH WV12 25 H3
Coppice Gdns HLYWD B47 192 C1
Coppice Hollow
RIDG/WDGT B32 157 F1
Coppice La ALDR WS9 29 H1
BRLYHL DY5 119 H3
BRWNH WS8 8 D4
DUNHL/THL/PER WV6 21 G3
POL/KGSB/FAZ B78 49 E3
SHHTH WV12 26 A4
Coppice Ri BRLYHL DY5 120 A2
Coppice Rd ALDR WS9 19 F3
BDMR/CCFT WV3 35 H5
BILS/COS WV14 68 A3
CDYHTH B64 121 E5
HIA/OLT B92 165 G3
MOS/BIL B13 144 C4
Coppice Side BRWNH WS8 8 D4
Coppice St TPTN/OCK DY4 69 E5
WBROM B70 87 E2
The Coppice
BFLD/HDSWWD B20 90 A4
NFLD/LBR B31 174 C3
SHHTH WV12 26 A4
STRBR DY8 152 B5
TPTN/OCK DY4 70 A2
Coppice View Rd
SCFLD/BOLD B73 60 C4
Coppice Wk SHLY B90 194 C4
Copplestone Cl
BKDE/SHDE B34 112 D3
Coppy Hall Gv ALDR WS9 30 B1
Copse Cl NFLD/LBR B31 175 G3
Copse Crs BLOX/PEL WS3 18 A3
Copse Rd DUDS DY2 120 B1
The Copse FOAKS/STRLY B74 46 D4
MOS/BIL B13 144 D5
Copson Cl WBROM B70 87 E3
Copstone Dr DOR/KN B93 196 D5
Copston Gv SLYOAK B29 158 D2
Copthall Rd HDSW B21 89 E4
Copt Heath Cft DOR/KN B93 183 F5
Copt Heath Dr DOR/KN B93 197 E1
Copthorne Rd
BDMR/CCFT WV3 51 G1
KGSTG B44 60 A5
Coralin Cl
CHWD/FDBR/MGN B37 132 B2
Corbett Crs STRBR DY8 118 C5
Corbett Rd BRLYHL DY5 119 G3
HLYWD B47 192 C1
Corbetts Cl HIA/OLT B92 167 H3
Corbett St SMTHWK B66 106 D5
Corbridge Av KGSTG B44 75 F2
Corbridge Rd SCFLD/BOLD B73 76 D1
Corbyn Rd BORD B9 129 F1
DUDN DY1 101 H1
Corbyns Cl BRLYHL DY5 100 D2
Corbyns Hall La BRLYHL DY5 100 D2
Corbyns Hall Rd BRLYHL DY5 100 D2
Cordley St WBROM B70 87 F2
Corfe Cl DUNHL/THL/PER WV6 34 D2
RIDG/WDGT B32 141 F2
Corfe Dr OLDBY B69 103 G1
Corfe Rd BILS/COS WV14 68 A3
Corfton Dr
DUNHL/THL/PER WV6 35 G2
Coriander Cl RBRY B45 174 B4
Corinne Cl RBRY B45 188 A2
Corinne Cft
CHWD/FDBR/MGN B37 114 A5
Corisande Rd SLYOAK B29 142 A5
Corley Av NFLD/LBR B31 175 H2
Corley Cl SHLY B90 179 G4
Cornbrook Rd SLYOAK B29 158 B4
Cornbury Gv SOLH B91 180 D1
Corncrake Cl
CSCFLD/WYGN B72 77 H1
Corncrake Dr CBROM B36 114 A1
Corncrake Rd DUDN DY1 83 G3
Cornel Cl
CHWD/FDBR/MGN B37 132 C4
Cornerway HWK/WKHTH B38 190 D1
Cornfield CDSL WV8 22 A1
Cornfield Cl KGSWFD DY6 99 E1
Cornfield Cft
CHWD/FDBR/MGN B37 132 D1
WALM/CURD B76 63 F5
Cornfield Rd
BLKHTH/ROWR B65 103 F5
NFLD/LBR B31 175 H1
WALM/CURD B76 78 B2
Cornflower Crs DUDS DY2 103 F1
Cornflower Rd BRWNH WS8 18 D1
Corngreaves Rd CDYHTH B64 120 D4
The Corngreaves
BKDE/SHDE B34 113 E3
Corngreaves Wk CDYHTH B64 121 E5
Corn Hl DSYBK/YTR WS5 43 G5
WOLV WV1 7 H4
Cornhill Gv BVILLE B30 160 C4
Corn Mill Cl RIDG/WDGT B32 158 A1
WALM/CURD B76 78 B2
Cornmill Cl WSL WS1 56 D1
Cornmill Gv
DUNHL/THL/PER WV6 34 B2
Cornovian Cl
DUNHL/THL/PER WV6 20 C5
Corns Gv WMBN WV5 80 D1
Cornwall Av LGLYGN/QTN B68 123 F4
Cornwall Cl ALDR WS9 30 A1
DARL/WED WS10 56 D5
KGSWFD DY6 99 H1
Cornwall Ga SHHTH WV12 25 H5
Cornwallis Rd WBROM B70 87 E5
Cornwall Pl WSLW WS2 40 C2
Cornwall Rd
BFLD/HDSWWD B20 89 H4
DSYBK/YTR WS5 57 H1
DUNHL/THL/PER WV6 35 G1
RBRY B45 173 G3
SMTHWK B66 106 D2
STRBR DY8 117 H4
Cornwall St CBHAMNW B3 2 E4
Cornwell Cl TPTN/OCK DY4 85 G1
Cornwood La SHLY B90 194 A3
Cornyx La SOLH B91 165 F4
Coronation Av WLNHL WV13 40 B3
Coronation Rd ALDR WS9 19 F4
BILS/COS WV14 53 G2
DARL/WED WS10 56 C5
GTB/HAM B43 58 C4
RUSH/SHEL WS4 18 B5
SLYOAK B29 142 D5
TPTN/OCK DY4 69 H3
WASH/WDE B8 110 D3
WNSFLD WV11 24 A5
Corporation Rd DUDS DY2 85 F5
Corporation St CBHAM B2 3 G5
DARL/WED WS10 71 E1
WOLV WV1 6 E4
WSL WS1 4 D7
Corporation St West WSLW WS2 4 B6
Corrie Cft
LGN/SDN/BHAMAIR B26 130
RIDG/WDGT B32 157
Corrin Gv KGSWFD DY6 99
Corron Hl HALE B63 * 138
Corser St DUDN DY1 83
STRBR DY8 135
WOLV WV1 37
Corsican Cl SHHTH WV12 26
Corvedale Rd SLYOAK B29 158
Corve Gdns
DUNHL/THL/PER WV6 22
Corve Vw SEDG DY3 * 67
Corville Gdns
LGN/SDN/BHAMAIR B26 147
Corville Rd RMSLY B62 139
Corwen Cft NFLD/LBR B31 157
Cory Cft TPTN/OCK DY4 85
Coseley Rd BILS/COS WV14 53
Cosford Crs CVALE B35 94
Cosford Dr DUDS DY2 103
Cossington Rd
ERDW/GRVHL B23 76
Costock Cl
CHWD/FDBR/MGN B37 132
Cosyll Gdns DUDN DY1 102
Cotford Rd
ALE/KHTH/YWD B14 178
Cotheridge Cl SHLY B90 196
Cot La KGSWFD DY6 99
Cotleigh Gv GTB/HAM B43 59
Cotman Cl GTB/HAM B43 59
Coton Gv SHLY B90 179
Coton La ERDW/GRVHL B23 92
Coton Rd
ETTPK/GDPK/PENN WV4 51
Cotsdale Rd
ETTPK/GDPK/PENN WV4 51
Cotsford SOLH B91 * 181
Cotswold Cl ALDR WS9 30
OLDBY B69 104
RBRY B45 174
Cotswold Ct BKHL/PFLD WV2 51
Cotswold Cft HALE B63 154
Cotswold Gv SHHTH WV12 25
Cotswold Rd BKHL/PFLD WV2 52
STRBR DY8 135
Cottage Cl WNSFLD WV11 24
Cottage Gdns RBRY B45 187
Cottage La WALM/CURD B76 79
WOLVN WV10 12
Cottage Ms ALDR WS9 * 30
Cottage St BRLYHL DY5 119
KGSWFD DY6 99
Cottage Vw CDSL WV8 10
Cotteridge Rd BVILLE B30 177
Cotterills Av WASH/WDE B8 111
Cotterills La WASH/WDE B8 111
Cotterills Rd TPTN/OCK DY4 69
Cottesbrook Rd ACGN B27 146
Cottesfield Cl WASH/WDE B8 111
Cottesmore Cl HHTH/SAND B71 72
Cottle Cl WSLW WS2 40
Cotton La MOS/BIL B13 144
Cottrell St HHTH/SAND B71 87
Cottsmeadow Dr
WASH/WDE B8 111
Cotwall End Rd SEDG DY3 82
Cotysmore Rd MGN/WHC B75 62
Couchman Rd WASH/WDE B8 110
Coulter Gv
DUNHL/THL/PER WV6 34
Counterfield Dr
BLKHTH/ROWR B65 103
Countess Dr RUSH/SHEL WS4 29
Countess St WSL WS1 56
Country Park Vw
WALM/CURD B76 78
County Cl BVILLE B30 160
RIDG/WDGT B32 140
County Park Av RMSLY B62 139
Court Crs KGSWFD DY6 99
Courtenay Gdns GTB/HAM B43 73
Courtenay Rd KGSTG B44 75
Court Farm Rd
ERDW/GRVHL B23 76
Courtland Rd KGSWFD DY6 100
Courtlands Cl DIG/EDG B5 143
The Courtlands
DUNHL/THL/PER WV6 36
Court La ERDW/GRVHL B23 76
Court Oak Gv RIDG/WDGT B32 141
Court Oak Rd RIDG/WDGT B32 141
Court Pas DUDN DY1 * 84
Court Rd BHTH/HG B12 144
DUNHL/THL/PER WV6 36
ETTPK/GDPK/PENN WV4 53
SPARK B11 145
Court St CDYHTH B64 121
Court Wy WSLW WS2 4
Courtway Av
ALE/KHTH/YWD B14 178
The Courtyard
CSHL/WTROR B46 * 97
Cousins St BKHL/PFLD WV2 52
Coveley Gv WSNGN B18 108
Coven Cl BLOX/PEL WS3 18
Coven Gv SLYOAK B29 141
Coven St WOLVN WV10 37
Coventry Rd
CSHL/WTROR B46 133
HIA/OLT B92 150
LGN/SDN/BHAMAIR B26 147
SMHTH B10 127
Coventry St DIG/EDG B5 3
STRBR DY8 135
WOLV WV1 38
Cover Cft WALM/CURD B76 78
Coverdale Rd HIA/OLT B92 147
Covers La KINVER DY7 116
The Covert CDSL WV8 22
Cowles Cft YDLY B25 130
Cowley Cl CBROM B36 95
Cowley Dr ACGN B27 146
DUDN DY1 83
Cowley Rd SPARK B11 145
Cowper Cl SHHTH WV12 26
Cowslip Cl HWK/WKHTH B38 176
SLYOAK B29 158
Coxcroft Av BRLYHL DY5 119

xmoor Cl BLOX/PEL WS3 * 16 B4
x Rd BILS/COS WV14 ....69 E2
x's La CDYHTH B64 ....121 F2
x St CBHAMNW B3 ....
xwell Av WOLVN WV10 ....23 E5
xwell Gdns
  LDYWD/EDGR B16 ....125 H2
yne Cl TPTN/OCK DY4 ....84 D1
x Rd WBROM B70 ....9 F2
abbe St HAG/WOL DY9 ....136 D2
aba La SHHTH WV12 ....26 B1
abmill Cl DOR/KN B93 ....137 C5
ab Mill Cl HWK/WKHTH B38 ..190 C1
abmill La HWK/WKHTH B38 ...177 C5
abourne Rd DUDS DY2 ....120 C2
abtree Cl HAG/WOL DY9 .....152 D4
HHTH/SAND B71 ....77 H1
NFLD/LBR B31 ....176 A3
abtree Dr
  CHWD/FDBR/MGN B37 ......131 H1
abtree Rd WSL WS1 ....5 J3
  WSNGN B18 ....108 A4
ackley Wy DUDS DY2 ....102 A3
adock Rd SMTHWKW B67 .....106 B5
addock St
  DUNHL/THL/PER WV6 ......36 C1
adley Cft HDSW B21 ....89 F3
adley Flds HALE B63 ....137 H2
adley Forge HALE B63 ....120 A4
adley Park Rd DUDS DY2 ....120 C2
adock Rd CDYHTH B64 ....110 C4
aig Cft
  CHWD/FDBR/MGN B37 ......53 D2
ail Gv GTB/HAM B43 ....59 F5
amlington Rd
  PBAR/PBCH B42 ....74 A3
anmore Cl TPTN/OCK DY4 ....69 G3
amp Hl DARL/WED WS10 .....55 F2
anbourne Av
  ETTPK/GDPK/PENN WV4 ....52 C5
anbourne Cl RBRY B45 ......174 B3
anbourne Rd KGSTG B44 ....75 G3
anbourne Pl
  HHTH/SAND B71 * 87 H2
  STRBR DY8 ....135 G3
anbrook Gv
  DUNHL/THL/PER WV6 ......34 D2
anbrook Rd HDSW B21 ......89 E5
anby St WASH/WDE B8 .....110 A4
aneberry Rd
  CHWD/FDBR/MGN B37 ......131 G1
ane Hollow WMBN WV5 * 80 C1
anehouse Rd KGSTG B44 ....75 C1
anmoor Cl
  VAUX/NECH B7 * 110 A3
ane Rd BILS/COS WV14 .....54 B5
anesbill Rd SLYOAK B29 ...158 C4
anes Park Rd
  LGN/SDN/BHAMAIR B26 ...148 A2
ane Ter
  DUNHL/THL/PER WV6 ......22 A5
anfield Gv
  LGN/SDN/BHAMAIR B26 ...130 B4
anfield Pl DSYBK/YTR WS5 ..57 F4
anford Gv SOLH B91 * 182 A4
anford Rd BDMR/CCFT WV3 ..107 F4
anford Wy SMTHWK B66 ....107 E4
annam Dr KGSWFD DY6 .....99 H4
annhill Cl HIA/OLT B92 .....164 D1
ankhall La DARL/WED WS10 .71 G1
anleigh Cl ALDR WS9 ....30 B5
  SHHTH WV11 ....26 A1
anleigh Pl KGSTG B44 ......91 E1
anleigh Rd CDSL WV8 ......20 B3
anmer Av SHHTH WV12 .....26 B3
anmer Gv
  DUNHL/THL/PER WV6 ......21 E4
anmore Av
  DUNHL/THL/PER WV6 * 21 E4
anmoor Gv FOAKS/STRLY B74 .32 D4
anmoor Crs HDSW B21 .....107 F2
  SHLY B90 ....181 H5
anmore Bvd SHLY B90 .....180 D5
anmore Rd Dr SHLY B90 ....181 E4
anmore Rd BDMR/CCFT WV3 .36 B2
  CBROM B36 ....95 G5
  SHLY B90 ....180 D5
ansley Gv SOLH B91 ....181 H1
antock Cl WNSFLD WV11 ....26 A1
antock Rd PBAR/PBCH B42 ..90 C2
anwell Gv WMBN WV5 ....80 D1
anwell Rd ERDE/BCHGN B24 .93 H3
anwell Wy CVALE B35 ....94 C3
athorne Av WOLVN WV10 ....23 E1
aufurst Ct STRBR DY8 .....135 G4
aren St
  ETTPK/GDPK/PENN WV4 ...52 D2
awford Av DARL/WED WS10 .54 D5
  ETTPK/GDPK/PENN WV4 ...52 D5
  SMTHWKW B67 ....106 A4
awford St WASH/WDE B8 ...110 A4
awshays Rd CBROM B36 ....95 E5
ayford Rd KGSTG B44 ....75 G2
aythorne Av
  BFLD/HDSWWD B20 ....89 G1
ecy Cl WALM/CURD B76 .....63 E4
edon Cl WBROM B70 ....87 E5
edon Gv EDG B15 ....142 D2
eed Wy WBROM B70 ....87 F5
egoe St EDG B15 ....126 C3
emore Av WASH/WDE B8 ....110 C4
emore Rd MGN/WHC B75 ....47 F5
emore Wk MGN/WHC B75 * ..47 F5
endon Rd
  BLKHTH/ROWR B65 ....103 G3
escent Ar SOLH B91 * 182 A1
e Crescent BRLYHL DY5 ....119 E2
ae Crescent Orange Rd
  HAG/WOL DY9 * 136 A3
escent Rd DARL/WED WS10 .54 D5
  DUDS DY2 ....102 B4
  WLNHL WV13 ....40 A5
escent Studios WSNGN B18 * .108 B5
e Crescent BILS/COS WV14 ..53 H2

CDYHTH B64 ....121 G5
CHWD/FDBR/MGN B37 ....133 E4
DARL/WED WS10 ....56 A4
DUDN DY1 ....94 C1
DUNHL/THL/PER WV6 ....35 F2
GTB/HAM B43 ....74 A2
HIA/OLT B92 ....167 H3
SHLY B90 ....180 A1
SOLH B91 ....181 H1
STRBR DY8 ....152 B5
WLNHL WV13 ....40 A4
WSL WS1 ....5 J3
WSNGN B18 ....108 A4
Cressage Av NFLD/LBR B31 .175 G4
Cressett Av BRLYHL DY5 ....101 H5
Cressett La BRLYHL DY5 ....101 C5
Cressington Dr
  FOAKS/STRLY B74 ....47 E4
Cresswell Crs BLOX/PEL WS3 ..16 B5
Cresswell Gv ERDE/BCHGN B24 .93 H2
Cressy Vw FOAKS/STRLY B74 .177 C1
The Crest NFLD/LBR B31 ....189 H2
Crest Vw FOAKS/STRLY B74 ..177 C1
Crestwood Av KGSTG B44 ...75 H6
Crestwood Gln
  DUNHL/THL/PER WV6 ......22 A3
Creswell Rd DUNHL/THL/PER WV6 * .87 B3
Creswick Gv RBRY B45 .....188 C1
Crew Cft TPTN/OCK DY4 ....85 E1
Crew Rd DARL/WED WS10 ...56 A5
Creynolds Cl SHLY B90 ....194 D4
Creynolds La SHLY B90 ....194 C4
Cricket Cl DSYBK/YTR WS5 ..57 H1
Cricketers Meadow
  CDYHTH B64 ....110 C5
Cricket Meadow SEDG DY5 ..83 C1
  WOLVN WV10 ....12 D3
Crick La BFLD/HDSWWD B20 .108 A1
Cricklewood Dr RMSLY B62 .139 F4
Crimmond Ri HALE B63 ....138 A2
Crimscote Cl SHLY B90 ....195 F2
Cripps Rd WSLW WS2 ......40 C2
Crockets Ct HDSW B21 * ...107 F2
Crockett's La SMTHWK B66 .106 C4
Crockett St HDSW B21 * 84 A4
Crockford Dr MGN/WHC B75 .47 E2
Crockford Rd HHTH/SAND B71 .71 G2
Crocus Cm COVEN WV9 .....12 A4
Croft Cl YDLY B25 ....124 B4
Croft Ct CBROM B36 * 112 D1
Croft Crs BRWNH WS8 ....8 D5
Croft Down Rd HIA/OLT B92 .148 B3
Croftdown Rd HRBN B17 ...141 F1
Crofters Cl STRBR DY8 .....135 H1
Crofters Ct EDG B15 ....142 C1
Crofters La MGN/WHC B75 ..48 A2
Croft La WOLVN WV10 ......23 H5
Croftleigh Gdns SOLH B91 * .181 E5
Croft Rd
  BFLD/HDSWWD B20 ....73 G5
Croftwood Rd HAG/WOL DY9 .136 B3
Cromdale Dr HALE B63 ....137 H4
Cromer Gdns
  DUNHL/THL/PER WV6 ......36 C1
Crome Rd GTB/HAM B43 ....59 H5
Cromer Rd BHTH/HG B12 ...144 A2
Crompton Av
  BFLD/HDSWWD B20 ....108 C1
  RBRY B45 ....175 F4
Crompton Cl DSYBK/YTR WS5 * .57 H1
Crompton Ct CDSL WV8 ....10 D3
Crompton Rd
  BFLD/HDSWWD B20 ....108 C1
  RBRY B45 ....175 F4
  VAUX/NECH B7 ....110 A1
Cromwell Cl
  BLKHTH/ROWR B65 ....103 F4
  WSLW WS2 ....40 C1
Cromwell Dr DUDS DY2 .....103 F1
Cromwell La NFLD/LBR B31 .189 E5
Cromwell Rd DUDS DY2 ....103 E1
  HHTH/SAND B71 ....87 G1
  WNSFLD WV11 ....109 H4
Crondal Pl EDG B15 ....126 B5
Cronehills Linkway
  WBROM B70 ....87 H3
Cronehills St WBROM B70 ...87 H3
Crookham Cl HRBN B17 ....124 B5
Crookhay La HHTH/SAND B71 .71 G1
Crook La ALDR WS9 ....59 E2
Croome Cl SPARK B11 .....144 D4
Cropredy Rd NFLD/LBR B31 .175 G5
Cropthorne Dr HLYWD B47 ..192 D1
Cropthorne Rd SHLY B90 ...180 A1
Crosbie Rd HRBN B17 .....141 H1
Crosby Cl CBHAMW B1 ....2 A4
  DUNHL/THL/PER WV6 ......22 B5
Cross Cl CDYHTH B64 ......121 F2
Cross Farm Rd HRBN B17 ..142 B3
Crossfield Rd STETCH B33 .130 C1
Crossfield Wy BILS/COS WV14 .54 A1
Crossgate Rd DUDS DY2 ...101 H5
Crosskey Cl STETCH B33 ...131 G2
Crossland Crs
  DUNHL/THL/PER WV6 ......22 B4
Cross La GTB/HAM B43 .....73 G2
  SEDG DY5 ....67 F3
Crossley Wk DUDS DY2 ....102 D5
Cross Pl SEDG DY5 ....67 G2
Cross St BILS/COS WV14 ...69 F1
  BLKHTH/ROWR B65 ....122 A3
  BLOX/PEL WS3 ....28 C1
  DARL/WED WS10 ....55 G5
  DUDN DY1 ....84 C5

HALE B63 ....138 C4
HDSW B21 ....107 E1
KGSWFD DY6 ....99 E5
LGLYGN/QTN B68 ....105 E5
SMTHWK B66 ....106 C3
STRBR DY8 ....135 E2
WLNHL WV13 ....39 G4
WOLV WV1 ....1 G4
Cross St North WOLV WV1 ..37 F1
Cross St South WOLV WV1 ..37 F1
Cross Walks Rd HAG/WOL DY9 .136 C2
Crossway La KGSTG B44 ....75 F5
Crossways Gn KGSTG B44 ...74 H4
Crosswells Rd
  LGLYGN/QTN B68 ....105 F4
Crowberry Cl BRWNH WS8 ..18 D1
Crowesbridge Ms
  BILS/COS WV14 ....68 B3
Crowhurst Rd NFLD/LBR B31 .189 E1
Crowland Av
  DUNHL/THL/PER WV6 ......34 C1
Crowle Dr HAG/WOL DY9 ...136 A2
Crown Cl BLKHTH/ROWR B65 .104 B5
  SEDG DY5 ....67 E3
Crown Ct DARL/WED WS10 ..40 A5
Crown La FOAKS/STRLY B74 .46 C3
  STRBR DY8 ....135 F1
Crownmeadow Dr
  TPTN/OCK DY4 ....70 B4
Crownoakes Dr STRBR DY8 .118 A2
Crown Rd BORD B9 ....128 B2
  BVILLE B30 ....177 E1
Crown St WOLV WV1 ....37 F1
Crown Wk TPTN/OCK DY4 ...85 G4
Crows Nest Cl WALM/CURD B76 .63 F5
Crowther Gdns HALE B63 ..120 C5
Crowther Gv
  DUNHL/THL/PER WV6 ......36 B1
Crowther Rd
  DUNHL/THL/PER WV6 ......22 B5
  ERDW/GRVHL B23 ....92 B1
Crowther St WOLVN WV10 ..37 G1
Croxall Wy SMTHWK B66 ...106 C4
Croxdene Av DUDS/PEL WS3 .26 D1
Croxley Gdns WLNHL WV13 .39 F5
Croxstalls Av BLOX/PEL WS3 .27 E2
Croxstalls Cl BLOX/PEL WS3 .27 E1
Croxstalls Pl BLOX/PEL WS3 .27 E2
Croxstalls Rd BLOX/PEL WS3 .27 E2
Croxton Gv STETCH B33 ...112 C5
Croyde Av PBAR/PBCH B42 .74 A3
Croydon Rd ERDE/BCHGN B24 .93 E5
  SLYOAK B29 ....142 D5
Croy Dr CVALE B35 ....94 D2
The Crucible BILS/COS WV14 .68 B1
Crusader Cl OLBY B69 .....104 C4
Crychan Cl RBRY B45 ......174 B3
Cryersoak Cl SHLY B90 ....195 F2
Crystal Av STRBR DY8 .....118 B3
Crystal Dr SMTHWK B66 ...105 G1
Cubley Rd HLGN/YWD B28 .162 C1
Cuckoo Cl STETCH B33 ....112 B5
Cuckoo Rd VAUX/NECH B7 ..110 B1
Cuin Rd SMTHWK B66 .....107 E4
Culey Gv STETCH B33 .....131 H1
Culford Dr RIDG/WDGT B32 .157 G2
Culham Cl ACGN B27 ......146 D5
Cullwick St WOLV WV1 .....53 E1
Culmington Gv NFLD/LBR B31 .175 F5
Culmington Rd NFLD/LBR B31 .175 F5
Culmore Cl SHHTH WV12 ...26 C3
Culmore Rd RMSLY B62 ...122 C3
Culverhouse Dr BRLYHL DY5 .118 C3
Culverley Crs DOR/KN B93 .196 D2
Culvert Wy SMTHWK B66 ...105 H2
Culwell St WOLVN WV10 ...37 G1
Cumberford Av STETCH B33 .131 G3
Cumberland Cl KGSWFD DY6 .100 A5
Cumberland Rd BILS/COS WV14 .53 H5
  HHTH/SAND B71 ....71 H5
  LGLYGN/QTN B68 ....105 G5
  WSLW WS2 ....40 B3
Cumberland St CBHAMW B1 ..2 C6
Cumbrian Cft HALE B63 ...137 H5
Cumbria Wy WASH/WDE B8 .110 B3
Cunningham Rd
  DUNHL/THL/PER WV6 ......34 C1
  WSLW WS2 ....40 C3
Cupfields Av TPTN/OCK DY4 .70 A4
Cupfields Crs TPTN/OCK DY4 .70 A4
Curbar Rd PBAR/PBCH B42 .74 C5
Curlew Cl DARL/WED WS10 ..54 D4
Curlew Dr BRWNH WS8 ....9 E5
Curlews Cl ERDW/GRVHL B23 .76 A3
Curral Rd BLKHTH/ROWR B65 .121 H4
Curtin Dr DARL/WED WS10 ..54 D4
Curtis Cl SMTHWK B66 ....107 E5
Curwborth La
  WALM/CURD B76 ....79 H2
Curzon Circ CBHAMNE B4 ..127 G1
Curzon St BKHL/PFLD WV2 ..52 B1
  CBHAMNE B4 ....3 K4
Cutbert Rd WSNGN B18 ....107 G5
Cutlers Rough Cl
  NFLD/LBR B31 ....158 B5
Cutler St SMTHWK B66 ....106 D4
Cutsdean Cl NFLD/LBR B31 .158 C3
Cutshill Cl CBROM B36 ....113 E1
The Cutting RUSH/SHEL WS4 .29 G5
Cutworth Cl WALM/CURD B76 .63 G5
Cygnet Cl WMBN WV5 ......80 D1
Cygnet Dr BRWNH WS8 ....9 E5
Cygnet Gv ERDW/GRVHL B23 .75 H5
Cygnet La BRLYHL DY5 ....101 E2
Cygnet Rd WBROM B70 .....87 E1
Cygnus Wy WBROM B70 .....86 D1
Cypress Av SEDG DY5 ......83 F1
Cypress Gdns
  FOAKS/STRLY B74 ....62 A1
  KGSWFD DY6 ....99 G5
Cypress Gv NFLD/LBR B31 .175 E4
Cypress Rd DSYBK/YTR WS5 .58 A4
  DUDS DY2 ....103 F4
Cypress Sq ACGN B27 ....146 C2
Cypress Wy NFLD/LBR B31 .175 F5
Cyprus Cl SLYOAK B29 ....158 C3
Cyprus St BKHL/PFLD WV2 ..51 H2
  OLBY B69 ....105 E1
Cyril Gv SMHTH B10 ......128 A4
Cyril Rd SMHTH B10 ......128 B4

D

Dacer Cl BVILLE B30 ....160 B5
Dace Rd WOLVN WV10 ......38 B1
Dadford Vw BRLYHL DY5 ...118 B2
Dad's La MOS/BIL B13 .....160 D1
Daffodil Cl SEDG DY5 ......67 G4
Daffodil Pl DSYBK/YTR WS5 .43 F5
Daffodil Rd DSYBK/YTR WS5 .43 F5
Daffodil Wy NFLD/LBR B31 .175 E5
Dagger La HHTH/SAND B71 .88 A1
Dagnall Rd ACGN B27 .....146 D4
Dahlia Cl WOLV WV1 ....38 C4
Daimler Cl CBROM B36 ....95 H5
Daimler Rd
  ALE/KHTH/YWD B14 ....179 F2
Dainton Gv RIDG/WDGT B32 .157 G1
Dairy Cl TPTN/OCK DY4 ....85 H1
Dairy Ct LGLYGN/QTN B68 .123 H5
Daisy Bank Crs DSYBK/YTR WS5 .43 F5
Daisy Dr ERDW/GRVHL B23 ..91 G1
Daisy Farm Rd
  ALE/KHTH/YWD B14 ....178 D3
Daisy Meadow TPTN/OCK DY4 .70 A5
Daisy Rd LDYWD/EDGR B16 .125 G3
Daisy St BILS/COS WV14 ...69 E1
  DUNHL/THL/PER WV6 ......36 C1
Daisy Wk COVEN WV9 ......12 A4
Dalbeg Cl CDSL WV8 ......22 A2
Dalbury Rd HLGN/YWD B28 .161 G3
Dalby Rd BORD B9 ....128 B4
Dale Cl GTB/HAM B43 .....73 F2
  SMTHWKW B67 ....124 C1
  TPTN/OCK DY4 ....86 B1
Dalecote Av HIA/OLT B92 ..165 G2
Dalewood Cft
  LGN/SDN/BHAMAIR B26 ...147 F1
Dalewood Rd
  CHWD/FDBR/MGN B37 .....113 H4
Daley Cl CBHAMW B1 ....2 A4
Daley Rd BILS/COS WV14 ..69 F1
Dalkeith Rd SCFLD/BOLD B73 .76 C1
Dalkeith St WSLW WS2 ......4 A1
Dallas Rd ERDW/GRVHL B23 .91 H4
Dallimore Cl HIA/OLT B92 .145 H1
Dalloway Cl DIG/EDG B5 ...143 H4
Dalston Cl DUDS DY2 .....102 D3
Dalston Rd ACGN B27 .....146 C3
Dalton Ct ERDW/GRVHL B23 .76 C5
Dalton Rd WSLW WS2 ......41 E2
Dalton St WBROM B70 .....87 E5
  CBHAMNE B4 ....3 H4
Dalton Wy CBHAMNE B4 ....3 G4
Dalvine Rd DUDS DY2 .....120 B2
Dalwood Cl BILS/COS WV14 .68 B4
Damar Cft
  ALE/KHTH/YWD B14 ....177 H1
Damien Cl SMTHWKW B67 ..106 B4
Dam Mill Cl CDSL WV8 .....21 G1
Damson Cl WNSFLD WV11 ..25 G4
Damson La HIA/OLT B92 ...165 H3
Damson Pkwy HIA/OLT B92 .165 H5
Damson Whf TPTN/OCK DY4 .85 G3
Danbury Cl WALM/CURD B76 .78 C1
Danbury Gdns WOLVN WV10 .12 D5
Danby Gv ERDE/BCHGN B24 .93 E4
Dando Rd DUDS DY2 ....102 D1
Dandy Bank Rd KGSWFD DY6 .100 C1
Dandy's Wk WSL WS1 ....5 F6
Dane Gv BVILLE B30 ....160 D2
Danescourt Rd
  DUNHL/THL/PER WV6 ....21 G4
Dane Ter BLKHTH/ROWR B65 .104 A1
Danevays Cl FOAKS/STRLY B74 .45 C5
Danford Cl STRBR DY8 .....135 G3
Danford Gdns SOLH B91 ...181 E2
Danford La SOLH B91 .....181 E2
Danford Rd HLYWD B47 ...192 B2
Danford Wy GTB/HAM B43 .73 F3
Dangerfield La
  DARL/WED WS10 ....55 E3
Daniels La ALDR WS9 ......44 C1
Daniels Rd BORD B9 ....129 E2
Danks St TPTN/OCK DY4 ...85 F5
Danzey Green Rd CBROM B36 .94 D5
Danzey Gv
  ALE/KHTH/YWD B14 ....177 G2
Darby Cl BILS/COS WV14 ..68 A1
Darby End Rd DUDS DY2 ...103 F1
Darby Rd DARL/WED WS10 ..56 B5
  LGLYGN/QTN B68 ....105 G4
Darbys Hill Rd OLDBY B69 .103 H2
Darby St BLKHTH/ROWR B65 .122 A3
Darby Wy TPTN/OCK DY4 ...85 H1
Darell Cft WALM/CURD B76 .95 E5
Daren Cl CBROM B36 .....113 H1
Dare Rd ERDW/GRVHL B23 ..92 C2
Darfield Wk BHTH/HG B12 ..127 F4
Darkhouse La BILS/COS WV14 .68 C1
Dark La HAG/WOL DY9 .....184 C1
  HWK/WKHTH B38 ....191 H1
  RMSLY B62 ....72 B1
Darlaston La BILS/COS WV14 .54 C1
Darlaston Rd DARL/WED WS10 .41 E5
  WSLW WS2 ....55 E5
Darley Av BKDE/SHDE B34 .112 B5
Darleydale Av KGSTG B44 ...75 E2

Darley Dr DUNHL/THL/PER WV6 .22 D5
Darley Green Rd DOR/KN B93 .199 F2
Darley Wy FOAKS/STRLY B74 .46 D4
Darlington St DARL/WED WS10 .55 F3
  WOLV WV1 ....6 E4
Darlington Yd WOLV WV1 ...6 E4
Darnel Cft SMHTH B10 ....127 H5
Darnel Hurst Rd MGN/WHC B75 .47 G2
Darnford Cl CSCFLD/WYGN B72 .77 H4
  HLGN/YWD B28 ....163 E5
Darnick Rd SCFLD/BOLD B73 .76 B1
Darnley Rd LDYWD/EDGR B16 .125 H2
Darris Rd SLYOAK B29 .....160 A2
Dartford Rd BLOX/PEL WS3 .28 A5
Dartmoor Cl RBRY B45 ....174 A3
Dartmouth Av BLOX/PEL WS3 .28 A5
  STRBR DY8 ....98 A3
  WLNHL WV13 ....39 F3
Dartmouth Circ AST/WIT B6 .109 F4
Dartmouth Cl BLOX/PEL WS3 .28 A5
Dartmouth Crs BILS/COS WV14 .54 C1
Dartmouth Dr ALDR WS9 ...29 H5
Dartmouth Middleway
  VAUX/NECH B7 ....3 K1
Dartmouth Pl BLOX/PEL WS3 .28 A5
Dartmouth Rd SLYOAK B29 .142 D5
  SMTHWK B66 ....106 B1
  WBROM B70 ....87 F3
Dart St BORD B9 ....127 H3
Darwall St WSL WS1 ....4 E5
Darwin Ct
  DUNHL/THL/PER WV6 ......34 C1
Darwin Pl WSLW WS2 ......27 F4
Darwin Rd WSLW WS2 .....27 F4
Darwin St DIG/EDG B5 ....127 F4
Dassett Gv BORD B9 ......129 G2
Dassett Rd DOR/KN B93 ..196 D4
Dauntsey Covert
  ALE/KHTH/YWD B14 ....177 H3
Davena Dr RIDG/WDGT B32 .141 E5
Davena Gv BILS/COS WV14 ..53 H5
Davenport Dr CVALE B35 ...95 G1
Davenport Rd
  DUNHL/THL/PER WV6 ......21 F5
  WNSFLD WV11 ....25 E4
Daventry Gv RIDG/WDGT B32 .140 C1
Davey Rd BFLD/HDSWWD B20 .91 E1
  WBROM B70 ....87 E2
David Harman Dr
  HHTH/SAND B71 ....72 B4
David Peacock Cl
  TPTN/OCK DY4 ....85 C1
David Rd BFLD/HDSWWD B20 .90 B4
  TPTN/OCK DY4 ....69 G4
The Davids NFLD/LBR B31 .159 E4
Davies Av BILS/COS WV14 ..53 H5
Davies Cv YDLY B25 ....124 C2
Davis Gv YDLY B25 ....124 C2
Davison Rd SMTHWKW B67 .124 D1
Davis Rd SHHTH WV12 .....26 B2
Davy Rd WSLW WS2 ....27 E5
Dawberry Cl
  ALE/KHTH/YWD B14 ....160 D5
Dawberry Fields Rd
  ALE/KHTH/YWD B14 ....160 D5
Dawberry Rd
  ALE/KHTH/YWD B14 ....160 C5
Daw End RUSH/SHEL WS4 ..29 G4
Daw End La RUSH/SHEL WS4 .29 G4
Dawes Av WBROM B70 .....87 G5
Dawes La BRWNH WS8 ......9 H2
Dawley Brook Rd KGSWFD DY6 .99 H2
Dawley Cl WSL WS1 ....56 B1
Dawley Crs
  CHWD/FDBR/MGN B37 .....132 B3
Dawley Rd KGSWFD DY6 ...99 G1
Dawlish Rd DUDN DY1 .....84 C1
  SLYOAK B29 ....143 E3
  SMTHWK B66 ....106 D4
Dawn Dr TPTN/OCK DY4 ....70 A1
Dawney Dr MGN/WHC B75 ..47 E1
Dawn Rd NFLD/LBR B31 ...158 A4
Dawson Av BILS/COS WV14 .67 H1
Dawson Rd HDSW B21 * 90 B1
Dawson Sq BILS/COS WV14 * .53 G3
Dawson St SMTHWK B66 ...106 D3
Day Av WNSFLD WV11 .....24 D2
Dayhouse Bank RMSLY B62 .172 D4
Daylesford Rd HIA/OLT B92 .147 G4
Day St WSLW WS2 ....4 D1
Deakin Av BRWNH WS8 .....8 C5
Deakin Rd ERDE/BCHGN B24 .92 D5
  MGN/WHC B75 ....48 A5
Deakins Rd YDLY B25 .....129 F5
Deal Dr OLDBY B69 ....85 F5
Deal Gv NFLD/LBR B31 ....175 G1
Deanbrook Cl SHLY B90 ...195 G2
Dean Cl CSCFLD/WYGN B72 .77 H4
  DUDN DY1 ....84 C2
  STRBR DY8 ....135 H1
Dean Ct DUNHL/THL/PER WV6 .35 E3
Deanery Rw WOLV WV1 .....7 F2
Dean Rd ERDW/GRVHL B23 .92 D1
  RUSH/SHEL WS4 ....29 H5
  WMBN WV5 ....80 D1
Deansfield Rd WOLV WV1 ..38 A3
Deans Ga WLNHL WV13 ....38 D5
Deans Pl BLOX/PEL WS3 ...28 B4
Dean's Rd WOLV WV1 ......38 B3
Dean St BILS/COS WV14 ...68 A4
  DIG/EDG B5 ....3 H7
  SEDG DY5 ....67 E4
Dearman Rd SPARK B11 ...127 H5
Dearmont Rd NFLD/LBR B31 .189 E1
Dearne Ct SEDG DY5 ......83 G1
Debden Cl DOR/KN B93 ...198 C1
Debenham Crs YDLY B25 ..129 H3
Debenham Rd YDLY B25 ...129 H3
Deblen Dr LDYWD/EDGR B16 .125 F1
Deborah Cl BKHL/PFLD WV2 .52 B3
Deelands Rd RBRY B45 ....155 E5
Deeley Cl CDYHTH B64 ....121 E5
  EDG B15 ....126 C5
Deeley Dr TPTN/OCK DY4 ..70 A5
Deeley Pl BLOX/PEL WS3 ..27 F2
Deeley St BLOX/PEL WS3 * .27 F2
  BRLYHL DY5 * 119 G3

Deepdale Av
LGN/SDN/BHAMAIR B26 147 H3
Deepdale La DUDN DY1 83 G3
Deepdales WMBN WV5 64 C5
Deeplow Cl
CSCFLD/WYGN B72 * 62 C4
Deepmoor Rd STETCH B33 130 B1
Deepmore Av WSLW WS2 41 F3
Deepwood Cl RUSH/SHEL WS4 28 D2
Deer Cl BLOX/PEL WS3 27 G1
Deerhurst Rd
BFLD/HDSWWD B20 89 H1
Dee Rd BLOX/PEL WS3 28 A1
Deer Park Wy SOLH B91 182 A4
Defford Av RUSH/SHEL WS4 29 E1
Defford Dr LGLYGN/QTN B68 105 F5
De Havilland Dr CVALE B35 94 C4
Deighton Rd DSYBK/YTR WS5 57 H4
Delamere Cl CBROM B36 95 F5
Delamere Dr DSYBK/YTR WS5 58 A5
Delamere Rd HLGN/YWD B28 162 D3
SHHTH WV12 26 A3
Delancey Keep MGN/WHC B75 63 G3
Delhurst Av
ETTPK/GDPK/PENN WV4 52 C5
Delhurst Rd KGSTG B44 74 D2
Della Dr RIDG/WDGT B32 157 H2
Dell Farm Cl DOR/KN B93 197 F2
Dellows Cl HWK/WKHTH B38 190 B1
Dell Rd BRLYHL DY5 100 D4
BVILLE B30 160 A5
The Dell HIA/OLT B92 164 C1
LDYWD/EDGR B16 * 125 H2
NFLD/LBR B31 157 H4
STRBR DY8 135 E1
Delmore Wy WALM/CURD B76 78 D5
Delph Dr BRLYHL DY5 119 G5
Delphinium Cl BORD B9 128 D1
Delph La BRLYHL DY5 119 F4
Delph Rd BRLYHL DY5 119 F3
Delrene Rd HLGN/YWD B28 179 H2
Delves Crs DSYBK/YTR WS5 57 G3
Delves Green Rd
DSYBK/YTR WS5 57 G2
Delves Rd WSL WS1 57 F1
Delville Rd DARL/WED WS10 55 H5
De Marnham Cl WBROM B70 88 A5
De Moram Gv HIA/OLT B92 165 H3
Demuth Wy OLDBY B69 104 D4
Denaby Gv
ALE/KHTH/YWD B14 179 F1
Denbigh Cl DUDN DY1 83 H4
Denbigh Crs HHTH/SAND B71 71 F5
Denbigh Dr DARL/WED WS10 56 D4
HHTH/SAND B71 71 F5
Denbigh Rd TPTN/OCK DY4 86 A2
Denbigh St BORD B9 128 B2
Denby Cl VAUX/NECH B7 109 H4
Denby Cft SHLY B90 195 H2
Dencer Cl RBRY B45 173 H5
Dencil Cl HALE B63 137 H2
Dene Av KGSWFD DY6 99 G5
Dene Court Rd HIA/OLT B92 164 B1
Denegate Cl WALM/CURD B76 78 D5
Dene Hollow MOS/BIL B13 162 A4
Dene Rd STRBR DY8 135 F4
Denewood Av
BFLD/HDSWWD B20 90 B4
Denford Gv
ALE/KHTH/YWD B14 160 D5
Denham Gdns
BDMR/CCFT WV3 35 F5
Denham Rd ACGN B27 146 B2
Denholme Gv
ALE/KHTH/YWD B14 178 C2
Denholm Rd SCFLD/BOLD B73 61 F5
Denise Dr BILS/COS WV14 68 B3
CHWD/FDBR/MGN B37 113 H5
HRBN B17 142 A3
Denleigh Rd KGSWFD DY6 100 B5
Denmark Cl
DUNHL/THL/PER WV6 36 C1
Denmead Dr WNSFLD WV11 25 F2
Denmore Gdns WOLV WV1 38 B3
Dennis Hall Rd STRBR DY8 118 C4
Dennis Rd BHTH/HG B12 144 D3
Dennis St STRBR DY8 118 B4
Denshaw Rd
ALE/KHTH/YWD B14 160 D4
Denton Cft DOR/KN B93 196 B5
Denton Gv GTB/HAM B43 73 F4
STETCH B33 129 H2
Denton Rd HAG/WOL DY9 137 E3
Denver Rd
ALE/KHTH/YWD B14 178 C3
Denville Cl BILS/COS WV14 54 A1
Denville Crs BORD B9 129 F1
Depwo Gv RIDG/WDGT B32 157 F2
Derby Av DUNHL/THL/PER WV6 22 A3
Derby Dr
CHWD/FDBR/MGN B37 132 B2
Derby St BORD B9 127 G2
WSLW WS2 41 H1
Dereham Cl WASH/WDE B8 110 A5
Dereham Wk BILS/COS WV14 69 E1
Dereton Cl DUDN DY1 101 G2
Derron Av
LGN/SDN/BHAMAIR B26 147 E2
Derry Cl HRBN B17 141 G4
Derrydown Cl
ERDW/GRVHL B23 92 C3
Derrydown Rd
PBAR/PBCH B42 90 B1
Derry St BKHL/PFLD WV2 37 F5
BRLYHL DY5 119 E2
Derwent Cl BRLYHL DY5 100 D3
FOAKS/STRLY B74 45 F3
WLNHL WV13 40 A3
Derwent Gv BVILLE B30 160 C1
Derwent Rd BVILLE B30 160 C2
DUNHL/THL/PER WV6 21 H2
Desford Av PBAR/PBCH B42 74 C4
Dettonford Rd
RIDG/WDGT B32 157 F2
Devereux Cl CBROM B36 113 E1
Devereux Rd MGN/WHC B75 47 G4
WBROM B70 88 A5
Devey Dr TPTN/OCK DY4 70 B5
Devine Cft TPTN/OCK DY4 85 G1
Devitts Cl SHLY B90 195 F1
Devon Crs ALDR WS9 30 A1
DUDS DY2 101 H2
HHTH/SAND B71 71 G5
Devon Rd DARL/WED WS10 56 C4
RBRY B45 173 H4
SMTHWKW B67 124 A5
STRBR DY8 117 H5
WLNHL WV13 40 B4
WOLV WV1 6 D1
Devonshire Av WSNGN B18 107 H3
Devonshire Dr WBROM B70 88 A3
Devonshire Rd
BFLD/HDSWWD B20 89 H4
SMTHWKW B67 106 A3
Devonshire St WSNGN B18 107 H3
Devon St VAUX/NECH B7 110 A5
Devoran Cl
DUNHL/THL/PER WV6 36 D1
Dewberry Dr DSYBK/YTR WS5 57 G5
Dewberry Rd STRBR DY8 118 B3
Dewhurst Cft STETCH B33 130 D1
Dewsbury Cl STRBR DY8 118 A1
Dewsbury Dr
ETTPK/GDPK/PENN WV4 51 G5
Dewsbury Gv PBAR/PBCH B42 90 C1
Deykin Av AST/WIT B6 91 G4
D'Eyncourt Rd WOLVN WV10 24 A3
Dial Cl ALE/KHTH/YWD B14 178 A3
Dial La STRBR DY8 118 A4
WBROM B70 70 D5
Diamond Park Dr STRBR DY8 118 A3
Diana Cl ALDR WS9 19 H4
Diane Cl TPTN/OCK DY4 69 H1
Dibble Cl SHHTH WV12 26 B5
Dibble Rd SMTHWKW B67 106 B3
Dibdale Rd DUDN DY1 83 H3
Dibdale Rd West DUDN DY1 83 G3
Dibdale St DUDN DY1 83 H4
Dice Pleck NFLD/LBR B31 176 A3
Dickens Cl SEDG DY3 82 D1
Dickens Heath Rd SHLY B90 193 G4
Dickens Rd BILS/COS WV14 68 D1
WOLVN WV10 24 A2
Dickinson Av WOLVN WV10 23 H5
Dickinson Dr WALM/CURD B76 63 E4
WSLW WS2 56 C2
Dickinson Rd WMBN WV5 81 E2
Dick Sheppard Av
TPTN/OCK DY4 69 H3
Diddington Av
HLGN/YWD B28 163 E5
Didgley Gv
CHWD/FDBR/MGN B37 114 A4
Digbeth DIG/EDG B5 3 J7
WSL WS1 4 E4
Digby Crs CSHL/WTROR B46 96 B3
Digby Dr
CHWD/FDBR/MGN B37 149 F1
Digby Rd CSHL/WTROR B46 115 F3
KGSWFD DY6 99 H1
SCFLD/BOLD B73 62 A5
Dilke Rd ALDR WS9 29 H5
Dilloways La WLNHL WV13 39 E4
Dimmingsdale Bank
RIDG/WDGT B32 140 C3
Dimminsdale WLNHL WV13 39 G4
Dimmocks Av BILS/COS WV14 68 D3
Dimmock St
ETTPK/GDPK/PENN WV4 52 C3
Dimsdale Gv NFLD/LBR B31 175 E2
Dimsdale Rd NFLD/LBR B31 174 D2
Dingle Av CDYHTH B64 121 E4
Dingle Cl BVILLE B30 159 F3
DUDS DY2 103 E2
Dingle Hollow OLDBY B69 104 B1
Dingle La SOLH B91 181 F3
WLNHL WV13 39 G1
Dingle Rd BRWNH WS8 19 E2
DUDS DY2 103 E2
HAG/WOL DY9 135 H5
KGSWFD DY6 100 C5
WMBN WV5 80 D1
Dingle St OLDBY B69 104 B1
The Dingle BDMR/CCFT WV3 35 H4
OLDBY B69 104 B1
SHLY B90 194 D3
SLYOAK B29 142 C5
Dingle Vw SEDG DY3 67 E4
Dingley Rd DARL/WED WS10 56 A3
Dinham Gdns DUDN DY1 83 G3
Dinmore Av NFLD/LBR B31 175 H1
Dippons Dr
DUNHL/THL/PER WV6 35 E3
Dippons Mill Cl
DUNHL/THL/PER WV6 35 E2
Dirtyfoot La
ETTPK/GDPK/PENN WV4 50 A3
Discovery Cl TPTN/OCK DY4 86 A1
The Ditch WSL WS1 5 F4
Ditton Gv NFLD/LBR B31 189 F2
Dixon Cl CVALE B35 94 C4
TPTN/OCK DY4 70 A5
Dixon Rd SMRTH B10 127 H4
Dixon's Green Rd DUDS DY2 103 E1
Dixon St BKHL/PFLD WV2 52 C2
Dobbins Oak Rd
HAG/WOL DY9 153 F1
Dobbs Mill Cl SLYOAK B29 143 F5
Dobbs St BKHL/PFLD WV2 7 F7
Dockar Rd NFLD/LBR B31 175 E3
Dock La DUDN DY1 84 B5
Dock Meadow Dr
ETTPK/GDPK/PENN WV4 53 E4
Dock Rd STRBR DY8 118 B2
The Dock HAG/WOL DY9 136 D2
Doctors Hl HAG/WOL DY9 136 A4
Doctors La KGSWFD DY6 98 D4
Doctor's Piece WLNHL WV13 39 H3
Doddington Gv
RIDG/WDGT B32 157 F2
Dodford Cl RBRY B45 187 H1
Doe Bank La ALDR WS9 59 H2
Doe Bank Rd TPTN/OCK DY4 70 A2
Dogge Lane Cft ACGN B27 146 B5
Dog Kennel La HALE B63 138 D4
Dogkennel La
LGLYGN/QTN B68 105 G4
Dog Kennel La SHLY B90 194 D1
WSL WS1 5 G3
Dogpool La BVILLE B30 160 B1
Doidge Rd ERDW/GRVHL B23 92 B3
Dollery Dr DIG/EDG B5 143 G2
Dollis Gv KGSTG B44 60 B5
Dollman St VAUX/NECH B7 127 H1
Dolman Rd AST/WIT B6 109 E1
Dolobran Rd SPARK B11 127 H5
Dolphin Cl BLOX/PEL WS3 28 B1
Dolphin La ACGN B27 163 G1
Dolphin Rd SPARK B11 145 F2
Dolton Wy TPTN/OCK DY4 69 E5
Dominic Cl BVILLE B30 176 B1
Doncaster Wy CBROM B36 111 G1
Don Cl EDG B15 125 F4
Donegal Rd FOAKS/STRLY B74 60 C3
Donibristle Cft CVALE B35 94 C2
Donovan Dr SCFLD/BOLD B73 62 A2
Dooley Cl WLNHL WV13 39 E3
Doran Cl HALE B63 154 D1
Doranda Wy HHTH/SAND B71 88 B5
Dora Rd HDSW B21 107 G2
SMHTH B10 128 C5
WBROM B70 87 G5
Dora St WSLW WS2 56 B1
Dorchester Cl SHHTH WV12 26 A2
Dorchester Ct SOLH B91 181 G1
Dorchester Dr HRBN B17 141 H3
Dorchester Rd HAG/WOL DY9 136 B5
SHHTH WV12 26 A2
SOLH B91 181 G1
Dordale Cl NFLD/LBR B31 174 C4
Dordale Rd HAG/WOL DY9 184 B5
Dordon Cl SHLY B90 179 G4
Doreen Gv ERDE/BCHGN B24 93 F4
Doris Rd BORD B9 128 B3
CSHL/WTROR B46 115 F1
SPARK B11 144 D3
Doricote Rd WASH/WDE B8 111 E5
Dormie Cl HWK/WKHTH B38 176 B4
Dormington Rd KGSTG B44 60 B5
Dormston Cl SOLH B91 182 A5
Dormston Dr SEDG DY3 67 F3
SLYOAK B29 141 F5
Dormy Dr NFLD/LBR B31 189 G1
Dorncliffe Av STETCH B33 131 F5
Dornie Dr HWK/WKHTH B38 176 D4
Dornton Rd BVILLE B30 160 C2
Dorothy Adams Cl
CDYHTH B64 121 E4
Dorothy Rd SMTHWKW B67 124 C1
SPARK B11 146 B2
Dorothy St WSL WS1 56 D1
Dorridge Cft DOR/KN B93 198 D1
Dorridge Rd DOR/KN B93 199 E1
Dorrington Gn PBAR/PBCH B42 90 A1
Dorrington Rd PBAR/PBCH B42 90 A1
Dorset Cl RBRY B45 173 H3
Dorset Dr ALDR WS9 30 A1
Dorset Rd HRBN B17 124 D1
STRBR DY8 117 H5
WASH/WDE B8 110 B3
Dorset Tower WSNGN B18 * 2 A2
Dorsett Pl BLOX/PEL WS3 27 G3
Dorsett Rd DARL/WED WS10 55 E2
Dorsett Road Ter
DARL/WED WS10 55 E2
Dorsheath Gdns
ERDW/GRVHL B23 92 D2
Dorsington Rd ACGN B27 163 H1
Dorstone Covert
ALE/KHTH/YWD B14 177 G3
Dorville Cl HWK/WKHTH B38 176 B5
Douay Rd ERDW/GRVHL B23 77 F5
Double Rw DUDS DY2 103 E5
Doughty St TPTN/OCK DY4 86 A1
Douglas Av CBROM B36 111 H3
LGLYGN/QTN B68 105 H4
Douglas Davies Cl SHHTH WV12 40 A1
Douglas Pl WOLVN WV10 23 E4
Douglas Rd ACGN B27 146 B3
BILS/COS WV14 68 D3
CSCFLD/WYGN B72 62 C5
HDSW B21 107 G1
HLYWD B47 192 C1
LGLYGN/QTN B68 105 H5
RMSLY B62 122 C3
Douglass Rd DUDS DY2 102 D1
Douglas Turner Wy
BDMR/CCFT WV3 36 A2
Doulton Cl RIDG/WDGT B32 141 F4
Doulton Dr SMTHWK B66 106 C3
Doulton Rd
BLKHTH/ROWR B65 103 G5
Dovebridge Cl
WALM/CURD B76 63 F4
Dove Cl DARL/WED WS10 56 B4
WSL WS1 5 H5
YDLY B25 130 A4
Dovecote Cl
DUNHL/THL/PER WV6 35 G1
SOLH B91 164 D2
TPTN/OCK DY4 86 A1
The Dovecotes MGN/WHC B75 47 F2
Dovedale Av BLOX/PEL WS3 18 A2
SHHTH WV12 39 G1
SHLY B90 180 B4
Dovedale Ct
ETTPK/GDPK/PENN WV4 67 H1
Dovedale Dr HLGN/YWD B28 162 D4
Dovedale Rd ERDW/GRVHL B23 76 A5
ETTPK/GDPK/PENN WV4 67 G1
KGSWFD DY6 100 A1
Dove Dr STRBR DY8 118 C4
Dove Gdns HWK/WKHTH B38 177 F3
Dove House La SOLH B91 164 B3
Dovehouse Pool Rd
AST/WIT B6 109 E1
Dover Cl RIDG/WDGT B32 157 E3
Dovercourt Rd
LGN/SDN/BHAMAIR B26 148 A2
Doverdale Cl HALE B63 137 H2
Dove Rdg STRBR DY8 118 C5
Doveridge Cl SOLH B91 164 A4
Doveridge Pl WSL WS1 5 F7
Doveridge Rd HLGN/YWD B28 162 C5
Doversley Rd
ALE/KHTH/YWD B14 160 C5
Dover St BILS/COS WV14 53 H2
WSNGN B18 107 H3
Dove Wy CBROM B36 113 H1
Dovey Dr WALM/CURD B76 78 C4
Dovey Gv BLKHTH/ROWR B65 121 H2
Dovey Rd MOS/BIL B13 145 F5
OLDBY B69 104 B1
Dovey Tower VAUX/NECH B7 * 109 G5
Dowar Rd RBRY B45 188 C1
Dowells Cl MOS/BIL B13 144 B5
Dowells Gdns STRBR DY8 117 H1
The Doweries RBRY B45 173 H5
Dower Rd MGN/WHC B75 47 G5
Dowles Cl SLYOAK B29 158 D4
Downcroft Av HWK/WKHTH B38 176 C3
Downend Cl WOLVN WV10 13 F3
Downes Ct TPTN/OCK DY4 85 E1
Downey Cl SPARK B11 127 H5
Downfield Cl BLOX/PEL WS3 16 C3
Downfield Dr SEDG DY3 67 G5
Downham Cl DSYBK/YTR WS5 43 G4
Downham Pl BDMR/CCFT WV3 36 B5
Downie Rd CDSL WV8 11 E4
Downing Cl
BLKHTH/ROWR B65 122 A3
DOR/KN B93 197 E4
WNSFLD WV11 25 G3
Downing St HALE B63 138 C2
SMTHWK B66 107 E2
Downland Cl
HWK/WKHTH B38 176 D4
Downsfield Rd
LGN/SDN/BHAMAIR B26 130 D5
Downside Rd
ERDE/BCHGN B24 92 C5
Downs Rd WLNHL WV13 40 A5
The Downs ALDR WS9 45 E3
WOLVN WV10 23 E4
Downton Crs STETCH B33 131 G1
Dowty Wy COVEN WV9 12 A4
Drake Cl BLOX/PEL WS3 27 F1
Drake Cft
CHWD/FDBR/MGN B37 114 D5
Drake Rd BLOX/PEL WS3 27 G1
ERDW/GRVHL B23 92 A3
SMTHWK B66 105 H2
Drakes Cl HLYWD B47 192 B3
Drakes Cross Pde HLYWD B47 192 C3
Drake's Gn BILS/COS WV14 54 B5
Drakes Hill Cl STRBR DY8 134 C3
Drake St HHTH/SAND B71 87 G1
Drancy Av SHHTH WV12 26 B4
Drawbridge Rd SHLY B90 179 G5
Draycote Cl HIA/OLT B92 165 F3
Draycott Av ERDW/GRVHL B23 92 B2
Draycott Cl
ETTPK/GDPK/PENN WV4 50 C3
Draycott Dr NFLD/LBR B31 158 A3
Draycott Rd SMTHWK B66 106 A2
Drayman Cl WSL WS1 5 F7
Drayton Cl MGN/WHC B75 47 F2
Drayton Rd
ALE/KHTH/YWD B14 161 E2
HAG/WOL DY9 184 B2
SHLY B90 181 E5
SMTHWK B66 124 C3
Drayton St BKHL/PFLD WV2 37 E5
WSLW WS2 41 G3
Dreadnought Rd BRLYHL DY5 100 D2
The Dreel EDG B15 125 G5
Dreghorn Rd CBROM B36 112 A1
Drem Cft CVALE B35 94 C4
Dresden Cl
ETTPK/GDPK/PENN WV4 53 E4
Drew Crs HAG/WOL DY9 136 B4
Drew Rd HAG/WOL DY9 136 B4
Drews Holloway HALE B63 137 H2
Drews Holloway South
HALE B63 137 H2
Drews La WASH/WDE B8 111 E3
Drews Meadow Cl
ALE/KHTH/YWD B14 177 G3
Driffold SCFLD/BOLD B73 62 B5
Driftwood Cl
HWK/WKHTH B38 190 B1
Drive Flds
ETTPK/GDPK/PENN WV4 50 B2
The Drive ALVE B48 189 H5
BFLD/HDSWWD B20 90 A4
BLOX/PEL WS3 17 G5
BRLYHL DY5 101 E4
CDSL WV8 10 B4
CSHL/WTROR B46 115 G3
DUNHL/THL/PER WV6 * 21 G5
ERDW/GRVHL B23 92 C4
HALE B63 137 H2
RUSH/SHEL WS4 29 E1
The Droveway COVEN WV9 11 H5
Druid Park Rd SHHTH WV12 26 A1
Druids Av ALDR WS9 30 C2
BLKHTH/ROWR B65 104 B5
Druids La ALE/KHTH/YWD B14 177 H4
Druids Wk ALDR WS9 19 G4
Drummond Cl WNSFLD WV11 15 E5
Drummond Gv GTB/HAM B43 59 G5
Drummond Rd BORD B9 128 D2
HAG/WOL DY9 136 D3
Drummond St WOLV WV1 6 E2
Drummond Wy
CHWD/FDBR/MGN B37 132 C2
Drury La CDSL WV8 10 B3
SOLH B91 182 A2
STRBR DY8 135 G2
Drybrook Cl HWK/WKHTH B38 176 C5
Dryden Cl SHHTH WV12 26 C2
TPTN/OCK DY4 69 G4
Dryden Gv ACGN B27 146 B5
Dryden Pl BLOX/PEL WS3 28 A3
Dryden Rd BLOX/PEL WS3 28 A3
WOLVN WV10 23 H1
Drylea Gv CBROM B36 112 B1
Dubarry Av KGSWFD DY6 99 G2
Duchess Pde WBROM B70 * 87 H3
Duchess Rd LDYWD/EDGR B16 126 A3
WSL WS1 56 D3
Duckhouse Rd WNSFLD WV11 24 D3
Duck La CDSL WV8 10 D5
Duddeston Dr WASH/WDE B8 110 B5
Duddeston Manor Rd
VAUX/NECH B7 109 G4
Duddeston Mill Rd
VAUX/NECH B7 109 H5
Dudding Rd
ETTPK/GDPK/PENN WV4 52 B3
Dudhill Rd BLKHTH/ROWR B65 121 G1
Dudley Cl BLKHTH/ROWR B65 103 F3
Dudley Crs WNSFLD WV11 25 E4
Dudley Park Rd ACGN B27 146 C4
Dudley Port TPTN/OCK DY4 85 G3
Dudley Rd BKHL/PFLD WV2 52 B1
BLKHTH/ROWR B65 103 F3
BRLYHL DY5 119 F1
HAG/WOL DY9 136 C1
HALE B63 138 D2
KGSWFD DY6 99 G1
OLDBY B69 104 C1
SEDG DY3 67 F4
TPTN/OCK DY4 84 D1
WSNGN B18 107 F5
Dudley Rd East OLDBY B69 86 A4
Dudley Rd West OLDBY B69 85 H4
Dudley Rw DUDS DY2 84 D5
Dudley Southern By-Pass
DUDS DY2 102 A2
Dudley St BILS/COS WV14 53 H4
DARL/WED WS10 70 C1
DIG/EDG B5 3 G6
SEDG DY3 67 F3
WBROM B70 87 E1
WOLV WV1 7 F4
WSL WS1 4 E5
Dudley Wk
ETTPK/GDPK/PENN WV4 52 A3
Dudley Wood Av DUDS DY2 120 C2
Dudley Wood Rd DUDS DY2 120 C3
Dudmaston Wy DUDN DY1 83 G3
Dudnill Gv RIDG/WDGT B32 157 E2
Duffield Cl CDSL WV8 22 B1
Dufton Rd RIDG/WDGT B32 141 E2
Dugdale Crs MGN/WHC B75 47 G2
Dugdale St WSNGN B18 107 F5
Dukes Rd BVILLE B30 177 E1
Duke St BDMR/CCFT WV3 51 G1
BLKHTH/ROWR B65 121 H2
CSCFLD/WYGN B72 62 B4
SEDG DY3 83 F1
STRBR DY8 135 G2
WBROM B70 87 F2
WNSFLD WV11 24 D5
WOLV WV1 7 J5
Dulvern Gv
ALE/KHTH/YWD B14 160 D5
Dulverton Rd AST/WIT B6 91 G5
Dulwich Gv KGSTG B44 75 H3
Dulwich Rd KGSTG B44 75 G3
Dumbleberry Av SEDG DY3 67 E4
Dumblederry La ALDR WS9 29 G2
Dunard Rd SHLY B90 179 H2
Dunbar Gv GTB/HAM B43 59 F4
Duncalfe Dr MGN/WHC B75 47 F2
Duncan Edwards Cl
DUDN DY1 102 A1
Duncan St BKHL/PFLD WV2 52 A1
Dunchurch Crs
SCFLD/BOLD B73 61 E5
Dunchurch Dr NFLD/LBR B31 158 A3
Duncombe Gn
CSHL/WTROR B46 115 F2
Duncombe Gv HRBN B17 124 B5
Duncombe St STRBR DY8 134 D1
Duncroft Rd
LGN/SDN/BHAMAIR B26 130 B4
Duncumb Rd MGN/WHC B75 63 G3
Dundas Av DUDS DY2 103 F1
Dunedin Rd KGSTG B44 60 A5
Dunham Cft DOR/KN B93 196 B5
Dunkirk Av WBROM B70 86 C2
Dunkley St WOLV WV1 6 E2
Dunley Cft SHLY B90 195 F2
Dunlin Cl ERDW/GRVHL B23 92 A4
KGSWFD DY6 100 C3
Dunlop Wy CVALE B35 94 A5
Dunnerdale Rd BRWNH WS8 18 D1
Dunnigan Rd RIDG/WDGT B32 141 F4
Dunns Bank BRLYHL DY5 119 H5
Dunoon Dr
ETTPK/GDPK/PENN WV4 52 D3
Dunsfold Cl BILS/COS WV14 53 E5
Dunsfold Cft AST/WIT B6 109 F3
Dunsford Cl BRLYHL DY5 118 D5
Dunsford Rd SMTHWK B66 124 C2
Dunsink Rd AST/WIT B6 91 F5
Dunslade Crs BRLYHL DY5 119 H4
Dunslade Rd ERDW/GRVHL B23 76 C4
Dunsley Dr STRBR DY8 118 A
Dunsley Gv
ETTPK/GDPK/PENN WV4 51 G
Dunsmore Dr BRLYHL DY5 119 H
Dunsmore Gv SOLH B91 164 B
Dunsmore Rd HLGN/YWD B28 162 C
Dunstall Av
DUNHL/THL/PER WV6 37 E
Dunstall Gv SLYOAK B29 158 B
Dunstall Hl
DUNHL/THL/PER WV6 23 E
Dunstall La
DUNHL/THL/PER WV6 22 D
Dunstall Rd
DUNHL/THL/PER WV6 36 D
HALE B63 137 H
Dunstan Cft SHLY B90 180 C
Dunster Cl BVILLE B30 177 F
Dunster Gv
DUNHL/THL/PER WV6 34 D
Dunster Rd
CHWD/FDBR/MGN B37 132 C
Dunston Cl KGSWFD DY6 99 H
Dunton Cl MGN/WHC B75 47 E
Dunton Hall Rd SHLY B90 180 A
Dunton Rd
CHWD/FDBR/MGN B37 113 H
Dunvegan Rd
ERDE/BCHGN B24 93 E
Durant Cl RBRY B45 173 F
Durban Rd SMTHWK B66 107 E
D'Urberville Rd
BKHL/PFLD WV2 52 D
Durham Av WLNHL WV13 40 A
Durham Cft
CHWD/FDBR/MGN B37 132 A
Durham Dr HHTH/SAND B71 71 H
Durham Pl WSLW WS2 41
Durham Rd
BLKHTH/ROWR B65 104

DARL/WED WS10 ...56 D4
DUDS DY2 ...120 D2
SPARK B11 ...144 D3
STRBR DY8 ...117 H4
WSLW WS2
Durley Dean Rd SLYOAK B29 ...142 A5
Durley Cl SCFLD/BOLD B73 ...61 E5
Durley Rd YDLY B25 ...146 C2
Durlston Gv HLGN/YWD B28 ...163 E2
Durnford Cft
  ALE/KHTH/YWD B14 ...178 A4
Dursley Cl HIA/OLT B92 ...164 D2
  SHHTH WV12 ...40 B1
Dutton's La MGN/WHC B75 ...48 A1
Duxford Rd FOAKS/STRLY B74 ...74 B5
Dwellings La RIDG/WDGT B32 ...140 B2
Dyas Av PBAR/PBCH B42 ...74 A4
Dyas Rd HLYWD B47 ...192 C1
  KGSTG B44 ...74 D3
Dyce Cl CVALE B35 ...94 C2
Dymoke St BKTH/HG B12 ...127 F4
Dynes Wk SMTHWKW B67 ...106 C4
Dyott Rd MOS/BIL B13 ...161 G1
Dyson Cl WSLW WS2 ...40 D2
Dysons Gdns WASH/WDE B8 ...110 C4

E

Eachelhurst Rd
  ERDE/BCHGN B24 ...94 A2
Eachus Rd BILS/COS WV14 ...68 D3
Eachway RBRY B45 ...187 H2
Eachway Farm Cl RBRY B45 ...188 A2
Eachway La RBRY B45 ...188 A2
Eagle Cl BDMR/CCFT WV3 * ...51 C1
Eagle Cft ALE/KHTH/YWD B14 ...178 A3
Eagle Gdns ERDE/BCHGN B24 ...95 E4
Eagle Gv TPTN/OCK DY4 ...114 A1
Eagle La TPTN/OCK DY4 ...70 B5
Eagle St BDMR/CCFT WV3 ...51 G1
  BKHL/PFLD WV2 ...7 K7
  TPTN/OCK DY4 ...70 A5
Ealing Gv KGSTG B44 ...75 G2
Earlsbury Gdns
  BFLD/HDSWWD B20 ...90 D5
Earls Court Rd HRBN B17 ...141 G1
Earls Ferry Gdns
  RIDG/WDGT B32 ...157 F3
Earlsmead Rd HDSW B21 ...107 E1
Earls Rd RUSH/SHEL WS4 ...29 E3
Earlston Wy GTB/HAM B43 ...73 F5
Earls St BILS/COS WV14 ...68 D3
  KGSWFD DY6 ...
  WBROM B70 ...87 F2
Earls Wy HALE B63 ...138 D3
Earlswood Ct
  BFLD/HDSWWD B20 ...90 A4
Earlswood Dr FOAKS/STRLY B74 ...
  KGSWFD DY6 ...
Earlswood Gv
  FOAKS/STRLY B74 ...62 C1
Earlswood Rd DOR/KN B93 ...198 B1
  KGSWFD DY6 ...100 A2
Easby Wy BLOX/PEL WS3 ...16 B5
  WASH/WDE B8 ...110 C4
Easenhall Cl DOR/KN B93 ...197 E4
Easmore Cl
  ALE/KHTH/YWD B14 ...177 H3
East Acre WLNHL WV13 ...39 G4
East Av OLDBY B69 ...104 A2
  WNSFLD WV11 ...24 C4
Eastbourne Gv
  BKDE/SHDE B34 ...111 H3
Eastbourne St
  RUSH/SHEL WS4 ...42 B2
Eastbrook Cl WALM/CURD B76 ...62 D4
Eastbury Dr HIA/OLT B92 ...145 E2
East Car Park Rd
  BHAMNEC B40 ...150 B3
Eastcote Cl SHLY B90 ...180 D2
Eastcote La HIA/OLT B92 ...167 G5
Eastcote Rd ACGN B27 ...163 E1
  WOLVN WV10 ...23 H5
East Cft Rd
  ETTPK/GDPK/PENN WV4 ...50 C4
Eastdean Cl ERDW/GRVHL B23 ...76 B5
East Dr DIG/EDG B5 ...143 G5
Eastern Av BRLYHL DY5 ...118 D2
Eastern Cl DARL/WED WS10 ...55 H3
Eastern Cl SCFLD/BOLD B73 ...77 F2
  SLYOAK B29 ...143 F4
Eastern Cft
  ALE/KHTH/YWD B14 ...178 A3
East Farm Cft SMHTH B10 ...128 B4
Eastfield Cl ALDR WS9 ...30 A4
Eastfield Dr HIA/OLT B92 ...165 G2
Eastfield Gv WOLV WV1 ...37 H3
Eastfield Retreat WOLV WV1 ...37 H3
Eastfield Rd BORD B9 ...129 G2
  TPTN/OCK DY4 ...69 G3
  WOLV WV1 ...37 H3
East Ga LDYWD/EDGR B16 ...125 G1
Eastgate St
  ETTPK/GDPK/PENN WV4 ...50 D2
Eastham Rd MOS/BIL B13 ...162 A4
East Holme BORD B9 ...128 A2
Easthope Rd STECH B33 ...112 C5
Eastlake Cl GTB/HAM B43 ...59 H5
Eastleigh Rd MOS/BIL B13 ...161 G1
Eastleigh SEDG DY3 ...66 D5
Eastleigh Cft WALM/CURD B76 ...78 C4
Eastleigh Dr RMSLY B62 ...172 C1
Eastleigh Gv HLGN/YWD B28 ...129 H4
East Meadway STETCH B33 ...131 F1
East Ms KGSTG B44 ...74 D1
Eastmoor Cl FOAKS/STRLY B74 ...45 H3
Eastney Crs COVEN WV9 ...22 A2
Easton Gdns WNSFLD WV11 ...25 F5
Easton Gv ACGN B27 ...163 G1
  HLYWD B47 ...192 D1
East Park Wy WOLV WV1 ...38 A4
East Pathway HRBN B17 ...142 A1
East Ri MGN/WHC B75 ...62 D2
East Rd
  TPK/GDPK/PENN WV4 ...52 D4

TPTN/OCK DY4 ...69 H5
  WOLV WV10 ...13 C1
East St BRLYHL DY5 ...120 A4
  DUDS DY2 ...103 E1
  SEDG DY3 ...83 E3
  WOLV WV1 ...7 J5
  WSL WS1 ...57 F1
East View Rd
  SCFLD/WYGN B72 ...62 D5
Eastville NFLD/LBR B31 ...175 H2
Eastward Gn CDSL WV8 ...21 G1
East Wy BHAMNEC B40 ...150 B4
Eastway HRBN B17 ...142 A1
Eastwood Rd BHTH/HG B12 ...143 H2
  DUDS DY2 ...103 E3
  PBAR B43 ...73 G3
Eatesbrook Rd STECH B33 ...131 E1
Eathorpe Cl BKDE/SHDE B34 ...113 F5
Eaton Av WBROM B70 ...87 E2
Eaton Crt FOAKS/STRLY B74 ...62 B1
Eaton Crs SEDG DY3 ...82 D3
Eaton Pl KGSWFD DY6 ...100 A4
Eaton Ri SHHTH WV12 ...25 H4
Eaton Wd ERDE/BCHGN B24 ...93 H5
Eaton Wood Dr
  LGN/SDN/BHAMAIR B26 ...146 D2
Eaves Court Dr SEDG DY3 ...67 E1
Eaves Green Gdns ACGN B27 ...146 B2
Ebenezer St BILS/COS WV14 ...68 B3
  WBROM B70 ...70 D5
Ebley Rd BFLD/HDSWWD B20 ...90 A2
Ebmore Dr
  ALE/KHTH/YWD B14 ...177 H3
Ebrington Av HHTH/SAND B71 ...71 H5
Ebrington Cl
  ALE/KHTH/YWD B14 ...177 H1
Ebrington Rd HHTH/SAND B71 ...71 H5
Ebrook Rd CSCFLD/WYGN B72 ...62 D5
Ebury Rd BVILLE S30 ...177 F1
Eccleshall Av WOLVN WV10 ...23 E2
Ecclestone Rd WNSFLD WV11 ...25 C2
Echo Wy
  ETTPK/GDPK/PENN WV4 ...53 E4
Eckersall Rd HWK/WKHTH B38 ...176 C2
Edale Cl
  ETTPK/GDPK/PENN WV4 ...52 C5
  KGSWFD DY6 ...99 F2
Edale Rd PBAR/PBCH B42 ...74 C4
Eddish Rd STETCH B33 ...112 D5
Eddison Rd CL/WTROR B46 * ...97 E2
Edelweiss Cl DSYBK/YTR WS5 ...57 H5
Edenbridge Rd
  HLGN/YWD B28 ...163 F2
Edenbridge Vw DUDN DY1 ...83 G3
Eden Cl NFLD/LBR B31 ...175 E5
  OLDBY B69 ...86 B4
Edendale Rd
  LGN/SDN/BHAMAIR B26 ...147 H3
Eden Gdns
  BLKHTH/ROWR B65 ...121 H2
  SEDG DY3 ...67 H3
Eden Gv
  CHWD/FDBR/MGN B37 ...132 D3
  HHTH/SAND B71 ...87 G1
Edenhall Rd RIDG/WDGT B32 ...140 B1
Edenhurst Rd NFLD/LBR B31 ...189 F2
Eden Pl CBHAMNW B3 ...2 E5
Eden Rd HIA/OLT B92 ...148 B4
Edensor Cl WOLVN WV10 ...37 G1
Edgbaston Park Rd EDG B15 ...143 E2
Edgbaston Rd BHTH/HG B12 ...144 A5
  DIG/EDG B5 ...143 G2
  SMTHWK B66 ...124 D1
Edgbaston East
  BHTH/HG B12 ...144 B3
Edgcombe Rd HLGN/YWD B28 ...162 D1
Edge Hill Av WOLVN WV10 ...24 B1
Edge Hill Dr
  DUNHL/THL/PER WV6 ...34 C2
  SEDG DY3 ...67 E1
Edge Hill Rd FOAKS/STRLY B74 ...46 C1
Edgehill Rd NFLD/LBR B31 ...175 G4
Edgemond Av
  ERDE/BCHGN B24 ...94 B2
Edge St BILS/COS WV14 ...68 C3
Edgewood Cl CDYHTH B64 ...121 F4
Edgewood Rd
  HWK/WKHTH B38 ...190 C1
  RBRY B45 ...188 B2
Edgeworth Cl SHHTH WV12 ...25 H2
Edgware Rd ERDW/GRVHL B23 ...92 B1
Edinburgh Av WSLW WS2 ...41 F1
Edinburgh Ct
  ERDW/GRVHL B23 * ...93 H2
Edinburgh Crs STRBR DY8 ...117 H3
Edinburgh Dr RUSH/SHEL WS4 ...29 E3
  SHHTH WV12 ...25 H5
Edinburgh La
Edinburgh Rd BILS/COS WV14 ...54 B5
  DSYBK/YTR WS5 ...42 D5
  DUDS DY2 ...102 D3
  LGLYGN/QTN B68 ...123 F4
Edison Gv RIDG/WDGT B32 ...140 D2
Edison Rd CSHL/WTROR B46 ...97 F3
  WSLW WS2 ...27 G5
Edith Rd SMTHWK B66 ...124 D1
Edith St WBROM B70 ...87 F3
Edmonds Cl STECH B33 ...130 D2
Edmonds Rd LGLYGN/QTN B68 ...125 G2
Edmonton Av KGSTG B44 ...75 H2
Edmoor Ct SHHTH WV12 ...26 A4
Edmund Rd SEDG DY3 ...67 G5
  WASH/WDE B8 ...110 C5
Edmund St CBHAMNW B3 ...3 F4
Ednam Cl HHTH/SAND B71 ...72 B3
Ednam Gv WMBN WV5 ...65 E2
Ednam Rd BILS/COS WV14 ...53 H2
  DUDS DY1 ...
  ETTPK/GDPK/PENN WV4 ...52 A2
Edsome Wy ERDE/BCHGN B36 ...112 B1
Edstone Cl BVILLE B30 ...177 H2
  DOR/KN B93 ...196 D5
Edstone Ms CBROM B36 ...112 B1
Edward Fisher Dr
  TPTN/OCK DY4 ...85 G1
Edward Rd
  ALE/KHTH/YWD B14 ...178 A4
  BHTH/HG B12 ...144 A2
  CSHL/WTROR B46 ...96 C3

DIG/EDG B5 ...143 H1
  DUNHL/THL/PER WV6 ...20 C5
  HALE B63 ...138 B3
  LGLYGN/QTN B68 ...123 C4
  SMTHWKW B67 ...106 B4
  TPTN/OCK DY4 ...69 G4
Edwards Rd DUDS DY2 ...102 C5
  ERDE/BCHGN B24 ...93 E1
  MGN/WHC B75 ...47 H2
Edward St CBHAMW B1 ...55 G2
  DARL/WED WS10 ...55 G2
  ETTPK/GDPK/PENN WV4 ...52 D2
  LGLYGN/QTN B68 ...105 E5
  WLSW WS2 ...41 F2
Edwin Phillips Dr
  HHTH/SAND B71 ...71 F3
Edwin Rd BVILLE B30 ...160 B3
Edwinstowe Cl BRLYHL DY5 ...120 A2
Eel St OLDBY B69 ...104 D2
Effingham Rd MOS/BIL B13 ...162 A4
Egbert Cl AST/WIT B6 ...109 H1
Egelwin Cl
  DUNHL/THL/PER WV6 ...20 C5
Egerton Rd ERDE/BCHGN B24 ...93 H3
  FOAKS/STRLY B74 ...45 H4
  WOLVN WV10 ...13 E4
Egghill La RBRY B45 ...174 A1
Eggington Rd STRBR DY8 ...117 H5
Egginton Rd HLGN/YWD B28 ...162 C5
Egmont Gdns WNSFLD WV11 ...25 F5
Elbow St CDYHTH B64 ...121 F2
Elbury Cft DOR/KN B93 ...196 D3
Elcock Dr PBAR/PBCH B42 ...90 D1
Eldalade Wy DARL/WED WS10 ...71 G2
Elderberry Cl DSYBK/YTR WS5 ...57 H5
  STRBR DY8 ...134 C4
Elderfield Rd BVILLE B30 ...177 F2
Elder Gv WMBN WV5 ...64 D5
  WNSFLD WV11 ...24 A4
Eldersfield Cl SOLH B91 ...195 H1
Eldersice Cl BRWNH WS8 ...9 F2
Elder Wy ERDW/GRVHL B23 ...92 B4
Eldon Dr WALM/CURD B76 ...78 A4
Eldon Rd LDYWD/EDGR B16 ...125 H1
  RMSLY B62 ...140 A4
Eldon St DARL/WED WS10 ...55 F1
  WSL WS1 ...
Eldridge Cl COVEN WV9 ...11 H5
Eleanor Rd BILS/COS WV14 ...53 H2
Electric Av AST/WIT B6 ...109 H1
Elford Cl ALE/KHTH/YWD B14 ...161 E5
  FOAKS/STRLY B74 ...45 G3
Elford Gv BILS/COS WV14 ...53 G4
  CHWD/FDBR/MGN B37 ...132 B3
Elford Rd HRBN B17 ...141 H4
  SLYOAK B29 ...159 F3
Elgar Crs BRLYHL DY5 ...101 F2
Elgin Cl SEDG DY3 ...66 D3
  STRBR DY8 ...118 C5
Elgin Ct DUNHL/THL/PER WV6 ...34 C1
Elgin Gv YDLY B25 ...129 G5
Elgin Rd BLOX/PEL WS3 ...16 C3
Eliot Cft BILS/COS WV14 ...68 C1
Eliot St VAUX/NECH B7 ...110 A1
Elizabeth Av BILS/COS WV14 ...54 B5
  DARL/WED WS10 ...55 H4
  ETTPK/GDPK/PENN WV4 ...51 H3
Elizabeth Crs
  LGLYGN/QTN B68 ...123 H2
Elizabeth Dr DUDS DY2 ...103 F2
  SHLY B90 ...180 D3
Elizabeth Ms OLDBY B69 ...85 G4
Elizabeth Rd DSYBK/YTR WS5 ...57 H1
  HALE B63 ...138 B4
  MOS/BIL B13 ...145 G5
  SCFLD/BOLD B73 ...76 A2
  STETCH B33 ...129 H1
  WBROM B70 ...86 B2
Elizabeth Wk TPTN/OCK DY4 ...69 G2
Elkington Cft SHLY B90 ...195 F3
Elkington St AST/WIT B6 ...109 E4
Elkstone Cl HIA/OLT B92 ...147 H4
Elkstone Covert
  ALE/KHTH/YWD B14 ...177 G3
Elland Gv ACGN B27 ...146 C5
Ellards Dr WNSFLD WV11 ...25 F5
Ellen St WSNGN B18 ...2 A1
Ellerby Gv ERDE/BCHGN B24 ...94 A2
Ellerside Gv NFLD/LBR B31 ...175 F3
Ellerslie Cl BRLYHL DY5 ...119 F4
Ellerslie Rd MOS/BIL B13 ...162 A5
Ellerton Rd KGSTG B44 ...75 H2
Ellerton Wk WOLVN WV10 ...37 H1
Ellesboro' Rd HRBN B17 ...124 D4
Ellesmere Rd WASH/WDE B8 ...110 B5
Ellice Dr CBROM B36 ...114 B2
Elliot Gdns RBRY B45 ...188 B3
Elliott Rd SLYOAK B29 ...142 C5
Elliotts La CDSL WV8 ...10 C4
Elliott's Rd TPTN/OCK DY4 ...85 E1
Elliott Wy AST/WIT B6 ...91 F2
Ellis Av BRLYHL DY5 ...118 C2
Ellison St WBROM B70 ...87 F4
Ellis St CBHAMW B1 ...2 E7
Elliston Av KGSTG B44 ...75 E3
Ellowes Rd SEDG DY3 ...82 C2
Elm Av BHTH/HG B12 ...144 C3
  BILS/COS WV14 ...53 H2
  DARL/WED WS10 ...55 H4
  WNSFLD WV11 ...24 B2
Elmay Rd
  LGN/SDN/BHAMAIR B26 ...130 C5
Elm Bank MOS/BIL B13 ...144 C4
Elmbank Gv
  BFLD/HDSWWD B20 ...89 G1
Elmbank Rd DSYBK/YTR WS5 ...58 A4
Elmbridge Cl HALE B63 ...137 H2
Elmbridge Dr SHLY B90 ...195 H2
Elmbridge Rd KGSTG B44 ...75 E5
Elmbridge Wy
  HWK/WKHTH B38 ...176 B3

SEDG DY3 ...67 G5
Elm Cl SEDG DY3 ...82 D4
Elm Cft LGLYGN/QTN B68 ...134 C5
Elmcroft Av NFLD/LBR B31 ...157 E1
Elmcroft Gdns WOLVN WV10 ...13 E4
Elmcroft Rd
  LGN/SDN/BHAMAIR B26 ...130 B5
Elmdale RMSLY B62 ...123 E5
Elmdale Crs NFLD/LBR B31 ...174 B4
Elmdale Dr ALDR WS9 ...30 C2
Elmdale Gv NFLD/LBR B31 ...175 E1
Elmdale Rd BILS/COS WV14 ...68 A4
Elmdon Cl
  ETTPK/GDPK/PENN WV4 ...51 G3
Elmdon Ct HIA/OLT B92 ...148 B5
  WOLVN WV10 ...22 C1
Elmdon Coppice HIA/OLT B92 ...165 H3
Elmdon La
  LGN/SDN/BHAMAIR B26 ...149 E4
Elmdon Park Rd HIA/OLT B92 ...148 B5
Elmdon Rd CBROM B36 ...113 G2
  CHWD/FDBR/MGN B37 ...149 G1
  SLYOAK B29 ...143 E5
  WOLVN WV10 ...22 C1
Elm Dr GTB/HAM B43 ...73 E2
  KIDD DY10 ...168 B3
  NFLD/LBR B31 ...174 C4
  RMSLY B62 ...122 C5
Elm Farm Av
  LGN/SDN/BHAMAIR B26 ...131 H5
Elm Farm Rd BKHL/PFLD WV2 ...52 B1
Elmfield Av ERDE/BCHGN B24 ...94 A2
Elmfield Crs MOS/BIL B13 ...144 B5
Elmfield Rd CBROM B36 ...113 G2
Elmfield Vw DUDN DY1 ...84 A1
Elm Gn DUDN DY1 ...84 A1
  CDSL WV8 ...10 C4
  ERDE/BCHGN B37 ...113 H3
Elmhurst Av
  BLKHTH/ROWR B65 ...122 A1
Elmhurst Dr KGSWFD DY6 ...100 B5
Elmhurst Rd HDSW B21 ...89 G5
Elmley Cl BILS/COS WV14 ...68 B4
Elm Gv BVILLE B30 ...177 F2
  DUNHL/THL/PER WV6 ...34 D2
  SLYOAK B29 ...167 G3
Elmore Cl
  CHWD/FDBR/MGN B37 ...131 A5
Elmore Gn Cl BLOX/PEL WS3 ...27 F2
Elmore Green Rd
  BLOX/PEL WS3 ...27 E1
Elmore Rd BLOX/PEL WS3 ...27 F1
Elm Rd BLOX/PEL WS3 ...27 H4
  BVILLE S30 ...159 H2
  DUDN DY1 ...84 C3
  KGSWFD DY6 ...100 A3
  WALM/CURD B76 ...78 B1
Elms Cl SOLH B91 ...165 F5
Elmsdale DUNHL/THL/PER WV6 ...34 A4
Elmsdale Ct WSL WS1 ...43 E3
Elmstead Av STETCH B33 ...131 F5
Elmstead Cl DSYBK/YTR WS5 ...43 G4
Elmstead Wd DSYBK/YTR WS5 ...43 G5
Elm St DUNHL/THL/PER WV6 ...125 H1
  WLNHL WV13 ...39 H5
Elmsworth Gv
  ALE/KHTH/YWD B14 ...178 B1
Elm Ter OLDBY B69 ...85 G5
Elm Tree Cl WMBN WV5 ...80 D1
Elm Tree Gv HALE B65 ...137 H1
Elm Tree Ri HRBN B17 ...141 C1
Elm Tree Rd HRBN B17 ...141 G1
  MOS/BIL B13 ...160 A4
Elmtree Rd FOAKS/STRLY B74 ...44 D5
Elm Tree Wy CDYHTH B64 ...121 E3
Elmwood Av WNSFLD WV11 ...25 E4
Elmwood Gdns
  BFLD/HDSWWD B20 ...90 B4
Elmwood Gv HLYWD B47 ...192 C2
Elmwood Ri SEDG DY3 ...66 B2
Elmwood Rd ERDE/BCHGN B24 ...93 G4
  FOAKS/STRLY B74 ...60 C2
  STETCH B33 ...130 C1
Elmwoods RIDG/WDGT B32 ...140 B5
Elphinstone End
  ERDE/BCHGN B24 ...78 G5
Elsma Rd LGLYGN/QTN B68 ...123 G5
Elston Hall La WOLVN WV10 ...23 G1
Elston Hall Ter WOLVN WV10 ...23 G1
Elstree Rd ERDW/GRVHL B23 ...92 B1
Elswick Gv KGSTG B44 ...75 H3
Elswick Rd KGSTG B44 ...75 H2
Elsworth Gv YDLY B25 ...146 C1
Eltham Gv KGSTG B44 ...75 H2
Elton Cl WOLVN WV10 ...13 E5
Elton Cft DOR/KN B93 ...197 H2
Eltonia Cft
  LGN/SDN/BHAMAIR B26 ...147 H1
Elva Cft CBROM B36 ...95 H5
Elvaston Wy SHLY B90 ...195 H4
Elvetham Rd EDG B15 ...126 C5
Elviron Dr
  DUNHL/THL/PER WV6 ...21 G5
Elwell Crs DUDN DY1 ...67 H5
Elwells Cl BILS/COS WV14 ...53 E5
Elwell St DARL/WED WS10 ...56 B2
  WBROM B70 ...71 G5
Elwyn Rd SCFLD/BOLD B73 ...62 A5
Ely Cl BLKHTH/ROWR B65 ...104 C5
  CHWD/FDBR/MGN B37 ...132 B2
Ely Crs HHTH/SAND B71 ...71 H1
Ely Pl WSLW WS2 ...41 F4
Ely Rd WSLW WS2 ...41 F4
Emay Cl WBROM B70 ...70 D3
The Embankment
  BRLYHL DY5 ...119 G2
Embassy Dr EDG B15 ...126 A4
  LGLYGN/QTN B68 ...105 F5
Embassy Rd OLDBY B69 ...105 F5
Embleton Gv BKDE/SHDE B34 ...112 C5
Emerald Ct WASH/WDE B8 ...111 G4
Emerson Cl SEDG DY3 ...82 C2
Emerson Gv WOLVN WV10 ...23 H2
Emerson Rd HRBN B17 ...142 A1
  WOLVN WV10 ...23 H1

Emery Cl ERDW/GRVHL B23 ...92 B5
  WSL WS1 ...5 F6
Emery St WSL WS1 ...5 G6
Emily Gdns LDYWD/EDGR B16 ...125 H1
Emily Rd
  LGN/SDN/BHAMAIR B26 ...146 D1
Emily St BHTH/HG B12 ...127 F5
  WBROM B70 ...87 F4
Emmanuel Rd SCFLD/BOLD B73 ...77 F4
Emmeline St BORD B9 ...127 H3
Empire Cl ALDR WS9 ...29 G4
Empress Wy DARL/WED WS10 ...40 B5
Emscote Dr SCFLD/BOLD B73 ...77 F4
Emscote Gn SOLH B91 ...181 E5
Emscote Rd AST/WIT B6 ...91 F5
Emsworth Crs COVEN WV9 ...12 A5
Emsworth Gv
  ALE/KHTH/YWD B14 ...160 D4
Enderby Cl DOR/KN B93 ...196 D4
Enderby Dr
  ETTPK/GDPK/PENN WV4 ...51 F4
Enderley Rd ERDW/GRVHL B23 ...76 A4
Enderley Cl BLOX/PEL WS3 * ...16 D4
Enderley Dr BLOX/PEL WS3 ...16 D4
End Hall Rd
  DUNHL/THL/PER WV6 ...35 E2
Endhill Rd KGSTG B44 ...60 C5
Endicott Rd AST/WIT B6 ...91 F5
Endmoor Gv ERDW/GRVHL B23 ...76 B5
Endsleigh Gv HLGN/YWD B28 ...163 E2
Endwood Court Rd
  BFLD/HDSWWD B20 ...90 A4
Endwood Dr FOAKS/STRLY B74 ...46 A1
  SOLH B91 ...181 F3
Enfield Cl ERDW/GRVHL B23 ...76 D5
Enfield Rd BLKHTH/ROWR B65 ...122 B1
  EDG B15 ...126 B5
Enford Cl BKDE/SHDE B34 ...113 F5
Engine La BRLYHL DY5 ...119 H1
  BRWNH WS8 ...8 C4
  DARL/WED WS10 ...54 C4
  HAG/WOL DY9 ...136 B2
Engine St OLDBY B69 ...105 E3
  SMTHWK B66 ...106 D3
Englestede Cl
  BFLD/HDSWWD B20 ...89 H3
Englewood Dr
  HLGN/YWD B28 ...163 E2
Ennerdale Cl BRWNH WS8 ...9 E5
Ennerdale Dr
  DUNHL/THL/PER WV6 ...34 D1
  HALE B65 ...137 H5
Ennerdale Rd
  DUNHL/THL/PER WV6 ...21 H2
  GTB/HAM B43 ...73 G2
Ennersdale Bungalows
  CSHL/WTROR B46 ...97 F5
Ennersdale Cl
  CSHL/WTROR B46 ...97 F5
Ennersdale Rd
  CSHL/WTROR B46 ...97 F5
Ensall Dr STRBR DY8 ...118 A3
Ensbury Cl SHHTH WV12 ...40 B1
Ensdale Rw WLNHL WV13 ...39 G4
Ensdon Gv KGSTG B44 ...75 H2
Ensford Cl FOAKS/STRLY B74 ...46 C1
Enstone Rd DUDN DY1 ...101 H1
  ERDW/GRVHL B23 ...77 E5
Enterprise Dr FOAKS/STRLY B74 ...60 A1
  HAG/WOL DY9 ...136 D1
Enterprise Gv BLOX/PEL WS3 ...18 B2
Enterprise Wy VAUX/NECH B7 ...3 J1
Enville Cl BLOX/PEL WS3 ...16 C4
  CHWD/FDBR/MGN B37 ...132 B3
Enville Gv SPARK B11 ...145 F2
Enville Pl STRBR DY8 * ...135 F2
Enville Rd
  ETTPK/GDPK/PENN WV4 ...50 C3
  KGSWFD DY6 ...99 F1
  SEDG DY3 ...83 G2
Enville St STRBR DY8 ...135 F2
Epping Cl BLOX/PEL WS3 ...28 B4
  RBRY B45 ...174 B3
Epping Gv KGSTG B44 ...75 H3
Epsom Cl DUNHL/THL/PER WV6 ...34 D1
Epsom Gv KGSTG B44 ...75 H3
Epwell Gv KGSTG B44 ...75 F5
Epwell Rd KGSTG B44 ...75 F5
Equipoint YDLY B25 ...146 D1
Erasmus Rd SPARK B11 ...127 G5
Ercall Cl ERDW/GRVHL B23 ...75 G5
Erdington Hall Rd
  ERDE/BCHGN B24 ...92 D4
Erdington Rd ALDR WS9 ...44 C4
Erica Cl SLYOAK B29 ...158 C2
Erica Rd DSYBK/YTR WS5 ...57 H5
Ermington Crs CBROM B36 ...112 A2
Ermington Rd
  ETTPK/GDPK/PENN WV4 ...52 C5
Ernest Clarke Cl SHHTH WV12 ...40 B1
Ernest Ct HWK/WKHTH B38 ...177 E4
Ernest Rd BHTH/HG B12 ...144 D3
  DUDS DY2 ...85 F5
  SMTHWKW B67 ...106 A3
Ernest St CBHAMW B1 ...2 E7
Ernsford Cl DOR/KN B93 ...198 D1
Erskine St VAUX/NECH B7 ...127 H1
Esher Rd HHTH/SAND B71 ...71 H5
  KGSTG B44 ...60 B4
Eskdale Cl WOLV WV1 ...38 A3
Eskdale Wk BRLYHL DY5 ...118 D4
Esme Rd SPARK B11 ...144 D3
Esmond Cl BVILLE B30 ...159 F5
Essendon Rd WASH/WDE B8 ...111 F5
Essex Av DARL/WED WS10 ...56 C4
  HHTH/SAND B71 ...71 G4
  KGSWFD DY6 ...99 F1
Essex Gdns STRBR DY8 ...117 H5
Essex Rd DUDS DY2 ...101 H3
  MGN/WHC B75 ...63 E5
Essex St DIG/EDG B5 ...127 E3
  WSLW WS2 ...27 H5
Essington Cl STRBR DY8 ...118 A4
Essington Rd SHHTH WV12 ...25 H1
Essington St LDYWD/EDGR B16 ...2 B7
Essington Wy WOLV WV1 ...38 B4
Este Rd
  LGN/SDN/BHAMAIR B26 ...130 C4
Estone Wk AST/WIT B6 ...109 F2
Estria Rd EDG B15 ...126 B5

Ethelfleda Ter DARL/WED WS10..55 H5
Ethelred Cl FOAKS/STRLY B74....47 E2
Ethel Rd HRBN B17 ....142 B2
Ethel St CBHAM B2 ....3 F5
  LGLYGN/QTN B68 ....105 E5
Etheridge Rd BILS/COS WV14 ....53 H1
Eton Cl SEDG DY3...................67 H4
Eton Dr STRBR DY8................135 G4
Eton Rd BHTH/HG B12 ....144 D3
Eton Wk HAG/WOL DY9 ....152 C4
Etruria Wy BILS/COS WV14 ....54 A1
Etta Gv KGSTG B44..................60 A4
Ettingshall Park Farm La
  ETTPK/GDPK/PENN WV4 ......52 B4
Ettingshall Rd BILS/COS WV14 ..68 A2
  BKHL/PFLD WV2 ....53 E1
Ettington Cl DOR/KN B93........198 B1
Ettington Rd AIT/WIT B6.........109 E1
Ettymore Cl SEDG DY3............67 F3
Ettymore Rd SEDG DY3 ....67 F3
Ettymore Rd West SEDG DY3 ..67 F3
Etwall Rd HLGN/YWD B28.......162 C5
Euan Cl WBRM B70 ....125 F4
Europa Av WBROM B70 ....88 B4
Evans Cl TPTN/OCK DY4...........84 C1
Evans Pl BILS/COS WV14 ....54 A1
Evans St BILS/COS WV14 ....67 H2
  DUNHL/THL/PER WV6 ....36 D1
  WLNHL WV13.......................38 D4
Eva Rd LGLYGN/QTN B68 ....123 G2
  WSNGN B18........................107 G3
Eve La DUDN DY1 ....83 H1
Evelyn Cft SCFLD/BOLD B73 ....77 E5
Evelyn Rd SPARK B11 ....145 E3
Evenlode Gv WLNHL WV13.......40 B4
Evenlode Rd HIA/OLT B92 ......147 G4
Everest Cl SMTHWK B66 ....106 B1
Everest Rd BFLD/HDSWWD B20 .90 A3
  WSLW WS2...........................40 D2
Evergreen Cl BILS/COS WV14 ...68 B3
Everitt Dr DOR/KN B93 ....197 G2
Eversley Dr ERDE/BCHGN B24 ..93 E4
Eversley Gv SEDG DY3 ....67 G1
  WNSFLD WV11......................24 C1
Eversley Rd BORD B9 ....128 B3
Evers St BRLYHL DY5 ....120 A4
Everton Rd WASH/WDE B8 .....111 G5
Eves Cft RIDG/WDGT B32.......157 G1
Evesham Crs BLOX/PEL WS3 ....16 B4
Evesham Ri DUDS DY2............120 D1
Eveson Cl STRBR DY8.............135 E4
Eveson Rd STRBR DY8 ....134 D5
Evington Pl YDLY B25 *...........129 E5
Ewart Rd WSLW WS2...............40 C2
Ewell Rd ERDE/BCHGN B24 .....93 F2
Ewhurst Av SLYOAK B29.........159 H1
Ewhurst Cl WLNHL WV13.........39 F5
Exbury Cl COVEN WV9............11 H5
Excelsior Gv BLOX/PEL WS3 .....6 B2
Exchange St BRLYHL DY5........101 F5
The Exchange BLOX/PEL WS3 * .27 F1
Exe Cft NFLD/LBR B31............175 H5
Exeter Dr
  CHWD/FDBR/MGN B37.......131 H4
Exeter Pas CBHAMW B1 ....126 D3
Exeter Pl WSLW WS2..............41 F4
Exeter Rd DUDS DY2..............120 D2
  SLYOAK B29........................142 D5
  SMTHWK B66 ....106 D4
Exeter St CBHAMW B1 ....2 F3
Exford Cl BRLYHL DY5............118 D5
Exhall Cl SOLH B91................181 E5
Exhibition Wy BHAMNEC B40...149 H5
Exmoor Gn WNSFLD WV11......24 C3
The Expressway WBROM B70....87 G2
Exton Cl WNSFLD WV11...........25 F2
Exton Gdns SMTHWK B66 * 107 F3
Exton Wy WASH/WDE B8........110 B4
Eyland Gv WSL WS1..................5 F3
Eymore Cl SLYOAK B29...........158 D4
Eyre St WSNGN B18................126 A1
Eyston Av TPTN/OCK DY4.........70 B3
Eyton Cft BHTH/HG B12.........127 F5
Ezekiel La SHHTH WV12...........26 A4

F

Fabian Cl RBRY B45................173 H3
Fabian Crs SHLY B90...............180 B4
Facet Rd HWK/WKHTH B38.....177 E3
Factory Rd TPTN/OCK DY4.......69 E5
  WSNGN B18.........................107 H3
Factory St DARL/WED WS10 .....5 G2
Fairbourne Av
  BLKHTH/ROWR B65.............104 C5
  KGSTG B44...........................75 E1
Fairburn Crs BLOX/PEL WS3 ....18 B2
Faircroft Av WALM/CURD B76...78 B5
Faircroft Rd CBROM B36 ....95 G5
Fairfax Rd MGN/WHC B75........63 F4
  NFLD/LBR B31.....................175 G5
  WOLVN WV10.......................12 D4
Fairfield Dr BLOX/PEL WS3 ......18 B3
  CDSL WV8.............................10 A4
  RMSLY B62..........................122 C3
Fairfield Gv RMSLY B62...........122 C3
Fairfield Mt WSL WS1................5 F7
Fairfield Ri STRBR DY8............134 C2
Fairfield Rd
  ALE/KHTH/YWD B14............161 E2
  DUDS DY2...........................102 C3
  HALE B63............................138 C5
  RMSLY B62..........................122 C3
  STRBR DY8...........................118 B2
Fairford Gdns STRBR DY8.......118 A1
Fairford Rd KGSTG B44............75 F5
Fairgreen Gdns BRLYHL DY5....101 F4
Fairgreen Wy
  FOAKS/STRLY B74.................45 G4
  SLYOAK B29........................159 H1
Fairground Wy WSL WS1..........4 C6
Fairhaven Cft RMSLY B62.........122 C3
Fairhills SEDG DY3...................67 E3
Fairhill Wy SPARK B11.............127 H5
Fairholme Rd CBROM B36.......111 F2

Fairlawn EDG B15 *................126 A5
Fairlawn Cl SHHTH WV12 ....26 A1
Fairlawn Dr KGSWFD DY6.......99 H5
Fairlawns
  LGN/SDN/BHAMAIR B26 .....130 B3
Fairlie Crs HWK/WKHTH B38...176 B4
Fairmead Ri HWK/WKHTH B38..176 C4
Fairmile Rd HALE B63.............138 B1
Fairoak Dr
  DUNHL/THL/PER WV6...........35 E2
Fairview Av PBAR/PBCH B42....74 B5
Fairview Cl WNSFLD WV11........24 B3
Fairview Crs KGSWFD DY6.......100 B3
  WNSFLD WV11 ....24 B3
Fairview Crs Gv WNSFLD WV11..24 B3
Fairview Ms
  CSHL/WTROR B46 * 115 F2
Fairview Rd DUDN DY1.............84 A4
  ETTPK/GDPK/PENN WV4 ......50 C4
  WNSFLD WV11 ....24 B3
Fairway NFLD/LBR B31............175 E3
  RUSH/SHEL WS4 ....29 F1
Fairway Av OLDBY B69............103 G1
Fairway Dr RBRY B45..............187 H2
Fairway Gn BILS/COS WV14 .....53 G1
Fairway Rd LGLYGN/QTN B68..122 D3
Fairways Av STRBR DY8...........135 E5
Fairways Cl STRBR DY8............135 E5
The Fairways WALM/CURD B76..78 B5
The Fairway HWK/WKHTH B38..176 B3
Fairyfield Av GTB/HAM B43.......75 F2
Fakenham Cft HRBN B17.........124 B5
Falcon Crs BILS/COS WV14 ....67 H1
Falcondale Rd SHHTH WV12.....26 A1
Falconhurst Rd SLYOAK B29....142 A5
Falcon Lodge Crs
  ....65 G3
Falcon Pl OLDBY B69 ....104 A2
Falcon Ri STRBR DY8..............134 C1
Falcon Rd LGLYGN/QTN B68....122 D2
The Falcons MGN/WHC B75 .....63 H5
Falcon Wy DUDN DY1 ....85 H5
Falfield Cl BLKHTH/ROWR B65..104 B3
Falfield Gv NFLD/LBR B31........189 E1
Falkland Cft BVILLE B30..........160 B4
Falklands Cl SEDG DY3 ....80 C4
Falkland Wy CBROM B36........114 B4
Falkwood Gv DOR/KN B93......196 D2
Fallindale Rd
  LGN/SDN/BHAMAIR B26......147 H1
Fallings Heath Cl
  DARL/WED WS10...................55 H1
Fallowfield CDSL WV8...............11 G5
  DUNHL/THL/PER WV6...........34 B1
Fallow Fld FOAKS/STRLY B74....45 H2
Fallowfield Av HLGN/YWD B28..162 D5
Fallow Field Rd
  BLKHTH/ROWR B65.............121 G1
  HALE B63............................137 H4
  HIA/OLT B92........................148 A5
Fallows Rd SPARK B11.............145 E1
Falmouth Rd BKDE/SHDE B34..112 A4
  DSYBK/YTR WS5 ....58 B1
Falstaff Av HLYWD B47...........192 C2
Falstaff Cl WALM/CURD B76.....78 C4
Falstaff Rd SHLY B90..............180 C3
Falstone Rd SCFLD/BOLD B73...76 B1
Fancott Rd NFLD/LBR B31.......158 C5
Fancourt Av
  ETTPK/GDPK/PENN WV4 ......50 D3
Fane Rd WNSFLD WV11............25 G1
Fanshawe Rd ACGN B27.........145 H3
Faraday Av RIDG/WDGT B32....100 D2
  WALM/CURD B76...................97 E1
Faraday Whf VAUX/NECH B7 * ...3 K1
Farbrook Wy SHHTH WV12......25 H4
Farcroft Av HDSW B21............107 F1
Farcroft Gv HDSW B21.............89 F5
Farcroft Rd HDSW B21.............89 F5
Fardon Wy ERDW/GRVHL B23..76 B3
Fareham Crs
  ETTPK/GDPK/PENN WV4 ......50 C2
Farfield Cl NFLD/LBR B31........175 H5
Far High Dr TPTN/OCK DY4.....85 H1
Far Highfield WALM/CURD B76..62 D4
Far Hill Cl HHTH/SAND B71......72 B5
Farlands Dr STRBR DY8...........135 G4
Farlands Gv GTB/HAM B43........73 H4
Farlands Rd STRBR DY8...........135 G4
Farleigh Dr BDMR/CCFT WV3 ...35 E5
Farleigh Rd
  DUNHL/THL/PER WV6...........35 E2
Farley La RMSLY B62...............172 B4
Farley Rd ERDW/GRVHL B23...91 H2
Farley St TPTN/OCK DY4...........86 B1
Farlow Cft
  CHWD/FDBR/MGN B37.......131 H5
Farlow Rd NFLD/LBR B31........176 A2
Farmacre BORD B9.................127 H2
Farm Av LGLYGN/QTN B68.....123 E1
Farmbridge Cl WSLW WS2........40 B2
Farmbridge Rd WLNHL WV13...40 B3
Farmbrook Av WOLVN WV10....12 D4
Farm Cl CDSL WV8...................10 D5
  HIA/OLT B92........................148 A5
  SEDG DY3............................66 D4
  STETCH B33........................130 B1
Farmcote Rd STETCH B33......112 D5
Farm Cft LOZ/NWT B19..........108 C3
Farmcroft Rd HAG/WOL DY9....136 C5
Farmdale Gv RBRY B45...........188 A2
Farm End Cl HHTH/SAND B71...72 B2
Farmers Cl WALM/CURD B76....63 E4
Farmers Ct HALE B63..............138 B3
Farmers Fold WOLV WV1..........7 F4
Farmers Wk HDSW B21...........107 F2
Farm House La MGN/WHC B75..48 A2
Farmhouse Rd SHHTH WV12....26 B5
Farm House Wy GTB/HAM B43..58 C4
Farmoor Gv SHLY B90.............195 H2
Farmoor Gv BKDE/SHDE B34..113 G3
Farmoor Wy WOLVN WV10.......1 J5
Farm Rd BDMR/CCFT WV3.......35 G5
  BLKHTH/ROWR B65..............103 G5
  BRLYHL DY5.........................119 G3

DUDS DY2.............................102 A5
LGLYGN/QTN B68 ....123 E1
SMTHWK B67 ....124 A1
SPARK B11............................144 D1
TPTN/OCK DY4.......................69 H4
Farmside Cl HAG/WOL DY9.....137 E4
Farmside Gn COVEN WV9 ....9 H3
Farmstead Cl WSL WS1 ....57 E3
Farmstead Rd HIA/OLT B92....148 A5
Farm St LOZ/NWT B19............108 C3
  WBROM B70 ....87 G5
  WSLW WS2............................42 A1
Farnborough Ct
  MGN/WHC B75......................47 G3
Farnborough Dr SHLY B90......195 F2
Farnborough Rd CVALE B35.....94 D3
Farnbury Cft
  HWK/WKHTH B38.................177 F3
Farncote Dr FOAKS/STRLY B74..46 D2
Farndale Av
  DUNHL/THL/PER WV6............36 C1
Farndale Cl BRLYHL DY5.........135 H1
Farndon Av
  CHWD/FDBR/MGN B37.......132 B5
Farndon Rd WASH/WDE B8....110 D4
Farnham Cl GTB/HAM B43........73 H5
Farnham Rd HDSW B21............89 F4
Farnhurst Rd WASH/WDE B8...111 F2
Farnol Rd
  LGN/SDN/BHAMAIR B26......130 B4
Farnworth Gv CBROM B36.......95 G5
Farquhar Rd EDG B15.............142 D1
  MOS/BIL B13.........................144 B4
Farquhar Rd East EDG B15.....142 D1
Farren Rd NFLD/LBR B31........174 D4
Farrier Cl WALM/CURD B76......78 B3
Farrier Rd GTB/HAM B43..........59 H5
Farriers MI BLOX/PEL WS3 ....17 G3
The Farriers
  LGN/SDN/BHAMAIR B26......147 H2
Farrier Wy KGSWFD DY6..........99 E2
Farringdon St WSLW WS2..........4 B2
Farrington Rd
  ERDW/GRVHL B23.................91 H1
  ETTPK/GDPK/PENN WV4 ......67 C1
Farrow Rd KGSTG B44...............60 A5
Farthing La CSCFLD/WYGN B72..62 G4
Farthing Pools Cl
  CSCFLD/WYGN B72...............62 C4
Farthings La DUDS DY2..........102 A2
The Farthings HRBN B17........142 B1
Farvale Rd WALM/CURD B76....79 E5
Far Vw ALDR WS9.....................19 H5
Farway Gdns CDSL WV8..........10 B5
Far Wood Rd NFLD/LBR B31...158 A2
Fashoda Rd SLYOAK B29.........160 A1
Fastlea Rd RIDG/WDGT B32...157 H1
Fastmoor Ov STETCH B33.......131 G3
Fast Pits Rd YDLY B25.............129 F4
Fatherless Barn Crs HALE B63..137 G5
Faulkland Crs WOLV WV1..........7 H2
Faulkner Cl STRBR DY8...........135 F5
Faulkner Rd HIA/OLT B92.......164 D1
Faulkners Farm Dr
  ERDW/GRVHL B23.................91 H1
Faulknor Dr BRLYHL DY5........100 D2
Faversham Cl CDSL WV8..........22 A2
  WSLW WS2...........................40 D2
Fawdry Cl SCFLD/BOLD B73.....77 E4
Fawdry St CBHAMNE B4 ....127 G2
  SMTHWK B66 ....107 E4
  WOLV WV1.............................6 D1
Fawley Cl WLNHL WV13...........39 F5
Fawley Gv BVILLE B30............160 B5
Fazeley St DIG/EDG D5..............3 K5
Fearon Pl SMTHWK B66 * 106 C3
Featherstone Cl SHLY B90......180 D3
Featherstone Crs SHLY B90....180 D4
Featherstone Rd
  ALE/KHTH/YWD B14............161 E4
Featherston Rd
  FOAKS/STRLY B74.................45 G3
Feiashill Rd SEDG DY3..............80 B3
Felbrigg Cl BRLYHL DY5..........119 F4
Feldings Croft BKDE/SHDE B34..93 G2
Feldon La RMSLY B62.............122 C5
Felgate Cl SHLY B90...............195 G2
Feilbrook Cl STETCH B33........112 B5
Fell Gv HDSW B21....................89 F3
Fellmeadow Rd STETCH B33....130 C2
Fellmeadow Wy SEDG DY3.......67 G5
Fellows Av KGSWFD DY6..........99 G1
Fellows La HRBN B17..............141 G1
Fellows Park Gdns
  WSLW WS2 * 56 B2
Fellows Rd BILS/COS WV14 ......53 H1
Fellows St BKHL/PFLD WV2......37 E5
Felsted Wy VAUX/NECH B7.....109 G5
Felstone Rd KGSTG B44............75 F2
Feltham Cl STETCH B33..........131 G3
Felton Crs STETCH B33..........130 C1
Felton Gv SOLH B91...............181 H4
Fenbourne Cl RUSH/SHEL WS4..29 E2
Fenchurch Cl WSLW WS2.........41 H1
Fencote Av
  CHWD/FDBR/MGN B37.......114 A5
Fenmere Cl
  ETTPK/GDPK/PENN WV4 ......52 B3
Fennel Cft BKDE/SHDE B34....117 G2
Fennel Rd BRLYHL DY5............119 E5
Fennis Cl DOR/KN B93............196 D5
Fenn Ri SHHTH WV12...............25 H4
  STRBR DY8..........................117 G1
Fens Crs BRLYHL DY5.............101 E4
Fens Pool Av BRLYHL DY5.......101 F4
The Fensway BKDE/SHDE B34..112 C4
Fenter Cl MOS/BIL B13............144 B3
Fentham Cl HIA/OLT B92........167 H4
Fentham Ct HIA/OLT B92........167 G3
Fentham Rd ACGN B27 ....146 B1
  ERDW/GRVHL B23 ....92 B3
  HIA/OLT B92........................167 G3
Fenton Rd ACGN B27 ....146 A2
  HLYWD B47..........................192 C1
Fenton St BRLYHL DY5............119 F1
  SMTHWK B66 ....106 A3
Fenton Wy ACGN B27.............146 A2
Fereday Rd ALDR WS9..............19 H4

Fereday's Cft SEDG DY3 ....67 F4
Fereday St TPTN/OCK DY4.......69 F3
Ferguson Dr TPTN/OCK DY4....69 H5
Ferguson Rd LGLYGN/QTN B68..105 H4
Ferguson St WNSFLD WV11.....25 C1
Fern Av TPTN/OCK DY4............69 H4
Fernbank Cl HALE B63.............137 H5
Fernbank Crs DSYBK/YTR WS5..58 A4
Fernbank Rd WASH/WDE B8....111 E5
Ferncliffe Rd HRBN B17...........141 H3
Fern Cl BILS/COS WV14............68 B5
  RUSH/SHEL WS4 ....29 E1
Ferndale Av GTB/HAM B43.......73 H4
Ferndale Cl CSHL/WTROR B46..115 C4
Ferndale Crs BHTH/HG B12.....127 G4
Ferndale Ms
  CSHL/WTROR B46................115 C4
Ferndale Pk HAG/WOL DY9....153 E2
Ferndale Rd CSHL/WTROR B46..115 C4
  FOAKS/STRLY B74..................45 F5
  HLGN/YWD B28....................162 C2
  LGLYGN/QTN B68.................123 E2
  WNSFLD WV11 ....15 F4
Ferndene Rd SPARK B11.........145 H4
Ferndown Av SEDG DY3...........67 E4
Ferndown Cl BLOX/PEL WS3.....16 C5
  LGN/SDN/BHAMAIR B26......130 C3
Ferndown Rd SOLH B91..........164 D4
Fernhill Gv KGSTG B44.............60 B5
Fernhill Rd HIA/OLT B92..........147 H3
Fernhurst Dr BRLYHL DY5.......100 D3
Fernhurst Rd WASH/WDE B8...129 E1
Fernleigh Gdns STRBR DY8.....117 G1
Fernleigh Rd RUSH/SHEL WS4..42 D2
Fernley Rd SPARK B11.............145 E3
Fern Leys BDMR/CCFT WV3.....35 H4
Fern Rd BDMR/CCFT WV3.......35 G4
  DUDN DY1 ....84 C2
  ERDE/BCHGN B24.................93 E2
Fernside Gdns MOS/BIL B13...144 D4
Fernside Rd WLNHL WV13.......39 F1
Fern Vlls DARL/WED WS10 * 55 C2
Fernwood Cft SCFLD/BOLD B73..76 C2
Fernwood Cft
  ALE/KHTH/YWD B14............161 E4
  TPTN/OCK DY4.......................85 F2
Fernwood Rd SCFLD/BOLD B73..76 C5
Fernwoods RIDG/WDGT B32...140 B5
Ferrers Cl MGN/WHC B75.........47 H3
Ferrie Gv BRWNH WS8...............9 E4
Ferris Gv ACGN B27................163 E1
Festival Av DARL/WED WS10....55 H4
Festival Wy
  DUNHL/THL/PER WV6 ....22 D5
Ffernfall Ct ERDW/GRVHL B23..92 C1
Fibbersley WLNHL WV13..........39 F1
Fibbersley Bank WLNHL WV13..39 F1
Fiddlers Gn HIA/OLT B92.........167 G3
Field Av NFLD/LBR B31...........158 B5
  LGN/SDN/BHAMAIR B26......147 G1
  RUSH/SHEL WS4 ....18 B5
  STRBR DY8..........................118 C2
Field Cottage Dr STRBR DY8...135 H4
Fieldfare Cl DUDS DY2............103 F5
Fieldfare Cft BCROM B36.........114 A1
Field Head Pl
  DUNHL/THL/PER WV6............35 F1
Fieldhouse La RMSLY B62.......172 A1
Fieldhouse Rd
  ETTPK/GDPK/PENN WV4 ......52 C4
  YDLY B25.............................129 G4
Field La HAG/WOL DY9...........170 A1
  RIDG/WDGT B32...................157 E2
  RUSH/SHEL WS4 ....18 B5
  SOLH B91............................166 A5
  STRBR DY8..........................135 C4
Field Maple Rd
  DUNHL/THL/PER WV6 ....60 B2
Field Ms DUDS DY2................121 E2
Fieldon Cl SHLY B90...............180 C2
Field Rd BLOX/PEL WS3 ....28 E5
  DUDS DY2.............................69 F3
  TPTN/OCK DY4.......................69 F3
The Fields CDSL WV8...............10 D3
Fieldside Vw SEDG DY3 ....83 E2
Field St BILS/COS WV14............54 A5
  WLNHL WV13.........................39 G3
  WOLVN WV10 ....7 J2
Fieldview Cl BILS/COS WV14....68 C1
Field View Dr
  BLKHTH/ROWR B65..............122 D2
Field Wk ALDR WS9..................30 B3
Field Wy HOCK/TIA B94..........198 A5
Fieldways Cl HLYWD B47.........192 C1
Fifield Gv STETCH B33............130 B1
Fifth Av BORD B9.....................128 D3
  WOLVN WV10 ....23 E3
Filey Rd WOLVN WV10 ....12 B5
Fillingham Cl
  CHWD/FDBR/MGN B37.......132 D3
Filton Cft CVALE B35................94 C2
Fimbrell Cl BRLYHL DY5.........118 C4
Finbury Cl HIA/OLT B92..........164 B1
Finchall Cft SOLH B91.............165 G3
Fincham Cl COVEN WV9..........11 G4
Finch Cl BLKHTH/ROWR B65...105 F5
Finchden Gv BDMR/CCFT WV3..35 H4
Finch Dr FOAKS/STRLY B74.......46 C5
Finches End BKDE/SHDE B34..115 E4
Finchfield Cl STRBR DY8.........134 C5
Finchfield Gdns
  BDMR/CCFT WV3....................36 A4
Finchley Av LOZ/NWT B19 * 108 D2
Finchley Cl SEDG DY3..............83 F4
Finchley Rd KGSTG B44............61 E5
Finchmead Rd STETCH B33....131 G2
Finchpath Rd WBROM B70......71 E5
Finch Rd LOZ/NWT B19..........108 C1
Findlay Rd
  ALE/KHTH/YWD B14............161 E1

Findon Rd WASH/WDE B8 111
Finger Post Dr BLOX/PEL WS3...18
Finlarigg Dr EDG B15 142
Finmere Rd BILS/COS WV14 B28..162
Finmere Wy SHLY B90 180
Finnemore Rd BORD B9 128
Finney Well Cl BILS/COS WV14...53
Finsbury Dr BRLYHL DY5..........119
Finsbury Gv ERDW/GRVHL B23..76
Finstall Cl CSCFLD/WYGN B72....77
  VAUX/NECH B7.....................109
Finwood Cl HIA/OLT B92..........165
Fir Av BHTH/HG B12.................144
Firbank Cl BVILLE B30..............159
Firbank Wy BLOX/PEL WS3.......17
Firbarn Cl WALM/CURD B76......62
Firbeck Gv KGSTG B44..............75
Firbeck Rd KGSTG B44..............75
Fircroft BILS/COS WV14 68
Fir Cft BRLYHL DY5..................119
Fircroft NFLD/LBR B31.............158
  SOLH B91............................164
Firecrest Cl ERDW/GRVHL B23..75
Fir Gv ALE/KHTH/YWD B14.......16
  BDMR/CCFT WV5
  STRBR DY8............................
Firhill Cft ALE/KHTH/YWD B14..177
Firmstone St STRBR DY8..........117
Firsbrook Cl
  DUNHL/THL/PER WV6............22
Firsby Rd RIDG/WDGT B32.......140
Firs Cl SMTHWK B67...............108
Firs Dr SHLY B90.....................180
Firs Farm Dr CBROM B36........111
Firsholm Cl SCFLD/BOLD B73.....7
Firs Rd KGSWFD DY6.................8
Firs St DUDS DY2......................8
First Av BORD B9.......................
  BRWNH WS8...........................8
  KGSWFD DY6..........................8
  SLYOAK B29.........................15
  WALM/CURD B76.....................9
First Exhibition Av
  BHAMNEC B40.......................14
First Meadow Piece
  RIDG/WDGT B32....................14
Fir St SEDG DY3.......................
Firsvale Rd WNSFLD WV11........2
Firsway DUNHL/THL/PER WV6....3
Firswood Rd STETCH B33..........
Firth Dr ALE/KHTH/YWD B14.....16
  RMSLY B62...........................
Firth Park Crs RMSLY B62........12
Fir Tree Cl KGSTG B44................7
Fir Tree Dr DSYBK/YTR WS5......
  SEDG DY3.............................
Fir Tree Gv SCFLD/BOLD B73.....
Fir Tree Rd BDMR/CCFT WV3.....
Firtree Rd ERDE/BCHGN B24.....9
Fisher Rd BLOX/PEL WS3..........
  OLDBY B69...........................10
Fishers Dr SHLY B90................19
Fisher St BDMR/CCFT WV3........
  BRLYHL DY5...........................
  DUDN DY1.............................
  TPTN/OCK DY4.......................
  WLNHL WV13.........................
Fishley Cl BLOX/PEL WS3..........
Fishley La BLOX/PEL WS3.........
Fishpool Cl CBROM B36...........
Fishpool La
  RCOVN/BALC/EX CV7...........
Fistral Gdns BDMR/CCFT WV3...
Fitters Mill Cl DIG/EDG D5 *......14
Fitton Av KGSWFD DY6.............10
Fitzgerald Pl BRLYHL DY5........13
Fitzguy Cl WBROM B70............
Fitzmaurice Rd WNSFLD WV11..2
Fitz Roy Av HRBN B17..............12
Fitzroy Rd NFLD/LBR B31........12
Five Broadway EDG B15 *.........12
Five Fields Rd SHHTH WV12.....
Five Oaks Rd WLNHL WV13......
Five Ways LDYWD/EDGR B16...12
Flackwell Rd ERDW/GRVHL B23..
Fladbury Cl DUDS DY2.............14
Fladbury Crs SLYOAK B29........14
Fladbury Gdns
  LOZ/NWT B19 *......................
Fladbury Pl LOZ/NWT B19 * ......
Flamborough Gv
  BKDE/SHDE B34....................11
Flamborough Wy
  BILS/COS WV14.....................
Flanders Dr KGSWFD DY6.........
Flash La
  ETTPK/GDPK/PENN WV4.........
Flash Rd OLDBY B69...................
The Flatts DARL/WED WS10......
Flavell Av BILS/COS WV14..........
Flavell Cl RIDG/WDGT B32.........
Flavells La SEDG DY3.................
  YDLY B25...............................
Flavell St DUDN DY1.................
Flax Cl HLYWD B47..................
Flax Gdns HWK/WKHTH B38....11
Flaxhall St WSLW WS2..............
Flaxley Pkwy STETCH B33.........
Flaxley Rd STETCH B33............
Flaxton Gv STETCH B33............
Flecknoe Cl CBROM B36............
Fledburgh Dr WALM/CURD B76..
Fleet St CBHAMW B1................
Fleetwood Gv
  LGN/SDN/BHAMAIR B26.........
Fleming Pl WSLW WS2..............
Fleming Rd RIDG/WDGT B32.....1
Flemmynge Cl CDSL WV8..........
Fletcher Gv DOR/KN B93..........
Fletcher Rd SHHTH WV12.........
Fletcher's La WLNHL WV13.......
Fletcher St HAG/WOL DY9........
Fletton Gv
  ALE/KHTH/YWD B14..............
Flinkford Cl DSYBK/YTR WS5.....
Flint Green Rd ACGN B27.........
Flintham Cl ACGN B27..............

Flintway STETCH B33 .... 112 A5
odgate St DIG/EDG B5 .... 3 K7
od St DUDS DY2 .... 84 D5
ra Rd YDLY B25 .... 129 F5
rence Av
ETTPK/GDPK/PENN WV4 .... 52 D4
SPARK B11 .... 144 D2
rence Gv HHTH/SAND B71 .... 72 A2
WSNGN B18 .... 107 G5
rence Rd ACGN B27 .... 146 D3
ALE/KHTH/YWD B14 .... 161 F2
CDSL WV8 .... 10 D4
ERDW/GRVHL B23 .... 77 F4
HDSW B21 .... 107 F1
OLDBY B69 .... 104 B2
SMTHWK B66 .... 106 D5
TPTN/OCK DY4 .... 69 G4
WBROM B70 .... 88 A5
rence St CBHAMW B1 .... 126 D3
WSL WS1 .... 5 H5
rence Vls SPARK B11 * 128 A5
rian Gv DARL/WED WS10 .... 55 G1
rida Wy KGSWFD DY6 .... 100 C4
werdale Cl BILS/COS WV14 .... 68 B3
yds La RUSH/SHEL WS4 .... 29 E4
yer Rd SMTHTH B10 .... 128 C3
ord Cft SLYOAK B29 .... 141 F5
en Rd PBAR/PBCH B42 .... 74 A3
navon Cl
BLKHTH/ROWR B65 .... 103 F3
d St WOLV WV1 .... 6 E5
Fold DARL/WED WS10 .... 55 F2
TTPK/GDPK/PENN WV4 .... 51 F4
dyard Cl WALM/CURD B76 .... 78 C3
ey Av DUNHL/THL/PER WV6 ... 35 F2
ey Church Cl
OAKS/STRLY B74 .... 45 G3
ey Dr DUNHL/THL/PER WV6 ... 35 G2
ey Gv WMBN WV5 .... 80 C1
ey Rd HAG/WOL DY9 .... 135 H5
WASH/WDE B8 .... 111 F3
ey Rd East
OAKS/STRLY B74 .... 45 F4
ey Rd West
OAKS/STRLY B74 .... 44 D4
ey St DARL/WED WS10 .... 56 A5
ey Wood Cl
OAKS/STRLY B74 .... 45 E4
ot Flds YDLY B25 .... 129 H4
kes Rd HAG/WOL DY9 .... 137 E1
kestone Cft CBROM B36 .... 112 A1
ott Rd STETCH B33 .... 130 C1
yhouse Cl WSL WS1 .... 57 F1
yhouse La WSL WS1 .... 5 F7
WSL WS1 .... 57 F1
tley Cl
GN/SDN/BHAMAIR B26 .... 130 C3
twell Rd WOLVN WV10 .... 12 D3
therley La LICHS WS14 .... 32 D1
dbridge Rd
HWD/FDBR/MGN B37 .... 113 H5
d Brook La BLOX/PEL WS3 ..... 28 D1
der Gv
LE/KHTH/YWD B14 .... 178 C3
de Way Gdns
WK/WKHTH B38 .... 190 B1
dfield Rd STETCH B33 .... 113 E5
dham Gv COVEN WV9 .... 12 A4
dhouse La BVILLE B30 .... 160 B4
dhouse Rd WOLVN WV10 .... 23 F1
draught La RMSLY B62 .... 172 D4
Fordrift
HWD/FDBR/MGN B37 .... 149 E2
drough YDLY B25 .... 128 D5
drough Av BORD B9 .... 128 C1
drough La BORD B9 .... 128 C2
Fordrough
OAKS/STRLY B74 .... 47 E4
FLD/LBR B31 .... 175 H5
HLY B90 .... 193 E1
ls Rd SHLY B90 .... 193 G1
St SMTHWKW B67 .... 106 B3
WSLW WS2 .... 56 C1
WSNGN B18 .... 108 B4
water Rd
OAKS/STRLY B74 .... 60 B2
draft Cl RIDG/WDGT B32 ..... 140 C5
draft St HALE B63 .... 137 G2
drove La HIA/OLT B92 .... 165 G4
est Av BLOX/PEL WS3 .... 27 H3
st Cl FOAKS/STRLY B74 .... 60 A1
MTHWK B66 .... 106 A2
est Ct DOR/KN B93 .... 196 D5
est Dl RBRY B45 .... 188 B2
st Dr CDYHTH B64 .... 121 F2
RBN B17 .... 142 B1
st Ga SHHTH WV12 .... 26 B2
st Hill Rd
GN/SDN/BHAMAIR B26 .... 148 A2
st La BLOX/PEL WS3 .... 28 A5
SLW WS2 .... 27 H5
st Pk WALM/CURD B76 .... 63 E4
st Pl BLOX/PEL WS3 .... 28 A4
St CBHAM B2 .... 3 G5
st Rd DOR/KN B93 .... 197 E5
UDN DY1 .... 84 C2
LGLYGN/QTN B68 .... 123 G5
OS/BIL B13 .... 144 C4
DLY B25 .... 146 C1
st Wy HLYWD B47 .... 192 D2
e Cl CDSL WV8 .... 22 A1
e Cft WALM/CURD B76 .... 78 D5
e La ALDR WS9 .... 31 F4
DYHTH B64 .... 120 B4
OAKS/STRLY B74 .... 32 A4
AG/WOL DY9 .... 184 B1
HTH/SAND B71 .... 72 C5
GSWFD DY6 .... 99 E1
DD DY10 .... 168 B4
MSLY B62 .... 139 E2
ALM/CURD B76 .... 94 D1
e Leys WMBN WV5 .... 64 C5
e Rd BLOX/PEL WS3 .... 17 H2
ARL/WED WS10 .... 54 D2
HHTH WV12 .... 40 A1
TRBR DY8 .... 135 F1
e St DARL/WED WS10 .... 55 G4
Forge HALE B63 .... 120 A4
e Valley Wy WMBN WV5 ..... 64 C5
e Wy OLDBY B69 .... 104 C3
Formans Rd SPARK B11 .... 145 G4
Formby Av
DUNHL/THL/PER WV6 .... 34 B1
Formby Wy BLOX/PEL WS3 .... 16 C4
Forrell Gv NFLD/LBR B31 .... 189 H1
Forrest Av WNSFLD WV11 .... 15 E3
Forrester St WSLW WS2 .... 4 A3
Forrester Street Prec
WSLW WS2 .... 4 A3
Forster St SMTHWKW B67 .... 106 A2
VAUX/NECH B7 .... 127 G1
Forsythia Cl NFLD/LBR B31 .... 158 B2
Forsythia Gv CDSL WV8 .... 10 C4
Fort Crs ALDR WS9 .... 19 G4
Forth Dr
CHWD/FDBR/MGN B37 .... 114 B5
Forth Gv HWK/WKHTH B38 .... 176 C5
Forth Wy RMSLY B62 .... 122 C4
Fortnum Cl STETCH B33 .... 131 E2
Forton Cl DUNHL/THL/PER WV6 .. 35 F3
Fort Pkwy ERDE/BCHGN B24 .... 93 H5
Forward Rd
LGN/SDN/BHAMAIR B26 .... 149 E4
Fosbrooke Rd SMHTH B10 .... 129 E4
Fosseway Dr ERDW/GRVHL B23 .. 76 C3
Fossil Dr RBRY B45 .... 188 A1
Foster Av BILS/COS WV14 .... 68 B2
Foster Gdns WSNGN B18 * 107 H3
Foster Gn
DUNHL/THL/PER WV6 .... 34 C2
Foster Pl STRBR DY8 .... 135 E1
Foster Rd WOLVN WV10 .... 23 G4
Foster St BLOX/PEL WS3 .... 27 H2
DARL/WED WS10 .... 55 F1
Foster St East STRBR DY8 .... 135 G2
Foster Wy DIG/EDG B5 .... 143 G2
Fotherley Brook Rd ALDR WS9 ... 31 F5
Foundry La BLOX/PEL WS3 .... 17 G4
SMTHWK B66 .... 107 F2
Foundry Rd KGSWFD DY6 .... 99 F1
WSNGN B18 .... 107 F4
Foundry St BILS/COS WV14 .... 68 C2
KGSWFD DY6 .... 99 G1
TPTN/OCK DY4 .... 69 E3
Fountain Arcade Chambers
DUDN DY1 * 84 C5
Fountain Cl NFLD/LBR B31 .... 189 E2
Fountain Ct CBHAMNE B4 * 3 G3
Fountain La BILS/COS WV14 .... 68 D3
OLDBY B69 .... 86 D5
Fountain Rd HRBN B17 .... 124 D3
Fountains Rd BLOX/PEL WS3 .... 16 A5
Fountains Wy BLOX/PEL WS3 .... 16 A5
Four Acres RIDG/WDGT B32 .... 140 C3
Four Ashes Rd DOR/KN B93 .... 196 C4
Four Crosses Rd
RUSH/SHEL WS4 .... 29 E1
Fourlands Av
CSCFLD/WYGN B72 .... 77 H4
Fourlands Rd NFLD/LBR B31 ..... 158 A4
Four Oaks Common Rd
FOAKS/STRLY B74 .... 46 C2
Four Oaks Rd FOAKS/STRLY B74 .. 46 D3
Four Stones Cl SOLH B91 .... 181 G4
Four Stones Gv DIG/EDG B5 .... 143 H1
Fourth Av BORD B9 .... 128 D2
BRWNH WS8 .... 9 G4
SLYOAK B29 .... 143 G4
WOLVN WV10 .... 23 F4
Four Winds Rd DUDS DY2 .... 103 E2
Fowey Cl WALM/CURD B76 .... 78 C4
Fowey Rd BKDE/SHDE B34 .... 112 B3
Fowgay Dr SOLH B91 .... 181 F4
Fowler Cl
DUNHL/THL/PER WV6 .... 20 C4
SMTHWK B66 .... 106 C1
Fowler Rd MGN/WHC B75 .... 63 G3
Fowler St BKHL/PFLD WV2 .... 52 A2
VAUX/NECH B7 .... 109 H4
Fowlmere Rd
PBAR/PBCH B42 .... 74 B3
Foxbury Dr DOR/KN B93 .... 197 E5
Fox Cl MGN/WHC B75 .... 63 F1
Foxcote Av HDSW B21 .... 107 G2
Foxcote Cl SHLY B90 .... 180 D5
Foxcote Dr SHLY B90 .... 180 D5
Foxcote La HAG/WOL DY9 .... 137 F4
Fox Covert STRBR DY8 .... 135 E2
Fox Crs SPARK B11 * 145 F3
Foxdale Dr BRLYHL DY5 .... 118 D1
Foxdale Gv STETCH B33 .... 131 E2
Foxes Meadow BVILLE B30 .... 176 D1
WALM/CURD B76 .... 78 C3
Foxes Rdg CDYHTH B64 .... 121 E4
Foxfield Dr STRBR DY8 .... 135 G4
Fox Foot Dr BRLYHL DY5 .... 101 E5
Foxford Cl CBROM B36 .... 95 F5
CSCFLD/WYGN B72 .... 77 G4
Foxglove Cl ACGN B27 .... 163 F1
BLOX/PEL WS3 .... 18 A2
WNSFLD WV11 .... 25 E5
Foxglove Crs
CHWD/FDBR/MGN B37 .... 131 G1
Foxglove Rd DUDN DY1 .... 83 H2
Foxglove Wy
ERDW/GRVHL B23 .... 75 H4
HDSW B21 .... 107 F2
Fox Green Crs ACGN B27 .... 146 A5
Fox Gv ACGN B27 .... 146 A5
Fox Hl SLYOAK B29 .... 159 E2
Fox Hill Cl SLYOAK B29 .... 159 E2
Fox Hill Rd MGN/WHC B75 .... 48 C3
Foxhills Pk DUDS DY2 .... 102 C5
Foxhills Rd
ETTPK/GDPK/PENN WV4 .... 50 C5
STRBR DY8 .... 117 H3
Foxhollies Dr HALE B63 .... 138 A3
Fox Hollies Rd ACGN B27 .... 146 B4
WALM/CURD B76 .... 78 B3
Fox Hollow
DUNHL/THL/PER WV6 .... 35 G3
Fox Hollow Cl RBRY B45 .... 188 C1
Foxhope Cl HWK/WKHTH B38 .... 177 F4
Foxhunt Rd HALE B63 .... 138 A5
Foxland Av RBRY B45 .... 188 C1
Foxland Cl
CHWD/FDBR/MGN B37 .... 132 D2
SHLY B90 .... 194 D4
Foxlands Av
ETTPK/GDPK/PENN WV4 .... 50 D5
Foxlands Crs
ETTPK/GDPK/PENN WV4 .... 50 C5
Foxlands Dr CSCFLD/WYGN B72 .. 77 H4
ETTPK/GDPK/PENN WV4 .... 50 C5
SEDG DY3 .... 83 F1
Foxlea Rd HALE B63 .... 154 D1
Foxley Dr SOLH B91 .... 166 B5
Foxmeadow Cl SEDG DY3 .... 67 G4
Foxoak St CDYHTH B64 .... 120 C3
Fox's La WOLV WV1 .... 23 F5
Fox St DIG/EDG B5 .... 3 J4
DUDN DY1 .... 68 C5
Foxton Rd WASH/WDE B8 .... 110 D4
Fox Wk ALDR WS9 .... 19 H4
Foxwell Gv BORD B9 .... 129 F2
Foxwell Rd BORD B9 .... 129 F2
Foxwood Av GTB/HAM B43 .... 59 F5
Foxwood Gv
CHWD/FDBR/MGN B37 .... 113 H4
Foxwood Rd
CHWD/FDBR/MGN B37 .... 113 H4
Foxyards Cl TPTN/OCK DY4 * 84 D1
Foxyards Rd TPTN/OCK DY4 .... 84 D1
Foyle Rd HWK/WKHTH B38 .... 176 D4
Fozdar Crs BILS/COS WV14 .... 68 A2
Fradley Cl BVILLE B30 .... 176 B1
Framefield Dr SOLH B91 .... 165 G4
Framlingham Gv
DUNHL/THL/PER WV6 .... 35 E2
Frampton Cl BVILLE B30 .... 159 F3
CHWD/FDBR/MGN B37 .... 132 D1
Frampton Wy GTB/HAM B43 .... 59 H4
Frances Dr BLOX/PEL WS3 .... 16 D5
Frances Rd BVILLE B30 .... 160 A5
ERDW/GRVHL B23 .... 92 B3
LOZ/NWT B19 .... 108 C1
Franchise Gdns
DARL/WED WS10 .... 55 H2
Franchise St DARL/WED WS10 ..... 55 G3
PBAR/PBCH B42 .... 91 E4
Francis Cl FOAKS/STRLY B74 .... 45 F5
KGSWFD DY6 .... 99 H1
Francis Rd LDYWD/EDGR B16 .... 126 A3
SMTHWKW B67 .... 105 H4
STETCH B33 .... 129 H1
STRBR DY8 .... 134 C2
YDLY B25 .... 146 A1
Francis St VAUX/NECH B7 .... 109 G5
WBROM B70 .... 87 H5
WOLV WV1 .... 37 E1
Francis Wk NFLD/LBR B31 .... 189 G1
Francis Ward Cl
HHTH/SAND B71 .... 71 E3
Frankburn Rd
FOAKS/STRLY B74 .... 45 E5
Frank Fisher Wy WBROM B70 ..... 87 G4
Frankfort St LOZ/NWT B19 .... 108 D4
Frankholmes Dr SHLY B90 .... 195 G2
Frankley Av RMSLY B62 .... 139 H2
Frankley Beeches Rd
NFLD/LBR B31 .... 174 D2
Frankley Gn RIDG/WDGT B32 .... 156 B5
Frankley Green La
RIDG/WDGT B32 .... 156 D5
Frankley Hill La
RIDG/WDGT B32 .... 173 H3
Frankley La RIDG/WDGT B32 ..... 157 G4
Frankley Lodge Rd
NFLD/LBR B31 .... 174 D1
Frankley Rd LGLYGN/QTN B68 ... 123 E4
Frankley Ter HRBN B17 * 141 H2
Franklin Rd BVILLE B30 .... 159 H5
Franklin St WSNGN B18 .... 107 G4
Franklin Wy BVILLE B30 .... 159 H3
Franklyn Cl
DUNHL/THL/PER WV6 .... 20 C5
Frank Rd SMTHWKW B67 .... 106 A3
Frank St BHTH/HG B12 .... 127 F5
Franks Wy STETCH B33 .... 130 A2
Frank Tommey Cl
BLKHTH/ROWR B65 * 122 A3
Frankton Cl HIA/OLT B92 .... 147 H5
Frankton Gv BORD B9 .... 129 F2
Fraser Rd SPARK B11 .... 145 E2
Fraser St BILS/COS WV14 .... 54 A2
Frayne Av KGSWFD DY6 .... 99 G2
Freasley Cl SHLY B90 .... 180 D2
Freasley Rd BKDE/SHDE B34 ..... 113 F4
Freda Ri OLDBY B69 .... 104 B1
Freda Rd WBROM B70 .... 87 H5
Fredas Gv HRBN B17 .... 141 G3
Frederick Rd AST/WIT B6 .... 109 F1
EDG B15 .... 126 B4
ERDW/GRVHL B23 .... 92 B4
LGLYGN/QTN B68 .... 123 H5
SCFLD/BOLD B73 .... 77 E1
SLYOAK B29 .... 142 B5
SPARK B11 .... 145 E3
STETCH B33 .... 129 H1
WNSFLD WV11 .... 24 C5
Fredericks Cl STRBR DY8 .... 135 E3
Frederick St BKHL/PFLD WV2 .... 7 F7
CBHAMW B1 .... 2 C2
WBROM B70 .... 87 G2
WSLW WS2 .... 4 B4
Frederick William St
WLNHL WV13 .... 39 H3
Fred Smith Cl DARL/WED WS10 ... 56 B3
Freeland Gv KGSWFD DY6 .... 100 B5
Freeman Dr WALM/CURD B76 ..... 63 F4
Freeman Pl BILS/COS WV14 .... 39 E5
Freeman Rd DARL/WED WS10 ..... 56 C5
VAUX/NECH B7 .... 109 H4
Freeman St DIG/EDG B5 .... 3 H5
WOLVN WV10 .... 37 H3
Freemantle Dr
BKDE/SHDE B34 .... 113 G3
Freer Rd AST/WIT B6 .... 108 D1
Freer St WSL WS1 .... 4 E3
Freeth Rd BRWNH WS8 .... 9 G3
Freeth St LDYWD/EDGR B16 .... 126 A2
OLDBY B69 .... 104 D1
Freezeland St BILS/COS WV14 ..... 53 F2
Fremont Dr DUDN DY1 .... 83 G3
French Rd DUDS DY2 .... 85 E5
Frensham Cl
CHWD/FDBR/MGN B37 .... 132 C2
Frensham Wy HRBN B17 .... 142 A1
Frenshaw Gv KGSTG B44 .... 75 F3
Freshwater Dr BRLYHL DY5 .... 118 D3
Friardale Cl DARL/WED WS10 ...... 56 D5
Friar Park Rd DARL/WED WS10 ... 56 C5
Friars Cl STRBR DY8 .... 117 G1
Friars Gorse KINVER DY7 .... 117 G5
Friar St DARL/WED WS10 .... 56 B5
Friary Av SHLY B90 .... 195 G2
Friary Crs RUSH/SHEL WS4 .... 29 E4
Friary Dr FOAKS/STRLY B74 .... 46 D2
Friary Gdns HDSW B21 .... 89 F4
Friary Rd BFLD/HDSWWD B20 ..... 89 G4
Friday La HIA/OLT B92 .... 183 H1
Friesland Dr WOLV WV1 .... 38 B2
Friezeland Rd WSLW WS2 .... 41 F3
Friezland La BRWNH WS8 .... 19 G2
Friezland Wy BRWNH WS8 .... 19 G2
Frinton Gv HDSW B21 .... 107 E2
Friston Av LDYWD/EDGR B16 .... 2 A7
Frodesley Rd
LGN/SDN/BHAMAIR B26 .... 130 D4
Froggatt Rd BILS/COS WV14 .... 53 H1
Froggatts Ride
WALM/CURD B76 .... 63 F5
Frogmill Rd RBRY B45 .... 174 B3
Frome Cl SEDG DY3 .... 83 F4
Frome Dr WNSFLD WV11 .... 24 C5
Frome Wy
ALE/KHTH/YWD B14 .... 160 D4
Frost St BKHL/PFLD WV2 .... 53 E2
Froxmere Cl SOLH B91 .... 181 H5
Froyle Cl DUNHL/THL/PER WV6 ... 21 G5
Froysell St WLNHL WV13 .... 39 H3
Fryer Rd NFLD/LBR B31 .... 189 H1
Fryers Cl BLOX/PEL WS3 .... 27 F3
Fryers Rd WSLW WS2 .... 27 E4
Fryer St WOLV WV1 .... 7 G3
Fuchsia Dr COVEN WV9 .... 11 H4
Fugelmere Cl HRBN B17 .... 124 B5
Fulbrook Gv SLYOAK B29 .... 158 B2
Fulbrook Rd DUDN DY1 .... 84 A5
Fulford Cl HLYWD B47 .... 193 E3
Fulford Dr WALM/CURD B76 .... 94 D1
Fulford Gv
LGN/SDN/BHAMAIR B26 .... 148 A1
Fulford Hall Rd HOCK/TIA B94 ... 193 F5
Fulham Rd SPARK B11 .... 144 D2
Fullbrook Cl SHLY B90 .... 195 G3
Fullbrook Rd DSYBK/YTR WS5 ..... 57 E3
Fullelove Rd BRWNH WS8 .... 19 G1
Fullerton Cl CDSL WV8 .... 22 A1
Fullwood Crs DUDS DY2 .... 101 G3
Fullwoods End BILS/COS WV14 ... 68 C3
Fulmer Wk WSNGN B18 * 126 A1
Fulwell Gv KGSTG B44 .... 75 G3
Fulwell Ms
CHWD/FDBR/MGN B37 .... 132 B4
Fulwood Av RMSLY B62 .... 122 D4
Furber Pl KGSWFD DY6 .... 100 B3
Furlong La HALE B63 .... 137 G1
Furlong Meadow
NFLD/LBR B31 .... 176 A3
Furlongs Rd SEDG DY3 .... 67 F5
The Furlongs STRBR DY8 .... 135 H4
WNSFLD WV11 .... 24 B5
The Furlong DARL/WED WS10 ..... 55 G3
Furlong Wk SEDG DY3 .... 83 F2
Furnace Cl WMBN WV5 .... 80 C1
Furnace Hl HALE B63 .... 138 D1
Furnace La HALE B63 .... 138 D2
Furnace Pde TPTN/OCK DY4 .... 69 E5
Furnace Rd DUDS DY2 .... 102 C1
Furness Cl BLOX/PEL WS3 .... 16 B4
Furst St BRWNH WS8 .... 9 G4
Furzebank Wy SHHTH WV12 .... 40 C1
Furze Wy DSYBK/YTR WS5 .... 43 F5

G

The Gables ERDE/BCHGN B24 ...... 93 H2
WNSFLD WV11 .... 15 E3
Gaddesby Rd
ALE/KHTH/YWD B14 .... 161 F2
Gadds Dr BLKHTH/ROWR B65 .... 104 B5
Gadsby Av WNSFLD WV11 .... 25 G3
Gads Gn DUDS DY2 .... 102 D4
Gads Green Crs DUDS DY2 .... 103 E3
Gads La DUDN DY1 .... 84 C5
WBROM B70 .... 87 E3
Gadwall Cft ERDW/GRVHL B23 .... 91 H3
Gail Cl ALDR WS9 .... 19 H3
Gailey Cft KGSTG B44 .... 60 A5
Gailey Pk WOLVN WV10 * 12 C1
Gail Pk BDMR/CCFT WV3 .... 50 D1
Gainford Cl CDSL WV8 .... 22 B1
Gainford Rd KGSTG B44 .... 76 A2
Gainsborough Crs
DOR/KN B93 .... 197 E2
GTB/HAM B43 .... 59 H4
Gainsborough Dr
DUNHL/THL/PER WV6 .... 34 D1
Gainsborough Hl STRBR DY8 ..... 135 G4
Gainsborough Pl DUDN DY1 .... 83 G4
Gainsborough Rd
PBAR/PBCH B42 .... 74 B5
Gainsford Dr RMSLY B62 .... 138 D1
Gairloch Rd SHHTH WV12 .... 25 H1
Gaitskell Ter OLDBY B69 .... 86 B4
Gaitswell Wy SMTHWK B66 .... 106 B2
Galahad Wy DARL/WED WS10 ...... 71 E1
Galbraith Cl BILS/COS WV14 .... 68 D3
Galena Wy AST/WIT B6 .... 109 E3
Gale Wk BLKHTH/ROWR B65 ...... 103 F4
Gallery Sq WSLW WS2 .... 4 D3
Galloway Av BKDE/SHDE B34 .... 112 B3
Galton Cl ERDE/BCHGN B24 .... 94 B2
TPTN/OCK DY4 .... 70 A5
Galton Dr DUDS DY2 .... 102 B3
GTB/HAM B43 .... 73 H2
Galton Rd SMTHWKW B67 .... 124 B3
Galtons La HAG/WOL DY9 .... 185 E1
Gamesfield Gn
BDMR/CCFT WV3 .... 36 B4
Gammage St DUDS DY2 .... 102 B1
Gandy Rd SHHTH WV12 .... 25 G4
Gannahs Farm Cl
WALM/CURD B76 .... 63 F5
Gannow Green La RBRY B45 ..... 173 E4
Gannow Manor Crs RBRY B45 ... 173 G4
Gannow Manor Gdns
RBRY B45 .... 173 H4
Gannow Rd RBRY B45 .... 187 G1
Gannow Wk RBRY B45 .... 187 G1
Ganton Rd BLOX/PEL WS3 .... 16 C3
Garden Cl DOR/KN B93 .... 196 D2
RBRY B45 .... 174 A3
WASH/WDE B8 .... 111 E4
Garden Crs BLOX/PEL WS3 .... 17 H4
Garden Cft ALDR WS9 .... 30 B3
Gardeners Wy WMBN WV5 .... 80 D2
Garden Gv BFLD/HDSWWD B20 ... 73 G5
The Gardens
CSCFLD/WYGN B72 .... 77 F3
ERDW/GRVHL B23 .... 92 C3
Garden St WSLW WS2 .... 4 D1
Garden Wk BILS/COS WV14 .... 54 B2
SEDG DY3 .... 83 E4
Garfield Rd
LGN/SDN/BHAMAIR B26 .... 130 D4
Garland Crs RMSLY B62 .... 122 C4
The Garlands WNSFLD WV11 .... 24 C3
Garland St BORD B9 .... 128 A1
Garland Wy NFLD/LBR B31 .... 175 H1
Garman Cl GTB/HAM B43 .... 73 G1
Garner Cl BILS/COS WV14 .... 53 H5
Garnet Av GTB/HAM B43 .... 59 F5
Garnett Dr MGN/WHC B75 .... 63 E2
Garrard Gdns SCFLD/BOLD B73 ... 62 B3
Garrat St BRLYHL DY5 .... 101 G4
Garratt Cl LGLYGN/QTN B68 ...... 105 G5
Garratt's La CDYHTH B64 .... 121 F2
Garret Cl KGSWFD DY6 .... 81 H5
Garretts Green La
LGN/SDN/BHAMAIR B26 .... 130 C5
Garrick Cl DUDN DY1 .... 83 H3
Garrick St WOLV WV1 .... 7 G5
Garrington St DARL/WED WS10 .. 55 E1
Garrison Circ CBHAMNE B4 .... 127 G2
Garrison La BORD B9 .... 127 H2
Garrison St BORD B9 .... 127 H2
The Garth ALE/KHTH/YWD B14 .. 179 F1
Garway Gv YDLY B25 .... 146 B1
Garwood Rd
LGN/SDN/BHAMAIR B26 .... 130 B2
Gas St CBHAMW B1 .... 2 C6
Gatacre St SEDG DY3 .... 83 F3
Gatcombe Cl WOLVN WV10 .... 13 F3
Gatcombe Rd DUDN DY1 .... 83 G4
Gatehouse Fold DUDS DY2 .... 84 D5
Gate La DOR/KN B93 .... 196 A5
SCFLD/BOLD B73 .... 76 D1
Gateley Rd LGLYGN/QTN B68 ..... 123 H5
Gate St SEDG DY3 .... 67 G4
TPTN/OCK DY4 .... 85 G4
WASH/WDE B8 .... 110 B4
Gatis St DUNHL/THL/PER WV6 ..... 36 C1
Gatwick Rd CVALE B35 .... 94 D2
Gauden Rd HAG/WOL DY9 .... 153 F1
Gavin Wy AST/WIT B6 .... 91 F2
Gawne La CDYHTH B64 .... 103 E5
Gaydon Cl
DUNHL/THL/PER WV6 .... 20 C5
Gaydon Gv SLYOAK B29 .... 141 G5
Gaydon Pl SCFLD/BOLD B73 .... 62 B4
Gaydon Rd ALDR WS9 .... 44 A1
HIA/OLT B92 .... 148 B4
Gayfield Av BRLYHL DY5 .... 119 F4
Gay Hill La HWK/WKHTH B38 ...... 177 F5
Gayhurst Dr YDLY B25 .... 130 A4
Gayle Gv ACGN B27 .... 163 G2
Gayton Rd HHTH/SAND B71 .... 71 H5
Geach St LOZ/NWT B19 .... 108 D3
Gedney Cl SHLY B90 .... 179 E2
Geeson Cl CVALE B35 .... 94 D2
Gee St LOZ/NWT B19 .... 108 D3
Gem Vls SPARK B11 * 128 A5
Geneva Rd TPTN/OCK DY4 .... 84 D2
Genge Av
ETTPK/GDPK/PENN WV4 .... 52 C4
Genners Ap NFLD/LBR B31 .... 157 H2
Genners La NFLD/LBR B31 .... 157 H3
Genthorn Cl
ETTPK/GDPK/PENN WV4 .... 52 D4
Gentian Cl NFLD/LBR B31 .... 158 B4
Geoffrey Cl WALM/CURD B76 ...... 78 D4
Geoffrey Pl SPARK B11 * 145 E4
Geoffrey Rd SHLY B90 .... 179 H2
SPARK B11 .... 145 E4
George Arthur Rd
WASH/WDE B8 .... 110 B5
George Av BLKHTH/ROWR B65 .. 122 B2
George Bird Cl SMTHWK B66 * ... 106 C3
George Cl DUDS DY2 .... 103 E1
George Frederick Rd
SCFLD/BOLD B73 .... 60 C4
George Henry Rd
TPTN/OCK DY4 .... 70 C4
George Rd CSHL/WTROR B46 ...... 96 C3
EDG B15 .... 126 B4
ERDW/GRVHL B23 .... 92 A3
GTB/HAM B43 .... 73 H1
HALE B63 .... 138 B3
LGLYGN/QTN B68 .... 123 G2
SCFLD/BOLD B73 .... 76 B2
SLYOAK B29 .... 142 C5
SOLH B91 .... 182 A2
TPTN/OCK DY4 .... 68 D5
YDLY B25 .... 146 A1
George St BHTH/HG B12 .... 144 B2
BKHL/PFLD WV2 .... 7 F6
CBHAMW B1 .... 2 C4
DUDN DY1 .... 68 B5
HDSW B21 .... 107 E1
LOZ/NWT B19 .... 108 B2
STRBR DY8 .... 118 B3
WBROM B70 .... 87 H4
WLNHL WV13 .... 39 G1
WSL WS1 .... 4 E5
George St West WSNGN B18 ...... 108 A5
Georgina Av BILS/COS WV14 ...... 53 H5
Geraldine Rd YDLY B25 .... 129 F5
Gerald Rd STRBR DY8 .... 118 A5
Geranium Gv BORD B9 .... 128 D1
Geranium Rd DUDS DY2 .... 103 F1
Gerardsfield Rd STETCH B33 ...... 131 F1
Germander Dr DSYBK/YTR WS5 .. 57 G5
Gerrard Cl LOZ/NWT B19 .... 108 D2
Gerrard Rd WLNHL WV13 .... 39 E4
Gerrard St LOZ/NWT B19 .... 108 C3

Gervase Dr *DUDN* DY1 .... 84 C3
Geston Rd *DUDN* DY1 .... 101 H1
Gibbet La *KINVER* DY7 .... 134 A3
Gibbins Rd *SLYOAK* B29 .... 159 E1
Gibbons Gv
  DUNHL/THL/PER WV6 .... 36 A1
Gibbons Hill Rd *SEDG* DY3 .... 67 F1
Gibbons La *BRLYHL* DY5 .... 100 C2
Gibbons Rd
  DUNHL/THL/PER WV6 .... 36 B1
  MGN/WHC B75 .... 47 F2
Gibbs Hill Rd *NFLD/LBR* B31 .... 189 H1
Gibbs Rd *HAG/WOL* DY9 .... 137 E2
Gibbs St *DUNHL/THL/PER* WV6 .... 36 C1
Gibb St *BORD* B9 .... 3 K7
Gibson Dr *BFLD/HDSWWD* B20 .... 108 B1
Gibson Rd
  BFLD/HDSWWD B20 .... 108 B1
  DUNHL/THL/PER WV6 .... 34 C2
Gideon Cl *YDLY* B25 .... 146 D1
Gideons Cl *SEDG* DY3 .... 83 F1
Giffard Rd *WOLV* WV1 .... 53 F1
  WOLVN WV10 .... 13 E4
Giggetty La *WMBN* WV5 .... 64 C5
Gigmill Wy *STRBR* DY8 .... 135 E3
Gilbanks Rd *STRBR* DY8 .... 117 H5
Gilberry Cl *DOR/KN* B93 .... 197 E3
Gilbert Av *OLDBY* B69 .... 103 H0
Gilbert Cl *WNSFLD* WV11 .... 40 B3
Gilbert La *WMBN* WV5 .... 65 F4
Gilbert Rd *SMTHWK* B66 .... 106 D5
Gilbertstone Av
  LGN/SDN/BHAMAIR B26 .... 147 E2
Gilbert St *TPTN/OCK* DY4 .... 85 F4
Gilbeys Cl *STRBR* DY8 .... 118 A3
Gilby Rd *LDYWD/EDGR* B16 .... 126 A3
Gilchrist Dr *EDG* B15 .... 125 C4
Gildas Av *HWK/WKHTH* B38 .... 174 B5
Giles Cl *HIA/OLT* B92 .... 165 H5
  STETCH B33 .... 130 A1
Giles Rd *LGLYGN/QTN* B68 .... 105 F4
Gilldown Pl *EDG* B15 .... 126 B5
Gilldown Wy *HRBN* B17 .... 124 D5
Gilling Gv *BKDE/SHDE* B34 .... 112 C3
Gillingham La *DARL/WED* WS10 .... 56 D4
Gillity Av *DSYBK/YTR* WS5 .... 42 D5
Gillity Cl *DSYBK/YTR* WS5 .... 42 D5
Gilliver Rd *SHLY* B90 .... 180 B3
Gillman Cl
  LGN/SDN/BHAMAIR B26 .... 148 B3
Gillott Cl *SOLH* B91 .... 182 C2
Gillott Rd *LDYWD/EDGR* B16 .... 125 F2
Gillows Cft *SHLY* B90 .... 195 G5
Gillscroft Rd *STETCH* B33 .... 130 C1
Gill St *DUDS* DY2 .... 121 E1
  WBROM B70 .... 87 G5
Gilmorton Cl *HRBN* B17 .... 124 D5
  SOLH B91 .... 182 A4
Gilpin Cl *WASH/WDE* B8 .... 111 G3
Gilpin Crs *BLOX/PEL* WS3 .... 18 A3
Gilson Dr *CSHL/WTROR* B46 .... 114 D1
Gilson Rd *CSHL/WTROR* B46 .... 115 E1
Gilson St *TPTN/OCK* DY4 .... 70 A3
Gilson Wy
  CHWD/FDBR/MGN B37 .... 114 A4
Gilwell Rd *BKDE/SHDE* B34 .... 113 G3
Gimble Wk *HRBN* B17 .... 124 B4
Gipsy La *ERW/CRVHL* B23 .... 69 H1
  WLNHL WV13 .... 39 H4
Gisborn Cl *SMHTH* B10 .... 127 H4
Gladeside Cl *RUSH/SHEL* WS4 .... 29 E2
The Glades *ALDR* WS9 .... 30 B3
The Glade *CDSL* WV8 .... 22 A1
  FOAKS/STRLY B74 .... 45 E4
  HAG/WOL DY9 .... 136 C2
  LGN/SDN/BHAMAIR B26 .... 148 B3
Gladstone Dr *OLDBY* B69 .... 86 A5
Gladstone Gv *KGSWFD* DY6 .... 99 H1
Gladstone Rd *DOR/KN* B93 .... 199 E1
  ERW/GRVHL B23 .... 92 B3
  LGN/SDN/BHAMAIR B26 .... 146 D1
  SPARK B11 .... 144 D1
  STRBR DY8 .... 134 D1
Gladstone St *AST/WIT* B6 .... 109 J1
  DARL/WED WS10 .... 55 G2
  HHTH/SAND B71 .... 87 G1
  WSLW WS2 .... 41 H1
Gladys Rd *SMTHWKW* B67 .... 124 B2
  YDLY B25 .... 129 F5
Gladys Ter *SMTHWKW* B67 * 124 C2
Glaisdale Gdns
  DUNHL/THL/PER WV6 .... 34 D1
Glaisdale Rd *HLGN/YWD* B28 .... 163 E2
Glaisher Gv *WLNHL* WV13 .... 40 A3
Glaisher Dr *WOLVN* WV10 .... 12 C5
Glamis Rd *SHHTH* WV12 .... 25 H3
Glanville Dr *MGN/WHC* B75 .... 47 H1
Glasbury Cft *HWK/WKHTH* B38 .... 190 C1
Glascote Cl *SHLY* B90 .... 180 A2
Glascote Gv *BKDE/SHDE* B34 .... 113 E3
Glaslyn Av *BLKHTH/ROWR* B65 .... 121 H2
Glassford Dr
  DUNHL/THL/PER WV6 .... 22 A4
Glasshouse Hi *STRBR* DY8 .... 135 H4
Glastonbury Crs *BLOX/PEL* WS3 .... 16 A5
Glastonbury Rd
  ALE/KHTH/YWD B14 .... 162 A5
  HHTH/SAND B71 .... 71 H5
Glastonbury Wy *BLOX/PEL* WS3 .... 26 C1
Glaston Dr *SOLH* B91 .... 181 G5
Gleads Cft *RMSLY* B62 .... 140 A4
Gleave Rd *SLYOAK* B29 .... 159 G1
Glebe Dr *SCFLD/BOLD* B73 .... 76 D3
Glebe Farm Rd
  BKDE/SHDE B34 .... 112 C4
Glebefields Rd *TPTN/OCK* DY4 .... 69 G3
Glebeland Cl *LDYWD/EDGR* B16 * 2 D7
Glebe La *STRBR* DY8 .... 135 E3
Glebe Pl *DARL/WED* WS10 .... 54 D2
Glebe Rd *SOLH* B91 .... 181 H2
  WLNHL WV13 .... 39 F5
The Glebe *WSL* WS1 .... 4 D6
The Glebe *HAG/WOL* DY9 .... 184 C2
Glenavon Rd
  ALE/KHTH/YWD B14 .... 178 C2
Glen Cl *RUSH/SHEL* WS4 .... 42 C2
Glencoe Rd *LDYWD/EDGR* B16 .... 107 E5
Glen Ct *BDMR/CCFT* WV3 .... 36 A3
  CDSL WV8 .... 10 C3

Glencroft Rd *HIA/OLT* B92 .... 148 B4
Glendale Cl *BDMR/CCFT* WV3 .... 35 G5
  HALE B63 .... 138 D3
Glendale Dr *STETCH* B33 .... 130 B1
  WMBN WV5 .... 65 E5
Glendene Crs
  HWK/WKHTH B38 .... 190 A1
Glen Devon Cl *RBRY* B45 .... 174 A3
Glendon Rd *ERW/GRVHL* B23 .... 76 B5
Glendon Wy *DOR/KN* B93 .... 196 C5
Glendower Rd *ALDR* WS9 .... 30 B1
  PBAR/PBCH B42 .... 90 C1
Gleneagles Dr *GTB/HAM* B43 .... 58 C5
  MGN/WHC B75 .... 48 B1
  OLDBY B69 .... 103 G2
Gleneagles Rd *BLOX/PEL* WS3 .... 16 B4
  DUNHL/THL/PER WV6 .... 20 D5
  LGN/SDN/BHAMAIR B26 .... 130 C4
Glenelg Dr *STRBR* DY8 .... 135 H5
Glenelg Ms *DSYBK/YTR* WS5 .... 58 B3
Glenfern Rd *BILS/COS* WV14 .... 68 A3
Glenfield *CDSL* WV8 .... 11 C5
Glenfield Cl *SOLH* B91 .... 182 A5
  WALM/CURD B76 .... 63 E5
Glenfield Gv *SLYOAK* B29 .... 160 A1
Glengarry Cl *WNSFLD* WV11 * 157 F3
Glengarry Gdns
  BDMR/CCFT WV3 .... 36 B4
Glenhill Dr *HWK/WKHTH* B38 .... 177 E5
Glenhurst Cl *WSLW* WS2 .... 40 B2
Glenmead Rd *KGSTG* B44 .... 74 D3
Glenmore Cl *BDMR/CCFT* WV3 .... 51 E1
Glenmore Dr *HWK/WKHTH* B38 .... 176 B4
Glen Park Rd *SEDG* DY3 .... 83 F4
Glenpark Rd *WASH/WDE* B8 .... 110 C4
Glen Ri *MOS/BIL* B13 .... 162 A4
Glen Rd *SEDG* DY3 .... 67 G5
  STRBR DY8 .... 135 F4
Glenroyde *HWK/WKHTH* B38 .... 190 C1
Glen Side *RIDG/WDGT* B32 .... 140 D5
Glenside Av *HIA/OLT* B92 .... 147 H4
Glenthorne Rd
  ERDE/BCHGN B24 .... 93 E4
Glentworth *HIA/OLT* B92 .... 148 B4
Glentworth Gdns
  DUNHL/THL/PER WV6 .... 22 D5
Glenville Dr *ERDW/GRVHL* B23 .... 92 C1
Glenwood Cl *BRLYHL* DY5 .... 119 F4
Glenwood Dr *SHLY* B90 .... 194 D4
Glenwood Rd
  HWK/WKHTH B38 .... 176 B5
Globe St *DARL/WED* WS10 .... 70 D2
Gloucester Pl *WNLHL* WV13 .... 40 B3
Gloucester Rd *DARL/WED* WS10 .... 56 C5
  DSYBK/YTR WS5 .... 42 D5
  DUDS DY2 .... 120 D2
Gloucester St
  DUNHL/THL/PER WV6 .... 36 D1
Gloucester Wy
  CHWD/FDBR/MGN B37 .... 132 A3
Glover Cl *HLGN/YWD* B28 .... 162 D4
Glover Rd *MGN/WHC* B75 .... 63 F3
Glovers Cft
  CHWD/FDBR/MGN B37 .... 131 H1
Glovers Field Dr
  VAUX/NECH B7 .... 110 A2
Glovers Rd *SMHTH* B10 .... 128 A4
Glover St *BORD* B9 .... 127 G2
  WBROM B70 .... 87 H5
Glyme Dr *DUNHL/THL/PER* WV6 .... 22 A5
Glyn Av *BILS/COS* WV14 .... 54 D5
Glyn Dr *BILS/COS* WV14 .... 54 D5
Glyn Farm Rd *RIDG/WDGT* B32 .... 140 C2
Glynn Crs *HALE* B63 .... 137 H5
Glynne Av *KGSWFD* DY6 .... 99 H5
Glyn Rd *RIDG/WDGT* B32 .... 140 D1
Glynside Av *RIDG/WDGT* B32 .... 140 C2
Goffs Cl *RIDG/WDGT* B32 .... 141 F4
Goldborough Ct
  BILS/COS WV14 .... 53 H5
Goldby Dr *DARL/WED* WS10 .... 55 G4
Goldcrest Cl *DUDS* DY2 .... 120 C2
Goldcrest Cft *CBROM* B36 .... 114 A1
Goldencrest Dr *OLDBY* B69 .... 104 C1
Golden Cft *BFLD/HDSWWD* B20 .... 89 H5
Goldencross Wy *BRLYHL* DY5 .... 118 D5
Golden End Dr *DOR/KN* B93 .... 197 H2
Golden Hillock Rd *DUDS* DY2 .... 120 C1
  SMHTH B10 .... 128 B5
  SPARK B11 .... 145 F2
Goldfinch Cl *BVILLE* B30 .... 159 F2
Goldfinch Rd *HAG/WOL* DY9 * 136 A4
Goldicroft Rd *DARL/WED* WS10 .... 56 A4
Goldieslie Cl *SCFLD/BOLD* B73 .... 77 F1
Goldieslie Rd *SCFLD/BOLD* B73 .... 77 F1
Golds Hill Gdns *HDSW* B21 .... 107 H2
Golds Hill Rd *HDSW* B21 .... 107 H1
Golds Hill Wy *TPTN/OCK* DY4 .... 70 B4
Goldsmith Rd
  ALE/KHTH/YWD B14 .... 161 F2
  BLOX/PEL WS3 .... 28 A2
Goldstar Wy *STETCH* B33 .... 131 E2
Goldthorn Av
  ETTPK/GDPK/PENN WV4 .... 51 H3
Goldthorn Crs
  ETTPK/GDPK/PENN WV4 .... 51 G2
Goldthorne Av
  LGN/SDN/BHAMAIR B26 .... 148 A3
Goldthorn Hi *BRLYHL* DY5 .... 119 F4
Goldthorn Hl *BKHL/PFLD* WV2 .... 51 H2
Goldthorn Rd *BKHL/PFLD* WV2 .... 51 H2
Golf La *BILS/COS* WV14 .... 53 H1
Golson Cl *MGN/WHC* B75 .... 63 E2
Gomeldon Av
  ALE/KHTH/YWD B14 .... 178 B2
Gomer St *WLNHL* WV13 .... 39 G3
Gomer St West *WLNHL* WV13 .... 39 G3
Gooch Cl *STRBR* DY8 .... 135 C1
Gooch St *DIG/EDG* B5 .... 127 E4
Gooch St North *DIG/EDG* B5 .... 127 E5
Goodall Gv *CTB/HAM* B43 .... 60 A5
Goodall St *WSL* WS1 .... 5 H4
Goodby Rd *MOS/BIL* B13 .... 143 H4
Goode Av *WSNGN* B18 .... 108 A4
Goode Cl *LGLYGN/QTN* B68 .... 105 G5
Goodeve Wk *MGN/WHC* B75 .... 63 H5
Goodison Gdns
  ERDE/BCHGN B24 .... 93 F1
Goodman Cl *HLGN/YWD* B28 .... 162 D4
Goodman St *CBHAMW* B1 .... 2 A4

Goodrest Av *RMSLY* B62 .... 140 A2
Goodrest Cft
  ALE/KHTH/YWD B14 .... 179 E1
Goodrest La *HWK/WKHTH* B38 .... 190 C2
Goodrich Av
  ALE/KHTH/YWD B14 .... 177 G3
Goodrich Covert
  ALE/KHTH/YWD B14 .... 177 C5
Goodrick Wy *VAUX/NECH* B7 * 109 H3
Goodway Ct *CBHAMNE* B4 .... 3 G2
Goodway Rd *HIA/OLT* B92 .... 148 C4
  KGSTG B44 .... 75 E3
Goodwood Cl *CBROM* B36 .... 111 H1
Goodwood Dr
  FOAKS/STRLY B74 .... 60 B2
Goodwyn Av *LGLYGN/QTN* B68 .... 123 H5
Goodyear Av *WOLVN* WV10 .... 23 C3
Goodyear Rd *SMTHWKW* B67 .... 123 H2
Goosemoor La
  ERDW/GRVHL B23 .... 76 D4
Gopsal St *CBHAMNE* B4 .... 127 C1
Gorcott La *SHLY* B90 .... 194 A3
Gordon Av
  ETTPK/GDPK/PENN WV4 .... 52 D5
  HHTH/SAND B71 .... 71 G3
  LOZ/NWT B19 .... 108 D2
Gordon Cl *OLDBY* B69 .... 86 B4
Gordon Crs *BRLYHL* DY5 .... 101 G4
Gordon Dr *TPTN/OCK* DY4 .... 86 A1
Gordon Pl *BILS/COS* WV14 .... 53 C5
Gordon Rd *HRBN* B17 .... 142 B1
  LOZ/NWT B19 .... 108 C1
Gordon St *BKHL/PFLD* WV2 * 7 H7
  BORD B9 .... 127 H2
  DARL/WED WS10 .... 55 F2
Gorey Cl *SHHTH* WV12 .... 25 H2
Gorge Rd *SEDG* DY3 .... 67 G3
Gorleston Gv
  ALE/KHTH/YWD B14 .... 178 D3
Gorleston Rd
  ALE/KHTH/YWD B14 .... 178 D3
Gorsebrook Rd
  WOLVN WV10 .... 23 E5
Gorse Cl
  CHWD/FDBR/MGN B37 .... 131 H2
  SLYOAK B29 .... 158 C2
Gorse Farm Rd *GTB/HAM* B43 .... 73 G3
Gorsefield Rd *BKDE/SHDE* B34 .... 113 E4
Gorse Green La *HAG/WOL* DY9 .... 171 F5
Gorsemoor Wy *WNSFLD* WV11 .... 15 F4
Gorse Rd *DUDN* DY1 .... 84 A2
  WNSFLD WV11 .... 25 G1
Gorsey La *CSHL/WTROR* B46 .... 97 E4
  HLYWD B47 .... 192 C4
Gorsey Wy *ALDR* WS9 .... 29 G5
Gorsly Piece *RIDG/WDGT* B32 .... 140 C3
Gorstie Cft *GTB/HAM* B43 .... 73 G5
Gorsty Av *BRLYHL* DY5 .... 101 E5
Gorsty Cl *HHTH/SAND* B71 .... 72 B5
Gorsty Hayes *CDSL* WV8 .... 10 B4
Gorsty Hill Rd *RMSLY* B62 .... 121 H4
Gorsymead Gv *NFLD/LBR* B31 .... 174 C3
Gorsy Rd *RIDG/WDGT* B32 .... 140 D3
Gorway Cl *WSL* WS1 .... 57 F1
Gorway Gdns *WSL* WS1 .... 57 G1
Gorway Rd *WSL* WS1 .... 57 F1
Goscote Cl *BLOX/PEL* WS3 .... 28 B3
Goscote La *BLOX/PEL* WS3 .... 28 B2
Goscote Lodge Crs
  BLOX/PEL WS3 .... 28 C3
Goscote Pl *BLOX/PEL* WS3 .... 28 C3
Goscote Rd *BLOX/PEL* WS3 .... 18 B5
Gosford St *BHTH/HG* B12 .... 144 B1
Gospel End Rd *SEDG* DY3 .... 66 C5
Gospel End St *SEDG* DY3 .... 67 F4
Gospel Farm Rd *ACGN* B27 .... 163 F2
Gospel La *ACGN* B27 .... 163 H2
Gospel Oak Rd *TPTN/OCK* DY4 .... 69 H2
Gosport Cl *WOLV* WV1 .... 53 F1
Goss Cft *SLYOAK* B29 .... 159 F1
Gossey La *STETCH* B33 .... 131 E2
The Goss *BRLYHL* DY5 .... 119 F3
Gotham Rd
  LGN/SDN/BHAMAIR B26 .... 147 E1
Gothersley La *KINVER* DY7 .... 116 B2
Goths Cl *BLKHTH/ROWR* B65 .... 104 A5
Gough Av *WNSFLD* WV11 .... 24 B2
Gough Dr *TPTN/OCK* DY4 .... 86 A1
Gough Rd *BILS/COS* WV14 .... 68 C5
  EDG B15 .... 126 C5
  SPARK B11 .... 145 F2
Gough St *CBHAMW* B1 .... 2 E7
  WLNHL WV13 .... 40 A3
  WLNHL WV13 .... 39 G2
  WSLW WS2 .... 56 B1
Gozzard St *BILS/COS* WV14 .... 54 A3
Gracemere Crs
  HLGN/YWD B28 .... 179 G1
Grace Rd *OLDBY* B69 .... 104 A1
  SPARK B11 .... 145 E1
  TPTN/OCK DY4 .... 69 E4
Gracewell Rd *MOS/BIL* B13 .... 162 B1
Grafton Dr *WLNHL* WV13 .... 38 D4
Grafton Gdns *SEDG* DY3 .... 82 D3
Grafton Pl *BILS/COS* WV14 .... 54 A1
Grafton Rd *HDSW* B21 .... 89 F5
  HHTH/SAND B71 .... 87 H2
  LGLYGN/QTN B68 .... 122 D2
  SHLY B90 .... 179 E3
Graham Cl *TPTN/OCK* DY4 .... 69 H2
Graham Crs *RBRY* B45 .... 187 H1
Graham Rd *HHTH/SAND* B71 .... 87 F2
  RMSLY B62 .... 122 A4
  STRBR DY8 .... 99 H5
  WASH/WDE B8 .... 128 C1
  YDLY B25 .... 146 C1
Graham St *CBHAMW* B1 .... 2 C3
  LOZ/NWT B19 .... 108 C2
Grainger Cl *TPTN/OCK* DY4 .... 70 B5

Gray St *BORD* B9 .... 12?
Graywood Park Rd
  RIDG/WDGT B32 .... 14?
Graywood Rd *NFLD/LBR* B31 .... 18?
Grazebrook Cft
  RIDG/WDGT B32 .... 15?
Grazebrook Rd *DUDS* DY2 .... 10?
Grazewood Cl *SHHTH* WV12 .... 2?
Greadier St *SHHTH* WV12 .... 1?
Great Arthur St *SMTHWK* B66 .... 10?
Great Barr St *BORD* B9 .... 12?
Great Brickkiln St
  BDMR/CCFT WV3 ....
Great Br *TPTN/OCK* DY4 .... 8?
Great Bridge Rd
  BILS/COS WV14 .... 5?
Great Bridge St *WBROM* B70 .... 8?
Great Brook St *VAUX/NECH* B7 .... 10?
Great Charles St *BRWNH* WS8 ....
Great Charles Street Queensway
  CBHAMNW B3 ....
Great Colmore St *DIG/EDG* B15 .... 12?
Great Combow *HALE* B63 .... 13?
Great Farley Dr *NFLD/LBR* B31 .... 17?
Great Francis St
  VAUX/NECH B7 ....
Great Hampton Rw
  LOZ/NWT B19 .... 10?
Great Hampton St *WOLV* WV1 ....
  WSNGN B18 .... 10?
Great King St *LOZ/NWT* B19 .... 10?
Great King St North
  LOZ/NWT B19 .... 10?
Great Lister St *VAUX/NECH* B7 ....
Great Meadow *TPTN/OCK* DY4 .... 8?
Great Moor Rd
  DUNHL/THL/PER WV6 ....
Great Stone Rd *NFLD/LBR* B31 .... 17?
Great Tindal St
  LDYWD/EDGR B16 ....
Great Western Ar *CBHAM* B2 ....
Great Western Cl *WSNGN* B18 .... 10?
Great Western Dr
  CDYHTH B64 .... 12?
Great Western St
  DARL/WED WS10 ....
  WOLV WV1 ....
Great Western Wy
  TPTN/OCK DY4 ....
Great Wood Rd *BORD* B9 .... 12?
Greaves Av *DSYBK/YTR* WS5 ....
Greaves Cl *DSYBK/YTR* WS5 ....
Greaves Crs *SHHTH* WV12 ....
Greaves Rd *DUDS* DY2 ....
Greaves Sq *HWK/WKHTH* B38 .... 1?
The Greaves *WALM/CURD* B76 ....
Grebe Cl *ERDW/GRVHL* B23 ....
Greenacre Dr *CDSL* WV8 ....
Greenacre Rd *TPTN/OCK* DY4 .... 14?
Green Acres *ACGN* B27 ....
Greenacres
  DUNHL/THL/PER WV6 ....
Green Acres *RIDG/WDGT* B32 .... 1?
Greenacres *SEDG* DY3 ....
  WALM/CURD B76 ....
Green Acres *WMBN* WV5 ....
Greenacres Av *WOLVN* WV10 ....
Greenacres Cl
  FOAKS/STRLY B74 ....
Green Acres Rd
  HWK/WKHTH B38 .... 1?
Greenaleigh Rd
  ALE/KHTH/YWD B14 ....
Green Av *HLGN/YWD* B28 ....
Greenaway Cl *GTB/HAM* B43 ....
Green Bank Av
  HLGN/YWD B28 ....
Greenbank Gdns *STRBR* DY8 .... 1?
Green Barns La *LICHS* WS14 ....
Greenbush Dr *HALE* B63 .... 1?
Green Cl *HLYWD* B47 .... 1?
Green Ct *WOLVN/WENSFLD* ....
Greencroft *BILS/COS* WV14 ....
Green Cft *BORD* B9 ....
Greencroft *KGSWFD* DY6 ....
Green Dr *RIDG/WDGT* B32 ....
  WOLVN WV10 ....
Greenend Rd *MOS/BIL* B13 .... 14?
Greenfels Ri *DUDS* DY2 ....
Greenfield Av *CDYHTH* B64 .... 1?
  STRBR DY8 ....
Greenfield Crs *EDG* B15 ....
Greenfield Cft *BILS/COS* WV14 ....
Greenfield La *WOLVN* WV10 ....
Greenfield Rd *GTB/HAM* B43 ....
  HRBN B17 ....
  SMTHWKW B67 ....
Greenfields ALDR* WS9 ....
Greenfields Rd *KGSWFD* DY6 .... 1?
  RUSH/SHEL WS4 ....
Greenfield Vw *SEDG* DY3 ....
Greenfinch Rd *CBROM* B36 ....
  HAG/WOL DY9 ....
Greenford Rd
  ALE/KHTH/YWD B14 ....
Green Gables
  FOAKS/STRLY B74 * ....
  HLYWD B47 ....
Green Gables Dr *HLYWD* B47 * .... 1?
Greenhill *WMBN* WV5 ....
Greenhill Cl *SHHTH* WV12 ....
Greenhill Dr *SLYOAK* B29 ....
Greenhill Gdns *GTB/HAM* B43 ....
  RMSLY B62 ....
  WMBN WV5 ....
Greenhill Rd
  CSCFLD/WYGN B72 ....
  HDSW B21 ....
  MOS/BIL B13 ....
  RMSLY B62 ....
  SEDG DY3 ....
Greenhill Vils *WSL* WS1 * ....
Greenhill Wy *ALDR* WS9 ....
Green Hill Wy *SHLY* B90 ....
Greenholm Rd *KGSTG* B44 ....
Greening Dr *EDG* B15 ....
Greenland Cl *KGSWFD* DY6 ....
Greenland Ri *HIA/OLT* B92 ....
Greenland Rd *SLYOAK* B29 ....
Greenlands *WMBN* WV5 ....

enlands Rd
CHWD/FDBR/MGN B37..........132 C2
en La ALDR WS9..........31 E5
BLOX/PEL WS3..........18 A3
BLOX/PEL WS3..........27 G4
BORD B9..........128 A3
BRWNH WS8..........9 G2
CBROM B36..........113 G1
CSHL/WTROR B46..........115 G4
DUDN DY1..........83 H1
DUNHL/THL/PER WV6..........22 A3
GTB/HAM B43..........73 F4
HAG/WOL DY9..........136 B2
HDSW B21..........107 E1
HWK/WKHTH B38..........176 C5
KGSWFD DY6..........99 H2
RIDG/WDGT B32..........140 C1
RMSLY B62..........122 B3
RUSH/SHEL WS4..........18 D4
SHLY B90..........179 G4
WSLW WS2..........4 C2
en Lanes BILS/COS WV14..........53 G1
SCFLD/BOLD B73..........77 F4
enleas Gdns HALE B63..........139 E4
en Leigh ERDW/GRVHL B23..76 D3
enleighs SEDG DY3..........52 B5
enly Rd
ETTPK/GDPK/PENN WV4..........52 B3
en Meadow HAG/WOL DY9..152 D2
WNSFLD WV11..........24 D5
en Meadow Cl WMBN WV5....64 C5
en Meadow Rd
SHHTH WV12..........25 H3
SLYOAK B29..........158 C3
enoak Crs BILS/COS WV14..........68 A5
BVILLE B30..........160 C2
en Oak Rd CDSL WV8..........10 D5
enock Crs
ETTPK/GDPK/PENN WV4..........52 D3
en Park Av BILS/COS WV14....38 B5
en Park Dr BILS/COS WV14....38 C5
en Park Rd DUDS DY2..........85 F5
FLD/LBR B31..........175 E3
enridge Rd
BFLD/HDSWWD B20..........89 G1
en Rd DUDS DY2..........102 D2
MOS/BIL B13..........162 B1
en Rock La BLOX/PEL WS3....27 H1
enroyde HAG/WOL DY9..........152 D1
ensand Dr BILS/COS WV14....68 C1
ensforge La KINVER DY7..........116 B4
enside HRBN B17..........142 A2
enside Rd
ERDE/BCHGN B24..........93 G1
enside Wy DSYBK/YTR WS5....57 G4
ensill Av TPTN/OCK DY4..........69 F3
enslade Cft NFLD/LBR B31....175 G3
enslade Rd DSYBK/YTR WS5....58 A1
SEDG DY3..........66 D1
SHLY B90..........179 E3
ensleeves FOAKS/STRLY B74..46 D3
enstead Rd MOS/BIL B13..........162 B1
Greens
DUNHL/THL/PER WV6 *..........34 C2
n St BTHH/HG B12..........127 F3
BILS/COS WV14..........68 C3
OLDBY B69..........105 E2
STRBR DY8..........135 F2
WBROM B70..........106 A1
WSLW WS2..........41 G2
nsway WNSFLD WV11..........24 B2
Green ALDR WS9..........30 C4
BLOX/PEL WS3..........27 F1
CBROM B36..........112 D2
SCFLD/WYGN B72..........77 H2
DARL/WED WS10..........55 F1
HWK/WKHTH B38..........176 D3
LGLYGN/QTN B68..........123 F2
NFLD/LBR B31..........174 C3
RIDG/WDGT B32..........140 A1
SOLH B91..........165 F5
STRBR DY8..........117 H2
nvale NFLD/LBR B31..........158 B5
nvale Av
LGN/SDN/BHAMAIR B26..........148 B1
n Wk HRBN B17..........124 B5
nway ALDR WS9..........19 H5
BFLD/HDSWWD B20..........73 H5
SEDG DY3..........67 G2
nway Av STRBR DY8..........118 A3
nway Dr SCFLD/BOLD B73....61 E5
nway Gdns
HWK/WKHTH B38..........190 C1
SEDG DY3..........67 G2
nway Rd BILS/COS WV14..........54 A4
nways HALE B63..........137 G2
NFLD/LBR B31..........158 B2
STRBR DY8..........117 G3
nway St BORD B9..........128 A3
Greenway
CHWD/FDBR/MGN B37..........149 E1
HAG/WOL DY9..........152 B5
SCFLD/BOLD B73..........60 D5
nwood YDLY B25..........129 H4
nwood Av ACGN B27..........146 A5
BLKHTH/ROWR B65..........122 B2
LGLYGN/QTN B68..........105 F4
nwood Cl
ALE/KHTH/YWD B14..........161 E5
nwood Pk ALDR WS9..........30 C1
nwood Pl KGSTG B44..........75 H2
nwood Rd ALDR WS9..........19 H5
HHTH/SAND B71..........71 F3
WOLVN WV10..........23 E3
Greenwoods STRBR DY8.....135 E2
thurst Dr MOS/BIL B13..........145 E5
s Green Rd WBROM B70..........86 C2
ville Cl STETCH B33..........112 C4
ory Av SLYOAK B29..........158 C2
ory Cl DARL/WED WS10..........70 D1
ory Dr DUDN DY1..........84 A4
ory Rd STRBR DY8..........134 C2
don Dr SCFLD/BOLD B73..........61 F5
don Gdns
BDMR/CCFT WV3..........50 D2
don Rd
ALE/KHTH/YWD B14..........178 C2
HIA/OLT B92..........164 A2
ell Dr EDG B15..........125 H4
ell Rd BLOX/PEL WS3..........17 F4
Grenville Cl WSLW WS2..........40 B2
Grenville Dr ERDW/GRVHL B23....91 H3
SMTHWK B66..........105 H1
Grenville Pl WBROM B70..........86 C3
Grenville Rd DUDN DY1..........83 G5
SHLY B90..........180 B3
Gresham Rd HLGN/YWD B28..........162 D4
LGLYGN/QTN B68..........105 F3
Gresley Cl FOAKS/STRLY B74..........47 E1
Gressel La STETCH B33..........131 E1
Grestone Av
BFLD/HDSWWD B20..........89 G3
Greswolde Dr
ERDE/BCHGN B24..........93 F2
Greswolde Park Rd ACGN B27....146 B4
Greswolde Rd SOLH B91..........164 A4
SPARK B11..........145 E4
Greswold Gdns
BKDE/SHDE B34..........112 C4
Greswold St HHTH/SAND B71......87 G1
Gretton Crs ALDR WS9..........29 H5
Gretton Rd ALDR WS9..........29 H5
ERDW/GRVHL B23..........76 B4
Greville Dr EDG B15..........143 G1
Grevis Cl MOS/BIL B13..........144 B3
Grevis Rd YDLY B25..........130 A3
Greyfort Crs HIA/OLT B92..........164 B1
Greyfriars Cl DUDN DY1..........83 G3
HIA/OLT B92..........163 H3
Greyhound La STRBR DY8..........134 D5
Greyhurst Cft SOLH B91..........181 H5
Grey Mill Cl SHLY B90..........195 F2
Greystoke Av CBROM B36..........111 H2
Greystoke Dr KGSWFD DY6..........99 H3
Greystone Pas DUDN DY1..........84 B5
Greystone St DUDN DY1..........84 C5
Grey Tree Crs DOR/KN B93..........196 C5
Grice St WBROM B70..........105 G1
Griffen La SHLY B90..........194 A4
Griffin Cl NFLD/LBR B31..........158 D4
Griffin Gdns HRBN B17..........142 B3
Griffin Rd ERDW/GRVHL B23..........92 A1
Griffins Brook Cl BVILLE B30..........159 F4
Griffins Brook La BVILLE B30......159 E4
Griffin St DUDS DY2..........102 C5
WBROM B70..........87 H3
WOLV WV1..........37 H4
Griffiths Dr WMBN WV5..........81 E1
WNSFLD WV11..........25 F2
Griffiths Rd DUDN DY1..........68 A5
HHTH/SAND B71..........71 G2
SHHTH WV12..........26 B2
Grigg Gv NFLD/LBR B31..........175 E4
Grimley Rd NFLD/LBR B31..........176 B3
Grimpits La HWK/WKHTH B38....191 E1
Grimshaw Rd HLGN/YWD B28....163 E1
Grimstock Hl
CSHL/WTROR B46 *..........115 E1
Grimstone St WOLVN WV10..........7 H2
Grindleford Rd
PBAR/PBCH B42..........74 D4
Gristhorpe Rd SLYOAK B29..........160 A2
Grizedale Cl RBRY B45..........174 B3
Grocott Rd DARL/WED WS10..........54 D4
Grosmont Av BTHH/HG B12..........144 C1
Grosvenor Av
BFLD/HDSWWD B20..........90 C4
FOAKS/STRLY B74..........45 F4
Grosvenor Cl MGN/WHC B75..........47 G4
WOLVN WV10..........12 D5
Grosvenor Crs WOLVN WV10..........12 D5
Grosvenor Pk
ETTPK/GDPK/PENN WV4..........51 F3
Grosvenor Rd AST/WIT B6..........109 H1
BFLD/HDSWWD B20..........90 C4
ETTPK/GDPK/PENN WV4..........52 C5
HRBN B17..........141 G1
LGLYGN/QTN B68..........105 E5
SEDG DY3..........83 F4
SOLH B91..........181 F4
WOLVN WV10..........12 D5
Grosvenor Sq HLGN/YWD B28....162 C5
Grosvenor St DIG/EDG B5..........3 J4
WOLVN WV10..........37 H2
Grosvenor St West EDG B15..........2 A7
Grosvenor Wy BRLYHL DY5..........119 F5
Grotto La
DUNHL/THL/PER WV6..........22 A5
Groucutt St BILS/COS WV14..........68 C3
Grounds Dr FOAKS/STRLY B74....46 D2
Grounds Rd FOAKS/STRLY B74....46 D2
Grout St WBROM B70..........86 C2
Grove Av HALE B63..........138 B4
HDSW B21 *..........107 H1
MOS/BIL B13..........144 C5
SLYOAK B29 *..........158 D3
SOLH B91..........165 E5
Grove Cottage Rd BORD B9..........128 B2
Grove Ct PBAR/PBCH B42 *..........73 H5
Grove Crs BLOX/PEL WS3..........17 H4
BRLYHL DY5..........101 E4
Grove Farm Dr MGN/WHC B75....63 F3
Grove Gdns HDSW B21..........89 H4
Grove Hl DSYBK/YTR WS5..........43 G5
Grove Hill Rd HDSW B21..........89 H5
Grove House WSL WS1 *..........5 F5
Groveland Rd TPTN/OCK DY4..........85 G4
Grovelands Crs WOLVN WV10..........12 D4
Grove La BFLD/HDSWWD B20..........89 H4
DUNHL/THL/PER WV6..........35 F3
HRBN B17..........142 A4
SMTHWK B66..........107 F5
WALM/CURD B76..........79 H1
Groveley La NFLD/LBR B31..........189 F2
RBRY B45..........188 C4
Grove Ms NFLD/LBR B31..........175 H5
Grove Pk KGSWFD DY6..........99 G1
Grove Rd ALE/KHTH/YWD B14....160 D3
DOR/KN B93..........197 F5
HAG/WOL DY9..........136 D3
LGLYGN/QTN B68..........123 H3
SOLH B91..........163 H5
SPARK B11..........145 E4
Groveside Wy BLOX/PEL WS3......18 A2
Grove St DUDS DY2..........103 E1
SMTHWK B66..........107 F5
WSNGN B18..........107 F5
Grove Ter WSL WS1..........5 F5
The Grove BLKHTH/ROWR B65....122 A2
BRLYHL DY5..........119 E3
CSHL/WTROR B46..........115 F5
DSYBK/YTR WS5..........57 H5
ETTPK/GDPK/PENN WV4..........52 C3
FOAKS/STRLY B74..........32 B5
GTB/HAM B43..........58 C4
HIA/OLT B92..........167 G2
LDYWD/EDGR B16 *..........125 H2
NFLD/LBR B31..........175 H5
RBRY B45..........188 D4
WASH/WDE B8..........110 A5
WNSFLD WV11..........24 B4
Grove Vale Av GTB/HAM B43..........73 E2
Grove Wy FOAKS/STRLY B74..........60 B1
Grovewood Dr
HWK/WKHTH B38..........176 C4
Guardian Ct NFLD/LBR B31..........174 D2
SOLH B91..........182 B2
Guardians Wy NFLD/LBR B31....158 A2
Guernsey Dr CBROM B36..........114 B3
Guest Av WNSFLD WV11..........24 C2
Guest Gv LOZ/NWT B19..........108 C3
Guild Av BLOX/PEL WS3..........27 H3
Guild Cl LDYWD/EDGR B16..........126 A2
Guild Cft LOZ/NWT B19..........108 D3
Guildford Cft
CHWD/FDBR/MGN B37..........131 H4
Guildford Dr LOZ/NWT B19..........108 D3
Guildford St LOZ/NWT B19..........108 B2
Guillane Cl HWK/WKHTH B38....176 B4
Gullswood Cl
ALE/KHTH/YWD B14..........177 H3
Gumbleberrys Cl
WASH/WDE B8..........111 G5
Gunmakers Wk LOZ/NWT B19....108 D2
Gunner Gv MGN/WHC B75..........63 G2
Gunner La RBRY B45..........187 F1
Gunns Wy HIA/OLT B92..........163 H3
Guns La WBROM B70..........87 F2
Gunstock Cl FOAKS/STRLY B74....60 A1
Gunstone La CDSL WV8..........10 B2
Gunter Rd ERDE/BCHGN B24..........94 A3
Gurnard Cl SHHTH WV12..........25 H1
Gurney Pl WSLW WS2..........27 E5
Gurney Rd WSLW WS2..........27 E5
Guthrum Cl
DUNHL/THL/PER WV6..........20 D5
ERDW/GRVHL B23..........76 C3
The Gutter HAG/WOL DY9..........186 A1
Guy Av WOLVN WV10..........23 G4
Guys Cliffe Av WALM/CURD B76..78 B2
Guys La SEDG DY3..........82 D4
Gwalia Gv ERDW/GRVHL B23 *....92 D2
Gwendoline Wy ALDR WS9..........19 H3
Gypsy La CSHL/WTROR B46..........96 D4

H

Habberley Rd
BLKHTH/ROWR B65..........122 B2
Habberly Cft SOLH B91..........181 H4
Hackett Cl BILS/COS WV14..........67 H2
Hackett Dr SMTHWK B66..........105 H2
Hackett Rd
BLKHTH/ROWR B65..........122 C1
Hackett St TPTN/OCK DY4..........70 A4
Hackford Rd
ETTPK/GDPK/PENN WV4..........52 D4
Hackman's Gate La
HAG/WOL DY9..........169 G5
Hack St BORD B9..........127 G3
Hackwood Rd DARL/WED WS10..71 F1
Hadcroft Gra HAG/WOL DY9..........136 B3
Hadcroft Rd HAG/WOL DY9..........136 A3
Haddock Rd BILS/COS WV14..........53 G1
Haddon Crs SHHTH WV12..........26 A3
Haddon Cft HALE B63..........154 C1
Haddon Rd PBAR/PBCH B42..........74 D4
Haden Circ BTHH/HG B12..........127 F5
Haden Cl CDYHTH B64..........121 F5
STRBR DY8..........117 H2
Haden Crs WNSFLD WV11..........25 F4
Haden Cross Dr CDYHTH B64......121 G5
Hadendale CDYHTH B64..........121 G5
Haden Hl BDMR/CCFT WV3..........6 A4
Haden Hill Rd CDYHTH B64..........121 G5
HALE B63..........138 D1
Haden Park Rd CDYHTH B64......121 E5
Haden Rd CDYHTH B64..........121 E2
TPTN/OCK DY4..........69 G2
Haden St BTHH/HG B12..........144 B1
Haden Wy BTHH/HG B12..........144 B1
Hadfield Cl ERDE/BCHGN B24......94 A3
Hadfield Cft LOZ/NWT B19..........108 C4
Hadfield Wy
CHWD/FDBR/MGN B37..........114 A5
Hadland Rd STETCH B33..........130 D3
Hadleigh Cft
WALM/CURD B76..........78 C5
Hadley Cl DUDS DY2..........103 E5
HLYWD B47..........192 C3
Hadley Cft SMTHWK B66..........106 C2
Hadley Pl BILS/COS WV14..........53 G1
Hadley Rd BILS/COS WV14..........53 G1
WSLW WS2..........26 D4
Hadley St LGLYGN/QTN B68..........105 E5
Hadlow Cft STETCH B33..........131 F5
Hadrian Dr CSHL/WTROR B46......97 E5
Hadyn Gv
LGN/SDN/BHAMAIR B26..........147 H1
Hadzor Rd LGLYGN/QTN B68..........123 H4
Hafren Cl RBRY B45..........174 B3
Hafton Gv BORD B9 *..........128 B3
Haggar St BKHL/PFLD WV2..........52 A2
Hagley Cswy HAG/WOL DY9..........153 H3
Hagley Cl HAG/WOL DY9..........153 E4
Hagley Gra HAG/WOL DY9..........152 D4
Hagley Ml HALE B63 *..........138 D4
Hagley Park Dr RBRY B45..........188 A2
Hagley Rd HAG/WOL DY9..........153 E2
HALE B63..........154 D1
HRBN B17..........125 E3
STRBR DY8..........135 H4
Hagley Rd West HRBN B17..........124 C3
RIDG/WDGT B32..........140 B1
RMSLY B62..........139 H1
Hagley View Rd DUDS DY2..........102 C1
Hagley Vls BTHH/HG B12 *..........144 D3
Hagley Wood La RMSLY B62..........154 B4
Haig Cl MGN/WHC B75..........62 C1
Haig Rd DUDS DY2..........85 F5
Haig St HHTH/SAND B71..........87 G1
Hailes Park Cl
ETTPK/GDPK/PENN WV4..........52 B2
Hailsham Rd ERDW/GRVHL B23..92 D1
Hailstone Cl
BLKHTH/ROWR B65..........103 G3
Haines Cl TPTN/OCK DY4..........85 H2
Haines St WBROM B70..........87 H4
Hainfield Dr SOLH B91..........165 G5
Hainge Rd OLDBY B69..........86 A4
Hainult Cl STRBR DY8..........99 H5
Halas Ct CDYHTH B64..........121 E2
Halberton St WSNGN B18..........107 F5
Haldon Gv NFLD/LBR B31..........189 E1
Hale Ct WSL WS1 *..........5 J6
Halecroft Av WNSFLD WV11..........24 D5
Hale Gv ERDE/BCHGN B24..........93 H2
Hales Crs SMTHWKW B67..........124 A1
Halescroft Sq NFLD/LBR B31....158 A4
Hales Gdns ERDW/GRVHL B23....76 A3
Hales La SMTHWKW B67..........106 B5
Halesmere Wy HALE B63 *..........139 E4
Halesowen Rd BRGRVW B61......186 D5
CDYHTH B64..........121 E3
DUDS DY2..........102 C4
RMSLY B62..........139 G1
Halesowen St
BLKHTH/ROWR B65..........122 A4
OLDBY B69..........104 D2
Hales Rd DARL/WED WS10..........56 A4
HALE B63..........138 C3
Hales Wy OLDBY B69..........104 D2
Halesworth Rd COVEN WV9..........11 H5
Halewood Gv HLGN/YWD B28....163 E3
Haley St SHHTH WV12..........26 A5
Halfcot Av HAG/WOL DY9..........136 A4
Halford Crs BLOX/PEL WS3..........28 B5
Halford Gv ERDE/BCHGN B24......94 A2
Halford Rd SOLH B91..........164 A4
Halfords La HHTH/SAND B71......88 C5
SMTHWK B66..........106 C2
Halfords Pk SMTHWK B66..........106 C1
Halfshire La KIDD DY10..........168 B4
Halfway Cl KGSTG B44..........75 E5
Halifax Gv WSNGN B18 *..........107 G5
Halifax Rd SHLY B90..........180 B3
Haliscombe Gv AST/WIT B6 *......109 E1
Halkett Gld STETCH B33..........129 H1
Halladale HWK/WKHTH B38......176 D4
Hallam Cl HHTH/SAND B71..........88 A2
Hallam Crs WOLVN WV10..........23 G4
Hallam Dr HHTH/SAND B71..........87 H1
Hallam St BTHH/HG B12..........144 A2
HHTH/SAND B71..........87 H2
Hallbridge Cl BLOX/PEL WS3..........17 H5
Hallbridge Wy OLDBY B69..........85 H4
Hallchurch Rd DUDS DY2..........101 H2
Hall Crs HHTH/SAND B71..........71 G5
Hallcroft Cl CSCFLD/WYGN B72....77 G4
Hallcroft Wy ALDR WS9..........30 C5
DOR/KN B93..........197 E2
Hall Dale Cl HLGN/YWD B28..........162 D5
Hall Dr CHWD/FDBR/MGN B37....132 A5
HAG/WOL DY9..........153 F4
Hall End DARL/WED WS10..........55 H5
Hallens Dr DARL/WED WS10..........55 F5
Hallet Dr BDMR/CCFT WV3..........6 D6
Hallewell Rd
LDYWD/EDGR B16..........125 F2
Hall Green Rd HHTH/SAND B71....71 H2
Hallgreen St BILS/COS WV14..........54 A5
Hall Gv BILS/COS WV14..........68 C2
Hall Hays Rd BKDE/SHDE B34....113 G2
Hall La ALDR WS9..........19 E5
BILS/COS WV14..........67 H2
BLOX/PEL WS3..........17 H4
HAG/WOL DY9..........153 F4
TPTN/OCK DY4..........69 H3
Hall Meadow HAG/WOL DY9..........153 F3
Hallmoor Rd STETCH B33..........130 D1
Hallot Cl ERDW/GRVHL B23..........76 B3
Halloughton Rd
FOAKS/STRLY B74..........62 A1
Hallow Cl NFLD/LBR B31..........176 B3
Hall Park St BILS/COS WV14..........53 F2
Hall Rd BFLD/HDSWWD B20..........108 A2
CBROM B36..........112 C1
SMTHWKW B67..........106 A5
WASH/WDE B8..........110 B5
Hallstead Rd MOS/BIL B13..........161 H5
Hall St BILS/COS WV14..........54 A3
CDYHTH B64..........121 F2
DUDS DY2..........84 D5
LGLYGN/QTN B68..........105 F4
SEDG DY3..........67 F3
STRBR DY8..........135 G4
TPTN/OCK DY4..........85 E1
WBROM B70..........87 G4
WLNHL WV13..........39 H4
WNSFLD WV11..........24 C5
WSLW WS2..........41 H2
WSNGN B18..........2 D1
Hall St East
DARL/WED WS10..........55 E1
Hall St South WBROM B70..........105 H1
Hallswelle Gv GTB/HAM B43..........60 A4
Hall Wk CSHL/WTROR B46..........115 F5
Halsbury Gv KGSTG B44..........75 H3
Halstead Gv SOLH B91..........181 G5
Halton Rd SCFLD/BOLD B73..........61 F5
Halton St DUDS DY2..........102 C4
Hamar Wy
CHWD/FDBR/MGN B37..........132 B4
Hamberley Ct WSNGN B18..........107 F5
Hamble Cl BRLYHL DY5..........100 C3
CBROM B36..........113 H1
Hambledon Cl COVEN WV9..........12 A5
Hamble Gv
DUNHL/THL/PER WV6..........34 C1
Hamble Rd
ETTPK/GDPK/PENN WV4..........50 C2
GTB/HAM B43..........73 H2
Hambleton Rd HALE B63..........137 H5
Hambletts Rd WBROM B70..........87 E3
Hambrook Cl
DUNHL/THL/PER WV6..........22 C5
Hambury Dr
ALE/KHTH/YWD B14..........160 D3
Hamilton Av HRBN B17..........124 C4
RMSLY B62..........139 E4
STRBR DY8..........134 D1
Hamilton Cl SEDG DY3..........67 E3
STRBR DY8..........117 G2
Hamilton Dr OLDBY B69..........86 A4
SLYOAK B29..........159 E2
STRBR DY8..........117 G2
Hamilton Gdns WOLVN WV10..........13 F4
Hamilton Rd HDSW B21..........107 F1
SMTHWKW B67..........124 A2
TPTN/OCK DY4..........70 A5
Hamilton St BLOX/PEL WS3..........27 G1
Ham La HAG/WOL DY9..........136 A5
KGSWFD DY6..........82 A5
Hamlet Gdns HLGN/YWD B28....162 D2
Hamlet Rd HLGN/YWD B28..........162 D3
Hammer Bank HALE B63..........120 A4
Hammersley Cl HALE B63..........120 C5
Hammond Av WOLVN WV10..........23 G2
Hammond Dr
ERDW/GRVHL B23..........92 D1
Hammond Wy STRBR DY8..........118 C5
Hampden Cl BRLYHL DY5..........120 A4
Hampden Retreat
BTHH/HG B12..........144 A1
Hampshire Dr EDG B15..........125 G4
Hampshire Rd HHTH/SAND B71..71 E2
Hampson Cl SPARK B11..........144 D1
Hampstead Cl WNSFLD WV11..........24 D4
Hampstead Gld HALE B63..........139 E4
Hampton Cl SCFLD/BOLD B73......76 A1
Hampton Ct WOLVN WV10 *..........13 H3
Hampton Court Rd HRBN B17....141 G1
Hampton Dr FOAKS/STRLY B74...47 F5
Hampton Gdns HAG/WOL DY9....136 A4
Hampton Gv BLOX/PEL WS3..........17 H3
Hampton La SOLH B91..........182 C1
Hampton Rd AST/WIT B6..........108 D1
DOR/KN B93..........197 G1
ERDW/GRVHL B23..........92 B2
WOLVN WV10..........22 D1
Hampton St BILS/COS WV14..........68 B3
DUDS DY2..........102 B4
LOZ/NWT B19..........2 E1
Hams La CSHL/WTROR B46..........97 F1
Hams Rd WASH/WDE B8..........110 B5
Hamstead Hall Av
BFLD/HDSWWD B20..........89 G1
Hamstead Hall Rd
BFLD/HDSWWD B20..........89 G2
Hamstead Hl
BFLD/HDSWWD B20..........89 H2
Hamstead Rd
BFLD/HDSWWD B20..........90 B5
GTB/HAM B43..........73 E4
Hamstead Ter DARL/WED WS10..71 E1
Hanam Cl MGN/WHC B75..........63 F2
Hanbury Cl HALE B63 *..........138 B5
Hanbury Crs
ETTPK/GDPK/PENN WV4..........51 E2
Hanbury Cft ACGN B27..........147 E4
Hanbury Dr OLDBY B69..........104 B5
Hanbury Hl STRBR DY8..........135 G3
Hanbury Rd BRWNH WS8..........9 E2
DOR/KN B93..........196 D5
WBROM B70..........87 E3
Hanch Pl WSL WS1..........5 G6
Hancock Rd WASH/WDE B8..........110 D5
Hancox St LGLYGN/QTN B68..........123 F2
Handley Gv NFLD/LBR B31..........174 C3
Handley St DARL/WED WS10..........56 A4
Handsworth Cl HDSW B21..........107 F2
Handsworth Dr GTB/HAM B43....74 A2
Handsworth New Rd
WSNGN B18..........107 G4
Handsworth Wood Rd
BFLD/HDSWWD B20..........89 H3
Hangar Rd
LGN/SDN/BHAMAIR B26..........149 E4
Hanging La NFLD/LBR B31..........175 E4
Hangleton Dr SPARK B11..........145 F1
Hanley Cl HALE B63..........138 A3
Hanley St LOZ/NWT B19..........3 F1
Hannafore Rd
LDYWD/EDGR B16..........125 F1
Hannah Rd BILS/COS WV14..........54 C5
Hanney Hay Rd BNTWD WS7..........9 H1
Hannon Rd
ALE/KHTH/YWD B14..........160 D5
Hanover Cl AST/WIT B6..........109 E2
Hanover Ct
DUNHL/THL/PER WV6..........35 G1
Hanover Dr ERDE/BCHGN B24....110 D1
Hanover Rd
BLKHTH/ROWR B65..........104 A5
Hansell Dr DOR/KN B93..........198 C1
Hansom Rd RIDG/WDGT B32..........140 C2
Hanson Cl SMTHWK B66..........106 C2
Hanson Gv HIA/OLT B92..........147 F2
Hanson's Bridge Rd
ERDE/BCHGN B24..........94 C2
Hanwell Cl WALM/CURD B76..........78 D4
Hanwood Cl BTHH/HG B12..........127 F4
Harald Cl DUNHL/THL/PER WV6..20 C5
Harbeck Av KGSTG B44..........75 F3
Harberrow Cl HAG/WOL DY9..........152 C4
Harbet Dr BHAMNEC B40..........150 A3
Harbinger Rd
HWK/WKHTH B38..........177 F3
Harborne La SLYOAK B29..........142 B5
Harborne Park Rd HRBN B17....142 B3
Harborne Rd EDG B15..........142 C1
LGLYGN/QTN B68..........123 H3
Harborough Dr ALDR WS9..........30 A5
CBROM B36..........95 F5
Harborough Wk
HAG/WOL DY9..........135 H5
Harbours Hl HAG/WOL DY9..........186 A2
Harbury Cl WALM/CURD B76..........78 D5
Harbury Rd BTHH/HG B12..........143 H2
Harby Cl
CHWD/FDBR/MGN B37..........132 B4
Harcourt Dr FOAKS/STRLY B74....46 C1
SEDG DY3..........83 F4
Harcourt Rd CDYHTH B64..........121 F4
DARL/WED WS10..........55 H4
ERDW/GRVHL B23..........76 C5

Harden Cl BLOX/PEL WS3 ....28 A3
Harden Gv BLOX/PEL WS3 ....28 A3
Harden Manor Ct HALE B63 * 139 E4
Harden Rd BLOX/PEL WS3 ....27 H3
Harden V HALE B63 * 138 A2
Harding St BILS/COS WV14 ....68 D2
Hardon Rd
ETTPK/GDPK/PENN WV4 ....52 D3
Hardware St WBROM B70 ....87 H2
Hardwick Dr CDYHTH B64 ....121 G5
Hardwicke Wy HAG/WOL DY9 ....136 B2
Hardwick Rd FOAKS/STRLY B74 ....45 F3
LGN/SDN/BHAMAIR B26 ....147 E3
Hardy Rd BLOX/PEL WS3 ....28 A2
DARL/WED WS10 ....56 A5
Hardy Sq BKHL/PFLD WV2 * 52 D2
Harebell Cl DSYBK/YTR WS5 ....57 G5
Harebell Crs DUDN DY1 ....84 A2
Harebell Gdns
HWK/WKHTH B38 ....176 D5
Hare Gv NFLD/LBR B31 ....174 D2
Hare St BILS/COS WV14 ....54 B3
Harewell Dr MGN/WHC B75 ....47 G4
Harewood Av DARL/WED WS10 ....56 C5
GTB/HAM B43 ....73 E1
Harewood Cl HLGN/YWD B28 ....162 C5
Harford St WSNGN B18 ....2 D1
Hargate La HHTH/SAND B71 ....87 G2
Hargrave Cl CSHL/WTROR B46 ....96 B3
Hargrave Rd SHLY B90 ....179 F3
Hargreave Cl WALM/CURD B76 ....78 B4
Hargreaves St BKHL/PFLD WV2 ....53 E1
Harland Rd FOAKS/STRLY B74 ....47 E2
Harlech Cl DUDS DY2 ....85 G5
RIDG/WDGT B32 ....157 E4
Harlech Rd SHHTH WV12 ....26 A4
Harlech Wy DUDN DY1 ....83 H4
Harlequin Dr MOS/BIL B13 ....144 A5
Harleston Rd KGSTG B44 ....75 F3
Harley Cl BRWNH WS8 ....19 G1
Harley Dr BILS/COS WV14 ....53 F4
Harley Gra DUDS DY2 ....102 D1
Harlow Gv HLGN/YWD B28 ....163 E4
Harlstones Cl STRBR DY8 ....118 C5
Harlyn Cl BILS/COS WV14 ....69 G1
Harman Rd ERDW/GRVHL B23 ....77 F4
Harmer St WSNGN B18 ....108 A4
Harmon Rd STRBR DY8 ....134 C2
Harnall Cl SHLY B90 ....195 E1
Harness Cl DSYBK/YTR WS5 ....57 E4
Harold Rd LDYWD/EDGR B16 ....125 H3
SMTHWKW B67 ....124 A1
Harold Ter LOZ/NWT B19 * 108 C1
Harper Av WNSFLD WV11 ....24 C3
Harper Gv TPTN/OCK DY4 ....84 D1
Harper Rd BILS/COS WV14 ....53 H2
Harpers Rd
ALE/KHTH/YWD B14 ....178 C4
NFLD/LBR B31 ....175 G3
Harper St WLNHL WV13 ....39 G3
Harpur Cl RUSH/SHEL WS4 ....42 C1
Harpur Rd RUSH/SHEL WS4 ....42 C1
Harrier Rd ACGN B27 ....146 D5
Harriet Cl BRLYHL DY5 ....100 D4
Harringay Dr STRBR DY8 ....135 E4
Harringay Rd KGSTG B44 ....75 F1
Harrington Cft
HHTH/SAND B71 ....72 B4
Harris Dr PBAR/PBCH B42 ....74 A3
SMTHWK B66 ....124 D1
Harrison Cl BLOX/PEL WS3 ....27 G1
Harrison Rd ERDE/BCHGN B24 ....92 D2
FOAKS/STRLY B74 ....32 C5
RUSH/SHEL WS4 ....18 C5
STRBR DY8 ....118 C3
Harrison's Fold DUDS DY2 ....102 C4
Harrisons Gn EDG B15 ....142 C1
Harrisons Pleck MOS/BIL B13 ....144 B4
Harrison's Rd EDG B15 ....142 C1
Harrison St BLOX/PEL WS3 ....27 G1
Harrold Av
BLKHTH/ROWR B65 ....122 C1
Harrold Rd
BLKHTH/ROWR B65 ....122 C1
Harrold St TPTN/OCK DY4 ....70 A4
Harrop Wy STRBR DY8 ....118 A4
Harrowby Dr TPTN/OCK DY4 ....85 G2
Harrowby Pl WLNHL WV13 ....40 A4
Harrowby Rd BILS/COS WV14 ....54 C4
WOLVN WV10 ....12 B4
Harrow Cl HAG/WOL DY9 ....152 C4
Harrowfield Rd STETCH B33 ....112 A5
Harrow Rd KGSWFD DY6 ....81 H5
SLYOAK B29 ....142 D4
Harrow St
DUNHL/THL/PER WV6 ....36 D1
Harry Perks St WLNHL WV13 ....39 G2
Hart Dr SCFLD/BOLD B73 ....77 E3
Hartfield Crs ACGN B27 ....163 E1
Hartford Cl HRBN B17 ....124 C5
Hartill Rd
ETTPK/GDPK/PENN WV4 ....50 D5
Hartill St WLNHL WV13 ....39 H5
Hartington Cl DOR/KN B93 ....196 C5
Hartington Rd LOZ/NWT B19 ....108 D1
Hartland Av BILS/COS WV14 ....68 A3
Hartland Rd HHTH/SAND B71 ....72 B4
NFLD/LBR B31 ....189 E2
TPTN/OCK DY4 ....84 D1
Hartland St BRLYHL DY5 ....101 F2
Hartlebury Cl DOR/KN B93 ....196 D5
Hartlebury Rd HALE B63 ....138 B5
OLDBY B69 ....104 B4
Hartledon Rd HRBN B17 ....141 H2
Hartle La HAG/WOL DY9 ....184 D2
Hartley Dr ALDR WS9 ....44 B1
Hartley Gv KGSTG B44 ....60 D5
Hartley Pl EDG B15 ....125 H4
Hartley Rd KGSTG B44 ....60 C5
Hartley St BDMR/CCFT WV3 ....6 A4
Harton Wy
ALE/KHTH/YWD B14 ....160 C5
Hartopp Rd FOAKS/STRLY B74 ....46 D5
WASH/WDE B8 ....110 C5
Hart Rd ERDE/BCHGN B24 ....93 E1
WNSFLD WV11 ....38 D1
Hartsbourne Dr RMSLY B62 ....139 F3
Harts Cl HRBN B17 ....142 B1
Harts Green Rd HRBN B17 ....141 G2
Hartshill Cl BKDE/SHDE B34 ....112 C3
Hartshill Rd ACGN B27 ....146 D5
BKDE/SHDE B34 ....112 C3
Hartshorn St BILS/COS WV14 ....53 H3
Hartside Cl HALE B63 ....137 G5
Harts Rd WASH/WDE B8 ....110 C4
Hart St WSL WS1 ....4 E6
Hartswell Dr MOS/BIL B13 ....161 F4
Hartwell Cl SOLH B91 ....181 H4
Hartwell Rd ERDE/BCHGN B24 ....93 F4
Hartwood Crs
ETTPK/GDPK/PENN WV4 ....51 F4
Harvard Cl DUDN DY1 ....83 H2
Harvard Rd HIA/OLT B92 ....147 H3
Harvest Cl BVILLE B30 ....160 B5
SEDG DY3 ....83 G1
Harvesters Cl ALDR WS9 ....45 E3
Harvesters Rd SHHTH WV12 ....26 B5
Harvester Wy KGSWFD DY6 ....99 E1
Harvest Fields Wy
MGN/WHC B75 ....47 H1
Harvest Rd
BLKHTH/ROWR B65 ....121 G1
SMTHWKW B67 ....123 H1
Harvey Ct STETCH B33 * 131 F1
Harvey Dr MGN/WHC B75 ....47 G3
Harvey Rd
LGN/SDN/BHAMAIR B26 ....129 H5
WSLW WS2 ....27 F5
Harvills Hawthorn WBROM B70 ....70 D4
Harvine Wk STRBR DY8 ....135 E4
Harvington Dr SHLY B90 ....195 H2
Harvington Rd BILS/COS WV14 ....68 B2
HALE B63 ....138 B5
LGLYGN/QTN B68 ....123 E4
SLYOAK B29 ....158 C2
Harvington Wy
WALM/CURD B76 ....78 B3
Harwin Cl
DUNHL/THL/PER WV6 ....22 B3
Harwood Gv SHLY B90 ....180 C5
Harwood St WBROM B70 ....87 F3
Hasbury Cl HALE B63 ....138 A5
Hasbury Rd RIDG/WDGT B32 ....157 E2
Haseley Rd HDSW B21 ....107 G2
SOLH B91 ....164 A4
Haselor Rd SCFLD/BOLD B73 ....76 C2
Haselour Rd
CHWD/FDBR/MGN B37 ....113 H4
Haselwell Dr BVILLE B30 ....177 H2
Haskell St WSL WS1 ....57 F1
Haslucks Cl SHLY B90 ....193 G1
Haslucks Cft SHLY B90 ....180 A2
Haslucks Green Rd SHLY B90 ....193 G1
Hassop Rd PBAR/PBCH B42 ....74 D4
Hastings Ct DUDN DY1 ....83 G4
Hastings Rd ERDW/GRVHL B23 ....75 H4
Haswell Rd HALE B63 ....137 H4
Hatcham Rd KGSTG B44 ....76 A1
Hatchett St LOZ/NWT B19 ....109 E4
Hatchford Av HIA/OLT B92 ....148 A4
Hatchford Brook Rd
HIA/OLT B92 ....148 A4
Hatch Heath Cl WMBN WV5 ....64 D4
Hateley Dr
ETTPK/GDPK/PENN WV4 ....52 C4
Hatfield Cl ERDW/GRVHL B23 ....76 B4
Hatfield Rd HAG/WOL DY9 ....136 A3
LOZ/NWT B19 ....108 D1
Hathaway Cl WLNHL WV13 ....39 F5
Hathaway Ms STRBR DY8 * 117 G1
Hathaway Rd MGN/WHC B75 ....47 E1
SHLY B90 ....180 B4
Hatherden Dr WALM/CURD B76 ....78 C1
Hathersage Rd
PBAR/PBCH B42 ....74 D4
Hatherton Gdns WOLVN WV10 ....13 E5
Hatherton Gv SLYOAK B29 ....158 B1
Hatherton Pl ALDR WS9 ....30 A3
Hatherton Rd BILS/COS WV14 ....54 B2
WSL WS1 ....4 E3
Hatherton St WSL WS1 ....4 E2
Hattersley Gv SPARK B11 ....146 A4
Hatton Crs WOLVN WV10 ....24 A3
Hatton Gdns PBAR/PBCH B42 ....74 B4
Hatton Rd
DUNHL/THL/PER WV6 * 36 B2
Hattons Gv CDSL WV8 ....10 D5
Hatton St BILS/COS WV14 ....54 A4
Haughton Rd
BFLD/HDSWWD B20 ....90 C5
Haunch La MOS/BIL B13 ....161 G5
Haunchwood Dr
WALM/CURD B76 ....78 B4
Havacre La BILS/COS WV14 ....68 C1
Havelock Cl BDMR/CCFT WV3 ....51 E1
Havelock Rd
BFLD/HDSWWD B20 ....90 C4
SPARK B11 ....145 G3
WASH/WDE B8 ....110 C4
Haven Cft GTB/HAM B43 ....73 F3
Haven Dr ACGN B27 ....146 B4
The Haven
ALE/KHTH/YWD B14 ....179 F1
BKHL/PFLD WV2 ....37 E5
STRBR DY8 ....117 H2
Haverford Dr RBRY B45 ....188 B2
Havergal Wk HALE B63 ....137 F3
Haverhill Cl BLOX/PEL WS3 ....16 C4
Hawbridge Cl SHLY B90 ....195 H2
Hawbush Gdns STRBR DY8 ....118 C3
Hawbush Rd BLOX/PEL WS3 ....28 A4
BRLYHL DY5 ....118 C2
Hawcroft Gv BKDE/SHDE B34 ....113 E3
Hawes Cl WSL WS1 ....57 F2
Hawes La BLKHTH/ROWR B65 ....103 H5
Hawes Rd WSL WS1 ....57 F2
Haweswater Dr KGSWFD DY6 ....99 H3
Hawfield Cl OLDBY B69 ....104 A2
Hawfield Gv
CSCFLD/WYGN B72 ....77 G4
Hawfield Rd OLDBY B69 ....104 A2
Hawker Dr CVALE B35 ....94 B4
Hawkesbury Rd SHLY B90 ....179 H4
Hawkes Cl BVILLE B30 ....160 A2
Hawkesford Cl CBROM B36 ....112 C1
FOAKS/STRLY B74 ....47 F4
Hawkesford Rd STETCH B33 ....131 F1
Hawkes La WBROM B70 ....71 E4
Hawkesley Crs NFLD/LBR B31 ....175 F4
Hawkesley Dr NFLD/LBR B31 ....175 F5
Hawkesley End
HWK/WKHTH B38 ....176 B5
Hawkesley Mill La
NFLD/LBR B31 ....175 F3
Hawkesley Rd DUDN DY1 ....101 H1
Hawkes St SMHTH B10 ....128 B4
Hawkestone Crs WBROM B70 ....70 D5
Hawkestone Rd SLYOAK B29 ....158 C3
Hawkeswell Cl HIA/OLT B92 ....164 A2
Hawkeswell Dr KGSWFD DY6 ....99 H1
Hawkeswell La
CSHL/WTROR B46 ....133 H1
Hawkesyard Rd
ERDE/BCHGN B24 ....92 C5
Hawkhurst Rd
ALE/KHTH/YWD B14 ....178 B3
Hawkinge Dr CVALE B35 ....94 C2
Hawkins Cl DIG/EDG B5 ....144 A1
Hawkins Cft TPTN/OCK DY4 ....85 G3
Hawkin's Pl BILS/COS WV14 ....54 B5
Hawkins St WBROM B70 ....71 E3
Hawkley Cl WOLV WV1 ....38 B3
Hawkley Rd WOLV WV1 ....38 B3
Hawkmoor Gdns
HWK/WKHTH B38 ....177 E5
Hawksford Crs WOLVN WV10 ....23 F3
Hawkshead Dr DOR/KN B93 ....196 D2
Hawksmoor Dr
DUNHL/THL/PER WV6 ....34 B2
Hawkstone Ct
DUNHL/THL/PER WV6 ....20 B5
Hawkswell Av WMBN WV5 ....81 E1
Hawkswell Dr WLNHL WV13 ....39 F5
Hawkswood Dr
BILS/COS WV14 ....54 D5
Hawkswood Gv
ALE/KHTH/YWD B14 ....178 D2
Hawksworth Crs
CHWD/FDBR/MGN B37 ....132 C1
Hawley Cl RUSH/SHEL WS4 ....42 B1
Hawnby Gv WALM/CURD B76 ....78 C1
Hawne Cl HALE B63 ....138 A1
The Hawnelands HALE B63 ....138 B2
Hawne La HALE B63 ....138 A1
Hawskford Crs WOLVN WV10 ....23 F3
Hawthorn Brook Wy
ERDW/GRVHL B23 ....76 C3
Hawthorn Cl BORD B9 ....127 H3
ERDW/GRVHL B23 ....76 D4
Hawthorn Coppice
HAG/WOL DY9 ....152 C4
Hawthorn Cft
LGLYGN/QTN B68 ....123 H5
Hawthorne Dr HLYWD B47 ....192 D2
Hawthorne Gv SEDG DY3 ....83 F4
Hawthorne La CDSL WV8 ....20 D1
Hawthorne Rd
BKHL/PFLD WV2 ....52 B2
BVILLE B30 ....159 F5
CBROM B36 ....113 G2
DUDN DY1 ....84 C2
EDG B15 ....125 G5
HALE B63 ....138 A5
SHHTH WV12 ....26 B3
WNSFLD WV11 ....15 E4
Hawthorn Gv LOZ/NWT B19 * 108 C1
Hawthorn Pk
BFLD/HDSWWD B20 ....89 G3
Hawthorn Pl WSLW WS2 ....40 C2
Hawthorn Rd BRLYHL DY5 ....119 G4
CSCFLD/WYGN B72 ....77 G2
DARL/WED WS10 ....55 H4
DSYBK/YTR WS5 ....57 F3
FOAKS/STRLY B74 ....45 G4
KGSTG B44 ....75 G4
RUSH/SHEL WS4 ....28 D2
TPTN/OCK DY4 ....69 G3
WOLV WV1 ....38 B5
The Hawthorns
HAG/WOL DY9 * 169 F1
MOS/BIL B13 * 144 B4
Hawthorn Ter DARL/WED WS10 ....55 H4
Haxby Av BKDE/SHDE B34 ....112 C3
The Haybarn WALM/CURD B76 ....78 C2
Haybridge Av STRBR DY8 ....152 B5
Haybrook Dr SPARK B11 ....145 H3
Haycock Pl DARL/WED WS10 ....55 E1
Haycroft Av WASH/WDE B8 ....110 C4
Haycroft Dr FOAKS/STRLY B74 ....47 E1
Haydn Sanders Sq WSL WS1 ....4 D6
Haydock Cl CBROM B36 ....111 G1
DUNHL/THL/PER WV6 ....22 D5
Haydon Cl DOR/KN B93 ....198 D1
Haydon Cft STETCH B33 ....130 C1
Haye House Gv CBROM B36 ....112 A2
Hayes Crs LGLYGN/QTN B68 ....105 H4
Hayes Cft HWK/WKHTH B38 ....190 C1
Hayes Dr ERDE/BCHGN B24 ....93 H1
Hayes Gv ERDE/BCHGN B24 ....77 H5
Hayes La HAG/WOL DY9 ....137 E1
Hayes Meadow
CSCFLD/WYGN B72 ....77 H4
Hayes Rd LGLYGN/QTN B68 ....105 H4
Hayes St WBROM B70 ....87 E2
The Hayes HAG/WOL DY9 ....137 E2
NFLD/LBR B31 ....190 A1
SHHTH WV12 ....25 H4
Hayfield Ct MOS/BIL B13 ....144 D5
Hayfield Gdns MOS/BIL B13 ....144 D5
Hayfield Rd MOS/BIL B13 ....144 D5
Hay Gn HAG/WOL DY9 ....136 B2
Hay Green La BVILLE B30 ....159 F4
Hay Hall Rd SPARK B11 ....145 H2
Hay Hl DSYBK/YTR WS5 ....43 G5
Hayland Rd ERDW/GRVHL B23 ....76 C5
Hay La SHLY B90 ....195 G2
Hayle Cl HWK/WKHTH B38 ....177 F3
Hayley Green Rd
RIDG/WDGT B32 ....157 F2
Hayley Park Rd HALE B63 ....154 C2
Hayling Cl RBRY B45 ....173 H4
Hayling Gv BDMR/CCFT WV3 ....51 H2
The Haylofts HALE B63 ....154 C1
Haynes La DSYBK/YTR WS5 ....57 H4
Hay Pk DIG/EDG B5 ....143 H1
Haypits Cl HHTH/SAND B71 ....72 A4
Hayrick Dr KGSWFD DY6 ....99 F2
Hay Rd YDLY B25 ....129 E5
Hayseech CDYHTH B64 ....121 G5
Hayseech Rd HALE B63 ....138 B1
The Hays Kent's Moat
LGN/SDN/BHAMAIR B26 ....130 C3
Haytor Av
ALE/KHTH/YWD B14 ....160 D5
Haywain Cl COVEN WV9 ....11 H5
Hayward Rd MGN/WHC B75 ....62 C1
Haywards Cl BLOX/PEL WS3 ....17 H4
ERDW/GRVHL B23 ....92 C1
Hayward St BILS/COS WV14 ....68 B3
Haywharf Rd BRLYHL DY5 ....100 D4
Haywood Dr
DUNHL/THL/PER WV6 ....35 G1
RMSLY B62 ....122 A4
Haywood Rd STETCH B33 ....131 F2
Haywood's Farm
HHTH/SAND B71 ....72 B1
Hazel Av DARL/WED WS10 ....56 A4
SCFLD/BOLD B73 ....76 A2
Hazelbank HWK/WKHTH B38 ....176 C3
Hazelbeach Rd WASH/WDE B8 ....110 D4
Hazelbeech Rd WBROM B70 ....87 F4
Hazel Cft
CHWD/FDBR/MGN B37 ....132 B3
NFLD/LBR B31 ....175 G2
Hazeldene Gv AST/WIT B6 * 109 E1
Hazeldene Rd HALE B63 ....138 A5
STETCH B33 ....131 F5
Hazel Dr HLYWD B47 ....192 D2
SLYOAK B29 ....158 B3
Hazeley Cl HRBN B17 ....124 B5
Hazel Gdns ACGN B27 * 146 C3
CDSL WV8 ....10 C3
Hazel Gv BILS/COS WV14 ....54 A1
HOCK/TIA B94 ....198 A5
STRBR DY8 ....134 C4
WBROM B70 ....87 G5
WMBN WV5 ....65 E4
Hazelhurst Rd
ALE/KHTH/YWD B14 ....161 E3
CBROM B36 ....113 G2
Hazelmere Dr BDMR/CCFT WV3 ....35 E4
Hazelmere Rd HLGN/YWD B28 ....162 D2
Hazeloak Rd SHLY B90 ....180 A4
Hazel Rd BDMR/CCFT WV3 ....51 E1
DUDN DY1 ....84 C4
KGSWFD DY6 ....100 A4
RBRY B45 ....187 H2
TPTN/OCK DY4 ....70 A2
Hazelton Cl SOLH B91 ....181 H4
Hazeltree Cft ACGN B27 ....146 B5
Hazeltree Gv DOR/KN B93 ....196 C5
Hazelville Gv HLGN/YWD B28 ....163 E4
Hazelville Rd HLGN/YWD B28 ....163 E4
Hazelwell Crs BVILLE B30 ....160 B4
Hazelwell Dr
ALE/KHTH/YWD B14 ....160 D4
Hazelwell Fordrough
BVILLE B30 ....160 B3
Hazelwell La BVILLE B30 ....160 A3
Hazelwell Rd BVILLE B30 ....160 A4
Hazelwood Dr WNSFLD WV11 ....24 A5
Hazelwood Gv SHHTH WV12 ....26 B5
Hazelwood Rd ACGN B27 ....146 B5
DUDN DY1 ....83 H1
FOAKS/STRLY B74 ....44 D4
Hazlemere Dr
FOAKS/STRLY B74 ....47 E4
Hazlitt Gv BVILLE B30 ....176 B1
Headborough Wk ALDR WS9 ....30 B1
Headingley Dr KINVER DY7 ....116 D3
Headingley Rd HDSW B21 ....89 G4
Headland Dr WASH/WDE B8 ....110 B4
Headland Rd BDMR/CCFT WV3 ....34 D4
The Headlands
FOAKS/STRLY B74 ....46 A2
Headley Cft HWK/WKHTH B38 ....176 B5
Headley Heath La
HWK/WKHTH B38 ....191 F1
Headley Ri SHLY B90 ....180 D3
Headway Rd WOLVN WV10 ....12 C4
Heale Cl HALE B63 ....120 A5
Heanor Cft AST/WIT B6 ....109 H1
Heantun Ri WOLV WV1 * 37 E1
Heantun Rw WNSFLD WV11 * 15 F5
Heartland Ms
BLKHTH/ROWR B65 ....121 H2
Heartlands Pkwy
WASH/WDE B8 ....110 A4
Heartlands Pl WASH/WDE B8 ....110 C5
Heath Acres DARL/WED WS10 ....55 E4
Heath Bridge Cl
RUSH/SHEL WS4 ....28 C2
Heathbrook Av KGSWFD DY6 ....99 F2
Heathcliff Rd DUDS DY2 ....103 F2
SPARK B11 ....145 H3
Heath Cl BVILLE B30 ....159 F5
MGN/WHC B75 ....63 F1
TPTN/OCK DY4 ....85 H1
Heathcote Av SOLH B91 ....181 E2
Heathcote Rd BVILLE B30 ....160 A5
Heath Cft NFLD/LBR B31 ....189 G1
Heath Croft Rd MGN/WHC B75 ....47 G4
Heath End Rd HAG/WOL DY9 ....185 G1
Heather Av DSYBK/YTR WS5 ....57 H4
Heather Cl CBROM B36 ....114 A1
WNSFLD WV11 ....25 E5
Heather Court Gdns
FOAKS/STRLY B74 ....47 E5
Heather Cft KGSTG B44 ....75 F2
Heather Dl MOS/BIL B13 ....143 G5
Heather Dr RBRY B45 ....187 H2
Heather Gv SHHTH WV12 ....40 C1
SOLH B91 ....165 G4
Heatherleigh Rd CBROM B36 ....113 H1
Heather Rd BLOX/PEL WS3 ....26 D2
DUDN DY1 ....84 C2
GTB/HAM B43 ....73 E3
SMHTH B10 ....128 D4
SMTHWKW B67 ....106 A4
Heath Farm Rd CDSL WV8 ....10 D5
STRBR DY8 ....135 E4
Heathfield Av
BFLD/HDSWWD B20 ....108 B1
Heathfield Cl CDYHTH B64 ....121 F2
DOR/KN B93 ....197 E3
Heathfield Dr BLOX/PEL WS3 ....16 D5
Heathfield Gdns STRBR DY8 ....135 F3
Heathfield La DARL/WED WS10 ....55 E2
Heathfield La West
DARL/WED WS10 ....54 D3
Heathfield Rd
ALE/KHTH/YWD B14 ....161 E2
FOAKS/STRLY B74 ....46 D2
HALE B63 ....138 A4
LOZ/NWT B19 ....108 B2
Heathfields CDSL WV8 ....20 C1
Heathfield Wy CDYHTH B64 ....121 F3
Heath Gdns SOLH B91 ....165 F4
Heath Gn DUDN DY1 ....83 H1
Heathgreen Cl
CHWD/FDBR/MGN B37 ....132 D1
Heath Green Gv WSNGN B18 * 107 G5
Heath Green Rd WSNGN B18 ....107 G5
Heath Gv CDSL WV8 ....10 D4
Heath Hill Rd
DUNHL/THL/PER WV6 ....34 C4
Heath House Dr WMBN WV5 ....80 B1
Heath House La CDSL WV8 ....20 C2
Heathland Av BKDE/SHDE B34 ....112 C2
Heathlands WMBN WV5 ....80 B1
Heathlands Cl KGSWFD DY6 ....100 A1
Heathlands Gv NFLD/LBR B31 ....175 G4
Heathlands Rd
SCFLD/BOLD B73 ....76 D1
The Heathlands
BLKHTH/ROWR B65 ....122 A3
STRBR DY8 ....135 H3
WMBN WV5 ....80 B1
Heath La HHTH/SAND B71 ....71 H4
STRBR DY8 ....135 G3
Heathleigh Rd
HWK/WKHTH B38 ....176 A5
Heathmere Av YDLY B25 ....129 H4
Heathmere Dr
CHWD/FDBR/MGN B37 ....131 H2
Heath Mill Cl WMBN WV5 ....80 B2
Heath Mill La BORD B9 ....127 G3
Heath Mill Rd WMBN WV5 ....80 B2
Heath Pk WOLVN WV10 * ....12 C
Heath Ri ALE/KHTH/YWD B14 ....178 C
Heath Rd BVILLE B30 ....176 A
DARL/WED WS10 ....40 C
DUDS DY2 ....120 B
HLYWD B47 ....192 C
SHHTH WV12 ....26 B
SOLH B91 ....165 F
Heath Rd South
NFLD/LBR B31 ....175 H
Heathside Dr BLOX/PEL WS3 ....18 A
HWK/WKHTH B38 ....177 F
Heath St BLKHTH/ROWR B65 ....122 A
STRBR DY8 ....135 F
WSNGN B18 ....107 F
Heath St South WSNGN B18 * ....107 H
Heath Wy BKDE/SHDE B34 ....112 E
Heathway Cl BKDE/SHDE B34 ....112 C
Heathy Farm Cl
RIDG/WDGT B32 ....157 F
Heathy Ri RIDG/WDGT B32 ....140 A
Heaton Cl WOLVN WV10 ....13 E
Heaton Dr EDG B15 ....125 H
Heaton Rd SOLH B91 ....164 E
Heaton St WSNGN B18 ....108 E
Hebden Gv HLGN/YWD B28 179
SHHTH WV12 25
Heddon Pl VAUX/NECH B7 * 127
Hedera Cl DSYBK/YTR WS5 57
Hedgefield Gv HALE B63 137
Hedgerow Dr KGSWFD DY6 81
The Hedgerows RMSLY B62 172
The Hedges WMBN WV5 64
Hedgetree Cft
CHWD/FDBR/MGN B37 132
Hedgley Gv STETCH B33 112
Hedingham Gv
CHWD/FDBR/MGN B37 132
Hedley Cft CVALE B35 94
Hednesford Rd BRWNH WS8 8
Heeley Rd SLYOAK B29 142
Hefford Dr SMTHWK B66 106
Helena St CBHAMW B1 2
Helenny Cl WNSFLD WV11 24
Helford Cl TPTN/OCK DY4 84
Hellaby Cl CSCFLD/WYGN B72 62
Hellier Av TPTN/OCK DY4 85
Hellier Dr WMBN WV5 64
Hellier Rd WOLVN WV10 13
Hellier St DUDS DY2 102
Helming Dr WOLV WV1 38
Helmsdale Wy SEDG DY3 68
Helmsley Cl BRLYHL DY5 119
Helmsley Rd WNSFLD WV11 24
Helmswood Dr
CHWD/FDBR/MGN B37 13
Helston Cl DSYBK/YTR WS5 5
STRBR DY8 11
Helstone Gv SPARK B11 14
Helston Rd DSYBK/YTR WS5 5
Hembs Crs GTB/HAM B43 7
Hemlingford Cft
CHWD/FDBR/MGN B37 13
Hemlingford Rd
CHWD/FDBR/MGN B37 11
WALM/CURD B76 7
Hemmings Cl STRBR DY8 13
WOLVN WV10
Hemmings St DARL/WED WS10 4
Hemplands Rd STRBR DY8 13
Hempole La TPTN/OCK DY4 7
Hemyock Rd SLYOAK B29 15
Henbury Dr
CHWD/FDBR/MGN B37 1
Henbury Rd ACGN B27 14
Henderson Wk TPTN/OCK DY4 6
Henderson Wy
BLKHTH/ROWR B65 1
Hendon Cl SEDG DY3
WOLVN WV10
Hendon Rd SPARK B11 1
Heneage Pl VAUX/NECH B7 * 1
Heneage St VAUX/NECH B7
Heneage St West
VAUX/NECH B7
Henfield Cl WNSFLD WV11
Hengham Rd
LGN/SDN/BHAMAIR B26 1
Henley Cl BLOX/PEL WS3
SCFLD/BOLD B73
TPTN/OCK DY4
Henley Crs SOLH B91 1

RMSLY B62	139 G1
Hollies Ri *CDYHTH* B64	121 F4
Hollies Rd *WED* B69	103 G1
Hollies St *BRLYHL* DY5	101 F2
The Hollies *AST/WIT* B6	109 H1
BKHL/PFLD WV2 *	6 E7
SMTHWK B66	107 E5
Hollin Brow Cl *DOR/KN* B95	197 F5
Hollingberry La	
WALM/CURD B76	65 F5
Hollings Gv *SOLH* B91	181 H5
Hollington Rd *WOLV* WV1	38 B5
Hollington Wy *SHLY* B90	196 A1
Hollinwell Cl *BLOX/PEL* WS3	16 C4
Hollister Dr *RIDG/WDGT* B32	141 F4
Holloway *NFLD/LBR* B31	158 A4
Holloway Bank	
DARL/WED WS10	70 D3
Holloway Circ Queensway	
CBHAMW B1 *	3 F7
Holloway Dr *WMBN* WV5	80 C1
Holloway Head *EDG* B15	2 D7
Holloway St *WOLV* WV1	53 E1
SEDG DY3	83 F2
Holloway St West *SEDG* DY3	68 A7
The Holloway	
DUNHL/THL/PER WV6	35 F5
SEDG DY8	80 B5
Hollow Cft *NFLD/LBR* B31	118 B5
Hollow Cft *NFLD/LBR* B31	175 H2
Hollow Croft Rd *SHHTH* WV12	25 H3
The Hollow *MOS/BIL* B13	144 A3
Holly Av *HIA/OLT* B12	144 C2
SLYOAK B29	143 H4
Hollybank Av *WNSFLD* WV11	15 E4
Hollybank Cl *BLOX/PEL* WS3	27 E1
Hollybank Gv *HALE* B63	154 D1
Hollybank Rd *MOS/BIL* B13	161 G4
Hollyberry Av *SOLH* B91	181 G5
Hollyberry Cl *HALE* B63	138 C4
Hollyberry Cft	
BKDE/SHDE B34	113 G3
Holly Bush Gv *SLYOAK* B29	158 C3
Holly Bush Gv	
RIDG/WDGT B32	123 H5
Hollybush La	
ETTPK/GDPK/PENN WV4	50 D4
STRBR DY8	118 B5
Holly Cl *SHHTH* WV12	26 A4
WALM/CURD B76	78 B1
Hollycot Gdns *BHTH/HG* B12	144 B2
Holly Ct *DSYBK/YTR* WS5	57 G4
Hollycroft Rd *HDSW* B21	89 F5
Hollydale Rd	
BLKHTH/ROWR B65	122 B1
ERDE/BCHGN B24	93 G3
Holly Dell *HWK/WKHTH* B38	177 F3
Holly Dr *ACGN* B27	146 B5
HLYWD B47	192 D1
Hollyfaste Rd *STECH* B33	130 D3
Hollyfield Av *SOLH* B91	181 E2
Hollyfield Crs *MGN/WHC* B75	63 E4
Hollyfield Crs *MGN/WHC* B75	63 E4
Hollyfield Rd *MGN/WHC* B75	63 E5
Hollyfield Rd *MGN/WHC* B75	63 E5
Holly Gv *BDMR/CCFT* WV3	159 H2
BVILLE B30	
LOZ/NWT B19	108 B1
STRBR DY8	102 A3
Holly Hall Rd *DUDS* DY2	
Hollyhedge Cl *NFLD/LBR* B31	157 H4
WSLW WS2	4 A2
Hollyhedge La *WSLW* WS2	4 A1
Hollyhedge Rd	
HHTH/SAND B71	72 A4
Holly Hill Rd *RBRY* B45	174 A3
Hollyhock Rd *ACGN* B27	162 D1
DUDS DY2	85 F5
Hollyhurst *CSHL/WTROR* B46	96 C4
Hollyhurst Dr *STRBR* DY8	118 A1
Hollyhurst Gv	
LGN/SDN/BHAMAIR B26	147 E1
SHLY B90	180 B5
Hollyhurst Rd *SCFLD/BOLD* B73	60 C5
Holly La *ALDR* WS9	
CHWD/FDBR/MGN B37	131 H4
ERDE/BCHGN B24	93 G4
FOAKS/STRLY B74	47 E2
SMTHWK B66	106 A2
SMTHWK B66	105 H5
Hollymoor Wy *NFLD/LBR* B31	174 C4
Hollymount *RMSLY* B62	123 E5
Hollyoak Cft *NFLD/LBR* B31	175 H5
Hollyoak Gv *SOLH* B91	181 G3
Hollyoake Cl *LGLYGN/QTN* B68	123 E2
Hollyoake Cl *LGLYGN/QTN* B68	123 E2
Hollyoak Rd *FOAKS/STRLY* B74	60 D2
Hollyoak St *HHTH/SAND* B71	72 B1
Holly Park Dr *ERDE/BCHGN* B24	93 F3
Holly Pl *AST/WIT* B6 *	
SLYOAK B29	
Holly Rd *BFLD/HDSWWD* B20	107 H1
BLKHTH/ROWR B65	121 H3
BVILLE B30	177 E1
DARL/WED WS10	55 H3
DUDN DY1	
HHTH/SAND B71	72 A3
LDYWD/EDGR B16	107 H6
LGLYGN/QTN B68	123 G4
Holly St *DUDN* DY1	101 G2
SMTHWK B66	107 E3
Hollywell Rd *DOR/KN* B93	197 E3
LGN/SDN/BHAMAIR B26	
Hollywell St *BILS/COS* WV14	68 A2
Holly Wy *GTB/HAM* B43	74 A2
Hollywood By-Pass	
HLYWD B47	192 A3
Hollywood Cft *PBAR/PBCH* B42	73 H3
Hollywood Gdns *HLYWD* B47	178 C5
Hollywood La *HLYWD* B47	192 D1
Holman Cl *WNLHL* WV13	39 E3
Holman Rd *WNLHL* WV13	39 E3
Holmbridge Gv	
RUSH/SHEL WS4	18 D5
Holme Ml *WOLV* WV10	12 D3
Holme Rd *RBRY* B45	187 H2
Holmes Dr *SHHTH* WV12	26 B4
The Holmes *WOLV* WV10	12 D4

Holme Wy *RUSH/SHEL* WS4	28 D3
Holmwood Rd *BORD* B9	128 B3
Holt Ct North *VAUX/NECH* B7 *	3 K2
Holt Ct South *VAUX/NECH* B7 *	3 K2
Holte Dr *MGN/WHC* B75	47 H5
Holte Rd *AST/WIT* B6	109 G1
HIA/OLT B11	145 F2
Holtes Wk *AST/WIT* B6 *	109 H1
Holt La *RMSLY* B62	171 H1
Holt Rd *RMSLY* B62	123 E5
Holtshill La *WSL* WS1	5 G3
Holt St *VAUX/NECH* B7	3 J1
Holy Cross Gn *HAG/WOL* DY9	170 C3
Holy Cross La *HAG/WOL* DY9	170 C5
Holyhead Rd *CDSL* WV8	20 B2
HDSW B21	107 E1
HDSW B21	107 H1
Holyoak Cl *AST/WIT* B6 *	91 F5
Holyrood Gv *AST/WIT* B6 *	109 E1
Holy Well Cl *LDYWD/EDGR* B16	126 A2
Holywell La *RBRY* B45	187 F2
Homecroft Rd *YDLY* B25	130 A4
Homedene Rd *NFLD/LBR* B31	158 A5
Homefield Rd *CDSL* WV8	10 D4
Homelands *PBAR/PBCH* B42	74 B4
The Homelands *WOLVN* WV10 *	12 C1
Homelea Rd *YDLY* B25	129 H4
Homemead Gv *RBRY* B45	187 H1
Homer Hill Rd *HALE* B63	120 B5
Homer Rd *MGN/WHC* B75	47 E4
SOLH B91	181 H2
Homers Fold *BILS/COS* WV14	53 H3
Homer St *BHTH/HG* B12	144 B2
Homerton Rd *KGSTG* B44	75 H2
Homestead Cl *SEDG* DY3	83 G1
Homestead Dr *MGN/WHC* B75	47 G2
Homestead Rd *STECH* B33	130 D3
Homewood Cl	
WALM/CURD B76	63 E5
Honesty Cl *BRWNH* WS8	8 D5
Honeswode Cl	
BFLD/HDSWWD B20	108 A1
Honeyborne Rd *MGN/WHC* B75	62 D1
Honeybourne Cl *HALE* B63	138 C4
Honeybourne Crs *WMBN* WV5	80 D1
Honeybourne Rd *HALE* B63	139 E4
STECH B33	131 E4
Honeybourne Wy	
WLNHL WV13	40 A3
Honeycomb Wy	
NFLD/LBR B31	175 E2
Honeysuckle Av *KGSWFD* DY6	100 A2
Honeysuckle Cl	
RIDG/WDGT B32	140 B2
Honeysuckle Dr	
DSYBK/YTR WS5	57 G5
Honeysuckle Gv *ACGN* B27	146 C2
Honeytree Cl *KGSWFD* DY6	118 B1
Honiley Dr *KGSTG* B44	76 A1
Honiley Rd *STECH* B33	130 C2
Honister Cl *BRLYHL* DY5	119 H3
Honiton Cl *NFLD/LBR* B31	175 H1
Honiton Crs *NFLD/LBR* B31	175 H1
Honiton Wy *ALDR* WS9	29 H5
Honnington Ct *SLYOAK* B29 *	158 B1
Honor Av	
ETTPK/GDPK/PENN WV4	52 A3
Hood Gv *BVILLE* B30	176 B1
Hook Dr *FOAKS/STRLY* B74	46 C1
Hooper St *WSNGN* B18	107 H5
Hoosen Cl *RMSLY* B62	140 A1
Hopedale Rd *RIDG/WDGT* B32	140 B2
Hope Rd *TPTN/OCK* DY4	70 A5
Hope St *DIG/EDG* B5	126 D4
DUDS DY2	102 D1
RMSLY B62	122 D4
STRBR DY8	117 H1
WBROM B70	88 A4
WSL WS1	4 E6
Hopkins Dr *HHTH/SAND* B71	72 A4
Hopkins St *TPTN/OCK* DY4	85 G4
Hopstone Gdns	
ETTPK/GDPK/PENN WV4	51 F3
Hopstone Rd *SLYOAK* B29 *	158 C1
Hopton Cl	
DUNHL/THL/PER WV6	34 D2
TPTN/OCK DY4	70 A1
Hopton Crs *WNSFLD* WV11	25 E4
Hopton Gdns *DUDN* DY1	84 A3
Hopton Gv *MOS/BIL* B13	162 A5
Hopwas Gv	
CHWD/FDBR/MGN B37	113 H4
Hopwood Cl *HALE* B63	138 C5
Hopwood Gv *NFLD/LBR* B31	189 E2
Hopyard Cl *SEDG* DY3	82 D3
Hopyard Gdns *BILS/COS* WV14	53 G5
Hopyard La *SEDG* DY3	82 D4
Hopyard Rd *WSLW* WS2	40 C3
Horace Partridge Rd	
DARL/WED WS10	54 C3
Horace St *BILS/COS* WV14	68 A3
Horatio Dr *MOS/BIL* B13	144 B3
Hordern Cl	
DUNHL/THL/PER WV6	22 B5
Hordern Crs *BRLYHL* DY5	119 F4
Hordern Gv	
DUNHL/THL/PER WV6	22 B5
Hordern Rd *H WOLVN* WV10 *	12 C1
Hordern Rd	
DUNHL/THL/PER WV6	36 C1
Hornbeam Cl *SLYOAK* B29	158 D3
Hornbeam Wk *BDMR/CCFT* WV3	6 B5
Hornbrook Gv *HIA/OLT* B92	163 G3
Hornby Gv	
ALE/KHTH/YWD B14	179 E1
Hornby Rd	
ETTPK/GDPK/PENN WV4	52 A4
Horne Wy *BKDE/SHDE* B34	113 G4
Horning Dr *BILS/COS* WV14	53 G5
Hornsey Gv *KGSTG* B44	75 G1
Hornsey Rd *KGSTG* B44	75 G1
Hornton Cl *FOAKS/STRLY* B74	32 B5
Horrell Rd	
LGN/SDN/BHAMAIR B26	147 H1
SHLY B90	179 H3
Horsecroft Dr *HHTH/SAND* B71	72 C3
Horsehills Dr *BDMR/CCFT* WV3	36 A3
Horselea Cft *WASH/WDE* B8	111 G5

Horseley Flds *WOLV* WV1	7 H4
Horseley Heath *TPTN/OCK* DY4	85 H2
Horseley Rd *TPTN/OCK* DY4	69 H5
Horseshoe Cl *WSLW* WS2	39 H5
Horse Shoes La	
LGN/SDN/BHAMAIR B26	147 H2
The Horseshoe	
LGLYGN/QTN B68	123 G2
Horsfall Rd *MGN/WHC* B75	63 G3
Horsham Av *STRBR* DY8	117 G1
Horsley Rd *FOAKS/STRLY* B74	45 H3
GTB/HAM B43	59 H4
Horton Cl *DARL/WED* WS10	55 F1
SEDG DY3	67 E5
Horton Gv *SHLY* B90	195 G5
Horton Pl *DARL/WED* WS10	55 F1
Horton Sq *BHTH/HG* B12	127 E5
Horton St *DARL/WED* WS10	55 F1
TPTN/OCK DY4	86 B1
WBROM B70	87 G5
Hospital La *BILS/COS* WV14	67 F4
Hospital St *BKHL/PFLD* WV2	7 F1
ERDW/CRVHL B23	92 C2
LOZ/NWT B19	3 F1
Hossil La *HAG/WOL* DY9	169 H5
Hothersall Dr *SCFLD/BOLD* B73	76 D3
Hotspur Rd *KGSTG* B44	75 F2
Hough Pl *WSLW* WS2	56 B1
Hough Rd	
ALE/KHTH/YWD B14	160 D4
WSLW WS2	55 H4
Houghton Ct *HLGN/YWD* B28	179 F1
Houghton St *OLDBY* B69	104 D3
WBROM B70	105 H1
Houldey Rd *NFLD/LBR* B31	175 H4
Houliston Cl *DARL/WED* WS10	56 B3
Houndel Gv *WMBN* WV5	64 D4
Houndsfield Cl *HLYWD* B47	195 E2
Houndsfield Gv *HLYWD* B47	192 C3
Houndsfield La *HLYWD* B47	192 D3
The Houx *STRBR* DY8	118 A4
Hove Rd *ACGN* B27	163 F1
Howard Rd	
ALE/KHTH/YWD B14	160 D3
BFLD/HDSWWD B20	90 B4
BILS/COS WV14	54 B5
GTB/HAM B43	73 E5
HIA/OLT B92	147 H4
WNSFLD WV11	25 F2
YDLY B25	146 C1
Howard Rd East	
ALE/KHTH/YWD B14	161 F2
Howard St *BKHL/PFLD* WV2	7 G7
LOZ/NWT B19	2 E1
WBROM B70	70 D4
Howarth Wy *AST/WIT* B6	109 G2
Howden Pl *BKDE/SHDE* B34	112 C4
Howdle's La *BRWNH* WS8	9 E2
Howe Crs *SHHTH* WV12	26 A4
Howell Rd *BKHL/PFLD* WV2	52 C1
Howes Cft *HALE* B35	94 C4
Howe St *CBHAMNE* B4	3 K3
Howford Gv *VAUX/NECH* B7	109 H5
Howland Cl *COVEN* WV9	11 H5
Howley Av *KGSTG* B44	75 E2
Howley Grange Rd	
RMSLY B62	139 H3
Hoylake Cl *BLOX/PEL* WS3	16 D4
Hoylake Dr *OLDBY* B69	103 G2
Hoylake Rd	
DUNHL/THL/PER WV6	20 B5
Hoyland Wy *BVILLE* B30	159 G2
Hubert Cl *BLOX/PEL* WS3	142 D5
Hubert Rd *SLYOAK* B29	142 D5
Hubert St *AST/WIT* B6	109 F4
The Hub *SOLH* B91 *	182 A2
Hucker Cl *WSLW* WS2	56 A1
Hucker Rd *WSLW* WS2	56 A1
Huddlestone Cl *WOLVN* WV10	13 G1
Huddleston Wy *SLYOAK* B29	158 B1
Huddocks Vw *BLOX/PEL* WS3	17 H2
Hudson Av *CSHL/WTROR* B46	115 F3
Hudson Gv	
DUNHL/THL/PER WV6	20 C5
Hudson's Dr *BVILLE* B30	177 E1
Hudswell Dr *BRLYHL* DY5	119 F4
Hughes Av *BDMR/CCFT* WV3	36 D5
Hughes Pl *BILS/COS* WV14	53 H1
Hughes Rd *BILS/COS* WV14	54 C3
DARL/WED WS10	54 C3
Hugh Porter Wy	
DUNHL/THL/PER WV6	22 B3
Hugh Rd *BHTH/HG* B10	128 C5
SMTHWK B67	105 H4
Hugh Vls *SMHTH* B10 *	128 C5
Hulbert Dr *DUDS* DY2	102 B5
Hulland Pl *BRLYHL* DY5	119 F4
Hullbrook Rd *MOS/BIL* B13	162 A5
Humber Av *WALM/CURD* B76	78 D4
Humber Gdns *HALE* B63	137 F2
Humber Gv *CBROM* B36	95 H5
Humber Rd *BDMR/CCFT* WV3	37 F5
Humberstone Rd	
ERDE/BCHGN B24	94 A2
Humpage Rd *BORD* B9	128 C2
Humphrey Middlemore Dr	
HRBN B17	142 B3
Humphreys St *SEDG* DY3	83 F3
Humphries Crs	
BILS/COS WV14	69 F1
Humphries Rd *WOLVN* WV10	25 F3
Hundred Acre Rd	
FOAKS/STRLY B74	60 B1
Hungary Cl *HAG/WOL* DY9	136 A2
Hungary Hi *HAG/WOL* DY9	136 A2
Hungerfield Rd *CBROM* B36	95 E5
Hungerford Rd *STRBR* DY8	135 E5
Hunningham Gv *SOLH* B91	181 H3
Hunnington Cl	
RIDG/WDGT B32	157 E1
Hunnington Crs *HALE* B63	138 D5
Hunscote Cl *SHLY* B90	179 H2
Hunslet Cl *RIDG/WDGT* B32	141 F3
Hunslet Rd *RIDG/WDGT* B32	141 F3
Hunstanton Av *HRBN* B17	124 B4

Hunstanton Cl *BRLYHL* DY5	119 E4
Hunter Crs *BLOX/PEL* WS3	28 B4
Hunters Cl *BILS/COS* WV14	54 C1
Hunter's Ride *KINVER* DY7	117 F2
Hunters Rd *LOZ/NWT* B19	108 B3
Hunter St	
DUNHL/THL/PER WV6	36 C1
Hunters V *LOZ/NWT* B19	108 C3
Huntingdon Rd	
HHTH/SAND B71	71 F4
Huntingtree Rd *HALE* B63	138 A5
Huntlands Rd *HALE* B63	138 A5
Huntley Dr *SOLH* B91	181 H3
Huntly Rd *LDYWD/EDGR* B16	126 A3
Hunton HI *ERDW/CRVHL* B23	92 B3
Hunton Rd *ERDW/CRVHL* B23	92 C5
Hunt's La *SHHTH* WV12	26 B4
Huntsman Cl *BILS/COS* WV14	68 D1
Hunts Mill Dr *BRLYHL* DY5	83 E5
Hunts Rd *BVILLE* B30	160 A3
Hurdis Rd *SHLY* B90	180 B1
Hurdlow Av *WSNGN* B18	108 B4
Hurley Cl *SCFLD/WYGN* B72	77 G1
DSYBK/YTR WS5	58 B2
Hurley Gv	
ERDW/CRVHL B23	76 A3
Hurleys Fold *DUDS* DY2	102 B4
Hurlingham Rd *KGSTG* B44	75 G2
Hurricane Wy *CVALE* B35	94 C4
Hursey Dr *TPTN/OCK* DY4	85 G1
Hurstbourne Crs *WOLV* WV1	113 G2
Hurstcroft Rd *STECH* B33	130 D1
Hurst Green Rd *DOR/KN* B93	122 C4
RMSLY B62	
WALM/CURD B76	73 F5
Hurst La North	
BKDE/SHDE B34	113 G1
Hurst Rd *BILS/COS* WV14	67 H2
SMTHWK B67	123 H2
Hurst St *DIG/EDG* B5	2 E7
The Hurst *HLGN/YWD* B47	192 C2
MOS/BIL B13	162 A3
The Hurstway	
ERDW/CRVHL B23	76 A3
Hurstwood Rd *KGSTG* B44	75 H4
Huskinson Cl *OLDBY* B69	85 H5
Hussey Rd *BRWNH* WS8	8 D4
Hutchings La *SHLY* B90	194 B3
Hutton Av *WASH/WDE* B8	110 D4
Hutton Rd *ERDW/CRVHL* B23	92 D5
WASH/WDE B8	110 D4
Huxbey Dr *HIA/OLT* B92	165 H2
Huxley Cl *COVEN* WV9	12 A4
Hyacinth Cl *DSYBK/YTR* WS5	57 F5
Hyatt Sq *BRLYHL* DY5	119 E5
Hyde Rd *WNSFLD* WV11	24 D4
Hydes Rd *DARL/WED* WS10	71 F2
The Hyde *HAG/WOL* DY9	136 B5
Hyett Wy *BILS/COS* WV14	69 H1
Hylda Rd *BFLD/HDSWWD* B20	90 B5
Hylstone Crs *WNSFLD* WV11	24 D4
Hylton St *WSNGN* B18	108 C4
Hyperion Dr	
ETTPK/GDPK/PENN WV4	51 G5
Hyperion Rd *CBROM* B36	94 A5
KINVER DY7	117 G5
Hyron Hall Rd *ACGN* B27	146 C5
Hyssop Cl *VAUX/NECH* B7	109 G4
Hytall Rd *SHLY* B90	179 E5
Hythe Gv *YDLY* B25	129 H4

I

Ibberton Rd	
ALE/KHTH/YWD B14	178 D2
Ibis Gdns *KGSWFD* DY6	100 D3
Ibstock Dr *STRBR* DY8	135 G3
Icknield Cl *FOAKS/STRLY* B74	45 G4
Icknield Port Rd	
LDYWD/EDGR B16	125 G1
Icknield Sq *LDYWD/EDGR* B16	126 A1
Icknield St *HWK/WKHTH* B38	191 E5
WSNGN B18	2 A2
Ida Rd *WBROM* B70	87 H5
WSLW WS2	41 G4
Idbury Rd *KGSTG* B44	75 G4
Idmiston Cft	
ALE/KHTH/YWD B14	178 B3
Idonia Rd	
DUNHL/THL/PER WV6	20 C5
Ilford Rd *ERDW/CRVHL* B23	76 B5
Iliffe Wy *HRBN* B17	142 B3
Ilkley Gv	
CHWD/FDBR/MGN B37	131 H2
Illey Cl *NFLD/LBR* B31	174 B4
Illey La *RMSLY* B62	156 A1
Illshaw *COVEN* WV9	12 A4
Illshaw Heath Rd	
HOCK/TIA B94	194 D5
Ilmington Dr *SCFLD/BOLD* B73	61 E5
Ilmington Rd *SLYOAK* B29	158 B1
Ilsham Gv *NFLD/LBR* B31	189 E2
Ilsley Rd *ERDW/CRVHL* B23	92 C1
Imperial Ri *CSHL/WTROR* B46	97 F4
Imperial Rd *BORD* B9	128 C3
Impsley Cl *CBROM* B36	112 D1
Ince Rd *DARL/WED* WS10	55 E1
Inchcape Av	
BFLD/HDSWWD B20	90 A3
Inchford Rd *HIA/OLT* B92	165 G3
Inchlaggan Rd *WOLVN* WV10	25 G2
Infantry Pl *MGN/WHC* B75	63 G2
Ingestre Dr *STRBR* DY8	117 G1
Ingestre Cl *BLOX/PEL* WS3	16 B4
Ingestre Rd *HLGN/YWD* B28	162 D3
WOLVN WV10	24 D1
Ingham Wy *HRBN* B17	124 B5
Ingleby Gdns	
DUNHL/THL/PER WV6	22 C5

Ingledew Cl *WSLW* WS2	40 D2
Inglefield Rd *STECH* B33	130 B1
Inglemere Gv *SLYOAK* B29	158 B3
Inglenook Dr	
BFLD/HDSWWD B20	90 B4
Ingleside Vls *SPARK* B11 *	145 E2
Ingleton Rd *WASH/WDE* B8	111 E2
Inglewood Av *BDMR/CCFT* WV3	36 B5
Inglewood Cl *KGSWFD* DY6 *	99 H4
Inglewood Gv	
FOAKS/STRLY B74	45 F4
Inglewood Rd *SPARK* B11	145 G2
Ingoldsby Rd *NFLD/LBR* B31	176 A2
Ingot Cl *WSLW* WS2	27 F4
Ingram Dr *GTB/HAM* B43	73 E3
Ingram Gv *ACGN* B27	146 A5
Ingram Pl *BLOX/PEL* WS3	27 F1
Ingram Rd *BLOX/PEL* WS3	27 F1
Inhedge St *SEDG* DY3	83 G1
The Inhedge *DUDN* DY1	
Inkberrow Cl *OLDBY* B69	
Inkberrow Rd *HALE* B63	138 B5
Inkerman St *VAUX/NECH* B7	127 H1
WOLV WV10	37 H2
Inland Rd *ERDE/BCHGN* B24	93 F4
Innage Rd *NFLD/LBR* B31	175 H1
The Innage *HLYWD* B47	192 C3
Innsworth Dr *CVALE* B35	94 C2
Inshaw Cl *STECH* B33	130 A1
Institute Rd	
ALE/KHTH/YWD B14	161 F2
KHL/VPK B14	138 B4
Instone Rd *HALE* B63	
Instow Cl *SHHTH* WV12	25 H2
Insull Av *ALE/KHTH/YWD* B14	178 D4
Intended St *HALE* B63	120 C5
International Dr	
LGN/SDN/BHAMAIR B26	149 G3
International Sq	
CHWD/FDBR/MGN B37 *	149 G1
Intown *WSL* WS1	5 F3
Intown Rw *WSL* WS1	5 F3
Inverclyde Dr	
ETTPK/GDPK/PENN WV4	52 D3
Inverclyde Rd	
BFLD/HDSWWD B20	90 A3
Inverkip Wk	
ETTPK/GDPK/PENN WV4	52 D3
Inverness Rd *NFLD/LBR* B31	175 F1
Inworth *COVEN* WV9	12 B4
Ipsley Gv *ERDW/CRVHL* B23	91 G5
Ipstones Av *STECH* B33	112 D1
Ireland Gn *WBROM* B70	87 F3
Ireland Green Rd *WBROM* B70	87 F3
Ireton Rd *BFLD/HDSWWD* B20	90 A1
WOLVN WV10	12 D1
Iris Cl *DUDS* DY2	85 G3
SLYOAK B29	158 D1
Iris Dr *ALE/KHTH/YWD* B14	177 H1
Irnham Rd *FOAKS/STRLY* B74	47 E1
Iron Bridge Wk *HAG/WOL* DY9	152 C2
Iron La *STECH* B33	111 H1
Irvan Av *WBROM* B70	86 C1
Irvine Cl *BLOX/PEL* WS3	27 F4
Irvine Rd *BLOX/PEL* WS3	27 F4
Irving Cl *SEDG* DY3	82 C4
Irving Rd *HIA/OLT* B92	148 A1
TPTN/OCK DY4	70 C2
Irving St *CBHAMW* B1	126 C4
Irwin Av *RBRY* B45	188 B3
Isaac Walton Pl *WBROM* B70	70 C4
Isbourne Wy *BORD* B9	127 H3
Isis Gv *CBROM* B36	113 F2
WLNHL WV13	40 B5
Island Rd *HDSW* B21	89 H4
Islington Hall B63	138 B4
Islington Rw *EDG* B15	126 A5
Ismere Rd *ERDE/BCHGN* B24	93 H4
Itchen Gv	
DUNHL/THL/PER WV6	34 B1
Ithon Gv *HWK/WKHTH* B38	190 D1
Ivanhoe Rd *BKHL/PFLD* WV2	52 C1
GTB/HAM B43	59 E2
Ivanhoe St *DUDS* DY2	102 B2
Ivatt Cl *RUSH/SHEL* WS4	28 D5
Iverley Rd *HALE* B63	139 G1
Iverley Wk *HAG/WOL* DY9	135 H5
Ivor Rd *SPARK* B11	144 D4
Ivy Av *BHTH/HG* B12	144 C2
Ivybridge Gv *PBAR/PBCH* B42	75 G4
Ivy Cft *COVEN* WV9	11 H5
Ivydale Av	
LGN/SDN/BHAMAIR B26	148 A1
Ivyfield Rd *ERDW/CRVHL* B23	91 H5
Ivy Gv *BRWNH* WS8	
Ivyhouse La *BILS/COS* WV14	68 A1
Ivyhouse Rd *HWK/WKHTH* B38	176 C1
Ivy House Rd *OLDBY* B69	104 A1
Ivy La *CBHAMNE* B4	
RMSLY B62	
Ivy Lodge Cl	
CHWD/FDBR/MGN B37	133
Ivy Rd *BVILLE* B30	160
DUDN DY1	
SCFLD/BOLD B73	
TPTN/OCK DY4	
Ivy Wy *SHLY* B90	
Izons La *WBROM* B70	
Izons Rd *WBROM* B70	

J

Jacamar Av *STECH* B33	
Jacey Rd *LDYWD/EDGR* B16	
SHLY B90	
Jackdaw Cl *SEDG* DY3	
Jackdaw Dr *CBROM* B36	
Jack Hayward Wy *WOLV* WV1	
Jack Holden Av *BILS/COS* WV14	
Jackson Cl *LGLYGN/QTN* B68	
SPARK B11 *	
TPTN/OCK DY4	
WOLVN WV10	
Jackson Dr *SMTHWK* B67	
Jackson Rd *WASH/WDE* B8	
Jackson St	
DUNHL/THL/PER WV6	

HAG/WOL DY9....................136 C2
LCLYGN/QTN B68..................105 F5
Jackson Wy RIDG/WDGT B32.....140 A2
Jacmar Crs SMTHWKW B67.......106 A3
Jacobean La DOR/KN DY5........183 F4
Jacoby Pl DIG/EDG B5.............143 G2
Jaffray Crs ERDE/BCHGN B24....92 D5
Jaffray Rd ERDE/BCHGN B24.....92 D5
Jakeman Rd BHTH/HG B12........144 A2
James Bridge Cl WSLW WS2.......56 B1
James Cl DARL/WED WS10........55 H1
James Dee Cl BRLYHL DY5.......119 H3
James Eaton Cl
  HHTH/SAND B71..................87 G1
James Rd CSHL/WTROR B46.....115 F1
Jameson St
  DUNHL/THL/PER WV6..............36 D1
  GTB/HAM B43.......................73 G4
  SPARK B11..........................145 H1
James Samuel Pl
  BHTH/HG B12.......................127 F5
James Scott Rd HALE B63.........137 E1
James St BILS/COS WV14.........54 A2
  CBHAMNW B3........................2 D3
  WLNHL WV13.........................39 G3
James Turner St WSNGN B18....107 G3
James Watt Dr LOZ/NWT B19....107 G3
James Watt Queensway
  CBHAMNE B4.........................3 J3
James Watt St HHTH/SAND B71..71 F3
Jane Lane Cl WSLW WS2...........40 D1
Janice Gv ALE/KHTH/YWD B14...178 D1
Janine Av WNSFLD WV11...........25 E3
Jaques Cl CVALE B35..............94 D4
Jardine Rd AST/WIT B6.............91 F5
Jarvis Crs OLDBY B69..............105 E5
Jarvis Rd ERDE/BCHGN B23.......92 D5
Jarvis Wy ERDE/BCHGN B24......110 C1
Jasmin Cft
  ALE/KHTH/YWD B14...............178 A2
Jasmine Cl COVEN WV9............11 H4
Jasmine Gv CDSL WV8..............85 G3
Jasmine Rd DUDS DY2..............85 F5
Jason Rd HAG/WOL DY9............136 D3
Javelin Av CVALE B35...............94 D4
Javelin PK DARL/WED WS10......70 B1
Jayne Cl HHTH/SAND B71..........71 G1
  WNSFLD WV11.......................24 D3
Jay Rd KGSWFD DY6................99 H1
Jays Av TPTN/OCK DY4..............85 H2
Jayshaw Av GTB/HAM B43.........73 G5
Jean Dr TPTN/OCK DY4.............79 F5
Jeavons Pl BILS/COS WV14........53 G3
Jedburgh Av
  DUNHL/THL/PER WV6...............34 C1
Jeddo St BKHL/PFLD WV2..........37 F5
Jeffcock Rd BDMR/CCFT WV3...36 C5
Jefferson Cl HHTH/SAND B71......71 F3
Jeffrey Av
  ETTPK/GDPK/PENN WV4...........52 D2
Jeffrey Rd BLKHTH/ROWR B65...122 C1
Jenkins Cl BILS/COS WV14.........53 G5
Jenkinson Rd DARL/WED WS10...70 B2
Jenks Av WMBN WV5................80 D1
Jennens Rd CBHAMNE B4............3 J3
Jenner Cl WSLW WS2................27 E4
Jenner Rd WSLW WS2...............26 D4
Jenner St BKHL/PFLD WV2...........7 J6
Jennings St CDYHTH B64..........121 F2
Jenny Cl BILS/COS WV14...........69 E2
Jenny Walkers La
  DUNHL/THL/PER WV6...............34 B5
Jephcott Rd WASH/WDE B8.......129 E1
Jephson Dr
  LGN/SDN/BHAMAIR B26..........130 D5
Jeremy Gv HIA/OLT B92............147 H3
Jeremy Rd
  ETTPK/GDPK/PENN WV4...........52 A3
Jerome Rd CSCFLD/WYGN B72...62 D4
  WSLW WS2............................41 E3
Jerrard Dr MGN/WHC B75..........62 C3
Jerrard Ms MGN/WHC B75..........62 C3
Jersey La ERDW/GRVHL B23.......76 B4
Jersey Cft CBROM B36.............114 B2
Jersey Rd WASH/WDE B8..........110 B5
Jervis Cl BRLYHL DY5...............101 E2
Jervis Crs FOAKS/STRLY B74......46 B2
Jervis Pk FOAKS/STRLY B74........46 A1
Jervis Ter HDSW B21 *...............87 G1
Jervoise Dr NFLD/LBR B31........158 D5
Jervoise La HHTH/SAND B71........72 A2
Jervoise St WBROM B70.............87 E2
Jesmond Gv ERDE/BCHGN B24....93 H2
Jessel Rd WSLW WS2................41 E3
Jessie Rd ALDR WS9..................30 A1
Jesson Cl WSL WS1..................57 G1
Jesson Rd MGN/WHC B75..........63 G5
Jevons Rd SCFLD/BOLD B73.......61 E5
Jevon St BILS/COS WV14...........68 C3
Jew's La CDSL WV8..................83 G2
Jiggins La EDG/WDGT B32........157 G2
Jill Av GTB/HAM B43.................73 E2
Jinscot Rd HALE B63...............147 H4
Joan Cl BHTH/HG B12..............127 F4
Joan St BKHL/PFLD WV2...........52 C2
Jockey Fld SEDG DY3................67 G5
Jockey La DARL/WED WS10........56 A4
Jockey Rd SCFLD/BOLD B73.......76 B1
Joeys La CDSL WV8.................11 E4
John Bright Cl TPTN/OCK DY4.....69 F5
John Bright St CBHAMW B1..........3 F7
John Fletcher Cl
  DARL/WED WS10....................56 B4
John Harper St WLNHL WV13......39 H3
John Howell Dr TPTN/OCK DY4....85 G1
Johns Kempe Wy
  BHTH/HG B12.......................127 G5
John Padden Cl
  BLKHTH/ROWR B65...............121 H3
John Riley Dr SHHTH WV12.........26 A2

John Rd RMSLY B62.................139 H5
Johns Gv GTB/HAM B43............75 E3
John's La OLDBY B69................85 H2
  TPTN/OCK DY4......................85 H2
Johnson Av WNSFLD WV11.......25 F3
Johnson Cl DARL/WED WS10.....55 F3
  DARL/WED B8......................145 E2
  WASH/WDE B8.....................111 G3
Johnson Dr CVALE B35.............94 B3
Johnson Pl BILS/COS WV14.......54 B1
Johnson Rd DARL/WED WS10...71 G1
  ERDW/GRVHL B23.................92 D1
  SHHTH WV12.........................26 B3
Johnsons Bridge Rd
  HHTH/SAND B71...................71 G5
Johnsons Gv LGLYGN/QTN B68..123 G4
Johnson St BILS/COS WV14.......67 H2
  BKHL/PFLD WV2.....................37 F5
  VAUX/NECH B7....................110 A3
Johnstone St HRBN B17..........108 D1
Johnston St WBROM B70..........87 H5
John St BKHL/PFLD WV2............53 E2
  BLKHTH/ROWR B65...............122 A3
  BRLYHL DY5...........................101 G5
  LOZ/NWT B19.......................108 B2
  OLDBY B69............................105 E2
  STRBR DY8...........................118 B3
  WBROM B70..........................86 D1
  WLNHL WV13.........................39 G1
  WSLW WS2............................4 D1
John St North HHTH/SAND B71...87 F1
John Wesley Wy
  DARL/WED WS10...................71 E2
Joiners Cft HIA/OLT B92...........165 G2
Joinings Bank
  LGLYGN/QTN B68..................105 F5
Jones Field Crs WOLV WV1.........38 B3
Jones Rd SHHTH WV12..............26 B1
  WOLV WV10...........................23 E4
Jones Wood Cl
  WALM/CURD B76....................78 B4
Jonquil Cl ERDW/GRVHL B23......76 A4
Jordan Cl MGN/WHC B75..........47 F4
Jordan Ho BDMR/CCFT WV3....106 D4
Jordan Leys TPTN/OCK DY4.......85 H1
Jordan Pl BILS/COS WV14..........54 A5
Jordan Rd MGN/WHC B75.........47 F4
Jordan Wy ALDR WS9...............30 B1
Joseph St OLDBY B69..............104 D3
Josiah Houses BILS/COS WV14 *...68 C3
Josiah Rd NFLD/LBR B31..........174 D5
Jowett's La HHTH/SAND B71......71 F3
Joyberry Dr STRBR DY8............135 F4
Joynson St DARL/WED WS10......55 G3
Jubilee Av HHTH/SAND B71........71 F4
Jubilee Cl BLOX/PEL WS3...........28 A4
Jubilee Rd BILS/COS WV14.........54 C4
  RBRY B45............................173 G5
  TPTN/OCK DY4.......................69 G4
Jubilee St HHTH/SAND B71........71 H4
Judge Cl OLDBY B69...............105 E2
Judge Rd BRLYHL DY5..............119 H5
Julia Av ERDE/BCHGN B24.........94 B2
Julia Gdns HHTH/SAND B71.......72 D3
Julian Cl WOLV WV1..................38 B3
Julian Rd WOLV WV1.................38 B3
Julie Cft BILS/COS WV14............69 E2
Juliet Rd RMSLY B62................139 G3
Julius Dr CSHL/WTROR B46......107 F3
Junction Rd BKHL/PFLD WV2......53 F1
  HDSW B21............................101 H1
  STRBR DY8...........................135 H3
Junction St DUDS DY2..............102 B1
  OLDBY B69.............................86 C5
  WSL WS1................................56 D1
Junction St South OLDBY B69...105 E4
The Junction STRBR DY8.........118 A4
June Cft
  LGN/SDN/BHAMAIR B26.........148 B2
Juniper Cl ACGN B27...............146 B2
  WALM/CURD B76.....................63 F5
Juniper Dr DYSBK/YTR WS5......57 H4
  WALM/CURD B76.....................78 C4
Juniper Ri HALE B63.................137 G2
Jury Rd BRLYHL DY5................119 H5
Jutland Rd MOS/BIL B13.........161 H5

K

Karen Wy BRLYHL DY5.............119 F4
Katherine Rd SMTHWKW B67...124 D3
Kathleen Rd
  CSCFLD/WYGN B72.................62 C4
  YDLY B25...............................129 G5
Katie Rd SLYOAK B29..............159 G1
Katsura Cl FOAKS/STRLY B74......60 B2
Kauri Cl KGSWFD DY6...............99 G2
Keanscott Dr
  LGLYGN/QTN B68..................105 G5
Keasdon Gv WALM/CURD WV13...40 A2
Keating Gdns MGN/WHC B75......47 E1
Keats Av SMHTH B10...............128 D5
Keats Cl FOAKS/STRLY B74.........32 D4
  SEDG DY3..............................82 C1
  STRBR DY8...........................118 C4
Keats Dr BILS/COS WV14...........68 D1
Keats Gv ACGN B27.................163 F1
  WOLV WV10...........................24 A3
Keats Rd BLOX/PEL WS3...........28 A3
  WOLV WV10...........................24 A1
Keble Gv
  LGN/SDN/BHAMAIR B26.........147 H1
  WSL WS1................................57 G1
Kedleston Cl BLOX/PEL WS3 *....16 C4
Kedleston Rd
  HLGN/YWD B28....................162 D4
Keel Dr MOS/BIL B13..............161 H3
Keeley St BORD DY8..............127 H2
Keelinge St TPTN/OCK DY4........85 H1
Keen St SMTHWK B66..............107 E5
Keepers Cl ALDR WS9................19 F4
  CSHL/WTROR B46.................115 G5
  KGSWFD DY6..........................99 F1
  WSNGN B18...........................107 H4

Keepers Gate Cl
  FOAKS/STRLY B74..................62 C1
Keepers La CDSL WV8................21 E1
Keepers Rd FOAKS/STRLY B74....32 A5
Keer Ct BORD B9 *...................127 H1
Kegworth Rd
  ERDW/GRVHL B23...................92 A4
Keir Pl STRBR DY8..................118 A4
Keir Rd DARL/WED WS10..........71 G4
Kelby Cl NFLD/LBR B31............175 E2
Kelby Rd NFLD/LBR B31...........175 E1
Keldy Cl DUNHL/THL/PER WV6....22 B5
Kelfield Av HRBN B17...............141 H3
Kelia Dr SMTHWKW B67..........106 B3
Kellett Rd VAUX/NECH B7..........91 H5
Kelling Cl BRLYHL DY5..............119 E4
Kellington Cl WASH/WDE B8.....110 D5
Kelmarsh Dr SOLH B91.............181 H4
Kelmscott Rd HRBN B17..........124 D5
Kelsall Cl WOLV WV1..................38 B3
Kelsall Cft CBHAMW B1..............2 B5
Kelsey Cl VAUX/NECH B7 *........109 H5
Kelso Gdns
  DUNHL/THL/PER WV6..............34 B1
Kelvin Cft
  CHWD/FDBR/MGN B37.............132 A2
Kelton Ct EDG B15..................126 A5
Kelvedon Gv SOLH B91............182 A1
Kelverdale Gv
  ALE/KHTH/YWD B14...............177 G1
Kelverley Gv HHTH/SAND B71....72 C2
Kelvin Pl WSLW WS2.................27 F4
Kelvin Rd NFLD/LBR B31..........175 G4
  WSLW WS2............................27 E4
Kelvin Wy WBROM B70..............87 G5
Kelway Av GTB/HAM B43...........59 F5
Kelwood Dr HALE B65..............138 D2
Kelynmead Rd STETCH B33......129 E5
Kemberton Cl BDMR/CCFT WV3...35 C4
Kemberton Rd
  BDMR/CCFT WV3.....................35 G4
  SLYOAK B29..........................141 G5
Kemble Cl SHHTH WV12............40 B1
Kemble Cft DIG/EDG B5...........127 E5
Kemble Dr CVALE B35...............94 C5
Kemelstowe Crs HALE B63.......154 C2
Kemerton Wy SHLY B90...........195 F3
Kempe Rd STETCH B33...........112 C5
Kempsey Cl HALE B63..............138 A3
  HIA/OLT B92.........................147 F4
  OLDBY B69............................104 B5
Kempsey Covert
  HWK/WKHTH B38...................190 C1
Kempson Av
  CSCFLD/WYGN B72.................77 G2
  HHTH/SAND B71......................87 F1
Kempson Rd CBROM B36.........112 B1
Kempsons Gv BILS/COS WV14....53 F3
Kempthorne Av WOLV WV10......23 G2
Kempthorne Gdns
  BLOX/PEL WS3........................16 C5
Kempthorne Rd
  BILS/COS WV14......................54 B1
Kempton Park Rd CBROM B36...111 H1
Kempton Wy STRBR DY8..........135 E4
Kemsey Dr BILS/COS WV14........54 B4
Kemshead Av NFLD/LBR B31.....175 G5
Kemsley Rd
  ALE/KHTH/YWD B14...............178 B3
Kendal Av CSHL/WTROR B46.....115 F2
Kendall Ri KGSWFD DY6...........100 B4
Kendal Cl DUNHL/THL/PER WV6...22 B4
Kendal Ct ALDR WS9 *...............19 F5
Kendall Gv HIA/OLT B92...........165 H2
Kendal Ri KGSWFD DY6...........100 B4
Kendal Rd
  DUNHL/THL/PER WV6..............22 B3
  LGLYGN/QTN B68..................123 F1
Kendal Rise Rd RBRY B45.........188 B1
Kendal Rd SPARK B11..............127 H5
Kendrick Av NFLD/LBR B31......175 E1
Kendrick Cl HIA/OLT B92..........165 H4
Kendrick Pl BILS/COS WV14.......54 C4
Kendrick Rd BILS/COS WV14......54 C4
  WALM/CURD B76....................63 G1
  WOLV WV10...........................23 G4
Kendricks Rd DARL/WED WS10...56 A1
Kenelm Ct RMSLY B62...............62 C2
Kenelm Rd BILS/COS WV14........68 C2
  LGLYGN/QTN B68..................123 E1
  SCFLD/BOLD B73.....................62 B4
  SMHTH B10..........................128 C4

Kensington Dr
  FOAKS/STRLY B74..................32 D5
Kensington Gdns STRBR DY8....117 G3
Kensington Rd SHHTH WV12.....52 C1
  SLYOAK B29..........................160 A1
Kensington St LOZ/NWT B19....108 D3
Kenswick Dr HALE B63.............138 C5
Kent Av ALDR WS9....................41 F2
Kent Cl ALDR WS9.....................30 B1
  HHTH/SAND B71.....................71 F4
  WSLW WS2............................28 A5
Kentish Rd HDSW B21...............107 E1
Kenton Av
  DUNHL/THL/PER WV6..............36 B1
Kent Rd DUDS DY2..................102 A3
Kent Rd BKHL/PFLD WV2...........52 C1
  DARL/WED WS10....................56 D4
  RBRY B45............................173 H4
  RMSLY B62..........................139 C1
  STRBR DY8...........................117 H4
  WSLW WS2............................40 D2
Kent's Cl HIA/OLT B92..............147 F4
Kent St DIG/EDG B5................127 E4
  SEDG DY3...............................83 G1
  WSLW WS2............................28 A5
Kent St North WSNGN B18.......107 F3
Kenward Cft HRBN B17............124 D5
Kenway HLYWD B47.................192 C1
Kenwick Rd HRBN B17.............141 H3
Kenwood Rd BORD B9.............129 F2
Kenyon Cl STRBR DY8..............135 G1
Kenyon St CBHAMNW B3...........2 D3
Kerby Rd ERDW/GRVHL B23.......92 A2
Keresley Cl SOLH B91..............165 G5
Keresley Gv SLYOAK B29..........158 B1
Kernthorpe Rd
  ALE/KHTH/YWD B14...............177 G1
Kerr Dr TPTN/OCK DY4..............69 E3
Kerridge Cl COVEN WV9............12 A5
Kerr La SHLY B90....................194 A2
Kerry Cl BRLYHL DY5...............101 E5
  NFLD/LBR B31......................158 D4
Kersley Gdns WNSFLD WV11......25 F4
Kerswell Dr SHLY B90..............195 G3
Kesterton Rd FOAKS/STRLY B74..32 C5
Kesteven Cl EDG B15...............143 F1
Kesteven Rd HHTH/SAND B71....71 G4
Keston Rd KGSTG B44..............74 B5
Kestrel Av YDLY B25................129 F4
Kestrel Cl CVALE B35................94 D3
  ERDW/GRVHL B23...................76 B5
Kestrel Dr FOAKS/STRLY B74.....32 C5
Kestrel Gv BVILLE B30.............159 F2
  SHHTH WV12.........................26 A2
Kestrel Rd
  DUNHL/THL/PER WV6..............22 B3
Kestrel Rd DUDS DY2...............102 A1
  HALE B65............................120 D5
  LGLYGN/QTN B68..................122 D2
Keswick Dr KGSWFD DY6...........99 H3
Keswick Gv FOAKS/STRLY B74....45 F3
Keswick Rd HIA/OLT B92..........147 F3
Ketley Cft BHTH/HG B12..........127 F5
Ketley Flds KGSWFD DY6.........100 C4
Kettlebrook Rd HILY B90..........195 H2
Kettlehouse Rd KGSTG B44........60 B5
Kettlesbank Rd SEDG DY3 *.......83 E4
Kettles Wood Dr
  RIDG/WDGT B32.....................140 C5
Kettlewell Wy
  CHWD/FDBR/MGN B37...........131 H2
Kestrel Rd DUDN DY1...............84 A4
Kew Cl CHWD/FDBR/MGN B37..131 H1
Kew Dr DUDN DY1....................84 A4
Kew Gdns STETCH B33............130 A3
Kewstoke Cl SHHTH WV12.........25 H1
Kewstoke Cft NFLD/LBR B31....158 B5
Kewstoke Rd SHHTH WV12........26 A1
Keyes Dr KGSWFD DY6...............81 H5
Key Hi WSNGN B18..................108 B4
Key Hill Circ WSNGN B18.........108 B4
Key Hill Dr WSNGN B18...........108 B4
Keynell Covert BVILLE B30.........177 G5
Keynes Dr BILS/COS WV14........54 A2
Keys Crs HHTH/SAND B71..........71 G5
Keyse Rd MGN/WHC B75..........63 F1
Keysmith Cl WLNHL WV13..........40 A4
Keyte Cl TPTN/OCK DY4.............85 G1
Keyway WLNHL WV13.................39 G5
Keyworth Cl TPTN/OCK DY4.......85 H1
Kidd Cft TPTN/OCK DY4.............70 A1
Kidderminster Rd
  KIDD DY11.............................169 E2
Kidderminster Rd South
  KIDD DY11.............................169 G5
Kielder Cl DYSBK/YTR WS5.......58 A5
Kielder Gdns HAG/WOL DY9.....152 D1
Kier's Bridge Cl TPTN/OCK DY4...85 H3
Kilburn Dr KGSWFD DY6...........82 A5
Kilburn Gv KGSTG B44..............60 B5
Kilburn Pl DUDS DY2...............102 D3
Kilburn Rd KGSTG B44.............60 B5
Kilby Av LDYWD/EDGR B16......126 A2
Kilbys Gv BFLD/HDSWWD B20....89 H4
Kilcote Rd SHLY B90................179 E3
Kilmet Wk SMTHWKW B67........106 B4
Kilmore Cft CBROM B36.............94 A5
Kilmorie Rd ACGN B27.............146 C2
Kiln Cl ERDW/GRVHL B23.........105 G5
Kiln La SHLY B90....................180 A5
  YDLY B25..............................146 D1
Kilsby Gv SOLH B91................182 A5
Kilvert Rd DARL/WED WS10........71 F1
Kimberley Av WASH/WDE B8....110 C4
Kimberley Cl FOAKS/STRLY B74...45 G3
Kimberley Pl BILS/COS WV14......68 B4
Kimberley Rd
  LGN/SDN/BHAMAIR B26.........130 B5
  SMTHWK B66........................106 C2
Kimberley St BDMR/CCFT WV3....6 A5
Kimble Gv ERDE/BCHGN B24......93 H3
Kimbley Ri HHTH/SAND B71......71 E4
Kimpton Cl
  ALE/KHTH/YWD B14...............178 A3
Kimsan Cft FOAKS/STRLY B74....60 C1
Kinchford Cl SOLH B91............181 H5

Kineton Cft RIDG/WDGT B32....157 H2
Kineton Green Rd
  HIA/OLT B92.........................163 H2
Kineton Ri SEDG DY3................67 E1
Kineton Rd RBRY B45...............187 G1
  SCFLD/BOLD B73.....................76 C2
Kinfare Dr
  DUNHL/THL/PER WV6..............35 F1
Kinfare Ri SEDG DY3..................83 G2
King Charles Av WSLW WS2.......40 C3
King Charles Ct KGSTG B44.......75 H1
King Charles Rd RMSLY B62......139 H3
King Edmund St DUDN DY1.......84 B4
King Edward Rd MOS/BIL B13....144 B4
King Edwards Cl
  BFLD/HDSWWD B20 *...............108 B1
King Edwards Gdns
  BFLD/HDSWWD B20 *...............108 B2
  CBHAMW B1...........................2 A3
King Edward's Rw
  CBHAMW B1............................2 C5
King Edward's Rw CBHAMW B1...37 E5
King Edward St
  DARL/WED WS10....................55 F3
King Edward VI Rd BRWHH WS8...9 E5
King Fisher Cl BRWHH WS8.........9 E5
  LGN/SDN/BHAMAIR B26.........147 G1
  SEDG DY3..............................67 E5
Kingfisher Ct ALE/KHTH/YWD B14..177 H3
  STRBR DY8...........................134 C3
Kingfisher Dr SHHTH WV12.......25 H2
Kingfisher Rd
  ERDW/GRVHL B23...................76 A4
Kingfisher Veiw
  BDE/SHDE B34......................112 C4
Kingfisher Wy BVILLE B30.........159 F2
King George Crs
  RUSH/SHEL WS4.....................28 D4
King George Pl
  RUSH/SHEL WS4.....................28 D4
King George Vi Av WSL WS1......45 E5
Kingham Cl SEDG DY3...............82 C1
Kingham Covert
  ALE/KHTH/YWD B14...............177 H3
King's Av OLDBY B69.................85 H4
Kingsbridge Rd
  RIDG/WDGT B32.....................157 H1
Kingsbrook Dr SOLH B91.........181 H5
Kingsbury Av
  ERDE/BCHGN B24...................93 H3
Kingsbury Cl RUSH/SHEL WS4....42 D1
  WALM/CURD B76.....................95 E1
Kingsbury Rd
  ERDE/BCHGN B24...................92 D4
  TPTN/OCK DY4.......................69 G3
  WALM/CURD B76.....................95 E1
Kingsclere Wk
  BDMR/CCFT WV3.....................50 C1
Kingscliff Rd SMHTH B10.........129 E4
Kings Cl ALE/KHTH/YWD B14....160 C4
Kingscote Rd DOR/KN B93......198 C1
  EDG B15..............................142 B1
King's Ct
  CHWD/FDBR/MGN B37...........133 E3
  STRBR DY8...........................135 E2
  LGN/SDN/BHAMAIR B26.........113 H2
Kingscroft Cl FOAKS/STRLY B74...45 G5
Kingsdene Av KGSWFD DY6.......99 G5
Kingsdown Av PBAR/PBCH B42...73 H5
Kingsdown Rd NFLD/LBR B31....158 A1
Kingsfield Rd
  ALE/KHTH/YWD B14...............161 E2
Kingsford Cl CBROM B36...........95 F5
Kingsford Nouveau
  KGSWFD DY6........................100 C4
Kings Gdn BVILLE B30.............176 C1
Kings Green Av
  HWK/WKHTH B38....................176 D3
Kingshayes Rd ALDR WS9..........30 B1
Kingshill Dr HWK/WKHTH B38...176 C3
Kings Hill Fld DARL/WED WS10...55 G3
Kingshurst Rd NFLD/LBR B31....158 C5
  SHLY B90.............................179 H4
Kingslow Av
  CHWD/FDBR/MGN B37...........113 H4
Kingsland Dr DOR/KN B93.......196 C5
Kingsland Rd KGSTG B44...........60 A4
  WOLV WV1.............................23 H1
Kingslea Rd SOLH B91.............181 E5
Kingsleigh Dr MGN/WHC B75....47 F5
Kingsleigh Dr CBROM B36.......112 B3
Kingsleigh Rd
  BFLD/HDSWWD B20.................90 B4
Kingsley Av
  DUNHL/THL/PER WV6..............35 F1
Kingsley Bank Wy
  LGN/SDN/BHAMAIR B26.........130 D5
Kingsley Gdns CDSL WV8...........10 A4
Kingsley Gv SEDG DY3...............82 C1
Kingsley Rd BHTH/HG B12........144 C2
  BVILLE B30..........................176 B1
  KGSWFD DY6..........................99 G4
Kingsley St DUDS DY2.............102 C4
  WSLW WS2............................56 B1
Kingslow Av
  CHWD/FDBR/MGN B37...........113 H4
Kings Meadow HAG/WOL DY9...170 C3
Kingsmere Cl CVALE B35...........94 C4
Kings Mill Cl DARL/WED WS10....55 G3
Kingsoak Gdns DUDS DY2.......102 B3
Kings Rd ALE/KHTH/YWD B14...160 C4
  ERDW/GRVHL B23...................92 A2
  KGSTG B44.............................75 H1
  RUSH/SHEL WS4.....................28 C3
  SEDG DY3..............................67 G3
  SPARK B11...........................146 A2
Kings Sq BILS/COS WV14 *.........68 A3
Kings Street Prec
  DARL/WED WS10....................55 F2
Kingstanding Rd KGSTG B44......60 C4
  KGSTG B44.............................75 F5
Kings Ter
  ALE/KHTH/YWD B14...............160 C4

Kingsthorpe Rd
ALE/KHTH/YWD B14.............178 C2
Kingston Rd BORD B9.................127 H5
Kingston Rw CBHAMNW B1 ....2 C5
Kingston Wy KGSWFD DY6..........99 G2
King St ALDR WS9..........................19 F5
BILS/COS WV14...............................68 A3
BRLYHL DY5..................................119 H4
CDYHTH B64..................................121 F3
DARL/WED WS10.............................70 C1
DUDS DY2......................................54 C5
HAG/WOL DY9................................136 D3
HALE B63......................................138 C3
SMTHWK B66................................106 D2
SPARK B11.......................................11 F5
STRBR DY8.....................................135 E1
WLNHL WV13..................................39 H3
WOLV WV1.......................................7 F4
WSL WS1..56 D1
King Street Pas BRLYHL DY5.......120 A5
DUDS DY2.......................................84 D5
Kingsway LGLYGN/QTN B68.......123 F5
STRBR DY8....................................117 H4
WNSFLD WV11................................15 E3
WOLVN WV10..................................24 A4
Kingsway Av TPTN/OCK DY4.......69 G5
Kingsway Dr
HWK/WKHTH B38...........................176 D3
Kingsway North WOLVN WV10 *...29 G4
Kingsway South ALDR WS9 *.......29 G4
Kingsway South WOLVN WV10 *...24 A4
Kingsway Ter WNSFLD WV11 *....15 E3
Kingswear Av
DUNHL/THL/PER WV6....................34 D2
Kingswinford Rd DUDN DY1......101 G2
Kingswood Cl BVILLE B30............178 A2
SHLY B90......................................180 D4
Kingswood Cft
VAUX/NECH B7...............................110 A2
Kingswood Dr BVILLE B30..........177 G2
FOAKS/STRLY B74...........................60 B4
Kingswood Gdns
ETTPK/GDPK/PENN WV4..................51 F2
MOS/BIL B13.................................144 C3
NFLD/LBR B31................................189 F2
Kingswood Ter YDLY B25 *.........129 F5
Kington Cl SHHTH WV12.............25 H2
Kington Gdns
CHWD/FDBR/MGN B37..................131 H2
Kington Wy STECH B33................130 A3
King William St STRBR DY8.........118 D4
Kiniths Crs HHTH/SAND B71........88 A2
Kiniths Wy HHTH/SAND B71........88 A2
RMSLY B62....................................122 C3
Kinlet Cl BDMR/CCFT WV3..........35 E5
Kinlet Gv NFLD/LBR B31...............176 A3
Kinloch Dr DUDN DY1...................83 H5
Kinnerley St WSL WS1....................5 H5
Kinnersley Crs OLDBY B69..........104 B4
Kinnerton Crs SLYOAK B29.........141 F5
Kinross Crs GTB/HAM B43...........59 F4
Kinsey Gv ALE/KHTH/YWD B14...178 D1
Kinsham Dr SOLH B91..................181 H5
Kintore Cft RIDG/WDGT B32........157 F3
Kintyre Cl RBRY B45....................173 G4
Kinver Av ALDR WS9....................30 C1
Kinver Cft BHTH/HG B12..............144 A1
WALM/CURD B76..............................78 B3
Kinver Dr
ETTPK/GDPK/PENN WV4..................50 C3
HAG/WOL DY9.................................153 E3
Kinver Rd NFLD/LBR B31..............176 B3
Kinver St STRBR DY8...................117 H3
Kinwarton Cl YDLY B25...............146 D1
Kipling Av BILS/COS WV14............68 B2
Kipling Cl TPTN/OCK DY4..............69 G3
Kipling Rd NFLD/LBR B31.............176 A1
SEDG DY3...82 C1
SHHTH WV12....................................25 H2
WOLVN WV10..................................12 D5
Kirby Cl BILS/COS WV14...............54 A5
Kirby Dr DUDN DY1.......................83 G5
Kirby Rd WSNGN B18...................107 G5
Kirkby Gn SCFLD/BOLD B73.........62 A5
Kirkham Gdns BRLYHL DY5.........101 E3
Kirkham Gv STECH B33.................112 B5
Kirkham Wy TPTN/OCK DY4..........85 C1
Kirkside Gv BRWNH WS8................9 F5
Kirkstall Cl BLOX/PEL WS3............16 B5
Kirkstall Crs BLOX/PEL WS3.........16 B5
Kirkstone Ct BRLYHL DY5............118 D4
Kirkstone Crs GTB/HAM B43........59 H5
WMBN WV5.....................................64 D5
Kirkstone Wy BRLYHL DY5...........119 E4
Kirkwall Rd RIDG/WDGT B32.......157 H1
Kirkwood Av ERDW/GRVHL B23...76 D4
Kirstead Gdns
DUNHL/THL/PER WV6......................35 F2
Kirton Gv
DUNHL/THL/PER WV6......................35 G1
SOLH B91......................................181 G4
STECH B33....................................112 C5
Kitchener Rd DUDS DY2...............85 F5
SLYOAK B29..................................142 D3
Kitchener St WSNGN B18...........107 F3
Kitchen La WNSFLD WV11.............26 C3
Kitebrook Cl SHLY B90.................195 G1
Kitegreen Cl
CHWD/FDBR/MGN B37..................114 D5
Kitsland Rd BKDE/SHDE B34.......114 D5
Kitswell Gdns RIDG/WDGT B32...157 E2
Kittiwake Dr BRLYHL DY5............119 G5
Kittoe Rd FOAKS/STRLY B74.........46 D2
Kitt's Green Rd STECH B33...........130 D1
Kitwell La RIDG/WDGT B32..........157 E2
Kitwood Dr HIA/OLT B92..............165 F3
Kixley La DOR/KN B93..................197 G2
Knaresdale Cl BVILLE B30...........119 E4
Knaves Castle Av BRWNH WS8......9 F2
Knebworth Cl KGSTG B44.............75 E3
Knightcote Dr SOLH B91..............181 H5
Knightley Rd SOLH B91................181 H5
Knightlow Rd HRBN B17..............142 B2
Knighton Cl FOAKS/STRLY B74....46 D2
Knighton Dr FOAKS/STRLY B74....46 B1
Knighton Rd DUDS DY2...............102 D5
FOAKS/STRLY B74............................46 B1

NFLD/LBR B31................................176 A1
Knights Av
DUNHL/THL/PER WV6......................22 A4
Knightsbridge Cl
FOAKS/STRLY B74............................46 D1
Knightsbridge La SHHTH WV12....25 H4
Knightsbridge Rd
HIA/OLT B92...................................164 B1
Knights Cl ERDW/GRVHL B23.......92 C4
WLNHL WV13.....................................39 H3
Knights Ct
CHWD/FDBR/MGN B37..................133 E4
Knights Crs
DUNHL/THL/PER WV6......................22 A3
Knightsfield Cl
SCFLD/BOLD B73..............................61 E5
Knights Hl ALDR WS9...................44 B2
Knights Rd SPARK B11.................146 A3
Knightstone Av WSNGN B18......108 A5
Knights Wood Cl
MGN/WHC B75.................................62 D1
Knightwick Crs
ERDW/GRVHL B23............................92 A1
Kniperley Rd
ERDW/GRVHL B23............................77 E5
Knoll Cft ALDR WS9.......................30 C1
LDYWD/EDGR B16 *.......................126 A2
SHLY B90.......................................194 D4
The Knoll KGSWFD DY6...............100 A4
RIDG/WDGT B32............................157 G1
Knottsall La LGLYGN/QTN B68....123 F1
Knotts Farm Rd KGSWFD DY6......100 C5
Knowlands Rd SHLY B90..............195 G1
Knowle Cl RBRY B45.....................188 D1
Knowle Hill Rd DUDS DY2...........102 B5
Knowle Rd
BLKHTH/ROWR B65........................103 F5
SPARK B11.....................................145 F4
Knowles Dr FOAKS/STRLY B74......62 A1
Knowles Rd DARL/WED WS10.......71 H4
Knowles St DARL/WED WS10.......56 A5
Knowle Wood Rd
DOR/KN B93..................................199 F1
Knox Rd BKHL/PFLD WV2..............52 A2
Knutswood Cl MOS/BIL B13 *......162 B3
Kohima Dr STRBR DY8.................118 A4
Kossuth Rd BILS/COS WV14..........68 A2
Kyle Cl WOLVN WV10.....................22 D1
Kyles Wy RIDG/WDGT B32............157 F3
Kynaston Crs CDSL WV8................10 D5
Kyngsford Rd STECH B33.............131 F2
Kyotts Lake Rd SPARK B11..........127 C5
Kyrwicks La BHTH/HG B12...........127 C5
SPARK B11.....................................144 C1
Kyter La CBROM B36....................112 D1

L

Laburnham Rd KGSWFD DY6........100 A3
Laburnum Av
CHWD/FDBR/MGN B37..................113 H3
SMTHWKW B67..............................106 A5
Laburnum Cl BLOX/PEL WS3.........17 H5
CHWD/FDBR/MGN B37..................113 H5
HLYWD B47...................................192 C5
Laburnum Ct OLDBY B69...............85 H4
Laburnum Dr WALM/CURD B76....78 B1
Laburnum Gv MOS/BIL B13 *........144 B4
WSLW WS2...40 D2
Laburnum Rd ALDR WS9................19 F3
BVILLE B30....................................159 H3
DARL/WED WS10..............................56 B5
DSYBK/YTR WS5...............................58 A3
DUDN DY1.......................................84 B2
ETTPK/GDPK/PENN WV4.................50 C5
TPTN/OCK DY4................................69 F4
WOLV WV1..38 B5
Laburnum Vls SPARK B11 *..........145 E2
Laburnum Wy NFLD/LBR B31.......175 G4
Ladbroke Dr WALM/CURD B76......78 B1
Ladbroke Gv ACGN B27................163 G2
Ladbrook Gv SOLH B91..................82 C3
Ladbrook Rd SOLH B91................182 A3
Ladbury Gv DSYBK/YTR WS5..........57 G4
Ladbury Rd DSYBK/YTR WS5..........57 G4
Ladeler Gv STECH B33...................131 F2
Ladies Wk SEDG DY3.......................67 F5
Lady Bank RIDG/WDGT B32.........157 F3
Lady Bracknell Ms
NFLD/LBR B31................................176 A1
Lady Byron La DOR/KN B93..........196 D1
Lady Grey's Wk STRBR DY8.........134 D2
Lady La SHLY B90..........................194 B5
Ladymoor Rd BILS/COS WV14........54 A3
Ladypool Av SPARK B11 *.............144 D1
Ladypool Cl RMSLY B62................139 E3
RUSH/SHEL WS4..............................28 C5
Ladypool Rd BHTH/HG B12..........144 C2
Ladysmith Rd HALE B63................137 G1
Ladywell Cl WMBN WV5................65 E3
Ladywell Wk DIG/EDG B5................3 H7
Ladywood Cl
LDYWD/EDGR B16.........................126 A2
Ladywood Cl BRLYHL DY5............119 H2
Ladywood Middleway
LDYWD/EDGR B16..........................126 A2
Ladywood Rd
FOAKS/STRLY B74............................47 E5
LDYWD/EDGR B16...........................125 H3
Lake Av DSYBK/YTR WS5................57 H1
Lake Cl DSYBK/YTR WS5.................58 A1
Lakedown Cl
ALE/KHTH/YWD B14......................178 A4
Lakefield Cl HLGN/YWD B28.........163 H1
Lakefield Rd WNSFLD WV11...........25 E5
Lakehouse Gv
HWK/WKHTH B38...........................175 G4
Lakehouse Rd SCFLD/BOLD B73....76 C3
Laker Cl STRBR DY8......................118 C5
Lakeside
CHWD/FDBR/MGN B37..................133 E4
FOAKS/STRLY B74............................31 H5
Lakeside Cl WLNHL WV13..............39 E2
Lakeside Ct BRLYHL DY5..............118 D4
Lakeside Dr ERDW/GRVHL B23......91 H1

SHLY B90.......................................195 F1
Lakeside Rd WBROM B70...............71 E5
Lakes Rd ERDW/GRVHL B23..........75 C5
Lake St SEDG DY3...........................83 F5
Lake View Cl BVILLE B30..............159 C5
Lakewood Dr RBRY B45................174 B4
Lakey La HLGN/YWD B28..............163 F5
Lambah Cl BILS/COS WV14............54 A1
Lamb Cl BKDE/SHDE B34..............113 G4
Lamb Crs WMBN WV5.....................80 D1
Lambert Cl ERDW/GRVHL B23.......76 B5
Lambert Ct KGSWFD DY6...............99 H1
Lambert End WBROM B70..............87 F5
Lambert Fold DUDS DY2...............103 E1
Lambert Rd DUDS DY2.................139 E4
Lambert St WBROM B70.................87 F5
Lambeth Cl
CHWD/FDBR/MGN B37..................114 D5
Lambeth Rd BILS/COS WV14..........53 F1
KGSTG B44.......................................60 A5
Lambourne Gv
CHWD/FDBR/MGN B37..................131 G2
Lambourn Rd WLNHL DY5............118 D4
Lambourn Rd
ERDW/GRVHL B23............................92 D2
WLNHL WV13....................................40 B4
Lambscote Cl SHLY B90................179 E3
Lammas Cl HIA/OLT B92...............165 H1
Lammas Rd STRBR DY8.................117 G1
Lammermoor Av GTB/HAM B43...59 H4
Lamont Av RIDG/WDGT B32.........141 F4
Lamorna Cl BDMR/CCFT WV3.......35 F5
Lanark Cl KGSWFD DY6................100 B4
Lanark Cft CVALE B35.....................94 B3
Lancaster Av ALDR WS9..................30 B2
DARL/WED WS10..............................56 C5
RBRY B45......................................174 A5
Lancaster Circ Queensway
CBHAMNE B4.....................................3 H2
Lancaster Cl BVILLE B30..............160 A4
Lancaster Dr CVALE B35................94 C4
Lancaster Gdns
ETTPK/GDPK/PENN WV4..................51 E5
Lancaster Pl BLOX/PEL WS3...........17 E5
Lancaster Rd BRLYHL DY5............119 F2
Lancelot Cl WASH/WDE B8...........128 C1
Lanchester Rd
HWK/WKHTH B38...........................177 E4
Lanchester Wy CBROM B36............95 H5
Landgate Rd RBRY B45.................188 A2
Landgate Rd HDSW B21..................89 E4
Land La
CHWD/FDBR/MGN B37..................132 A5
Landor Rd DOR/KN B93.................197 G2
Landor St BORD B9.......................127 H1
Landport Rd BKHL/PFLD WV2.......37 H5
Landrake Rd KGSWFD DY6............100 B4
Landsdown Pl WSNGN B18...........108 A4
Landseer Gv GTB/HAM B43............59 H4
Landsgate STRBR DY8..................152 C1
Landswood Cl KGSTG B44.............75 G2
Landswood Rd
LGLYGN/QTN B68...........................105 G5
Lane Av WSLW WS2........................41 F2
Lane Cl WSLW WS2..........................41 F2
Lane Cft WALM/CURD B76..............78 C3
Lane Green Av CDSL WV8...............21 G1
Lane Green Rd CDSL WV8..............11 E5
Lane Rd
ETTPK/GDPK/PENN WV4..................53 E5
Lanes Cl WMBN WV5......................80 B1
Lanesfield Dr
ETTPK/GDPK/PENN WV4..................53 E4
Laneside Av FOAKS/STRLY B74......60 B1
Laneside Gdns WSLW WS2............41 H3
Lane St BILS/COS WV14..................53 H5
Langcomb Rd SHLY B90...............180 A5
Langdale Cl BRWNH WS8...............19 E1
Langdale Cft BRWNH WS8 *.........107 G2
Langdale Dr BILS/COS WV14..........53 H5
Langdale Rd GTB/HAM B43...........73 H4
Langfield Rd DOR/KN B93.............197 E1
Langford Av GTB/HAM B43...........73 C5
Langford Cl WSL WS1......................5 C5
Langford Cft SOLH B91.................182 A3
Langford Gv HRBN B17.................142 A4
Langham Cl
LGLYGN/BHAMAIR B26..................130 C5
Langham Gn FOAKS/STRLY B74....45 H1
Langholm Dr KGSTG B44................76 B2
Langland Dr SEDG DY3...................67 E3
Langley Av BILS/COS WV14............68 C3
Langley Cl ALDR WS9......................19 G4
Langley Crs LGLYGN/QTN B68......105 H5
Langley Dr BILS/COS WV14............94 C5
Langley Gdns BDMR/CCFT WV3....50 D1
Langley Green Rd OLDBY B69......105 E5
Langley Gv SMHTH B10.................128 B4
Langley Hall Dr MGN/WHC B75.....63 H2
Langley Hall Rd HIA/OLT B92........163 C3
MGN/WHC B75..................................63 H3
Langley Heath Dr
WALM/CURD B76..............................63 F5
Langley High St LGLYGN/QTN B69.105 E4
Langley Pkwy MGN/WHC B75.......63 F2
Langley Rd BILS/COS WV14...........148 B4
Langley Rd
ERDW/GRVHL B23............................75 H4
LGLYGN/QTN B68............................105 E5
SMHTH B10...................................128 B4
Langleys Rd SLYOAK B29..............159 G1
Langmead Cl WSLW WS2...............40 B2
Langsett Rd WOLVN WV10.............37 G1
Langstone Rd
ALE/KHTH/YWD B14......................178 D3
DUDN DY1..85 G5
Langton Cl CBROM B36.................114 B3
Langton Pl BILS/COS WV14............54 C2
Langton Rd WASH/WDE B8..........110 C5
Langtree Av SOLH B91..................181 H4
Langwood Ct CBROM B36.............112 D1
Langwood Ct WALM/CURD B76.....78 A4
Lannacombe Rd
NFLD/LBR B31................................189 E2
Lansbury Av DARL/WED WS10.......55 E4
Lansbury Gn CDYHTH B64............121 H4
Lansbury Rd CDYHTH B64.............121 H4

Lansdale Av HIA/OLT B92.............165 H2
Lansdowne Av CDSL WV8................10 A5
Lansdowne Cl BILS/COS WV14.......68 A4
DUDS DY2.....................................103 F3
Lansdowne Rd BILS/COS WV14......54 A1
ERDW/GRVHL B23............................92 D2
HALE B63.......................................137 H5
HDSW B21.....................................108 A2
RMSLY B62....................................122 D4
WOLV WV1...6 D2
Lansdowne St WSNGN B18..........107 H5
Lansdown Pl WSNGN B18 *..........108 C2
Lantern Rd DUDS DY2...................120 C2
Lanton Cl BLOX/PEL WS3...............16 C5
Lapal La North RMSLY B62...........139 G4
Lapal La South RMSLY B62...........139 G4
Lapley Cl WOLV WV1........................38 B3
Lapper Av
ETTPK/GDPK/PENN WV4..................67 H1
Lapwing Cl BRWNH WS8..................9 E5
Lapwing Cft ERDW/GRVHL B23.....76 A4
Lapwing Dr HIA/OLT B92..............167 H5
Lapwood Av KGSWFD DY6............100 C4
Lapworth Gv SCFLD/BOLD B73.....61 E5
Lapworth Gv BHTH/HG B12.........144 B1
Lara Cl HRBN B17.........................124 D4
Lara Gv TPTN/OCK DY4..................85 G4
Larch Av HDSW B21.........................89 F4
Larch Cft
CHWD/FDBR/MGN B37..................132 B2
OLDBY B69..85 H4
Larch Dr NFLD/LBR B31................174 C4
Larches La BDMR/CCFT WV3............6 A4
Larches St SPARK B11...................144 C1
Larchfield Cl
BFLD/HDSWWD B20........................90 B3
Larch Gdns BILS/COS WV14...........54 B4
Larch Gv SEDG DY3..........................67 E4
Larchmere Dr HLGN/YWD B28......162 D2
WNSFLD WV11..................................15 E4
Larch Rd KGSWFD DY6..................100 A2
Larchwood Crs
FOAKS/STRLY B74............................45 E5
Larchwood Rd DSYBK/YTR WS5.....57 C4
Larcombe Dr
ETTPK/GDPK/PENN WV4..................52 B3
Large Av DARL/WED WS10.............55 E4
Lark Cl ALE/KHTH/YWD B14.........178 C5
Larkfield Av CBROM B36...............112 D1
Larkhill Rd STRBR DY8.................134 C3
Larkin Cl WOLVN WV10..................24 A1
Lark Meadow Dr
BFLD/HDSWWD B20........................131 G1
Larksfield Ms BRLYHL DY5...........119 E5
Larks Ml BLOX/PEL WS3...............17 G3
Larkspur Cft CBROM B36..............111 H1
Larkspur Rd DUDS DY2................103 F1
Larkswood Dr
ETTPK/GDPK/PENN WV4..................50 C5
SEDG DY3..67 F4
Larne Rd
LGN/SDN/BHAMAIR B26.................130 C5
Latches Cl DARL/WED WS10...........55 G2
Latelow Rd STECH B33...................130 C2
Latham Av GTB/HAM B43................73 G4
Latham Crs TPTN/OCK DY4............85 G5
Lath La SMTHWK B66.....................88 A5
Lathom Gv STECH B33...................131 E1
Latimer Gdns EDG B15..................126 D5
Latimer Pl WSNGN B18.................107 G3
Latimer St WLNHL WV13................53 H2
Latymer Cl WALM/CURD B76..........78 C4
Lauder Cl SEDG DY3........................67 E2
WLNHL WV13....................................39 E2
Lauderdale Cl BRWNH WS8...........19 E1
Lauderdale Gdns WOLVN WV10.....11 E5
Laughton Cl NFLD/LBR B31...........189 H1
Launceston Cl DSYBK/YTR WS5.....58 B1
Launceston Rd
DSYBK/YTR WS5................................58 B1
The Launde HLGN/YWD B28.........179 F3
Laundry Rd SMTHWK B66.............106 D1
Laural Dr SMTHWK B66.................106 D1
Laurakers Wk
FOAKS/STRLY B74............................47 E4
Laurel Av BHTH/HG B12..................144 B1
Laurel Cl FOAKS/STRLY B74............45 E5
SMTHWK B66..................................106 C1
Laurel Gdns ACGN B27..................146 C2
HDSW B21..89 G5
Laurel Gv BDMR/CCFT WV3............51 E2
BILS/COS WV14..................................54 C2
BVILLE B30....................................159 G4
Laurel La HALE B63........................138 D4
Laurel Rd BVILLE B30.....................159 H4
DSYBK/YTR WS5................................58 A3
DUDN DY1..84 B3
SMTHWK B66..................................106 A2
TPTN/OCK DY4.................................69 F4
The Laurels
LGN/SDN/BHAMAIR B26..................148 A2
SMTHWK B66 *..............................107 E5
Laurence Gv
DUNHL/THL/PER WV6......................22 A3
Lauriston Cl DUDN DY1..................83 H4
Lavender Cl COVEN WV9................11 H4
Lavender Gdns
ERDW/GRVHL B23............................75 H4
Lavender Gv BILS/COS WV14..........54 B2
BLOX/PEL WS3..................................18 A5
Lavender La STRBR DY8................134 C4
Lavender Rd DUDN DY1..................84 B3
Lavendon Rd PBAR/PBCH B42......90 B3
Lavinia Rd RMSLY B62...................122 D4
Law Cliff Rd PBAR/PBCH B42.........74 B5
Law Ct OLDBY B69...........................86 B4
Lawden Rd SMHTH B10.................127 C1
Lawford Cl VAUX/NECH B7...........127 G1
Lawford Gv DIG/EDG B5................179 F2
SHLY B90.......................................179 F3
Lawfred Av WNSFLD WV11.............24 D5
Lawley Cl RUSH/SHEL WS4.............28 A5
Lawley Middleway
CBHAMNE B4.................................127 G1
Lawley Rd BILS/COS WV14..............53 F2
Lawley St DUDN DY1.......................68 A5
WBROM B70......................................86 D3

The Lawley HALE B63...................154 C1
Lawn Av STRBR DY8.....................135 E3
Lawn La COVEN WV9......................11 H2
Lawnoaks Cl BRWNH WS8..............9 E2
Lawn Rd BKHL/PFLD WV2...............52 C2
Lawnsdale Cl
CSHL/WTROR B46..........................115 F5
Lawnsdown Rd BRLYHL DY5........119 H5
Lawnsfield Gv
ERDW/GRVHL B23............................76 B4
Lawnside Gn BILS/COS WV14........38 D5
Lawn St STRBR DY8......................135 E3
Lawnswood KINVER DY7..............117 E2
WALM/CURD B76..............................78 C3
Lawnswood Av
DUNHL/THL/PER WV6......................22 A2
ETTPK/GDPK/PENN WV4..................52 A2
SHLY B90......................................180 D2
STRBR DY8......................................99 C5
Lawnswood Dr ALDR WS9...............19 G4
KINVER DY7....................................117 E2
Lawnswood Gv HDSW B21............89 E5
Lawnswood Rd
DUNHL/THL/PER WV6......................22 B2
SEDG DY3...83 F1
STRBR DY8......................................117 C1
Lawnwood Rd DUDS DY2.............102 C5
Lawrence Av WNSFLD WV11...........25 F4
WOLVN WV10....................................38 A1
Lawrence Dr WALM/CURD B76......78 C5
Lawrence La CDYHTH B64.............121 F3
Lawrence St HAG/WOL DY9..........136 A1
WLNHL WV13....................................39 G2
Lawrence Wk GTB/HAM B43..........59 H4
Lawson Cl ALDR WS9.......................44 B1
Lawson St CBHAMNE B4....................3 H2
Lawton Cl BLKHTH/ROWR B65......104 A1
Laxey Rd LDYWD/EDGR B16.........125 E1
Laxford Cl BHTH/HG B12...............144 A1
Laxton Cl KGSWFD DY6................100 C4
Laxton Gv SOLH B91.....................165 E3
YDLY B25......................................129 H3
Lazy Hl HWK/WKHTH B38.............177 F3
Lazy Hill Rd ALDR WS9...................30 C1
Lea Av DARL/WED WS10.................70 B2
Lea Bank Rd DUDS DY2................120 B1
Leabon Gv HRBN B17...................142 A3
Leabrook
LGN/SDN/BHAMAIR B26.................130 B4
Leabrook Rd DARL/WED WS10......70 B2
Leabrook Rd North
DARL/WED WS10..............................70 B2
Leach Green La RBRY B45.............188 A1
Leach Heath La RBRY B45.............187 H1
Leacliffe Wy ALDR WS9...................45 F2
Leacote Dr
DUNHL/THL/PER WV6......................35 G1
Leacroft SHHTH WV12.....................26 A3
Leacroft Av WOLVN WV10..............23 C2
Leacroft Cl ALDR WS9......................30 B1
Leacroft Gv HHTH/SAND B71........71 F4
Leacroft Rd KGSWFD DY6.............100 A1
Lea Dr LGN/SDN/BHAMAIR B26....147 G1
Lea End La ALVE B48......................190 A4
HWK/WKHTH B38...........................191 E5
Leafield Crs STECH B33.................112 A5
Leafield Gdns RMSLY B62.............122 B4
Leafield Rd HIA/OLT B92...............164 D1
Lea Ford Rd STECH B33.................113 E5
Leaford Wy KGSWFD DY6.............100 B4
Leafy Glade FOAKS/STRLY B74.......45 G2
Leafy Ri SEDG DY3...........................82 A5
Lea Gdns BDMR/CCFT WV3..........36 D5
Lea Green Av TPTN/OCK DY4.........84 C5
Lea Green La HLYWD B47..............193 E5
Lea Green La HLYWD B47..............193 E5
Lea Hall Rd STECH B33..................130 C1
Leahill Cft
BFLD/HDSWWD B20........................131 H1
Lea Hill Rd BFLD/HDSWWD B20....90 C1
Leaholme Gdns HAG/WOL DY9....135 H1
Leahouse Gdns
LGLYGN/QTN B68............................123 E1
Lea House Rd BVILLE B30.............160 A3
Leahouse Rd LGLYGN/QTN B68....123 F1
Leahurst Crs HRBN B17.................142 A3
Lea Manor Dr
ETTPK/GDPK/PENN WV4..................51 E5
Leam Crs HIA/OLT B92...................164 D1
Leamington Rd BHTH/HG B12......144 D1
Leamore Cl WSLW WS2....................27 E1
Leamore La WSLW WS2....................27 E1
Leamount Dr KGSTG B44................84 A4
Leander Gdns
ALE/KHTH/YWD B14......................161 F1
Leander Rd HAG/WOL DY9............136 D2
Lea Rd BDMR/CCFT WV3.................51 E1
SPARK B11.....................................145 F1
Lear Rd WMBN WV5........................65 H5
Leason La WOLVN WV10.................24 A1
Leasow Dr EDG B15......................142 A1
Leasow Dr RBRY B45.....................173 F1
TPTN/OCK DY4.................................85 E5
Leasowe Cft HALE B63..................138 C4
Leasowes Dr
DUNHL/THL/PER WV6......................34 C5
ETTPK/GDPK/PENN WV4..................51 E5
Leasowes La RMSLY B62...............139 G2
Leasowes Rd
ALE/KHTH/YWD B14......................161 G4
The Leasowes TPTN/OCK DY4........85 E5
The Leasow ALDR WS9...................29 H5
The Lea STETCH B33.....................130 C1
Leatherhead Cl AST/WIT B6..........109 H5
Lea Vale Rd STRBR DY8................135 E3
Leavesden Gv
LGN/SDN/BHAMAIR B26.................130 B5
Lea Vw ALDR WS9............................29 H5
SHHTH WV12....................................25 H2
Lea Village STECH B33..................130 D1
Lea Wk RBRY B45..........................173 H5
Lea Yield Cl BVILLE B30................159 H3
Lechlade Rd GTB/HAM B43............73 E2
Leckie Rd WSLW WS2........................5 K2
Ledbury Cl ALDR WS9......................45 E5
LDYWD/EDGR B16..........................126 A2
Ledbury Dr WOLV WV1......................7 M3
Ledbury Wy WALM/CURD B76........78 D1

Ledsam Gv RIDG/WDGT B32 ....141 F1
Ledsam St LDYWD/EDGR B16 ...126 C4
Ledwell SHLY B90 ......194 A3
Lee Bank Middleway EDG B15..126 C4
Leebank Rd HALE B63 .....138 A5
Leech St TPTN/OCK DY4 .....86 A1
Lee Crs EDG B15 * 126 C4
Lee Mt EDG B15 * 126 C4
Lee Rd CDYHTH B64 .....121 F4
   HLYWD B47 ....192 C1
Leeson Wk HRBN B17 .....142 B2
Lees Rd BILS/COS WV14 .....54 B5
Lees St WSNGN B18 .....107 H4
Lees Ter BILS/COS WV14 .....54 B5
Lee St WBROM B70 .....71 E5
Legge La BILS/COS WV14......68 D3
   CBHAMNW B1 .....2 C3
Legge St BKHL/PFLD WV2 .....52 C2
   CBHAMNE B4 .....3 J1
   WBROM B70 .....87 G3
Legion Rd RBRY B45 .....187 G1
Leges La WOLVN WV10 .....13 F4
Leicester Cl SMTHWKW B67 ..124 A3
Leicester Pl HHTH/SAND B71 ..71 C4
Leicester Sq
   DUNHL/THL/PER WV6......36 D1
   WSL WS1 .....4 E5
Leigham Dr HRBN B17 .....124 B5
Leigh Cl RUSH/SHEL WS4 .....42 C1
Leigh Rd MGN/WHC B75......63 H2
   RUSH/SHEL WS4 .....42 C1
   WASH/WDE B8 .....110 C3
Leighs Cl RUSH/SHEL WS4 .....29 E1
Leighs Rd RUSH/SHEL WS4 .....28 D1
Leighswood Av ALDR WS9 .....30 B3
Leighswood Gv ALDR WS9 .....30 A3
Leighswood Rd ALDR WS9......30 A3
Leighton Cl DUDN DY1 .....83 G4
   GTB/HAM B43 .....59 G5
Leighton Rd BILS/COS WV14 ..54 C4
   ETTPK/GDPK/PENN WV4 ....51 F2
   MOS/BIL B13 .....144 B5
Leith Gv HWK/WKHTH B38....176 C5
Lelant Gv HRBN B17
Lellow St HHTH/SAND B71 .....71 G3
Le More FOAKS/STRLY B74 .....47 E5
Lemox Rd WBROM B70 .....71 E5
Lench Cl RMSLY B62 .....122 A3
Lench's Cl MOS/BIL B13 ...144 B5
Lench Cl on DIG/EDG B5 .....127 E5
Lench St CBHAMNE B4 ....3 G2
Lenchs Trust Houses
   BHTH/HG B12 * 127 F5
Len Davies Rd SHHTH WV12...25 C3
Lennard Gdns SMTHWK B66 *..107 F3
Lennox Gdns BDMR/CCFT WV3 ....6 A2
Lennox St LOZ/NWT B19......108 D1
Lenton Cft SOLH B91 .....182 A5
Lenwade Rd OLGLYGN/QTN B68..123 H4
Leominster Rd SPARK B11 .....145 G4
Leominster Wk RBRY B45 .....175 H5
Leonard Gv LOZ/NWT B19......108 D1
Leonard Rd LOZ/NWT B19......108 D1
   STRBR DY8 .....134 C2
Leopold Av BFLD/HDSWWD B20..89 C1
Leopold St BHTH/HG B12 ....127 F4
Lepid Gv SLYOAK B29 .....142 B5
Lerryn Cl KGSWFD DY6......100 B4
Lercik Cl KGSWFD DY6 ....100 B4
Lesley Dr KGSWFD DY6......100 A5
Leslie Dr TPTN/OCK DY4......69 C2
Leslie Ri OLDBY B69 .....104 A1
Leslie Rd BDMR/CCFT WV3 ....90 D4
   FOAKS/STRLY B74 .....45 H3
   LDYWD/EDGR B16......125 H2
   WOLVN WV10 .....37 H1
Lesscroft Cl COVEN WV9 .....12 A4
Lester Gv ALDR WS9 .....45 E5
Lester St BILS/COS WV14......54 B5
Levante Gdns STETCH B33 ....129 H2
Leve La WLNHL WV13 .....39 H4
Level St BRLYHL DY5......119 G1
Leven Dr SHHTH WV12 .....25 H1
Leven Wy KGSWFD DY6......100 C4
Le Leverets HDSW B21 .....89 E3
Lever St BKHL/PFLD WV2......7 G7
Leverton Ri WOLVN WV10 .....23 E4
Leveson Cl DUDLEY DY2 ....103 E1
Leveson Dr TPTN/OCK DY4 ....69 C1
Leveson Rd WOLVN WV10 .....25 F2
Leveson St WLNHL WV13 .....39 G3
Levington Cl
   DUNHL/THL/PER WV6......20 D5
Levis Av WOLV WV1 .....38 B2
Levis Cl SHHTH WV12 .....26 B5
Levis Gv WNSFLD WV11......24 D4
Levisham Rd SMTHWK B66....106 C1
   WOLVN WV10 .....12 B5
Lewis Av WOLV WV1 .....39 E1
   HHTH/SAND B71 * 87 H2
Lewis Gv BVILLE B30

Leysdown Gv ACGN B27 ......163 G2
Leysdown Rd ACGN B27 ......163 G2
Leys Rd BRLYHL DY5 .....118 C1
The Leys DUDLEY DY2 .....85 H4
   NFLD/LBR B31 .....158 D5
Leys Wood Cft
   LGN/SDN/BHAMAIR B26 ...147 G1
Leyton Cl BRLYHL DY5 .....119 F4
Leyton Gv KGSTG B44 .....75 G2
Leyton Rd HDSW B21 .....107 H1
Libbards Ga SOLH B91 .....182 A5
Libbards Wy SOLH B91 .....181 H5
Library Wy RBRY B45 .....187 H1
Lich Av WNSFLD WV11 .....25 E3
Lichfield Rd ALDR WS9 .....18 C5
   AST/WIT B6 .....109 G3
   BLOX/PEL WS3 .....17 E5
   BRWNH W8 .....9 F4
   CSHL/WTROR B46 .....115 F1
   FOAKS/STRLY B74 .....62 B1
   RUSH/SHEL WS4 .....29 F1
   WLNHL WV13 .....24 D5
Lichwood Rd WNSFLD WV11...25 F3
Lickey Coppice RBRY B45 .....188 C4
Lickey Rd RBRY B45 .....188 C2
   STRBR DY8 .....135 H1
Liddon Gv ACGN B27 .....163 G2
Liddon Rd ACGN B27 .....163 G2
Lifford Cl ALE/KHTH/YWD B14..177 F1
Lifford La BVILLE B30 .....177 F1
Lifton Cft KGSWFD DY6 .....100 B4
Lighthorne Av
   LDYWD/EDGR B16 .....126 A1
Lighthorne Rd SOLH B91 .....164 D4
Lightning Wy NFLD/LBR B31....189 H1
Lightwood Cl DOR/KN B93 ....185 F5
Lightwood Rd DUDN DY1 .....84 A3
Lightwoods HI HAG/WOL DY9 ..124 A4
Lightwoods Rd HAG/WOL DY9 ..153 C1
   SMTHWKW B67 .....124 B3
Lilac Av BHTH/HG B12 .....144 C2
   DSYBK/YTR WS5 .....57 G4
   FOAKS/STRLY B74 .....60 A1
   KGSTG B44 .....75 E4
   TPTN/OCK DY4 .....69 G4
Lilac Dr WMBN WV5 .....64 D5
Lilac Gv DARL/WED WS10 .....71 E1
   SHHTH WV12 .....26 C3
   WOLV WV1 .....38 B5
Lilac Wy RMSLY B62 .....122 D4
Lilian Gv BILS/COS WV14 .....69 E2
Lilleshall Crs BKHL/PFLD WV2..52 B1
Lilleshall Rd
   LGN/SDN/BHAMAIR B26 ...130 D5
Lilley La NFLD/LBR B31 .....175 H5
Lillington Gv BORD/SHDE B34..113 F4
Lillington Rd SHLY B90 .....180 D5
Lilycroft La HWK/WKHTH B38..191 E1
Lily Rd
   LGN/SDN/BHAMAIR B26 ...146 D1
Lily St HHTH/SAND B71 .....87 G1
Limberlost Cl
   BFLD/HDSWWD B20 .....90 A3
Limbrick Cl SHLY B90 .....179 H3
Limbury Gv HIA/OLT B92 .....165 H2
Lime Av BLOX/PEL WS3 * 40 C2
   TPTN/OCK DY4 .....85 E1
   WBROM B70 * 87 E2
Lime Ct SPARK B11 .....145 E3
Lime Gv BHTH/HG B12 .....144 B2
   BILS/COS WV14 .....38 C5
   CHWD/FDBR/MGN B37 .....132 B3
   LGN/SDN/BHAMAIR B26 ...146 D1
   LOZ/NWT B19 .....108 C1
   RUSH/SHEL WS4 .....29 E4
   SCFLD/BOLD B73 .....77 F4
   WBROM B70 * 106 D5
Limehurst Av BDMR/CCFT WV3..35 G4
Limehurst Rd RUSH/SHEL WS4..29 E5
Lime Kiln Cl HWK/WKHTH B38..190 B1
Limekiln La
   ALE/KHTH/YWD B14.....178 C1
Lime La BLOX/PEL WS3 .....8 A3
Limepit La DUDN DY1 .....84 A3
Lime Rd DARL/WED WS10 .....55 H4
   SEDG DY3 .....67 H2
Limes Av BLKHTH/ROWR B65..122 A2
   BRLYHL DY5 .....101 G4
Limes Ct CDYHTH B64 * 120 D5
Limes Rd DUDN DY1 .....84 B3
   DUNHL/THL/PER WV6.....35 G1
The Limes ERDE/BCHGN B24 ..92 D3
   LDYWD/EDGR B16 * 125 H1
   SPARK B11 .....145 E1
Lime St BDMR/CCFT WV3 .....6 B7
   BILS/COS WV14 * 68 A3
   WSL WS1 .....5 G4
Limes Vw SEDG DY3 .....67 F4
Lime Tree Av
   DUNHL/THL/PER WV6.....35 E2
Lime Tree Gdns CDSL WV8 .....10 D4
Lime Tree Gv NFLD/LBR B31 ..176 A3
Lime Tree Rd ACGN B27 .....146 C2
   CDSL WV8 .....10 D4
   DSYBK/YTR WS5 * 57 G4
   WASH/WDE B8 .....110 D3
Limetree Rd FOAKS/STRLY B74..44 D4
Linchmere Rd HDSW B21 .....89 E4
Lincoln Av WLNHL WV13 .....40 B3
Lincoln Cl ACGN B27 .....147 G1
Lincoln Gv WOLVN WV10 .....12 D5
Lincoln Gv
   CHWD/FDBR/MGN B37 .....132 A4
Lincoln Rd ACGN B27 .....147 G1
   DUDS DY2 * 120 D1
   HHTH/SAND B71 .....71 H2
   SMTHWKW B67 .....124 A2
   WSL WS1 .....43 F2
Lincoln Rd North ACGN B27 ..147 G4
Lincoln St BHTH/HG B12 .....144 A1

   WOLV WV10 .....7 K2
Lindale Av CBROM B36 .....111 G3
Lindale Crs BRLYHL DY5 .....135 H1
Linden Av HWK/WKHTH B38...177 F3
   OLDBY B69 .....104 B1
   RMSLY B62 .....122 D3
Linden Cl WSLW WS2 * 40 B3
Linden Dr STRBR DY8 .....135 G4
Linden La SHHTH WV12 .....26 C3
Linden Lea BDMR/CCFT WV3 ..35 H4
Linden Rd BVILLE B30 .....159 G3
   DUDN DY1 .....84 A5
Lindens Dr FOAKS/STRLY B74..46 D5
The Lindens
   DUNHL/THL/PER WV6......36 A2
   RIDG/WDGT B32 .....124 A5
Lindenwood SCFLD/BOLD B73 ..62 D2
Lindford Wy HWK/WKHTH B38..177 F3
Lindley Av TPTN/OCK DY4 .....85 F3
Lindon Cl BRWNH WS8 .....19 G1
Lindon Dr BRWNH WS8 .....19 G1
Lindon Rd BRWNH WS8 .....19 G1
Lindon Vw BRWNH WS8 .....19 G1
Lindrick Cl BLOX/PEL WS3 .....16 B4
Lindridge Dr MGN/WHC B76....63 H2
Lindridge Rd ERDW/GRVHL B23..92 A1
   MGN/WHC B75 .....63 C2
   SHLY B90 .....179 H4
Lindrosa Rd FOAKS/STRLY B74..45 F2
Lindsay Rd PBAR/PBCH B42....74 B2
Lindsey Av NFLD/LBR B31 .....176 A1
Lindsey Pl BRLYHL DY5 .....119 E1
Lindsey Rd HHTH/SAND B71 ..71 C4
Lindsworth Ap BVILLE B30 ....177 G2
Lindsworth Cl BVILLE B30 ....177 H2
Lindsworth Rd BVILLE B30 ....177 F2
Linfield Gdns SEDG DY3 .....67 E2
Linford Gv YDLY B25 .....129 H5
Linforth Dr FOAKS/STRLY B74..62 A1
Lingard Cl VAUX/NECH B7 ....109 H4
Lingard Rd MGN/WHC B75......63 F3
Lingfield Av KGSTG B44 .....75 E2
   WOLVN WV10 .....12 D2
Lingfield Gdns
   BKDE/SHDE B34 .....112 D3
Lingfield Gv
   DUNHL/THL/PER WV6......34 D1
Lingfield Wy KGSWFD DY6....100 C4
Lingham Cl HIA/OLT B92 .....165 H5
Lingmoor Gv ALDR WS9 .....30 A3
Linhope Dr KGSWFD DY6......100 C4
Link Rd ALDR WS9 .....19 H4
   LDYWD/EDGR B16 .....125 G1
   WMBN WV5 .....65 E4
Links Av DUNHL/THL/PER WV6..21 H3
Links Dr RBRY B45 .....188 A2
   SOLH B91 .....164 D1
   STRBR DY8 .....135 E5
Links End ACGN B27 .....162 D1
Linley Cl ALDR WS9 .....29 G5
Linley Dr WOLVN WV10 .....23 H5
Linley Gv ALE/KHTH/YWD B14..160 C4
   SEDG DY3 .....82 B5
Linley Rd RUSH/SHEL WS4......29 F5
Linley Wood Rd ALDR WS9 ....29 G5
Linnet Cl HWK/WKHTH B38....159 G2
   RMSLY B62 .....138 D1
Linnet Gv ERDW/GRVHL B23 ..75 H5
   SHHTH WV12 .....26 A2
Linsey Rd HIA/OLT B92 .....148 A5
Linslade Cl
   ETTPK/GDPK/PENN WV4......52 B4
Linthouse La WNSFLD WV11 ..24 D2
Lint Meadow HLYWD B47 ....192 D1
Linton Av SOLH B91 .....181 H4
Linton Cl HALE B63 .....137 G2
Linton Crt BILS/COS WV14 .....53 H4
Linton Rd BILS/COS WV14 ....121 F1
   ETTPK/GDPK/PENN WV4......51 E5
   GTB/HAM B43 .....59 G4
   SPARK B11 .....146 A3
Linwood Rd DUDN DY1 .....84 B1
   HDSW B21 .....107 G1
   SOLH B91 .....163 H5
Lionel St CBHAMNW B3 .....2 E5
Lion Pas STRBR DY8 .....135 F2
Lion St STRBR DY8 .....135 F2
Liskeard Rd DSYBK/YTR WS5..58 B1
Lisko Cl BRLYHL DY5 .....118 C4
Lismore Cl RBRY B45 .....173 G4
Lismore Dr HRBN B17 .....141 G4
Lissimore Dr TPTN/OCK DY4 ..85 E4
Lisson Gv KGSTG B44 .....60 B4
Lister Cl TPTN/OCK DY4 .....85 C2
   WSLW WS2 .....27 F5
Lister Rd DUDS DY2 .....102 C2
   WSLW WS2 .....27 F5
Lister St VAUX/NECH B7 .....3 J1
   WLNHL WV13 .....39 H4
Listowel Rd
   ALE/KHTH/YWD B14.....160 D4
Lisures Dr WALM/CURD B76....76 D2
Little Albert St WSL WS2 * 4 E2
Little Ann St DIG/EDG B5 .....3 K6
Little Aston Hall Dr
   FOAKS/STRLY B74 .....31 G5
Little Aston La
   FOAKS/STRLY B74 .....32 C4
Little Aston Park Rd
   FOAKS/STRLY B74 .....45 G2
Little Aston Rd ALDR WS9 .....30 D4
Little Barr St BORD B9 .....127 G2
Little Bell Hall Cottages
   HAG/WOL DY9 * 184 B2
Little Birches BDMR/CCFT WV3..36 B5
Little Brickiln St
   BDMR/CCFT WV3 .....6 E6
Little Bromwich Rd BORD B9 ..129 F3
Little Broom St BHTH/HG B12 ..127 G4
Little Caldmore WSL WS1 .....4 E6

Little Checkhill La KINVER DY7..98 B5
Little Clothier St WLNHL WV13..39 H2
Little Clover Cl VAUX/NECH B7..110 A3
Little Cornbow HALE B63 .....138 D4
Littlecote Cft
   ALE/KHTH/YWD B14.....178 C2
Littlecote Dr ERDW/GRVHL B23..76 D4
Little Cottage St BRLYHL DY5..119 F2
Little Cft GTB/HAM B43 .....73 E2
Little Cross St DARL/WED WS10..55 G3
Little Edward St BORD B9 .....127 G2
Little Fields Wy OLDBY B69....104 D2
Little Francis Gv
   VAUX/NECH B7 .....109 H4
Little Gorway WSL WS1 .....57 F1
Little Green La BORD B9 .....128 B3
Little Gn Lanes
   SCFLD/BOLD B73 .....77 F4
Little Hall Rd VAUX/NECH B7 ..109 H4
Little Hardwick Rd ALDR WS9..44 D3
Little Hay La LICHS WS14 .....33 F3
Little Heath Cft
   BKDE/SHDE B34 .....112 D3
Little HI DARL/WED WS10 .....55 H3
Littlehill Crs CDYHTH B64......120 C5
Little Hill Gv HWK/WKHTH B38..177 E4
Little Hill Wy RIDG/WDGT B32..140 D5
Little Johnson's La ALDR WS9..44 B4
Little Lawns Cl BRWNH WS8 ..19 G2
Little London WSL WS1 .....57 F1
Littlemead Av NFLD/LBR B31 ..159 H4
Little Meadow Cft
   NFLD/LBR B31 .....158 B5
Littlemead Rd SHLY B90 .....179 C5
Little Moor HI SMTHWK B67 ..106 B4
Little Newport St WSL WS1 ....4 D4
Little Oaks Rd AST/WIT B6 ....109 F1
Little Pk RIDG/WDGT B32 .....140 B3
Little Park St WOLV WV1 * 7 H4
Little Pitts Cl ERDE/BCHGN B24..93 H1
Little Potter St BRLYHL DY5 ..119 F3
Little Pountney St
   BKHL/PFLD WV2 * 7 F7
Little Shadwell St
   CBHAMNE B4 * 3 G2
Littleshaw Cft HLYWD B47 ....195 E4
Littleshaw La HLYWD B47 .....195 E4
Little's La WOLV WV1 * 7 G2
Little Station St WSLW WS2 ....4 D3
Little Sutton La MGN/WHC B75..47 H4
Little Sutton Rd MGN/WHC B75..47 H5
Littleton Cl WALM/CURD B76 ..78 C1
Littleton Cft SOLH B91 .....182 A5
Littleton St East WSL WS1 .....4 E2
Littleton St West WSLW WS2 ..4 D2
Littlewood Cl SOLH B91 .....181 H5
Little Wood St WLNHL WV13 ..39 G3
Littleworth Dr DUDN DY1 .....68 B5
Littleworth Gv
   WALM/CURD B76 .....63 F4
Liveridge Cl DOR/KN B93 ....196 D2
Liverpool Cft
   CHWD/FDBR/MGN B37 .....131 H3
Liverpool St BORD B9 .....127 G2
Livery St CBHAMNW B3 .....2 E2
Livingstone Av
   DUNHL/THL/PER WV6......20 C5
Livingstone Rd
   ALE/KHTH/YWD B14.....161 E4
   BFLD/HDSWWD B20 .....90 C5
   BILS/COS WV14 .....54 B5
   BLOX/PEL WS3 .....17 G5
   WBROM B70 .....87 F5
Lloyd Dr
   ETTPK/GDPK/PENN WV4......65 G1
Lloyd HI
   ETTPK/GDPK/PENN WV4 * 50 C5
Lloyd Rd BFLD/HDSWWD B20..90 A2
   DUNHL/THL/PER WV6......21 H5
Lloyd Sq EDG B15 * 125 G4
Lloyds Rd RMSLY B62 .....122 A5
Lloyd St DARL/WED WS10 .....55 G5
   DUDS DY2 * 102 D1
   DUNHL/THL/PER WV6......36 B1
   HHTH/SAND B71 .....88 A2
   WOLV WV1 .....7 K5
Locarno Rd TPTN/OCK DY4 ....69 F4
Lochalsh Gv SHHTH WV12......25 H1
Lochranza Cft GTB/HAM B43 ..72 C1
Lock Dr STETCH B33 .....129 H1
Locke Pl VAUX/NECH B7 * 127 G1
Locket Cl WSLW WS2 .....40 D1
Lockfield Cl STRBR DY8 .....118 B2
Lockhart Dr MGN/WHC B75 ....47 G4
Locking Cft CDYHTH B64 .....120 D5
Lockington Cft RMSLY B62 ....139 H1
Lockley Cl WOLVN WV10 .....37 H1
Lockside ALDR WS9 .....29 H1
Locksmith Cl WLNHL WV13 ....39 H3
Lockton Rd STETCH B33 .....129 G1
Lockwood Rd NFLD/LBR B31 ..175 H2
Lode La SOLH B91 .....181 H1
Lode Mill Ct SOLH B91 .....164 D3
Lodge Cl DSYBK/YTR WS5 .....58 B2
   HALE B63 .....137 G3
Lodge Crs DUDS DY2 .....102 D5
   HAG/WOL DY9 .....152 D5
Lodge Cft DOR/KN B93 .....197 F2
   NFLD/LBR B31 .....158 A5
Lodge Dr
   LGN/SDN/BHAMAIR B26 ...130 A4
Lodge Farm Cl
   WALM/CURD B76 .....63 F5
Lodgefield Rd RMSLY B62 ....121 H5
Lodge Gv ALDR WS9 .....30 A5
Lodge Hill Rd SLYOAK B29 ....159 F1
Lodge La KGSWFD DY6 .....99 G4
Lodgepool Cl KGSTG B44 .....75 E5
Lodge Rd AST/WIT B6 .....109 E1
   BILS/COS WV14 .....54 B4
   DARL/WED WS10 .....55 F3

   DOR/KN B93 .....197 F2
   DSYBK/YTR WS5 .....58 B3
   RUSH/SHEL WS4 .....28 D1
   SMTHWKW B67 .....106 A2
   WBROM B70 .....87 F3
   WOLVN WV10 .....22 D2
   WSNGN B18 .....107 G4
Lodge St OLDBY B69 .....105 E2
   SMTHWKW B67 .....26 A5
Loeless Rd STETCH B33 .....130 C1
Lofthouse Crs NFLD/LBR B31 ..175 F2
Lofthouse Gv NFLD/LBR B31 ..175 F2
Lofthouse Rd
   BFLD/HDSWWD B20 .....89 H4
Loftus Cl SLYOAK B29 .....158 D2
Logan Cl WOLVN WV10 .....23 E4
Lomaine Dr BVILLE B30 .....176 C1
Lomas Dr NFLD/LBR B31 .....175 E2
Lomas St WOLV WV1 .....37 E1
Lombard Av DUDS DY2 .....120 D1
Lombard St BHTH/HG B12 ....127 F4
   WBROM B70 .....87 G3
Lombard St West
   WBROM B70 * 87 G3
Lombardy Gdns SHHTH WV12..26 C3
Lomond Cl BKDE/SHDE B34 ..113 G3
Lomond Rd SEDG DY3 .....67 E2
Londonderry Gv
   SMTHWKW B67 .....106 B4
Londonderry La
   SMTHWKW B67 .....105 H5
London Hts DUDN DY1 .....84 A4
London Pl BFLD/HDSWWD B20..91 E4
   MGN/WHC B75
London St SMTHWK B66 .....107 E4
Lones Rd HHTH/SAND B71 ....106 D1
Long Acre CDSL WV8 .....10 A5
   VAUX/NECH B7 .....109 H3
Longacre WLNHL WV13 .....39 G5
Long Acre St WSLW WS2 .....4 C1
Longbank Rd OLDBY B69 .....104 A1
Longboat La STRBR DY8 .....118 A4
Longboat Quay DUDS DY2 ....102 D5
Longbow Rd SLYOAK B29 .....158 B3
Longbridge La NFLD/LBR B31 ..175 F5
Long Cl Av RIDG/WDGT B31 ..189 F1
Long Cl HAG/WOL DY9 .....169 G1
Long Close Wk CVALE B35 .....94 C3
Long Compton Dr
   HAG/WOL DY9 .....152 C4
Longcroft Cl CVALE B35 .....94 C3
The Longcroft HALE B63 .....138 A3
   RUSH/SHEL WS4 .....29 E5
Longdales Rd
   HWK/WKHTH B38 .....190 B1
Longdon Av
   ETTPK/GDPK/PENN WV4......52 B3
Longdon Cft DOR/KN B93 ....183 G5
Longdon Dr FOAKS/STRLY B74..46 A4
Longdon Rd DOR/KN B93 .....197 E2
Longfellow Rd NFLD/LBR B31..176 B2
   SEDG DY3 .....82 C1
Longfield Cl HLGN/YWD B28 ..162 D4
Longfield Dr FOAKS/STRLY B74..46 A5
Longfield Rd HAG/WOL DY9 ..136 B2
   NFLD/LBR B31 .....158 A3
Longford Cl DOR/KN B93 .....197 F5
   RIDG/WDGT B32 .....157 E3
   WMBN WV5 .....80 C5
Longham Cft RIDG/WDGT B32..141 F3
Longhurst Cft NFLD/LBR B31 ..189 G1
Long Hyde Rd SMTHWKW B67..124 B3
Long Innage HALE B63 .....137 F1
Long Knowle La WNSFLD WV11..24 B2
Longlake Av
   DUNHL/THL/PER WV6......35 E2
The Longlands WMBN WV5 ....65 E5
Long La BLKHTH/ROWR B65 ..122 A3
   GTWY WS6 .....16 B1
   WNSFLD WV11 .....15 H2
Long Leasow SLYOAK B29 ....158 B3
Longleat GTB/HAM B43 .....73 E1
Longleat Av EDG B15 .....126 C4
Longleat Dr DUDN DY1 .....83 G4
   SHLY B90 .....195 E3
Longleat Rd ALDR WS9 .....19 F5
Long Ley WOLVN WV10 .....37 H2
Longley Av WALM/CURD B76 ..95 F1
Longley Crs
   LGN/SDN/BHAMAIR B26 ...147 E3
Long Leys Cft
   CSHL/WTROR B46 * 96 B4
Long Leys Cft
   CSHL/WTROR B46 .....96 B4

Longmeadow Cl
   MGN/WHC B75 .....63 E3
Longmeadow Crs
   BKDE/SHDE B34 .....113 G3
Long Meadow Dr SEDG DY3 ..66 D2
Longmeadow Gv
   NFLD/LBR B31 .....189 G5
Longmeadow Rd
   DSYBK/YTR WS5 .....58 B3
Long MI North WNSFLD WV11..24 B3
Long MI South WNSFLD WV11..24 B3
Longmoor Cl WNSFLD WV11 ..25 F5
Longmoor Rd HALE B63 .....139 H4
   SCFLD/BOLD B73 .....60 D5
Longmore Av WSLW WS2 .....40 D4
Longmore Cl SCFLD/BOLD B73..60 D4
Longmore Rd SHLY B90 .....180 D4
Longmore St BHTH/HG B12 ..127 E5
   DARL/WED WS10 .....55 F3
Longshaw Gv BKDE/SHDE B34..113 F3
Longstone Cl SHLY B90 .....195 H2
Longstone Rd PBAR/PBCH B42..74 C4
Long St SPARK B11 .....144 C1

WOLV WV1.......7 G3
WSLW WS2.......4 C4
Long Wd BVILLE B30....159 C5
Longwood La RUSH/SHEL WS4..43 C3
Longwood Ri SHHTH WV12...26 B5
Longwood Rd ALDR WS9....44 B3
RBRY B45.......188 A1
Lonicera CI DSYBK/YTR WS5..57 H5
Lonsdale CI SHHTH WV12....25 H5
STECH B33.......129 H5
Lonsdale Rd BDMR/CCFT WV3..36 D5
BILS/COS WV14....54 B2
DSYBK/YTR WS5....58 A2
HRBN B17.......141 H1
Lord's Dr WSLW WS2....4 E1
Lords La KINVER DY7....116 C3
Lordsmore CI BILS/COS WV14..68 D2
Lord St BDMR/CCFT WV3....6 C5
BILS/COS WV14....6 C5
DSYBK/YTR WS5....57 E5
VAUX/NECH B7....3 K1
WSL WS1.......56 D2
Lord St West BILS/COS WV14..54 A5
Lordswood Rd HRBN B17....141 H1
Lordswood Sq HRBN B17 *...124 D5
Lorimer Wy GTB/HAM B43...59 H3
Lorne St TPTN/OCK DY4...69 F3
Lorrainer Av BRLYHL DY5...118 C4
Lothians Rd BLOX/PEL WS3...18 A2
DUNHL/THL/PER WV6....21 H4
Lottie Rd SLYOAK B29....159 G1
Lotus CI DUDN DY1....84 A3
Lotus Ct BDMR/CCFT WV3...6 C5
Lotus Dr BRLYHL DY5....119 H3
Lotus Wy BLKHTH/ROWR B65..103 F5
Loughton Gv HALE B63....138 B3
Louisa St CBHAMW B1....2 C4
Louise Cft
  ALE/KHTH/YWD B14....178 A3
Louise Lorne Rd MOS/BIL B13..144 B3
Louise Rd HSW B21....107 H2
Louise St SEDG DY3....82 D3
Lount Wk LOZ/NWT B19....109 E4
Lovat St BDMR/CCFT WV3....6 D4
Loveday St CBHAMNE B4....3 G2
Lovelace Av SOLH B91....182 B5
Love La DUNHL/THL/PER WV6..21 H4
  HAG/WOL DY9....136 C2
  HLYWD B47.......192 A1
  RBRY B45.......169 E3
  STRBR DY8.......135 G4
  VAUX/NECH B7.......3 J1
  WSL WS1.......57 E1
Lovell CI SLYOAK B29....158 C4
Loveridge CI CDSL WV8....10 A4
Lovett Av OLDBY B69....104 B4
Low Av GTB/HAM B43....73 H1
Lowbridge CI SHHTH WV12...26 A5
Lowbrook La SHLY B90....193 F4
Lowden Cft
  LGN/SDN/BHAMAIR B26...147 E3
Lowe Av DARL/WED WS10...54 D1
Lowe Dr KGSWFD DY6....100 A5
  SCFLD/BOLD B73....61 F5
Lower Beeches Rd RBRY B45...174 C3
Lower Chapel St OLDBY B69...86 A4
Lower Church La
  TPTN/OCK DY4....85 H1
Lower City Rd OLDBY B69...86 A5
Lowercroft Wy
  FOAKS/STRLY B74....32 C4
Lower Dartmouth St
  BORD B9.......127 H2
Lower Darwin St
  BHTH/HG B12....127 F4
Lower Derry St BRLYHL DY5...119 F2
Lower Essex St DIG/EDG B5...127 E5
Lower Forster St WSL WS1....5 F2
Lower Gn
  DUNHL/THL/PER WV6....21 E4
  TPTN/OCK DY4 *....91 F5
Lower Ground Ct AST/WIT B6 *..91 F5
Lower Hall La WSL WS1....4 E5
Lower High St CDYHTH B64...120 C4
  DARL/WED WS10....70 D1
  STRBR DY8.......135 F1
Lower Higley Ct
  RIDG/WDGT B32....141 E3
Lower Horseley Flds WOLV WV1..7 K4
Lower Lichfield St
  WLNHL WV13....39 H3
Lower Loveday St LOZ/NWT B19..3 F1
Lower Moor BVILLE B30 *....159 G2
Lower North St
  RUSH/SHEL WS4....42 B2
The Lower Pde
  CSCFLD/WYGN B72....62 C3
Lower Prestwood Rd
  WNSFLD WV11....24 C3
Lower Queen St
  CSCFLD/WYGN B72....62 C4
Lower Reddicroft
  SCFLD/BOLD B73....62 C3
Lower Rushall St WSL WS1....5 F3
Lower Severn St CBHAMW B1...2 C6
Lowerstack Cft
  CHWD/FDBR/MGN B37...131 H1
Lower St
  DUNHL/THL/PER WV6....21 F3
Lower Temple St CBHAM B2....3 F5
Lower Tower St LOZ/NWT B19..108 D4
Lower Trinity St BORD B9....127 G3
Lower Valley Rd BRLYHL DY5...118 C2
Lower Vauxhall WOLV WV1....6 A3
Lower Villiers St
  BKHL/PFLD WV2....6 C5
Lower Walsall St WOLV WV1...37 H4
Lower White Rd
  RIDG/WDGT B32....140 D2
Lowesmoor Rd
  LGN/SDN/BHAMAIR B26...130 D5
Lowe St BHTH/HG B12....127 F4
  DUNHL/THL/PER WV6....36 C1
Lowewater Dr SEDG DY3....83 F3
Lowfield CI RMSLY B62....140 A4
Low Hill Crs WOLV WV10....23 G2
Lowhill La RBRY B45....188 C2
Lowland Cft CDYHTH B64....121 F3

Lowlands Av
  DUNHL/THL/PER WV6....22 A4
  FOAKS/STRLY B74....45 E5
Lowry CI DUNHL/THL/PER WV6..34 D1
  SMTHWKW B67....106 B3
  WLNHL WV13....38 D3
Low Thatch HWK/WKHTH B38..190 C1
Low Wood Rd
  ERDW/GRVHL B23....92 C2
Loxdale Sidings BILS/COS WV14..54 B4
Loxdale St BILS/COS WV14....54 B4
Loxley Av SHLY B90....179 H4
Loxley CI NFLD/LBR B31....158 A2
Loxley Rd MGN/WHC B75....47 H2
  SMTHWKW B67....124 B3
Loxton CI FOAKS/STRLY B74....32 B5
Loynells Rd RBRY B45....188 A1
Loyns CI
  CHWD/FDBR/MGN B37...131 G1
Lozells La LOZ/NWT B19....108 B2
Lozells St LOZ/NWT B19....108 C2
Lozells Wood CI LOZ/NWT B19..108 B2
Luanne CI CDYHTH B64....121 G3
Lucas Circ LOZ/NWT B19....108 C3
Luce CI CVALE B35....94 D2
Luce Rd WOLV WV10....23 G4
Lucknow Rd SHHTH WV12....25 H5
Luddington Rd HIA/OLT B92...165 G5
Ludford CI SMHTH B10....63 E1
Ludford Rd RIDG/WDGT B32...157 E1
Ludgate CI CSHL/WTROR B46...96 A3
  OLDBY B69.......103 H1
Ludgate Hi CBHAMNW B3....2 E3
Ludgate St DUDN DY1 *....84 B5
Ludlow CI
  CHWD/FDBR/MGN B37...132 C2
  SHHTH WV12....12 D2
Ludlow La WSLW WS2....41 E1
Ludlow Rd WASH/WDE B8....128 D1
Ludlow Wy DUDN DY1....83 C4
Ludmer Wy
  BFLD/HDSWWD B20....90 C4
Ludstone Av
  ETTPK/GDPK/PENN WV4...50 D3
Ludstone Rd SLYOAK B29...158 B1
Ludworth Av
  CHWD/FDBR/MGN B37...132 B4
Lugtrout La SOLH B91....165 H4
The Lukes DUDS DY2....120 C3
Lulworth CI HALE B63....137 G1
Lulworth Rd HLGN/YWD B28..163 E2
Lumley Gv
  CHWD/FDBR/MGN B37...132 D2
Lumley Rd WSL WS1....5 H4
Lundy Vw CBROM B36....114 B3
Lunt Gv RIDG/WDGT B32....140 D2
Lunt PI BILS/COS WV14....54 C2
Lunt Rd BILS/COS WV14....54 C2
Lupin Gv BORD B9....128 D1
  DSYBK/YTR WS5....57 H4
Lupin Rd DUDS DY2....85 F5
Lusbridge CI HALE B63....137 F3
Lutley Av HALE B63....137 G3
Lutley CI BDMR/CCFT WV3....51 E1
Lutley Dr HAG/WOL DY9....136 A4
Lutley Gv RIDG/WDGT B32....157 F1
Lutley La HAG/WOL DY9....136 A5
Lutley Mill Rd HALE B63....138 A3
Luton Rd SLYOAK B29....142 D4
Lyall Gdns FOAKS/STRLY B74..32 C4
Lyall Gdns RBRY B45....173 G4
Lyall Gv ACGN B27....146 A5
Lychgate Av HAG/WOL DY9...153 E1
Lydate Rd RMSLY B62....139 H3
Lydbrook Covert
  HWK/WKHTH B38....176 C5
Lydbury Gv STECH B33....112 C5
Lyd CI WNSFLD WV11....24 B5
Lydd Cft CVALE B35....94 D2
Lyddington Dr RMSLY B62....121 H5
Lyde Gn HALE B63....120 C5
Lydford Gv ERDE/BCHGN B24...93 E4
Lydford Rd BLOX/PEL WS3....16 B5
Lydgate Rd KGSWFD DY6....100 B4
Lydget Gv ERDW/GRVHL B23..76 B4
Lydham CI BILS/COS WV14....53 F4
  KGSTG B44.......75 C5
Lydia Cft FOAKS/STRLY B74....32 C4
Lydian CI DUNHL/THL/PER WV6..36 D1
Lydiate Ash Rd BRCRVW B61...187 C5
Lydiate Av NFLD/LBR B31....174 D4
Lydiates CI SEDG DY3....66 D4
Lydney CI SHHTH WV12....40 B1
Lydney Rd NFLD/LBR B31....175 F2
Lye Av RIDG/WDGT B32....140 B4
Lye By-Pass HAG/WOL DY9...136 C1
Lye Close La RIDG/WDGT B32..139 H5
Lyecroft Av
  CHWD/FDBR/MGN B37...132 D2
Lye Cross Rd OLDBY B69....103 H2
Lygon Gv RIDG/WDGT B32....141 E3
Lymedene Rd PBAR/PBCH B42..90 B1
Lyme Green Rd STECH B33....112 B5
Lymer Rd WOLV WV10....23 E1
Lymington Rd WLNHL WV13...40 B3
Lymsey Cft STRBR DY8....97 H5
Lynbrook CI DUDS DY2....102 D5
  HLYWD B47.......192 D1
Lyncourt Gv RIDG/WDGT B32..140 B1
Lyncroft Rd SPARK B11....145 H5
Lyndale Dr WNSFLD WV11....25 E5
Lyndale Rd DUDS DY2....103 E5
  SEDG DY3.......66 D1
Lyndhurst Dr STRBR DY8....118 B3
Lyndhurst Rd BDMR/CCFT WV3..51 G1
  ERDE/BCHGN B24....92 A4
  HHTH/SAND B71....72 A4
Lyndon HHTH/SAND B71....87 H1
Lyndon CI BFLD/HDSWWD B20..90 C4
  CBROM B36.......113 E1
  HALE B63.......138 A2
  SEDG DY3.......66 C3
Lyndon Cft
  CHWD/FDBR/MGN B37...132 B5
Lyndon Gv HHTH/SAND B71...87 H2
  KGSWFD DY6....99 F1
Lyndon Rd HIA/OLT B92....147 F5

RBRY B45.......187 G1
SCFLD/BOLD B73....62 B3
STETCH B33.......130 A1
Lyndworth Rd BRLYHL B30....160 C3
Lyneham Gdns
  WALM/CURD B76....78 D5
Lyneham Wy CVALE B35....94 C3
Lynfield CI HWK/WKHTH B38...190 D1
Lyng La WBROM B70....87 G4
Lynmouth CI ALDR WS9....29 H5
Lynn Gv SLYOAK B29....142 A4
Lynton Av
  DUNHL/THL/PER WV6....22 A3
  HHTH/SAND B71....71 G4
  SMTHWK B66.......106 C5
Lynton Rd AST/WIT B6....109 G2
Lynval Rd BRLYHL DY5....119 H5
Lynwood Av KGSWFD DY6....99 F1
Lynwood CI SHHTH WV12....26 C2
Lynwood Dr KIDD DY10....168 B5
Lynwood Wk HRBN B17....142 A3
Lynwood Wy RBRY B45....188 A5
Lyons Gv SPARK B11....145 E4
Lysander Rd RBRY B45....174 A3
Lysander Wy CVALE B35....94 C4
Lysways St WSL WS1....5 H6
Lytham CI STRBR DY8....135 C5
  WALM/CURD B76....78 D5
Lytham Cft EDG B15....126 D3
Lytham Gv BLOX/PEL WS3....16 C3
Lytham Rd
  DUNHL/THL/PER WV6....34 B1
Lythwood Dr BRLYHL DY5....119 E4
Lyttelton Rd
  ERDW/GRVHL B23....75 H4
  STECH B33.......129 H2
  STRBR DY8.......134 D2
Lyttleton Av RMSLY B62....122 C5
Lyttleton CI DUDS DY2....102 C5
Lyttleton St WBROM B70....87 G4
Lytton Av
  ETTPK/GDPK/PENN WV4...50 A5
Lytton Gv ACGN B27....163 F1
Lytton La RIDG/WDGT B32....141 F4

M

Maas Rd NFLD/LBR B31....175 G1
Macarthur Rd CDYHTH B64...120 C4
Macdonald CI OLDBY B69....86 B4
Macdonald St DIG/EDG B5....127 E4
Mace St CDYHTH B64....121 E3
Machin Rd ERDW/GRVHL B23..92 D2
Mackadown La STETCH B33....131 F5
Mackay Rd BLOX/PEL WS3....17 F5
Mackenzie Rd SPARK B11....145 E5
Mackmillan Rd
  BLKHTH/ROWR B65....122 A2
Macmillan CI OLDBY B69....86 A4
Macrome Rd
  DUNHL/THL/PER WV6....21 G5
Madam's Hill Rd SHLY B90....194 D1
Maddocks Hi
  CSCFLD/WYGN B72....77 F1
Madehurst Rd
  ERDW/GRVHL B23....76 C5
Madeira Av CDSL WV8....10 C5
Madeley Rd HAG/WOL DY9....186 A1
  KGSWFD DY6....101 G5
  SPARK B11.......145 C2
Madin Rd TPTN/OCK DY4....85 E2
Madison Av WASH/WDE B8....111 H3
  CBROM B36.......111 H3
  WSLW WS3.......41 F3
Madley CI RBRY B45....173 G5
Madresfield Dr HALE B63....138 D5
Maer CI BLKHTH/ROWR B65...122 A1
Mafeking Rd SMTHWK B66...106 C2
Mafeking Vls RMSLY B62....121 H5
Magdala St WSNGN B18....107 G4
Magdalen CI DUDN DY1....84 A4
Magdalene Rd WSL WS1....57 G1
Magness Crs SHHTH WV12....26 A5
Magnolia CI SLYOAK B29....158 C3
Magnolia Dr DSYBK/YTR WS5..57 H3
Magnolia Gv CDSL WV8....10 C4
  SHHTH WV12....39 H1
Magnolia Wy STRBR DY8....118 B4
Magnum CI FOAKS/STRLY B74 *..60 B1
Maguire CI DUDS DY2....121 E1
Maidendale Rd KGSWFD DY6..99 F2
Maidenbridge Gdns
  KGSWFD DY6....99 F5
Maidenbridge Rd
  KGSWFD DY6....99 F5
Maidstone Dr STRBR DY8....118 A1
Maidstone Rd
  BFLD/HDSWWD B20....91 E5
Maidwell Dr SHLY B90....181 E5
Mainstream Wy
  VAUX/NECH B7....110 A5
Main St SHLY B90....194 A3
  SPARK B11.......127 G5
Main Ter SPARK B11 *....127 G5
Mainwaring Dr MGN/WHC B75..48 A3
Maisonettes CDSL WV8 *....10 D4
The Maisonettes
  ERDE/BCHGN B24....92 C4
Maitland Dr BKDE/SHDE B34..113 G3
Maitland Rd DUDN DY1....88 B3
  WASH/WDE B8....110 D5
Majestic Wy
  BLKHTH/ROWR B65....104 A5
Major St BKHL/PFLD WV2....52 C1
Majuba Rd LDYWD/EDGR B16..107 F5
Malins Rd
  ETTPK/GDPK/PENN WV4...52 B3
  HRBN B17.......142 B2
Malkit CI WSLW WS2....40 C1
Mallaby CI SHLY B90....180 A5
Mallard CI ACGN B27....146 C4

BLOX/PEL WS3....18 A1
BRLYHL DY5.......119 E5
Mallard Dr ERDW/GRVHL B23..91 E5
OLDBY B69.......104 B1
Mallender Dr DOR/KN B93....196 D1
Mallin Dr OLDBY B69....85 H5
Mallin Gdns DUDN DY1....101 C1
Mallin St SMTHWK B66....105 H2
Mallory Crs BLOX/PEL WS3....17 F5
Mallory Ri MOS/BIL B13....162 A1
Malt CI HRBN B17....142 B1
Malthouse Cft AST/WIT B6....109 F1
Malthouse Dr DUDN DY1....84 A4
Malthouse Gdns
  LOZ/NWT B19....108 D2
Malthouse Gv YDLY B25....130 A4
Malthouse La
  DUNHL/THL/PER WV6....21 H4
  PBAR/PBCH B42....74 D1
  WASH/WDE B8....110 C1
Malthouse Meadow SOLH B91..181 H4
Malthouse Rw TPTN/OCK DY4..85 E1
The Maltings ALDR WS9 *....30 C4
WMBN WV5.......65 E5
WOLV WV1.......7 G1
Malt Mill La RMSLY B62....122 A4
Malton Av OLDBY B69....104 B5
Malton Gv MOS/BIL B13....161 H5
Malvern Av HAG/WOL DY9....136 A2
Malvern CI EDG B15....125 E4
  HHTH/SAND B71....87 H1
  SHHTH WV12....26 C2
Malvern Ct ACGN B27 *....146 C3
  WOLN WV10....23 F2
Malvern Crs DUDS DY2....101 H5
Malvern Dr ALDR WS9....30 C2
  WALM/CURD B76....78 C5
  WOLV WV1.......38 B4
Malvern Hill Rd
  VAUX/NECH B7....110 A2
Malvern Park Av SOLH B91....182 B2
Malvern Rd ACGN B27....146 C3
  LGLYGN/QTN B68....123 F4
Malvern St BHTH/HG B12....144 C2
Malvern View Rd SEDG DY3....83 F2
Mamble Rd STRBR DY8....135 E2
Mammoth Dr WOLN WV10....23 E4
Manby CI DUNHL/THL/PER WV6..36 C1
Manby Rd CVALE B35....94 C2
Manby St TPTN/OCK DY4....69 F3
Mancetter Rd SHLY B90....180 C2
Manchester St AST/WIT B6....109 E4
  OLDBY B69.......105 F2
Mancroft CI KGSWFD DY6....99 F2
Mancroft Gdns
  DUNHL/THL/PER WV6....21 G5
Mancroft Rd
  DUNHL/THL/PER WV6....21 G5
Mandale Rd WOLN WV10....23 H4
Manderley CI SEDG DY3....67 E1
Manders St WOLV WV1....37 H2
Manderston CI DUDN DY1....83 C3
Mander St BDMR/CCFT WV3....6 D7
Man Der Ville Gdns
  KGSWFD DY6....99 G3
Mandeville Gdns WSL WS1....5 G6
Manfield Rd WLNHL WV13....38 C2
Manifold CI DARL/WED WS10...57 E5
Manilla Rd BVILLE B30....160 B1
Manitoba Cft
  HWK/WKHTH B38....176 D5
Manley CI WBROM B70....87 E3
Manlove St BDMR/CCFT WV3....6 A7
Manningford Rd
  ALE/KHTH/YWD B14....178 B3
Manor Abbey Dr RMSLY B62...139 G4
Manor Abbey Rd RMSLY B62...139 G3
Manor CI CDSL WV8....10 D4
  ETTPK/GDPK/PENN WV4...51 F4
  WLNHL WV13....39 F2
Manor Ct DOR/KN B93 *....198 D1
  WSLW WS2 *....4 E4
Manor Dr NFLD/LBR B31 *....158 D3
  SCFLD/BOLD B73....62 B4
  SEDG DY3.......80 C4
  TPTN/OCK DY4....69 G2
Manor Farm Dr SHHTH WV12...26 B5
Manor Farm Rd SPARK B11....145 G3
Manorford Av HHTH/SAND B71..72 C2
Manor Gdns STECH B33....129 H5
  WMBN WV5.......65 H4
Manor Gv DARL/WED WS10....71 H1
  RIDG/WDGT B32....140 A3
Manor Hi SCFLD/BOLD B73....62 B4
Manor House CI SLYOAK B29...158 B1
Manor House Dr
  NFLD/LBR B31....158 D3
Manor House La
  CSHL/WTROR B46....96 B3
  LGN/SDN/BHAMAIR B26...147 E1
Manor House Pk CDSL WV8....10 D3
Manor House Rd
  DARL/WED WS10....55 H4
Manor Houses RMSLY B62....139 H2
Manorial Rd MGN/WHC B75...48 A2
Manor La BRGRVW B61....187 E5
  RMSLY B62.......139 G3
  STRBR DY8.......134 D4
Manor Pk KGSWFD DY6....99 F1
  NFLD/LBR B31....174 C1
Manor Park CI NFLD/LBR B31...144 C5
Manor Park Rd CBROM B36....113 F2
Manor Rd AST/WIT B6....91 H5
  DARL/WED WS10....71 H1

DOR/KN B93.......196 D5
ETTPK/GDPK/PENN WV4...51 F4
ETTPK/GDPK/PENN WV4...45 C5
FOAKS/STRLY B74....45 C5
HLYWD B47.......192 C5
LDYWD/EDGR B16....125 F3
SCFLD/BOLD B73....62 B3
SMTHWKW B67....105 H2
SOLH B91.......164 D5
STECH B33.......130 A1
STRBR DY8.......117 H2
TPTN/OCK DY4....69 G3
WOLV WV10.......23 E3
WSLW WS2.......41 G3
Manor North
  LDYWD/EDGR B16....125 F3
Manor Road Prec WSLW WS2..41 G5
Manor St DUNHL/THL/PER WV6..21 G5
Manor Wy HALE B63....155 F1
RMSLY B62.......139 F4
Mansard Ct BDMR/CCFT WV3..36 B5
WOLN WV10.......24 B2
Mansell CI HALE B63....138 C2
Mansell Rd TPTN/OCK DY4....69 G2
Mansel Rd SMHTH B10....128 C4
Mansfield Rd AST/WIT B6....108 D1
YDLY B25.......145 E2
Mansion CI DUDN DY1....84 A3
Mansion Crs SMTHWKW B67...106 A5
Mansion Dr TPTN/OCK DY4....86 A1
Manson Dr CDYHTH B64....121 G3
Manston Dr
  DUNHL/THL/PER WV6....20 C5
Manston Rd
  BKDE/SHDE B34....130 D5
Manton Cft DOR/KN B93....196 C5
Manway CI BFLD/HDSWWD B20..90 B4
Manwoods CI
  BFLD/HDSWWD B20....90 B4
Maple Av DARL/WED WS10....56 C4
Maple Bank EDG B15 *....126 A5
Maplebeck Ct SOLH B91 *....165 E5
Maple CI BILS/COS WV14....68 A4
HDSW B21.......89 G5
STRBR DY8.......134 D5
Maple Cft MOS/BIL B13....161 F4
Mapledene Rd
  LGN/SDN/BHAMAIR B26...148 B3
Maple Dr DSYBK/YTR WS5....57 H4
KGSTG B44.......75 H4
RUSH/SHEL WS4....28 D2
SEDG DY3.......82 D5
Maple Gn DUDN DY1....83 H3
Maple Gv BDMR/CCFT WV3....35 G5
BILS/COS WV14....68 A4
CHWD/FDBR/MGN B37...113 H4
KGSWFD DY6....100 C5
LOZ/NWT B19.......108 C2
Maple Leaf Dr
  CHWD/FDBR/MGN B37...132 B5
Maple Leaf Rd
  DARL/WED WS10....71 E1
Maple Ri DSYBK/YTR WS5....57 H4
KGSTG B44.......75 H4
RUSH/SHEL WS4....28 D2
SEDG DY3.......82 D5
Maple Rd BDMR/CCFT WV3....35 G5
BLOX/PEL WS3....17 H3
BVILLE B30.......159 G5
CSCFLD/WYGN B72....62 C2
DUDN DY1.......83 H3
RBRY B45.......187 H4
RMSLY B62.......122 C5
Maple St BLOX/PEL WS3....18 D1
Mapleton Gv HLGN/YWD B28..163 H3
Mapleton Rd HLGN/YWD B28..163 H3
Maple Tree La HALE B63....137 H1
Maple Wy NFLD/LBR B31....175 F5
Maplewood WALM/CURD B76..78 A4
Mapperley Gdns MOS/BIL B13..143 E5
Mappleborough Rd SHLY B90..179 H1
Mapps CI HALE B63....137 E5
Marans Cft HWK/WKHTH B38..190 C2
Marbury CI HWK/WKHTH B38..176 B5
Marbury Dr BILS/COS WV14....54 B1
Marbury Ms BRLYHL DY5....119 F3
Marchant Rd BDMR/CCFT WV3..36 C5
BILS/COS WV14....53 F5
March End Rd WNSFLD WV11..25 E5
Marchmont Rd BORD B9....129 E1
Marchmount Rd
  CSCFLD/WYGN B72....77 F1
Marclift Crs WSL WS1....8 C1
Marcos Dr CBROM B36....96 D5
Marcot Rd HIA/OLT B92....147 E5
Marden CI WLNHL WV13....39 E3
Marden Gv NFLD/LBR B31....175 F3
Mardon Rd
  LGN/SDN/BHAMAIR B26...147 H2
Mare CI CBROM B36....96 D5
Marfield CI WALM/CURD B76...78 B5
Margam Crs BLOX/PEL WS3....16 B2
Margam Ter BLOX/PEL WS3....16 B2
Margam Wy BLOX/PEL WS3....16 B2
Margaret Av HALE B63....138 B2
CSCFLD/WYGN B72....62 C1
Margaret CI BRLYHL DY5....119 H4
Margaret Dr STRBR DY8....135 F2
Margaret Gdns SMTHWKW B67..106 A5
Margaret Gv HRBN B17....124 B5
Margaret Rd DARL/WED WS10..55 H2
HRBN B17.......141 G1
SCFLD/BOLD B73....62 A4
WSLW WS2.......4 A5
Margaret St CBHAMNW B3....2 E3
WBROM B70.......87 F4
Margaret's Ter TPTN/OCK DY4..70 A3
Marholm CI COVEN WV9....11 H2
Marian Cft
  LGN/SDN/BHAMAIR B26...148 A3
Maria St WBROM B70....104 C1
Marie Dr ACGN B27....163 F1
Marigold Crs DUDN DY1....84 A1
Marine Crs STRBR DY8....117 H3
Marine Dr KGSTG B44....74 C4
Marine Gdns STRBR DY8....117 H3
Mariner Av LDYWD/EDGR B16..124 D2
Marion CI BRLYHL DY5....119 H1
Marion Rd SMTHWK B66....106 D2
Marita CI DUDS DY2....121 E1
Marjoram CI HWK/WKHTH B38..176 D5
Marjorie Av BVILLE B30....175 H1

Av DARL/WED WS10 .....55 C5
kby Rd WSNGN B18 ....107 C5
ket Pl
  LKHTH/ROWR B65 * 122 A3
  LOX/PEL WS3 ....27 F1
ket Rd WSNLO 70 D1
  PTN/OCK DY4 ....86 B1
  LNHL WV13 ....39 C3
ket Sq CDYHTH B64 * ...120 C4
ket St KGSWFD DY6 .....99 H5
  LDBY B69 ....105 E1
  TRBR DY8 ....135 C2
  VOLV WV1 ....7 C4
ket Wy HAG/WOL DY9 ...154 B3
kfield Rd
  GN/SDN/BHAMAIR B26 ..130 D4
kford Wk LGLYGN WV9 ..108 C5
kham Crs HIA/OLT B92 ..165 H1
kham Cft COVEN WV9 ....12 A2
kham Dr KGSWFD DY6 ...100 A5
klew Cl BRWNH WS8 ....19 G2
klin Av WOLVN WV10 ....2 A2
k Rd DARL/WED WS10 ...55 C5
ksbury Cl
  UNHL/THL/PER WV6......22 C5
kbank Rd STRBR DY8 ...118 C3
borough Cl
  FOAKS/STRLY B74 .....32 C4
borough Dr STRBR DY8 ..135 C4
borough Gdns
  UNHL/THL/PER WV6.....36 A1
  TRBR B10 ....128 C3
borough Gv YDLY B25 ..129 H3
rook Cl HIA/OLT B92 ...165 C3
brook Dr
  TTPK/GDPK/PENN WV4 ..51 H2
burn Wy WMBN WV5 ....64 C5
cliff Gv MOS/BIL B15 ...161 C4
don Rd
  ALE/KHTH/YWD B14 ...160 D4
one Cft
  CHWD/FDBR/MGN B37 ..132 C3
ny Rd KGSWFD DY6 ....100 C5
ning Cft HIA/OLT B92 ...165 C3
owe Cl DUDS DY2 ......25 D1
owe Dr SHHTH WV12 ...25 C5
owe Rd ERDW/GRVHL B23 ...92 A1
owe St BLKHTH/ROWR B65 ..121 H5
VSLW WS2 ...
pit La MGN/WHC B75 ...47 F1
pit Rd MGN/WHC B75 ...48 A2
pool Dr BLOX/PEL WS3 ..28 B1
pool Rd DUDS DY2 ......102 B5
Top HWK/WKHTH B38 ...176 D4
mion Dr GTB/HAM B43 ...78 H1
mion Gv DUDN DY1 ......102 A1
mion Wy WBROM B70.....70 D5
mion Rd BDMR/CCFT WV3 ..35 H5
uis Dr CDYHTH B64 .....121 G5
iott Rd DUDS DY2 ......102 C5
MTHWK B66 ....105 H2
roway St
  DYWD/EDGR B16 ....125 H1
rowfat La HDSW B21 ...107 H2
l Cl BILS/COS WV14 ....68 A2
sden Cl HIA/OLT B92 ...164 A1
shall Cl ALDR WS9 .....44 B4
shall Gv KGSTG B44 ...75 F3
shall Lake Rd SHLY B90 ..180 D4
shall Rd LGLYGN/QTN B68 ..123 C4
LNHL WV13 ....38 C4
shall St CBHAMW B1 ....2 E7
shall Wr HAG/WOL DY9 ..154 B3
ham Court Rd SOLH B91 ..164 B3
mont Wy
  RDW/GRVHL B23 ......96 B5
sh St WSLW WS2 ....4 C3
Marsh DARL/WED WS10 ...55 C5
hwood Cft RMSLY B62 ..140 A4
land Cl HRBN B17 .....125 E4
land Rd HIA/OLT B92 ..164 A3
ton Av DARL/WED WS10 ..55 C5
ton Cl STRBR DY8 .....134 C3
ton Cft
  WD/FDBR/MGN B37 ....131 H4
ton Dr
  WD/FDBR/MGN B37 ....114 A4
ton Gv GTB/HAM DY5 ..99 C2
ton Rd BKHL/PFLD WV2 ..52 A1
UDN DY1 ....101 F1
OLD/BOLD B73 ....77 E4
YOAK B29 ....158 C2
ton St WLNHL WV13.....40 A3
ham Dr
  UNHL/THL/PER WV6.....35 F3
n Cl BILS/COS WV14 ....68 D4
LY B25 ....146 D1
indale Wk BRLYHL DY5 ..135 H4
n Dr SHHTH WV12......26 A5
neau Pl CBHAM B2 * 3 C5
neau Sq CBHAM B2 * 3 C5
ngale Cl DSYBK/YTR WS5 ..57 F4
in Hill St DUDS DY2 ....102 C5

Martin Ri
  CHWD/FDBR/MGN B37 ..131 H4
Martin Rd BILS/COS WV14 ..54 B5
  DSYBK/YTR WS5 ....43 E5
  TPTN/OCK DY4 ....85 C1
Martin St
  ETTPK/GDPK/PENN WV4 ..52 D2
Martlesham Sq CVALE B35 ..94 C2
Martley Cft RIDG/WDGT B32 ..141 E3
  SOLH B91 ....181 H5
Martley Dr HAG/WOL DY9 ..136 A3
Martley Rd OLDBY B69 ....104 B5
  RUSH/SHEL WS4 ....29 E1
Marton Cl VAUX/NECH B7 ..109 H5
Marwood Cft FOAKS/STRLY B74..45 C3
Mary Ann St CBHAMNW B3 ..2 E3
  WOLV WV1 * 7 J5
Maryland Av BKDE/SHDE B34 ..112 A4
Maryland Dr NFLD/LBR B31 ..158 D5
Maryland Rd BRLYHL DY5 ..119 H5
Marylebone Cl STRBR DY8 ..118 C5
Mary Macarthur Dr
  CDYHTH B64 ....120 C3
Mary Rd HDSW B21 ......107 G2
  OLDBY B69 ....104 A1
  STETCH B33 ....129 H1
  WBROM B70 ....87 H5
Mary St BHTH/HG B12 .....144 C3
  CBHAMNW B3 ....2 D2
  WSLW WS2 ....41 H2
Mary Vale Rd BVILLE B30 ..159 C4
Maryvell Cl RIDG/WDGT B32 ..157 F5
Masefield Av DUDN DY1 ...68 C4
Masefield Cl BILS/COS WV14 ..69 F1
Masefield Rd RMSLY B62 ..139 F4
  BLOX/PEL WS3 ....28 A2
  SEDG DY3 ....82 C2
  WOLVN WV10 ....10 A5
Masefield Sq NFLD/LBR B31 ..176 A1
Masham Cl STETCH B33 ...130 A2
Mashie Gdns
  HWK/WKHTH B38 ......176 B4
Maslen Pl HALE B63 ......138 D4
Maslin Dr BILS/COS WV14 ..68 A2
Mason Crs
  ETTPK/GDPK/PENN WV4 ..51 E3
Masonieys Rd NFLD/LBR B31 ..174 D2
Masons Cl HALE B63 ......137 C1
Masons Cottages
  ERDE/BCHGN B24 * 93 F1
Masons St BILS/COS WV14 ..68 B4
  BKHL/PFLD WV2 ......80 B7
  WBROM B70 ....87 F2
Masons Wy HIA/OLT B92 ..147 E5
Massbrook Gv WOLVN WV10 ..23 H4
Massbrook Rd WOLVN WV10 ..23 H4
Masshouse La DIG/EDG B5....3 J4
  HWK/WKHTH B38 ......176 D4
Masters La RMSLY B62 ....122 C3
Matchlock Cl FOAKS/STRLY B74 ..60 A1
Matfen Av SCFLD/BOLD B73 ..76 D1
Matt Meadow
  RIDG/WDGT B32 ......141 F2
Matlock Cl BLOX/PEL WS3 ..17 E4
  DUDS DY2 ....120 D1
Matlock Rd BLOX/PEL WS3 ..17 E4
  SPARK B11 ....145 H4
Matlock Vils BHTH/HG B12 * ..144 D2
Matthews Cl
  BLKHTH/ROWR B65 ....121 H5
Mattox Rd WNSFLD WV11 ..24 D4
Matty Rd LGLYGN/QTN B68 ..105 C5
Maud Rd CSHL/WTROR B46 ..96 D3
  SOLH B91 * 87 C5
Maughan St BRLYHL DY5 ..120 A4
Maurce Gv WOLVN WV10 ..24 A4
Maurice Rd
  ALE/KHTH/YWD B14 ...161 E4
  SMTHWKW B67 ....124 A2
Mavis Gdns LGLYGN/QTN B68 ..123 F4
Mavis Rd NFLD/LBR B31 ...175 E4
Maw St WSL WS1 ....7 J7
Maxholm Rd FOAKS/STRLY B74..45 E5
Max Rd RIDG/WDGT B32 ..140 D2
Maxstoke Cl BLOX/PEL WS3 ..16 C4
Maxstoke Cft SHLY B90 ...180 C5
Maxstoke La
  CSHL/WTROR B46 ......115 C3
Maxstoke Rd SCFLD/BOLD B73 ..76 C1
Maxstoke St BORD B9.....127 H2
Maxted Rd ERDW/GRVHL B23 ..76 A3
Maxwell Av
  BFLD/HDSWWD B20.....90 B5
Maxwell Rd BKHL/PFLD WV2 ..7 H7
Mayall Dr MGN/WHC B75 ..47 C1
May Av BHTH/HG B12 .....144 C2
Maybank BORD B9 ....128 C1
Maybank Pl KGSTG B44 ...75 E5
Maybank Rd DUDS DY2 ...120 C1
Mayberry Cl
  ALE/KHTH/YWD B14 ...178 D3
Maybridge Dr SOLH B91 ..181 H5
Maybrook Rd BRWNH WS8 ..19 F2
  WALM/CURD B76 ....94 C1
Maybury Cl CDSL WV8.....10 A3
Maybush Gdns WOLVN WV10 ..23 E1
Maydene Cft BHTH/HG B12 ..144 B1
Mayfair HAG/WOL DY9 ....136 A5
Mayfair Cl DUDN DY1 .....84 A4
  KGSTG B44 ....75 H4
Mayfair Dr KGSWFD DY6 ..99 G2
Mayfair Gdns BDMR/CCFT WV3 ..35 H2
May Farm Cl HLYWD B47 ..192 B2
Mayfield Cl SOLH B91 ....182 A4
Mayfield Crs
  BLKHTH/ROWR B65 ....121 C1
Mayfield Rd BVILLE B30 ...160 C3
  DUDN DY1 ....84 B2
  FOAKS/STRLY B74 .....45 F5
  HALE B63 ....137 H5
  LOZ/NWT B19 ....108 C1
  MOS/BIL B13 ....144 D5
  RMSLY B62 ....122 D3
  SCFLD/BOLD B73 ......77 E1
  SPARK B11 ....146 A3
  WOLV WV1 ....38 B4

Mayfields Dr BRWNH WS8...8 B2
Mayflower Cl LOZ/NWT B19 ..108 D3
Mayflower Dr BRLYHL DY5 ..100 C2
Mayford Gv MOS/BIL B13 ..161 H4
Maygrove Rd KGSWFD DY6 ..99 C2
Mayhurst Cl HLYWD B47 ..193 C2
  TPTN/OCK DY4 ....69 C3
Mayhurst Rd HLYWD B47 ..192 D1
Mayland Dr FOAKS/STRLY B74..60 B3
Mayland Rd
  EDGBE B16 ....125 C2
May La ALE/KHTH/YWD B14..161 F5
  HLYWD B47 ....192 C1
Maynard Av STRBR DY8 ...134 D4
Maypole Cl CDYHTH B64 ..120 B4
Maypole Ct WMBN WV5 ...65 E5
Maypole Dr STRBR DY8 ...135 E2
Maypole Flds HALE B63 ...120 A4
Maypole Gv
  ALE/KHTH/YWD B14 ...178 D3
Maypole Hi HALE B63 ....120 A4
Maypole La
  ALE/KHTH/YWD B14 ...178 C3
Maypole Rd LGLYGN/QTN B68 ..123 F3
Maypole St WMBN WV5 ...65 F4
May St BLOX/PEL WS3 .....27 H4
Maywood Dr
  RIDG/WDGT B32 ......140 D3
Maywood Gv
  RIDG/WDGT B32 ......140 D3
Maywood Rd HIA/OLT B92 ..148 A5
Maythorn Av WALM/CURD B76 ..78 C5
Maythorn Gdns CDSL WV8 ..10 C3
  DUNHL/THL/PER WV6 ...35 C1
Maythorn Gv SOLH B91 ...181 H5
Maytree Cl
  CHWD/FDBR/MGN B37 ..132 A2
May Tree Gv
  BFLD/HDSWWD B20.....89 H3
Maywell Dr HIA/OLT B92 ..165 H2
Maywood Cl KGSWFD DY6 ..99 F4
McBean Rd
  DUNHL/THL/PER WV6 ...36 B1
McDougall Rd DARL/WED WS10..56 C5
McGregor Cl AST/WIT B6 ..91 F5
McKean Rd OLDBY B69 ...105 E1
McKen Ct WBROM B70 * ..87 G4
McLean Rd WOLVN WV10 ..15 C5
Meaburn Cl SLYOAK B29 ..158 C3
Mead Cl ALDR WS9 ....30 B4
Mead Crs BORD B9 ....129 F1
Meadfoot Av
  ALE/KHTH/YWD B14 ...178 D2
Meadfoot Dr KGSWFD DY6 ..99 F2
The Meadlands WMBN WV5 ..64 C5
Meadow Av HHTH/SAND B71 ..72 B2
Meadowbrook Gdns CDSL WV8 ..10 D3
Meadowbrook Rd HALE B63 ..137 H4
Meadow Brook Rd
  NFLD/LBR B31 ....158 B5
Meadow Cl FOAKS/STRLY B74..45 F4
  HOCK/TIA B94 ....198 A5
  HRBN B17 ....124 D5
  RUSH/SHEL WS4 * 29 E2
  WALM/CURD B76 ......70 A4
Meadow Cft
  DUNHL/THL/PER WV6 ...34 B2
  HAG/WOL DY9 ....169 F1
  HLYWD B47 ....192 C5
Meadow Dr HIA/OLT B92 ..167 G4
Meadowfield Rd RBRY B45 ..188 A1
Meadowfields Cl STRBR DY8 ..118 A1
Meadow Ga NFLD/LBR B31 ..175 E3
Meadow Grange Dr
  SHHTH WV12 ....25 H3
Meadow Gv HIA/OLT B92 ..163 H1
Meadowhill Dr STRBR DY8 ..118 A1
Meadow Hill Rd
  HWK/WKHTH B38 ......176 C3
Meadowlands Dr
  RUSH/SHEL WS4 ....29 E2
Meadow La BILS/COS WV14 ..68 B1
  SHHTH WV12 ....65 E5
  WMBN WV5 ....65 E5
  WOLVN WV10 ....12 B5
Meadowpark Rd STRBR DY8..117 H4
Meadow Pleck La SHLY B90 ..193 H2
Meadow Ri ALDR WS9 ....44 A4
  BDMR/CCFT WV3 ......35 C1
  DUDN DY1 * 84 A2
  HLYWD B47 ....192 C5
  LGLYGN/QTN B68 ......123 F2
  RMSLY B62 ....140 A1
  SMTHWKW B67 ....106 D5
Meadows Gv CDSL WV8 ...10 A5
Meadowside Rd GTB/HAM B43 ..73 C2
Meadowsweet Av
  HWK/WKHTH B38 ......176 C3
Meadowsweet Wy
  FOAKS/STRLY B74 .....46 D1
Meadow V CDSL WV8.......21 F1
Meadow Vw MOS/BIL B13 ..162 A2
  SEDG DY3 ....67 E2
Meadow View Whf
  DUNHL/THL/PER WV6 * ..36 A1
Meadow Vw Wy WOLVN WV10 ..10 A5
  STRBR DY8 ....117 G2
Mead Rd EDG B15 ....142 D1
The Mead SEDG DY3 .....135 C3
Meadthorpe Rd KGSTG B44 ..74 D3
Meadvale Rd RBRY B45 ...188 B2
Meadway STETCH B33 ....130 C2
The Meadway
  DUNHL/THL/PER WV6 ...21 E5
Mears Cl ERDW/GRVHL B23 ..76 B3
Mears Coppice BRLYHL DY5 ..136 C1
Mears Dr STETCH B33 ....111 H5
Mearse La HAG/WOL DY9 ..184 D2

Mease Cft BORD B9 ....127 H2
Measham Gv
  LGN/SDN/BHAMAIR B26 ..147 E2
Measham Wy WNSFLD WV11..25 E3
Medcroft Av
  BFLD/HDSWWD B20.....89 C2
Medina Rd SPARK B11 ....145 G3
Medina Wy KGSWFD DY6 ..99 C3
Medley Rd SPARK B11 ....145 F2
Medlicott Rd SPARK B11 ..145 E2
Medway Cl KGSWFD DY6 ..98 C3
Medway Cft CBROM B36 ..113 H2
Medway Gv HWK/WKHTH B38 ..176 C5
Medway Rd BRWNH WS8...9 H2
Medwin Gv ERDW/GRVHL B23 ..76 B4
Meer End HWK/WKHTH B38 ..190 C1
Meerhill Av SHLY B90 ....195 F2
Meeting House La
  NFLD/LBR B31 ....175 C1
Meeting St DARL/WED WS10..55 C5
  DUDS DY2 ....102 C5
  TPTN/OCK DY4 ....85 C4
Mehdi Rd OLDBY B69 .....104 C3
Melbourne Av
  SMTHWK B66 ....106 D2
Melbourne Cl KGSWFD DY6 ..100 A5
  WBROM B70 ....71 E3
Melbourne Gdns
  DSYBK/YTR WS5 ....57 H2
Melbourne Rd
  BKDE/SHDE B34 ......113 G3
  HALE B63 ....138 D2
  SMTHWK B66 ....106 C2
Melbourne St BKHL/PFLD WV2 ..7 G6
Melbury Cl BDMR/CCFT WV3 * ..6 C6
Melbury Gv
  ALE/KHTH/YWD B14 ...161 E5
Melchett Rd BVILLE B30 ..176 D2
Melcote Gv KGSTG B44 ....75 F3
Meldon Dr BILS/COS WV14 ..69 F1
Melford Cl SEDG DY3 .....67 E1
Melford Hall Rd SOLH B91 ..164 B3
Melfort Gv
  ALE/KHTH/YWD B14 ...178 C2
Melksham Sq CVALE B35 ..94 C3
Mellis Gv ERDW/GRVHL B23 ..91 C1
Mellish Dr RUSH/SHEL WS4 ..42 D2
Mellish Rd RUSH/SHEL WS4 ..42 D2
Mellor Dr FOAKS/STRLY B74 ..46 C2
Mellors Cl HRBN B17 .....141 H4
Mellowdew Rd STRBR DY8 ..117 G1
Mells Sq SOLH B91 ....182 A1
Melplash Av SOLH B91 ...181 C1
Melrose Av BHTH/HG B12 ..144 C1
  HHTH/SAND B71 ....71 H2
  SCFLD/BOLD B73 ......76 C1
  STRBR DY8 ....134 C1
Melrose Dr
  DUNHL/THL/PER WV6 ...34 B1
Melrose Gv LOZ/NWT B19 ..108 B2
Melrose Pl SMTHWK B66 ..105 H1
Melrose Rd
  BFLD/HDSWWD B20.....91 E5
Melstock Cl TPTN/OCK DY4 ..84 D1
Melstock Rd
  ALE/KHTH/YWD B14 ...160 D3
Melton Av HIA/OLT B92 ...147 C3
Melton Dr EDG B15 ....126 C5
Melton Rd
  ALE/KHTH/YWD B14 ...161 F2
  MOS/BIL B13 ....161 H1
Melverley Gv KGSTG B44 ..75 F4
Melverton Av WOLVN WV10 ..23 C2
Melville Hall
  LDYWD/EDGR B16 * 125 F3
Melville Rd LDYWD/EDGR B16 ..125 F3
Melvina Rd VAUX/NECH B7 ..109 H5
Membury Rd WASH/WDE B8 ..110 B3
Memorial Cl WLNHL WV13 ..39 C1
Memory La DARL/WED WS10 ..40 D5
  WNSFLD WV11 ....24 B5
Menai Cl SHHTH WV12 ....26 A4
Mendip Av WASH/WDE B8 ..110 C4
Mendip Cl BKHL/PFLD WV2 ..52 D2
  SEDG DY3 ....83 F3
Mendip Rd HALE B63 ......154 D1
  STRBR DY8 ....135 H1
  WASH/WDE B8 ....110 C5
Menin Crs MOS/BIL B13 ...161 H1
Menin Rd MOS/BIL B13 ...161 H1
  TPTN/OCK DY4 ....84 D1
Meon Gv
  DUNHL/THL/PER WV6 ...34 C1
  STETCH B33 ....130 D4
Meon Rd HAG/WOL DY9 ..136 A5
Meon Wy WNSFLD WV11 ..25 F3
Meranti Cl SHHTH WV12 ..26 A4
Mercer Av CSHL/WTROR B46 ..96 A3
Mercer Gv WNSFLD WV11 ..25 G5
Merchants Wy ALDR WS9 ..30 A3
Mercia Dr
  ALE/KHTH/YWD B14 ...160 D4
  DUNHL/THL/PER WV6 ...20 C5
Mere Av CVALE B35 ....94 C3
Mere Cl SHHTH WV12 .....25 G5
Merecote Rd HIA/OLT B92 ..163 H5
Meredith Pool Cl
  WSNGN B18 ....107 H3
Meredith Rd SEDG DY3 ...82 C1
  WNSFLD WV11 ....25 F4
Meredith St CDYHTH B64 ..120 C5
Mere Gn Cl MGN/WHC B75 ..47 F3
Mere Green Cl MGN/WHC B75 ..47 F3
Mere Green Rd MGN/WHC B75..47 F3
Mere Oak Rd
  DUNHL/THL/PER WV6 ...20 C5
Mere Pool Rd MGN/WHC B75 ..47 H3
Mere Rd ERDW/GRVHL B23 ..92 C3
  STRBR DY8 ....135 E3
Mereside Wy HIA/OLT B92 ..164 A2
Meres Rd HALE B63 ....137 H2
Merevale Rd HIA/OLT B92 ..147 H5
Mere Vw RUSH/SHEL WS4 ..29 E2
Mereways SHLY B90 ......194 A3
Meriden Av STRBR DY8 ...134 D1
Meriden Cl STRBR DY8 ....134 D1
  YDLY B25 ....129 F5
Meriden Dr
  CHWD/FDBR/MGN B37 ..114 A4

Meriden Ri HIA/OLT B92 ..148 B4
Meriden Rd HIA/OLT B92 ..167 H3
  WOLVN WV10 ....22 C2
Meriden St DIG/EDG B5 ....3 J6
Merino Av NFLD/LBR B31 ..175 C5
Merlin Cl CVALE B35 ......94 C3
  DUDN DY1 ....101 H1
Merlin Gv
  LGN/SDN/BHAMAIR B26 ..147 H2
Merrick Cl HALE B63 ......137 H5
Merrick Rd WNSFLD WV11 ..25 C4
Merridale Av BDMR/CCFT WV3 ..36 B5
Merridale Gv BDMR/CCFT WV3..6 A4
Merridale Gdns
  BDMR/CCFT WV3 ......6 A5
Merridale Gv BDMR/CCFT WV3 ..36 A4
Merridale La BDMR/CCFT WV3 ..6 A4
Merridale Rd BDMR/CCFT WV3 ..6 A4
Merridale St BDMR/CCFT WV3 ..6 D6
Merridale St West
  BDMR/CCFT WV3 ......6 A7
Merrill's Hall La WNSFLD WV11 ..24 B4
Merrington Cl SOLH B91 ..182 A5
Merrion's Cl GTB/HAM B43 ..58 C4
Merrishaw Rd NFLD/LBR B31 ..175 C5
Merritts Brook Cl SLYOAK B29 ..158 C5
Merritt's Brook La
  NFLD/LBR B31 ....158 A5
Merritt's Hill NFLD/LBR B31 ..158 A4
Merrivale Rd RMSLY B62 ..122 D4
Merry Hl BRLYHL DY5 .....119 H5
Merryhill Dr WSNGN B18 ..107 H3
Mersey Gv HWK/WKHTH B38 ..176 C5
Mersey Rd BLOX/PEL WS3 ..29 E3
Merstal Dr HIA/OLT B92 ...165 H3
Merstone Cl BILS/COS WV14 ..53 C2
Merstowe Cl ACGN B27 ...146 B4
Merton Cl LGLYGN/QTN B68 ..123 F2
Merton Rd MOS/BIL B13 ..144 D5
Mervyn Pl BILS/COS WV14 ..54 B5
Mervyn Rd BILS/COS WV14 ..54 B5
  HDSW B21 ....89 F5
Meryhurst Rd DARL/WED WS10..56 A5
Messenger La WBROM B70 ..87 H5
Messenger Rd SMTHWK B66 ..106 D3
Metchley Crt HRBN B17 ..142 B5
Metchley Cft SHLY B90 ...195 F2
Metchley Dr HRBN B17 ...142 A2
Metchley La HRBN B17 ...142 A2
Metchley Park Rd EDG B15 ..142 C2
Metchley Ri HRBN B17 ...142 A2
Metfield Cft HRBN B17 ...142 B3
  KGSWFD DY6 ....100 B3
Metlin Gv STETCH B33 ...131 G1
Metric Wk SMTHWKW B67 ..106 C4
Metro Wy SMTHWK B66 ...107 E2
The Mews BLKHTH/ROWR B65 ..121 H2
Meyrick Rd WBROM B70 ..71 E5
Meysham Ct NFLD/LBR B31 ..176 A1
Miall Park Rd SOLH B91 ...164 A5
Miall Rd HLGN/YWD B28 ..163 E2
Michael Dr EDG B15 ......126 C5
Michael Rd DARL/WED WS10 ..54 D1
  SMTHWKW B67 ....106 A3
Michelle Cl MOS/BIL B13 ..161 C5
Micklehill Dr SHLY B90 ...180 B5
Mickle Meadow
  CSHL/WTROR B46 ......96 B3
Mickleover Rd WASH/WDE B8 ..111 G4
Mickleton Av STETCH B33 ..131 E4
Mickleton Rd HIA/OLT B92 ..163 H2
Mickley Av WOLVN WV10 ..23 C5
Midacre WLNHL WV13 ....39 G4
Middle Acre Rd
  RIDG/WDGT B32 ......141 E5
Middle Av WLNHL WV13 ..39 E5
Middle Bickenhill La
  HIA/OLT B92 ....150 C3
Middle Crs BLOX/PEL WS3 ..28 B3
Middle Cross WOLV WV1 * ..7 H4
Middle Dr RBRY B45 ......188 D4
Middlefield CDSL WV8 ....11 C5
Middlefield Av DOR/KN B93 ..197 H4
  RMSLY B62 ....122 D4
Middlefield Cl RMSLY B62 ..122 D3
Middlefield La HAG/WOL DY9 ..152 D4
Middle Field Rd NFLD/LBR B31 ..176 A3
Middlefield Rd OLDBY B69 ..105 C1
Middle Gdns WLNHL WV13 ..39 H3
Middlehill Ri RIDG/WDGT B32 ..140 B5
Middle La HLYWD B47 ....192 B5
  HWK/WKHTH B38 ......190 C1
Middle Leaford
  BKDE/SHDE B34 ......112 C4
Middle Leasowe
  RIDG/WDGT B32 ......140 C3
Middle Meadow Av
  RIDG/WDGT B32 ......140 C2
Middlemist Gv GTB/HAM B43 ..75 H3
Middlemore Cl FOAKS/STRLY B74..45 E5
Middlemore La ALDR WS9 ..29 C4
Middlemore La West ALDR WS9 ..29 C4
Middlemore Rd NFLD/LBR B31 ..175 H3
  SMTHWK B66 ....106 D2
Middle Park Cl SLYOAK B29 ..158 D2
Middlepark Dr NFLD/LBR B31 ..158 D2
Middlepark Rd DUDN DY1 ..101 C1
Middle Park Rd SLYOAK B29 ..158 D2
Middle Rd BRGRVW B61 ..186 B4
Middleton Cl DSYBK/YTR WS5 ..57 F3
Middleton Gdns BVILLE B30 ..176 C1
Middleton Gra NFLD/LBR B31 ..176 A1
Middleton Hall Rd BVILLE B30 ..176 C1
Middleton Rd
  ALE/KHTH/YWD B14 ...161 E3
  BRWNH WS8 ....9 E4
  FOAKS/STRLY B74 .....45 G4
  SHLY B90 ....180 C3
Middletree Rd HALE B63 ..120 C5
Middle Vauxhall WOLV WV1 * ..6 B5
Middleway Av STRBR DY8 ..117 C1
Middleway Gn BILS/COS WV14 ..53 C5
Middleway Rd BILS/COS WV14 ..38 C5
Middleway Vw WSNGN B18 ..126 A1
Middlewood Cl SOLH B91 ..165 F4

Midgley Dr FOAKS/STRLY B74 47 E3
Midhill Dr BLKHTH/ROWR B65 104 A3
Midhurst Gv
DUNHL/THL/PER WV6 21 G5
Midhurst Rd BVILLE B30 177 F2
Midland Cl HDSW B21 107 H2
Midland Cft STETCH B33 131 F1
Midland Dr CSCFLD/WYGN B72 62 C3
Midland Rd BVILLE B30 159 H5
DARL/WED WS10 40 A5
FOAKS/STRLY B74 62 B2
WSL WS1 4 D5
Midland St BORD B9 128 A1
Midpoint Bvd WALM/CURD B76 95 E1
Midpoint Pk WALM/CURD B76 * 95 E1
Midvale Dr
ALE/KHTH/YWD B14 177 H3
Milburn Rd KGSTG B44 60 C5
Milcote Dr SCFLD/BOLD B73 61 E5
WLNHL WV13 38 D4
Milcote Rd SLYOAK B29 158 C2
SMTHWKW B67 124 B2
SOLH B91 181 H1
Milcote Wy KGSWFD DY6 99 F2
Mildenhall Rd PBAR/PBCH B42 74 A2
Mildred Rd CDYHTH B64 121 E2
Mildred Wy
BLKHTH/ROWR B65 104 A3
Milebrook Gv RIDG/WDGT B32 157 F2
Milebush Av CBROM B36 95 F5
Mile Flat KGSWFD DY6 98 D2
Miles Gv DUDS DY2 103 F2
Miles Meadow Cl SHHTH WV12 26 A2
Milestone Dr HAG/WOL DY9 169 G1
Milestone La HDSW B21 107 F1
Milestone Wy SHHTH WV12 25 H2
Milford Av SHHTH WV12 25 G5
Milford Cl STRBR DY8 118 A1
Milford Copse HRBN B17 141 H2
Milford Ct LOZ/NWT B19 108 D4
Milford Cft
BLKHTH/ROWR B65 103 F3
Milford Gv SHLY B90 196 A1
Milford Pl
ALE/KHTH/YWD B14 * 161 E2
Milford Rd BKHL/PFLD WV2 52 A1
HRBN B17 141 H2
Milholme Gn HIA/OLT B92 165 F3
Milking Bank DUDN DY1 83 G4
Milk St DIG/EDG B5 3 K7
Millard Rd BILS/COS WV14 68 B2
Mill Bank SEDG DY3 67 F3
Millbank Gv ERDW/GRVHL B23 75 H5
Millbank St WNSFLD WV11 25 F1
Millbrook Dr NFLD/LBR B31 175 E5
Millbrook Rd
ALE/KHTH/YWD B14 160 C4
Millbrook Wy BRLYHL DY5 118 D4
Mill Burn Wy BORD B9 127 H2
Mill Cl HLYWD B47 192 C1
KIDD DY10 168 B3
SEDG DY3 67 F5
Mill Cft BILS/COS WV14 54 A2
Millcroft Cl RIDG/WDGT B32 141 E5
Millcroft Rd FOAKS/STRLY B74 45 G5
Milldale Crs WOLVN WV10 12 D4
Milldale Rd WOLVN WV10 12 D3
Mill Dr SMTHWK B66 106 D4
Millenium Pk WBROM B70 87 E1
Millennium Cl BLOX/PEL WS3 18 A3
Millennium Gdns CDYHTH B64 121 F2
Millennium Pk WBROM B70 * 87 E1
Millennium Wy CDSL WV8 10 D3
Miller Crs BILS/COS WV14 68 A2
Millers Cl WSLW WS2 40 D4
Millersdale Dr HHTH/SAND B71 72 B1
Millers Green Dr KGSWFD DY6 99 E1
Miller St AST/WIT B6 109 E4
Millers V WMBN WV5 80 B1
Millers Wk BLOX/PEL WS3 17 G4
Mill Farm Rd HRBN B17 142 A4
Millfield NFLD/LBR B31 * 175 G1
Millfield Av BLOX/PEL WS3 17 F5
RUSH/SHEL WS4 28 D1
Millfield Rd
BFLD/HDSWWD B20 89 H1
BRWNH WS8 9 G5
Millfields STETCH B33 131 G1
Millfields Rd
ETTPK/GDPK/PENN WV4 53 E3
HHTH/SAND B71 71 F2
Millfields Wy WMBN WV5 80 B1
Millfield Vw HALE B63 138 A3
Millford Cl HLGN/YWD B28 163 E5
Mill Gdns SMTHWKW B67 * 124 B2
Mill Gn WOLVN WV10 12 D3
Mill Gv CDSL WV8 11 E4
Millhaven Av BVILLE B30 160 B4
Mill Hl SMTHWKW B67 124 B1
Millhouse Rd YDLY B25 129 G4
Millichip Rd WLNHL WV13 39 E4
Millington Rd CBROM B36 112 A1
TPTN/OCK DY4 69 F2
WOLVN WV10 23 G4
Millison Gv SHLY B90 195 G1
Mill La ALDR WS9 31 G4
BRGRVW B61 186 B5
CDSL WV8 10 B2
DIG/EDG B5 3 J7
DOR/KN B93 196 D4
DUNHL/THL/PER WV6 35 E3
HALE B63 139 E3
KIDD DY10 168 B3
NFLD/LBR B31 175 F3
OLDBY B69 105 E5
RIDG/WDGT B32 141 E5
RUSH/SHEL WS4 42 B1
SEDG DY3 80 B3
SHHTH WV12 26 A5
SOLH B91 182 A2
WMBN WV5 65 F4
WNSFLD WV11 24 B3
Mill Lane Ar SOLH B91 * 182 A2
Millmead Rd
RIDG/WDGT B32 141 E5
Mill Pl BLOX/PEL WS3 42 A1
Mill Pool Cl HAG/WOL DY9 169 G1
WMBN WV5 80 B1
Millpool Gdns
ALE/KHTH/YWD B14 178 B2
Millpool Hill Alcester Rd South
ALE/KHTH/YWD B14 178 B1
Mill Pool La DOR/KN B93 199 E3
Millpool Wy SMTHWK B66 106 C5
Mill Race La STRBR DY8 135 G1
Mill Rd BRWNH WS8 9 G5
CDYHTH B64 121 E5
RUSH/SHEL WS4 28 D1
Mills Av WALM/CURD B76 63 E4
Mills Cl WNSFLD WV11 24 B2
Mills Crs BKHL/PFLD WV2 37 G5
Millside HLGN/YWD B28 179 G2
WMBN WV5 * 80 C1
Mills Rd BKHL/PFLD WV2 37 G5
Millstone Cl WALM/CURD B76 78 B2
Mill Stream Cl CDSL WV8 10 D3
Mill St AST/WIT B6 109 F4
BILS/COS WV14 53 G3
BRLYHL DY5 119 F2
CDYHTH B64 120 C5
CSCFLD/WYGN B72 62 C3
DARL/WED WS10 55 E2
STRBR DY8 118 A2
TPTN/OCK DY4 86 B1
WBROM B70 87 G2
WLNHL WV13 40 A3
WSLW WS2 42 A2
Millthorpe Cl WASH/WDE B8 110 D4
Mill Vw STETCH B33 113 E5
Millwalk Dr COVEN WV9 12 A4
The Mill Wk NFLD/LBR B31 175 F4
Millward St BORD B9 128 A3
WBROM B70 87 E3
Millwright Cl TPTN/OCK DY4 85 H1
Milner Rd SLYOAK B29 160 A1
Milner Wy MOS/BIL B13 162 B2
Milsom Gv BKDE/SHDE B34 113 F3
Milstead Rd
LGN/SDN/BHAMAIR B26 130 C3
Milston Cl ALE/KHTH/YWD B14 178 A4
Milton Cl DOR/KN B93 196 D4
SHHTH WV12 26 C3
STRBR DY8 118 C5
WSL WS1 56 D2
Milton Ct DUNHL/THL/PER WV6 34 C1
Milton Crs SEDG DY3 82 C1
YDLY B25 129 H5
Milton Dr HAG/WOL DY9 153 F3
Milton Gv HDSW B21 * 107 E1
Milton Pl WSL WS1 56 D2
Milton Rd BILS/COS WV14 68 D4
DOR/KN B93 196 D4
SMTHWKW B67 105 H4
WOLVN WV10 24 A5
Milton St BRLYHL DY5 101 F2
HHTH/SAND B71 87 F1
LOZ/NWT B19 109 E3
WSL WS1 4 C7
Milverton Cl HALE B63 138 C1
WALM/CURD B76 78 B4
Milverton Rd DOR/KN B93 197 G3
ERDW/GRVHL B23 92 C1
Mimosa Cl SLYOAK B29 158 D2
Mimosa Wk KGSWFD DY6 100 A1
Mincing La
BLKHTH/ROWR B65 122 A1
Mindelsohn Wy HRBN B17 142 B3
Minden Gv SLYOAK B29 158 D1
Minehead Rd DUDN DY1 101 F1
WOLVN WV10 12 B5
Miner St WSLW WS2 41 G2
Minerva Cl SHHTH WV12 40 C1
Minewood Cl BLOX/PEL WS3 16 B4
Minith Rd BILS/COS WV14 68 D3
Miniva Dr WALM/CURD B76 78 C1
Minivet Dr BTHH/HG B12 144 A1
Minley Av HRBN B17 124 B5
The Minories CBHAMNE B4 3 G4
DUDS DY2 84 D5
Minstead Rd ERDE/BCHGN B24 92 B5
Minster Cl BLKHTH/ROWR B65 122 C1
DOR/KN B93 183 F5
Minster Ct MOS/BIL B13 * 144 C3
Minster Dr SMHTH B10 128 A5
Minsterley Cl BDMR/CCFT WV3 36 A5
The Minster BDMR/CCFT WV3 51 F1
Mintern Rd YDLY B25 129 G3
Minton Cl WOLV WV1 38 A4
Minton Rd RIDG/WDGT B32 141 F3
Minworth Rd CSHL/WTROR B46 96 B3
Miranda Cl RBRY B45 174 A3
Mirfield Cl COVEN WV9 12 A4
Mirfield Rd SOLH B91 164 C4
STETCH B33 130 D2
Mission Cl CDYHTH B64 121 G3
Mission Dr TPTN/OCK DY4 85 E2
Mistletoe Dr DSYBK/YTR WS5 57 G5
Mitcham Gv KGSTG B44 75 H2
Mitcheldean Covert
ALE/KHTH/YWD B14 177 H3
Mitchell Av BILS/COS WV14 68 B4
Mitchel Rd KGSWFD DY6 100 B5
Mitford Dr HIA/OLT B92 165 F3
Mitre Cl SHHTH WV12 26 B3
WNSFLD WV11 15 E4
Mitre Fold WOLV WV1 6 E3
Mitre Rd HAG/WOL DY9 136 C2
Mitten Av RBRY B45 173 H4
Mitton Rd BFLD/HDSWWD B20 89 G4
Moat Brook Av CDSL WV8 10 A3
Moat Coppice
RIDG/WDGT B32 157 E1
Moat Cft
CHWD/FDBR/MGN B37 132 A2
WALM/CURD B76 78 D4
Moat Dr BKDE/SHDE B34 112 C3
RMSLY B62 122 D3
Moat Farm Dr RIDG/WDGT B32 157 E1
Moat Farm Wy BLOX/PEL WS3 18 A2
Moatfield Ter DARL/WED WS10 56 A5
Moat Green Av WNSFLD WV11 25 E3
Moat House La East
WNSFLD WV11 24 D3
Moathouse La West
WNSFLD WV11 24 D3
Moat House Rd
WASH/WDE B8 111 E5
Moat La DIG/EDG B5 3 H6
LGN/SDN/BHAMAIR B26 130 A5
SOLH B91 165 E4
Moat Mdw RIDG/WDGT B32 141 E3
Moat Rd LGLYGN/QTN B68 123 F1
TPTN/OCK DY4 69 G4
WSLW WS2 41 G3
Moatside Cl BLOX/PEL WS3 18 A2
Moat St WLNHL WV13 39 G3
The Moatway
HWK/WKHTH B38 190 C1
Mobberley Rd BILS/COS WV14 68 A2
Mob La RUSH/SHEL WS4 18 C5
Mockley Wood Rd
DOR/KN B93 197 F1
Modbury Av RIDG/WDGT B32 157 H1
Moden Cl SEDG DY3 83 F1
Moden Hl SEDG DY3 67 E5
Mogul La HALE B63 120 A5
Moillett St WSNGN B18 107 F5
Moilliett Ct SMTHWK B66 107 E3
Moira Crs ALE/KHTH/YWD B14 179 E1
Moises Hall Rd WMBN WV5 65 F5
Moland St CBHAMNE B4 3 H1
Mole St BTHH/HG B12 144 D1
Molineux St WOLV WV1 7 F2
Mollington Crs SHLY B90 180 C2
Molyneux Rd DUDS DY2 121 E2
Monarch Dr TPTN/OCK DY4 70 A5
Monarch's Wy
BLKHTH/ROWR B65 121 G2
BRGRVW B61 186 B5
CDSL WV8 20 A5
CDYHTH B64 121 F1
COVEN WV9 11 G2
DARL/WED WS10 54 D3
ETTPK/GDPK/PENN WV4 64 D1
HAG/WOL DY9 153 F2
KGSWFD DY6 98 C3
KIDD DY10 168 D4
KINVER DY7 116 C2
OLDBY B69 86 A4
RBRY B45 187 E2
RMSLY B62 173 E2
SEDG DY3 80 C4
SHHTH WV12 26 C4
STRBR DY8 135 E1
TPTN/OCK DY4 70 B5
WMBN WV5 80 C1
WNSFLD WV11 24 D2
WOLVN WV10 12 C1
WSLW WS2 41 E2
Monarch Wy DUDS DY2 102 B5
Mona Rd ERDW/GRVHL B23 92 D1
Monastery Dr SOLH B91 164 A4
Monckton Rd
LGLYGN/QTN B68 123 E5
Moncrieffe Cl DUDS DY2 103 E1
Moncrieffe St WSL WS1 5 H5
Money La BRGRVW B61 186 C2
Monica Rd SMHTH B10 128 D4
Monins Av TPTN/OCK DY4 85 G3
Monk Cl TPTN/OCK DY4 85 H3
Monkgate Dr HHTH/SAND B71 71 F5
Monk Rd WASH/WDE B8 111 F4
Monks Cl WMBN WV5 64 C5
Monkseaton Rd
CSCFLD/WYGN B72 77 F1
Monksfield Av GTB/HAM B43 73 F2
Monkshood Ms
ERDW/GRVHL B23 75 H4
Monkshood Retreat
HWK/WKHTH B38 176 D5
Monks Kirby Rd
WALM/CURD B76 63 F5
Monkspath SHLY B90 195 G2
WALM/CURD B76 78 B3
Monkspath Cl SHLY B90 194 D1
Monkspath Hall Rd SHLY B90 195 F2
Monksway HWK/WKHTH B38 177 F3
Monkswell Cl BRLYHL DY5 119 F3
SMHTH B10 128 B5
Monkswood Rd
NFLD/LBR B31 176 A3
Monkton Rd SLYOAK B29 141 G4
Monmer Cl WLNHL WV13 39 H2
Monmer La WLNHL WV13 39 H2
Monmore Rd WOLV WV1 38 A5
Monmouth Dr
HHTH/SAND B71 71 F4
SCFLD/BOLD B73 61 E4
Monmouth Rd
RIDG/WDGT B32 157 H2
SMTHWKW B67 124 A4
WSLW WS2 40 C2
Monsal Av WOLVN WV10 37 G1
Monsaldale Cl BRWNH WS8 18 D1
Monsal Rd PBAR/PBCH B42 74 C4
Mons Rd DUDS DY2 85 E5
Montague Rd
ERDE/BCHGN B24 93 E5
HDSW B21 107 H1
LDYWD/EDGR B16 125 G3
SMTHWK B66 124 D1
Montague St AST/WIT B6 109 H1
BORD B9 127 G1
Montana Av PBAR/PBCH B42 90 A1
Monteagle Dr KGSWFD DY6 81 H5
Montfort Gv SEDG DY3 * 67 F4
Montfort Rd
CSHL/WTROR B46 115 F4
WSLW WS2 56 B2
Montgomery Crs BRLYHL DY5 119 H5
Montgomery Cft SPARK B11 128 A5
Montgomery Rd WSLW WS2 40 C3
Montgomery St SPARK B11 127 H5
Montgomery Wy
WASH/WDE B8 111 E5
Montpelier Rd
ERDE/BCHGN B24 93 E5
Montpellier Gdns DUDN DY1 83 G4
Montpellier St BTHH/HG B12 144 C1
Montrose Dr CVALE B35 94 C3
DUDN DY1 102 A1
Montsford Cl DOR/KN B93 196 D2
Monument Av HAG/WOL DY9 136 C3
Monument La HAG/WOL DY9 153 F3
RBRY B45 187 H4
SEDG DY3 67 G2
Monument Rd
LDYWD/EDGR B16 125 H3
Monway Ter DARL/WED WS10 55 G5
Monwood Gv SOLH B91 181 F3
Monyhull Hall Rd BVILLE B30 177 F2
Moodyscroft Rd STETCH B33 131 E1
Moorcroft Dr DARL/WED WS10 70 A1
Moorcroft Pl VAUX/NECH B7 * 109 G5
Moorcroft Rd MOS/BIL B13 143 H4
Moordown Av HIA/OLT B92 147 G5
Moore Cl DUNHL/THL/PER WV6 34 D1
FOAKS/STRLY B74 32 D4
Moore Crs LGLYGN/QTN B68 123 G1
Moorend Av
CHWD/FDBR/MGN B37 132 A3
Moor End La ERDE/BCHGN B24 93 E2
Moore Rd SHHTH WV12 26 B2
Moore's Rw DIG/EDG B5 3 K7
Moore St WOLV WV1 37 H4
Moorfield Av DOR/KN B93 196 D2
Moorfield Dr HALE B63 138 C2
SCFLD/BOLD B73 76 D3
Moorfield Rd BKDE/SHDE B34 112 C3
BKHL/PFLD WV2 51 H1
Moorfields Cl ALDR WS9 30 A3
Moorfoot Av HALE B63 154 C1
Moor Green La MOS/BIL B13 160 C1
Moor Hall Dr HAG/WOL DY9 171 E4
MGN/WHC B75 47 G4
Moorhen Cl BRWNH WS8 9 E5
Moorhills Cft SHLY B90 180 B5
The Moorings BRLYHL DY5 101 H5
COVEN WV9 * 11 H5
OLDBY B69 104 C1
WSNGN B18 107 H4
Moorland Av WOLVN WV10 23 E4
Moorland Rd BLOX/PEL WS3 27 E2
LDYWD/EDGR B16 125 F3
Moorlands Dr SHLY B90 180 C3
Moorlands Rd HHTH/SAND B71 71 G2
The Moorlands
FOAKS/STRLY B74 46 D5
Moor La AST/WIT B6 91 G3
BLKHTH/ROWR B65 121 G1
LICHS WS14 32 C1
Moor Leasow NFLD/LBR B31 176 A3
Moor Meadow Rd
MGN/WHC B75 62 D1
Moor Pk BLOX/PEL WS3 16 D4
DUNHL/THL/PER WV6 20 B5
Moorpark Rd NFLD/LBR B31 175 G4
Moor Pool Av HRBN B17 142 A1
Moors Cft RIDG/WDGT B32 157 F1
Moorside Gdns WSLW WS2 41 F2
Moorside Rd
ALE/KHTH/YWD B14 179 E1
Moors La NFLD/LBR B31 158 A2
Moors Mill La TPTN/OCK DY4 70 A4
Moorsom St AST/WIT B6 109 E4
The Moors CBROM B36 112 B1
Moor St BRLYHL DY5 118 C1
CBHAMNE B4 3 H6
DARL/WED WS10 71 F1
WBROM B70 87 G4
Moor St Queensway
CBHAMNE B4 3 H5
Moor St South BKHL/PFLD WV2 52 A1
The Moor WALM/CURD B76 78 C3
Moorville Wk SPARK B11 127 G5
Morar Cl CVALE B35 94 D2
Moray Cl RMSLY B62 122 C4
Morcom Rd SPARK B11 145 G2
Morcroft BILS/COS WV14 54 C5
Mordaunt Dr MGN/WHC B75 47 H3
Morden Rd STETCH B33 129 H1
Moreland Cft WALM/CURD B76 78 D5
The Morelands NFLD/LBR B31 175 H4
Morestead Av
LGN/SDN/BHAMAIR B26 148 A2
Moreton Av
ETTPK/GDPK/PENN WV4 52 C4
GTB/HAM B43 74 C1
Moreton Cl RIDG/WDGT B32 141 F2
TPTN/OCK DY4 69 H1
YDLY B25 129 F5
Moreton Rd SHLY B90 180 C3
WOLVN WV10 23 F1
Moreton St CBHAMW B1 2 A2
Morford Rd ALDR WS9 30 A3
Morgan Cl CDYHTH B64 121 E3
OLDBY B69 104 B1
SHHTH WV12 39 H1
Morgan Gv CBROM B36 95 H5
Morgrove Av DOR/KN B93 196 D2
Morjon Dr GTB/HAM B43 73 H1
Morland Rd GTB/HAM B43 59 G4
Morley Gv
DUNHL/THL/PER WV6 37 E1
Morley Rd WASH/WDE B8 111 F3
Morlich Ri BRLYHL DY5 118 D4
Morning Pines STRBR DY8 135 E3
Morningside SCFLD/BOLD B73 62 B2
Mornington Rd SMTHWK B66 106 D2
Morris Av WSLW WS2 40 C3
Morris Cl ACGN B27 146 D3
Morris Cft CBROM B36 95 G5
Morris Field Cft
HLGN/YWD B28 179 G1
Morrison Av WOLVN WV10 23 F2
Morrison Rd TPTN/OCK DY4 86 A2
Morris Rd WASH/WDE B8 111 F3
Morris St WBROM B70 87 G5
Mortimers Cl
ALE/KHTH/YWD B14 178 D4
Morton Rd BRLYHL DY5 119 F5
Morvale Gdns HAG/WOL DY9 136 C2
Morvale St HAG/WOL DY9 136 C2
Morven Rd SCFLD/BOLD B73 76 D1
Morville Cl DOR/KN B93 196 B5
Morville Cft BILS/COS WV14 53 F4
Morville Rd DUDS DY2 102 D5
Morville St LDYWD/EDGR B16 2 A7
Mosborough Crs
LOZ/NWT B19 108 C4
Mosedale Dr WNSFLD WV11 25 F5
Moseley Ct WNSFLD WV11 14 D4
Moseley Dr
CHWD/FDBR/MGN B37 131 H4
Moseley Old Hall La
WOLVN WV10 13 G2
Moseley Rd BTHH/HG B12 144 B2
BILS/COS WV14 39 E5
WLNHL WV13 38 D4
WOLVN WV10 13 H2
Moseley St DIG/EDG B5 127 F3
TPTN/OCK DY4 70 A4
WOLVN WV10 37 E1
Moss Cl ALDR WS9 30 A5
RUSH/SHEL WS4 42 C2
Mossdale Wy SEDG DY3 67 G4
Moss Dr CSCFLD/WYGN B72 62 C5
Mossfield Rd
ALE/KHTH/YWD B14 161 E3
Moss Gdns BILS/COS WV14 53 F5
Moss Gv ALE/KHTH/YWD B14 160 D4
KGSWFD DY6 99 H2
Moss House Cl EDG B15 126 B3
Mossley Cl BLOX/PEL WS3 26 D1
Mossley La BLOX/PEL WS3 16 B5
Mossvale Cl CDYHTH B64 121 E3
Mossvale Gv WASH/WDE B8 110 D4
Moss Wy FOAKS/STRLY B74 60 B1
Mostyn Crs HHTH/SAND B71 71 E4
Mostyn Rd HDSW B21 107 H1
LDYWD/EDGR B16 125 H3
Mostyn St WOLV WV1 36 D1
Mott Cl TPTN/OCK DY4 * 70 A3
Mottram Cl WBROM B70 87 E4
Mottrams Cl
CSCFLD/WYGN B72 77 G1
Mott St LOZ/NWT B19 2 E1
Mott's Wy CSHL/WTROR B46 115 G3
Moundsley Gv
ALE/KHTH/YWD B14 178 C2
Mountain Ash Dr
HAG/WOL DY9 136 A5
Mountain Ash Rd BRWNH WS8 19 E2
Mount Av BRLYHL DY5 101 E5
Mountbatten Cl WBROM B70 88 B4
Mountbatten Rd WSLW WS2 40 D3
Mount Cl MOS/BIL B13 144 B3
SEDG DY3 83 E4
WMBN WV5 65 E4
Mount Cottages
ETTPK/GDPK/PENN WV4 * 51 F
Mount Ct
DUNHL/THL/PER WV6 * 35 F
Mount Dr WMBN WV5 65 E
Mountfield Cl
ALE/KHTH/YWD B14 178 C
Mountford Cl
BLKHTH/ROWR B65 122 A
Mountford Crs ALDR WS9 30 B
Mountford Dr MGN/WHC B75 47 G
Mountford La BILS/COS WV14 53 H
Mountford Rd SHLY B90 179 F
Mountford St SPARK B11 145 F
Mount Gdns CDSL WV8 10 B
Mountjoy Crs HIA/OLT B92 148 A
Mount La HAG/WOL DY9 170 C
SEDG DY3 83 E
Mount Pleasant
ALE/KHTH/YWD B14 161 E
BILS/COS WV14 54 A
BKHL/PFLD WV2 * 52 D
BRLYHL DY5 119 C
ETTPK/GDPK/PENN WV4 * 51 F
KGSWFD DY6 99 C
LGLYGN/QTN B68 * 105 F
SMHTH B10 127 H
Mount Pleasant Av HDSW B21 89
WMBN WV5 64 D
Mount Pleasant St
BILS/COS WV14 68
WBROM B70 87
Mountrath St WSL WS1 4 D
Mount Rd BLKHTH/ROWR B65 122
BLOX/PEL WS3 18
DUNHL/THL/PER WV6 35
ETTPK/GDPK/PENN WV4 67
HDSW B21 107
OLDBY B69 104
STRBR DY8 135
WLNHL WV13 39
WMBN WV5 65
Mounts Rd DARL/WED WS10 70
Mount St HALE B63 138
STRBR DY8 135
TPTN/OCK DY4 70
VAUX/NECH B7 110
WSL WS1 4
Mounts Wy VAUX/NECH B7 110
The Mount CDYHTH B64 121
ERDW/GRVHL B23 92
WALM/CURD B76 96
Mount Vw MGN/WHC B75 63
Mountwood Covert
DUNHL/THL/PER WV6 35
Mousehall Farm Rd
BRLYHL DY5 119
Mouse Hl BLOX/PEL WS3 17
Mousesweet Cl DUDS DY2 103
Mousesweet La DUDS DY2 121
Mowbray Cl RBRY B45 174
Mowbray St DIG/EDG B5 127
Mowe Cft
CHWD/FDBR/MGN B37 132
Moxhull Cl SHHTH WV12 26
Moxhull Dr WALM/CURD B76 78
Moxhull Gdns SHHTH WV12 26
Moxhull Rd
CHWD/FDBR/MGN B37 114
Moxley Rd DARL/WED WS10 54
Moyle Dr HALE B63 120
Moyses Cft SMTHWK B66 106
Muchall Rd
ETTPK/GDPK/PENN WV4 5
Mucklow Hl RMSLY B62 13
Muirfield Cl BLOX/PEL WS3 1
Muirfield Crs OLDBY B69 10
Muirfield Gdns
HWK/WKHTH B38 17
Muirville Cl STRBR DY8 11
Mulberry Dr MOS/BIL B13 16
Mulberry Gn DUDN DY1 8
Mulberry Pl BLOX/PEL WS3 2
Mulberry Rd BLOX/PEL WS3 2
NFLD/LBR B31 15
Mull Cl RBRY B45 17
Mull Cft CBROM B36 11
Mullensgrove Rd
CHWD/FDBR/MGN B37 11
Mullett Rd WNSFLD WV11 2
Mullett St BRLYHL DY5 1

Mulliners Cl
CHWD/FDBR/MGN B37 * 132 D2
Mullion Cft HWKWKHTH B38 ... 176 C4
Mulroy Rd FOAKS/STRLY B74 .... 62 D2
Mulwych Rd STETCH B33 .... 131 C2
Munches La ANSLY B62 .... 171 C5
Munslow Gv NFLD/LBR B31 .... 175 F5
Muntz Crs HOCK/TIA B94 .... 198 A5
Muntz St SMHTH B10 .... 128 B4
Murcroft Rd MGN/WHC DY9 .... 153 F1
Murdoch Dr KGSWFD DY6 .... 99 G2
Murdock Rd BILS/COS WV14 .... 54 B2
Murdock Gv WSLW WS2 .... 84 B5
Murdock Rd SMTHWK B66 .... 107 F3
Murdock Wy ACGN B27 .... 26 D5
Murray ct SCFLD/BOLD B73 .... 62 A5
Murrell Cl DIG/EDG B5 .... 126 D5
Musborough Cl CBROM B36 .... 95 E5
Muscott Gv HRBN B17 .... 141 G2
Muscovy Rd ERDW/GRVHL B23 .. 92 A3
Musgrave Cl WALM/CURD B76 .. 63 E5
Musgrave Rd WSNGN B18 .... 107 H4
Mushroom Hall Rd
    LGLYGN/QTN B68 .... 105 G4
Musk La SEDG DY3 .... 82 D3
Musk La West SEDG DY3 .... 82 D3
Musson Cl
    CHWD/FDBR/MGN B37 .... 132 D4
Muswell Cl SOLH B91 .... 165 F5
Muxloe Cl BLOX/PEL WS3 .... 16 C4
Myatt Av ALDR WS9 .... 29 H5
    BKHL/PFLD WV2 .... 52 C2
Myatt Cl BKHL/PFLD WV2 .... 52 C2
Myddleton St WSNGN B18 .... 108 A5
Myles Ct BRYLHL DY5 .... 101 F5
Mynors Crs HLYWD B47 .... 192 C3
Myring Dr MGN/WHC BC75 .... 63 F5
Myrtle Av KA/KHTH/YWD B14..178 B3
    BHTH/HG B12 .... 144 C2
Myrtle Cl SHHTH WV12 .... 26 C3
Myrtle Gv BDMR/CCFT WV3 .... 51 E2
    LOZ/NWT B19 * 108 C1
Myrtle Pl SLYOAK B29 * 143 E5
Myrtle Rd DUDN DY1 .... 84 A5
Myrtle St BKHL/PFLD WV2 .... 52 D2
Myrtle Ter TPTN/OCK DY4 .... 69 H1
Myton Dr SHLY B90 .... 179 F3
Mytton Cl DUDS DY2 .... 85 E5
Mytton Gv TPTN/OCK DY4 .... 85 E1
Mytton Rd BVILLE B30 .... 159 E5
    CSHL/WTROR B46 .... 95 H3
Myvod Rd DARL/WED WS10 .. 56 A3

N

Naden Rd LOZ/NWT B19 .... 108 B3
Nadin Rd SCFLD/BOLD B73.... 77 E3
Naesby Rd
    DUNHL/THL/PER WV6 .... 34 D2
Nafford Gv
    ALE/KHTH/YWD B14 .... 178 B3
Nagersfield Rd BRLYHL DY5 .. 118 C1
Nailers Cl RIDG/WDGT B32 .. 139 H5
Nailors Fold BILS/COS WV14 .. 68 C1
Nailors Rw WMBN WV5 .... 80 D1
Nailstone Crs ACGN B27 .. 163 G2
Nailsworth Rd DOR/KN B93 .. 198 B1
Nairn Cl HLGN/YWD B28 .... 162 D5
Nairn Rd BLOX/PEL WS3 .... 16 C5
Nair Dr BILS/COS WV14 .... 68 A1
Nanaimo Wy KGSWFD DY6 .... 100 C5
Nansen Rd EAST B 145 E4
    WASH/WDE B8 .... 110 C4
Nantmel Gv RIDG/WDGT B32 .157 G2
Naomi Wy ALDR WS9 .... 19 H3
Napier Gv BKHL/PFLD WV2 .. 70 A5
Napier Rd BKHL/PFLD WV2 .. 70 A5
    WSLW WS2 .... 27 E5
Napton Gv SLYOAK B29 .... 141 F5
Narraway Gv TPTN/OCK DY4 .. 70 B3
Narrowboat Wy BRLYHL DY5 .. 102 A4
Narrow La BRWNH WS8 .... 9 F4
    RMSLY B62 .... 122 C5
Naseby Dr HALE B63 .... 137 H5
Naseby Rd SOLH B91 .... 165 H4
    WASH/WDE B8 .... 110 D4
Nash Av DUNHL/THL/PER WV6 .34 C2
Nash Cl BLKHTH/ROWR B65 .122 A3
Nash Cft
    CHWD/FDBR/MGN B37 .. 132 B4
Nash La HAG/WOL DY9 .... 184 B1
Nash Sq PBAR/PBCH B42 .... 90 D2
Nash Wk SMTHWK B66 * .. 107 F4
Nately Gv SLYOAK B29 .... 141 H4
Nathan Cl MGN/WHC B75 .... 47 G5
Naunton Cl SLYOAK B29 .... 158 C3
Naunton Rd WSLW WS2 .... 42 C1
Navenby Cl
    CHWD/FDBR/MGN B37 .132 B4
Navigation La HHTH/SAND B71 .72 B1
Navigation St CBHAMW B1 .. 2 E6
    WOLV WV1 .... 7 J6
    WSLW WS2 .... 42 A2
Navigation Wy WBROM B70 .. 86 D4
    WSNGN B18 .... 107 H4
Nayland Cft HLGN/YWD B28 .. 163 E5
Naylors Gv SEDG DY3 .... 83 C2
Nechells Ct WLNHL WV13 .... 38 D2
Nechells La WLNHL WV13 .... 58 D2
Nechells Pk Rd NECH B7 * 110 C1
Neale Av HWK/WKHTH WS4 .. 6 A4
Neale St TPTN/OCK DY4 .... 85 E1
Nearmoor Rd BKDE/SHDE B34 ..113 F4
Neander Cl KGSTG B44 .... 75 H3
Neath Rd BLOX/PEL WS3 .... 16 B5
    EDG DY3 .... 68 A5
Neath Wy SHLY B90 .... 110 A2

Nechells Pkwy VAUX/NECH B7.. 109 G5
Nechells Pl VAUX/NECH B7 .... 109 H3
Needham St VAUX/NECH B7 .. 110 A2
Needhill Cl DOR/KN B93.... 196 D2
Needless Aly CBHAM B2 * 3 C5
Needwood Cl BKHL/PFLD WV2..51 H2
Needwood Dr
    ETTPK/GDPK/PENN WV4 .. 52 D4
Nelson Av BILS/COS WV14 .... 53 C1
Nelson Rd AST/WIT B6 .... 91 F5
    DUDN DY1 .... 84 B5
Nelson St CBHAMW B1.... 2 B4
    HHTH/SAND B71 .... 87 G1
    OLDBY B69 .... 105 F3
    WLNHL WV13 .... 39 H2
Nene Cl STRBR DY8 .... 135 G3
Nene Wy CBROM B36 .... 113 H1
Neptune St TPTN/OCK DY4 .... 84 D1
Nesbit Gv BORD B9 .... 129 F1
Nesfield Cl HWK/WKHTH B38 .176 A4
Nesfield Gv HIA/OLT B92 .... 167 H3
Nesscliffe Gv ERDW/GRVHL B23..76 B4
Nest Common BLOX/PEL WS3 .. 17 F2
Neston Gv STECH B33 .... 129 H2
Netheravon Cl
    ALE/KHTH/YWD B14 .... 177 H4
Netherby Rd SEDG DY3 .... 67 E3
Nethercote Gdns SHLY B90 .. 179 G2
Netherdale Cl
    CSCFLD/WYGN B72 .... 77 G4
Netherdale Rd
    ALE/KHTH/YWD B14 .... 178 C4
Netherend Cl HALE B63 .... 120 A5
Netherend La HALE B63 .... 120 B5
Netherend Sq HALE B63 .... 120 A5
Netherfield Gdns ACGN B27 .. 146 B4
Nethergate SEDG DY3.... 83 H1
Netherstone Gv
    FOAKS/STRLY B74 .... 32 D5
Netherton Gv STETCH B33 .. 131 E1
Netherwood Cl SOLH B91 .... 164 A4
Nethy Dr DUNHL/THL/PER WV6..5 F5
Netley Gv SPARK B11 .... 145 H4
Netley Rd BLOX/PEL WS3 .... 16 A5
Netley Wy BLOX/PEL WS3 .... 16 A5
Nevada Wy
    CHWD/FDBR/MGN B37 .132 C3
Neve Av WOLVN WV10 .... 23 H1
Neville Av
    ETTPK/GDPK/PENN WV4 .. 52 B2
Neville Rd CBROM B36 .... 95 G5
    ERDW/GRVHL B23 .... 92 A3
    SHLY B90 .... 179 H4
Nevin Gv PBAR/PBCH B42 .... 90 C1
Nevis Ct BDMR/CCFT WV3 .... 36 A3
Nevis Gv SHHTH WV12 .... 25 H1
Nevison Gv GTB/HAM B43 .... 59 F4
Newark Cft
    LGN/SDN/BHAMAIR B26 ..147 H1
Newark Rd DUDS DY2 .... 120 D2
    SHHTH WV12 .... 26 A3
Newbank Gv BORD B9 .... 129 E1
New Bartholomew St
    DIG/EDG B5 .... 3 J5
New Birmingham Rd
    DUDS DY2 .... 85 G5
    OLDBY B69 .... 104 D5
Newbold Cl DOR/KN B93 .. 196 D3
Newbold Cft VAUX/NECH B7 .. 109 H4
Newbolds Rd WOLVN WV10 .. 24 A4
Newbolt Rd BILS/COS WV14 .. 54 A2
Newbolt St DSYBK/YTR WS5 .. 57 E3
New Bond St BORD B9 .... 127 H3
    DUDS DY2 .... 102 D1
Newborough Gv
    HLGN/YWD B28 .... 179 H1
Newborough Rd
    HLGN/YWD B28 .... 179 H1
Newbridge Av
    BDMR/CCFT WV3 .... 36 A2
Newbridge Crs
    DUNHL/THL/PER WV6 .. 36 A1
Newbridge Gdns
    DUNHL/THL/PER WV6 .. 36 A1
Newbridge Ms
    DUNHL/THL/PER WV6 * .36 A1
Newbridge Rd BORD B9 .. 129 F4
    WOLV WV1 .... 99 G1
Newbridge St
    DUNHL/THL/PER WV6 .. 36 A1
Newburn Cft RIDG/WDGT B32 .140 B2
Newbury Cl RMSLY B62 .... 139 F4
Newbury La OLDBY B69 .... 104 B3
Newbury Rd STRBR DY8 .... 117 G2
    WOLVN WV10 .... 12 C5
Newby Gv
    CHWD/FDBR/MGN B37 .. 114 B5
New Canal St DIG/EDG B5 .... 3 J6
Newcastle Cft CVALE B35 .... 95 E1
New Church Rd
    SCFLD/BOLD B73 .... 77 E3
New College Cl WSL WS1 .... 57 G1
Newcombe Rd HDSW B21 .. 89 F4
Newcomen Dr TPTN/OCK DY4 .. 93 H2
Newcott Cl COVEN WV9 .... 11 H5
New Coventry Rd
    LGN/SDN/BHAMAIR B26 ..147 F2
New Ct LOZ/NWT B19 .... 109 C2
Newcroft Gv
    LGN/SDN/BHAMAIR B26 .. 130 A5
New Cross Av WOLVN WV10 .. 38 B1
New Cross St DARL/WED WS10..85 E1
New Crown St DUDN DY1 .. 102 B1
Newdigate Rd MGN/WHC B75 .. 63 G4
New Dudley Rd KGSWFD DY6 ..99 F4
Newells Dr TPTN/OCK DY4 .... 70 B4
Newells Rd
    LGN/SDN/BHAMAIR B26 .. 130 C4
New England RMSLY B62 .... 122 C5
New England Cl OLDBY B69.. 86 C5
Newent Cl WLNHL WV13 .... 40 B1
Newent Rd NFLD/LBR B31 .. 176 A1
Newey Cl RBRY B45 .... 188 A2
Newey Rd HLGN/YWD B28 .. 162 D4
    WNSFLD WV11 .... 25 C2
Newey St DUDN DY1 .... 84 A4

New Farm Rd HAG/WOL DY9 .. 136 A2
Newfield Cl SOLH B91 .... 165 H4
    WSLW WS2 .... 27 G5
Newfield Crs HALE B63 .... 138 C2
Newfield Dr KGSWFD DY6.... 100 A5
Newfield Gdns HAG/WOL DY9 .. 169 G1
Newfield La HALE B63 .... 138 C2
Newfield Rd HALE B63 .... 169 G1
    OLDBY B69 .... 104 D1
New Forest Rd BLOX/PEL WS3 .. 28 A4
New Gas St WBROM B70 .... 71 E5
Newhall Ct CBHAMNW B3 * .. 2 C3
Newhall Farm Cl
    WALM/CURD B76 .... 62 D4
Newhall Hill CBHAMW B1 .... 2 C3
Newhall Rd BLKHTH/ROWR B65 .122 A4
New Hall St WLNHL WV13 .... 39 G3
Newhall St CBHAMNW B3 * .. 2 E4
    TPTN/OCK DY4 .... 69 E3
    WBROM B70 .... 87 G4
    WSL WS1 .... 15 F5
New Hampton Rd East
    WOLV WV1 .... 6 C1
New Hampton Rd West
    DUNHL/THL/PER WV6 .. 36 C1
Newhaven Cl VAUX/NECH B7 .. 109 C5
Newhay Cft LOZ/NWT B19 .. 108 C2
New Heath Cl WNSFLD WV11.. 24 B5
New Henry St
    LGLYGN/QTN B68 .... 105 E5
Newhome Wy BLOX/PEL WS3 .. 27 H5
Newhope Cl EDG B15.... 126 D5
New Hope Rd SMTHWK B66 .. 107 E5
Newhouse Farm Cl
    WALM/CURD B76 * 63 F5
Newhouse Farm Dr
    NFLD/LBR B31 .... 158 D4
Newick Av FOAKS/STRLY B74 .. 45 H2
Newick Gv
    ALE/KHTH/YWD B14 * .. 160 C5
Newick St DUDS DY2 .... 102 C5
Newington Rd
    CHWD/FDBR/MGN B37 .. 132 B4
New Inn Rd LOZ/NWT B19 .. 108 D1
New Inns La NFLD/LBR B31 .. 157 H1
New Inns La RBRY B45.... 173 G4
New John St AST/WIT B6 .... 109 E4
    RMSLY B62 .... 122 A3
New John St West
    LOZ/NWT B19 .... 108 D1
New King St DUDS DY2 * 84 C5
Newland Cl RUSH/SHEL WS4 .. 18 C5
Newland Gdns CDYHTH B64 .. 121 E4
Newland Gv DUDS DY2 .... 119 G3
Newland Rd BORD B9 .... 128 D5
    HAG/WOL DY9 .... 153 E4
Newlands Cl
    CHWD/FDBR/MGN B37 .. 149 E1
    WLNHL WV13 .... 39 G4
Newlands Dr RMSLY B62 .. 122 C5
Newlands La
    CHWD/FDBR/MGN B37 .. 131 E4
Newlands Rd BVILLE B30 .. 160 B3
    DOR/KN B93 .... 196 C4
Newlands Wk
    LGLYGN/QTN B68 * 105 F5
New Landywood La
    WNSFLD WV11 .... 16 A1
Newlyn Rd CDYHTH B64 .... 120 D4
    NFLD/LBR B31 .... 175 F2
Newman Av
    ETTPK/GDPK/PENN WV4 .. 52 D4
Newman College Cl
    RIDG/WDGT B32 * 157 G2
Newman Pl BILS/COS WV14 .. 54 B1
Newman Rd
    ERDE/BCHGN B24 .... 92 D2
    TPTN/OCK DY4 .... 70 A2
    WOLVN WV10 .... 24 A1
Newman Wy RBRY B45 .... 188 A1
Newmarket Cl
    DUNHL/THL/PER WV6 .. 22 C5
New Market St CBHAMW B3 .. 2 E4
Newmarket Wy CBROM B36..111 F2
Newmarsh Rd
    WALM/CURD B76 .... 78 C5
New Meadow Cl
    NFLD/LBR B31 .... 175 H3
New Meeting St OLDBY B69 .. 105 E1
New Mills St WSL WS1 .... 42 A1
New Mill St DUDS DY2 .... 84 C5
Newmore Gdns
    DSYBK/YTR WS5 .... 58 A2
New Moseley Rd
    BHTH/HG B12 .... 127 G4
Newnham Gv
    ERDW/GRVHL B23 .... 76 C5
Newnham Ri SHLY B90 .... 180 D2
Newnham Rd
    LDYWD/EDGR B16 .... 125 E2
New Pool Rd CDYHTH B64 .. 120 B4
Newport Rd BHTH/HG B12 .. 144 C3
    CBROM B36 .... 112 B1
Newport St WOLVN WV10 .. 37 G1
Newquay Cl DSYBK/YTR WS5 .. 58 C1
Newquay Rd DSYBK/YTR WS5 .. 58 C1
New Railway St WLNHL WV13..39 H5
New Rd ALDR WS9 .... 30 A5
    BRWNH WS8 .... 9 C5
    CSHL/WTROR B46 .... 96 B3
    DUDS DY2 .... 102 C2
    DUNHL/THL/PER WV6 .. 36 A1
    HALE B63 .... 138 D3
    HLYWD B47 .... 192 C5
    RBRY B45 .... 187 G1
    SEDG DY3 .... 80 A3
    SOLH B91 .... 180 C2
    STRBR DY8 .... 135 G2
    TPTN/OCK DY4 .... 69 H3
    WLNHL WV13 .... 39 G4
    WOLVN WV10 .... 24 B2
New Rowley Rd DUDS DY2 .. 103 E2
New Shipton Cl
    WALM/CURD B76 .... 78 B2
New Spring Gdns WSNGN B18..108 A5

New Spring St WSNGN B18 .... 108 A5
New Spring St North
    WSNGN B18 .... 108 A4
Newstead Rd KGSTG B44.... 60 D5
New St BDMR/CCFT WV3 .... 50 D2
    BKHL/PFLD WV2 .... 53 E2
    BLOX/PEL WS3 .... 27 F1
    BRLYHL DY5 .... 120 A4
    CBHAM B2 .... 3 G5
    CBROM B36 .... 112 D1
    DARL/WED WS10 .... 70 D2
    DUDN DY1 .... 84 C5
    ERDW/GRVHL B23 .... 92 D1
    ETTPK/GDPK/PENN WV4 .. 52 C5
    KGSWFD DY6 .... 99 G1
    RBRY B45 .... 174 A3
    RUSH/SHEL WS4 .... 28 D5
    SEDG DY3 .... 83 E5
    SMTHWK B66 .... 106 D3
    STRBR DY8 .... 135 G2
    TPTN/OCK DY4 .... 85 E1
    WBROM B70 .... 87 G4
    WLNHL WV13 .... 39 G4
    WNSFLD WV11 .... 15 F4
    WSL WS1 .... 15 F5
New St North HHTH/SAND B71..87 F1
New Summer St LOZ/NWT B19 .. 3 F1
New Swan La WBROM B70 .... 87 E1
Newton Cl GTB/HAM B43 .... 73 F3
Newton Gdns GTB/HAM B43 .. 72 D3
Newton Gv SLYOAK B29 * .. 142 D5
Newton Manor Cl
    GTB/HAM B43 .... 73 F3
Newton Pl WSLW WS2 .... 27 F4
    WSNGN B18 .... 107 H2
Newton Rd DOR/KN B93 .. 197 F1
    GTB/HAM B43 .... 73 F3
    SPARK B11 .... 144 D2
    WSLW WS2 .... 27 F5
Newton Sq GTB/HAM B43 .... 73 G2
Newton St BRLYHL DY5 .... 100 D5
    DUDS DY2 .... 120 D5
    HHTH/SAND B71 .... 72 A4
Newtown Dr LOZ/NWT B19 .. 108 C3
Newtown La CDYHTH B64 .. 120 D5
    HAG/WOL DY9 .... 171 H5
    RMSLY B62 .... 173 F3
Newtown Middleway
    AST/WIT B6 .... 109 E4
New Town Rw AST/WIT B6 .. 109 E4
New Village DUDS DY2 .... 120 D2
Newtown Rd SLYOAK B29 * .. 142 D5
New Vis WNSFLD WV11 * .. 24 A5
New Wood Dr NFLD/LBR B31 .. 174 D4
New Wood Gv ALDR WS9 .. 19 G4
New Wood La HDSW DY9 .. 169 F2
Niall Cl EDG B15.... 125 H4
Nicholas Rd FOAKS/STRLY B74.. 45 E5
Nicholds Cl BILS/COS WV14 .. 68 B2
Nicholls Fold WNSFLD WV11 .. 24 D5
Nicholls Rd TPTN/OCK DY4 .. 69 E2
Nicholls St WBROM B70 .... 87 H4
Nichols Cl HIA/OLT B92 .. 165 H3
Nigel Av NFLD/LBR B31 .. 158 C5
Nigel Rd DUDN DY1 .... 83 H4
    WASH/WDE B8 .... 110 C3
Nightingale Av CBROM B36 .. 114 A1
Nightingale Cl
    ERDW/GRVHL B23 .... 76 A4
Nightingale Crs BRLYHL DY5 .. 119 F5
    SHHTH WV12 .... 25 H2
Nightingale Dr TPTN/OCK DY4..86 A1
Nightingale La EDG B15.... 126 C5
Nightingale Pl BILS/COS WV14 .. 53 H1
Nightgate Gv ERDW/GRVHL B23..76 A5
Nightingale Wlk EDG B15 * .. 126 B5
Nighwood Dr FOAKS/STRLY B74..60 D1
Nijon Cl HDSW B21 * 89 F5
Nimmings Cl NFLD/LBR B31 .. 189 F2
Nimmings Rd RMSLY B62 .. 122 B3
Nineacres Dr
    CHWD/FDBR/MGN B37 .. 132 A2
Nine Elms La WOLVN WV10 .. 37 C1
Nine Leasowes SMTHWK B66 .. 106 A2
Nine Locks Rdg BRLYHL DY5 .. 119 F2
Nineveh Av HDSW B21 .... 107 H1
Nineveh Rd HDSW B21 .... 107 G2
Ninfield Rd ACGN B27 .... 145 H4
Nith Pl DUDN DY1 .... 84 B4
Nocke Rd WNSFLD WV11 .... 25 F1
Nock St TPTN/OCK DY4 * .. 70 A4
Noddy Pk ALDR WS9 .... 30 B3
Noddy Park Rd ALDR WS9 .. 30 B3
Noele Gordon Gdns WSL WS1 * .. 4 D7
Noel Rd LDYWD/EDGR B16 .. 125 H3
Nolton Cl GTB/HAM B43 .... 73 F3
Nooklands Cft STETCH B33 .. 130 D4
The Nook BRLYHL DY5 .... 100 D4
Noose Cres WLNHL WV13 .... 39 E3
Noose La WLNHL WV13 .... 39 F2
Nora Rd SPARK B11 .... 145 E4
Norbiton Rd KGSTG B44.... 75 G3
Norbreck Cl GTB/HAM B43 .. 73 F3
Norbury Av BLOX/PEL WS3 .. 18 C3
Norbury Crs
    ETTPK/GDPK/PENN WV4 .. 52 D4
Norbury Dr BRLYHL DY5 .... 119 F3
Norbury Gv HIA/OLT B92 .. 147 C4
Norbury Rd BILS/COS WV14 .. 54 B2
    KGSTG B44 .... 60 B5
    WBROM B70 .... 70 D4
    WOLVN WV10 .... 12 A5

Norgrave Rd HIA/OLT B92 .... 148 B2
Norlan Dr ALE/KHTH/YWD B14..178 B2
Norland Rd ACGN B27 .... 162 C1
Norley Gv MOS/BIL B13 .... 162 A3
Norman Av RIDG/WDGT B32 .. 124 A5
Normandy Rd
    BFLD/HDSWWD B20 .... 90 D5
Norman Rd DSYBK/YTR WS5 .. 58 A1
    NFLD/LBR B31 .... 175 H2
    SMTHWKW B67 .... 123 H5
Norman St DUDS DY2 .... 102 D1
    WSNGN B18 .... 107 G4
Norman Ter
    BLKHTH/ROWR B65 .... 104 A5
Normanton Av
    LGN/SDN/BHAMAIR B26 .. 148 B2
Norrington Gv RBRY B45 .... 174 C2
Norrington Rd NFLD/LBR B31 .. 174 C2
Norris Dr STETCH B33 .... 130 A1
Norris Rd AST/WIT B6 .... 91 F5
Norris Wy MGN/WHC B75 .... 62 D3
Northampton St WSNGN B18 .. 2 C1
Northam Wk
    DUNHL/THL/PER WV6 .... 36 D1
Northanger Rd ACGN B27 .. 146 B5
North Av BHAMNEC B40 .... 150 B2
    WNSFLD WV11 .... 24 C4
Northbrook Rd SHLY B90 .. 163 G5
Northbrook St
    LDYWD/EDGR B16 .... 107 H5
Northcote Rd STETCH B33 .. 111 H5
Northcote St WSLW WS2 .... 41 H1
Northcott Rd BILS/COS WV14 .. 54 A4
    DUDS DY2 .... 102 D5
Northcroft Wy
    ERDW/GRVHL B23 .... 92 B3
Northdown Rd SOLH B91 .. 181 F4
North Dr BFLD/HDSWWD B20..91 E4
    MGN/WHC B75 .... 143 C2
Northfield Gv BDMR/CCFT WV3..50 C1
North St BVILLE B30 .... 176 C1
    DUDS DY2 .... 102 D4
    HRBN B17 .... 140 D3
Northfields Wy BRWNH WS8 .. 8 D5
Northgate ALDR WS9 .... 30 A3
    CDYHTH B64 .... 120 D4
North Ga HRBN B17 .... 125 E5
Northgate Wy ALDR WS9 .... 30 A2
North cn
    ETTPK/GDPK/PENN WV4 .. 50 D2
North Holme BORD B9 .... 128 A2
North Rd BFLD/HDSWWD B20..91 E3
    DARL/WED WS10 .... 55 H5
    DUDS DY2 .... 84 D5
    SMTHWKW B67 .... 106 B4
    WOLV WV1 .... 7 F3
    WSL WS1 * 42 A1
Northumberland St
    VAUX/NECH B7 .... 127 G1
North View Dr BRLYHL DY5 .. 101 G4
North Warwick St BORD B9 * .. 128 B3
Northway BHAMNEC B40 .... 150 B2
    SEDG DY3 .... 66 D2
North Western Ar
    SMTHWK B66 .... 106 B3
North Western Ter
    WSNGN B18 .... 107 H2
Northwick Crs SOLH B91 .. 181 H4
Northwood Park Cl
    WOLVN WV10 .... 13 E4
Northwood Park Rd
    WOLVN WV10 .... 13 E5
Northwood St CBHAMW B1 .. 2 D2
North Wood St CBHAMW B1 .. 2 C3
Northwood Wy BRLYHL DY5 ..118 D4
North Worcestershire Pth
    ALVE B48 .... 191 F5
    RBRY B45 .... 187 F1
    SHLY B90 .... 193 E1
Northycote La WOLVN WV10 .. 13 E2
Norton Cl
    ETTPK/GDPK/PENN WV4 .. 50 C5
    SMTHWK B66 .... 107 E4
Norton Crs BILS/COS WV14 .. 69 C1
    BORD B9 .... 129 F1
    DUDS DY2 .... 121 E1
Norton Ga HWK/WKHTH B38 .. 176 C4
Norton Green La DOR/KN B93 .199 F1
Norton La SHLY B90 .... 193 F4
Norton Rd BLOX/PEL WS3 .... 16 B5
    CSHL/WTROR B46 .... 115 F1
    STRBR DY8 .... 135 E5
Norton St WSNGN B18 .... 107 H4
Norton Ter BVILLE B30 * 160 A4
Norton Vw
    ALE/KHTH/YWD B14 .... 160 D4
Norton Wy HWK/WKHTH B38 .. 176 B3
Norwich Cft
    CHWD/FDBR/MGN B37 .. 131 H3
Norwich Dr HRBN B17 .... 124 B4
Norwich Rd DUDS DY2 .... 120 D2
    WSLW WS2 .... 41 F4
Norwood Av CDYHTH B64 .. 121 E5
Norwood Gv LOZ/NWT B19 .. 108 D2
Norwood Rd BORD B9 .... 128 C2
    BRLYHL DY5 .... 119 E1
Nottingham Dr SHHTH WV12..26 A3
Nottingham Wy BRLYHL DY5 .. 119 H2

Packington La
 CSHL/WTROR B46............115 G5
 RCOVN/BALC/EX CV7 ......150 D2
Packmores SHLY B90..........194 A3
Packwood Cl
 BFLD/HDSWWD B20........90 A4
 DOR/KN B93......................196 C4
 WLNHL WV13........................39 F5
Packwood Ct SLYOAK B29....198 D2
Packwood Dr GTB/HAM B43....73 F2
Packwood Rd HOCK/TIA B94..199 F4
 LGN/SDN/BHAMAIR B26....130 D4
 OLDBY B69..........................85 G5
Padarn Cl SEDG DY3............93 H5
Padbury COVEN WV9..............12 B4
Paddington Rd HDSW B21....199 E1
Paddock Dr DOR/KN B93......199 E1
 LGN/SDN/BHAMAIR B26....130 C5
Paddock La ALDR WS9............30 A5
 WSL WS1...............................5 G4
Paddocks Gn WSNCN B18....108 A4
Paddocks Rd HLYWD B47....192 B2
The Paddock BILS/COS WW14..68 D2
 CDSL WV8.............................10 C5
 DUNHL/THL/PER WV6..........34 B1
 HAG/WOL DY9..................152 D2
 SEDG DY3..............................83 G1
 WMBN WV5............................64 C5
Paddock Vw
 DUNHL/THL/PER WV6..........22 D5
Padgate Cl CVALE B35..........94 D3
Padstow Rd ERDE/BCHGN B24..93 H2
Paganal Dr WBROM B70..........88 A5
Paganel Dr DUDN DY1............84 C3
Paganel Rd SLYOAK B29......141 G5
Pages Cl CSCFLO/WYGN B72..62 A3
Pages La GTB/HAM B43............73 G2
Paget Cl BILS/COS WW14........68 D2
Paget Rd DUNHL/THL/PER WV6..36 B2
 ERDE/BCHGN B24..............93 H5
Paget St WOLV WV1..................6 D1
Pagham Cl COVEN WV9..........11 H5
Pagnell Gv MOS/BIL B13......162 A1
Pagoda Cl FOAKS/STRLY B74..60 B2
Paignton Rd
 LDYWD/EDGR B16..............125 F1
Pailton Cl SLYOAK B29..........158 D1
Pailton Rd SHLY B90..............163 F5
Painswick Cl DSYBK/YTR WS5..57 H5
Painswick Rd HLGN/YWD B28..162 C5
Paint Cup Rw DUDS DY1........120 C2
Painters Crt BILS/COS WW14....69 E2
Pakefield Rd BVILLE B30......177 F2
Pakenham Cl WALM/CURD B76..76 B3
Pakenham Dr WALM/CURD B76..76 B3
Pakenham Rd EDG B15..........126 C5
Pakfield Wk AST/WIT B6 * 71 F1
Palace Cl BLKHTH/ROWR B65..104 B5
Palace Dr SMTHWK B66..........105 G1
Palace Rd BORD B9................128 C3
Palefield Rd SHLY B90..........195 F2
Pale La HRBN B17..................123 E1
Pale St SEDG DY3....................83 G1
Palethorpe Rd TPTN/OCK DY4..69 G3
Palfrey Rd STRBR DY8..........134 D2
Palmcourt Av HLGN/YWD B28..162 C3
Palmers Cl SPARK B11..........128 C2
Palmer Cl WNSFLD WV11........25 F1
Palmer Cl CDSL WV8................11 E5
 SHLY B90............................163 F5
Palmers Gv CBROM B36........112 A4
Palmerston Dr OLDBY B69......86 B4
Palmerston Rd SPARK B11....144 D1
Palmer St BORD B9................127 G2
Palmers Wy CDSL WV8............21 G1
Painvale Cft
 LGN/SDN/BHAMAIR B26....147 G1
Palomino Pl
 LDYWD/EDGR B16..............125 H2
Pamela Rd NFLD/LBR B31......175 G3
Pan Cft CBROM B36................111 G2
Panjab Gdns SMTHWK B67 *..106 C1
Pannel Cft LOZ/NWT B19......108 D3
Panther Cft BKDE/SHDE B34..113 F4
Paper Mill End ACGN B27........74 D5
Papyrus Vy CBROM B36..........94 B5
The Parade BRWNH WS8..........9 E4
 CDYHTH B64........................121 E4
 DUDN DY1..............................84 B4
 KGSWFD DY6........................99 F2
 WNSFLD WV11 *......................24 A2
Paradise DUDS DY1..............102 D1
Paradise Cir Queensway
 CBHAMNW B3.........................2 D4
Paradise La BLOX/PEL WS3....17 H4
Paradise La BLOX/PEL WS3....17 H4
Paradise Pl CBHAMNW B3 * 2 E3
Paradise St CBHAMW B1..........2 E5
Pardington Cl HIA/OLT B92....165 G2
Pargeter Rd SMTHWK B67....124 B2
Pargeter St STRBR DY8..........135 F3
 WSLW WS2..............................4 C5
Par Gn WH/WKHTH B58........176 A4
Parish Gdns HAG/WOL DY9..152 D1
Park Ap ERDW/GRVHL B23......94 A4
Park Av BLKHTH/ROWR B65..122 A1
 BVILLE B30..........................160 A5
 CSHL/WTROR B46..............115 G3
 ETTPK/GDPK/PENN WV4....52 A5
 LGLYGN/QTN B68................123 F1
 SMTHWK B67 *......................106 B5
 SOLH B91............................182 B2
 TPTN/OCK DY4......................85 E1
 WLNHL WV13..........................39 F5
 WMBN WV5............................80 D1
 WOLV WV1..............................10 B3
 WSNCN B18..........................108 A2
Park Av BRWNH WS8................9 F4
 DUDN DY1..............................68 B4
 ERDE/BCHGN B24................93 H1
 HIA/OLT B92........................165 H4
 OLDBY B69............................104 A2
Park Cft HHTH/SAND B71........87 H2
 WOLV WV1............................10 B3
'kdale Av DARL/WED WS10....56 A4
'kdale Cl ERDE/BCHGN B24..92 D4

Park Dale Ct WOLV WV1..........6 A2
Parkdale Dr NFLD/LBR B31..189 C1
Park Dl East WOLV WV1..........6 A2
Parkdale Rd
 LGN/SDN/BHAMAIR B26....148 A1
Park Dl West WOLV WV1..........6 A2
Park Dr
 ETTPK/GDPK/PENN WV4....52 A3
 FOAKS/STRLY B74................46 A1
Park Edge HRBN B17............125 E5
Park End Dr RIDG/WDGT B32..157 H1
Parker Rd WNSFLD WV11........25 F1
Parker St BLOX/PEL WS3......17 F3
 LDYWD/EDGR B16..............125 H5
Parkes Av CDSL WV8................10 D5
Parkes Hall Rd DUDN DY1......84 A1
Parkes La SEDG DY3..................68 A4
 TPTN/OCK DY4......................69 G5
Parkes St BRLYHL DY5..........119 F1
 SMTHWK B67 *......................106 B5
 WLNHL WV13..........................39 H4
Parkeston Crs KGSTG B44......75 H2
Park Farm Rd GTB/HAM B43....59 F5
Parkfield RIDG/WDGT B32....139 H5
Parkfield Chalet Land
 BKHL/PFLD WV2 * 52 B2
Parkfield Cl EDG B15............126 C5
 RMSLY B62..........................140 A2
Parkfield Colliery
 ETTPK/GDPK/PENN WV4....52 D3
Parkfield Crs BKHL/PFLD WV2..52 C2
Parkfield Dr CBROM B36..........95 E5
Parkfield Gv BKHL/PFLD WV2..52 C2
Parkfield Rd
 CSHL/WTROR B46..............115 F2
 DUDS DY2............................102 D3
 ETTPK/GDPK/PENN WV4....52 C2
 LGLYGN/QTN B68................123 F1
 STRBR DY8..........................135 F3
 WASH/WDE B8......................128 C1
Park Gv CSHL/WTROR B46......96 C3
 SMHTH B10 *........................128 B4
Park Hall Crs CBROM B36......58 A2
Park Hall Crs CBROM B36....112 D1
Parkhall Cft BKDE/SHDE B34..113 E2
Park Hall Rd DSYBK/YTR WS5..58 B2
 ETTPK/GDPK/PENN WV4......52 B4
Park Head Crs DUDS DY2 *....102 B1
Parkhead Locks DUDS DY2 *..102 A3
Park Hill BLKHTH/ROWR B65..121 H5
 DARL/WED WS10....................56 C4
 MOS/BIL B13........................144 A3
Park Hill Dr
 BFLD/HDSWWD B20..............89 H2
Park Hill Rd HRBN B17..........142 A1
 SMTHWK B67........................106 C4
Parkhill Rd WALM/CURD B76..78 B5
Park Hill St DUDS DY2..........103 E1
Parkhouse Av WNSFLD WV11..24 B4
Parkhouse Dr
 ERDW/GRVHL B23................91 G1
Parkhouse Gdns SEDG DY3....83 E2
Parklands Av
 BFLD/HDSWWD B20..............90 A5
Parklands Dr FOAKS/STRLY B74..46 D5
Parklands Gdns WSL WS1........5 J7
Parklands Rd HLGN/YWD B28..53 H5
 DARL/WED WS10....................56 A4
 WOLV WV1..............................38 B5
The Parklands
 BDMR/CCFT WV3..................35 H3
 ERDW/GRVHL B23................76 B5
 HAG/WOL DY9......................136 B4
Park La ASH/WIT B6................109 E2
 CVALE B35..............................94 D1
 DARL/WED WS10..................137 E1
 HALE B63..............................137 E1
 NECH B7................................88 D2
 KGSWFD DY6........................100 A2
 OLDBY B69............................105 E3
 WOLVN WV10..........................23 H5
Park La East TPTN/OCK DY4....85 H2
Park La West TPTN/OCK DY4..85 E2
Park Lime Dr RUSH/SHEL WS4..42 D1
Park Meadow Av
 BILS/COS WW14....................53 G5
Park Ms SLYOAK B29............158 D1
Park Pl VAUX/NECH B7..........110 A5
Park Retreat SMTHWK B66....106 D5
Park Rdtg FOAKS/STRLY B74....62 A1
Park Ridge Dr HALE B63......137 F1
Park Ri BDMR/CCFT WV3..........36 A3
Park Rd AST/WIT B6................109 G2
 BILS/COS WW14......................53 G3
 BLOX/PEL WS3......................27 F1
 BRLYHL DY5........................119 H4
 CSHL/WTROR B46..............115 F3
 DARL/WED WS10....................54 D1
 DSYBK/YTR WS5....................58 B3
 DUDN DY1..............................68 B5
 DUDS DY2............................102 C3
 ERDW/GRVHL B23................92 A4
 HAG/WOL DY9......................152 D5
 HALE B63..............................137 F1
 MOS/BIL B13........................144 B3
 OLDBY B69............................104 A1
 RUSH/SHEL WS4....................29 E5
 SCFLD/BOLD B73..................62 D2
 SEDG DY3..............................82 D2
 SMTHWK B67........................124 B3
 SOLH B91............................182 A2
 SPARK B11..........................145 E4
 STRBR DY8..........................134 D2
 WLNHL WV13..........................39 F2
 WSNGN B18............................108 A1
Park Rd East WSNCN B18......108 B4
Park Rd South WSNCN B18....108 A4
Park Rd West STRBR DY8......134 C3
 WOLV WV1..............................6 B2
Park Rd Crs WNSFLD WV11....15 E3
Parkside DARL/WED WS10......56 B5
Parkside Av WLNHL WV13......39 E3
Parkside Rd
 BFLD/HDSWWD B20..............89 G1
 HALE B63..............................137 H2
Parkside Wy
 FOAKS/STRLY B74................45 G4
 NFLD/LBR B31......................174 C4

Park Sq
 CHWD/FDBR/MGN B37......132 D4
Parkstone Cl RUSH/SHEL WS4..29 E1
Park St AST/WIT B6................109 G2
 BLKHTH/ROWR B65............122 B3
 CDYHTH B64........................120 D2
 DARL/WED WS10....................55 E3
 HAG/WOL DY9......................136 C4
 KGSWFD DY6........................100 A3
 OLDBY B69............................104 D3
 STRBR DY8..........................135 G4
 TPTN/OCK DY4......................85 G1
 WBROM B70............................87 H3
 WSL WS1................................4 D5
Park St South BKHL/PFLD WV2..52 A2
Park St West
 BLKHTH/ROWR B65............122 B3
Park Ter DARL/WED WS10......107 G1
 HDSW B21............................107 G1
Park Tree Wk
 ERDE/BCHGN B24................93 H2
Park Vw DARL/WED WS10......55 E2
 HOCK/TIA B94......................199 F1
 SCFLD/BOLD B73..................62 A2
Parkview Cl KGSWFD DY6......99 F1
Parkview Crs WSLW WS2........41 E1
Parkview Dr BRWNH WS8..........9 F2
 WASH/WDE B8......................128 B1
Parkview Rd BILS/COS WW14..38 C5
 HAG/WOL DY9......................136 D3
 NFLD/LBR B31......................175 F3
Park View Rd FOAKS/STRLY B74..46 B2
Parkville Av HRBN B17..........127 H2
Park Vis BORD B9 *..................127 H5
Park Wk BRLYHL DY5............119 H4
Parkway RBRY B45................174 B5
Parkway WASH/WDE B8........111 E4
Park Wy WNSFLD WV11..........84 A4
The Parkway
 DUNHL/THL/PER WV6..........34 C2
 RUSH/SHEL WS4....................29 E2
Parkwood Cl BRWNH WS8........9 E4
Parkwood Cft GTB/HAM B43....76 A1
Parkyn St BKHL/PFLD WV2......37 G5
Parliament Cl AST/WIT B6......109 F5
Parliament St
 SMHTH B10..........................128 A4
 WBROM B70............................87 H5
Parlows End
 HWK/WKHTH B38................190 B1
Parry Rd WNSFLD WV11..........25 G2
Parsonage Dr HALE B63......120 A5
 RBRY B45............................174 A4
Parsonage St HHTH/SAND B71..71 H5
 OLDBY B69............................105 F3
Parson's Hl BVILLE B30........177 F3
 LGLYGN/QTN B68................123 F3
Parsons St DUDS DY2............84 C5
Partons Rd
 ALE/KHTH/YWD B14............160 D4
Partridge Av DARL/WED WS10..54 D2
Partridge Cl
 CHWD/FDBR/MGN B37......132 C1
Partridge Mill BLOX/PEL WS3..17 G4
Partridge Rd
 LGN/SDN/BHAMAIR B26....130 C3
 STRBR DY8..........................134 C3
Passey Rd MOS/BIL B13........145 F5
Passfield Rd STETCH B33......130 B1
The Pastures
 DUNHL/THL/PER WV6..........34 B1
Pasture Vw BLOX/PEL WS3....28 A5
Patent Dr DARL/WED WS10....70 A1
Paternoster Rw DIG/EDG B5 *..3 H5
 WOLV WV1..............................6 E3
Paterson Pl BRWNH WS8........19 H2
Pathlow Crs SHLY B90..........180 A4
Patina Cl BRLYHL DY5..........119 H4
Paton Gv MOS/BIL B13..........144 B5
Patricia Av
 ALE/KHTH/YWD B14............179 E1
 ETTPK/GDPK/PENN WV4....52 A3
Patricia Crs DUDN DY1............68 B5
Patricia Dr TPTN/OCK DY4......85 G4
Patrick Gregory Rd
 WNSFLD WV11......................25 F3
Patrick Rd
 LGN/SDN/BHAMAIR B26....130 A5
Patshull Av WOLVN WV10........55 D3
Patshull Cl GTB/HAM B43........73 F2
Patshull Gv WOLVN WV10........72 B4
Patshull Pl LOZ/NWT B19......108 C2
Pattenham Cl SHHTH WV12....40 B1
Patterdale Rd
 ERDW/GRVHL B23................92 B2
Patterdale Wy BRLYHL DY5..119 H3
Patterton Dr WALM/CURD B76..78 B3
Pattingham Rd
 DUNHL/THL/PER WV6..........34 A3
Pattison Gdns
 ERDW/GRVHL B23................92 B4
Pattison St DSYBK/YTR WS5..57 E3
Paul Byrne Ct
 BFLD/HDSWWD B20..............90 B3
Paul Pursehouse Rd
 BILS/COS WW14......................53 H5
Pauls Coppice BRWNH WS8....19 F2
Paul St BILS/COS WW14..........68 A2
 DARL/WED WS10....................56 A4
Paul V TPTN/OCK DY4..............85 H1
Pavenham Dr DIG/EDG B5....143 G3
Pavilion Av SMTHWK B67......124 A1
Pavilion Cl SHHTH WV12..........26 B3
Pavilion End KNWVR DY7........116 C3
Pavilion Gdns DUDS DY2......120 C2
Pavilion Rd AST/WIT B6..........91 F3
The Pavilions CBHAMNE B4 * ..3 H5
 CHWD/FDBR/MGN B37......132 D4
Pavilion Cl ALDR WS9..............30 B2
Paxford Wy NFLD/LBR B31....158 B4
Paxton Av
 DUNHL/THL/PER WV6..........34 C2
Paxton Gdns SLYOAK B29....157 E3
Paxton Rd HAG/WOL DY9......137 E3
 WSNGN B18..........................108 A4
Payne St BLKHTH/ROWR B65..122 A3
Payton Cl OLDBY B69..............86 C5

Payton Rd HDSW B21............107 F1
Peach Av DARL/WED WS10......55 E2
Peachley Cl HALE B63............138 D5
Peach Ley Rd SLYOAK B29..158 B3
Peach Rd SHHTH WV12..........25 G4
Peacock Av WNSFLD WV11......25 G2
Peacock Cl TPTN/OCK DY4......85 G4
Peacock Rd DARL/WED WS10..54 D1
 MOS/BIL B13........................161 F4
Peacocks Est CDYHTH B64 *..120 C5
Peak Cft CBROM B36............111 H1
Peak Dr SEDG DY3..................83 F3
Peake Crs BRWNH WS8..........19 F2
Peake Dr TPTN/OCK DY4........85 G4
Peake Rd BRWNH WS8..........19 F2
Peak House Rd GTB/HAM B43..58 B5
Peakman Cl RBRY B45..........188 A2
Peak Rd STRBR DY8..............135 H1
Peal St WSL WS1......................5 F4
Pearce Cl DUDN DY1................84 A4
Pearl Gv ACGN B27................146 B4
 WSNGN B18..........................107 G5
Pearman Rd DARL/WED WS10..173 F4
 SMTHWK B66........................124 C1
Pearmans Cft HLYWD B47....192 C2
Pearsall Dr OLDBY B69..........104 C1
Pearson St BKHL/PFLD WV2..37 F5
 BRLYHL DY5........................119 F1
 CDYHTH B64........................121 E3
 STRBR DY8..........................135 E4
 WBROM B70............................87 H5
Pear Tree Av TPTN/OCK DY4..85 F1
Peartree Av WLNHL WV13......39 H4
Pear Tree Cl GTB/HAM B43....72 D2
 SHLY B90............................179 F3
 STETCH B33........................129 H2
Pear Tree Cr
 BLKHTH/ROWR B65............122 B1
Pear Tree Crs SHLY B90......179 E2
Pear Tree Dr
 BLKHTH/ROWR B65............122 B1
 GTB/HAM B43........................73 E2
Peartree Dr STRBR DY8........135 G5
Pear Tree Gv SHLY B90......179 F3
Pear Tree La BILS/COS WW14..68 D3
 BRWNH WS8............................9 E3
Peartree La CDYHTH B64......121 E3
 DUDS DY2............................101 H4
Peartree La WOLVN WV10......10 A3
Peascroft La BILS/COS WW14..54 A2
Peasefield Cl HDSW B21........107 E1
Pebble Cl STRBR DY8............135 H2
Pebble Mill Rd DIG/EDG B5..143 F5
Pebworth Av SHLY B90..........195 G2
Pebworth Cl DUDN DY1..........84 A3
 STETCH B33........................131 E4
Peckham Rd KGSTG B44........75 G1
Peckover Cl
 BLKHTH/ROWR B65............121 H3
Peddimore La
 WALM/CURD B76..................79 F5
Pedmore Court Rd STRBR DY8..152 D1
Pedmore Gv KGSTG B44..........75 F1
Pedmore Hall La
 HAG/WOL DY9......................153 G2
Pedmore La HAG/WOL DY9..153 E1
Pedmore Rd BRLYHL DY5......119 H1
 DUDS DY2............................101 H5
 HAG/WOL DY9......................119 G1
Peel Cl DARL/WED WS10..........40 B5
 HIA/OLT B92........................167 H4
 WLNHL WV13..........................39 G4
Peel St BDMR/CCFT WV3..........6 E5
 DUDS DY2............................101 F1
 HHTH/SAND B71....................87 G1
 TPTN/OCK DY4......................85 G2
 WLNHL WV13..........................39 G4
 WSNGN B18..........................107 G4
Peel Wk HRBN B17................123 G4
Peel Wy OLDBY B69................86 A4
Pegasus Wk SLYOAK B29....159 F1
Pelham Dr DUDN DY1..............84 A4
Pelham Rd WASH/WDE B8....111 F5
Pelham St BDMR/CCFT WV3....36 A4
Pelsall La BLOX/PEL WS3......17 F4
 RUSH/SHEL WS4....................28 C2
Pelsall Rd BRWNH WS8............8 D5
Pemberly Rd ACGN B27........163 E1
Pemberton Cl SMTHWK B66..124 D1
Pemberton Crs
 DARL/WED WS10....................56 C4
Pemberton Rd BILS/COS WW14..68 D2
 WBROM B70............................71 E5
Pemberton St WSNCN B18......2 B2
Pembridge Cl BRLYHL DY5..119 H3
 RIDG/WDGT B32................157 E5
Pembridge Rd DOR/KN B93..196 C5
Pembroke Av BKHL/PFLD WV2..53 E1
Pembroke Cl SHHTH WV12......25 H4
 HLGN/YWD B28......................163 E5
Pembroke Gdns STRBR DY8..117 G2
Pembroke Rd BHTH/HG B12..144 C3
 HHTH/SAND B71....................71 F2
Pembroke Wy HHTH/SAND B71..71 F4
 HLGN/YWD B28......................163 E5
Pembury Cl FOAKS/STRLY B74..60 B2
Pembury Cft KGSTG B44........75 G2
Pencombe Dr
 ETTPK/GDPK/PENN WV4....52 A4
Pencroft Rd BKDE/SHDE B34..112 D2
Penda Gv
 DUNHL/THL/PER WV6..........20 D5
Pendeen Rd
 ALE/KHTH/YWD B14............179 E1
Pendeford Av
 DUNHL/THL/PER WV6..........22 A2
Pendeford Cl
 DUNHL/THL/PER WV6..........22 A2
Pendeford Hall La COVEN WV9..11 F2
Pendeford Mill La CDSL WV8..11 E3
Pendennis Cl BVILLE B30......159 F5
Pendennis Dr OLDBY B69......103 G1
Penderel St BLOX/PEL WS3....27 G1
Pendigo Wy BHAMNEC B40..150 B4

Pendinas Dr CDSL WV8..........10 D4
Pendleton Gv ACGN B27......163 F2
Pendragon Rd PBAR/PBCH B42..90 C2
Pendrell Cl
 CHWD/FDBR/MGN B37......132 A1
Pendrell Ct CDSL WV8 *..........10 C5
Pendrill Rd WOLVN WV10........13 F4
Penfields Rd STRBR DY8......135 G1
Penge Gv KGSTG B44............60 A5
Penhallow Dr
 ETTPK/GDPK/PENN WV4....52 C3
Penhurst Av
 BFLD/HDSWWD B20..............90 D5
Penkridge Cl WSLW WS2........41 H1
Penkridge Gv STETCH B33..112 B5
Penkridge St WSLW WS2..........41 H2
Penk Ri CSHL/WTROR B46......35 F1
Penleigh Gdns WMBN WV5....64 D4
Penley Gv WASH/WDE B8......111 F3
Pennant Cft BDMR/CCFT WV3..36 D5
Pennant Gv SLYOAK B29......141 G5
Pennant Rd
 BLKHTH/ROWR B65............121 H1
 CDYHTH B64........................120 D3
Pennard Gv RIDG/WDGT B32..141 F3
Penn Cl BLOX/PEL WS3..........27 G1
Penn Common Rd
 ETTPK/GDPK/PENN WV4....66 A2
Penncricket La
 BLKHTH/ROWR B65............122 C1
Penn Cft La
 ETTPK/GDPK/PENN WV4....66 C2
Penndale Cl ERDE/BCHGN B24..77 C5
Pennhouse Av
 ETTPK/GDPK/PENN WV4....51 F5
Pennine Dr SEDG DY3............83 F5
Pennine Wy SHHTH WV12......40 B1
 STRBR DY8..........................135 G1
 WASH/WDE B8......................110 D3
Pennington Cl WBROM B70....87 E4
Penn Rd BLKHTH/ROWR B65..122 C1
 ETTPK/GDPK/PENN WV4....51 E4
 SEDG DY3..............................66 B2
Penn Road Island
 BDMR/CCFT WV3....................6 E6
Penns Lake Rd
 WALM/CURD B76..................78 A4
Penns La CSCFLD/WYGN B72..77 H4
Penn St BDMR/CCFT WV3........6 D7
 CBHAMNE B4......................127 G1
 CDYHTH B64........................121 F4
Penns Wood Cl SEDG DY3......67 E1
Penns Wood Dr
 WALM/CURD B76..................78 B4
Pennwood La
 ETTPK/GDPK/PENN WV4....51 F5
Pennyacre Rd
 ALE/KHTH/YWD B14............177 H3
Pennyfield Cft STETCH B33..130 A1
Pennyhill La HHTH/SAND B71..72 A4
Pennyroyal Cl DSYBK/YTR WS5..57 G5
Penny Royal Cl SEDG DY3......83 F4
Penrice Dr OLDBY B69............85 F5
Penrith Cl BRLYHL DY5..........118 D4
Penrith Cft RIDG/WDGT B32..157 H1
Penrith Gv
 CHWD/FDBR/MGN B37......132 C2
Penryn Cl DSYBK/YTR WS5....58 B1
Penryn Rd DSYBK/YTR WS5..58 B1
Pensarn Vls DARL/WED WS10 *..55 F2
Pensby Cl MOS/BIL B13........162 A2
Pens Cl SMTHWK B66............106 C5
Pensford Rd NFLD/LBR B31..176 A2
Pensham Cft SHLY B90..........195 G2
Penshaw Cl COVEN WV9........12 A5
Penshaw Gv MOS/BIL B13....162 B1
Pensnett Rd DUDN DY1........101 G2
Penstock Dr OLDBY B69........104 D5
Pentland Cft BHTH/HG B12..127 F5
Pentland Dr BDMR/CCFT WV3..36 A3
Pentos Dr SPARK B11............145 F3
Pentridge Cl WALM/CURD B76..94 B1
Penwood Gdns BILS/COS WW14..68 A3
Penzance Wy CBROM B36......99 H2
Peolsford Rd BLOX/PEL WS3..18 A3
Peplins Wy BVILLE B30..........177 F2
Peplow Rd STETCH B33........112 C5
Pepperbox Dr TPTN/OCK DY4..85 G1
Pepper Hl STRBR DY8............135 G3
Pepperwood Cl BRGRVW B61..185 H5
Pepper Wood Dr
 NFLD/LBR B31......................174 C4
Perch Av
 CHWD/FDBR/MGN B37......132 A1
Perch Cl WOLVN WV10..........38 B1
Perch Rd WSLW WS2..............41 E1
Percival Rd LDYWD/EDGR B16..125 E3
Percy Rd SPARK B11..............145 F4
Peregrine Cl DUDN DY1..........83 H5
Pereira Rd HRBN B17............125 F5
Perimeter Rd BHAMNEC B40..149 H5
Perivale Gv BILS/COS WW14..68 D3
Perivale Wy STRBR DY8........118 C4
Periwinkle Cl BRWNH WS8......18 D1
Perkins Cl DUDN DY1..............68 C5
Perks Rd WNSFLD WV11..........25 G1
Perott Dr MGN/WHC B75..........47 H5
Perrins Gv WASH/WDE B8....111 E3
Perrins La HAG/WOL DY9......136 D5
Perrins Ri HAG/WOL DY9......136 D5
Perrott Gdns BRLYHL DY5....118 D5
Perrott St WSNCN B18............107 F3
Perry Av PBAR/PBCH B42........90 C2
 WOLVN WV10..........................23 H2
Perry Barr Locks
 PBAR/PBCH B42 * 74 B5
Perry Cl DUDS DY2................102 D1
Perry Common Rd
 ERDW/GRVHL B23................75 H5
Perry Ct LGLYGN/QTN B68....123 F1
Perryford Dr SOLH B91..........181 H5
Perry Hall Dr SHHTH WV12....25 F5
Perry Hall Rd WNSFLD WV11..25 F1
Perry Hill Crs LGLYGN/QTN B68..123 F5
Perry Hill La
 LGLYGN/QTN B68................123 F5
Perry Hill Rd LGLYGN/QTN B68..125 G5
Perry Park Crs PBAR/PBCH B42..74 B5
Perry Park Rd
 BLKHTH/ROWR B65............121 H3

Perry St BILS/COS WV14 .... 54 A5
  DARL/WED WS10 .... 40 B5
  DARL/WED WS10 .... 70 D2
  SMTHWK B66 .... 86 C5
  TPTN/OCK DY4 .... 85 G2
Perry Villa Dr PBAR/PBCH B42 .... 20 D1
Perry Wk ERDW/GRVHL B23 .... 75 H5
Perrywell Rd AST/WIT B6 .... 91 G2
Perry Wood Rd
  PBAR/PBCH B42 .... 74 A3
Pershore St BILS/COS WV14 .... 5 G3
Pershore Cl BLOX/PEL WS3 .... 16 B5
Pershore Rd BLOX/PEL WS3 .... 16 B5
  BVILLE B30 .... 176 D1
  HALE B63 .... 138 C5
Pershore Rd South
  BVILLE B30 .... 176 D2
Pershore Rd DIG/EDG B5 .... 3 G7
Pershore Wy BLOX/PEL WS3 .... 16 B5
Perth Rd SHHTH WV12 .... 25 H4
Perton Brook V
  DUNHL/THL/PER WV6 .... 34 D3
Perton Gv
  DUNHL/THL/PER WV6 .... 34 D3
  SLYOAK B29 .... 158 C1
Perton Rd
  DUNHL/THL/PER WV6 .... 34 D3
Petchells Cl BRLYHL DY5 .... 100 D4
Peter Av BILS/COS WV14 .... 69 F1
Peterbrook Ri SHLY B90 .... 179 F4
Peterbrook Rd SHLY B90 .... 179 F4
Peterdale Dr
  ETTPK/GDPK/PENN WV4 .... 51 F5
Peters Av NFLD/LBR B31 .... 175 F3
Petersfield Ct
  HLGN/YWD B28 * 162 D2
Petersfield Dr
  BLKHTH/ROWR B65 .... 122 C1
Petersfield Rd HLGN/YWD B28... 162 C3
Petersham Pl EDG B15 .... 142 C1
Petersham Rd KGSTG B44 .... 76 A2
Peter's Hill Rd BRLYHL DY5 .... 119 E5
Petershouse Dr
  FOAKS/STRLY B74 .... 32 D5
Petford St CDYHTH B64 .... 121 E3
Pettyfield Cl
  LGN/SDN/BHAMAIR B26 .... 147 G1
Pettyfields Cl DOR/KN B93 .... 197 E3
Petworth Cl WLNHL WV13 .... 39 F5
Petworth Gv
  LGN/SDN/BHAMAIR B26 .... 147 E1
Pevensey Cl OLDBY B69 .... 103 F1
Peverell Dr HLGN/YWD B28 .... 162 C3
Peveril Gv WALM/CURD B76 .... 63 E4
Peverill Rd
  DUNHL/THL/PER WV6 .... 34 D1
  ETTPK/GDPK/PENN WV4 .... 52 C5
Peveril Wy GTB/HAM B43 .... 59 E5
Pheasant Cl CBROM B36 .... 114 A1
Pheasant Rd SMTHWK B67 .... 123 H2
Pheasant St BRLYHL DY5 .... 119 E1
Philip Rd HALE B63 .... 138 C1
  TPTN/OCK DY4 .... 86 B1
Philip Sidney Rd SPARK B11 .... 144 D4
Philip St BILS/COS WV14 .... 68 D2
Philip Victor Rd
  BFLD/HDSWWD B20 .... 89 H5
Phillimore Rd WASH/WDE B8 .... 110 B4
Phillip Rd WSLW WS2 .... 56 C2
Phillips Av WNSFLD WV11 .... 25 F1
Phillips St AST/WIT B6 .... 109 E3
Phipson Rd MOS/BIL B13 .... 144 D4
Phoenix Gn EDG B15 .... 125 G5
Phoenix Ri
  BLKHTH/ROWR B65 .... 122 B3
  DARL/WED WS10 .... 55 F4
  ERDW/GRVHL B23 .... 69 F5
  WNSFLD WV11 .... 38 D2
Phoenix St BKHL/PFLD WV2 .... 86 D1
  WBROM B70 .... 86 D1
Piccadilly Av CBHAM B2 .... 3 H5
Piccadilly Cl
  CHWD/FDBR/MGN B37 .... 132 C3
Pickenham Rd
  ALE/KHTH/YWD B14 .... 178 C4
Pickering Crs RIDG/WDGT B32... 157 G1
Pickering Rd WNSFLD WV11 .... 24 D5
Pickersleigh Cl HALE B63 .... 138 C4
Pickford St DIG/EDG B5 .... 3 K6
Pickrell Rd BILS/COS WV14 .... 68 B2
Pickwick Gv MOS/BIL B13 .... 145 E5
Pickwick Pl BILS/COS WV14 .... 54 A4
Picton Cft
  CHWD/FDBR/MGN B37 .... 132 B4
Picton Gv MOS/BIL B13 .... 161 H5
Picturedrome Wy
  DARL/WED WS10 .... 55 F2
Piddock Rd SMTHWK B66 .... 106 C4
Pierce Av HIA/OLT B92 .... 147 E4
Piercy St WBROM B70 .... 87 E3
Piers Rd HDSW B21 .... 108 A2
Piggots Cft
  CHWD/FDBR/MGN B37 .... 131 H1
Pike Cl BFLD/HDSWWD B20 .... 89 H5
Pike Dr CHWD/FDBR/MGN B37 .. 132 C1
Pikehelve St TPTN/OCK DY4 .... 70 C4
Pikehorne Cft CBROM B36 .... 95 F4
Pike Rd WSLW WS2 .... 42 B1
The Pikes RBRY B45 .... 173 H5
Pikewater Rd BORD B9 .... 128 B2
Pilkington Av
  CSCFLD/WYGN B72 .... 62 B5
Pilson Cl CBROM B36 .... 112 D1
Pimbury Rd SHHTH WV12 .... 26 B3
Pimlico Ct DUDS DY2 .... 83 F3
Pimpernel Dr DSYBK/YTR WS5 ..... 57 G5
Pinbury Cft
  CHWD/FDBR/MGN B37 .... 132 B1
Pinchers Cl HAG/WOL DY9 .... 184 C1
Pineapple Cl
  ALE/KHTH/YWD B14 .... 160 C4
Pineapple Gv BVILLE B30 .... 160 C2
Pineapple Rd BVILLE B30 .... 160 C3
Pine Av DARL/WED WS10 .... 55 H5
  SMTHWK B66 .... 106 A2
Pine Cl BDMR/CCFT WV3 .... 6 A5
  KGSWFD DY6 .... 99 H4
  SOLH B91 .... 181 F3

Pine Gn DUDN DY1 .... 84 A1
Pine Gv ALE/KHTH/YWD B14.... 161 G5
Pinehurst Dr
  HWK/WKHTH B38 .... 176 D2
Pine Leigh FOAKS/STRLY B74 .... 47 F4
Pineneedle Cft SHHTH WV12 .... 40 C1
Pine Rd DUDN DY1 .... 84 C1
  OLDBY B69 .... 103 G1
The Pines BDMR/CCFT WV3 .... 35 H4
  RBRY B45 .... 174 A4
  SHLY B90 .... 194 D3
  WSL WS1 .... 5 F6
Pine St BLOX/PEL WS3 .... 27 G1
Pinetree Dr FOAKS/STRLY B74 .... 44 C5
Pineview NFLD/LBR B31 .... 175 F5
Pine Wk CDSL WV8 .... 10 B5
  WOLV WV10 .... 136 B4
  NFLD/LBR B31 .... 175 H2
Pinewall Av HWK/WKHTH B38 ... 176 D4
Pineways FOAKS/STRLY B74 .... 46 A2
  STRBR DY8 .... 117 G2
Pineways Dr
  DUNHL/THL/PER WV6 .... 36 A2
The Pineways OLDBY B69 .... 104 A4
Pinewood Cl BDMR/CCFT WV3... 35 E5
  BRWNH WS8 .... 9 E2
  DSYBK/YTR WS5 .... 57 H4
  KGSTG B44 .... 75 E4
  RBRY B45 .... 173 F5
  SHHTH WV12 .... 26 B3
  WMBN WV5 .... 65 E5
Pinewood Dr RIDG/WDGT B32 .. 157 E2
Pinewood Gv SOLH B91 .... 181 F3
Pine Woods NFLD/LBR B31 .... 157 G5
Pinewoods CI HAG/WOL DY9 ... 169 F1
Pinewoods Cl HAG/WOL DY9 ... 169 F1
Pinewoods Cl BILS/COS WV14 .... 53 H3
  CBHAM B2 .... 3 F5
  OLDBY B69 .... 105 E1
Pinfold CI
  ETTPK/GDPK/PENN WV4 .... 50 D2
Pinfold Gdns WNSFLD WV11 .... 24 D5
Pinfold Gv
  ETTPK/GDPK/PENN WV4 .... 50 D2
Pinfold La ALDR WS9 .... 59 F3
  ETTPK/GDPK/PENN WV4 .... 51 E3
Pinfold St BILS/COS WV14 .... 53 H3
  CBHAM B2 .... 3 F5
  OLDBY B69 .... 105 E1
Pingle Cl HHTH/SAND B71 .... 72 B2
Pinkney PI LGLYGN/QTN B68... 123 G1
Pinley Gv GTB/HAM B43 .... 59 F5
Pinley Wy SOLH B91 .... 181 G5
Pinner Gv RIDG/WDGT B32 .... 141 E3
Pinson Rd WLNHL WV13 .... 39 F4
Pintail Dr ERDW/GRVHL B23 .... 92 A4
Pinto Cl LDYWD/EDGR B16 .... 125 H2
Pinza Cft CBROM B36 .... 111 H1
Pioli PI WSLW WS2 * 41 H5
Pioneer Wy CBROM B36 .... 94 D4
Piper Cl DUNHL/THL/PER WV6... 34 D1
Piper PI STRBR DY8 .... 118 B4
Piper Rd BDMR/CCFT WV3 .... 35 F5
Pipers Gn HLGN/YWD B28 .... 162 D5
Piper's Rw WOLV WV1 .... 7 H4
Pipes Meadow
  BILS/COS WV14 .... 54 A3
Pippin Av HALE B63 .... 120 B5
Pidright CI BILS/COS WV14 .... 54 A5
Pirrey Cl BILS/COS WV14 .... 68 D2
Pitcairn Cl BVILLE B30 .... 160 B4
Pitcairn Dr RMSLY B62 .... 138 C1
Pitclose Rd NFLD/LBR B31 .... 175 H4
Pitfield Rd STETCH B33 .... 131 F3
Pitfield Rw DUDN DY1 .... 84 B5
Pitfields CI LGLYGN/QTN B68... 123 E4
Pitfields Rd LGLYGN/QTN B68... 123 E4
Pitt St DUDN DY1 .... 84 B5
Pithall Rd BKDE/SHDE B34 .... 113 F4
Pit Leasow Cl BVILLE B30 .... 160 B2
Pitman Rd RIDG/WDGT B32 .... 140 C2
Pitmaston Rd HLGN/YWD B28.. 163 E2
Pitsford St WSNGN B18 .... 2 B1
Pitt La HIA/OLT B92 .... 149 H5
Pitts Farm Rd
  ERDE/BCHGN B24 .... 93 G1
Pitt St CBHAM B4 .... 127 G1
Pixall Dr EDG B15 .... 143 F1
Pixhall Wk CVALE B35 .... 94 D3
Plaistow Av ALDR WS9 .... 45 E3
Plaistow Av ALDR WS9 .... 111 G2
Plane Av
  CHWD/FDBR/MGN B37 .... 132 B3
Planetary Rd WLNHL WV13 .... 38 C2
Plane Tree Rd DSYBK/YTR WS5 .. 57 H4
Planetree Rd FOAKS/STRLY B74.. 44 D5
Planet Rd BRLYHL DY5 .... 101 F5
Plank La CSHL/WTROR B46 .... 96 A4
Planks La WMBN WV5 .... 64 D5
Plantation Dr MGN/WHC B75 .... 65 F2
Plantation La DUDS DY2 .... 81 F2
Plantation Rd DSYBK/YTR WS5 .. 57 H4
The Plantation SHLY B90 .... 100 D2
Plants Brook Rd
  WALM/CURD B76 .... 78 B5
Plants Cl SCFLD/BOLD D73 .... 76 B2
Plants Gv ERDE/BCHGN B24 .... 77 H5
Plants Hollow BRLYHL DY5 .... 119 F5
Plant St CDYHTH B64 .... 120 D5
  STRBR DY8 .... 118 A2
Plant Wy BLOX/PEL WS3 .... 17 H3
Plascom Rd WOLV WV1 .... 38 A4
Platts Crs STRBR DY8 .... 118 A4
Platts Dr STRBR DY8 .... 118 A4
Platts Rd STRBR DY8 .... 118 A4
Platt St DARL/WED WS10 .... 55 F3
Playdon Gv
  ALE/KHTH/YWD B14 .... 178 C2
Pleasant Cl KGSWFD DY6 .... 99 G5
Pleasant St BLKHTH/ROWR B65... 87 G5
Pleasant Vw SEDG DY3 .... 83 F4
Pleck Rd WSLW WS2 .... 41 G5
Pleck Wk HWK/WKHTH B38 ... 177 E4
Plestowes Cl SHLY B90 .... 163 F5
Plimsoll Gv RIDG/WDGT B32 ... 140 C2
Plough & Harrow Rd
  LDYWD/EDGR B16 .... 125 G4

Plough & Harrow Rd
  LDYWD/EDGR B16 .... 125 H3
Ploughmans Pl MGN/WHC B75... 47 H1
Ploughmans Wk KGSWFD DY6 ... 99 E2
Ploverdale Crs KGSWFD DY6..... 100 C1
Plowden Rd STETCH B33 .... 112 B5
Plume St AST/WIT B6 .... 109 H2
Plumstead Rd KGSTG B44 .... 75 G4
Plym Cl WNSFLD WV11 .... 24 C5
Plymouth Cl BRLYHL DY5 .... 189 G1
Plymouth Rd BVILLE B30 .... 160 B5
Pocklington Pl
  NFLD/LBR B31 * 159 E4
Pointon Cl BILS/COS WV14 .... 68 A1
Polden Cl HALE B63 .... 154 C1
Polesworth Gv
  BKDE/SHDE B34 .... 112 D3
Pollard Rd ACGN B27 .... 163 G1
The Pollards ERDW/GRVHL B23.. 76 C3
Polo Flds HAG/WOL DY9 .... 185 G1
Pomeroy Rd GTB/HAM B43 .... 59 H4
  RIDG/WDGT B32 .... 157 G1
Pommel Cl DSYBK/YTR WS5 .... 57 H4
Pomphrey Hl RUSH/SHEL WS4 ... 43 G4
Pond Cv BKHL/PFLD WV2 .... 52 C1
Pond Gv BKHL/PFLD WV2 .... 52 C1
Pond La BKHL/PFLD WV2 .... 52 C1
Poole Crs BILS/COS WV14 .... 68 D1
  BRWNH WS8 .... 8 C2
  HRBN B17 .... 142 A4
Poolehouse Rd GTB/HAM B43... 58 D5
Pool End Cl DOR/KN B93 .... 196 D2
Pooles La SHHTH WV12 .... 26 C3
Poole St STRBR DY8 .... 135 E1
Pool Farm Rd ACGN B27 .... 163 G1
Poolfield Dr SOLH B91 .... 181 E2
Pool Furlong HAG/WOL DY9 ... 170 C4
Pool Gn ALDR WS9 .... 30 A5
Pool Hall Crs BDMR/CCFT WV3... 34 B3
Pool Hall Rd BDMR/CCFT WV3... 34 B3
Pool Hayes La SHHTH WV12 .... 25 G5
Pool House Rd WMBN WV5 .... 64 B5
Pool La OLDBY B69 .... 104 D5
Pool Meadow WALM/CURD B76 .. 78 C3
Pool Meadow Cl MOS/BIL B13.. 162 A1
  SOLH B91 .... 182 D4
Pool Rd BRWNH WS8 .... 9 E2
  HALE B63 .... 138 D4
  SMTHWK B66 .... 106 D4
  WNSFLD WV11 .... 25 G4
Pool St AST/WIT B6 .... 109 F3
  BKHL/PFLD WV2 .... 6 E6
  DUDN DY1 .... 68 A5
  WSL WS1 .... 5 G5
Pool Vw RUSH/SHEL WS4 .... 29 F3
Popes Cr BKHL/PFLD WV2 * 7 F7
Popes La DUNHL/THL/PER WV6 .. 21 E4
  HWK/WKHTH B38 .... 176 B2
  OLDBY B69 .... 105 E3
Pope St SMTHWK B66 .... 106 D2
  WSNGN B18 .... 2 A1
Poplar Av B12 .... 182 A1
Poplar Av ALE/KHTH/YWD B14.. 161 E2
  BHTH/HG B12 .... 144 C3
  BRWNH WS8 .... 9 G4
  CHWD/FDBR/MGN B37 .... 132 C4
  ERDW/GRVHL B23 * 92 D2
  HRBN B17 .... 124 D2
  LOZ/NWT B19 * 108 C1
  MGN/WHC B75 .... 47 H5
  OLDBY B69 .... 85 H5
  TPTN/OCK DY4 .... 84 D1
  WBROM B70 .... 88 A4
  WNSFLD WV11 .... 40 B1
Poplar Crs DUDN DY1 .... 84 D1
  STRBR DY8 .... 135 E4
Poplar Dr BORD B9 .... 91 F1
  WASH/WDE B8 .... 110 D3
Poplar Gn DUDN DY1 .... 68 A5
Poplar Gv LOZ/NWT B19 * 108 C1
  SMTHWK B66 .... 106 B3
Poplar La RMSLY B62 .... 172 C2
Poplar Ri FOAKS/STRLY B74 .... 32 B5
  OLDBY B69 .... 104 A1
  PBAR/PBCH B42 .... 74 B4
Poplar Rd CBROM B36 .... 112 D1
  WSL WS1 .... 10 B5
The Poplars
  LDYWD/EDGR B16 * 125 H1
  STRBR DY8 .... 118 B2
Poplar St BKHL/PFLD WV2 .... 52 B2
  SMTHWK B66 .... 107 E4
Poplarwoods RIDG/WDGT B32.. 140 B5
Poppy Dr DSYBK/YTR WS5 .... 57 F5
Poppy Gv WASH/WDE B8 .... 110 D5
Poppy La ERDE/BCHGN B24 .... 77 H5
Popymead ERDW/GRVHL B23.. 75 H3
Porchester Cl ALDR WS9 .... 19 G5
Porchester Dr LOZ/NWT B19.... 108 D3
Porchester St LOZ/NWT B19.... 108 D3
Porlock Crs NFLD/LBR B31 .... 174 D2
Porlock Rd STRBR DY8 .... 135 H1
Portal Rd WSLW WS2 .... 40 D5
Portchester Dr WNSFLD WV11... 24 D5
Porter Cl CSCFLD/WYGN B72.... 77 F4
Porters Cft HRBN B17 .... 124 C4
Porters Fld DUDS DY2 .... 84 D5
Porters Rd CDYHTH B64 .... 120 C4
Portershill Dr SHLY B90 .... 180 C5
Porter St DUDS DY2 .... 84 D5
Porter St South DUDS DY2 .... 84 D5
Porters Wy BORD B9 .... 128 C2

Portfield Dr TPTN/OCK DY4 .... 85 G3
Portfield Gv ERDW/GRVHL B23... 77 E5
Porthkerry Gv SEDG DY3 .... 66 D4
Port Hope Rd SPARK B11 .... 127 G5
Porthouse Gv BILS/COS WV14 * .. 53 F5
Portia Av SHLY B90 .... 180 B3
Portland Av ALDR WS9 .... 30 B5
Portland Av HAG/WOL DY9 .... 152 D1
Portland Dr HAG/WOL DY9 .... 152 D1
  OLDBY B69 .... 86 B3
Portland Pl BILS/COS WV14 .... 68 B4
Portland Rd AST/WIT B6 .... 90 B4
  LDYWD/EDGR B16 .... 125 E2
Portland St AST/WIT B6 .... 109 G2
  WSLW WS2 .... 4 D1
Portland Ter WSNGN B18 .... 108 A1
Port La COVEN WV9 .... 10 D1
Portman Rd MOS/BIL B13 .... 161 F3
Portobello Cl WLNHL WV13 .... 38 C4
Portobello Rd WBROM B70 .... 70 D5
Portrush Av HWK/WKHTH B38 ... 176 A4
Portrush Rd
  DUNHL/THL/PER WV6 .... 34 B1
Portsdown Cl WOLV WV10 .... 23 H3
Portsdown Rd HALE B63 .... 154 D1
Portsea St BLOX/PEL WS3 .... 27 G4
Portswood Cl COVEN WV9 .... 22 B1
Portway Cl KGSWFD DY6 .... 100 A4
  SOLH B91 .... 181 E4
Portway Hl OLDBY B69 .... 103 H3
Portway Rd BILS/COS WV14 .... 54 A1
  BLKHTH/ROWR B65 .... 87 F5
  DARL/WED WS10 .... 55 E2
  OLDBY B69 .... 104 D2
The Portway KGSWFD DY6 .... 100 A4
Posey Cl HDSW B21 .... 89 E3
Poston Cft
  ALE/KHTH/YWD B14 .... 177 H1
Potter Cl ERDW/GRVHL B23 .... 76 B3
Potters La AST/WIT B6 .... 109 E2
  DARL/WED WS10 .... 70 C1
Potterton Wy SMTHWK B66 .... 106 B1
Pottery Rd LGLYGN/QTN B68... 123 F4
Pouk Hill Cl WSLW WS2 .... 41 E2
Poultney St WBROM B70 .... 70 D4
Poulton Cl LGLYGN/QTN B68... 144 C5
Pound Cl LGLYGN/QTN B68... 122 D1
Pound La CSHL/WTROR B46 .... 115 G5
  RIDG/WDGT B32 .... 175 H2
Pound Rd BILS/COS WV14 .... 54 A1
  DARL/WED WS10 .... 56 A5
  LGLYGN/QTN B68 .... 122 D1
Poundley Cl CBROM B36 .... 113 E1
Pountney St BKHL/PFLD WV2 *.... 7 F7
Powell Av RIDG/WDGT B32 .... 140 A1
Powell PI BILS/COS WV14 .... 54 A5
  TPTN/OCK DY4 .... 86 A1
Powells Cl CSCFLD/WYGN B72... 77 F1
Powell St HALE B63 .... 138 D4
  WOLV WV10 .... 37 H1
Power Crs
  LDYWD/EDGR B16 * 126 A3
Power Wy TPTN/OCK DY4 .... 70 B5
Pownall Rd LOZ/NWT B19 * 108 C2
Powick Rd ERDW/GRVHL B23... 92 B5
Powis Av TPTN/OCK DY4 .... 69 H4
Powke La CDYHTH B64 .... 121 F1
Powlers Cl HAG/WOL DY9 .... 136 C5
Powlett St BKHL/PFLD WV2 .... 7 G6
Poxon Rd ALDR WS9 .... 19 G4
The Poynings
  DUNHL/THL/PER WV6 .... 21 G3
The Precinct SHHTH WV12 * 25 H5
Premier Ct BVILLE B30 .... 177 G2
Premier St VAUX/NECH B7 .... 110 B1
Prescot Rd HAG/WOL DY9 .... 136 A4
Prestbury Rd AST/WIT B6 .... 109 E1
Presthope Rd SLYOAK B29 .... 158 D3
Preston Av WALM/CURD B76 .... 63 E1
Preston Rd
  LGN/SDN/BHAMAIR B26 .... 146 D1
  WSNGN B18 .... 107 G3
Prestons Rw BILS/COS WV14 .... 53 E5
Prestwick Cl MGN/WHC B75 .... 48 B3
Prestwick Rd CVALE B35 .... 94 D2
  KGSWFD DY6 .... 99 G3
Prestwood Av WNSFLD WV11 .... 24 D2
Prestwood Dr KINVER DY7 .... 158 D2
  WNSFLD WV11 .... 24 A5
Prestwood Rd West
  WNSFLD WV11 .... 24 A5
Pretoria Rd BORD B9 .... 128 C1
Priam Gv BLOX/PEL WS3 .... 18 B2
Price Crs BILS/COS WV14 .... 53 H1
Price Rd DARL/WED WS10 .... 56 C5
  HAG/WOL DY9 .... 137 E1
Prices Rd SEDG DY3 .... 66 C4
Price St BILS/COS WV14 .... 54 B5
  CBHAMNE B4 .... 3 G2
  DUDS DY2 .... 84 D4
  SMTHWK B66 .... 106 D4
  WBROM B70 .... 87 G3
Priestfield Cl KGSTG B44 .... 74 D1
Priestfield St BILS/COS WV14 .... 53 F5
Priestland Rd BKDE/SHDE B34.. 112 D2
Priestley Cl
  BFLD/HDSWWD B20 .... 90 A5
  HALE B63 .... 137 F1
Priestley Rd SPARK B11 .... 27 E5
  WSLW WS2 .... 41 E1
Priest St CDYHTH B64 .... 121 F3
Primley Av CBROM B36 .... 111 H2
  WSLW WS2 .... 41 F3
Primley Cl WSLW WS2 .... 41 F3
Primrose Av SPARK B11 .... 145 E2
  TPTN/OCK DY4 .... 70 A3
  WOLV WV10 .... 23 H1
Primrose Bank
  LGLYGN/QTN B68 .... 105 F5
Primrose Cl DUDS DY2 * 18 A2
  CDYHTH B64 .... 120 B4
Primrose Crs DUDN DY1 .... 84 C2
Primrose Cft ERDW/GRVHL B23.. 76 A4
  HLGN/YWD B28 .... 162 D5
Primrose Gdns CDSL WV8 .... 10 C4
  HWK/WKHTH B38 .... 176 D5
Primrose Hl HWK/WKHTH B38.. 176 D4
  SMTHWKW B67 .... 105 H5

STRBR DY8 .... 118 A2
Primrose La HLGN/YWD B28.... 162 D5
  WOLV WV10 .... 23 H2
Primrose Pk BRLYHL DY5 .... 101 E2
Primrose Rd DUDS DY2 .... 102 C5
The Primroses DSYBK/YTR WS5 .. 57 H4
Primrose Woods
  RIDG/WDGT B32 .... 140 B5
Primsland Cl SHLY B90 .... 196 A1
Prince Albert St BORD B9 .... 128 B3
Prince Andrew Crs RBRY B45.... 173 G3
Prince Charles Cl RBRY B45 .... 173 G3
Prince Charles Rd
  BILS/COS WV14 .... 54 B5
Prince Edward Dr RBRY B45 ..... 173 G3
Prince George Rd
  DARL/WED WS10 .... 56 A3
Prince of Wales La
  ALE/KHTH/YWD B14 .... 179 G5
Princep Cl GTB/HAM B43 .... 59 H4
Prince Philip Cl RBRY B45 .... 173 G3
Prince Ri BVILLE B30 .... 176 D2
Prince's Av WSL WS1 .... 5 J6
Princes Dr CDSL WV8 .... 10 C4
Princes Gdns CDSL WV8 .... 10 B4
Princes Ga SOLH B91 .... 181 H1
  WBROM B70 .... 88 A4
Prince's Rd OLDBY B69 .... 85 G4
  STRBR DY8 .... 134 D5
Princess Alice Dr
  SCFLD/BOLD D73 .... 76 B1
Princess Aly WOLV WV1 .... 7 G4
Princess Anne Rd
  BILS/COS WV14 .... 54 B5
  WSLW WS2 .... 40 D2
Princess Crs HALE B63 .... 138 A1
Princess Gv HHTH/SAND B71 ..... 71 H4
Princess Pde WBROM B70 * 87 H3
Princess Rd DIG/EDG B5 .... 144 A1
  LGLYGN/QTN B68 .... 123 H2
Princess Sq BILS/COS WV14 .... 54 B5
Princess St WOLV WV1 .... 7 G4
Princess Wy DARL/WED WS10.... 40 A5
Prince St ALDR WS9 .... 19 F5
  CDYHTH B64 .... 120 D5
  DUDS DY2 .... 102 C5
  WSL WS1 .... 41 G5
Prince's Wy SOLH B91 .... 181 H2
Princethorpe Cl
  BKDE/SHDE B34 .... 113 F2
  SHLY B90 .... 180 A5
Princethorpe Rd SLYOAK B29... 158 D3
Prince Thorpe Rd WLNHL WV13... 39 H5
Princeton Gdns COVEN WV9 .... 11 H5
Prince William Cl
  ERDW/GRVHL B23 .... 92 B4
Princip St CBHAMNE B4 .... 3 G2
Printing House St CBHAMNE B4.. 3 G2
Priors Ml SEDG DY3 .... 67 G5
Priors Wy ERDW/GRVHL B23.... 76 A3
Priory Chambers DUDN DY1 *... 84 B5
Priory Ci CSHL/WTROR B46 * 115 G4
  DUDN DY1 .... 84 B5
  SMTHWK B66 .... 107 E5
  WBROM B70 .... 88 B4
Priory Dr LGLYGN/QTN B68 .... 105 G4
Priory Fields Cl BILS/COS WV14.. 67 H1
Priory Gdns HLGN/YWD B28 .... 179 E1
Prioryate Wy BORD B9 .... 128 C2
Priory La SEDG DY3 .... 67 F4
The Priory Queensway
  CBHAMNE B4 .... 3 H
Priory Rd ALE/KHTH/YWD B14 .. 160 C
  AST/WIT B6 .... 109 H
  DUDN DY1 .... 84 C
  EDG B15 .... 143 F
  HLGN/YWD B28 .... 179 E
  RMSLY B62 .... 138 C
  STRBR DY8 .... 135 H
Priory Sq CBHAMNE B4 .... 3 H
Priory St DUDN DY1 .... 84 C
The Priory SEDG DY3 .... 67 F
Priory Wk CBHAMNE B4 .... 3 H
  CSCFLD/WYGN B72 .... 77 G
Pritchard Av WNSFLD WV11 .... 25 E
Pritchard Cl SMTHWK B66 .... 106 D
Pritchard St BRLYHL DY5 .... 118 D
  DARL/WED WS10 .... 55 H
Pritchatts Rd EDG B15 .... 142 D
Pritchett Av
  ETTPK/GDPK/PENN WV4 .... 52 D
Pritchett Rd NFLD/LBR B31 .... 189 H
Pritchett St AST/WIT B6 .... 109 H
Private Wy RBRY B45 .... 188 C
Privet Cl KGSTG B44 .... 60 D
Probert Rd WOLV WV10 .... 22 D
Proctor St VAUX/NECH B7 .... 109 G
Proffitt Cl WSLW WS2 .... 42 C
Proffitt St WSLW WS2 .... 42 C
Profitt St WOLV WV10 .... 37 G
The Promenade BRLYHL DY5 .... 119 F
Prospect Gdns STRBR DY8 .... 135 H
Prospect Hl STRBR DY8 .... 135 H
Prospect La SOLH B91 .... 164 D
Prospect Pl BHTH/HG B12 * .... 144 C
Prospect Rd MOS/BIL B13 .... 161 H
  RMSLY B62 .... 139 F
  SEDG DY3 .... 82 D
Prospect Row DUDS DY2 .... 102 D
  STRBR DY8 .... 135 H
Prospect St BILS/COS WV14 .... 54 D
  TPTN/OCK DY4 .... 70 B
Prosper Meadow
  KGSWFD DY6 .... 100 A
Prospero Cl RBRY B45 .... 174 A
Prosser St BILS/COS WV14 .... 53 H
  WOLV WV10 .... 23 H
Prossers Wk
  CSHL/WTROR B46 .... 115 H
Prouds La BILS/COS WV14 .... 53 H
Provence Cl WOLV WV10 .... 37 G
Providence Cl BLOX/PEL WS3 ..... 27 H
Providence Dr HAG/WOL DY9 ... 169 H
Providence La BLOX/PEL WS3 ..... 27 H
Providence Rw
  BILS/COS WV14 .... 68 C
Providence St CDYHTH B64 .... 120 B
  HAG/WOL DY9 .... 137 E
  TPTN/OCK DY4 .... 69 H

Providence Ter
DARL/WED WS10 * 55 G2
Pruden Av
ETTPK/GDPK/PENN WV4 52 D5
Pryor Rd LGLYGN/QTN B68 123 G1
Pudsey Dr MGN/WHC B75 47 G2
Pugh Crs WSLW WS2 40 C3
Pugh Rd AST/WIT B6 109 G2
BILS/COS WV14 67 H1
Pugin Cl DUNHL/THL/PER WV6 34 B2
Pugin Gdns ERDW/GRVHL B23 76 B3
Pumphouse Wy OLDBY B69 104 D5
Pump St BKHL/PFLD WV2 53 F2
Puppy Gn TPTN/OCK DY4 85 H1
Purbeck Cl HALE B63 154 D1
Purbeck Cft RIDG/WDGT B32 141 F2
Purbrook Rd WOLV WV1 38 A5
Purcell Rd WOLVN WV10 23 G2
Purdy Rd BILS/COS WV14 69 E2
Purefoy Rd MOS/BIL B13 162 A5
Purley Gv ERDW/GRVHL B23 91 G1
Purlin Whf DUDS DY2 121 E1
Purnells Wy DOR/KN B93 197 E3
Purslet Rd WOLV WV1 38 A4
Purslow Gv NFLD/LBR B31 175 G4
Putney Av BFLD/HDSWWD B20 90 C5
Putney La RMSLY B62 172 D3
Putney Rd BFLD/HDSWWD B20 90 C5
Pype Hayes Cl
ERDE/BCHGN B24 93 H2
Pype Hayes Rd
ERDE/BCHGN B24 93 H2
Pytman Dr WALM/CURD B76 78 C4

Q

The Quadrangle BVILLE B30 * 159 H4
The Quadrant SEDG DY3 67 F2
Quadrille Lawns COVEN WV9 11 H5
Quail Gn DUNHL/THL/PER WV6 34 D3
Qualcast Rd WOLV WV1 37 H3
Quantock Cl BRWNH WS8 19 G2
HALE B63 137 H5
RBRY B45 174 B3
Quantock Rd STRBR DY8 135 H1
Quantry La HAG/WOL DY9 186 A1
Quarrington Gv
ALE/KHTH/YWD B14 178 C2
Quarry Brow SEDG DY3 83 G1
Quarry Hl HALE B63 138 B5
Quarry House Cl RBRY B45 173 H4
Quarry La HALE B63 138 B5
NFLD/LBR B31 175 F2
Quarry Park Rd STRBR DY8 152 C2
Quarry Ri OLDBY B69 103 H1
Quarry Rd DUDS DY2 120 B2
SLYOAK B29 158 B1
Quarry Wk RBRY B45 188 A1
Quasar Centre WSL WS1 4 D3
Quayle Gv STRBR DY8 117 H1
Quayside WSNGN B18 108 A4
Quayside Cl OLDBY B69 104 C1
Quayside Dr WSLW WS2 4 A6
Queen Eleanors Dr
DOR/KN B93 183 F5
Queen Elizabeth Av WSLW WS2 40 D3
Queen Elizabeth Rd RBRY B45 173 G3
Queen Mary St WSL WS1 56 D2
Queens Ar WOLV WV1 7 F4
Queens Av
ALE/KHTH/YWD B14 * 161 E2
OLDBY B69 85 H5
SHLY B90 180 B3
WSNGN B18 * 107 H3
Queensbridge Rd MOS/BIL B13 143 H5
Queens Cl ERDE/BCHGN B24 92 D4
SMTHWKW B67 106 C4
Queens Ct RIDG/WDGT B32 141 G2
SOLH B91 * 182 C1
Queens Crs BILS/COS WV14 68 A2
STRBR DY8 118 C5
Queen's Cross DUDN DY1 102 B1
Queens Dr BLKHTH/ROWR B65 104 B5
BVILLE B30 177 E1
DIG/EDG B5 3 G6
Queens Gdns BILS/COS WV14 53 H1
CDSL WV8 10 B4
DUDS DY2 102 B5
ERDW/GRVHL B23 75 H4
Queens Head Rd HDSW B21 107 G2
Queens Hl HAG/WOL DY9 184 B1
Queens Hospital Cl EDG B15 126 C3
Queen's Lea SHHTH WV12 26 A5
Queens Md SMTHWKW B67 * 106 C4
Queen's Park Rd
RIDG/WDGT B32 141 F1
Queen Sq WOLV WV1 7 F4
Queen's Ride DIG/EDG B5 143 G3
Queens Rd AST/WIT B6 109 G1
DSYBK/YTR WS5 57 H2
ERDW/GRVHL B23 92 A3
LGN/SDN/BHAMAIR B26 130 B3
RUSH/SHEL WS4 29 E3
SEDG DY3 67 G3
SMTHWKW B67 105 H5
STRBR DY8 135 F1
Queens Tower
VAUX/NECH B7 * 109 H4
Queen St ALDR WS9 19 F5
BHTH/HG B12 144 D2
BILS/COS WV14 54 A3
BRLYHL DY5 120 A4
CSCFLD/WYGN B72 62 B4
HALE B63 138 C3
KGSWFD DY6 99 H2
OLDBY B69 105 E1
STRBR DY8 135 F1
TPTN/OCK DY4 69 F3
WBROM B70 87 H3
WOLV WV1 7 G4
WSLW WS2 4 B5
Queensway FOAKS/STRLY B74 45 G5
HAG/WOL DY9 136 C5
HALE B63 138 D4
LGLYGN/QTN B68 123 F4
Queensway Cl
LGLYGN/QTN B68 123 F4
Queensway Ml HALE B63 * 138 D4
Queenswood Rd
MGN/WHC B75 47 F4
MOS/BIL B13 144 C3
Quenby Dr DUDN DY1 84 A3
Quendale WMBN WV5 64 C5
Quentin Dr DUDN DY1 101 H2
Queslade Cl GTB/HAM B43 73 H2
Queslett Rd GTB/HAM B43 74 B2
Queslett Rd East
FOAKS/STRLY B74 60 A3
Quicksand La ALDR WS9 43 H1
Quigley Av BORD B9 127 H2
Quillets Rd STRBR DY8 117 G1
Quilter Cl BILS/COS WV14 68 A3
WSLW WS2 40 D2
Quilter Rd ERDE/BCHGN B24 93 F4
Quincey Dr ERDE/BCHGN B24 93 G3
Quincy Ri BRLYHL DY5 119 E5
Quinton Cl HIA/OLT B92 148 B3
Quinton Expy
RIDG/WDGT B32 140 B3
Quinton La RIDG/WDGT B32 140 D1
Quinton Rd HRBN B17 141 H4
Quinton Rd West RIDG/WDGT B32 140 B2
Quorn Crs STRBR DY8 117 G1
Quorn Gv ERDE/BCHGN B24 93 F4

R

Rabone La SMTHWK B66 106 D3
Raby Cl OLDBY B69 103 F1
Raby St BKHL/PFLD WV2 7 H7
Racecourse La STRBR DY8 152 A1
Racecourse Rd
DUNHL/THL/PER WV6 22 C5
Racemeadow Crs DUDS DY2 120 C3
Rachael Gdns DARL/WED WS10 56 C4
Rachel Cl TPTN/OCK DY4 70 A2
Rachel Gdns SLYOAK B29 142 B5
Radbourn Dr FOAKS/STRLY B74 62 C2
Radbourne Dr HALE B63 120 A5
Radbourne Rd SHLY B90 180 D2
Radcliffe Dr RMSLY B62 139 G1
Raddens Rd RMSLY B62 139 H4
Raddington Dr HIA/OLT B92 163 H2
Raddlebarn Farm Dr
SLYOAK B29 159 H1
Raddlebarn Rd SLYOAK B29 159 H1
Radford Cl DSYBK/YTR WS5 57 G5
Radford Dr RUSH/SHEL WS4 18 C5
Radford Ri SOLH B91 165 G5
Radford Rd SLYOAK B29 158 C3
Radley Gv SLYOAK B29 141 G5
Radley Rd HAG/WOL DY9 136 D3
RUSH/SHEL WS4 29 E4
The Radleys STETCH B33 131 G4
Radlow Crs
CHWD/FDBR/MGN B37 132 B4
Radnor Cl RBRY B45 174 B3
Radnor Cft DSYBK/YTR WS5 58 A5
Radnor Gn HHTH/SAND B71 71 G4
Radnor Rd
BFLD/HDSWWD B20 108 B1
LGLYGN/QTN B68 123 F5
SEDG DY3 67 E3
Radnor St WSNGN B18 107 H3
Radstock Av CBROM B36 111 G2
Radstock Rd SHHTH WV12 26 A1
Radway Rd SHLY B90 195 E1
Raeburn Rd GTB/HAM B43 59 G4
Raford Rd ERDW/GRVHL B23 76 B5
Ragees Rd KGSWFD DY6 118 B1
Raglan Av
DUNHL/THL/PER WV6 34 D2
SMTHWK B66 107 E5
Raglan Cl ALDR WS9 45 F2
SEDG DY3 66 D4
Raglan Rd DIG/EDG B5 143 H1
SMTHWK B66 107 E5
Raglan St BDMR/CCFT WV3 6 D4
BRLYHL DY5 101 E5
Raglan Wy
CHWD/FDBR/MGN B37 132 D2
Ragley Cl BLOX/PEL WS3 27 E1
DOR/KN B93 197 F1
Ragley Dr GTB/HAM B43 73 F1
LGN/SDN/BHAMAIR B26 148 A1
WLNHL WV13 39 F5
Ragnall Av STETCH B33 131 F5
Railswood Dr BLOX/PEL WS3 18 A4
Railway Dr BILS/COS WV14 54 A3
WOLV WV1 7 H3
Railway Rd
BFLD/HDSWWD B20 91 F4
SCFLD/BOLD B73 62 B3
Railwayside Cl SMTHWK B66 106 A2
Railway St BILS/COS WV14 54 A3
TPTN/OCK DY4 86 A1
WBROM B70 87 F2
WOLV WV1 7 H3
Railway Ter DARL/WED WS10 70 D1
PBAR/PBCH B42 * 73 H5
VAUX/NECH B7 109 H2
Railwharf Sidings DUDS DY2 102 D5
Rainbow St BILS/COS WV14 53 H5
BKHL/PFLD WV2 52 B1
Rainham Cl TPTN/OCK DY4 84 D1
Rainsbrook Dr SHLY B90 195 F2
Rake Wy EDG B15 2 B7
Raleigh Cl HDSW B21 88 D5
Raleigh Cft GTB/HAM B43 58 C5
Raleigh Rd BILS/COS WV14 54 B5
BORD B9 128 B2
Raleigh St HHTH/SAND B71 87 G2
WSLW WS2 41 G3
Ralph Rd SHLY B90 180 D1
WASH/WDE B8 110 B5
Ralphs Meadow
RIDG/WDGT B32 140 D5
Ralston Cl BLOX/PEL WS3 16 C3
Ramp Rd
CHWD/FDBR/MGN B37 149 G2
Ramsay Cl HHTH/SAND B71 72 B3
Ramsay Rd LGLYGN/QTN B68 123 G4
TPTN/OCK DY4 69 E4
WSLW WS2 27 E5
Ramsden Cl SLYOAK B29 158 D3
Ramsey Cl RBRY B45 173 G4
Ramsey Rd VAUX/NECH B7 110 A2
Randall Cl KGSWFD DY6 100 B5
Randle Dr MGN/WHC B75 47 G2
Randle Rd HAG/WOL DY9 136 A3
Randwick Gv KGSTG B44 74 D2
Ranelagh Rd BKHL/PFLD WV2 52 A2
Rangeview Cl
FOAKS/STRLY B74 60 B2
Rangeways Rd KGSWFD DY6 118 B1
Rangoon Rd HIA/OLT B92 148 C3
Ranleigh Av KGSWFD DY6 100 B5
Rann Cl LDYWD/EDGR B16 126 A3
Rannoch Cl BRLYHL DY5 118 D4
Ranscombe Dr SEDG DY3 83 E4
Ransom Rd ERDW/GRVHL B23 92 A2
Ranworth Ri
ETTPK/GDPK/PENN WV4 52 B4
Ratcliffe Av BVILLE B30 177 H2
Ratcliffe Cl SEDG DY3 67 H4
Ratcliffe Dr WLNHL WV13 39 G5
Ratcliffe Rd SOLH B91 165 E3
WNSFLD WV11 25 G4
Ratcliff Wk OLDBY B69 * 104 D2
Ratcliff Wy TPTN/OCK DY4 70 A5
Rathbone Cl BILS/COS WV14 53 H3
DIG/EDG B5 127 E5
Rathbone Rd SMTHWKW B67 124 B2
Rathlin Cl COVEN WV9 12 A4
Rathlin Cft CBROM B36 114 B4
Rathmore Cl STRBR DY8 135 E5
Rathwell Cl COVEN WV9 12 A5
Rattle Cft STETCH B33 130 A1
Ravenall Cl BKDE/SHDE B34 112 D2
Raven Crs WNSFLD WV11 25 F2
Ravenfield Cl WASH/WDE B8 110 D4
Ravenhayes La
RIDG/WDGT B32 157 E4
Raven Hays Rd NFLD/LBR B31 174 C3
Ravenhill Dr CDSL WV8 10 C4
Ravenhurst Dr GTB/HAM B43 58 C5
Ravenhurst Ms
ERDW/GRVHL B23 92 C3
Ravenhurst Rd HRBN B17 125 E5
Ravenhurst St BHTH/HG B12 127 G4
Raven Rd DSYBK/YTR WS5 57 H2
Ravensbourne Gv
WLNHL WV13 40 A3
Ravenscroft STRBR DY8 134 C1
Ravenscroft Rd HIA/OLT B92 164 C2
SHHTH WV12 25 H5
Ravensdale Cl DSYBK/YTR WS5 57 H1
Ravensdale Gdns
DSYBK/YTR WS5 57 H2
Ravensdale Rd SMHTH B10 128 D5
Ravenshaw La SOLH B91 183 E1
Ravenshaw Rd
LDYWD/EDGR B16 125 E2
Ravenshaw Wy DOR/KN B93 183 E3
Ravenshill Rd
ALE/KHTH/YWD B14 179 E1
Ravensholme
DUNHL/THL/PER WV6 34 D3
Ravensitch Wk BRLYHL DY5 119 G3
Ravenswood EDG B15 125 G4
Ravenswood Cl
FOAKS/STRLY B74 47 F5
Ravenswood Dr SOLH B91 181 E4
Ravenswood Hl
CSHL/WTROR B46 115 F2
Rawdon Gv KGSTG B44 75 H3
Rawlings Rd SMTHWKW B67 124 C2
Rawlins Cft CVALE B35 94 D3
Rawlins St LDYWD/EDGR B16 126 A3
Raybolds Bridge Rd WSLW WS2 41 G1
Raybolds Bridge St WSLW WS2 41 G1
Raybon Cft RBRY B45 * 188 A2
Raybould's Fold DUDS DY2 102 C4
Rayford Dr HHTH/SAND B71 72 B1
Ray Hall La GTB/HAM B43 72 D3
Rayleigh Rd BDMR/CCFT WV3 36 C5
Raymond Av PBAR/PBCH B42 74 B5
Raymond Cl WSLW WS2 27 H5
Raymond Gdns WNSFLD WV11 25 E5
Raymond Rd WASH/WDE B8 110 C5
Raymont Gv GTB/HAM B43 59 F4
Rayners Cft
LGN/SDN/BHAMAIR B26 130 B2
Raynor Rd WOLVN WV10 23 H4
Rea Av RBRY B45 173 G5
Reabrook Rd NFLD/LBR B31 175 F5
Rea Cl NFLD/LBR B31 189 G1
Readers Wk GTB/HAM B43 73 H2
Rea Fordway RBRY B45 173 H4
Reansway Sq
DUNHL/THL/PER WV6 36 C1
Reapers Cl SHHTH WV12 26 B5
Reaside Crs
ALE/KHTH/YWD B14 160 B5
Reaside Cft BHTH/HG B12 * 144 A1
Reaside Dr RBRY B45 174 B5
Rea St DIG/EDG B5 127 F3
Rea St South DIG/EDG B5 127 E4
Rea Ter DIG/EDG B5 3 K6
Rea Valley Dr NFLD/LBR B31 175 H3
Reaview Dr SLYOAK B29 143 F5
Reaymer Cl WSLW WS2 27 F4
Reay Nadin Dr
SCFLD/BOLD B73 60 D4
Rebecca Dr SLYOAK B29 142 C5
Rebecca Gdns
ETTPK/GDPK/PENN WV4 51 F4
Recreation St DUDS DY2 102 D4
Rectory Av DARL/WED WS10 55 F2
Rectory Cl STRBR DY8 135 H4
Rectory Gdns SOLH B91 182 B2
STRBR DY8 135 H4
Rectory Gv WSNGN B18 107 G3
Rectory La CBROM B36 112 C1
Rectory Park Av
MGN/WHC B75 63 E4
Rectory Park Cl MGN/WHC B75 63 E4
Rectory Park Rd
LGN/SDN/BHAMAIR B26 148 A2
Rectory Rd MGN/WHC B75 62 C3
NFLD/LBR B31 175 H2
SOLH B91 182 A2
STRBR DY8 135 H4
Rectory St STRBR DY8 117 H1
Redacre Rd SCFLD/BOLD B73 76 D1
Redacres DUNHL/THL/PER WV6 22 A4
Redbank Av ERDW/GRVHL B23 92 A3
Redbourn Rd BLOX/PEL WS3 16 C3
Red Brick Cl CDYHTH B64 120 D5
Redbrook Covert
HWK/WKHTH B38 190 C1
Red Brook Rd WSLW WS2 27 E5
Redbrooks Cl SOLH B91 181 G4
Redburn Dr
ALE/KHTH/YWD B14 177 H3
Redcar Cft CBROM B36 111 G1
Redcar Rd WOLVN WV10 12 D3
Redcliffe Dr WMBN WV5 65 F5
Redcotts Cl WOLVN WV10 24 A3
Redcroft Dr ERDE/BCHGN B24 93 G1
Redcroft Rd DUDS DY2 103 E3
Reddal Hill Rd CDYHTH B64 121 E3
Reddicap Heath Rd
MGN/WHC B75 63 F4
Reddicap Hl WALM/CURD B76 62 D4
Reddicroft SCFLD/BOLD B73 62 C3
Reddings La HLGN/YWD B28 145 G5
Reddings Rd MOS/BIL B13 143 H5
The Reddings HLYWD B47 192 C3
Redditch Rd ALVE B48 189 H5
HWK/WKHTH B38 176 C4
NFLD/LBR B31 190 A2
Redfern Cl HIA/OLT B92 164 D1
Redfern Park Wy SPARK B11 146 A2
Redfern Rd SPARK B11 146 A2
Redfly La BRLYHL DY5 101 E3
Redford Cl MOS/BIL B13 144 D5
Redgate Cl HWK/WKHTH B38 176 B3
Redhall Rd RIDG/WDGT B32 124 A5
SEDG DY3 83 E4
Red Hl STRBR DY8 135 H3
Redhill Av WMBN WV5 65 E5
Redhill Cl STRBR DY8 135 H3
Redhill Gdns NFLD/LBR B31 190 A1
Red Hill Gv HWK/WKHTH B38 190 D1
Redhill La BRGRVW B61 187 E3
Red Hill Pl RMSLY B62 155 G3
Redhill Rd HWK/WKHTH B38 190 B1
NFLD/LBR B31 175 H5
YDLY B25 146 A1
Red Hill St WOLV WV1 7 F1
Red House Av DARL/WED WS10 56 B5
Redhouse Cl DOR/KN B93 196 C3
Red House La ALDR WS9 29 G5
Red House Park Rd
GTB/HAM B43 73 G1
Redhouse Rd
DUNHL/THL/PER WV6 21 F5
Red House Rd STETCH B33 130 A1
Redhouse St WSL WS1 57 E1
Redhurst Dr WOLVN WV10 12 B4
Redlake Dr HAG/WOL DY9 152 D2
Redlake Rd HAG/WOL DY9 152 D1
Redlands Cl SOLH B91 165 F5
Redlands Rd SOLH B91 165 E5
Redlands Wy FOAKS/STRLY B74 45 G4
Red La SEDG DY3 66 D3
WNSFLD WV11 15 G5
Red Leasowes Rd HALE B63 138 B4
Redliff Av CBROM B36 95 F5
Red Lion Cl OLDBY B69 85 G5
Red Lion St WOLV WV1 6 E3
Redmead Cl NFLD/LBR B31 176 A1
Redmoor Gdns
ETTPK/GDPK/PENN WV4 51 G3
Redmoor Wy WALM/CURD B76 79 F5
Rednal Hill La RBRY B45 188 A2
Rednall Dr MGN/WHC B75 47 G2
Rednal Mill Dr RBRY B45 188 C1
Rednal Rd HWK/WKHTH B38 176 A5
Redpine Crest SHHTH WV12 40 B1
Red River Rd WSLW WS2 27 E5
Red Rock Dr CDSL WV8 10 B5
Redruth Cl DSYBK/YTR WS5 58 B1
KGSWFD DY6 99 H1
Redruth Rd DSYBK/YTR WS5 58 B1
Redstone Dr WNSFLD WV11 25 F5
Redstone Farm Rd
HLGN/YWD B28 163 F4
Redthorn Gv STETCH B33 129 H1
Redvers Rd BORD B9 128 C3
Redwing Gv ERDW/GRVHL B23 75 H4
Redwood Av DUDN DY1 83 H1
Redwood Cl BVILLE B30 176 C1
FOAKS/STRLY B74 45 F3
Redwood Cft
ALE/KHTH/YWD B14 161 E3
Redwood Dr OLDBY B69 85 H4
Redwood Gdns ACGN B27 146 B2
Redwood Rd BILS/COS WV14 68 D1
BVILLE B30 176 C1
DSYBK/YTR WS5 57 H4
Redwood Wy SHHTH WV12 25 H2
Reedham Gdns
ETTPK/GDPK/PENN WV4 50 D2
Reedly Rd SHHTH WV12 26 A1
Reedmace Cl
HWK/WKHTH B38 176 D5
Reedswood Cl WSLW WS2 41 G2
Reedswood Gdns WSLW WS2 41 G2
Reedswood La WSLW WS2 41 G2
Reedswood Wy WSLW WS2 41 E1
Rees Dr WMBN WV5 65 F4
Reeves Cl TPTN/OCK DY4 85 H4
Reeves Gdns CDSL WV8 10 C3
Reeves Rd
ALE/KHTH/YWD B14 160 C4
Reeves St BLOX/PEL WS3 27 F2
Reform St WBROM B70 87 H3
Regal Cft CBROM B36 111 F1
Regal Dr WSLW WS2 4 A7
Regan Av SHLY B90 180 A4
Regan Crs ERDW/GRVHL B23 76 C5
Regan Dr OLDBY B69 104 B1
Regency Cl BORD B9 128 B3
Regency Ct WSL WS1 57 G1
Regency Dr HWK/WKHTH B38 176 C3
Regency Gdns
ALE/KHTH/YWD B14 179 E2
Regency Wk FOAKS/STRLY B74 32 B5
Regent Av OLDBY B69 85 G5
Regent Cl DIG/EDG B5 143 H1
HALE B63 138 C3
KGSWFD DY6 99 G3
OLDBY B69 103 G1
Regent Ct SMTHWK B66 106 C4
Regent Dr OLDBY B69 85 G5
Regent Pde CBHAMW B1 2 C2
Regent Park Rd SMHTH B10 128 A4
Regent Pl CBHAMW B1 2 C2
OLDBY B69 85 H4
Regent Rd
ETTPK/GDPK/PENN WV4 51 E3
HDSW B21 107 F1
HRBN B17 142 A1
OLDBY B69 85 G5
Regents Ct BKHL/PFLD WV2 * 7 F6
Regent St BILS/COS WV14 53 H2
BVILLE B30 160 A3
CBHAMW B1 2 C2
CDYHTH B64 121 F2
DUDN DY1 68 C5
SMTHWK B66 106 C3
TPTN/OCK DY4 69 E3
WLNHL WV13 39 G2
Regents Wy MGN/WHC B75 63 F2
Regina Av KGSTG B44 74 D3
Regina Cl RBRY B45 173 G4
Regina Crs
DUNHL/THL/PER WV6 35 F1
Regina Dr PBAR/PBCH B42 90 D3
RUSH/SHEL WS4 42 C1
Reginald Rd SMTHWKW B67 124 B2
WASH/WDE B8 110 B5
Regis Beeches
DUNHL/THL/PER WV6 * 21 G5
Regis Gdns
BLKHTH/ROWR B65 122 A3
Regis Heath Rd
BLKHTH/ROWR B65 122 B2
Regis Rd BLKHTH/ROWR B65 122 A2
DUNHL/THL/PER WV6 21 F5
Reid Av SHHTH WV12 26 B4
Reid Rd LGLYGN/QTN B68 123 G3
Reigate Av WASH/WDE B8 111 G5
Relko Dr CBROM B36 111 G2
Remembrance Rd
DARL/WED WS10 56 C5
Remington Pl WSLW WS2 27 G5
Remington Rd WSLW WS2 27 F4
Renfrew Cl STRBR DY8 117 G1
Renfrew Sq CVALE B35 94 D2
Rennie Gv RIDG/WDGT B32 140 D2
Rennison Dr WMBN WV5 65 E5
Renown Cl BRLYHL DY5 100 D2
Renton Gv WOLVN WV10 22 C1
Renton Rd WOLVN WV10 22 C1
Repington Wy MGN/WHC B75 63 H3
Repton Av
DUNHL/THL/PER WV6 34 B2
Repton Gv BORD B9 129 F1
Repton Rd BORD B9 129 F1
Reservoir Cl WSLW WS2 41 F5
Reservoir Pas DARL/WED WS10 55 H5
Reservoir Pl WSLW WS2 41 F5
Reservoir Retreat
LDYWD/EDGR B16 125 H3
Reservoir Rd
BLKHTH/ROWR B65 122 B1
ERDW/GRVHL B23 92 B2
HIA/OLT B92 164 B2
LDYWD/EDGR B16 125 H2
LGLYGN/QTN B68 105 G5
RBRY B45 188 C5
SLYOAK B29 142 A4
Reservoir St WSLW WS2 41 F5
Retallack Cl SMTHWK B66 106 D1
Retford Dr WALM/CURD B76 63 E4
Retford Gv YDLY B25 146 C1
Retreat Gdns SEDG DY3 67 G4
The Retreat CDYHTH B64 121 E5
Revesby Wk VAUX/NECH B7 109 G5
Revival St BLOX/PEL WS3 27 F1
Reynards Cl SEDG DY3 68 A4
Reynolds Cl SEDG DY3 80 C5
Reynolds Gv
DUNHL/THL/PER WV6 20 D5
Reynolds Rd HDSW B21 107 G2
Reynoldstown Rd
CBROM B36 111 G1
Reynolds Wk WNSFLD WV11 25 G2
Rhayader Rd NFLD/LBR B31 158 A5
Rhodes Cl SEDG DY3 82 C2
Rhone Cl SPARK B11 145 E4
Rhoose Cft CVALE B35 94 D4
Rhys Thomas Cl SHHTH WV12 40 B1
Rian Ct CDYHTH B64 120 D4
Ribbesford Av WOLVN WV10 22 D2
Ribbesford Cl HALE B63 137 H2
Ribbesford Crs BILS/COS WV14 68 D2
Ribblesdale Rd BVILLE B30 160 A3
Richard Pl DSYBK/YTR WS5 43 E5
Richard Rd DSYBK/YTR WS5 43 E5
Richards Cl
BLKHTH/ROWR B65 104 C5
NFLD/LBR B31 189 F2
Richardson Dr STRBR DY8 118 A4
Richards Rd TPTN/OCK DY4 69 F2
Richards St DARL/WED WS10 55 F1
Richard St VAUX/NECH B7 109 F4
WBROM B70 87 F3
Richard St West WBROM B70 87 F4
Richard Watts Dr
DARL/WED WS10 55 H3
Richard Williams Rd
DARL/WED WS10 71 F1
Richborough Dr DUDN DY1 83 G3
Riches St DUNHL/THL/PER WV6 36 B2
Richford Gv STETCH B33 131 F2
Richmond Aston Dr
TPTN/OCK DY4 85 G1
Richmond Av BDMR/CCFT WV3 36 B4
BHTH/HG B12 * 144 B2
Richmond Cl
BFLD/HDSWWD B20 90 A4
Richmond Cft PBAR/PBCH B42 73 H5
Richmond Dr BDMR/CCFT WV3 36 A4
DUNHL/THL/PER WV6 34 D2
MGN/WHC B75 63 F2
Richmond Gdns WMBN WV5 81 E1
Richmond Gv STRBR DY8 118 A4
Richmond Hl LGLYGN/QTN B68 105 G4
Richmond Hill Gdns EDG B15 142 C1

Richmond Hill Rd EDG B15 142 D1
Richmond Pk KGSWFD DY6 99 G1
Richmond Pl
ALE/KHTH/YWD B14 161 F2
Richmond Rd
BDMR/CCFT WV3 36 A4
DUDN DY1 102 B1
HIA/OLT B92 147 E5
HLYWD B47 193 E1
RBRY B45 187 G1
SCFLD/BOLD B73 62 B2
SEDG DY3 67 G4
SMTHWK B66 124 C2
STETCH B33 129 H2
WSNGN B18 108 B3
Richmond St HALE B63 138 C3
WBROM B70 86 C1
WSL WS1 5 G5
Richmond St South
WBROM B70 86 C1
Richmond Wy
CHWD/FDBR/MGN B37 132 C1
Rickard Cl DOR/KN B93 196 C3
Rickman Dr EDG B15 126 D4
Rickyard Cl SLYOAK B29 158 C4
YDLY B25 129 H3
Rickyard Piece
RIDG/WDGT B32 141 E3
Riddfield Rd CBROM B36 112 A1
Ridding La DARL/WED WS10 70 D1
Riddings Crs BLOX/PEL WS3 17 H3
The Riddings HAG/WOL DY9 136 B5
STETCH B33 112 A5
WALM/CURD B76 78 D3
WOLVN WV10 24 A3
Ridgacre La RIDG/WDGT B32 140 C2
Ridgacre Rd HHTH/SAND B71 71 F5
RIDG/WDGT B32 140 B1
Ridgacre Rd West
RIDG/WDGT B32 140 A1
Ridge Cl MOS/BIL B13 162 A4
WSLW WS2 40 B2
Ridgefield Rd RMSLY B62 122 A4
Ridge Gv HAG/WOL DY9 136 A2
Ridge La WNSFLD WV11 24 D3
Ridgemount Dr
HWK/WKHTH B38 190 B1
Ridge Rd KGSWFD DY6 99 G4
Ridge St STRBR DY8 134 C1
Ridgewater Cl RBRY B45 188 B2
Ridge Wy ALDR WS9 44 B1
Ridgeway HRBN B17 124 D2
RIDG/WDGT B32 140 A2
SEDG DY3 67 F4
Ridgeway Av RMSLY B62 140 A1
Ridgeway Ct WSLW WS2 40 D4
Ridgeway Dr
ETTPK/GDPK/PENN WV4 51 F5
Ridgeway Rd STRBR DY8 118 B2
TPTN/OCK DY4 69 G3
The Ridgeway
ERDW/GRVHL B23 91 G1
Ridgewood BKDE/SHDE B34 112 D3
Ridgewood Av STRBR DY8 134 C1
Ridgewood Cl WSL WS1 5 F6
Ridgewood Dr MGN/WHC B75 47 F4
Ridgewood Gdns KGSTG B44 75 F4
Ridgmont Cft RIDG/WDGT B32 141 E2
Riding Cl HHTH/SAND B71 72 B4
Riding Wy SHHTH WV12 26 B4
Ridley St CBHAMW B1 126 C3
Ridpool Rd STETCH B33 130 D1
Rifle St BILS/COS WV14 68 A3
Rigby St DARL/WED WS10 70 D2
Riland Rd MGN/WHC B75 62 D3
Riley Crs BDMR/CCFT WV3 51 G2
Riley Dr CBROM B36 96 A5
Riley Rd ALE/KHTH/YWD B14 179 F2
Riley St WLNHL WV13 39 H3
Rilstone Rd RIDG/WDGT B32 141 F2
Rindleford Av
ETTPK/GDPK/PENN WV4 50 C2
Ringhills Rd CDSL WV8 10 D5
Ringinglow Rd KGSTG B44 74 C1
Ringmere Av CBROM B36 112 D1
Ring Rd North EDG B15 142 D3
Ring Road St Andrews
WOLV WV1 6 D4
Ring Road St Davids
WOLV WV1 7 H3
Ring Road St Georges
BKHL/PFLD WV2 7 G6
Ring Road St Johns
BKHL/PFLD WV2 6 E6
Ring Road St Marks
BDMR/CCFT WV3 6 D5
Ring Road St Patricks
WOLV WV1 7 G2
Ring Rd South EDG B15 142 D4
Ringswood Rd HIA/OLT B92 147 E3
The Ring YDLY B25 129 G4
Ringwood Av ALDR WS9 30 B5
Ringwood Dr RBRY B45 174 A4
Ringwood Rd WOLVN WV10 23 F1
Ripley Cl OLDBY B69 103 F1
Ripley Gv ERDW/GRVHL B23 91 H1
Ripon Dr HHTH/SAND B71 71 H2
Ripon Rd ALE/KHTH/YWD B14 179 E1
WOLVN WV10 23 E3
WSLW WS2 41 F3
Rippingille Rd GTB/HAM B43 59 G4
Ripple Rd BVILLE B30 160 B3
Rischale Wy RUSH/SHEL WS4 29 E2
Rise Av RBRY B45 188 A1
Riseley Crs DIG/EDG B5 143 H1
The Rise ALVE B48 189 H4
CHWD/FDBR/MGN B37 132 A5
KGSWFD DY6 100 A4
PBAR/PBCH B42 74 A3
Rising Brook
DUNHL/THL/PER WV6 35 F1
Rissington Av SLYOAK B29 160 A2
Ritchie Cl MOS/BIL B13 161 G1
Rivendell Gdns
DUNHL/THL/PER WV6 21 F5
Riverbank Rd WLNHL WV13 40 B3
River Brook Dr BVILLE B30 160 B3
River Lee Rd SPARK B11 * 145 G2
Rivermead Pk
BKDE/SHDE B34 112 C4
Riversdale Rd
ALE/KHTH/YWD B14 179 F2
Riverside Ct HWK/WKHTH B38 176 B2
Riverside Crs HLGN/YWD B28 179 F1
Riverside Dr SOLH B91 182 C3
STETCH B33 111 H5
Riverside Gdns CDSL WV8 10 D2
Riversleigh Dr STRBR DY8 118 A4
River St DIG/EDG B5 127 G2
River Wk DARL/WED WS10 71 E2
Riverway DARL/WED WS10 71 F1
Rivington Cl STRBR DY8 135 E3
Rivington Crs KGSTG B44 76 A2
Roach Cl BRLYHL DY5 101 F4
CHWD/FDBR/MGN B37 132 C1
Roach Crs WNSFLD WV11 * 25 F2
Roach Pool Cft
LDYWD/EDGR B16 125 E2
Robert Av ERDW/GRVHL B23 76 C5
Robert Rd BFLD/HDSWWD B20 90 B5
TPTN/OCK DY4 69 F5
Roberts Cl ALDR WS9 19 F5
Roberts Green Rd SEDG DY3 83 G2
Roberts La HAG/WOL DY9 152 D2
Robertson Knoll CBROM B36 112 B2
Robertsons Gdns
VAUX/NECH B7 110 A2
Roberts Rd ACGN B27 146 C4
BLOX/PEL WS3 28 B5
DARL/WED WS10 57 E5
Robert St SEDG DY3 83 G2
Robert Wynd BILS/COS WV14 67 H2
Robeson Cl TPTN/OCK DY4 84 D1
Robin Cl CBROM B36 114 A1
KGSWFD DY6 100 C3
Robin Gv WNSFLD WV11 24 C3
Robin Hood Crs
HLGN/YWD B28 162 C3
Robin Hood Cft
HLGN/YWD B28 162 D5
Robin Hood La
HLGN/YWD B28 162 C3
Robin Hood Rd BRLYHL DY5 119 H2
Robin Rd ERDW/GRVHL B23 92 C2
Robin's Cl STRBR DY8 135 G4
Robinsfield Dr NFLD/LBR B31 189 G1
Robinson's Wy
WALM/CURD B76 95 F1
Robottom Cl WSLW WS2 27 F4
Rocester Av WNSFLD WV11 25 E3
Rochdale Wk SMTHWK B10 128 A5
Roche Rd BLOX/PEL WS3 26 D1
Rochester Cft WSLW WS2 41 E1
Rochester Rd NFLD/LBR B31 175 G1
Roche Wy BLOX/PEL WS3 26 D1
Rochford Cl HALE B63 138 B5
RBRY B45 187 G1
WALM/CURD B76 78 C3
WSLW WS2 56 C1
Rochford Ct SHLY B90 195 G2
Rochford Gv
ETTPK/GDPK/PENN WV4 50 D3
Rock Av RBRY B45 188 C1
Rocket Pool Dr BILS/COS WV14 69 G1
Rockford Rd PBAR/PBCH B42 74 A4
Rock Gv HIA/OLT B92 147 E4
Rockingham Cl
BLOX/PEL WS3 * 27 F1
DOR/KN B93 198 B1
SEDG DY3 82 D3
Rockingham Dr
DUNHL/THL/PER WV6 34 C2
Rockingham Gdns
FOAKS/STRLY B74 62 B2
Rockingham Hall Gdns
HAG/WOL DY9 153 F3
Rockingham Rd YDLY B25 129 H4
Rockland Dr STETCH B33 112 A5
Rockland Gdns WLNHL WV13 39 F5
Rocklands Dr MGN/WHC B75 47 F5
Rockley Gv RBRY B45 188 B1
Rockley Rd
BLKHTH/ROWR B65 103 G3
Rockmead Av KGSTG B44 75 F1
Rockmoor Cl
CHWD/FDBR/MGN B37 131 G1
Rock Rd BILS/COS WV14 67 H3
HIA/OLT B92 147 E4
Rock St SEDG DY3 83 G1
The Rock DUNHL/THL/PER WV6 21 H5
Rockville Rd WASH/WDE B8 111 E5
Rockwood Rd ACGN B27 146 B3
Rocky La AST/WIT B6 109 G3
PBAR/PBCH B42 73 H5
Rodborough Rd DOR/KN B93 198 C1
LGN/SDN/BHAMAIR B26 147 H1
Rodbourne Rd HRBN B17 142 A4
Roddis Cl ERDW/GRVHL B23 76 B3
Roderick Dr WNSFLD WV11 24 D3
Roderick Rd SPARK B11 145 E2
Rodlington Av KGSTG B44 75 F2
Rodman Cl EDG B15 125 F4
Rodney Cl HIA/OLT B92 * 164 D1
LDYWD/EDGR B16 126 A2
Rodney Rd HIA/OLT B92 164 D1
Rodway Cl BRLYHL DY5 119 F5
ETTPK/GDPK/PENN WV4 52 B5
LOZ/NWT B19 108 D2
Rodwell Gv KGSTG B44 75 F3
Roebuck Cl BKDE/SHDE B34 113 G5
Roebuck Gld SHHTH WV12 40 C1
Roebuck La SMTHWK B66 106 B2
WBROM B70 88 A5
Roebuck Pl BLOX/PEL WS3 28 A4
Roebuck Rd BLOX/PEL WS3 28 A4
Roebuck St WBROM B70 88 B5
Roedean Cl KGSTG B44 75 H4
Roford Ct SEDG DY3 83 G1
Rogerfield Rd
ERDW/GRVHL B23 77 E5
Rogers Cl WNSFLD WV11 25 G1
Rogers Rd WASH/WDE B8 111 F4
Rokeby Cl WALM/CURD B76 63 E4
Rokeby Rd GTB/HAM B43 73 H1
Rokewood Cl KGSWFD DY6 81 H5
Rolan Dr SHLY B90 179 G5
Roland Rd LOZ/NWT B19 108 C1
Roland Vernon Wy
TPTN/OCK DY4 70 A4
Rolfe St SMTHWK B66 106 C3
Rollason Rd DUDS DY2 102 D1
ERDE/BCHGN B24 93 E3
Rollesby Dr WLNHL WV13 39 F5
Rolling Mill Cl DIG/EDG B5 * 127 E5
Rolling Mill Rd CNCK/NC WS11 8 A1
Rollingmill St WSLW WS2 4 A5
Rollswood Dr SOLH B91 181 F1
Roman Cl BRWNH WS8 9 E2
Roman Gra FOAKS/STRLY B74 32 A5
Roman La FOAKS/STRLY B74 45 H2
Roman Pk FOAKS/STRLY B74 45 H1
Roman Rd FOAKS/STRLY B74 46 A2
STRBR DY8 134 D3
Roman Wy
BLKHTH/ROWR B65 122 A1
CSHL/WTROR B46 97 E4
EDG B15 142 B4
Romany Rd RBRY B45 173 F4
Romany Wy STRBR DY8 134 C4
Roma Rd SPARK B11 145 G2
Romford Cl
LGN/SDN/BHAMAIR B26 147 H1
Romilly Av BFLD/HDSWWD B20 90 B4
Romilly Cl STRBR DY8 135 E1
WALM/CURD B76 63 G4
Romney Cl HLGN/YWD B28 162 D3
Romney Wy GTB/HAM B43 59 H4
Romsey Gv WOLVN WV10 12 C4
Romsey Rd WOLVN WV10 12 C4
Romsey Wy BLOX/PEL WS3 16 B4
Romsley Cl HALE B63 138 D5
RBRY B45 173 G5
RUSH/SHEL WS4 18 C5
Romsley Rd HAG/WOL DY9 136 A2
LGLYGN/QTN B68 123 F2
RIDG/WDGT B32 157 F2
Romulus Cl
BFLD/HDSWWD B20 90 B3
Ronald Gv CBROM B36 95 F5
Ronald Pl BORD B9 128 C2
Ronald Rd BORD B9 128 B2
Ron Davis Cl SMTHWK B66 * 106 D4
Rood End Rd
LGLYGN/QTN B68 105 G3
Rooker Av BKHL/PFLD WV2 52 C2
Rooker Crs BKHL/PFLD WV2 52 D2
Rookery Av BRLYHL DY5 118 C2
ETTPK/GDPK/PENN WV4 53 E5
Rookery La BKHL/PFLD WV2 51 G2
Rookery Pk BRLYHL DY5 100 D4
Rookery Ri WMBN WV5 65 F5
Rookery Rd
ETTPK/GDPK/PENN WV4 53 E5
HDSW B21 89 G5
SLYOAK B29 142 D5
WMBN WV5 65 F5
Rookery St WNSFLD WV11 24 C5
The Rookery RMSLY B62 140 A5
Rooks Meadow HAG/WOL DY9 152 D4
Rookwood Dr
DUNHL/THL/PER WV6 34 D4
Rooth St DARL/WED WS10 56 B4
Roper Wy SEDG DY3 67 H5
Rosafield Av RMSLY B62 139 H1
Rosalind Av DUDN DY1 68 B5
Rosalind Gv WNSFLD WV11 25 G5
Rosamond St WSL WS1 56 D1
Rosary Rd ERDW/GRVHL B23 92 B4
Rosary Vls SPARK B11 * 145 E2
Rose Av KGSWFD DY6 100 B4
LGLYGN/QTN B68 123 G5
Rose Bank Dr BLOX/PEL WS3 * 42 A1
Rosebay Av HWK/WKHTH B38 176 D5
Rosebery Rd SMTHWK B66 107 E5
Rosebery St BDMR/CCFT WV3 6 C6
WSNGN B18 108 A5
Rosebury Gv WMBN WV5 64 C5
Rose Cl SMTHWK B66 107 E4
Rose Cottage Dr STRBR DY8 117 H1
Rose Cottages SLYOAK B29 * 142 D5
Rosecroft Rd
LGN/SDN/BHAMAIR B26 148 A1
Rosedale Av ERDW/GRVHL B23 92 C3
SMTHWK B66 107 E4
Rosedale Gv YDLY B25 129 G4
Rosedale Pl WLNHL WV13 39 G5
Rosedene Dr
BFLD/HDSWWD B20 89 H4
Rose Dr BRWNH WS8 19 E2
Rosefield Cft AST/WIT B6 109 F2
Rosefield Rd SMTHWKW B67 106 C5
Rosehall Cl SOLH B91 181 F4
Rose Hl BRLYHL DY5 120 A3
RBRY B45 188 A4
WLNHL WV13 39 G4
Rose Hill Cl CBROM B36 112 D1
Rose Hill Gdns WLNHL WV13 39 G4
Rose Hill Rd HDSW B21 108 A2
Rosehip Cl DSYBK/YTR WS5 57 G5
Roseland Av DUDS DY2 85 F5
Roseland Wy EDG B15 126 B3
Roseleigh Rd RBRY B45 188 B2
Rosemary Av BILS/COS WV14 54 B2
ETTPK/GDPK/PENN WV4 52 A3
Rosemary Cl BRWNH WS8 18 D1
Rosemary Ct WNSFLD WV11 25 F3
Rosemary Crs DUDN DY1 67 H5
ETTPK/GDPK/PENN WV4 52 A3
Rosemary Crs West
ETTPK/GDPK/PENN WV4 51 H3
Rosemary Dr FOAKS/STRLY B74 46 A2
Rosemary Hill Rd
FOAKS/STRLY B74 46 A3
Rosemary La STRBR DY8 134 D4
Rosemary Nook
FOAKS/STRLY B74 32 B5
Rosemary Rd HALE B63 137 H5
STETCH B33 130 B2
TPTN/OCK DY4 85 G1
Rosemoor Dr BRLYHL DY5 118 D5
Rose Rd CSHL/WTROR B46 115 F1
HRBN B17 142 B1
Rose St BILS/COS WV14 69 F1
Rose Vls YDLY B25 * 129 E5
Roseville Gdns CDSL WV8 10 B3
Roseville Prec BILS/COS WV14 * 68 C3
Rosewood Dr
ERDW/GRVHL B23 92 B4
SHHTH WV12 25 H2
Rosewood Gdns WNSFLD WV11 15 F4
Rosewood Rd DUDN DY1 84 B1
Roshven Rd BHTH/HG B12 144 C3
Roslin Gv LOZ/NWT B19 108 C2
Roslyn Cl SMTHWK B66 106 C3
Ross BLKHTH/ROWR B65 121 H2
Ross Cl BDMR/CCFT WV3 36 A3
Ross Dr KGSWFD DY6 99 G2
Rosse Ct HIA/OLT B92 165 H2
Rossendale Cl HALE B63 137 H1
Ross Hts BLKHTH/ROWR B65 121 H1
Rosslyn Rd WALM/CURD B76 78 B5
Ross Rd BLOX/PEL WS3 28 B4
Rostrevor Rd SMTHWK B10 128 D3
Rotherby Gv
CHWD/FDBR/MGN B37 132 B5
Rotherfield Rd
LGN/SDN/BHAMAIR B26 130 D4
Rothesay Cft RIDG/WDGT B32 157 F3
Rothesay Dr STRBR DY8 117 G1
Rothesay Gdns
ETTPK/GDPK/PENN WV4 52 C3
Rothesay Wy SHHTH WV12 25 H4
Rothwell Dr SOLH B91 180 D1
Rotton Park Rd
LDYWD/EDGR B16 125 F3
Rotton Park St
LDYWD/EDGR B16 125 H1
Rough Hay Pl DARL/WED WS10 55 E1
Rough Hay Rd
DARL/WED WS10 55 E1
Rough Hill Dr
BLKHTH/ROWR B65 103 F3
Rough Hills Rd BKHL/PFLD WV2 52 D2
Roughlea Av CBROM B36 112 B2
Roughley Dr MGN/WHC B75 47 G3
Roughley Farm Rd
MGN/WHC B75 48 A2
Rough Rd KGSTG B44 60 C5
Rouncil Cl HIA/OLT B92 165 F3
The Roundabout
NFLD/LBR B31 174 D4
Round Cft WLNHL WV13 39 F3
Round Hl SEDG DY3 67 F1
Round Hill Av HAG/WOL DY9 153 E1
Roundhill Cl WALM/CURD B76 63 E4
Roundhills Rd RMSLY B62 122 D4
Roundhill Ter RMSLY B62 122 C3
Roundhill Wy BRWNH WS8 9 G2
Round House Rd SEDG DY3 83 G2
Roundlea Cl SHHTH WV12 25 H3
Roundlea Rd NFLD/LBR B31 158 A3
Round Rd ERDE/BCHGN B24 93 F4
Round Saw Cft RBRY B45 173 H5
Rounds Green Rd OLDBY B69 104 D2
Rounds Hill Rd BILS/COS WV14 68 D3
Rounds Rd BILS/COS WV14 53 H5
Round St DUDS DY2 102 C3
Roundway Down
DUNHL/THL/PER WV6 34 C2
Rounton Cl FOAKS/STRLY B74 46 B1
Rousay Cl RBRY B45 173 H4
Rousdon Gv GTB/HAM B43 73 F3
Rover Dr ACGN B27 146 D3
CBROM B36 95 H5
Rowallan Rd MGN/WHC B75 47 H3
Rowan Cl HLYWD B47 192 D3
WALM/CURD B76 78 B1
Rowan Ct BVILLE B30 177 E3
Rowan Crs BDMR/CCFT WV3 51 E1
BILS/COS WV14 68 B2
Rowan Dr HLGN/YWD B28 163 E5
WNSFLD WV11 15 F4
Rowan Ri KGSWFD DY6 100 A3
Rowan Rd CSCFLD/WYGN B72 77 G1
DSYBK/YTR WS5 57 F4
SEDG DY3 67 H2
Rowantrees RBRY B45 188 B3
Rowan Wy
CHWD/FDBR/MGN B37 132 C3
NFLD/LBR B31 175 F4
Roway La OLDBY B69 86 C5
Rowbrook Cl SHLY B90 179 G5
Rowchester Ct CBHAMNE B4 * 3 G3
Rowcroft Covert
ALE/KHTH/YWD B14 177 G2
Rowdale Rd PBAR/PBCH B42 74 C4
Rowden Dr ERDW/GRVHL B23 77 E5
SOLH B91 181 E3
Rowena Gdns SEDG DY3 67 E1
Rowheath Rd BVILLE B30 176 D1
Rowington Av
BLKHTH/ROWR B65 122 B1
Rowington Rd
BKDE/SHDE B34 113 G3
Rowington Ter YDLY B25 * 129 F5
Rowland Gdns WSLW WS2 41 G2
Rowland Hill Dr
TPTN/OCK DY4 * 86 A2
Rowlands Av WOLV WV1 38 B3
WSLW WS2 40 C2
Rowlands Cl WSLW WS2 40 C1
Rowlands Crs SOLH B91 164 D2
Rowlands Rd
LGN/SDN/BHAMAIR B26 130 A5
Rowland St WSLW WS2 41 G2
Rowley Gv STETCH B33 131 F1
Rowley Hall Av
BLKHTH/ROWR B65 122 A1
Rowley Hill Vw CDYHTH B64 121 F4
Rowley Pl RUSH/SHEL WS4 28 D3
Rowley St WSL WS1 5 G3
Rowley Vw BILS/COS WV14 54 C5
DARL/WED WS10 55 E4
WBROM B70 87 F3
Rowley Village
BLKHTH/ROWR B65 122 A1
Rowney Cft HLGN/YWD B28 179 G1
Rowood Dr HIA/OLT B92 165 E3
Rowthorn Cl FOAKS/STRLY B74 60 C1
Rowthorn Dr SHLY B90 195 G2
Rowton Av
DUNHL/THL/PER WV6 34 C2
Rowton Dr FOAKS/STRLY B74 60 B3
Roxall Cl KIDD DY10 168 C3
Roxburgh Gv GTB/HAM B43 59 G4
Roxburgh Rd SCFLD/BOLD B73 62 A5
Roxby Gdns
DUNHL/THL/PER WV6 22 C5
Royal Cl BLKHTH/ROWR B65 104 A4
BRLYHL DY5 119 E4
Royal Gv ERDW/GRVHL B23 75 H4
Royal Mail St CBHAMW B1 2 E6
Royal Oak Rd
BLKHTH/ROWR B65 103 F4
RMSLY B62 139 H3
Royal Rd CSCFLD/WYGN B72 62 C3
Royal Scot Gv WSL WS1 56 D3
Royal Star Cl STETCH B33 131 E2
Royal Wy TPTN/OCK DY4 85 G4
Roydon Rd ACGN B27 163 G2
Roylesden Crs
SCFLD/BOLD B73 76 A1
Royston Cha FOAKS/STRLY B74 45 G2
Royston Cft BHTH/HG B12 144 B1
Royston Wy SEDG DY3 67 E3
Rubens Cl SEDG DY3 83 F1
Rubery Farm Gv RBRY B45 173 H5
Rubery Field Cl RBRY B45 174 A4
Rubery La RBRY B45 173 H4
Rubery La South RBRY B45 173 H5
Rubery St DARL/WED WS10 40 B5
Ruckley Av LOZ/NWT B19 * 108 C2
Ruckley Rd SLYOAK B29 158 D2
Rudd Gdns WOLVN WV10 38 B1
Ruddington Wy LOZ/NWT B19 109 E4
Rudge Av WOLV WV1 38 B2
Rudge Cl SHHTH WV12 40 A1
Rudge Cft STETCH B33 112 C5
Rudge Wk WSNGN B18 * 126 A1
Rudgewick Cft AST/WIT B6 109 F3
Rudyard Cl WOLVN WV10 13 E3
Rudyard Gv STETCH B33 130 D1
Rudyngfield Dr STETCH B33 130 B1
Rufford Cl ERDW/GRVHL B23 76 B3
Rufford Rd HAG/WOL DY9 136 A3
Rufford St HAG/WOL DY9 136 B1
Rufford Wy ALDR WS9 29 G3
Rugby Rd STRBR DY8 117 H5
Rugby St WOLV WV1 6 C1
Rugeley Av SHHTH WV12 26 B2
Rugeley Cl TPTN/OCK DY4 85 E1
Ruislip Cl CVALE B35 94 C2
Ruiton St SEDG DY3 83 F2
Rumbow HALE B63 138 D3
Rumbow La RMSLY B62 171 H1
Rumbush La HOCK/TIA B94 193 H5
Runcorn Cl
CHWD/FDBR/MGN B37 114 C5
Runcorn Rd BHTH/HG B12 144 C2
Runnymede Rd SPARK B11 145 G4
Rupert St BDMR/CCFT WV3 6 A3
VAUX/NECH B7 109 G4
Rushall Cl RUSH/SHEL WS4 42 D1
STRBR DY8 118 A4
Rushall Manor Cl
RUSH/SHEL WS4 42 D1
Rushall Manor Rd
RUSH/SHEL WS4 42 D1
Rushall Rd WOLVN WV10 13 E5
Rushbrook Cl BRWNH WS8 19 E1
HIA/OLT B92 147 E5
Rushbrooke Cl MOS/BIL B13 144 B3
Rushbrooke Dr
SCFLD/BOLD B73 61 E4
Rushbrook Gv
ALE/KHTH/YWD B14 177 G2
Rushbury Cl BILS/COS WV14 53 F3
SHLY B90 180 D
Rushden Cft KGSTG B44 75 F2
Rushes Ml BLOX/PEL WS3 17 G4
Rushey La SPARK B11 146 A2
Rushford Av WMBN WV5 65 E5
Rushford Cl SHLY B90 195 G
Rush Gn RIDG/WDGT B32 141 E5
Rushleigh Rd SHLY B90 179 G5
Rushmead Gv RBRY B45 188 A
Rushmere Rd TPTN/OCK DY4 69 G3
Rushmoor Cl FOAKS/STRLY B74 62 B2
Rushwater Cl WMBN WV5 64 C
Rushwick Gv SHLY B90 195 G
Rushwood Cl RUSH/SHEL WS4 42 C
Rushy Piece RIDG/WDGT B32 140 D
Ruskin Av BLKHTH/ROWR B65 122 B
ETTPK/GDPK/PENN WV4 67 H
SEDG DY3 82 C
Ruskin Cl AST/WIT B6 109 F
Ruskin Gv ACGN B27 146 B
Ruskin Hall Gv AST/WIT B6 109 F
Ruskin Rd WOLVN WV10 23 H
Ruskin St HHTH/SAND B71 87 C
Russell Bank Rd
FOAKS/STRLY B74 46 C
Russell Cl OLDBY B69 86 E
TPTN/OCK DY4 70 A
WNSFLD WV11 25 F
Russell Rd BILS/COS WV14 54 E
HLGN/YWD B28 145 C
MOS/BIL B13 143 H
Russell's Hall Rd DUDN DY1 83 C
The Russells MOS/BIL B13 143 H
Russell St BDMR/CCFT WV3 6 D
DARL/WED WS10 70 D
DUDN DY1 84 E
WLNHL WV13 39
Russett Cl DSYBK/YTR WS5 43
Russett Wy BRLYHL DY5 100
Russet Wy NFLD/LBR B31 158
Ruston St LDYWD/EDGR B16 126
Ruthall Cl SLYOAK B29 159
Ruth Cl TPTN/OCK DY4 70
Rutherford Rd
ERDW/GRVHL B23 76
WSLW WS2 27
Rutland Av
ETTPK/GDPK/PENN WV4 50
Rutland Crs ALDR WS9 30
BILS/COS WV14 53
Rutland Dr
LGN/SDN/BHAMAIR B26 130
Rutland Pl STRBR DY8 117
Rutland Rd DARL/WED WS10 56
HHTH/SAND B71 71
SMTHWK B66 124
Rutland St BLOX/PEL WS3 28
Rutland Ter WSNGN B18 * 108
Rutley Gv RIDG/WDGT B32 141
Rutters Meadow
RIDG/WDGT B32 140
Rutter St WSL WS1 57
Ryan Av WNSFLD WV11 25

Ryan Pl DUDS DY2 .... 102 C3
Rycroft Gv STETCH B33 .... 131 E2
Rydal Cl FOAKS/STRLY B74 .... 45 F3
WNSFLD WV11 .... 24 C5
Rydal Dr DUNHL/THL/PER WV6 ... 34 D1
Rydding La HHTH/SAND B71 .... 71 G3
Rydding Sq HHTH/SAND B71 .... 71 F3
Ryde Gv ACGN B27 .... 163 E1
Ryde Park Rd RBRY B45 .... 188 C2
Ryders Green Rd WBROM B70 .... 86 C1
Ryders Hayes La
 BLOX/PEL WS3 .... 18 A3
Ryder St CBHAMNE B4 * 3 H3
 STRBR DY8 .... 117 H2
 WBROM B70 .... 86 D1
Ryebank Cl BVILLE B30 .... 159 E5
Ryeclose Cft
 CHWD/FDBR/MGN B37 .... 132 D1
Rye Cft ACGN B27 .... 162 A1
 HAG/WOL DY9 .... 136 C5
 HLYWD B47 .... 192 C3
Ryecroft Av
 ETTPK/GDPK/PENN WV4 .... 51 H3
Ryecroft Cl SEDG DY3 .... 67 E3
Ryecroft Pk WSLW WS2 .... 42 A2
Ryecroft Pl BLOX/PEL WS3 .... 28 B4
Ryecroft St WSLW WS2 .... 42 A2
Ryefield CDSL WV8 .... 22 A1
Ryefield Cl HAG/WOL DY9 .... 169 C1
 SOLH B91 .... 164 A5
Rye Grass Wk CVALE B35 .... 99 C3
Rye Gv SPARK B11 .... 145 H3
Ryknild Cl FOAKS/STRLY B74 .... 32 C4
Ryknild Dr FOAKS/STRLY B74 .... 60 C1
Ryland Cl HALE B63 .... 138 A5
 TPTN/OCK DY4 .... 85 H1
Ryland Rd EDG B15 .... 126 C5
 ERDE/BCHGN B24 .... 92 D5
 SPARK B11 .... 145 G4
Rylands Dr
 ETTPK/GDPK/PENN WV4 .... 51 G4
Ryland St LDYWD/EDGR B16 .... 2 A7
Ryle St BLOX/PEL WS3 .... 17 F5
Rymond Rd BKDE/SHDE B34 .... 112 A3
Ryton Cl SCFLD/BOLD B73 .... 62 B3
 WNSFLD WV11 .... 24 A5
Ryton Gv BKDE/SHDE B34 .... 113 F2

S

Sabell Rd SMTHWKW B67 .... 106 B3
Sabrina Dr
 DUNHL/THL/PER WV6 .... 34 C4
Saddlers Cl HALE B63 .... 137 F2
Saddlers Ms SOLH B91 .... 182 A4
The Saddlestones
 DUNHL/THL/PER WV6 .... 34 B1
Saddleworth Rd
 BLOX/PEL WS3 .... 16 C3
Sadler Gdns BRWNH WS8 .... 9 G4
Sadler Rd BRWNH WS8 .... 9 G4
Sadlers Ct WSLW WS2 .... 56 B1
Sadlers Mi BRWNH WS8 * 9 G5
Sadlers Wk LDYWD/EDGR B16 .... 126 A3
Saffron Gdns
 ETTPK/GDPK/PENN WV4 .... 51 G4
Sage Cft NFLD/LBR B31 .... 185 F1
St Agatha's Rd WASH/WDE B8 .... 111 F4
St Agnes Cl MOS/BIL B13 .... 144 D5
St Aidans Wk SMHTH B10 * 128 A4
St Albans Cl SMTHWKW B67 .... 106 A3
 WNSFLD WV11 .... 25 E1
St Albans Rd MOS/BIL B13 .... 144 C5
 SMTHWKW B67 .... 106 A3
St Alphege Cl SOLH B91 * 182 A2
St Ambrose Cl RMSLY B62 .... 121 H4
St Andrews Av BLOX/PEL WS3 .... 18 A2
St Andrews Cl
 DUNHL/THL/PER WV6 .... 36 C1
 RIDG/WDGT B32 .... 141 G4
 SEDG DY3 .... 82 C3
 STRBR DY8 .... 135 F5
St Andrews Dr
 DUNHL/THL/PER WV6 .... 34 B1
 OLDBY B69 .... 103 H2
St Andrew's Rd BORD B9 .... 127 H2
 MGN/WHC B75 .... 62 C1
St Andrew's St BORD B9 .... 127 H2
 DUDS DY2 .... 102 C4
Annes Ct
 BFLD/HDSWWD B20 .... 89 H2
Anne's Ct MOS/BIL B13 .... 144 A5
Annes Gv DOR/KN B93 .... 197 E2
Anne's Rd DUDS DY2 .... 120 C5
 WLNHL WS13 .... 39 H2
 WOLVN WV10 .... 22 D1
Annes Wy KGSTG B44 .... 75 C4
Anthonys Dr BLOX/PEL WS3 .... 18 B2
Athan Cft CVALE B35 .... 94 D3
Augustine's Rd
 LDYWD/EDGR B16 .... 125 F3
Augustus Cl WBROM B70 .... 88 B4
Austell Rd DSYBR/YTR WS5 .... 58 B1
Bartholomew Ter
 DARL/WED WED10 .... 55 H5
Benedict's Cl WBROM B70 .... 88 B4
Benedicts Rd SMHTH B10 .... 128 D4
nt Benedicts Rd WMBN WV5 ..... 65 E4
Bernards Rd
 CSCFLD/WYGN B72 .... 77 C1
 HIA/OLT B92 .... 163 H5
Blaise Av CSHL/WTROR B46 .... 96 C4
Blaise Rd MGN/WHC B75 .... 62 C5
Brades Cl OLDBY B69 .... 104 A2
Brides Cl SEDG DY3 .... 67 E3
WMBN WV5 .... 64 D5
ntbury Dr SOLH B91 .... 196 A1
Caroline Cl WBROM B70 .... 88 B4
Benedicts Rd SMHTH B10 .... 93 C1
atherines Cl WSL WS1 * 85 C5
atherines Cl DUDS DY2 * 85 C5
MGN/WHC B75 .... 63 F1
Catherine's Crs
 ETTPK/GDPK/PENN WV4 .... 51 F4
had's Circ CBHAMNW B3 * 3 D3
had's Cl SEDG DY3 .... 82 D3

St Chads Queensway
 CBHAMNE B4 .... 3 G2
St Chads Rd BILS/COS WV14 .... 54 B1
St Loye's Cl RMSLY B62 .... 122 B5
St Lukes Cl
 CHWD/FDBR/MGN B37 .... 132 A5
 BLKHTH/ROWR B65 .... 103 H5
St Lukes Rd DARL/WED WS10 .... 56 B5
Saint Lukes Rd
 DARL/WED WS10 .... 71 E1
St Luke's St DIG/EDG B5 .... 127 E5
St Lukes St CDYHTH B64 .... 120 D3
St Margaret's FOAKS/STRLY B74 .. 46 A2
St Margarets Av
 WASH/WDE B8 .... 111 F3
St Margarets Dr HALE B63 .... 138 B5
St Margarets Rd BLOX/PEL WS3 .. 17 H5
 CTB/HAM B43 .... 73 H1
 HIA/OLT B92 .... 162 A1
 WASH/WDE B8 .... 111 E3
St Marks Crs CBHAMW B1 .... 126 A1
St Mark's Rd BDMR/CCFT WV3 .... 6 C5
 BLOX/PEL WS3 .... 18 A3
 BRWNH WS8 .... 9 C4
 DUDS DY2 .... 85 F5
 HAG/WOL DY9 .... 136 B2
 SMTHWKW B67 .... 123 H1
 TPTN/OCK DY4 .... 69 G3
St Mark's St BDMR/CCFT WV3 ...... 6 D5
 CBHAMW B1 .... 88 B4
 WBROM B70 .... 88 B4
St Martin's Cl BKHL/PFLD WV2 .. 52 C2
 St Martin's Dr TPTN/OCK DY4 ... 85 G1
St Martin's Queensway (Below)
 .... 3 G6
St Martins Rd MGN/WHC B75 ... 46 B5
St Martin's St EDG B15 .... 126 B3
St Martin's Ter BILS/COS WV14 .. 54 A5
St Martins Ter
 ERDE/BCHGN B24 .... 146 B4
 SEDG DY3 .... 93 H2
St Marys Cl WLNHL WV13 * 39 C3
St Mary's La STRBR DY8 .... 135 H4
St Marys Rd DARL/WED WS10 .... 55 H5
 HRBN B17 .... 142 B2
St Mary's Rw CBHAMNE B4 .... 3 C3
St Marys Vw ERDW/CRVHL B23 .. 76 B3
St Mary's Wy WALM/CURD B76 .. 30 A5
St Matthews Cl
 BLOX/PEL WS3 * 18 B2
 WSL WS1 .... 5 F5
Saint Matthews Rd
 LGLYCN/QTN B68 .... 123 E2
St Matthews Rd SMTHWK B66 .. 107 E4
St Mawes Rd
 DUNHL/THL/PER WV6 .... 34 D2
St Mawgan Cl CVALE B35 .... 95 E2
St Michael's Cl BLOX/PEL WS3 .. 17 H5
St Michael's Cr
 DUNHL/THL/PER WV6 .... 22 A5
St Michael's Crs OLDBY B69 ...... 104 D5
St Michael's Rd
 SCFLD/BOLD B73 .... 76 D3
 SEDG DY3 .... 80 D2
 WSNGN B18 .... 108 A2
St Michael St WSL WS1 .... 4 E7
St Michael St West
 WBROM B70 .... 87 G3
St Michaels Wy TPTN/OCK DY4 .. 85 C3
St Nicholas Cl BLOX/PEL WS3 ... 18 A3
St Nicolas Gdns
 HWK/WKHTH B38 .... 176 D3
St Oswalds Rd SMHTH B10 .... 128 C4
St Patricks Cl
 ALE/KHTH/YWD B14 .... 161 E4
St Paul's Av BHTH/HG B12 .... 144 C2
St Pauls Crs BLOX/PEL WS3 .... 18 B2
 CSHL/WTROR B46 .... 115 C2
 WBROM B70 .... 70 C4
St Pauls Dr RMSLY B62 .... 122 B3
 TPTN/OCK DY4 .... 85 H2
St Paul's Rd BHTH/HG B12 .... 144 B1
 DARL/WED WS10 .... 56 B5
 DUDS DY2 .... 102 D4
 SMTHWK B66 .... 106 D5
St Paul's Sq CBHAMNW B3 .... 3 E3
St Paul's St WSL WS1 .... 4 E3
St Peters Cl CSCFLD/WYGN B72 .. 62 B5
 CSHL/WTROR B46 .... 96 B4
Saint Peters Cft
 HLGN/YWD B28 .... 162 B4
St Peters Cl TPTN/OCK DY4 .... 86 B2
St Peters La BLOX/PEL WS3 .... 27 F1
St Peters Crt
 SCFLD/BOLD B73 * 62 B5
St Peters La HIA/OLT B92 .... 166 D2
St Peter's Rd
 BFLD/HDSWWD B20 .... 90 C5
 DUDS DY2 .... 102 D4
 HAG/WOL DY9 .... 153 H1
 SMTHWK B66 .... 141 H2
St Peters Sq WLNHL WV1 .... 7 F3
St Peters Ter WSL WS1 .... 5 H1
St Philips Av BDMR/CCFT WV3 .. 51 F1
St Philips Gv BDMR/CCFT WV3 .. 51 F1
St Quentin St WSLW WS2 .... 41 G5
St Saviour's Cl BKHL/PFLD WV2 .. 52 D2
St Saviour's Rd WASH/WDE B8 .. 128 C1
St Silas' Sq LOZ/NWT B19 .... 108 B2
St Simons Cl MGN/WHC B75 ...... 63 F2
St Stephens Gdns
 WLNHL WV13 .... 39 F3
St Stephens Rd
 HHTH/SAND B71 .... 106 D1
 SLYOAK B29 .... 160 B2
St Thomas' St ALDR WS9 .... 30 B1
 BLOX/PEL WS3 .... 28 A4
 MGN/WHC B75 .... 63 F3
St Thomas' Rd
 ERDW/CRVHL B23 .... 92 B4
St Thomas St DUDS DY2 .... 102 C4
St Valentines Cl WBROM B70 .... 88 B4
St Vincent Crs WBROM B70 .... 70 D5
St Vincent St LDYWD/EDGR B16 .. 2 A5

St Vincent St West
 LDYWD/EDGR B16 .... 126 A2
Saladin Av OLDBY B69 .... 104 C4
Salcombe Av
 LGN/SDN/BHAMAIR B26 .... 130 B1
Salcombe Dr BRLYHL DY5 .... 119 E4
Salcombe Gv BILS/COS WV14 ..... 68 D2
Salcombe Rd SMTHWK B66 .... 106 D4
Salem St TPTN/OCK DY4 .... 86 B1
Salford St AST/WIT B6 .... 110 A1
Salisbury Chambers
 MOS/BIL B13 * 144 B3
Salisbury Cl DUDN DY1 .... 83 H3
 MOS/BIL B13 .... 144 B3
Salisbury Dr CSHL/WTROR B46 .. 96 C3
Salisbury Gv
 CSCFLD/WYGN B72 .... 77 G4
Salisbury Rd LOZ/NWT B19 .... 108 D1
 MOS/BIL B13 .... 144 A4
 SMTHWK B66 .... 106 D5
 WASH/WDE B8 .... 110 C4
 WBROM B70 .... 88 A5
Salisbury St BDMR/CCFT WV3 ...... 6 C6
 DARL/WED WS10 .... 55 G1
Sally Ward Dr ALDR WS9 .... 19 G3
Salop Cl HHTH/SAND B71 .... 87 G4
Salop Dr LGLYCN/QTN B68 .... 123 G2
Salop Rd LGLYCN/QTN B68 .... 123 G1
 OLDBY B69 .... 104 C5
Salop St BHTH/HG B12 .... 127 H5
 BILS/COS WV14 .... 54 A4
 DUDN DY1 .... 84 C5
 WOLV WV1 .... 6 E5
Salstar Cl AST/WIT B6 .... 109 E3
Saltash Gv YDLY B25 .... 129 G5
Saltbrook Rd HALE B63 .... 120 A3
Salter Rd TPTN/OCK DY4 .... 69 F4
Salter's La HHTH/SAND B71 .... 88 B2
Salters Rd ALDR WS9 .... 19 C4
Salters V WBROM B70 .... 88 A5
Saltley Cottages
 ERDE/BCHGN B24 * 110 D1
Saltley Rd VAUX/NECH B7 .... 110 H4
Saltley Vaid VAUX/NECH B7 .... 110 A4
Saltney Cl ERDE/BCHGN B24 .... 93 H1
Saltwells La BRLYHL DY5 .... 120 A2
Saltwells Rd DUDS DY2 .... 120 B2
Salwarpe Gv SLYOAK B29 .... 159 F2
Sambourn Cl SOLH B91 .... 165 G4
Sambourne Dr
 BKDE/SHDE B34 .... 113 F2
Sampson Cl OLDBY B69 .... 89 E5
 SMHTH B10 .... 104 A2
Sampson Cl HDSW B21 .... 127 H5
Sampson Rd North
 SPARK B11 .... 127 G4
Sampson St West SPARK B11 ..... 127 G4
Sampson St DARL/WED WS10 ..... 56 D5
Sams La WBROM B70 .... 87 G4
Samuels Rd RIDG/WDGT B32 .... 140 A2
Samuel Rd BLOX/PEL WS3 .... 27 F1
Sanda Cft CBROM B36 .... 114 B3
Sandal Ri SOLH B91 .... 182 D4
Sandal St SPARK B11 .... 127 G5
Sandals Ri RMSLY B62 .... 139 F4
Sandalwood Cl SHHTH WV12 ..... 25 H2
Sand Bank BLOX/PEL WS3 .... 27 F1
Sandbeds Rd SHLY B90 .... 195 F2
Sandbourne Rd
 WASH/WDE B8 .... 111 G5
Sanderling Ri KGSWFD DY6 ...... 100 C3
Sanders Cl DUDS DY2 .... 103 E2
Sanders Crs TPTN/OCK DY4 .... 86 A2
Sandfield Bl BRLYHL DY5 .... 82 D5
Sandfield Gv SEDG DY3 .... 82 D4
Sandfield Rd HHTH/SAND B71 .. 72 A2
 STRBR DY8 .... 118 B2
Sandfields Rd
 LGLYCN/QTN B68 .... 123 G2
Sandford Av
 BLKHTH/ROWR B65 .... 122 A1
Sandford Ri
 DUNHL/THL/PER WV6 .... 22 A4
Sandford Rd DUDN DY1 .... 83 G5
 MOS/BIL B13 .... 144 C4
Sandgate Rd HLGN/YWD B28 ... 179 H1
 TPTN/OCK DY4 .... 69 G2
Sandhills La HLGN/YWD B28 ..... 181 H5
Sandhill St BLOX/PEL WS3 .... 27 E1
Sandhurst Av CBROM B36 .... 111 H3
 HAG/WOL DY9 .... 136 B5
Sandhurst Rd
 FOAKS/STRLY B74 .... 32 D5
 KGSWFD DY6 .... 100 C5
 MOS/BIL B13 .... 144 A5
Sandland Cl BILS/COS WV14 ...... 54 B2
Sandland Rd SHHTH WV12 .... 26 A2
Sandmartin Cl DUDS DY2 .... 120 C2
Sandmeadow Pl KGSWFD DY6 ... 99 G4
Sandmere Gv
 ALE/KHTH/YWD B14 .... 179 F2
Sandmere Rd WOLVN WV10 ...... 23 G1
Sandon Gv ERDE/BCHGN B24 .... 93 E2
Sandon Rd HAG/WOL DY9 .... 136 B5
 HRBN B17 .... 124 D3
 SMTHWK B66 .... 124 A2
 WOLVN WV10 .... 23 G1
Sandown Dr
 DUNHL/THL/PER WV6 .... 34 D1
Sandown Rd CBROM B36 .... 111 H1
Sandpiper Cl HAG/WOL DY9 ..... 136 D2
Sandpiper Gdns
 HWK/WKHTH B38 .... 190 D1
Sandpiper Wy
 ERDW/CRVHL B23 .... 76 A5
Sand Pits Pde CBHAMW B1 .... 2 B4
The Sandpits BVILLE B30 .... 159 G2
Sandra Cl ALDR WS9 .... 31 E1
Sandringham Av SHHTH WV12 .. 25 H4
Sandringham Dr ALDR WS9 .... 30 B1

 BLKHTH/ROWR B65 .... 104 A5
Sandringham Pl STRBR DY8 ...... 117 H3
Sandringham Rd
 ETTPK/GDPK/PENN WV4 .... 51 G4
 PBAR/PBCH B42 .... 74 B3
 RMSLY B62 .... 121 H5
 STRBR DY8 .... 117 G3
 WMBN WV5 .... 64 D5
Sandringham Wy BRLYHL DY5 ... 119 E4
Sandstone Av RBRY B45 .... 174 A5
Sandstone Cl SEDG DY3 .... 66 D3
Sand St WBROM B70 .... 86 C2
Sandway Gdns WASH/WDE B8 .. 110 B3
Sandway Gv MOS/BIL B13 .... 162 A3
Sandwell Av DARL/WED WS10 ... 54 C5
Sandwell Pl SHHTH WV12 .... 26 B5
Sandwell Rd HDSW B21 .... 89 F5
 WBROM B70 .... 87 G2
 WOLV WV10 .... 22 D1
Sandwell Rd North
 HHTH/SAND B71 .... 87 H2
Sandwell St WSL WS1 .... 5 F6
Sandwell Wk WSL WS1 .... 5 F7
Sandwood Dr KGSTG B44 .... 74 D3
Sandyacre Wy STRBR DY8 .... 135 H2
Sandy Crs WNSFLD WV11 .... 25 F2
Sandy Cft CSCFLD/WYGN B72 .. 62 C5
 MOS/BIL B13 .... 162 A3
Sandyfields Rd SEDG DY3 .... 82 B1
Sandy Hill Gv SHLY B90 .... 194 C3
Sandy Hill Ri SHLY B90 .... 180 A1
Sandy Hill Rd SHLY B90 .... 180 A1
Sandy Hollow
 DUNHL/THL/PER WV6 .... 35 G3
Sandy La AST/WIT B6 .... 109 G2
 BRGRVW B61 .... 186 B5
 CDSL WV8 .... 10 B5
 DSYBR/YTR WS5 .... 57 E4
 DUNHL/THL/PER WV6 .... 22 A4
 PBAR/PBCH B42 .... 74 D3
 WOLVN WV10 .... 12 D5
Sandy wth WMBN WV5 .... 65 F4
Sandys Gv TPTN/OCK DY4 .... 85 E1
Sandy Wy EDG B15 .... 2 C7
Sangwin Rd BILS/COS WV14 ..... 68 C4
Sansome Ri SHLY B90 .... 179 H5
Sansome Rd SHLY B90 .... 179 H5
Sanstone Cl BLOX/PEL WS3 .... 17 E4
Sanstone Rd BLOX/PEL WS3 ...... 16 D4
Santolina Dr DSYBR/YTR WS5 .. 105 G3
Sant Rd NFLD/LBR B31 .... 189 H1
The Saplings WALM/CURD B76 ... 78 C3
Saracen Dr MGN/WHC B75 .... 63 F2
Sara Cl FOAKS/STRLY B74 .... 47 E2
Sarah Cl BILS/COS WV14 .... 69 E2
Sarah Gdns DSYBR/YTR WS5 ...... 57 F4
Sarah St BORD B9 .... 127 H2
Saredon Cl BLOX/PEL WS3 .... 28 C1
Sarehole Rd HLGN/YWD B28 .... 162 C2
Sargent Cl CTB/HAM B43 .... 59 H4
Sark Dr CBROM B36 .... 114 B4
Saunton Wy SLYOAK B29 .... 159 E1
Saveker Dr WALM/CURD B76 .... 63 E4
Savernake Cl RBRY B45 .... 174 A3
Saville Cl RBRY B45 .... 188 B1
Savoy Cl RIDG/WDGT B32 .... 141 F2
Saw Mill Cl RUSH/SHEL WS4 .... 4 E1
Saxelby Cl
 ALE/KHTH/YWD B14 .... 178 A3
Saxoncourt
 DUNHL/THL/PER WV6 .... 21 G5
Saxondale Av
 LGN/SDN/BHAMAIR B26 .... 147 F1
Saxon Dr BLKHTH/ROWR B65 .. 104 A5
Saxonfields
 DUNHL/THL/PER WV6 .... 21 G5
Saxons Wy
 ALE/KHTH/YWD B14 .... 178 C3
Saxon Wy
 CHWD/FDBR/MGN B37 .... 131 H1
Saxon Wood Cl NFLD/LBR B31 . 175 G1
Saxon Wood Rd SHLY B90 .... 194 D3
Saxton Dr FOAKS/STRLY B74 ...... 32 C4
Scafell Dr BILS/COS WV14 .... 54 B1
 ERDW/CRVHL B23 .... 92 A1
Scafell Rd STRBR DY8 .... 135 H1
Scampton Cl
 DUNHL/THL/PER WV6 .... 20 C5
Scarborough Cl WSLW WS2 .... 41 F5
Scarborough Rd WSLW WS2 .... 41 G5
Scarecrow La MGN/WHC B75 ...... 48 A1
Scarsdale Rd PBAR/PBCH B42 .... 74 D3
Schofield Av HHTH/SAND B71 .... 71 F3
Schofield Rd
 CHWD/FDBR/MGN B37 .... 113 H4
Scholars Ga STETCH B33 .... 130 D2
Scholars Rd HDSW B21 .... 107 F3
Schoolacre Ri
 FOAKS/STRLY B74 .... 45 E4
Schoolacre Rd
 BKDE/SHDE B34 .... 112 D5
School Av BRWNH WS8 .... 9 E3
School Cl BDMR/CCFT WV3 .... 50 C5
 CDSL WV8 .... 10 C5
 CHWD/FDBR/MGN B37 .... 114 A3
 CVALE B35 .... 94 D3
 OLDBY B69 .... 104 A2
 WMBN WV5 .... 64 A2
School Cottages
 WOLVN WV10 .... 12 B5
School Dr BILS/COS WV14 * 68 C2
 BKDE/SHDE B34 .... 113 C4
 HLYWD B47 .... 192 C5
 STRBR DY8 .... 118 B4
The School Dr DUDS DY2 .... 102 D2
 WASH/WDE B8 .... 111 E3
School Gn BILS/COS WV14 .... 54 A5
Schoolhouse Cl
 HWK/WKHTH B38 .... 177 F3
School La BKDE/SHDE B34 .... 112 D2
 BLOX/PEL WS3 .... 17 H5
 BRLYHL DY5 .... 100 D5
 HAG/WOL DY9 .... 153 H4
 HALE B63 .... 138 B5
 SOLH B91 .... 182 B1
 STETCH B33 .... 130 B3
 WOLVN WV10 .... 12 D5

School Rd
BRLYHL DY5......120 A2
DARL/WED B71......11 H4
CDYHTH/THL/PER WV6......35 E1
HLGN/YWD B28......162 D2
MOS/BIL B13......161 F1
RBRY B45......187 G2
SEDG DY3......81 F3
SHLY B90......180 B3
WMBN WV5......64 A2
WNSFLD WV11......24 C4
School St BDMR/CCFT WV3......6 E6
BRLYHL DY5......101 F2
CDYHTH B64......120 D3
DARL/WED WS10......55 F3
DUDN DY1......84 B5
RUSH/SHEL WS4......29 F1
SEDG DY3......67 G3
WLNHL WV13......39 F3
School St West BILS/COS WV14......58 C3
School Wk BILS/COS WV14......38 C5
Scorers Cl SHLY B90......
The Scotchings CBROM B36......112 A1
Scotland La RIDG/WDGT B32......157 G3
Scotland St CBHAMW B1......2 C4
Scott Av WAL/WED WS10......71 F1
Scott Cl WAL/CURD B76......
 ETTPK/GDPK/PENN WV4......51 E4
Scott Rd DSYBK/YTR WS5......58 B2
 GTB/HAM B43......73 H1
 HIA/OLT B92......147 E5
Scott's Green Cl DUDN DY1......101 H1
Scott's Rd STRBR DY8......135 F1
Scott St TPTN/OCK DY4......86 A1
Scotwell Cl
 BLKHTH/ROWR B65......121 H1
Scout Cl STETCH B33......131 E2
Scribbans Cl SMTHWK B66......106 D5
Scribers La HLGN/YWD B28......179 G1
Scribers Meadow
 HLGN/YWD B28......179 G1
Sculthorpe La KIDD DY10......168 B3
Seacroft Av YDLY B25......160 A4
Seafield Cl KGSWFD DY6......100 A5
Seaforth Gv SHHTH WV12......25 H1
Seagar St WHTH/SAND B71......87 H2
Seager's La BRLYHL DY5......119 F2
Seagull Bay Dr BILS/COS WV14......62 A5
Seal Cl WALM/CURD B76......63 E5
Seals Gn HWK/WKHTH B38......190 B1
Seamless Dr WNSFLD WV11......38 D1
Seaton Cl WNSFLD WV11......25 H5
Seaton Gv MOS/BIL B13......160 D1
Seaton Pl STRBR DY8......117 G2
Seaton Rd SMTHWK B66......106 D4
Second Av BORD B9......128 C3
 BRWNH WS8......9 G4
 KGSWFD DY6......100 C2
 SLYOAK B29......143 F4
 WOLVN WV10......23 H4
Second Exhibition Av
 BHAMNEC B40......149 H3
Sedge Av HWK/WKHTH B38......176 D2
Sedgeberrow Covert
 HWK/WKHTH B38......176 C5
Sedgeberrow Rd HALE B63......138 C1
Sedgeborne Wy
 NFLD/LBR B31......
Sedgefield Cl DUDN DY1......83 C3
Sedgefield Gv
 DUNHL/THL/PER WV6......34 D1
Sedgeford Cl BRLYHL DY5......119 F4
Sedgehill Av HRBN B17......141 H5
Sedgemere Gv RUSH/SHEL WS4......29 E2
Sedgemere Rd
 LGN/SDN/BHAMAIR B26......130 B3
Sedgley Gv BFLD/HDSWWD B20......89 G2
Sedgley Hall Av SEDG DY3......67 E3
Sedgley Rd
 ETTPK/GDPK/PENN WV4......66 B1
Sedgley Rd East TPTN/OCK DY4......85 G2
Sedgley Rd West
 TPTN/OCK DY4......68 C5
Sedgley St BKHL/PFLD WV2......52 A1
Seedhouse Ct COYHTH B64......121 G4
Seeds La BRWNH WS8......9 F4
Seeleys Rd SPARK B11......145 G2
Sefton Dr BLKHTH/ROWR B65......103 F5
Sefton Gv TPTN/OCK DY4......
Segbourne Rd RBRY B45......175 G5
Segundo Cl DSYBK/YTR WS5......57 E4
Segundo Rd DSYBK/YTR WS5......57 F4
Selborne Cl WSL WS1......5 H4
Selborne Gv MOS/BIL B13......162 A5
Selborne Rd
 BFLD/HDSWWD B20......90 A4
 DUDS DY2......102 D2
Selborne St WSL WS1......5 H4
Selbourne Crs WOLVN WV1......38 B4
Selby Cl
 LGN/SDN/BHAMAIR B26......130 B3
Selby Gv MOS/BIL B13......162 A5
Selby Wy BLOX/PEL WS3......16 A5
Selcombe Wy
 HWK/WKHTH B38......190 D1
Selco Wy WALM/CURD B76......94 C1
Selcroft Av RIDG/WDGT B32......141 F2
Selecta Av KGSTG B44......74 D1
Selkirk Cl WHTH/SAND B71......71 G5
Selly Av SLYOAK B29......143 F5
Selly Cl SLYOAK B29......143 F5
Selly Hall Cft BVILLE B30......159 H4
Selly Hill Rd SLYOAK B29......142 D5
Selly Oak Rd BVILLE B30......159 G5
Selly Park Rd SLYOAK B29......143 G5
Selly St SLYOAK B29......159 G1
Selly Wick Dr SLYOAK B29......143 F5
Selly Wick Rd SLYOAK B29......143 E5
Sellywood Rd BVILLE B30......159 G5
Selma Gv ALE/KHTH/YWD B14......161 H1
Selmans Hl BLOX/PEL WS3......17 E4
Selmans Pde BLOX/PEL WS3......17 E5
Selsdon Cl HLYWD B47......193 E3
Selsdon Rd BLOX/PEL WS3......16 B4
Selsey Av HRBN B17......124 D1
Selsey Rd HRBN B17......124 D1

Selston Rd AST/WIT B6......109 E2
Selvey Av GTB/HAM B43......59 F5
Selworthy Rd CBROM B36......115 H2
Selwyn Cl BKHL/PFLD WV2......52 A1
Selwyn Rd BILS/COS WV14......54 B2
 LDYWD/EDGR B16......125 F1
Selwyn Wk FOAKS/STRLY B74......46 A1
Sennelays Park Rd
 NFLD/LBR B31......158 B1
Senneth Cl WLNHL WV13......39 F4
Sensall Rd HAG/WOL DY9......136 D4
Sentry Wy MGN/WHC B75......63 G2
Serpentine Rd AST/WIT B6......91 C5
 BRWNH B17......142 A2
 SLYOAK B29......143 E4
Settle Av BKDE/SHDE B34......112 B3
Settle Cft
 CHWD/FDBR/MGN B37......131 H3
Setton Dr SEDG DY3......67 G2
Seven Acres Av......30 B5
Seven Acres Rd NFLD/LBR B31......176 A4
 RMSLY B62......140 A2
Sevendwellings Vw......119 E3
Seven Star Rd SOLH B91......164 D5
Seven Stars Rd OLDBY B69......105 G2
Severn Cl CBROM B36......113 H2
 SHHTH WV12......85 F1
Severn Dr BRLYHL DY5......100 D2
 DUNHL/THL/PER WV6......34 C1
Severne Gv ACGN B27......163 G1
Severne Rd ACGN B27......165 G2
Severn Gv LOZ/NWT B19......108 C2
 SPARK B11......145 E1
Severn Rd BLOX/PEL WS3......27 H2
 BRWNH WS8......9 H4
 HALE B63......137 F2
 STRBR DY8......135 F4
Severn St CBHAMW B1......2 D6
Sevington Cl SOLH B91......182 A5
Seymour Cl SLYOAK B29......143 F5
Seymour Gdns
 FOAKS/STRLY B74......46 C3
Seymour Rd HAG/WOL DY9......136 D2
 OLDBY B69......105 G2
 TPTN/OCK DY4......70 A2
Seymour St DIG/EDG B5......3 J5
Shackleton Dr
 DUNHL/THL/PER WV6......20 B5
Shackleton Rd BLOX/PEL WS3......17 F5
Shadowbrook La HIA/OLT B92......166 D3
Shadwell Dr SEDG DY3......83 F4
Shadwell St CBHAMNE B4......2 E3
Shady La KGSTG B44......74 D1
Shadymoor Dr BRLYHL DY5......119 E4
Shaftesbury Av HAG/WOL DY9......136 A4
Shaftesbury Rd
 DARL/WED WS10......71 F1
Shaftesbury Sq......87 G1
Shaftesbury St
 HHTH/SAND B71......87 G2
Shaftmoor La HLGN/YWD B28......145 G5
Shaftsbury Cl HALE B63......120 B5
Shaftsbury Cl BILS/COS WV14......54 B1
Shaftsbury Rd
 LGN/SDN/BHAMAIR B26......148 A2
Shahjalal Rd WASH/WDE B8......110 B4
Shakespeare Cl BILS/COS WV14......68 D1
Shakespeare Dr
 BLOX/PEL WS3......28 A2
Shakespeare Dr SHLY B90......180 B4
Shakespeare Pl BLOX/PEL WS3......28 A3
Shakespeare Rd
 ERDW/GRVHL B23......91 H5
 SEDG DY3......82 C2
 SHLY B90......180 D4
 SMTHWKW B67......105 H5
 TPTN/OCK DY4......69 G5
Shakespeare St SPARK B11......145 E2
 WOLV WV1......7 F6
Shaldon Wk SMTHWK B66......106 D4
The Shales WMBN WV5 *......80 C1
Shale Ct BILS/COS WV14......53 G3
Shalford Rd HIA/OLT B92......147 E3
Shallcross La SEDG DY3......83 F3
Shalnecote Gv
 ALE/KHTH/YWD B14......160 C5
Shambles DARL/WED WS10......70 D1
Shandon Cl RIDG/WDGT B32......141 F4
Shannon Dr BRWNH WS8......9 E2
Shannon Rd HWK/WKHTH B38......190 C1
Shapinsay Dr RBRY B45......173 H4
Shard End Crs
 BKDE/SHDE B34......113 E4
Shardlow Rd WNSFLD WV11......25 E2
The Shardway
 BKDE/SHDE B34......113 E4
Sharesacre St WLNHL WV13......39 H2
Sharington Cl DUDS DY2......103 E1
Sharman Rd WOLVN WV10......23 G4
Sharmans Cross Rd SOLH B91......181 F1
Sharon Cl
 ETTPK/GDPK/PENN WV4......52 C3
Sharps Cl RBRY B45......188 A1
Sharrat Fld MGN/WHC B75......47 H3
Sharrocks St WOLV WV1......7 J6
Shawberry Av CVALE B35......94 D3
Shawberry Rd
 CHWD/FDBR/MGN B37 *......113 H4
Shawbrook Cl
 ALE/KHTH/YWD B14......178 C2
Shawbury Gv BHTH/HG B12......127 H1
 DUNHL/THL/PER WV6......20 C5
Shawbury Rd WOLVN WV10......20 C5
Shawfield HLYWD B47......192 C3
Shawhellier Av BRLYHL DY5......119 G2
Shaw Hill Rd WASH/WDE B8......111 E5
Shawhurst Cft HLYWD B47......192 C1
Shawhurst Gdns HLYWD B47......192 C1
Shawhurst La HLYWD B47......192 C2
Shaw La DUNHL/THL/PER WV6......35 F2
Shawley Cft ACGN B27......147 E3
Shaw Rd BILS/COS WV14......54 A3
 BKHL/PFLD WV2......52 A2
 DUDS DY2......102 D2
 TPTN/OCK DY4......86 A2
 WOLVN WV10......23 F4

Shawsdale Rd CBROM B36......112 B2
Shaw's Pas DIG/EDG B5......3 J5
Shaw St WBROM B70......70 C3
 WSLW WS2......4 D3
Shayler Gv BKHL/PFLD WV2......52 B1
Sheaf La
 LGN/SDN/BHAMAIR B26......147 H3
Shearers Pl MGN/WHC B75......48 A2
Shearwater Cl RBRY B45......187 H2
Shearwater Wk
 ERDW/GRVHL B23......75 H5
 BILS/COS WV14......53 E5
Shedden St DUDS DY2......102 D1
Sheddington Rd
 ERDW/GRVHL B23......76 B4
Sheen Rd KGSTG B44......60 A4
Sheepclose Dr
 CHWD/FDBR/MGN B37......132 A1
Sheepcote St LDYWD/EDGR B16......2 A5
Sheepfold Cl
 BLKHTH/ROWR B65......103 G5
Sheepmoor Dr HRBN B17......124 B4
Sheepwash La TPTN/OCK DY4......86 B3
Sheepwater Dr BRLYHL DY5......119 E5
Sheffield Rd SCFLD/BOLD B73......77 E4
Sheffield St BRLYHL DY5......120 A3
Shefford Rd AST/WIT B6......108 B5
Sheila Av WNSFLD WV11......25 E5
Shelah Rd HALE B63......138 C1
Shelbourne Av DARL/WED WS10......56 A4
Sheldon Cl BILS/COS WV14......53 H5
Sheldon Dr NFLD/LBR B31......174 D4
Sheldonfield Rd
 LGN/SDN/BHAMAIR B26......148 B3
Sheldon Gv
 LGN/SDN/BHAMAIR B26......147 H2
Sheldon Hall Av STETCH B33......131 F1
Sheldon Heath Rd
 LGN/SDN/BHAMAIR B26......130 C2
 WOLVN WV10......22 C1
Shelfield Cl HOCK/TIA B24......198 A5
Shelfield Rd
 ALE/KHTH/YWD B14......177 G2
Shelley Av TPTN/OCK DY4......69 G5
Shelley Cl SEDG DY3......82 C1
 STRBR DY8......118 C4
Shelley Dr ERDW/GRVHL B23......91 H5
 FOAKS/STRLY B74......32 D4
Shelley Rd SHHTH WV12......25 H1
 WOLVN WV10......12 D5
Shelly Cl
 CHWD/FDBR/MGN B37......131 H2
Shelly Crs SHLY B90......195 H2
Shelly Cft STETCH B33......130 C1
Shelly La SHLY B90......195 H2
Shelsley Av OLDBY B69......104 B4
Shelsley Dr MOS/BIL B13......161 H1
Shelsley Wy SOLH B91......181 H4
Shelton Cl DARL/WED WS10......56 D1
Shelton La HALE B63......138 A2
Shelwick Gv DOR/KN B93......196 D4
Shenley Av DUDN DY1......84 B5
Shenley Fields Dr
 NFLD/LBR B31......158 A2
Shenley Fields Rd SLYOAK B29......158 B3
Shenley Gdns SLYOAK B29......158 C4
Shenley Hl NFLD/LBR B31......158 B3
Shenley La NFLD/LBR B31......158 B3
Shenstone Av RMSLY B62......139 G3
 HALE B63......138 C1
Shenstone Cl BDMR/CCFT WV3 *......51 G2
Shenstone Dr ALDR WS9......30 A2
Shenstone Rd
 ALE/KHTH/YWD B14......178 C4
 GTB/HAM B43......73 G3
 LDYWD/EDGR B16......125 E1
Shenstone Valley Rd
 RMSLY B62......139 H1
Shenton Wk
 CHWD/FDBR/MGN B37......113 H4
Shephearad Rd
 LGN/SDN/BHAMAIR B26......148 B2
Shepherd Dr SHHTH WV12......25 H5
Shepherds Brook Rd
 HAG/WOL DY9......136 B2
Shepherds Fold
 BLKHTH/ROWR B65......121 H2
Shepherds Gdns EDG B15......126 B3
Shepherds Green Rd
 ERDE/BCHGN B24......92 D4
Shepherds Pool Rd
 MGN/WHC B75......48 A3
Shepherds Standing
 BKDE/SHDE B34......112 D3
Shepherds Wy
 ERDW/GRVHL B23......76 A3
Shepley Rd RBRY B45......188 B2
Sheppey Dr CBROM B36......114 B4
Shepwell Gn WLNHL WV13......40 A4
Sherard Cl CBROM B36......114 B3
Sheraton Cl ALDR WS9......30 B4
Sheraton Gra STRBR DY8......135 H5
Sherborne Cl BLOX/PEL WS3......27 G5
 CSHL/WTROR B46......115 G5
Sherborne Gdns WOLVN WV10......10 C4
Sherborne Gv CBHAMW B1......2 A3
Sherborne Rd WOLVN WV10......23 F1
Sherborne St LDYWD/EDGR B16......2 A4
Sherbourne Rd ACGN B27......146 C3
 ACGN B27......146 B3
 BHTH/HG B12......144 B1
 CDYHTH B64......121 G4
Sherbourne Rd East
 BHTH/HG B12......144 C1
Sherdmore Cft SHLY B90......195 F2
Sheridan Cl WSLW WS2......56 B1
Sheridan Gdns SEDG DY3......82 B1
Sheridan St HHTH/SAND B71......56 B1
 WSLW WS2......56 B1
Sheridan Wk CVALE B35......94 C3
Sherifoot La MGN/WHC B75......47 F2
Sheringham EDG B15......125 G4
Sheringham Rd BVILLE B30......177 F2
Sherington Dr
 ETTPK/GDPK/PENN WV4......52 B3
Sherlock Cl SHHTH WV12......25 H1
Sherlock St DIG/EDG B5......127 E4

Sherrans Dell
 ETTPK/GDPK/PENN WV4......52 B5
Sherratt Cl WALM/CURD B76......78 B3
Sherringham Dr WNSFLD WV11......26 A1
Sherron Gdns BHTH/HG B12......144 B2
Sherston Covert BVILLE B30......177 G3
Shervale Cl
 ETTPK/GDPK/PENN WV4......51 G2
Sherwin Av BILS/COS WV14......85 F2
Sherwood Av TPTN/OCK DY4......85 G2
Sherwood Cl HIA/OLT B92......164 B2
 HLGN/YWD B28......162 D5
Sherwood Dr BRLYHL DY5......119 H5
Sherwood Ms HLGN/YWD B28......162 C3
Sherwood Rd HLGN/YWD B28......162 C5
 SMTHWKW B67......124 C3
 STRBR DY8......118 A5
Sherwood St WOLV WV1......6 E1
Sherwood Wk ALDR WS9......29 F5
Shetland Cl
 DUNHL/THL/PER WV6......22 D4
 LDYWD/EDGR B16......125 H2
Shetland Dr SMTHWK B66......105 H2
Shidas La OLDBY B69......104 A5
Shifnall Wy MGN/WHC B75......63 F1
Shillcock Gv LOZ/NWT B19......109 E4
Shilton Cl SHLY B90......195 F2
Shilton Gv SLYOAK B29......158 B2
Shinwell Crs OLDBY B69......86 B4
Shipbourne Cl
 RIDG/WDGT B32......141 F2
Shipley Flds ERDE/BCHGN B24......93 E3
Shipley Gv SLYOAK B29......158 C2
Shipston Rd NFLD/LBR B31......175 H4
Shipton Cl DUDN DY1......83 H3
Shipton Rd SCSFLD/WYGN B72......62 C5
Shipway Rd YDLY B25......129 E5
Shirebrook Cl AST/WIT B6......109 E1
Shire Cl LDYWD/EDGR B16......125 H2
 LGLYGN/QTN B68......123 F2
Shireland Brook Gdns
 WSNCN S18 *......107 F5
Shireland Cl
 BFLD/HDSWWD B20......89 G3
Shireland Rd SMTHWK B66......106 D5
Shire Rdg ALDR WS9......19 G5
Shireston Rd STETCH B33......131 G2
Shireview Gdns
 BLOX/PEL WS3......18 B5
Shireview Rd BLOX/PEL WS3......18 B5
Shirland Rd
 CHWD/FDBR/MGN B37......132 A3
Shirley Dr SCSFLD/WYGN B72......62 C4
Shirley Park Rd SHLY B90......180 B3
Shirley Rd ACGN B27......146 B5
 BVILLE B30......160 A5
 DUDS DY2......85 E5
 HLGN/YWD B28......163 E2
 LGLYGN/QTN B68......105 G3
Shirral Dr POL/KGSB/FAZ B78......49 H1
Shirral Gv
 CHWD/FDBR/MGN B37......113 H4
Shirrall Dr MGN/WHC B75......49 F1
Sholing Cl CDSL WV8......22 B1
Shooters Cl DIG/EDG B5......143 H1
Shooters Hl CSCFLD/WYGN B72......77 H1
Shop La CDSL WV8......20 B1
Shopton Rd BKDE/SHDE B34......112 C2
Shoreham Cl WLNHL WV13......38 D4
Short Acre St WSLW WS2......4 E1
Shorters Av
 ALE/KHTH/YWD B14......178 D1
Short Heath Rd
 ERDW/GRVHL B23......76 C5
Shortland Cl DOR/KN B93......197 E2
Shortlands Cl BVILLE B30......177 G3
Shortlands La BLOX/PEL WS3......17 H5
Short Rd SMTHWK B67......123 H1
 WOLVN WV10......23 C1
Short St BILS/COS WV14......53 H2
 BLKHTH/ROWR B65......122 A3
 BRWNH WS8......9 G5
 DARL/WED WS10......55 C5
 DUDN DY1......84 A4
 HALE B63......138 B3
 SHHTH WV12......26 A5
 SHLY B90......194 A3
 STRBR DY8......135 F2
 TPTN/OCK DY4......69 E3
 WOLV WV1......4 B4
 WSLW WS2......4 E1
Shorwell Pl BRLYHL DY5......119 E3
Shottery Gv WALM/CURD B76......78 B2
Shottery Rd SHLY B90......194 B1
Shotteswell Rd SHLY B90......194 B1
Showell Circ WOLVN WV10......23 G3
Showell Green La
 SPARK B11......145 E3
Showell La
 ETTPK/GDPK/PENN WV4......50 A5
Showell Rd WOLVN WV10......23 G3
Showells Gdns VAUX/NECH B7......110 A2
Shrawley Cl HALE B63......138 C5
 RBRY B45......188 A1
Shrawley Rd NFLD/LBR B31......176 A3
Shrewley Crs STETCH B33......131 G3
Shrewsbury Cl BLOX/PEL WS3......26 D1
Shrewton Av
 ALE/KHTH/YWD B14......177 H3
Shrubbery Av TPTN/OCK DY4......84 D1
Shrubbery Cl WALM/CURD B76......77 H5
The Shrubbery DUDN DY1......84 B4
 LDYWD/EDGR B16......125 H1
Shrublands Av
 LGLYGN/QTN B68......123 F5
Shrub La ERDE/BCHGN B24......93 E2
Shugborough Dr DUDN DY1......83 G4
Shustoke La DSYBK/YTR WS5......57 H4
Shustoke Rd BKDE/SHDE B34......113 E3
 SOLH B91......165 F5
Shutlock La MOS/BIL B13......160 D1
Shut Mill La RMSLY B62......171 H2
Sibdon Gv NFLD/LBR B31......175 H5
Sidaway Cl
 BLKHTH/ROWR B65......104 A3
Sidaway St CDYHTH B64......121 E3
Sidbury Gv DOR/KN B93......196 C5
Sidcup Cl BILS/COS WV14......53 F5
Sidcup Rd KGSTG B44......75 C2
Siddons Cl BILS/COS WV14......68 D1
Siddons Wy WBROM B70......71 E4

Sidenhill Cl SHLY B90......180 B5
Sidestrand COVEN WV9......11 H4
The Sidings STRBR DY8......117 H3
The Sidlaw Cl HALE B63......137 H5
 WBROM B70......87 G4
 WOLVN WV10......22 D4
Sidney St BKHL/PFLD WV2......6 E7
 BKHL/PFLD WV2......55 F2
Sigmund Cl WOLV WV1......38 B2
Signal Gv BLOX/PEL WS3......26 C5
Signal Hayes Rd
 WALM/CURD B76......95 E5
Silhill Hall Rd SOLH B91......164 C5
Silva Av KGSWFD DY6......100 B5
Silver Birch Coppice
 FOAKS/STRLY B74......32 B5
Silver Birch Dr HLYWD B47......192 D2
Silver Birch Rd BKHL/PFLD WV2......52 C1
 CHWD/FDBR/MGN B37......113 H3
 ERDW/GRVHL B23......77 F5
 FOAKS/STRLY B74......45 F4
Silverbirch Rd SOLH B91......182 C2
Silvercroft Av HDSW B21......89 E2
Silverdale Dr WOLVN WV10......23 F3
Silverdale Gdns STRBR DY8......117 G1
Silverdale Rd ERDE/BCHGN B24......93 F1
Silver Hayes Rd
 ALE/KHTH/YWD B14......161 E2
Silver Innage HALE B63......120 C5
Silverlands Av
 LGLYGN/QTN B68......123 F1
Silverlands Cl HLGN/YWD B28......162 D1
Silvermead Ct HLYWD B47......193 G3
Silvermead Rd
 SCFLD/BOLD B73......77 E2
Silvermere Rd
 LGN/SDN/BHAMAIR B26......148 B1
Silver's Cl BLOX/PEL WS3......17 H2
Silverstone Cl WSLW WS2......40 B2
Silverstone Dr
 FOAKS/STRLY B74......60 B2
Silver St ALE/KHTH/YWD B14......161 E2
 BRLYHL DY5......119 H5
 BRWNH WS8......9 E5
 HLYWD B47......192 A3
Silverthorne Av TPTN/OCK DY4......84 D1
Silverthorne La CDYHTH B64......120 B5
Silverton Crs MOS/BIL B13......162 D1
Silverton Hts SMTHWKW B67 *......106 B3
Silverton Rd SMTHWKW B67......106 A3
Silvertrees Rd TPTN/OCK DY4......85 E4
Silvester Rd BILS/COS WV14......54 A2
Silvester Wy BRLYHL DY5......118 D4
Silvington Cl SLYOAK B29......159 E3
Simcox Gdns RIDG/WDGT B32......140 D5
Simcox Rd DARL/WED WS10......55 H3
Simeon Bissell Cl
 TPTN/OCK DY4......85 G2
Simeon's Wk BRLYHL DY5......119 H5
Simmonds Pl DARL/WED WS10......55 H1
Simmonds Rd BLOX/PEL WS3......17 H1
Simmonds Wy BRWNH WS8......19 G2
Simmons Dr RIDG/WDGT B32......140 D5
Simmons Leasow
 RIDG/WDGT B32......140 D5
Simmons Rd WNSFLD WV11......25 H1
Simms La DUDS DY2......102 C4
 HLYWD B47......192 C1
Simon Cl WHTH/SAND B71......72 A1
Simon Rd HLYWD B47......192 C1
Simpkins Cl ALDR WS9......19 G3
Simpson Gv WOLVN WV10......23 G4
Simpson Rd CSCFLD/WYGN B72......77 G1
 WOLVN WV10......23 G4
 WSLW WS2......27 F1
Simpson St OLDBY B69......105 E1
Singer Cft CBROM B36......95 H1
Sir Alfreds Wy
 WALM/CURD B76......63 E1
Sir Harrys Rd DIG/EDG B5......143 C2
Sir Hilton's Rd NFLD/LBR B31......189 H1
Sir John's Rd SLYOAK B29......143 G1
Sirdar Av DUNHL/THL/PER WV6......124 E1
Sisefield Rd HWK/WKHTH B38......177 F1
Siskin Cl LGLYGN/QTN B68......106 A4
Siskin Dr BHTH/HG B12......
Siskin Rd HAG/WOL DY9......136 A1
Sister Dora Buildings WSL WS1 *......4 E3
Sister Dora Gdns WSL WS1......4 E3
Siviter's Cl BLKHTH/ROWR B65......121 H3
Siviter's La
 BLKHTH/ROWR B65......121 H3
Sivitter St HALE B63......138 B1
Six Acres RIDG/WDGT B32......140 B3
Skelcher Rd SHLY B90......180 C2
Skemp Cl BILS/COS WV14......53 H3
Sketchley Cl SMTHWK B66......106 D4
Skidmore Av BDMR/CCFT WV3......36 C4
Skidmore Dr WBROM B70......70 C3
Skidmore Rd BILS/COS WV14......68 A1
Skinner La DIG/EDG B5......127 E1
Skinner St WOLV WV1......6 D4
Skip La DSYBK/YTR WS5......58 B3
Skipton Gn
 DUNHL/THL/PER WV6......22 D3
Skipton Rd LDYWD/EDGR B16......126 A1
Skomer Cl RBRY B45......173 H4
Skye Cl CBROM B36......114 B1
Skylark Cl BRLYHL DY5......83 G5
 ERDW/GRVHL B23......76 A3
Slack La BFLD/HDSWWD B20......89 E1
Slacky La BLOX/PEL WS3......27 G4
Sladefield Rd WASH/WDE B8......111 F4
Slade Gdns CDSL WV8......10 D3
Slade Gv DOR/KN B93......196 B4
Slade Hl
 DUNHL/THL/PER WV6......22 D4
Slade La MGN/WHC B75......47 H4
 MGN/WHC B75......177 F1
Slade Lanker BKDE/SHDE B34......112 D3
Sladepool Farm Rd
 ALE/KHTH/YWD B14......178 B2
Slade Rd ERDW/GRVHL B23......77 E5
 HALE B63......138 C1
 MGN/WHC B75......47 H4
 WOLVN WV10......11 H4

Slaithwaite Rd
HHTH/SAND B71 87 H2
Slaney Ct WSLW WS2 56 C1
Slaney Rd WSLW WS2 56 B2
Slatch House Rd
SMTHWKW B67 124 A2
Slateley Crs SHLY B90 195 F2
Slater Cl CDYHTH B64 121 F3
Slater Rd DOR/KN B93 196 C4
Slaters La WSLW WS2 56 B1
Slaters Pl WSLW WS2 56 C1
Slater St BILS/COS WV14 54 A5
DARL/WED WS10 55 F2
TPTN/OCK DY4 85 G2
WLNHL WV13 40 A2
Sleaford Gv HLGN/YWD B28 163 E3
Sleaford Rd HLGN/YWD B28 163 E3
Sledmore Rd DUDS DY2 102 D2
The Slieve BFLD/HDSWWD B20 90 A3
Slim Av BILS/COS WV14 54 A5
Slimbridge Cl SHLY B90 195 G2
Slim Rd WSLW WS2 40 C3
Slims Ga HALE B63 138 C3
Slingfield Rd NFLD/LBR B31 176 A4
The Sling DUDS DY2 102 C3
Sloane St CBHAMW B1 2 C4
Smallbrook La WMBN WV5 65 F4
Smallbrook Queensway
DIG/EDG B5 3 G7
Small Cl SMTHWKW B67 105 H4
Smalldale Rd PBAR/PBCH B42 74 D4
Small Heath Br SPARK B11 127 H5
Small Heath Hwy SMHTH B10 145 H1
Smallshire Cl WNSFLD WV11 25 F5
Smallshire Wy STRBR DY8 117 H4
Small St HHTH/SAND B71 87 F1
WSL WS1 4 D6
mallwood Cl
ERDE/BCHGN B24 93 H3
WALM/CURD B76 63 E5
mallwood Rd CDSL WV8 11 G5
marts Av LICHS WS14 33 E3
meaton Gdns WSNGN B18 107 G5
meed Gv ERDE/BCHGN B24 93 F3
mestow La SEDG DY3 80 A2
mestow St WOLVN WV10 37 F1
mirrells Rd HLGN/YWD B28 162 C5
mith Av DARL/WED WS10 55 F4
mith Cl BILS/COS WV14 68 A2
SMTHWKW B67 123 H1
mithfield Rd BLOX/PEL WS3 27 H1
mithmoor Crs
HHTH/SAND B71 72 B3
mith Pl TPTN/OCK DY4 85 H2
mith Rd DARL/WED WS10 70 D2
WSLW WS2 56 C2
miths Cl RIDG/WDGT B32 157 F1
miths La DOR/KN B93 196 C2
mith St BILS/COS WV14 53 H3
DUDS DY2 102 D2
LOZ/NWT B19 108 C4
miths Wy CSHL/WTROR B46 96 A3
mithy Dr BLOX/PEL WS3 18 A3
mithy La BRLYHL DY5 100 D1
e Smithy
LGN/SDN/BHAMAIR B26 147 H1
nout Crs BILS/COS WV14 67 H1
apdragon Dr
DSYBK/YTR WS5 57 F5
ape Rd WNSFLD WV11 25 G1
eyd Hall Cl BLOX/PEL WS3 * 27 E2
eyd Hall Rd BLOX/PEL WS3 26 D1
eyd La WNSFLD WV11 26 A1
owberry Dr BRLYHL DY5 83 E5
owberry Gdns ACGN B27 * 146 C2
owdon Gv HALE B63 154 D1
owdon Ri SEDG DY3 67 F5
owdon Rd STRBR DY8 135 H1
owdon Wy SHHTH WV12 25 H1
WOLVN WV10 22 D4
owdrop Cl BRWNH WS8 18 D1
owford Cl SHLY B90 179 H4
ow Hl BKHL/PFLD WV2 7 G5
ow Hill Jct BKHL/PFLD WV2 7 G6
ow Hl Queensway
CBHAMNE B4 3 F3
ows Hill Dr SHLY B90 194 D3
owshill Gdns DUDN DY1 83 H2
erton Cl WNSFLD WV11 25 F3
o Av WSNGN B18 108 A2
o Cl SMTHWK B66 107 E3
o Hl HDSW B21 108 A2
opoolway WSNGN B18 108 A3
o Rd HDSW B21 107 H2
o Wy SMTHWK B66 106 D3
ari Cl TPTN/OCK DY4 70 A3
ent Cl COVEN WV9 11 H5
hull By-Pass SOLH B91 182 D2
hull La HLGN/YWD B28 163 E4
hull Pkwy
HWD/FDBR/MGN B37 133 E5
hull Rd HIA/OLT B92 166 D4
HLY B90 180 D2
PARK B11 145 F4
hull Wy CBROM B36 112 C1
IA/OLT B92 165 E1
HLY B90 194 D3
y Gv TPTN/OCK DY4 70 B4
a Cl WOLV WV1 38 B4
ay Cl DARL/WED WS10 56 C4
erby Dr SOLH B91 181 G5
ercotes Rd
BAR/PBCH B42 74 D3
erdale Rd NFLD/LBR B31 176 A1
erfield Cl RUSH/SHEL WS4 29 E1
erfield Rd BLOX/PEL WS3 27 F2
erford Gdns WOLVN WV10 13 E5
erford Pl WLNHL WV13 39 F4
erford Rd SLYOAK B29 158 B2
erford Wy BILS/COS WV14 68 B3
erland Rd
N/SDN/BHAMAIR B26 130 C3
erset Crs DARL/WED WS10 56 D4
erset Dr NFLD/LBR B31 189 F1
RBR DY8 117 H5
erset Rd
LD/HDSWWD B20 89 H4
G B15 142 C1
OW/GRVHL B23 76 C5
TH/SAND B71 71 H5
RUSH/SHEL WS4 42 C1
WLNHL WV13 40 B3
Somers Rd RMSLY B62 139 E2
WSLW WS2 56 A1
Somerton Dr
CHWD/FDBR/MGN B37 132 B5
ERDW/GRVHL B23 77 E5
Somerville Rd SCFLD/BOLD B73 62 A4
SMHTH B10 128 D4
Somery Rd DUDN DY1 84 C3
RIDG/WDGT B32 141 G5
Sommerfield Rd
RIDG/WDGT B32 140 D4
Sommerville Dr
SCFLD/BOLD B73 62 A4
Sonning Dr COVEN WV9 11 H5
Sopwith Cft CVALE B35 94 C4
Sorrel Cl OLDBY B69 85 H4
Sorrel Dr ACGN B27 146 B5
DSYBK/YTR WS5 57 G5
Sorrel Gv ERDE/BCHGN B24 93 H3
Sorrell Dr ACGN B27 * 146 B5
Southacre Av DIG/EDG B5 127 E4
Southall Crs BILS/COS WV14 68 C2
Southall Rd WNSFLD WV11 25 G2
Southall's La DUDN DY1 84 B5
Southam Cl HLGN/YWD B28 162 C2
Southam Dr SCFLD/BOLD B73 77 F2
Southampton St WOLV WV1 7 G2
Southam Rd HLGN/YWD B28 162 C2
South Av STRBR DY8 135 F3
WNSFLD WV11 24 C5
South Bank Rd CDYHTH B64 121 F4
Southbank Vw KGSWFD DY6 100 A5
Southbourne Av
BKDE/SHDE B34 111 H3
WSLW WS2 41 F4
Southbourne Cl SLYOAK B29 143 E5
Southbourne Rd WOLVN WV10 12 C4
South Car Park Rd
BHAMNEC B40 150 B4
Southcote Gv
HWK/WKHTH B38 176 B4
Southcott Av BRLYHL DY5 119 F4
South Crs WOLVN WV10 14 A1
Southcroft Rd
ERDW/GRVHL B23 92 C3
South Dene SMTHWKW B67 * 106 B4
Southdown Av WSNGN B18 108 A3
South Dr CSHL/WTROR B46 115 E3
DIG/EDG B5 143 G3
MGN/WHC B75 62 C2
Southern Cl KGSWFD DY6 118 B1
Southerndown Rd SEDG DY3 66 D3
Southern Dr
ALE/KHTH/YWD B14 177 H3
Southern Rd WASH/WDE B8 111 G4
Southern Wy DARL/WED WS10 55 E5
Southey Cl SHHTH WV12 26 C2
SOLH B91 181 H5
Southfield Av CBROM B36 112 D1
LDYWD/EDGR B16 125 F1
Southfield Cl ALDR WS9 30 A5
Southfield Dr HLGN/YWD B28 163 E5
Southfield Gv BDMR/CCFT WV3 50 C1
Southfield Rd
LDYWD/EDGR B16 125 F1
WNSFLD WV11 25 F5
Southfields Cl
CSHL/WTROR B46 115 G4
Southfields Rd SOLH B91 181 F4
South Gdns HAG/WOL DY9 169 G1
Southgate CDYHTH B64 120 D4
WOLV WV1 6 D3
Southgate Rd KGSTG B44 75 E1
South Gn
ETTPK/GDPK/PENN WV4 50 D3
South Gv ERDW/GRVHL B23 92 D1
LOZ/NWT B19 108 B1
South Holme BORD B9 128 A3
Southlands Rd MOS/BIL B13 161 G1
Southminster Dr
ALE/KHTH/YWD B14 161 E4
South Ov SEDG DY3 83 G1
South Pde CSCFLD/WYGN B72 62 C4
South Park Ms BRLYHL DY5 119 E2
South Range SPARK B11 144 D1
South Rd ALE/KHTH/YWD B14 161 E2
ERDW/GRVHL B23 92 D2
ETTPK/GDPK/PENN WV4 52 D4
HAG/WOL DY9 169 G1
NFLD/LBR B31 175 F3
SMTHWKW B67 106 B4
SPARK B11 127 H5
STRBR DY8 135 F3
TPTN/OCK DY4 69 H3
WSNGN B18 108 A3
South Road Av WSNGN B18 108 A3
South Roundhay STETCH B33 130 C1
South St BRLYHL DY5 119 E2
HRBN B17 142 B1
WLNHL WV13 39 E4
WOLVN WV10 23 E4
WSL WS1 4 C7
South Street Gdns WSL WS1 4 C7
South Tower VAUX/NECH B7 * 109 H5
South Vw GTB/HAM B43 73 G4
South View Cl CDSL WV8 10 D5
WOLVN WV10 13 H1
Southview Rdg BRLYHL DY5 119 F5
South View Rd SEDG DY3 66 D3
Southville Bungalows
ALE/KHTH/YWD B14 * 178 D1
South Wy BHAMNEC B40 150 B4
Southway Ct KGSWFD DY6 100 B5
Southwick Pl BILS/COS WV14 53 H1
Southwick Rd RMSLY B62 122 B4
Southwold Av BVILLE B30 177 G2
Southwood Av
BKDE/SHDE B34 112 C2
Southwood Cl KGSWFD DY6 100 A4
Southwood Covert
ALE/KHTH/YWD B14 177 G3
Sovereign Dr DUDN DY1 83 F4
Sovereign Hts NFLD/LBR B31 174 C4
Sovereign Rd BVILLE B30 176 D1
Sovereign Wk WSL WS1 5 G3
Sovereign Wy MOS/BIL B13 144 B3
Sowerby March
ERDE/BCHGN B24 93 H2
Sowers Cl SHHTH WV12 26 B5
Sowers Ct MGN/WHC B75 47 H1
Sowers Gdns SHHTH WV12 26 B5
Spa Gv BVILLE B30 160 C2
Spark St SPARK B11 144 A1
Sparrey Dr BVILLE B30 160 A2
Sparrow Cl DARL/WED WS10 56 B3
Speakers Cl OLDBY B69 103 H2
Speed Rd TPTN/OCK DY4 69 E5
Speedwell Cl ALDR WS9 29 H5
WNSFLD WV11 25 E5
Speedwell Gdns BRLYHL DY5 135 H1
Speedwell Rd DIG/EDG B5 143 H1
YDLY B25 146 A1
Spencer Av BILS/COS WV14 68 C3
Spencer Cl ERDE/BCHGN B24 93 H2
HHTH/SAND B71 72 B3
OLDBY B69 103 H1
SEDG DY3 82 C2
Spencer St WSNGN B18 2 C1
Spenser Av
DUNHL/THL/PER WV6 34 C1
Spernall Gv SLYOAK B29 158 C1
Spey Cl DIG/EDG B5 143 H1
Spiceland Rd NFLD/LBR B31 158 B4
Spiers Cl DOR/KN B93 197 E2
Spies Cl RMSLY B62 139 H1
Spies La RMSLY B62 139 H2
Spills Meadow SEDG DY3 83 G1
Spilsbury Cft SOLH B91 181 G5
Spindle La SHLY B90 194 A2
Spinners End Dr CDYHTH B64 120 D3
Spinney Cl BLOX/PEL WS3 18 A5
NFLD/LBR B31 175 G2
STRBR DY8 117 F1
Spinney Dr SHLY B90 194 D4
The Spinney BDMR/CCFT WV3 35 H4
BFLD/HDSWWD B20 89 G2
FOAKS/STRLY B74 31 H4
HLYWD B47 192 D4
SEDG DY3 83 E4
SOLH B91 182 A5
Spiral Cl RMSLY B62 122 C4
Spiral Gn ERDE/BCHGN B24 93 G2
Spitfire Rd ERDE/BCHGN B24 93 G4
Spitfire Wy CVALE B35 94 C4
Spondon Gv BKDE/SHDE B34 113 E4
Spondon Rd WNSFLD WV11 25 E2
Spon La WBROM B70 87 H5
Spon La South SMTHWK B66 105 H1
Spoon Dr HWK/WKHTH B38 176 B3
Spooner Cft DIG/EDG B5 127 E4
Spooners Cl HIA/OLT B92 165 H3
Spouthouse La GTB/HAM B43 73 G4
Spout La WSL WS1 4 E7
Spreadbury Cl HRBN B17 124 B4
Sprig Cft CBROM B36 111 G1
Spring Av BLKHTH/ROWR B65 122 B2
Springavon Cft HRBN B17 141 H1
Springbank BORD B9 128 D1
Springbank Rd EDG B15 126 C5
Springbrook Cl CBROM B36 95 F5
Spring Cl HAG/WOL DY9 169 F1
RUSH/SHEL WS4 18 C5
SOLH B91 181 F2
Spring Coppice Dr
DOR/KN B93 197 E5
Spring Ct WSL WS1 5 J7
Spring Crs CDYHTH B64 121 F5
Springcroft Rd SPARK B11 145 H5
Springfield ERDW/GRVHL B23 92 B3
Springfield Av BHTH/HG B12 144 C1
HAG/WOL DY9 136 C3
SEDG DY3 67 G2
Springfield Cl
BLKHTH/ROWR B65 103 G4
Springfield Ct
HLGN/YWD B28 * 162 D2
Springfield Crs DUDS DY2 103 F1
HIA/OLT B92 148 A4
WALM/CURD B76 63 G4
WBROM B70 88 A5
Springfield Dr
ALE/KHTH/YWD B14 * 161 E1
Springfield Gv SEDG DY3 67 F2
Springfield La
BLKHTH/ROWR B65 103 F4
WOLVN WV10 12 D3
Springfield Rd
ALE/KHTH/YWD B14 161 F2
BILS/COS WV14 54 A1
CBROM B36 113 F1
LGLYGN/QTN B68 105 G5
MOS/BIL B13 162 B1
RMSLY B62 122 B5
WALM/CURD B76 78 B1
WOLVN WV10 37 G1
Springfields
CSHL/WTROR B46 115 F4
RUSH/SHEL WS4 28 D3
Springfields Rd BRLYHL DY5 118 D2
Springfield St WSNGN B18 126 A1
Springfield Ter
BLKHTH/ROWR B65 103 F4
Spring Gdns DUDS DY2 102 D1
HDSW B21 * 107 H2
Spring Gv LOZ/NWT B19 * 108 B3
Spring Grove Gdns
WSNGN B18 107 H3
Spring Head DARL/WED WS10 70 D1
Spring Hl ERDE/BCHGN B24 92 D3
WSNGN B18 108 A5
Springhill Av
ETTPK/GDPK/PENN WV4 50 C5
Spring Hill Circ WSNGN B18 2 A3
Springhill Cl RUSH/SHEL WS4 29 F1
SHHTH WV12 26 B3
Springhill Gv
ETTPK/GDPK/PENN WV4 50 C4
Springhill La
ETTPK/GDPK/PENN WV4 50 A4
Springhill Pk
ETTPK/GDPK/PENN WV4 50 B5
Spring Hill Pas WSNGN B18 126 A1
Springhill Rd BRWNH WS8 9 G5
WNSFLD WV11 24 D3
WSL WS1 5 G5
Spring La ERDE/BCHGN B24 93 E3
RMSLY B62 171 H1
RUSH/SHEL WS4 18 C5
SHHTH WV12 39 H1
Spring Meadow CDYHTH B64 121 F3
HALE B63 138 B5
TPTN/OCK DY4 70 A5
Springmeadow Gv
LOZ/NWT B19 108 D3
Spring Meadow Rd DUDS DY2 120 C2
Springmeadow Rd EDG B15 126 D5
Spring Meadows Cl CDSL WV8 10 D3
Spring Parklands DUDN DY1 102 A1
Spring Rd DUDS DY2 102 D3
EDG B15 126 D5
ETTPK/GDPK/PENN WV4 53 E4
RUSH/SHEL WS4 29 F1
SMTHWK B66 105 H1
SPARK B11 145 H4
Springslade RIDG/WDGT B32 141 F2
Springslade Dr
ERDE/BCHGN B24 93 H3
The Springs CDYHTH B64 121 G3
Spring St EDG B15 126 D4
HAG/WOL DY9 136 C3
HALE B63 137 G1
TPTN/OCK DY4 85 G1
Springthorpe Gn
ERDE/BCHGN B24 93 G2
Springthorpe Rd
ERDE/BCHGN B24 93 H3
Springvale Av BILS/COS WV14 53 F4
DSYBK/YTR WS5 58 A1
Spring Vale Cl BILS/COS WV14 68 A2
Spring Vale Rd
BLKHTH/ROWR B65 * 103 G4
Springvale St WLNHL WV13 39 H2
Springvale Wy BILS/COS WV14 53 G4
Spring Wk HALE B63 154 D1
OLDBY B69 105 E4
WSLW WS2 41 F2
Sproat Av DARL/WED WS10 55 E3
Spruce Gv ERDE/BCHGN B24 93 F4
Spruce Rd DSYBK/YTR WS5 57 H5
Spruce Wy BDMR/CCFT WV3 35 H4
Spur Tree Av BDMR/CCFT WV3 35 E4
Squadron Cl CVALE B35 95 E2
Square Cl RIDG/WDGT B32 140 C4
The Square BKHL/PFLD WV2 37 F5
CDSL WV8 10 B3
HRBN B17 141 H1
SHHTH WV12 * 26 B2
SOLH B91 182 A2
TPTN/OCK DY4 70 B4
Squires Ct BRLYHL DY5 119 E3
Squires Cft WALM/CURD B76 78 C2
Squires Gate Rd WLNHL WV13 39 H3
Squirrel Hollow
WALM/CURD B76 78 C1
Squirrels Hollow
LGLYGN/QTN B68 123 H5
Squirrel Wk
ETTPK/GDPK/PENN WV4 51 G4
FOAKS/STRLY B74 32 A5
Stable Cl SEDG DY3 67 G5
Stable Cft HHTH/SAND B71 72 B4
Stableford Cl RIDG/WDGT B32 141 F4
The Stables SLYOAK B29 143 E5
Stacey Cl CDYHTH B64 121 E3
Stacey Grange Gdns
RBRY B45 * 188 A2
Stackhouse Cl ALDR WS9 19 G4
Stackhouse Dr BLOX/PEL WS3 18 A3
Stadium Cl WLNHL WV13 39 H2
Stadium Dr DUDS DY2 120 C3
Stafford Cl BLOX/PEL WS3 17 E5
Stafford Dr HHTH/SAND B71 71 F4
Stafford La CDSL WV8 20 B1
Stafford Rd DARL/WED WS10 54 D2
GTWY WS6 16 C1
HDSW B21 107 H1
WOLVN WV10 23 E3
Staffordshire Pool Cl
AST/WIT B6 91 F5
Staffordshire Wy CDSL WV8 10 B2
Stafford St BILS/COS WV14 53 H3
DARL/WED WS10 70 C1
DUDN DY1 84 B5
WLNHL WV13 39 G3
WOLV WV1 7 G3
WSLW WS2 4 D2
Stafford Street Jct WOLV WV1 7 F2
Stafford Wy GTB/HAM B43 73 G4
Staff Wy ERDW/GRVHL B23 92 C2
Stag Crs BLOX/PEL WS3 28 A4
Stag Hill Rd BLOX/PEL WS3 28 A3
Stag Wk WALM/CURD B76 77 H4
Stainsby Av LOZ/NWT B19 108 C4
Stainsby Cft SHLY B90 195 H3
Stakenbridge La KIDD DY10 168 C1
Stalling's La KGSWFD DY6 82 C5
Stambermill Cl HAG/WOL DY9 136 B2
Stamford Cft SOLH B91 181 H3
Stamford Gv
BFLD/HDSWWD B20 90 C4
Stamford Rd
BFLD/HDSWWD B20 90 C5
BRLYHL DY5 136 A1
STRBR DY8 135 H2
Stamford St STRBR DY8 118 B5
Stanbrook Rd SHLY B90 195 G3
Stanbury Av DARL/WED WS10 54 D2
Stanbury Rd
ALE/KHTH/YWD B14 178 D1
Stancroft Gv
LGN/SDN/BHAMAIR B26 130 C4
Standard Wy
ERDE/BCHGN B24 110 D1
Standbridge Wy
TPTN/OCK DY4 85 G1
Standhills Rd KGSWFD DY6 100 B4
Standlake Av CBROM B36 111 H2
Stanfield Rd GTB/HAM B43 59 H3
RIDG/WDGT B32 124 A5
Stanford Av PBAR/PBCH B42 74 A4
Stanford Gv HALE B63 154 C1
Stanford Rd BKHL/PFLD WV2 52 A1
BLKHTH/ROWR B65 121 H1
Stanhoe Cl BRLYHL DY5 119 F4
Stanhope Rd SMTHWKW B67 124 B1
Stanhope St BDMR/CCFT WV3 6 D5
BHTH/HG B12 127 F5
DUDS DY2 103 E5
Stanhope Wy GTB/HAM B43 59 H4
Stanhurst Wy HHTH/SAND B71 72 C1
Stanier Cl RUSH/SHEL WS4 28 D3
Stanier Gv BFLD/HDSWWD B20 90 B4
Staniforth St CBHAMNE B4 3 H1
Stanley Av MGN/WHC B75 63 F4
RIDG/WDGT B32 124 A5
SHLY B90 180 B1
Stanley Cl HLGN/YWD B28 163 E5
WNSFLD WV11 25 F2
Stanley Ct
DUNHL/THL/PER WV6 34 C1
Stanley Dr SEDG DY3 80 C4
Stanley Pl BILS/COS WV14 53 F3
MOS/BIL B13 * 144 B4
RUSH/SHEL WS4 28 D4
Stanley Rd
ALE/KHTH/YWD B14 160 D3
DARL/WED WS10 55 F3
HHTH/SAND B71 72 A4
LGLYGN/QTN B68 123 G5
RUSH/SHEL WS4 28 D4
STRBR DY8 135 F4
VAUX/NECH B7 110 A2
WOLVN WV10 23 G2
Stanley St BLOX/PEL WS3 27 G2
Stanmore Gv RMSLY B62 140 A4
Stanmore Rd
LDYWD/EDGR B16 125 E3
Stanton Av DUDN DY1 67 H5
Stanton Gv
LGN/SDN/BHAMAIR B26 130 B4
SHLY B90 180 A1
TPTN/OCK DY4 85 G1
Stanton Rd GTB/HAM B43 73 F3
SHLY B90 180 A1
WOLV WV1 37 H3
Stanville Rd
LGN/SDN/BHAMAIR B26 148 A1
Stanway Gdns HHTH/SAND B71 71 H5
Stanway Gv KGSTG B44 60 B5
Stanway Rd HHTH/SAND B71 71 H5
SHLY B90 180 D1
Stanwell Gv ERDW/GRVHL B23 76 C5
Stanwick Av STETCH B33 131 G1
Stapenhall Rd SHLY B90 195 G3
Stapleford Cft
ALE/KHTH/YWD B14 177 G3
Stapleford Gv STRBR DY8 118 A2
Staple Hall Rd NFLD/LBR B31 175 H3
Staplehurst Rd
HLGN/YWD B28 162 D2
Staple Lodge Rd
NFLD/LBR B31 175 H4
Stapleton Cl WALM/CURD B76 78 D5
Stapleton Dr
CHWD/FDBR/MGN B37 132 A1
Stapleton Rd ALDR WS9 29 H5
Stapylton Av HRBN B17 141 H2
Starbank Rd SMHTH B10 129 E4
Starbold Crs DOR/KN B93 197 F3
Star Cl TPTN/OCK DY4 86 A1
WSLW WS2 40 D1
Starcross Rd ACGN B27 146 C5
Star Hl EDG B15 126 B4
Starkey Cft
CHWD/FDBR/MGN B37 132 C2
Starkie Dr LGLYGN/QTN B68 105 G5
Starley Wy
CHWD/FDBR/MGN B37 149 G1
Star St BDMR/CCFT WV3 36 A5
HAG/WOL DY9 136 D2
Statham Dr LDYWD/EDGR B16 125 E2
Station Ap DOR/KN B93 196 D5
FOAKS/STRLY B74 32 D4
SCFLD/BOLD B73 62 B2
SOLH B91 181 G1
Station Av LDYWD/EDGR B16 125 E3
Station Buildings
DUNHL/THL/PER WV6 * 36 A1
Station Cl BLOX/PEL WS3 27 F2
CDSL WV8 10 A4
Station Dr BRLYHL DY5 118 D3
FOAKS/STRLY B74 47 F5
HAG/WOL DY9 152 C5
HIA/OLT B92 164 A1
KIDD DY10 168 B3
TPTN/OCK DY4 85 H2
Station Link Rd
CHWD/FDBR/MGN B37 149 H3
Station Pl BLOX/PEL WS3 27 F2
Station Rd ACGN B27 146 C4
ALDR WS9 30 A5
ALE/KHTH/YWD B14 160 D2
AST/WIT B6 91 F5
BILS/COS WV14 54 A3
BLKHTH/ROWR B65 122 B2
BLOX/PEL WS3 18 A4
BRLYHL DY5 101 E5
BVILLE B30 176 C1
CDSL WV8 10 A4
CDYHTH B64 121 G4
CHWD/FDBR/MGN B37 131 H5
CSHL/WTROR B46 115 F1
DOR/KN B93 197 F4
ERDW/GRVHL B23 92 D1
HAG/WOL DY9 152 C4
HDSW B21 107 E1
HIA/OLT B92 167 G3
HLYWD B47 192 B5
HRBN B17 142 A1
HWK/WKHTH B38 176 D1
NFLD/LBR B31 175 G3
OLDBY B69 105 E4
RUSH/SHEL WS4 28 C4
SCFLD/BOLD B73 77 E2
SOLH B91 181 H1
STETCH B33 129 H1
WMBN WV5 65 E3
Station St BLOX/PEL WS3 27 F2
CBHAMW B1 3 F7
CDYHTH B64 120 C4
DARL/WED WS10 55 G2
SCFLD/BOLD B73 62 C3
TPTN/OCK DY4 85 H1
WSLW WS2 4 D3
Staunton Rd BLOX/PEL WS3 16 C4
Staveley Rd
ALE/KHTH/YWD B14 160 D4
WOLV WV1 37 E1

Stead Cl *TPTN/OCK* DY4 ....69 H2
WSLW WS2 ....27 G5
Steadman Cft *TPTN/OCK* DY4 *..70 B3
Stechford La *WMBN* WS8 ....111 H4
Stechford Rd *BKDE/SHDE* B34 ..111 H4
Steel Bright Rd *PBAR/PBCH* B42 .107 E3
Steel Dr *WOLVN* WV10 ....23 F2
Steelhouse La *BRWNH* B4 ....7 J7
CBHAMNE B4 ....3 H5
Steelmans Rd *DARL/WED* WS10 ..15 H1
Steelpark Rd *RMSLY* B62 ....121 H5
Steelpark Wy *WNSFLD* WV11 ....38 D1
Steel Rd *NFLD/LBR* B31 ....175 F5
The Steeples *STRBR* DY8 ....135 H4
Steepwood Cft *BVILLE* B30 ....176 B1

Stella Cft
CHWD/FDBR/MGN B37 ....132 C2
Stella Gv *CTB/HAM* B43 ....73 E3
Stella Rd *TPTN/OCK* DY4 ....69 F5
Stenbury Cl *WOLVN* WV10 ....11 J5
Stencills Dr *RUSH/SHEL* WS4 ....42 D2
Stencills Rd *RUSH/SHEL* WS4 ....42 D1
Stennels Av *RMSLY* B62 ....139 G5
Stennels Crs *HALE* B62 ....139 G5
Stephens Cl *WNSFLD* WV11 ....24 D1
Stephenson Av *WSLW* WS2 ....27 E4

Stephenson Dr
CHWD/FDBR/MGN B37 ....132 B2
Stephenson Pl *CBHAM* B2 ....3 C6
Stephenson Sq *WSLW* WS2 ....27 F5
Stephenson St *BRWNH* WS7 ....6 D5
CBHAM B2 ....3 F6
Stephens Rd *WALM/CURD* B76 ....63 C4
Stepping Stone Cl *WSLW* WS2 ....40 D1
Stepping Stones *STRBR* DY8 ....135 H2
Steppingstone St *DUDN* DY1 ....84 B5
Sterling Pk *BRLYHL* DY5 *..............101 H5
Sterndale Rd *PBAR/PBCH* B42 ....74 C5
Steven Dr *BILS/COS* WV14 ....69 E2
Stevens Av *RIDG/WDGT* B32 ....140 D5
Stevens Ga *BKHL/PFLD* WV2 ....37 J3
Stevens Rd *HAG/WOL* DY9 ....136 B5
Steward St *WBROM* B18 ....126 A1
Stewart Rd *ALDR* WS9 ....19 G4
KGSWFD DY6 ....99 H5
Stewarts Rd *WALM/CURD* B76 ....63 C4
Stewart Rd *BKHL/PFLD* WV2 ....7 F7
Stewkins *STRBR* DY8 ....118 A4

Steyning Rd
LGN/SDN/BHAMAIR B26 ....147 E2
Stickley La *SEDG* DY3 ....83 E2
Stilehouse Crs
BLKHTH/ROWR B65 ....122 A2
Stilthouse Gv *RBRY* B45 ....188 A1
Stirling Crs *SMHTH* WV12 ....25 H5
Stirling Rd *BILS/COS* WV14 ....54 B5
DUDS DY2 ....103 G3
LDYWD/EDGR B16 ....125 H5
SCFLD/BOLD B73 ....181 E5
SHLY B90 ....181 E5
Stirrup Cl *DSYBK/YTR* WS5 ....57 F4

Stockbridge Cl
DUNHL/THL/PER WV6 ....34 D3
Stockdale Pl *EDG* B15 ....125 F4
Stock Exchange Buildings
CBHAMNW B3 *..............2 E4
Stockfield Rd *ACGN* B27 ....146 B3
Stockhill Dr *RBRY* B45 ....187 H2
Stocking St *HAG/WOL* DY9 ....136 D2

Stockland Rd
ERDW/GRVHL B23 ....92 B2
Stockley Crs *SHLY* B90 ....180 D2

Stockmans Cl
HWK/WKHTH B38 ....176 C5
Stockton Cl *DOR/KN* B93 ....197 H4
WALM/CURD B76 ....95 E1
WSLW WS2 ....41 H1
Stockton Gv *STETCH* B33 ....131 F5
Stockwell Av *BRLYHL* DY5 ....119 F4
Stockwell End
DUNHL/THL/PER WV6 ....21 H4
Stockwell Ri *HIA/OLT* B92 ....165 F3

Stockwell Rd
DUNHL/THL/PER WV6 ....21 H5
HDSW B21 ....89 G4
Stokes Av *TPTN/OCK* DY4 ....69 G3
WLNHL WV13 ....39 F5

Stokesay Av
DUNHL/THL/PER WV6 ....34 D2
Stokesay Cl *OLDBY* B69 ....103 G1
Stokesay Gv *NFLD/LBR* B31 ....175 F5
Stokesay Ri *DUDN* DY1 ....83 G3
Stokes St *BLOX/PEL* WS3 ....27 F2
Stoke Wy *EDG* B15 *..............125 F4
Stoneacre Cl *BDMR/CCFT* WV3 ....35 E4
Stone Av *MGN/WHC* B75 ....63 G3
Stonebow Av *SOLH* B91 ....181 H5

Stonebridge Crs
CHWD/FDBR/MGN B37 ....113 H5
Stonebridge Rd
Stonebrook Wy *SLYOAK* B29 ....141 H5

Stonechat Dr
ERDW/GRVHL B23 ....92 A4
Stone Cl *HWK/WKHTH* B38 ....176 D3
Stonecroft Av *RBRY* B45 ....188 A1
Stonecrop Cl *BRWNH* WS8 ....9 K5
HWK/WKHTH B38 ....176 D5
Stone Cross *CSHL/WTROR* B46 ....96 B3
Stonecross *BILS/COS* WV14 ....53 H5
Stonefield Dr *BRLYHL* DY5 ....100 C3
Stonefield Rd *BILS/COS* WV14 *..............53 H1
Stoneford Rd *SHLY* B90 ....180 A1

Stonehaven Gv
HLGN/YWD B28 ....163 F2

Stonehenge Cft
ALE/KHTH/YWD B14 ....177 H4
Stonehill Cft *SHLY* B90 ....195 F2
Stonehouse Av *WLNHL* WV13 ....39 F2

Stonehouse Cl
DARL/WED WS10 ....71 F1
Stonehouse Dr
FOAKS/STRLY B74 ....45 H1
Stonehouse Hl *SLYOAK* B29 ....141 G5

Stonehouse La
RIDG/WDGT B32 ....140 D5

Stonehouse Rd
SCFLD/BOLD B73 ....61 H5
Stonehurst Rd *GTB/HAM* B43 ....59 C5
Stonelea *ALDR* WS9 ....30 B5
Stonelea Cl *HHTH/SAND* B71 ....72 A3
Stoneleigh Cl *FOAKS/STRLY* B74 ....46 D5
Stoneleigh Gdns *CDSL* WV8 ....10 B5

Stoneleigh Rd
BFLD/HDSWWD B20 ....91 E5
SOLH B91 ....163 H5
Stoneleigh Wy *SEDG* DY3 ....67 F5
Stonepine Pl *SEDG* DY3 ....67 F5
Stone Rd *EDG* B15 ....126 D5

Stonerwood Av
HLGN/YWD B28 ....162 C3
Stones Gn *ERDW/GRVHL* B23 ....76 D5
Stone St *DUDN* DY1 ....84 C5
OLDBY B69 ....104 B1
Stone St *SLYOAK* B29 ....158 C2
Stone Yd *BHTH/HG* B12 ....3 K7

Stoneyford Gv
ALE/KHTH/YWD B14 ....178 D1

Stoneymoor Dr *CBROM* B36 ....95 F5
Stoneythorpe Cl *SOLH* B91 ....181 H4
Stonnal Gv *ERDW/GRVHL* B23 ....77 E5
Stonnall Ga *ALDR* WS9 ....30 B2
Stonnall Rd *ALDR* WS9 ....30 C2
Stonor Park Rd *SOLH* B91 ....164 B4
Stonor Rd *HLGN/YWD* B28 ....180 A1
Stony La *SMTHWK* B67 ....106 B3
Stony St *SMTHWK* B67 ....106 B3
Stornoway Rd *CVALE* B35 ....94 D2
Storrs Cl *BORD* B9 ....128 A3
Storrs Pl *SMHTH* B10 ....128 B3
The Storrs Wy
RIDG/WDGT B32 ....157 F3

Stot Fold Rd
ALE/KHTH/YWD B14 ....178 D3
Stourbridge Rd *BRGRVW* B61 ....185 H3
BRLYHL DY5 ....101 C4
DUDN DY1 ....102 A1
ETTPK/GDPK/PENN WV4 ....50 C5
HAG/WOL DY9 ....98 D3
HALE B63 ....138 B3
WOLV WV1 ....81 C2
Stour Cl *HALE* B63 ....138 A1
Stourdale Rd *CDYHTH* B64 ....120 C5
Stourdell Rd *HALE* B63 ....138 A1
Stour Hl *BRLYHL* DY5 ....120 A5
Stourmore Cl *SMHTH* WV12 ....26 B4
Stour St *WBROM* B70 ....86 C3
WSNGN B18 ....126 A1
Stourton Cl *DOR/KN* B93 ....197 F1
WALM/CURD B76 ....63 F4

Stourton Dr
ETTPK/GDPK/PENN WV4 ....50 C5
Stourton Rd *RIDG/WDGT* B32 ....140 B2
Stour Vale Rd *HAG/WOL* DY9 ....135 G5
Stour Valley Cl *BRLYHL* DY5 ....119 F5
Stow Dr *BRLYHL* DY5 ....135 H1
Stowell Rd *KGSTG* B44 ....75 F4
Stowe St *BLOX/PEL* WS3 ....27 C3
Stow Gv *CBROM* B36 ....112 A2
Stow Heath La *WOLV* WV1 ....53 F1
Stow Heath Rd *WOLV* WV1 ....53 F1
Stowmans Cl *BILS/COS* WV14 ....53 F5
Straight Rd *SHHTH* WV12 ....26 A4
Straits Gn *SEDG* DY3 ....82 D2
Straits Rd *SEDG* DY3 ....82 D3
The Straits *SEDG* DY3 ....82 C2
Stratford Cl *DUDN* DY1 ....83 G4
Stratford Dr *ALDR* WS9 ....30 C2
Stratford Pl *BHTH/HG* B12 ....127 G4
Stratford Rd *HLGN/YWD* B28 ....198 A5
HOCK/TIA B94 ....198 A5
SHLY B90 ....194 D1
SPARK B11 ....144 D1
Stratford St North *SPARK* B11 ....127 G4
Strathdene Rd *SLYOAK* B29 ....142 A5
Strathern Dr *BILS/COS* WV14 ....68 A2
Strathmore Crs *WMBN* WV5 ....65 E2
Strathmore Rd *TPTN/OCK* DY4 ....69 G3
Stratton St *WOLVN* WV10 ....37 G1
Strawberry Cl *OLDBY* B69 ....104 A2
Streamside Wy *HIA/OLT* B92 ....148 B3

Stream Meadow
RUSH/SHEL WS4 ....29 E1
Stream Pk *KGSWFD* DY6 ....99 H5
Stream Rd *KGSWFD* DY6 ....99 H5
Streamside Wy *HIA/OLT* B92 ....148 B3
RUSH/SHEL WS4 ....29 F2
Streatham Gv *KGSTG* B44 ....75 G1
Streather Rd *MGN/WHC* B75 ....47 G4
Streetly Crs *FOAKS/STRLY* B74 ....46 B2
Streetly Dr *FOAKS/STRLY* B74 ....46 B2
Streetly La *FOAKS/STRLY* B74 ....46 C3
Streetly Rd *ERDW/GRVHL* B23 ....92 B1
Streetly Wd *FOAKS/STRLY* B74 ....45 G5
Streetsbrook Rd *SOLH* B91 ....181 G1
Streets Corner Gdns *ALDR* WS9 ....19 G3
Strensham Hl *BHTH/HG* B12 ....144 A3
Strensham Rd *BHTH/HG* B12 ....144 A3
Stretton Gdns *CDSL* WV8 ....10 B3

Stretton Gv
LOZ/NWT B19 *..............108 A1
SPARK B11 ....145 E1
Stretton Pl *BILS/COS* WV14 ....68 A2
DUDS DY2 ....102 D5

Stretton Rd
SHHTH WV12 ....26 A2
SHLY B90 ....179 H5
Stringer Cl *MGN/WHC* B75 ....47 E1
Stringes Cl *WLNHL* WV13 ....39 H2
Stringes La *WLNHL* WV13 ....39 H3
Strode Rd *BKHL/PFLD* WV2 ....52 A2
Stronsay Cl *RBRY* B45 ....174 D5
Stroud Av *SHHTH* WV12 ....40 A1
Stroud Cl *SHHTH* WV12 ....40 A1
Stroud Rd *SHLY* B90 ....179 H3

Strutt Cl *EDG* B15 ....125 F4
Stuart Crs *DUDS* DY2 ....85 E5

Stuart Rd
BLKHTH/ROWR B65 ....104 A5
RMSLY B62 ....139 H2
Stuart's Dr *STCH* B33 ....129 H5
Stuart's Rd *STETCH* B33 ....129 H2
Stuart St *BLOX/PEL* WS3 ....27 F2
VAUX/NECH B7 ....110 A2
Stuarts Wy *RIDG/WDGT* B32 ....157 F3

Stubbers Green Rd
RUSH/SHEL WS4 ....29 G5
Stubbington Cl *WLNHL* WV13 ....38 D4
Stubbs Rd *BDMR/CCFT* WV3 ....51 H1
Stubby La *WNSFLD* WV11 ....25 C4
Studland Rd *HLGN/YWD* B28 ....163 E1
Stud La *STETCH* B33 ....130 B1
Studley Cft *HIA/OLT* B92 ....148 A4
Studley Dr *BRLYHL* DY5 ....119 E4
Studley Ga *STRBR* DY8 ....134 D2
Studley Rd *BHTH/HG* B12 ....144 D2

Sturman Dr
BLKHTH/ROWR B65 ....121 H3
Suckling Green La *CDSL* WV8 ....10 B5
Sudbury Cl *WNSFLD* WV11 ....25 E2
Sudbury Gv *KGSTG* B44 ....75 H1
Sudeley Cl *CBROM* B36 ....94 D5
Sudeley Gdns *DUDN* DY1 ....83 F3
Suffield Gv *ERDW/GRVHL* B23 ....91 H1
Suffolk Cl *LGLYGN/QTN* B68 ....105 E5
WNSFLD WV11 ....24 C4
Suffolk Dr *BRLYHL* DY5 ....135 G5
Suffolk Gv *ALDR* WS9 ....30 B2
Suffolk Pl *CBHAMW* B1 *..............5 F7
WSLW WS1 ....27 H5
Suffolk Rd *DARL/WED* WS10 ....56 C5
DUDS DY2 ....102 A2

Suffolk St Queensway
CBHAMW B1 ....2 E6
Suffrage St *SMTHWK* B66 ....106 D4
Sugden Gv *DIG/EDG* B5 ....127 E4
Sulgrave Cl *DUDN* DY1 ....84 A3
Sumburgh Cft *CVALE* B35 ....94 C3
Summercourt Dr *KGSWFD* DY6 ....99 G4
Summercourt Sq *KGSWFD* DY6 ....99 G4
Summer Cft *LOZ/NWT* B19 ....108 D3
Summer Dr *SEDG* DY3 ....83 E3
Summerfield Crs
LDYWD/EDGR B16 ....125 G1
Summerfield Dr *SLYOAK* B29 ....158 C3
Summerfield Gv *WSNGN* B18 *..............107 G5
Summerfield Rd *DUDS* DY2 ....102 D2
HAG/WOL DY9 ....170 C3
HIA/OLT B92 ....164 C1
LDYWD/EDGR B16 ....125 G1
WOLV WV1 ....6 C4
Summerfields Av *RMSLY* B62 ....122 D4
Summergate *SEDG* DY3 ....82 B4
Summer Hl *HALE* B63 ....138 D4
KGSWFD DY6 ....99 G3
Summer Hill Rd *CBHAMW* B1 ....2 A3
Summerhill Rd *BILS/COS* WV14 ....68 C2
TPTN/OCK DY4 ....69 F3
Summer Hill St *CBHAMW* B1 ....2 A4
Summer Hill Ter *CBHAMW* B1 ....2 B4

Summerhouse Rd
BILS/COS WV14 ....68 A2

Summerlee Rd
ERDE/BCHGN B24 ....93 F4
Summer Rd *ACGN* B27 ....146 A5
BLKHTH/ROWR B65 ....122 B1
DUDN DY1 ....84 A2
EDG B15 ....126 C5
ERDW/GRVHL B23 ....92 D2

Summer Rw
BRLYHL DY5 ....136 C2
HHTH/SAND B71 ....87 H2
KGSWFD DY6 ....99 H3
WSLW WS4 ....15 H5
Summer St *HALE* B63 ....138 D4
KGSWFD DY6 ....99 G3
WALM/CURD B76 ....79 E5
Summerton Rd *OLDBY* B69 ....104 B1
Summervale Cl *HAG/WOL* DY9 ....152 C5

Summervale Rd
HAG/WOL DY9 ....152 C5
Summerville Ter *HRBN* B17 *..............142 A2
Summit Crs *SMTHWK* B66 ....106 A1
Summit Gdns *HALE* B63 ....138 B4
Summit Pl *SEDG* DY3 ....82 D4
The Summit *HAG/WOL* DY9 ....136 B3
Sumbleam Cl *CBROM* B36 ....95 H5
Sunbeam Cl *CBROM* B36 ....95 H5
Sunbeam St *BKHL/PFLD* WV2 ....52 A1
Sunbeam Wy *STETCH* B33 ....131 E2
Sunbury Cl *BILS/COS* WV14 ....68 D2
Sunbury Rd *HALE* B63 ....158 B3
NFLD/LBR B31 ....189 F1
Suncroft *RIDG/WDGT* B32 ....140 D3
Sundbury Ri *NFLD/LBR* B31 ....158 C5
Sunderland Dr *STRBR* DY8 ....118 C4

Sunderton Rd
ALE/KHTH/YWD B14 ....178 A1
Sundew Cft *CBROM* B36 ....111 H1
Sundial La *GTB/HAM* B43 ....73 H2
Sundour Crs *WNSFLD* WV11 ....24 B4
Sundridge Rd *KGSTG* B44 ....60 A4
Sunleigh Gv *ACGN* B27 ....147 E3
Sunningdale *RMSLY* B62 ....139 G3

Sunningdale Av
DUNHL/THL/PER WV6 ....20 D1
Sunningdale Cl
BFLD/HDSWWD B20 ....89 G2
SCFLD/BOLD B73 ....62 A5
STRBR DY8 ....135 F5
Sunningdale Dr *OLDBY* B69 ....103 G2
Sunningdale Rd *SEDG* DY3 ....66 D2
SPARK B11 ....146 A4

Sunningdale Wy
BLOX/PEL WS3 ....16 C4
Sunny Av *BHTH/HG* B12 ....144 C2
Sunnybank Av *KGSTG* B44 ....75 H4

Sunnybank Cl *ALDR* WS9 ....45 E3

Sunny Bank Rd
LGLYGN/QTN B68 ....123 C5

Sunnybank Rd
SCFLD/BOLD B73 ....77 E5
Sun Cl *SEDG* DY3 ....83 G1
Sunnydene *WASH/WDE* B8 ....111 E4
Sunny Hill Cl *WMBN* WV5 ....65 F5

Sunnymead Rd
FOAKS/STRLY B74 ....60 B1
Sunnymead Wy *KGSWFD* DY6 ....100 C5
Sunnymede Rd *KGSWFD* DY6 ....100 C5
Sunnyside *ALDR* WS9 ....19 F5
SEDG DY3 ....103 H2

Sunnyside Av
ERDW/GRVHL B23 ....92 C3
Sunridge Av *LOZ/NWT* B19 ....108 D3
WMBN WV5 ....65 E4
Sunset Pl
ETTPK/GDPK/PENN WV4 ....52 D5
Surfeit Hl *CDYHTH* B64 ....121 E4
Surfeit Hill Rd *CDYHTH* B64 ....120 D4
Surrey Crs *HHTH/SAND* B71 ....71 E3
Surrey Dr *BDMR/CCFT* WV3 ....36 A4
KGSWFD DY6 ....100 A5
Surrey Rd *DUDS* DY2 ....102 A2
KGSTG B44 ....60 A4
Surrey Wk *ALDR* WS9 ....30 A2
Sussex Av *ALDR* WS9 ....30 A2
DARL/WED WS10 ....56 D4
HHTH/SAND B71 ....71 G5
Sussex Dr *BDMR/CCFT* WV3 ....36 A4
Sutherland Av *BKHL/PFLD* WV2 ....37 H5
SHLY B90 ....181 G4
Sutherland Cl *GTB/HAM* B43 ....59 H4
Sutherland Dr *MOS/BIL* B13 ....144 B5
WMBN WV5 ....65 E3

Sutherland Gv
DUNHL/THL/PER WV6 ....34 D1
Sutherland Pl *BKHL/PFLD* WV2 ....7 H6
Sutherland Rd *CDYHTH* B64 ....121 E4
ETTPK/GDPK/PENN WV4 ....51 H5
Sutherland St *AST/WIT* B6 ....109 H1
Sutton Ap *WASH/WDE* B8 ....111 E5

Sutton Ct
ETTPK/GDPK/PENN WV4 ....67 C1
MGN/WHC B75 ....62 B1
Sutton Crs *WBROM* B70 ....87 E2
Sutton New Rd
ERDW/GRVHL B23 ....92 D2

Sutton Oak Rd
SCFLD/BOLD B73 ....60 C4
Sutton Rd *ALDR* WS9 ....44 B4
DARL/WED WS10 ....54 C5
ERDW/GRVHL B23 ....93 E1
WSL WS1 ....5 H6
Sutton's Dr *GTB/HAM* B43 ....60 D4
Sutton Sq *WALM/CURD* B76 ....79 C5
Sutton St *AST/WIT* B6 ....126 D3
CBHAMW B1 ....2 D7
STRBR DY8 ....118 B5

Swains Gv *KGSTG* B44 ....60 B4
Swale Gv *HWK/WKHTH* B38 ....176 D5
WLNHL WV13 ....40 B3
Swale Rd *WALM/CURD* B76 ....78 C2
Swallow Av *CBROM* B36 ....114 A1
Swallow Cl *BHTH/HG* B12 ....144 B2
DARL/WED WS10 ....56 B4
DUDS DY2 ....120 D2
Swallow Ct *WOLVN* WV10 ....23 F5
Swallowdale *ALDR* WS9 ....19 G5
DUNHL/THL/PER WV6 ....34 D4
Swallowfall Av *STRBR* DY8 ....134 C5
Swallowfields Rd *SEDG* DY3 ....52 A5
Swallows Cl *BLOX/PEL* WS3 ....18 A2
Swallow's Meadow *SHLY* B90 ....180 D5
Swallow St *CBHAMW* B1 ....2 E6
WBROM B70 ....86 B2
Swanage Rd *SMHTH* B10 ....128 B4
Swan Av *SMTHWK* B66 ....106 A2

Swan Bank
ETTPK/GDPK/PENN WV4 ....51 F4
Swan Cl *KIDD* DY10 ....168 B4
WASH/WDE B8 ....110 D5
Swan Copse *YDLY* B25 ....146 B2

Swancote Dr
ETTPK/GDPK/PENN WV4 ....50 C3
Swancote Rd *DUDN* DY1 ....102 A1
STETCH B33 ....112 B4
Swan Ctyd
LGN/SDN/BHAMAIR B26 *..............146 D1
Swan Crs *OLDBY* B69 ....104 D5
Swancroft Rd *TPTN/OCK* DY4 ....69 F5
Swan Dr *BRWNH* WS8 ....9 C5
Swanfield Rd *STRBR* DY8 ....118 C5
Swan Gdns *ERDW/GRVHL* B23 ....92 D2
Swan La *BRGRVW* B61 ....185 H5
STRBR DY8 ....118 C2
WBROM B70 ....86 D3
Swanley Cl *RMSLY* B62 ....140 A4
Swanmore Cl *BDMR/CCFT* WV3 ....51 E1
Swann Rd *BILS/COS* WV14 ....68 A1
Swan Pool Gv *RUSH/SHEL* WS4 ....29 F1

Swansbrook Gdns
ALE/KHTH/YWD B14 ....177 G3
Swanshurst La *MOS/BIL* B13 ....162 A2
Swan St *BRLYHL* DY5 ....101 E3
DUDS DY2 ....102 C3
STRBR DY8 ....117 H3
Swanswell Rd *HIA/OLT* B92 ....163 H3

Swanswood Gv
CHWD/FDBR/MGN B37 *..............132 C1
Swarthmore Rd *SLYOAK* B29 ....158 D5
Sweetbriar La *SHHTH* WV12 ....26 B5
Sweetbriar Rd *BKHL/PFLD* WV2 ....53 E1
Sweetbrier Dr *STRBR* DY8 ....118 A3

Sweetman Pl
DUNHL/THL/PER WV6 ....6 B1

Sweetman St
DUNHL/THL/PER WV6 ....36 C1
Sweetmoor Cl *CBROM* B36 ....113 E1
Sweetpool La *STRBR* DY8 ....152 B5
Swift Cl *CBROM* B36 ....114 A1
Swinbrook Gv *KGSTG* B44 ....75 E2
Swinbrook Wy *SHLY* B90 ....180 D1

Swincross Rd *STRBR* DY8 ....135 H4
Swindell Rd *HAG/WOL* DY9 ....153 E1
Swinford Rd HR *BN* B17 ....124 D1
KGSWFD DY6 ....98 D1
Swinford Gv *DOR/KN* B93 ....196 C5
Swinford Leys *WMBN* WV5 ....80 C5
Swinford Rd *SLYOAK* B29 ....141 G4
STRBR DY8 ....135 G5
WOLVN WV10 ....23 G5
Swin Forge Wy *SEDG* DY3 ....66 A5
Swiss Dr *STRBR* DY8 ....118 B2
Swynnerton Dr *WNSFLD* WV11 ....11 G3
Sycamore Cl *ERDE/BCHGN* B24 ....92 D3
RUSH/SHEL WS4 ....28 D2
STRBR DY8 ....134 D5
WALM/CURD B76 ....78 D1

Sycamore Crs
CHWD/FDBR/MGN B37 ....132 A4
ERDE/BCHGN B24 ....92 D5
Sycamore Dr *BDMR/CCFT* WV3 ....35 H4
HLYWD B47 ....192 D5
Sycamore Gn *DUDN* DY1 ....83 H1

Sycamore Paddock
STRBR DY8 ....118 C5
Sycamore Pl *BILS/COS* WV14 ....54 C5
Sycamore Rd *AST/WIT* B6 ....109 C1
BVILLE B30 ....159 H5
DARL/WED WS10 ....71 E1
DSYBK/YTR WS5 ....57 F5
ERDW/GRVHL B23 ....76 D4
GTB/HAM B43 ....58 C5
HDSW B21 ....107 F1
KGSWFD DY6 ....100 A3
OLDBY B69 ....105 E5
RUSH/SHEL WS4 ....28 D2
SMTHWK B66 ....124 D1
TPTN/OCK DY4 ....69 F4
The Sycamores *STRBR* DY8 ....152 B5
WOLVN WV10 ....23 H2

Sycamore Ter
ALE/KHTH/YWD B14 *..............160 C5
Sydenham Rd *SMTHWK* B66 ....106 D1
SPARK B11 ....145 E2
WOLV WV1 ....38 B3
Sydney Cl *WBROM* B70 ....71 E4
Sydney Rd *BORD* B9 ....128 A2
CDYHTH B64 ....120 B4
SMTHWK B67 ....124 A1
Sydney Wy *BKDE/SHDE* B34 ....113 G1
Sylvan Av *NFLD/LBR* B31 ....175 F4
Sylvan Gn *RMSLY* B62 ....139 F1
Sylvia Av *NFLD/LBR* B31 ....175 H4

Symphony Ct
LDYWD/EDGR B16 ....2 E1
Sytch La *WMBN* WV5 ....81 E4

T

Tack Farm Rd *STRBR* DY8 ....117 H4
Tackford Cl *CBROM* B36 ....113 H1
Tackley Cl *SHLY* B90 ....180 D1
Tadmore Cl *BILS/COS* WV14 ....53 H5
Tadworth Cl *WOLV* WV1 ....38 A4
Tait Cft *HIA/OLT* B92 ....165 H1
Talaton Cl *COVEN* WV9 ....12 A5
Talbot Av *FOAKS/STRLY* B74 ....45 H3
Talbot Cl *ERDW/GRVHL* B23 ....76 D4
WSLW WS2 ....41 H1
Talbot Pl *BILS/COS* WV14 ....53 H5

Talbot Rd *BKHL/PFLD* WV2 ....52 A2
DUDS DY2 ....120 B1
SMTHWK B66 ....124 A2
Talbots La *BRLYHL* DY5 ....119 H2
Talbot St *BRLYHL* DY5 ....136 B1
HAG/WOL DY9 ....136 D3
HALE B63 ....135 H5
WSNGN B18 ....107 H5
Talbot Wy *SMHTH* B10 ....128 D4
Talfourd St *BORD* B9 ....128 D1
Talgarth Covert
HWK/WKHTH B38 ....190 A1
Talke Rd *DSYBK/YTR* WS5 ....57 E1
Talladale *RIDG/WDGT* B32 ....157 F3
Tallington Rd *STETCH* B33 ....131 G4
Tall Trees Cl *FOAKS/STRLY* B74 ....46 A3
SHHTH WV12 ....26 C4
Tall Trees Dr *HAG/WOL* DY9 ....136 A5
Talton Cl *SHLY* B90 ....195 F3
Tamar Cl *BRWNH* WS8 ....9 H4
Tamar Dr *CBROM* B36 ....112 A1
SEDG DY3 ....67 E2
WALM/CURD B76 ....78 D3
Tamar Gv *DUNHL/THL/PER* WV6 *..............34 D4
WLNHL WV13 ....39 H5
Tamarisk Cl *SLYOAK* B29 ....159 E2
Tamar Ri *STRBR* DY8 ....135 G1
Tame Av *DARL/WED* WS10 ....56 D3
Tame Cl *WSL* WS1 ....5 K6
Tame Crs *HHTH/SAND* B71 ....72 A3
Tame Dr *BLOX/PEL* WS3 ....18 A3
Tame Ri *LGLYGN/QTN* B68 ....123 F1
Tame Rd *AST/WIT* B6 ....109 H2
ERDE/BCHGN B24 ....93 H5
TPTN/OCK DY4 ....85 C1
Tamerton Rd *RIDG/WDGT* B32 ....157 H3
Tameside Cl *WLNHL* WV13 ....38 C4
Tameside Dr *AST/WIT* B6 ....91 H5
CVALE B35 ....93 H5
Tame St East *WSL* WS1 ....5 K5
Tamworth Cl *BRWNH* WS8 ....9 K4
Tamworth Rd *MGN/WHC* B75 ....47 H5
Tanacetum Dr *DSYBK/YTR* WS5 ....58 A2
Tandy Dr *ALE/KHTH/YWD* B14 ....177 H3
Tanfield Cl
DUNHL/THL/PER WV6 ....34 B1
Tanfield Dr *DUDS* DY2 ....102 A5
Tanfield Rd *DUDS* DY2 ....85 E4
STETCH B33 ....130 C3
Tanford Rd *HIA/OLT* B92 ....148 A2
Tanglewood Cl
BKDE/SHDE B34 ....96 A3
RIDG/WDGT B32 ....139 H5
Tanglewood Gv *SEDG* DY3 ....66 D3

SCFLD/BOLD B73 ....76 B1
Tudor Ct *TPTN/OCK* DY4 .....85 C2
WNSFLD WV11 ....14 D5
Tudor Crs *BKHL/PFLD* WV2 ...51 H2
Tudor Cft
CHWD/FDBR/MGN B37 ....131 H3
Tudor Gdns *ERDW/GRVHL* B23 ..92 C3
STRBR DY8 ....135 E2
Tudor Gv *FOAKS/STRLY* B74 ...45 G5
Tudor HI *SCFLD/BOLD* B73 .....62 A2
Tudor Pl *SEDG* DY3 ....67 G5
Tudor Rd *BILS/COS* WV14 .....104 A4
BKHTH/ROWR B65 ....105 C5
LGLYGN/QTN B68 ....144 B4
MOS/BIL B13 ....62 B3
SCFLD/BOLD B73 ....62 B3
SEDG DY3 ....53 A1
Tudors Cl *SMTH* B10 * 128 A4
Tudor St *TPTN/OCK* DY4 ....85 C2
WSNGN B18 ....107 F5
Tudor Ter *DUDS* DY2 ....142 A1
Tudor Wy *CSCFLD/WYGN* B72 ..77 F1
Tufnell Gv *WASH/WDE* B8 .....111 G2
Tugford Rd *SLYOAK* B29 ....159 E3
Tulip Gv *FOAKS/STRLY* B74 ....60 B2
Tunnel La *ALE/KHTH/YWD* B14..177 C1
Tunnel Rd *WBROM* B70 ....71 E3
Tunnel St *BILS/COS* WV14 .....68 C3
Tunstall Rd *KGSWFD* DY6 .....100 C4
Turchill Dr *WALM/CURD* B76 ...78 C5
Turfpits La *ERDW/GRVHL* B23 ..76 B5
Turf Pitts La *MGN/WHC* B75 ...87 G4
Turks Headway *WBROM* B70 ....87 C4
Turley St *DUDN* DY1 ....68 A5
Turls Hill Rd *BILS/COS* WV14 ...67 H5
Turls St *SEDG* DY3 ....67 G4
Turnberry Gv
DUNHL/THL/PER WV6 ....20 D1
Turnberry Rd *BLOX/PEL* WS3 ...16 D3
PBAR/PBCH B42 ....74 B3
Turner Dr *BRLYHL* DY5 ....119 F5
Turner Gv
DUNHL/THL/PER WV6 ....35 E1
Turners Cft *HHTH/SAND* B71 ...72 C3
Turner's Gv *SEDG* DY3 ....66 B5
Turner's HI
BLKHTH/ROWR B65 ....103 H3
Turners Hill Rd *SEDG* DY3 .....85 C2
Turner's La *BRLYHL* DY5 .....119 E4
Turner St *DUDN* DY1 ....102 B1
SEDG DY3 ....85 F3
SPARK B11 ....144 C1
TPTN/OCK DY4 ....69 F4
WBROM B70 ....87 F3
Turney Rd *STRBR* DY8 ....135 F1
Turnham Gn
DUNHL/THL/PER WV6 ....34 C2
Turnhouse Rd *CVALE* B35 ......94 D2
Turnley Rd *BKDE/SHDE* B34 ..113 E3
Turnpike Cl *SPARK* B11 ....144 C1
Turnpike Dr *CSHL/WTROR* B46 ..96 C5
Turton Cl *BLOX/PEL* WS3 ......16 C3
Turton Rd *TPTN/OCK* DY4 .....69 E2
WBROM B70 ....87 F4
Turtons Cft *BILS/COS* WV14 ...53 F5
Turves Gn *NFLD/LBR* B31 .....175 G4
Turville Rd
BFLD/HDSWWD B20 ....90 C5
Tustin Gv *ACGN* B27 ....163 G2
Tutbury Av
DUNHL/THL/PER WV6 ....34 D2
Tuxford Cl *WOLV* WV10 ....37 H2
Tweeds Well *RIDG/WDGT* B32 .157 F3
Twickenham Ct *STRBR* DY8 ...117 G5
Twickenham Dr *MOS/BIL* B13 ..144 A5
Twickenham Rd *KGSTG* B44 ....75 H2
Two Gates *HALE* B63 ....137 F2
Two Gates La *HALE* B63 ......137 G2
Two Locks *BRLYHL* DY5 ....105 H5
Two Woods La *BRLYHL* DY5 ...119 C5
Twycross Gv *CBROM* B36 ......111 H2
Twydale Av *OLDBY* B69 ....85 H5
Twyford Cl *ALDR* WS9 ....30 B5
Twyford Gv *WNSFLD* WV11 ....25 H4
Twyford Rd *WASH/WDE* B8 ....111 G4
Twyning Rd *BVILLE* B30 ......160 B3
WSNGN B18 ....107 F5
Tyber Dr *BFLD/HDSWWD* B20 ..90 B3
Tyberry Cl *SHLY* B90 ....179 H2
Tyburn Gv *ERDE/BCHGN* B24 ..93 H5
Tyburn Rd *ERDE/BCHGN* B24 ..92 B5
WOLV WV10 ....38 C4
Tyburn Sq *ERDE/BCHGN* B24 ..93 H5
Tyebeams *BKDE/SHDE* B34 ...113 G4
Tye Gdns *HAG/WOL* DY9 ......152 D1
Tye Rd *ERDE/BCHGN* B24 ......92 D3
Tyler Gdns *WLNHL* WV13 ......39 H4
Tyler Gv *GTB/HAM* B43 ....74 A2
Tyler Rd *WLNHL* WV13 ....39 G5
Tylers Gv *HWK/WKHTH* B38 ..199 F1
Tylney Cl *DIG/EDG* B5 ....126 D5
Tyndale Crs *GTB/HAM* B43 ....59 G5
Tyne Cl *BRWNH* WS8 ....8 C2
Tynedale Crs
ETTPK/GDPK/PENN WV4 ......52 C5
Tynedale Rd *SPARK* B11 ......145 H4
Tyne Gv *YDLY* B25 ....129 H4
Tyne Pl *BRLYHL* DY5 ....119 H2
Tyne Rd *COVEN* WV9 ....12 A5
Tyninghame Av
DUNHL/THL/PER WV6 ....21 H4
Tynings La *ALDR* WS9 ....30 A5
Tyrley Cl *DUNHL/THL/PER* WV6 ..35 F3
Tyrol Cl *STRBR* DY8 ....116 A3
Tyseley Hill Rd *SPARK* B11 ...146 A3
Tyseley La *SPARK* B11 ....146 A3
Tysoe Cl *HOCK/TIA* B94 .....198 A5
Tysoe Dr *WALM/CURD* B76 ....63 F4
Tysoe Rd *KGSTG* B44 ....75 G2
Tytheham Dr *KGSWFD* DY6 .....99 E2
The Barn La *SHLY* B90 ....193 G2
SHLY B90 ....194 A2
Tythebarn La *SHLY* B90 ......194 A2
Tyzack Cl *BRLYHL* DY5 ....119 E2

U

Udall Rd *BILS/COS* WV14 ....53 H5
Uffculme Rd *BVILLE* B30 ......160 D2
Uffmoor Est *HALE* B63 ....155 E1
Uffmoor La *HALE* B65 ....155 E1
RMSLY B62 ....154 D4
Ufton Cl *SHLY* B90 ....181 E2
Ufton Crs *SHLY* B90 ....180 D2
Ullenhall Rd *DOR/KN* B93 .....197 E2
WALM/CURD B76 ....78 B3
Ullenwood *HDSW* B21 ....107 F2
Ulleries Rd *HIA/OLT* B92 .....147 G5
Ullrik Gn *ERDE/BCHGN* B24 ...92 C4
Ullswater Cl *RIDG/WDGT* B32 .141 F5
Ullswater Gdns *KGSWFD* DY6 ..99 F5
Ullswater Ri *BRLYHL* DY5 .....101 F4
Ullswater Rd *SHHTH* WV12 ....25 H1
Ulster Dr *KGSWFD* DY6 ....100 A5
Ulverley Green Rd
HIA/OLT B92 ....164 C2
Ulwine Dr *NFLD/LBR* B31 .....175 G1
Umberslade Rd *SLYOAK* B29 ..160 A2
Uncle Ben's Cl *OLDBY* B69 ....13 G5
Underhill La *WOLV* WV10 .....24 A5
Underhill Rd *TPTN/OCK* DY4 ...70 A5
WASH/WDE B8 ....128 D1
Underhill St *OLDBY* B69 ......85 H5
Underley Cl *KGSWFD* DY6 .....99 F2
The Underpass *BHAMNEC* B40 .190 A3
Underwood Cl *BVILLE* B30 ....142 B4
ERDW/GRVHL B23 ....92 A2
Underwood Rd
BFLD/HDSWWD B20 ....89 G1
Unett Ct *LOZ/NWT* B19 ......108 C4
Unett St *LOZ/NWT* B19 ....108 C4
Unett St North *LOZ/NWT* B19 ..108 C4
Unett Wk *LOZ/NWT* B19 ......108 C4
Union La *WMBN* WV5 ....64 B2
Union Mill St *WOLV* WV1 ....7 J4
Union Pas *CBHAM* B2 ....3 G5
Union Rd *SLYOAK* B29 ....143 F5
Union St *AST/WIT* B6 ....109 H1
OLDBY B69 ....86 C4
SHLY B90 ....180 B5
STRBR DY8 ....182 A1
TPTN/OCK DY4 ....107 H1
Union Rw *HDSW* B21 ....107 H1
Union St *BILS/COS* WV14 .....53 C5
BLKHTH/ROWR B65 ....122 A3
CBHAM B2 ....3 G5
DUDN DY1 ....70 D1
HAG/WOL DY9 ....136 C2
STRBR DY8 ....135 G3
TPTN/OCK DY4 ....69 E4
WSL WS1 ....5 J3
Unitt Cl *CDYTH* B64 ....121 E4
Unity Cl *DARL/WED* WS10 .....55 E4
Unity Pl *OLDBY* B69 * 105 E1
SLYOAK B29 * 142 D5
Unketts Rd *SMTHWKW* B67 ...124 A1
Unwin Crs *STRBR* DY8 ....134 C2
Upavon Cl *CVALE* B35 ....94 C2
Upland Rd *SLYOAK* B29 ....143 E5
Uplands *HALE* B63 ....137 H5
Uplands Av *BDMR/CCFT* WV3 ..35 H5
BLKHTH/ROWR B65 ....122 A3
WLNHL WV13 ....38 D4
Uplands Cl *DUDS* DY2 ....103 E2
Uplands Dr *BDMR/CCFT* WV3 ..36 A5
SEDG DY3 ....67 F3
Uplands Gv *WLNHL* WV13 .....38 C4
Uplands Rd *DUDS* DY2 ....103 F2
WLNHL WV13 ....38 C4
The Uplands *SMTHWKW* B67 ..106 B5
Upper Ashley St *RMSLY* B62 ..122 A3
Upper Balsall Heath Rd
BHTH/HG B12 ....144 B1
Upper Brook St *WSLW* WS2 ....54 D3
Upper Chapel St *OLDBY* B69 ..85 H4
Upper Church La *TPTN/OCK* DY4 ..69 E5
Upper Clifton Rd
SCFLD/BOLD B73 ....62 B3
Upper Conybere St
BHTH/HG B12 ....127 F5
Upper Dean St *DIG/EDG* B5 ....3 G7
Upper Ettingshall Rd
BHTH/HG B12 ....68 A3
Upper Forster St
RUSH/SHEL WS4 ....5 F1
Upper Gough St *CBHAMW* B1 ..126 D5
Upper Gn on
DUNHL/THL/PER WV6 ....21 H5
Upper Green La *WSLW* WS2 ...41 G1
Upper Grosvenor Rd
BFLD/HDSWWD B20 ....90 B4
Upper Hall La *WSL* WS1 ......42 A2
Upper Highgate St
BHTH/HG B12 ....127 F5
Upper High St *CDYTH* B64 ...120 D3
DARL/WED WS10 ....55 H5
Upper Holland Rd
CSCFLD/WYGN B72 ....62 C4
Upper Lichfield St
WLNHL WV13 ....39 G3
Upper Marshall St
CBHAM B1 ....2 E7
Upper Meadow Rd
RIDG/WDGT B32 ....140 C2
Upper Navigation St
WSLW WS2 ....4 C3
Upper Rushall St *WSL* WS1 ....5 F4
Upper Russell St
DARL/WED WS10 ....70 D1
Upper St Mary's Rd
SMTHWKW B67 ....124 B3
Upper Short St *WSLW* WS2 ....4 B4
Upper Sneyd Rd *WNSFLD* WV11 ..15 F5

Upper Stone Cl
WALM/CURD B76 ....63 E4
Upper St
DUNHL/THL/PER WV6 ....21 H5
Upper Sutton St *AST/WIT* B6 ..109 F2
Upper Thomas St *AST/WIT* B6 .109 F1
Upper Trinity St *BORD* B9 ....127 G5
Upper Vauxhall *WOLV* WV1 .....6 B5
Upper Villiers St
BKHL/PFLD WV2 ....51 H2
Upper William St *CBHAMW* B1 ..2 C7
Upper Zoar St
BDMR/CCFT WV3 ....6 C7
Upton Cl *SOLH* B91 ....53 G3
Upton Gn *WOLV* WV10 ....12 B4
Upton Gv *STETCH* B33 ....129 G3
Upton Rd *STETCH* B33 ....129 G2
Upton St *DUDS* DY2 ....102 C4
Upwey Av *SOLH* B91 ....181 G1
Uttoxeter Cl
DUNHL/THL/PER WV6 ....22 D5
Uxbridge Cl *SEDG* DY3 ....83 F4
Uxbridge St *LOZ/NWT* B19 ...108 D4

V

Valbourne Rd
ALE/KHTH/YWD B14 ....177 G1
Vale Av *ALDR* WS9 ....44 D3
Vale Cl *RIDG/WDGT* B32 .....141 F4
Vale Ct *CDYHTH* B64 * 120 D5
Vale Head Dr
DUNHL/THL/PER WV6 ....35 E3
Valencia Cft *CVALE* B35 ......94 D2
Valentine Cl *FOAKS/STRLY* B74 ..60 B2
Valentine Rd
ALE/KHTH/YWD B14 ....161 E1
LGLYGN/QTN B68 ....123 G2
Valepits Rd *STETCH* B33 .....131 E3
Vale Rw *SEDG* DY3 ....85 H1
Vale St *BKHL/PFLD* WV2 ....53 E2
HHTH/SAND B71 ....72 A5
SEDG DY3 ....85 F1
STRBR DY8 ....118 B4
The Vale *SPARK* B11 ....144 B2
Vale Vw *ALDR* WS9 ....44 B2
Valley Farm Rd *RBRY* B45 ....187 H2
Valley La *HOCK/TIA* B94 .....199 H4
Valley Rd *BLOX/PEL* WS3 .....27 H2
CDYHTH B64 ....121 E5
FOAKS/STRLY B74 ....60 B1
HAG/WOL DY9 ....136 D1
HIA/OLT B92 ....148 A3
RMSLY B62 ....122 D4
SEDG DY3 ....67 G3
SMTHWKW B67 ....124 B1
SMTHWKW B67 ....117 H5
WBROM B70 ....24 B4
WSNGN B18 ....108 A2
YDLY B25 ....130 A3
Vicarage Rd West *LGLYGN/QTN* B68 ..105 D3
Vicarage St *LGLYGN/QTN* B68 ..105 D4
KGSWFD DY6 ....100 C4
Victor Cl *BKHL/PFLD* WV2 ....53 F2
Victoria Av *BLOX/PEL* WS3 ....27 C1
RMSLY B62 ....128 B5
SMTH B10 ....127 H1
SMTHWK B66 ....106 D4
Victoria Gdns *CDYHTH* B64 * ..121 F2
Victoria Gv *WMBN* WV5 ....7 F4
WSNGN B18 ....108 A2
Victoria Ms *OLDBY* B69 ....122 D1
RUSH/SHEL WS4 ....54 A1
Victoriana Wy
BFLD/HDSWWD B20 ....90 A5
Victoria Park Rd
SMTHWK B66 ....106 D4
Victoria Pas *WOLV* WV1 ....7 F4
Victoria Pl *DARL/WED* WS10 * ..55 H2
Victoria Rd *ACGN* B27 ....146 C5
AST/WIT B6 ....109 E2
BDMR/CCFT WV3 ....36 B3
BLOX/PEL WS3 ....18 A4
BRLYHL DY5 ....120 A3
BVILLE B30 ....160 B1
CDYHTH B64 ....121 F2
CSCFLD/WYGN B72 ....62 C4
DARL/WED WS10 ....55 F2
DUNHL/THL/PER WV6 ....35 E3
ERDW/GRVHL B23 ....107 G2
HDSW B21 ....141 H2
HRBN B17 ....124 D1
LGLYGN/QTN B68 ....105 G3
RMSLY B62 ....122 B4
SEDG DY3 ....85 F1
STETCH B33 ....129 H1
TPTN/OCK DY4 ....85 F1
WNSFLD WV11 ....24 B4
WOLV WV10 ....23 H5
Victoria Sq *CBHAMNW* B3 ....2 E4
Victoria St *BORD* B9 ....128 B2
BRLYHL DY5 ....119 F1
DARL/WED WS10 ....70 C1
HALE B63 ....138 C3
KGSWFD DY6 ....99 F1
SEDG DY3 ....86 D1
WLNHL WV13 ....39 G2
WOLV WV1 ....7 F5
Victoria Ter *RUSH/SHEL* WS4 ..42 B2
Victor Rd *HIA/OLT* B92 ......148 A2
WSNGN B18 ....107 G3
Victor St *BLOX/PEL* WS3 .....28 C1
WSL WS1 ....57 E1
Victory Av *DARL/WED* WS10 ...54 A4
Victory La *WSLW* WS2 ....41 E1
Victory Ri *HHTH/SAND* B71 ...72 C1
View Dr *DUDS* DY2 ....103 E1
Viewfield Crs *SEDG* DY3 ......67 F4
Viewlands Dr
DUNHL/THL/PER WV6 ....35 E3
View Point *OLDBY* B69 ....104 D1
Vigo Cl *WSL* WS1 ....19 F5
Vigo Pl *ALDR* WS9 ....30 A3
Vigo Rd *ALDR* WS9 ....19 F5
Vigo Ter *ALDR* WS9 ....19 F4

LCLYGN/QTN B68 ....105 C3
RMSLY B62 ....122 A4
Vernon St *WBROM* B70 ....86 C5
Vernon Wy *BLOX/PEL* WS3 .....26 C1
Veronica Av
ETTPK/GDPK/PENN WV4 ......52 C3
Veronica Cl *SLYOAK* B29 .....158 B4
Veronica Rd *KGSWFD* DY6 ....100 C3
Verstone Cft *NFLD/LBR* B31 ..175 G3
Verstone Rd *SHLY* B90 ....180 C5
Verwood Cl *WLNHL* WV13 ......38 A4
Vesey Cl *CSHL/WTROR* B46 ...96 B4
FOAKS/STRLY B74 ....46 D5
Vesey Rd *SCFLD/BOLD* B73 ....77 F2
Vesey St *CBHAMNE* B4 ....3 G2
Vestry Cl *CDYHTH* B64 ....121 F3
Vestry Ct *STRBR* DY8 ....135 E1
Viaduct Dr
DUNHL/THL/PER WV6 ....22 D4
Viaduct St *VAUX/NECH* B7 ...127 G1
Vibart Rd
BHTH/HG B12 ....127 H1
Vicarage Cl *BRLYHL* DY5 .....119 E5
BRWNH WS8 ....9 G4
BVILLE B30 ....160 B3
PBAR/PBCH B42 ....74 D4
Vicarage Gdns *RMSLY* B62 ...122 B3
WALM/CURD B76 ....78 B4
Vicarage Gv *ACGN* B27 ....163 F2
Vicarage La *BRLYHL* DY5 .....101 F1
CSHL/WTROR B46 ....96 B4
Vicarage Pl *WSL* WS1 ....5 F3
Vicarage Prospect *DUDN* DY1 ..84 B5
Vicarage Rd
ALE/KHTH/YWD B14 ....160 D3
AST/WIT B6 ....68 C4
BKHL/PFLD WV2 ....7 H7
BLOX/PEL WS3 ....18 A5
BRWNH WS8 ....9 F5
DARL/WED WS10 ....55 E5
DUDS DY2 ....125 H4
ERDW/GRVHL B23 ....51 E5
HAG/WOL DY9 ....136 D2
HHTH/SAND B71 ....71 H5
HRBN B17 ....141 H2
LGLYGN/QTN B68 ....105 G4
RMSLY B62 ....122 A4
SEDG DY3 ....83 G1
SMTHWK B66 ....106 C4
SMTHWKW B67 ....117 H5
SMTHWK B67 ....24 B4
STRBR DY8 ....108 A2
YDLY B25 ....130 A3

Viking Ri *BLKHTH/ROWR* B65 ..104 A5
Village Ms *RIDG/WDGT* B32 ...140 A1
Village Rd *AST/WIT* B6 ....91 C5
The Village *KGSWFD* DY6 .....100 A2
Villa Cl *BILS/COS* WV14 ......68 C2
Villa Rd *LOZ/NWT* B19 ....108 B3
STRBR DY8 ....118 C4
Villa Wk *LOZ/NWT* B19 ......108 C3
Villette Gv
ALE/KHTH/YWD B14 ....179 E1
Villiers Av *BILS/COS* WV14 ...53 H2
Villiers Sq *BILS/COS* WV14 ...53 H1
Villiers St *WLNHL* WV13 ......39 C3
WSL WS1 ....57 E1
WSNGN B18 ....107 G4
Vimy Rd *DARL/WED* WS10 .....56 A4
MOS/BIL B13 ....161 H2
Vincent Cl *BHTH/HG* B12 ....144 D2
Vincent Dr *EDG* B15 ....142 D4
Vincent Pde *BHTH/HG* B12 ...144 D2
Vincent Rd *MGN/WHC* B75 .....63 E1
Vincent St *BHTH/HG* B12 ....144 B2
WSL WS1 ....5 J3
Vinculum Wy *WLNHL* WV13 ...39 H4
Vine Av *BHTH/HG* B12 ....144 C2
Vine Cl *WOLV* WV10 ....11 C5
Vine Crs *HHTH/SAND* B71 ....72 A2
Vine Gdns *CDYHTH* B64 ......121 F3
Vine La *CDYHTH* B64 ....121 G3
HALE B63 ....138 D4
STRBR DY8 ....117 H3
The Vineries *ACGN* B27 ......147 E3
Vine St *AST/WIT* B6 ....109 E1
BRLYHL DY5 ....119 F1
STRBR DY8 ....108 A3
Vineyard Rd *NFLD/LBR* B31 ..175 F3
Vinnall Gv *RIDG/WDGT* B32 ..157 F2
Vintage Cl *BKDE/SHDE* B34 ..112 C4
Vinyard Cl *HDSW* B21 ....107 H2
Violet Cft *TPTN/OCK* DY4 .....69 H2
Violet La *HAG/WOL* DY9 .....170 C1
Virginia Dr
ETTPK/GDPK/PENN WV4 ......51 F4
Viscount Cl *CVALE* B35 ....94 C4
Viscount Dr *CVALE* B35 ....94 D4
Vista Gn *HWK/WKHTH* B38 ...178 A4
The Vista *SEDG* DY3 ....67 F2
Vittoria St *CBHAMW* B1 ....2 C1
SMTHWK B66 ....107 F1
Vivian Cl *HRBN* B17 ....142 A2
Vivian Rd *HRBN* B17 ....142 A1
Vixen Cl *WALM/CURD* B76 .....77 H4
Vowles Rd *HHTH/SAND* B71 ...71 H5
Vulcan Rd *BILS/COS* WV14 ...68 D5
SOLH B91 ....165 E4
Vyrnwy Gv *HWK/WKHTH* B38 ..176 D3
Vyse St *AST/WIT* B6 ....109 H1
WSNGN B18 ....108 A1

W

Wadbarn *SHLY* B90 ....194 A4
Waddams Pool *DUDS* DY2 ......84 C1
Waddell Cl *BILS/COS* WV14 ...67 H5
Waddens Brook La
WNSFLD WV11 ....25 G5
Waddington Av *GTB/HAM* B43 ..73 G1
Wades Cl *TPTN/OCK* DY4 ......85 E1
Wadesmill Lawns *WOLV* WV10 ..13 E4
Wadham Cl
BLKHTH/ROWR B65 ....104 A3
Wadhurst Rd *HRBN* B17 ......124 D1
Wadleys Rd *SOLH* B91 ....164 D1
Waen Cl *TPTN/OCK* DY4 ....69 F2
Waggon La *KIDD* DY10 ....168 D5
Waggon St *CDYHTH* B64 .....121 F2
Waggon Wk *HWK/WKHTH* B38 ..176 D1
Wagoners Cl *WASH/WDE* B8 ...92 B4
Wagon La *HIA/OLT* B92 ......147 G2
Wagstaff Cl *BILS/COS* WV14 ..68 D4
Wainscott Cl *HRBN* B17 .....124 D1
Wakefield Gdns *GTB/HAM* B43 ..73 H1
Wainwright St *KGSWFD* DY6 ...99 E3
Wainwright St *AST/WIT* B6 ..109 F1
Waite Rd *WLNHL* WV13 ....39 H5
Wakefield Cl *SCFLD/BOLD* B73 ..77 E3
Wakefield Ct *MOS/BIL* B13 ..162 A2
Wakefield Gv *CSHL/WTROR* B46 ..96 B4
Wakeford Rd *NFLD/LBR* B31 ..175 H1
Wake Green Pk *MOS/BIL* B13 ..144 D5
Wake Green Rd *MOS/BIL* B13 ..144 C5
MOS/BIL B13 ....162 A1
TPTN/OCK DY4 ....69 E2
Wakelam Gdns *GTB/HAM* B43 ..73 G1
Wakeley Hl
ETTPK/GDPK/PENN WV4 ......51 F5
Wakelin Rd *SHLY* B90 ....194 A1
Wakeman Ct *WNSFLD* WV11 ...10 D5
Wakeman Dr *OLDBY* B69 ......105 E1
Wakeman Gv *STETCH* B33 ....131 G3
Wakes Cl *WLNHL* WV13 ....39 H3
Wakes Rd *DARL/WED* WS10 ....56 C1
Walcot Cl *MGN/WHC* B75 ......63 G1
Walcot Dr *GTB/HAM* B43 .....59 H5
Walcot Gdns *BILS/COS* WV14 ..53 F5
Walcot Gn *DOR/KN* B93 ......197 H2
Waldale Cl *SHHTH* WV12 ......25 H2
Walden Gdns
ETTPK/GDPK/PENN WV4 ......51 F5
Walden Rd *SPARK* B11 ....146 B2
Waldeve Gv *HIA/OLT* B92 ....166 A2
Waldley Gv *ERDE/BCHGN* B24 ..92 D5
Waldron Av *BRLYHL* DY5 .....119 E2
Waldron Cl *DARL/WED* WS10 ..56 C4
Waldrons Moor
ALE/KHTH/YWD B14 ....160 C5
Walford Av *DUNHL/THL/PER* WV6 ..35 E4
Walford Dr *HIA/OLT* B92 ....148 B2
Walford Gv *MGN/WHC* B75 ....63 H1
Walford Rd *SPARK* B11 ....144 D2
Walford St *OLDBY* B69 ....85 E5
Walhouse Cl *WSL* WS1 ....5 G3
Walhouse Rd *WSL* WS1 ....5 G3
Walker Av *BRLYHL* DY5 ......119 E5
HAG/WOL DY9 ....153 E2
OLDBY B69 ....85 H5

WOLVN WV10 23 G2
Walker Dr *ERDE/BCHGN* B24 110 C1
Walker Pl *BLOX/PEL* WS3 28 A2
Walker Rd *BLOX/PEL* WS3 27 H2
Walkers Fold *SHHTH* WV12 26 B4
Walkers Heath Rd
HWK/WKHTH B38 177 F4
Walker St *DUDS* DY2 102 C5
TPTN/OCK DY4 70 A4
Walkers Wy *CSHL/WTROR* B46 115 G3
Walk La *WMBN* WV5 65 E5
The Walk *SEDG* DY3 67 F2
Wallace Cl *OLDBY* B69 104 B3
Wallace Ri *CDYHTH* B64 121 E5
Wallace Rd *BILS/COS* WV14 54 C5
BILS/COS WV14 69 F1
BRWNH WS8 9 E4
OLDBY B69 104 B3
SLYOAK B29 143 F5
Wall Av *CSHL/WTROR* B46 115 F4
Wallbank Rd *WASH/WDE* B8 111 E3
Wallbrook St *BILS/COS* WV14 68 D3
Wall Cl *SMTHWKW* B67 105 H5
Wall Cft *ALDR* WS9 30 B3
Wall Dr *FOAKS/STRLY* B74 46 D1
Wall End Cl *WSLW* WS2 27 E3
Wallface *HHTH/SAND* B71 71 E4
Walling Cft *BILS/COS* WV14 53 F5
Wallington Cl *BLOX/PEL* WS3 16 D5
Wallington Heath
BLOX/PEL WS3 16 D5
Wallows La *WSL* WS1 56 C2
Wallows Pl *BRLYHL* DY5 101 E4
Wallows Rd *BRLYHL* DY5 101 E5
Wallows Wd *SEDG* DY3 82 C2
Wall St *WOLV* WV1 38 A3
Wall Well *HALE* B63 138 B4
Wall Well La *HALE* B63 138 B4
Walmead Cft *HRBN* B17 124 B5
Walmer Gv *ERDW/GRVHL* B23 91 H1
Walmer Meadow *ALDR* WS9 30 B3
The Walmers *ALDR* WS9 30 B3
Walmer Wy
CHWD/FDBR/MGN B37 132 C1
Walmesley Wy *NFLD/LBR* B31 175 E2
Walmley Ash Rd
WALM/CURD B76 78 B4
Walmley Cl *HALE* B63 120 B5
WALM/CURD B76 78 B3
Walmley Rd *WALM/CURD* B76 63 F5
Walnut Av *CDSL* WV8 10 D4
Walnut Cl
CHWD/FDBR/MGN B37 132 B3
HAG/WOL DY9 152 D1
Walnut Dr *BDMR/CCFT* WV3 35 H4
SMTHWK B66 106 D4
Walnut La *DARL/WED* WS10 71 E1
Walnut Rd *DSYBK/YTR* WS5 57 G5
Walnut Wy *NFLD/LBR* B31 175 F5
Walpole St
DUNHL/THL/PER WV6 6 B1
Walpole Wk *WBROM* B70 87 H5
Walsall Rd *ALDR* WS9 30 A5
ALDR WS9 43 H1
BLOX/PEL WS3 18 A5
DARL/WED WS10 55 G2
DSYBK/YTR WS5 57 F4
FOAKS/STRLY B74 46 C2
HHTH/SAND B71 72 A4
PBAR/PBCH B42 74 A3
RUSH/SHEL WS4 19 E5
WLNHL WV13 40 A3
Walsall St *BILS/COS* WV14 53 H3
DARL/WED WS10 55 F2
WBROM B70 87 H3
WLNHL WV13 39 H4
WOLV WV1 7 J5
alsall Wood Rd *ALDR* WS9 30 B3
alsgrave Dr *HIA/OLT* B92 165 F3
alsham Cft *BKDE/SHDE* B34 113 E4
alsh Dr *WALM/CURD* B76 63 F4
alsh Gv *ERDW/GRVHL* B23 76 B3
alsingham St *WSL* WS1 5 H5
alstead Rd *DSYBK/YTR* WS5 57 H3
alstead Rd West
DSYBK/YTR WS5 57 E3
altdene Cl *GTB/HAM* B43 73 G1
alter Cobb Dr
SCFLD/BOLD B73 77 E2
alter Rd *BILS/COS* WV14 54 A5
SMTHWKW B67 106 A3
alters Cl *NFLD/LBR* B31 189 F2
alters Rd *LGLYGN/QTN* B68 123 E5
alters Rw *DUDN* DY1 84 A5
alter St *BLOX/PEL* WS3 28 C1
VAUX/NECH B7 109 H3
WBROM B70 87 H4
ltham Gv *KGSTG* B44 75 H1
lthamstow Ct *BRLYHL* DY5 119 F3
lton Av *BLKHTH/ROWR* B65 121 H4
lton Cl *BLKHTH/ROWR* B65 103 G5
HALE B63 138 B5
lton Crs
ETTPK/GDPK/PENN WV4 52 C3
lton Cft *SOLH* B91 181 H4
lton Dr *HAG/WOL* DY9 136 A2
lton Gdns *CDSL* WV8 10 B3
lton Gv *BVILLE* B30 177 F3
lton Heath *BLOX/PEL* WS3 16 B4
lton Pool La *HAG/WOL* DY9 170 D3
lton Ri *HAG/WOL* DY9 171 E2
lton Rd *ALDR* WS9 30 A1
DARL/WED WS10 71 G1
ETTPK/GDPK/PENN WV4 52 D3
LGLYGN/QTN B68 123 G3
STRBR DY8 135 G1
ton St *TPTN/OCK* DY4 85 F1
nderers Av *BKHL/PFLD* WV2 52 A2
nderer Wk *CBROM* B36 94 A5
ndle Gv *SPARK* B11 146 A4
ndsworth Rd *KGSTG* B44 60 A5
nerton Rd *KIDD* DY10 168 B4
sbeck Gv
WK/WKHTH B38 176 C5
sbeck Wk *SEDG* DY3 67 H5
stead Gv *KGSTG* B44 75 G2
tage Rd
SHL/WTROR B46 97 E5
d Cl *WASH/WDE* B8 111 E4
den Av *SCFLD/BOLD* B73 76 D3
Ward End Cl *WASH/WDE* B8 110 D3
Ward End Hall Gv
WASH/WDE B8 111 E3
Ward End Park Rd
WASH/WDE B8 110 D4
Wardend Rd *WASH/WDE* B8 111 E3
Warden Rd *SCFLD/BOLD* B73 76 D3
Ward Gv
ETTPK/GDPK/PENN WV4 52 D5
Wardle Cl *MGN/WHC* B75 47 E1
Wardlow Cl
ETTPK/GDPK/PENN WV4 51 H2
Wardlow Rd *VAUX/NECH* B7 109 G4
Wardour Dr
CHWD/FDBR/MGN B37 132 C2
Wardour Gv *KGSTG* B44 76 A3
Ward Rd *CDSL* WV8 10 B4
ETTPK/GDPK/PENN WV4 52 B3
Ward St *BILS/COS* WV14 68 B3
BKHL/PFLD WV2 53 F2
ERDW/GRVHL B23 92 C2
LOZ/NWT B19 3 G1
WLNHL WV13 39 H2
WOLV WV1 7 J4
WSL WS1 5 G2
Wareham Cl *BLOX/PEL* WS3 28 B5
Wareham Rd *RBRY* B45 174 B3
Wareing Dr *ERDW/GRVHL* B23 76 B3
Warewell Cl *WSL* WS1 5 F3
Warewell St *WSL* WS1 5 F4
Waring Cl *TPTN/OCK* DY4 69 E3
Waring Rd *TPTN/OCK* DY4 69 G3
The Warings *WMBN* WV5 80 D2
War La *HRBN* B17 141 H2
Warley Cft *LGLYGN/QTN* B68 123 H4
Warley Hall Rd
LGLYGN/QTN B68 123 H3
Warley Rd *LGLYGN/QTN* B68 105 G4
Warmington Dr
SCFLD/BOLD B73 62 B4
Warmington Rd *HLYWD* B47 192 C2
LGN/SDN/BHAMAIR B26 148 A2
Warmley Cl
DUNHL/THL/PER WV6 22 D5
SOLH B91 165 F5
Warner Dr *BRLYHL* DY5 119 F3
Warner Pl *BLOX/PEL* WS3 28 B4
Warner Rd *BLOX/PEL* WS3 28 C4
CDSL WV8 10 B4
DARL/WED WS10 71 G1
Warner St *BHTH/HG* B12 127 G4
Warners Wk *SMTHH* B10 128 A4
Warple Rd *RIDG/WDGT* B32 140 C2
Warren Av *WOLVN* WV10 23 H5
Warren Cl *TPTN/OCK* DY4 69 F4
Warren Dr *BLKHTH/ROWR* B65 103 F4
DOR/KN B93 197 E5
SEDG DY3 67 E1
Warren Farm Rd *KGSTG* B44 75 F3
Warren Gdns *KGSWFD* DY6 99 G3
Warren Gv *WASH/WDE* B8 * 110 C3
Warren Hill Rd *KGSTG* B44 75 G4
Warren House Wk
WALM/CURD B76 78 B2
Warren La *RBRY* B45 188 B5
Warren Pl *BRWNH* WS8 9 G5
Warren Rd *BVILLE* B30 160 A3
KGSTG B44 75 G5
WASH/WDE B8 110 C3
Warrens Cft *DSYBK/YTR* WS5 58 B3
Warrens End
HWK/WKHTH B38 176 D5
Warrens Hall Rd *DUDS* DY2 103 E2
Warrington Cl
WALM/CURD B76 78 C2
Warrington Dr
ERDW/GRVHL B23 76 B4
Warsash Cl *WOLV* WV1 38 B5
Warstock La
ALE/KHTH/YWD B14 178 C1
Warstock Rd
ALE/KHTH/YWD B14 178 C1
Warston Av *RIDG/WDGT* B32 140 D4
Warstone Dr *HHTH/SAND* B71 88 A2
Warstone La *WSNGN* B18 2 C2
Warstone Ms *WSNGN* B18 * 2 C2
Warstone Pde East *WSNGN* B18 2 B2
Warstones Crs
ETTPK/GDPK/PENN WV4 50 D3
Warstones Dr
ETTPK/GDPK/PENN WV4 50 C3
Warstones Gdns
ETTPK/GDPK/PENN WV4 50 C2
Warstones Rd
ETTPK/GDPK/PENN WV4 50 D4
Warstone Ter *HDSW* B21 107 G1
Wartell Bank *KGSWFD* DY6 99 H2
Warwards La *SLYOAK* B29 160 A1
Warwell La
LGN/SDN/BHAMAIR B26 146 D1
Warwick Av *DARL/WED* WS10 56 C5
DUNHL/THL/PER WV6 34 D2
WLNHL WV13 40 B3
Warwick Cl *LGLYGN/QTN* B68 123 F2
WBROM B70 70 C4
Warwick Crest *EDG* B15 * 126 B5
Warwick Dr *CDSL* WV8 10 A4
Warwick Gdns *OLDBY* B69 86 A4
Warwick Gra *SOLH* B91 164 B3
Warwick Gv *HIA/OLT* B92 163 H1
Warwick Pas *CBHAM* B2 3 G5
Warwick Rd *DOR/KN* B93 183 F5
DOR/KN B93 197 F1
DUDS DY2 121 E1
LGLYGN/QTN B68 123 H5
SCFLD/BOLD B73 76 A1
SOLH B91 164 B3
SPARK B11 145 G3
STRBR DY8 117 H3
Warwick St *BHTH/HG* B12 127 G3
BILS/COS WV14 54 A3
RUSH/SHEL WS4 5 F1
WOLV WV1 7 J5
Warwick Wy *ALDR* WS9 30 A1
Wasdale Dr *KGSWFD* DY6 100 A3
Wasdale Rd *BRWNH* WS8 * 18 D1
NFLD/LBR B31 175 F1
Waseley Rd *RBRY* B45 173 G5
Washbrook Rd
WASH/WDE B8 111 E3
Washford Gv *YDLY* B25 129 F4
Washington Dr
BFLD/HDSWWD B20 90 B3
Washington St *CBHAMW* B1 2 D7
DUDS DY2 120 D1
Washington Whf *CBHAMW* B1 2 D7
Wash La *YDLY* B25 129 G5
Washwood Heath Rd
WASH/WDE B8 110 C3
Wasperton Cl *CBROM* B36 112 D1
Wassell Ct *HALE* B63 138 A5
Wassell Grove La
HAG/WOL DY9 137 E5
Wassell Grove Rd
HAG/WOL DY9 153 H1
Wassell Rd *BILS/COS* WV14 53 H1
HAG/WOL DY9 136 C5
HALE B63 138 A5
Wast Hill Gv *HWK/WKHTH* B38 190 D1
Wasthill La *HWK/WKHTH* B38 190 B3
Wastwater Ct
DUNHL/THL/PER WV6 34 D1
Watchbury Cl *CBROM* B36 95 E5
Watchman Av *BRLYHL* DY5 119 H5
Waterbridge La *WMBN* WV5 64 C4
Water Dl *BDMR/CCFT* WV3 36 A3
Waterdale *SHLY* B90 194 D3
WMBN WV5 80 C1
Waterfall Cl *SMTHWK* B66 106 A2
Waterfall La *CDYHTH* B64 121 G3
Waterfall Rd *BRLYHL* DY5 119 E5
Waterfield Cl *TPTN/OCK* DY4 84 C1
Waterfield Wy
LGN/SDN/BHAMAIR B26 131 E5
Waterford Pl *STETCH* B33 131 E1
Waterford Rd *KGSWFD* DY6 99 H2
Waterfront East *BRLYHL* DY5 101 G5
The Waterfront *BRLYHL* DY5 * 101 G5
Waterfront Wy *BRLYHL* DY5 119 G1
WSLW WS2 4 B3
Waterfront West *BRLYHL* DY5 119 G1
Waterglade La *WLNHL* WV13 39 G4
Waterhaynes Cl *RBRY* B45 188 A2
Waterhead Cl *WOLVN* WV10 13 G5
Waterhead Dr *WOLVN* WV10 13 H5
Water La *HHTH/SAND* B71 72 B4
Water Lily Gv *BRWNH* WS8 8 D5
Waterlinks Bvd *AST/WIT* B6 109 G2
Waterloo Av
CHWD/FDBR/MGN B37 114 B5
Waterloo Rd
ALE/KHTH/YWD B14 161 E2
SMTHWK B66 124 D1
WOLV WV1 6 E3
YDLY B25 146 B1
Waterloo St *CBHAM* B2 3 F5
DUDN DY1 102 A1
TPTN/OCK DY4 85 F1
Waterloo St East
TPTN/OCK DY4 85 F1
Watermead Gra *BRWNH* WS8 9 E5
Watermeadow Dr
RUSH/SHEL WS4 29 F1
Watermere *RUSH/SHEL* WS4 29 F2
Water Mill Cl *SLYOAK* B29 142 B4
Watermill Cl *WOLVN* WV10 12 D4
Water Mill Crs *WALM/CURD* B76 78 B2
Water Orton La
WALM/CURD B76 95 F1
Water Orton Rd *CBROM* B36 113 F1
Water Rd *SEDG* DY3 83 E4
Waters Dr *FOAKS/STRLY* B74 46 B2
The Waters Edge *CBHAMW* B1 2 B6
Waterside *GTB/HAM* B43 73 G4
Waterside Av *DARL/WED* WS10 71 E2
Waterside Cl *BKHL/PFLD* WV2 52 B1
BORD B9 127 H2
ERDE/BCHGN B24 94 C2
Waterside Ct *OLDBY* B69 104 D5
Waterside Dr *WSNGN* B18 107 H4
Waterside Orch *ALVE* B48 * 189 H5
Waterside Pk *TPTN/OCK* DY4 * 70 B4
Waterside Vw *BRLYHL* DY5 118 D3
WSNGN B18 108 A4
Waterside Wy *BRWNH* WS8 8 C2
Water Side Wy *COVEN* WV9 12 A5
Waterson Cft
CHWD/FDBR/MGN B37 132 D1
Water St *CBHAMNW* B3 2 E3
KGSWFD DY6 99 H2
WBROM B70 87 H4
WOLVN WV10 7 H1
Waters Vw *BLOX/PEL* WS3 18 B2
Waterward Cl *HRBN* B17 142 A2
Waterway Ct
ALE/KHTH/YWD B14 179 E2
Waterways Dr *OLDBY* B69 86 C5
Waterways Gdns *STRBR* DY8 118 A3
Waterworks Dr *NFLD/LBR* B31 157 H5
Waterworks Rd
LDYWD/EDGR B16 125 H3
Waterworks St *AST/WIT* B6 109 H1
Watery La *CDSL* WV8 10 C2
SHLY B90 194 C4
SMTHWKW B67 106 C4
STRBR DY8 118 A2
TPTN/OCK DY4 85 F1
WLNHL WV13 39 E2
WSL WS1 4 D7
Watery La Middleway
BORD B9 127 H3
Watford Gap Rd *LICHS* WS14 33 E3
Watford Rd *BVILLE* B30 159 H5
Wathan Av *BILS/COS* WV14 67 H1
The Wathecroft *HRBN* B17 141 H1
Watkins Gdns *NFLD/LBR* B31 175 H2
Watkins Rd *SHHTH* WV12 26 A5
Watland Gn *BKDE/SHDE* B34 112 C4
Watling St *CNCK/NC* WS11 8 A2
Watney Gv *KGSTG* B44 76 A3
Watson Cl *CSCFLD/WYGN* B72 77 F1
Watson Rd *BILS/COS* WV14 67 H1
DARL/WED WS10 54 C3
WASH/WDE B8 110 B2
WOLVN WV10 12 B5
Watson Rd East
VAUX/NECH B7 110 B2
Watsons Cl *DUDS* DY2 103 E1
Watson's Green Flds
DUDS DY2 103 F1
Watson's Green Rd *DUDS* DY2 103 E1
Wattisham Sq *CVALE* B35 94 C2
Wattis Rd *SMTHWKW* B67 124 C2
Wattle Rd *WBROM* B70 87 E3
Watton Cl *BILS/COS* WV14 68 A2
Watton Gn *CVALE* B35 94 C4
Watton La *CSHL/WTROR* B46 96 C4
Watton St *WBROM* B70 87 G4
Watt Rd *ERDW/GRVHL* B23 92 C2
TPTN/OCK DY4 69 H3
Watts Cl *TPTN/OCK* DY4 84 C1
Watt's Rd *SMTHH* B10 128 B4
Watt St *HDSW* B21 107 F2
SMTHWK B66 106 D3
Wattville Av *HDSW* B21 * 107 E1
Wattville Rd *HDSW* B21 107 E1
Watwood Rd *HLGN/YWD* B28 179 H2
Waugh Cl
CHWD/FDBR/MGN B37 132 B2
Waugh Dr *HALE* B63 154 D2
Wavell Rd *BRLYHL* DY5 119 H5
WASH/WDE B8 110 C4
WSLW WS2 40 C3
Waveney Av
DUNHL/THL/PER WV6 34 C1
Waveney Cft *CBROM* B36 113 H1
Waverhill Rd *HDSW* B21 107 H2
Waverley Av *GTB/HAM* B43 59 F4
Waverley Crs *BKHL/PFLD* WV2 51 H2
ETTPK/GDPK/PENN WV4 52 D5
RMSLY B62 172 B1
Waverley Gv *SOLH* B91 181 E2
Waverley Rd *BLOX/PEL* WS3 16 B5
DARL/WED WS10 55 F2
SMTHH B10 145 G1
Waverley St *DUDN* DY1 102 A1
Wavers Marston *CHWD/FDBR/MGN*
B37 132 A4
Waxland Rd *HALE* B63 138 D5
Wayfield Cl *SHLY* B90 180 C2
Wayfield Rd *SHLY* B90 180 C2
Wayford Dr *CSCFLD/WYGN* B72 77 H4
Wayford Gld *WLNHL* WV13 39 F5
Waynecroft Rd *GTB/HAM* B43 73 G1
Wayside
CHWD/FDBR/MGN B37 132 A4
Wayside Acres *CDSL* WV8 10 B5
Wayside Dr *FOAKS/STRLY* B74 46 A2
Wayside Gdns *SHHTH* WV12 26 C5
Wayside Wk *WSLW* WS2 41 E2
Waystone La *HAG/WOL* DY9 184 B5
Wealden Hatch *WOLVN* WV10 13 E3
Wealdstone Dr *SEDG* DY3 83 F4
Weaman St *CBHAMNE* B4 3 G3
Weatheroak Rd *SPARK* B11 145 E2
Weatheroaks *ALDR* WS9 19 H3
Weather Oaks *HRBN* B17 141 H2
Weatheroaks *RMSLY* B62 123 E5
Weaver Av
LGN/SDN/BHAMAIR B26 147 H1
WALM/CURD B76 78 C2
Weaver Cl *BRLYHL* DY5 100 D3
Weaver Gv *WLNHL* WV13 40 B3
Weavers Ri *DUDS* DY2 120 D1
Webb Av *DUNHL/THL/PER* WV6 20 C5
Webbcroft Rd *STETCH* B33 112 A5
Webb La *HLGN/YWD* B28 162 C4
Webb Rd *TPTN/OCK* DY4 70 A4
Webb St *BILS/COS* WV14 68 C1
WLNHL WV13 39 F3
Webley Ri *WOLVN* WV10 13 F3
Webster Cl *CSCFLD/WYGN* B72 77 F4
SPARK B11 144 D1
Webster Rd *WLNHL* WV13 39 G2
WSLW WS2 27 H5
Webster Wy *WALM/CURD* B76 78 D4
Weddell Wynd *BILS/COS* WV14 69 E2
Wedgbury Cl *DARL/WED* WS10 71 E2
Wedgbury Wy *BRLYHL* DY5 118 D3
Wedge St *WSL* WS1 5 G3
Wedgewood Av *WBROM* B70 70 D4
Wedgewood Dr
BFLD/HDSWWD B20 90 B4
Wedgewood Pl *WBROM* B70 70 D4
Wedgewood Rd
RIDG/WDGT B32 140 C2
Wedgwood Cl *WMBN* WV5 64 D4
WOLV WV1 38 A4
Wedmore Rd *SCFLD/BOLD* B73 76 D3
Wednesbury Oak Rd
TPTN/OCK DY4 69 G2
Wednesbury One
DARL/WED WS10 * 55 F5
Wednesbury Rd *WSL* WS1 4 C6
WSLW WS2 56 C1
Wednesfield Rd *WLNHL* WV13 39 G2
WOLVN WV10 7 K2
Wednesfield Wy *WNSFLD* WV11 25 E5
WOLVN WV10 38 A1
Weeford Dell *MGN/WHC* B75 48 A2
Weeford Dr
BFLD/HDSWWD B20 89 H2
Weeford Rd *MGN/WHC* B75 48 A4
Weirbrook Cl *SLYOAK* B29 158 D3
Welbeck Av *WOLVN* WV10 23 F3
Welbeck Cl *RMSLY* B62 139 G2
Welbeck Dr *RUSH/SHEL* WS4 29 F3
Welbeck Gv *ERDW/GRVHL* B23 91 H1
Welbury Gdns
DUNHL/THL/PER WV6 22 B5
Welby Rd *HLGN/YWD* B28 162 D1
Welch Cl *TPTN/OCK* DY4 69 H4
Welches Cl *NFLD/LBR* B31 158 D5
Welcombe Dr *WALM/CURD* B76 78 A3
Welcombe Gv *SOLH* B91 181 F2
Welford Av
LGN/SDN/BHAMAIR B26 130 B4
Welford Gv *FOAKS/STRLY* B74 46 D2
Welford Rd
BFLD/HDSWWD B20 108 A1
SCFLD/BOLD B73 76 C2
SHLY B90 180 C1
Welham Cft *SHLY* B90 195 G2
Welland Cl *CSHL/WTROR* B46 96 B4
Welland Dr *STRBR* DY8 118 C4
Welland Gv *ERDE/BCHGN* B24 93 G3
WLNHL WV13 40 A3
Welland Rd *HALE* B63 138 C5
Welland Wy *WALM/CURD* B76 78 C4
Well Cl *CBROM* B36 * 112 A1
Wellcroft Rd *BKDE/SHDE* B34 112 C2
Wellcroft St *DARL/WED* WS10 55 H5
Wellesbourne Cl
BDMR/CCFT WV3 35 F5
Wellesbourne Dr
BILS/COS WV14 68 B4
Wellesbourne Rd
BFLD/HDSWWD B20 90 B5
Wellesley Dr *TPTN/OCK* DY4 85 F1
Wellesley Gdns *MOS/BIL* B13 162 B1
Wellesley Rd *LGLYGN/QTN* B68 105 F3
Wellfield Gdns *DUDS* DY2 103 E3
Wellfield Rd *ALDR* WS9 30 B2
HLGN/YWD B28 163 F4
Wellhead La *PBAR/PBCH* B42 91 E4
Wellington Av
BDMR/CCFT WV3 51 F1
Wellington Cl *KGSWFD* DY6 100 A5
Wellington Gv *SOLH* B91 164 B4
Wellington Pl *WLNHL* WV13 39 F2
Wellington Rd
BFLD/HDSWWD B20 90 B4
BILS/COS WV14 53 G2
DSYBK/YTR WS5 58 A2
DUDN DY1 84 B5
EDG B15 143 G1
SMTHWKW B67 124 C1
TPTN/OCK DY4 85 G1
Wellington St *CDYHTH* B64 121 F2
HHTH/SAND B71 87 G2
OLDBY B69 105 F3
SMTHWK B66 107 F4
WSLW WS2 56 B1
Wellington St South
WBROM B70 87 G2
Wellington Ter
LOZ/NWT B19 * 108 B2
WLNHL WV13 * 39 G2
Wellington Wy *CVALE* B35 94 D4
Well La *BLOX/PEL* WS3 28 A3
DIG/EDG B5 3 H6
WNSFLD WV11 38 C1
Wellman Cft *SLYOAK* B29 159 F1
Wellman's Rd *WLNHL* WV13 40 A4
Well Meadow *RBRY* B45 188 A2
Well Pl *BLOX/PEL* WS3 28 A2
Wells Av *DARL/WED* WS10 54 D2
Wells Cl *DUNHL/THL/PER* WV6 34 B1
HHTH/SAND B71 71 H3
TPTN/OCK DY4 69 G2
Wellsford Av *HIA/OLT* B92 147 G3
Wells Green Rd *HIA/OLT* B92 147 G3
Wells Rd *BILS/COS* WV14 54 A5
BLKHTH/ROWR B65 122 C1
BRLYHL DY5 118 D1
ETTPK/GDPK/PENN WV4 51 F3
HIA/OLT B92 148 A3
Well St *DARL/WED* WS10 55 G2
LOZ/NWT B19 108 C4
Welney Gdns *COVEN* WV9 12 A4
Welsby Av *GTB/HAM* B43 73 G4
Welsh House Farm Rd
RIDG/WDGT B32 141 F3
Welshmans Hl *KGSTG* B44 75 H1
SCFLD/BOLD B73 61 E5
Welton Cl *WALM/CURD* B76 78 C1
Welwyndale Rd
CSCFLD/WYGN B72 77 G5
Wembley Gv *YDLY* B25 129 G4
Wem Gdns *WNSFLD* WV11 24 D4
Wendell Crest *WOLVN* WV10 13 F4
Wendover Rd
BLKHTH/ROWR B65 103 G3
ERDW/GRVHL B23 76 A4
ETTPK/GDPK/PENN WV4 67 G1
Wendron Gv
ALE/KHTH/YWD B14 177 H1
Wenlock Av *BDMR/CCFT* WV3 36 A5
Wenlock Cl *HALE* B63 137 H5
SEDG DY3 67 E4
Wenlock Gdns *BLOX/PEL* WS3 28 A5
Wenlock Rd
BFLD/HDSWWD B20 91 E5
STRBR DY8 135 H1
Wenman St *BHTH/HG* B12 144 B1
Wensley Cft *HLGN/YWD* B28 163 F4
Wensleydale Rd
PBAR/PBCH B42 74 B5
Wensley Rd
LGN/SDN/BHAMAIR B26 147 F1
Wentbridge Rd *WOLV* WV1 38 C4
Wentworth Av *CBROM* B36 112 D1
Wentworth Dr *OLDBY* B69 103 G2
Wentworth Ga *HRBN* B17 141 H1
Wentworth Gv
DUNHL/THL/PER WV6 20 B5
Wentworth Park Av
HRBN B17 141 H1
Wentworth Ri *RMSLY* B62 139 F4
Wentworth Rd *BLOX/PEL* WS3 16 B3
FOAKS/STRLY B74 47 E5
HIA/OLT B92 147 F4
HRBN B17 141 H1
STRBR DY8 117 H5
WOLVN WV10 13 F5
Wentworth Wy
RIDG/WDGT B32 141 F4
Wenyon Cl *TPTN/OCK* DY4 85 H2
Weoley Av *SLYOAK* B29 142 A5
Weoley Castle Rd *SLYOAK* B29 158 C1
Weoley Hl *SLYOAK* B29 159 E2
Weoley Park Rd *SLYOAK* B29 158 D1
Wergs Dr *DUNHL/THL/PER* WV6 21 E3
Wergs Gdns *CDSL* WV8 * 20 D1
Wergs Hall Rd *CDSL* WV8 20 D1
Wergs Rd
DUNHL/THL/PER WV6 21 E4
Werneth Gv *BLOX/PEL* WS3 16 C3
Wesley Av *CDSL* WV8 10 D5
HALE B63 120 B5
Wesley Cl *CDYHTH* B64 121 F3
Wesley Gv *DARL/WED* WS10 55 G5
Wesley Pl *TPTN/OCK* DY4 70 A4
Wesley Rd *BRLYHL* DY5 100 D4
CDSL WV8 10 D5
ERDW/GRVHL B23 92 D1
Wesleys Fold *DARL/WED* WS10 55 F2
Wesley St *BILS/COS* WV14 69 E1
BKHL/PFLD WV2 53 E2
OLDBY B69 105 E1

WBROM B70 .... 87 F3
Wessex Cl BRWNH WS8 .... 9 F5
Wessex Rd BKHL/PFLD WV2 ...... 52 D2
Wesson Gdns HALE B63 .... 138 C4
Wesson Rd DARL/WED WS10 ...... 55 E1
West Acre WLNHL WV13 .... 39 F4
Westacre Crs BDMR/CCFT WV5 .. 35 F5
Westacre Dr BRLYHL DY5 .... 119 H4
Westacre Rd BFLD/HDSWWD B20 ....
CBROM B36 .... 113 F1
OLDBY B69 .... 103 H1
WNSFLD WV11 .... 24 C4
Westbook Wy WMBN WV5 .... 80 D1
West Bvd RIDG/WDGT B32 ...... 141 E1
Westbourne Av
BKDE/SHDE B34 .... 112 A3
Westbourne Crs EDG B15 .... 126 A4
Westbourne Gdns EDG B15 ...... 126 A5
Westbourne Rd DARL/WED WS10 .. 55 H2
Westbourne Rd HDSW B21 * ... 107 H2
Westbourne Rd
DARL/WED WS10 .... 55 H1
EDG B15 .... 125 H4
ETTPK/GDPK/PENN WV4 .... 51 C3
HLGN/YWD B28 .... 164 B5
RMSLY B62 .... 139 C1
RUSH/SHEL WS4 .... 42 B1
WBROM B70 .... 87 F5
Westbourne St
RUSH/SHEL WS4 .... 42 B2
Westbrook Av ALDR WS9 .... 29 H5
Westbury Av DARL/WED WS10 .... 55 H2
Westbury Rd Da HDSW B21 * 107 H2
HRBN B17 .... 124 D1
Westbury St WOLV WV1 .... 2 A3
Westcliff Pl NFLD/LBR B31 ... 175 F1
Westcombe Gv
RIDG/WDGT B32 .... 157 C1
West Coppice Rd BRWNH WS8 ..... 8 C4
Westcote Av NFLD/LBR B31 ... 174 C3
Westcote Cl HIA/OLT B92 ...... 147 C5
Westcott Cl KGSWFD DY6 ...... 118 B1
Westcott Rd
HWK/WKHTH B38 .... 176 A2
Westcroft Av
DUNHL/THL/PER WV6 .... 20 D4
SDGG D1 .... 66 D1
Westcroft Wy
ALE/KHTH/YWD B14 .... 178 D4
Westdean Cl RMSLY B62 .... 139 F3
West Dr BFLD/HDSWWD B20 .... 108 B1
DIG/EDG B5 .... 143 G1
West End Av SMTHWK B66 ...... 105 H2
Westerdale Cl SEDG D3 .... 68 A4
Westerham Cl DOR/KN B93 ...... 196 D2
Westeria Cl CBROM B36 .... 113 E1
Westering Pkwy WOLV WV10 .... 13 E3
Westerings
BFLD/HDSWWD B20 .... 90 C4
Western Av BRLYHL DY5 ...... 118 D2
RMSLY B62 .... 139 C3
SEDG D3 .... 66 D3
WSLW WS2 .... 41 G1
Western Cl WSLW WS2 .... 40 B2
Western Rd CDYHTH B64 ...... 120 D4
ERDE/BCHGN B24 .... 93 E3
HDSW B21 .... 169 H1
OLDBY B69 .... 105 F4
SCFLD/BOLD B73 .... 73 F2
STRBR DY8 .... 135 F3
WSNGN B18 .... 107 H5
Western Wy DARL/WED WS10 ... 55 E5
Westfield Av
ALE/KHTH/YWD B14 .... 178 D3
Westfield Cl DOR/KN B93 .... 198 C1
West Dr ALDR WS9 .... 30 A4
WMBN WV5 .... 64 D4
Westfield Gra
ALE/KHTH/YWD B14 .... 161 E1
Westfield Gv BDMR/CCFT WV5 .. 35 G5
Westfield Mnr BDMR/CCFT WV5 . 47 F1
Westfield Rd ACGN B27 ...... 146 B4
ALE/KHTH/YWD B14 .... 160 D2
BILS/COS WV14 .... 54 C5
BRLYHL DY5 .... 119 H4
DUDS DY2 .... 102 D2
EDG B15 .... 125 F5
RMSLY B62 .... 122 C3
SEDG DY3 .... 82 C2
SMTHWKW B67 .... 106 B5
WLNHL WV13 .... 39 G1
Westford Gv HLGN/YWD B28 ... 179 G2
Westgate ALDR WS9 .... 29 H3
EDG B15 .... 142 D5
West Ga LDYWD/EDGR B16 ...... 125 G1
Westgate Cl SEDG DY3 .... 67 G4
West Gn
ETTPK/GDPK/PENN WV4 .... 50 C3
West Green Cl EDG B15 .... 126 B4
Westgrove Av SHLY B90 .... 195 F2
Westhaven Dr NFLD/LBR B31 .. 158 A3
Westhaven Rd
SCFLD/WYGN B72 .... 62 C2
West Heath Rd NFLD/LBR B31 . 175 H4
WSNGN B18 .... 107 F5
Westhill BDMR/CCFT WV3 .... 35 G5
Westhill Cl HIA/OLT B92 .... 164 A2
SLYOAK B29 .... 159 G3
Westhill Rd HWK/WKHTH B38 .. 176 D2
West Holme BORD B9 .... 128 A2
Westhorne Cft BVILLE B30 ... 159 G3
Westhouse Gv
ALE/KHTH/YWD B14 .... 177 H1
Westland Av BDMR/CCFT WV5 .. 36 B5
Westland Cl ERDW/GRVHL B23 .. 92 D1
Westland Gdns
BDMR/CCFT WV5 .... 36 B5
STRBR DY8 .... 118 B5
Westland Rd BDMR/CCFT WV5 .. 36 B5

Westlands Rd MOS/BIL B13 ... 161 G1
WALM/CURD B76 .... 78 B5
Westleigh Rd WMBN WV5 .... 80 D1
Westley Brook Cl
LGN/SDN/BHAMAIR B26 .... 147 H2
Westley Cl HLGN/YWD B28 .... 163 F4
Westley Rd ACGN B27 .... 146 B4
Westley St BORD B9 .... 127 G2
DUDN DY1 .... 102 B1
Westmead Crs
ERDE/BCHGN B24 .... 93 G2
West Mead Dr
ALE/KHTH/YWD B14 .... 161 E4
Westmead Dr
OLGYGN/QTN B68 .... 105 F5
West Ms KGSTG B44 .... 74 D1
West Mill Cft
HWK/WKHTH B38 .... 190 C1
Westminster Av
ETTPK/GDPK/PENN WV4 .... 51 H3
Westminster Cl DUDN DY1 ..... 84 A4
Westminster Dr
ALE/KHTH/YWD B14 .... 160 D4
Westminster Rd
BFLD/HDSWWD B20 .... 90 C4
HHTH/SAND B71 .... 71 H2
RUSH/SHEL WS4 .... 28 D3
SLYOAK B29 .... 160 A1
STRBR DY8 .... 117 G2
Westmore Wy
DARL/WED WS10 .... 56 D3
Westmorland Rd
HHTH/SAND B71 .... 71 G5
Weston Av LOZ/NWT B19 * 108 C2
OLDBY B69 .... 85 H5
Weston Cl DOR/KN B93 .... 199 E1
WSL WS1 .... 57 E2
Weston Crs ALDR WS9 .... 44 B1
Weston Dr BILS/COS WV14 ..... 53 G4
TPTN/OCK DY4 .... 70 A1
Weston La SPARK B11 .... 145 G5
Weston Rd LOZ/NWT B19 ...... 108 B2
SMTHWKW B67 .... 124 B3
Weston St WSL WS1 .... 57 E2
Weston Ter LOZ/NWT B19 * ... 108 C1
Westover Rd
BFLD/HDSWWD B20 .... 89 C2
West Park Av NFLD/LBR B31 .. 175 E3
West Park Cl ALDR WS9 .... 29 G5
West Park Rd SMTHWKW B67 ... 105 H3
West Pathway HRBN B17 ...... 142 A1
Westport Crs WNSFLD WV11 .... 25 G5
Westray Cl RBRY B45 .... 173 G4
Westridge SEDC DY3 .... 67 E3
Westridge Rd MOS/BIL B13 ... 162 A4
West Ri MGN/WHC B75 .... 52 C2
West Rd
ETTPK/GDPK/PENN WV4 .... 50 D3
GTB/HAM B43 .... 73 F2
HALE B63 .... 137 F1
TPTN/OCK DY4 .... 69 H3
West Rd South HALE B63 ..... 137 F1
Westside Dr RIDG/WDGT B32 . 157 H1
West St BLKHTH/ROWR B65 ... 122 A3
BLOX/PEL WS3 .... 27 G3
BRLYHL DY5 .... 119 H4
DUDN DY1 .... 84 B4
DUNHL/THL/PER WV6 .... 23 E5
STRBR DY8 .... 135 F2
VAUX/NECH B7 * 3 K2
Westthorpe Gv LOZ/NWT B19 . 108 C4
West Vw WASH/WDE D8 .... 111 G5
West View Cl MGN/WHC B75 ... 63 E2
West View Dr KGSWFD DY6 .... 100 A4
West View Rd MGN/WHC B75 ... 63 E2
Westville Rd WSLW WS2 .... 41 E2
Westward Cl KGSTG B44 .... 75 E1
West Wy RUSH/SHEL WS4 .... 18 B5
Westwood Av SPARK B11 ...... 145 G3
STRBR DY8 .... 134 D4
Westwood Dr RBRY B45 ...... 174 B4
Westwood Gv SOLH B91 .... 181 F2
Westwood Rd AST/WIT B6 ...... 91 G4
SCFLD/BOLD B73 .... 60 C4
Westwood St BRLYHL DY5 .... 118 C3
Westwood Vw
ERDE/BCHGN B24 .... 93 G3
Wetherby Cl CBROM B36 ...... 111 H1
WOLV WV10 .... 12 C5
Wetherby Rd ACGN B27 .... 146 C5
BLOX/PEL WS3 .... 16 C3
Wetherfield Rd SPARK B11 ... 146 A4
Wexford Cl DUDN DY1 .... 83 H4
Weybourne Rd KGSTG B44 ...... 75 E1
Weycroft Rd ERDW/GRVHL B23 . 75 H4
Weyhill Cl COVEN WV9 .... 11 H1
Weymoor Rd HRBN B17 .... 141 G4
Weymouth Dr
FOAKS/STRLY B74 .... 46 D1
Wharf Ap ALDR WS9 .... 29 H3
Wharfdale Rd SPARK B11 ..... 146 B2
Wharfedale Cl KGSWFD DY6 .... 99 F2
Wharfedale St
DARL/WED WS10 .... 70 D1
Wharf La SOLH B91 .... 165 F4
WSNGN B18 .... 108 A3
Wharf Rd BVILLE B30 .... 177 E3
SPARK B11 .... 146 B2
Wharfside OLDBY B69 .... 104 D2
Wharfside St CBHAMW B1 .... 2 D7
Wharf St AST/WIT B6 .... 109 G2
WOLV WV1 .... 7 J5
WSNGN B18 .... 108 A3
Wharton Av HIA/OLT B92 ..... 165 G2
Wharton Rd SMTHWK B66 ...... 106 C4
Wharton St VAUX/NECH B7 .... 110 B1
Whatcote Gn HIA/OLT B92 .... 165 G2
Whateley Av BLOX/PEL WS3 ... 28 B4
Whateley Crs CBROM B36 .... 113 F1
Whateley Gn FOAKS/STRLY B74 . 47 E5
Whateley Hall Cl
DOR/KN B93 * 197 G1
Whateley Hall Rd
DOR/KN B93 .... 197 G1
Whateley Pl BLOX/PEL WS3 * .. 28 B4
Whateley Rd BLOX/PEL WS3 ... 28 B4
HDSW B21 .... 107 G1
Wheatcroft Cl MGN/WHC B75 .. 48 A2
RMSLY B62 .... 122 D3

Wheatcroft Dr
CHWD/FDBR/MGN B37 .... 132 C3
Wheatcroft Gv DUDS DY2 .... 85 F5
Wheatcroft Rd STETCH B33 ... 130 B2
Wheaten Ct
CHWD/FDBR/MGN B37 .... 132 D1
Wheatfield Cl CBROM B36 .... 114 A2
Wheatfield Vw NFLD/LBR B31 . 157 H5
Wheathill Cl
ETTPK/GDPK/PENN WV4 .... 51 E5
Wheatland Gv ALDR WS9 .... 44 C1
Wheatlands Cft STETCH B33 . 131 C1
The Wheatlands
DUNHL/THL/PER WV6 .... 34 B2
Wheatley Cl HIA/OLT B92 .... 165 G2
LGLYGN/QTN B68 .... 123 G4
MGN/WHC B75 .... 47 G2
Wheatley Gra
CSHL/WTROR B46 .... 115 F3
Wheatley Rd LGLYGN/QTN B68 . 123 G4
Wheatley St BKHL/PFLD WV2 .. 52 C2
WBROM B70 .... 87 E2
Wheatmill Cl KIDD DY10 ..... 168 B3
Wheatmoor Ri MGN/WHC B75 ... 48 B2
Wheatmoor Rd MGN/WHC B75 ... 63 F1
Wheaton Cl WOLV WV10 .... 23 E3
Wheaton V
BFLD/HDSWWD B20 .... 89 C3
Wheatridge Cl KGSWFD DY6 .... 99 E2
Wheats Av HRBN B17 .... 141 H4
Wheatsheaf Cl MGN/WHC B75 .. 48 A1
Wheatsheaf Rd CDSL WV8 ..... 22 A1
LDYWD/EDGR B16 .... 125 F2
OLDBY B69 .... 103 G1
Wheatstone Cl SEDG DY3 ...... 67 G5
Wheatstone Gv STETCH B33 .. 112 B4
Wheel Av CDSL WV8 .... 10 B4
The Wheel Ct CDSL WV8 .... 10 B4
Wheeler Cl CDSL WV8 .... 10 A5
Wheeler Rd WNSFLD WV11 ..... 24 C2
Wheeler's Fold WOLV WV1 ...... 7 G4
Wheeler St LOZ/NWT B19 ..... 108 D3
Wheeler St WSNGN B18 .... 108 C3
Wheeley's La EDG B15 .... 125 H4
Wheeleys Rd EDG B15 .... 126 B5
Wheelock Cl FOAKS/STRLY B74 . 46 B1
Wheelwright Cl
DARL/WED WS10 .... 55 E2
Wheelwright Rd
ERDE/BCHGN B24 .... 92 C4
Wheldrake Av
BKDE/SHDE B34 .... 113 E4
Whernside Dr
DUNHL/THL/PER WV6 .... 22 C5
Wherretts Well La SOLH B91 . 165 G5
Whetstone Cl EDG B15 * 142 D2
Whetstone Gn WOLV WV10 * ... 23 F1
Whetstone La ALDR WS9 .... 44 B1
Whetstone Rd WOLV WV10 ...... 23 F2
Whettybridge Rd RBRY B45 .. 187 G2
Whetty La RBRY B45 .... 187 G2
Whichford Cl WALM/CURD B76 . 77 H5
Whichford Gv BORD B9 .... 129 F2
While Rd CSCFLD/WYGN B72 ... 62 B4
Whilmot Cl WOLV WV10 .... 13 H1
Whinberry Ri BRLYHL DY5 .... 83 E5
Whisley Brook La
HLGN/YWD B28 .... 145 H5
Whiston Av WNSFLD WV11 ...... 25 G3
Whiston Gv SLYOAK B29 ..... 158 D2
Whitacre Rd BORD B9 .... 128 D2
DOR/KN B93 .... 197 F1
Whitbourne Cl BHTH/HG B12 . 144 D2
Whitburn Av PBAR/PBCH B42 .. 90 A1
Whitburn Cl COVEN WV9 .... 12 A5
Whitby Cl BLOX/PEL WS3 ...... 16 B4
Whitby Rd BHTH/HG B12 ..... 144 C5
Whitchurch La SHLY B90 .... 194 B1
Whitcot Gv NFLD/LBR B31 * . 175 F5
Whitebeam Cl BRWNH WS8 ...... 19 F1
Whitebeam Cl SEDG DY3 .... 83 E2
Whitebeam Cft
HWK/WKHTH B38 .... 176 C5
White Beam Rd
CHWD/FDBR/MGN B37 .... 132 D3
White City Rd BRLYHL DY5 .. 120 A3
White Cl HAG/WOL DY9 .... 136 A5
Whitecrest GTB/HAM B43 ...... 73 H1
Whitecroft Rd
LGN/SDN/BHAMAIR B26 .... 148 B2
White Falcon Ct SOLH B91 .. 181 F3
White Farm Rd
FOAKS/STRLY B74 .... 46 C1
White Field Av HRBN B17 ... 141 G1
Whitefield Cl CDSL WV8 ...... 10 D5
Whitefields Crs SOLH B91 .. 181 H4
Whitefields Gd SOLH B91 ... 181 G4
Whitefields Rd SOLH B91 ... 181 H5
Whitefriars Dr HALE B63 ... 138 C3
Whitegates Rd BILS/COS WV14 . 68 C1
Whitehall Dr DUDN DY1 .... 84 A4
HALE B63 .... 138 D3
Whitehall Rd BORD B9 .... 128 B3
CDYHTH B64 .... 120 C3
ETTPK/GDPK/PENN WV4 .... 51 H4
HALE B63 .... 138 D3
RBRY B45 .... 99 G3
STRBR DY8 .... 135 H5
TPTN/OCK DY4 .... 86 B1
WSL WS1 .... 57 E1
Whitehead Dr
WALM/CURD B76 .... 76 D1
Whitehead Rd AST/WIT B6 .... 109 E2
White Hl NFLD/LBR B31 ..... 158 D5
Whitehill La SLYOAK B29 ... 158 C5
White Hollies BLOX/PEL WS3 . 17 G3
White Horse Rd BRWNH WS8 ... 8 D3
Whitehouse Av
BDMR/CCFT WV3 .... 34 B4
DARL/WED WS10 .... 54 D1
White House Wy
WNSFLD WV11 .... 25 F3
White House Gn SOLH B91 ... 181 F2

Whitehouse Common Rd
MGN/WHC B75 .... 63 E1
Whitehouse Crs MGN/WHC B75 . 48 A4
WNSFLD WV11 .... 25 F1
Whitehouse Dr SMTHWK B66 .. 106 C2
White House Gn SOLH B91 ... 181 F2
Whitehouse La CDSL WV8 ...... 10 C2
Whitehouse Pl RBRY B45 .... 187 H2
White Houses La WOLV WV10 .. 13 C1
Whitehouse St AST/WIT B6 .. 109 F3
BILS/COS WV14 .... 68 C3
TPTN/OCK DY4 .... 85 G4
Whitehouse Wy ALDR WS9 ...... 43 H1
White House Wy SOLH B91 ... 181 G2
Whitemoor Dr SHLY B90 ..... 195 G1
White Oak Dr BDMR/CCFT WV3 . 35 G4
KGSWFD DY6 .... 99 C3
Whitepoplars Cl BRLYHL DY5 . 101 E5
White Rd RIDG/WDGT B32 .... 140 D1
SMTHWKW B67 .... 106 B3
SPARK B11 .... 128 A5
White Rw WMBN WV5 .... 64 A2
White's Dr SEDG DY3 .... 67 G5
Whitesladie Cl DOR/KN B93 . 197 E5
Whitesmith Cl SEDG DY3 ...... 67 F3
White's Rd HHTH/SAND B71 ... 71 G5
Whitestone Rd HALE B63 .... 138 C1
White St BHTH/HG B12 ...... 144 C2
WSL WS1 .... 57 E1
Whites Wd WMBN WV5 .... 81 E1
Whitethorn Crs
FOAKS/STRLY B74 .... 44 D4
Whitethorn Rd STRBR DY8 ... 118 C3
Whitewood Gld SMHTH WV12 .. 48 A1
Whitford Dr SHLY B90 ...... 195 H1
Whitgreave Av WOLV WV10 .... 23 C2
Whitgreave Ct WBROM B70 .... 86 C3
WOLV WV10 * 13 H1
Whitgreave St WBROM B70 ... 86 C3
Whitland Dr
ALE/KHTH/YWD B14 .... 178 B2
Whitley Cl
DUNHL/THL/PER WV6 .... 35 F3
Whitley Court Rd
RIDG/WDGT B32 .... 140 C1
Whitley Dr FOAKS/STRLY B74 . 45 G5
Whitley St DARL/WED WS10 ... 55 C5
Whitlock Gv
ALE/KHTH/YWD B14 .... 178 C2
Whitminster Av
ERDE/BCHGN B24 .... 93 F3
Whitmore Hl WOLV WV1 .... 6 E5
Whitmore Rd SMHTH B10 ..... 128 B3
STRBR DY8 .... 134 D2
Whitmore St WOLV WV1 .... 7 G3
WSL WS1 .... 56 D1
WSNGN B18 .... 108 B4
Whitney Av STRBR DY8 .... 134 D1
Whittaker St BKHL/PFLD WV2 . 52 C1
Whittall St CBHAMNE B4 .... 3 F5
Whittimere St WSL WS1 .... 5 F3
Whittingham Gv
WNSFLD WV11 .... 25 F4
Whittingham Rd HALE B63 .. 138 C2
Whittington Cl
ALE/KHTH/YWD B14 .... 161 E5
HHTH/SAND B71 .... 72 B3
Whittington Gv STETCH B33 . 130 B2
Whittington Hall La
KINVER CY7 .... 134 B4
Whittington Ov STETCH B33 . 130 C2
Whittington Rd STRBR DY8 . 134 D4
Whittle Cft CVALE B35 ...... 94 B5
Whittleford Gv CBROM B36 .. 95 H5
Whitton St DARL/WED WS10 ... 55 C2
Whitwell Cl SHLY B90 ...... 195 G2
Whitworth Cl DARL/WED WS10 . 55 E5
Whitworth Dr HHTH/SAND B71 . 72 A2
Whitworth St WBROM B70 ..... 87 E3
Whyley St WBROM B70 * 86 C3
Whyley Wk OLDBY B69 .... 105 E4
Whynot St HALE B63 .... 137 F2
Wibert Cl SOLH B91 .... 181 H4
Wichnor Rd HIA/OLT B92 .... 147 F2
Wicket La KINVER DY7 .... 116 C3
Wickham Gdns WNSFLD WV11 ... 24 A4
Wicklow Cl HALE B63 .... 154 D1
Wideacre Dr KGSTG B44 .... 75 E4
Wide Acres RBRY B45 .... 173 H4
Widney Av ALDR WS9 .... 30 B1
SLYOAK B29 .... 142 A5
Widney Cl DOR/KN B93 ...... 196 D3
Widney La SOLH B91 .... 181 F4
Widney Manor Rd
DOR/KN B93 .... 196 B3
SOLH B91 .... 182 A3
Widney Rd DOR/KN B93 ...... 196 D4
Wiggins Cft WALM/CURD B76 .. 63 F5
Wiggins Hill Rd
WALM/CURD B76 .... 79 H3
Wigginsmill Rd
DARL/WED WS10 .... 70 B2
Wiggin St LDYWD/EDGR B16 .. 125 H1
Wight Cft CBROM B36 .... 114 B3
Wightman Bank
DUNHL/THL/PER WV6 .... 34 D3
Wightwick Cl BLOX/PEL WS3 .. 27 F1
Wightwick Gv
DUNHL/THL/PER WV6 .... 35 E3
Wightwick Hall Rd
DUNHL/THL/PER WV6 .... 34 C4
Wigmore Gv KGSTG B44 .... 75 H3
Wigmore La HHTH/SAND B71 ... 72 C3
Wigorn La HAG/WOL DY9 ..... 152 D2
Wigorn Rd SMTHWKW B67 ..... 124 B3
Wilberforce Wy HIA/OLT B92 . 165 G3
Wilbraham Rd WSLW WS2 ...... 41 C4
Wilcote Gv ACGN B27 .... 165 G2
Wildacres STRBR DY8 .... 134 C1
Wilday Cl TPTN/OCK DY4 ...... 85 G3
Wilde Cl ALE/KHTH/YWD B14 . 177 H1
Wilderness La GTB/HAM B43 ... 58 B5
Wildfell Rd ACGN B27 ...... 146 D5
Wildmoor La SHLY B90 ...... 186 C4
Wildmoor Rd SHLY B90 ...... 163 F5
Wildtree Av WOLV WV10 .... 13 G5
Wiley Av DARL/WED WS10 ...... 55 E2

Wiley Av South
DARL/WED WS10 .... 55 E3
Wilford Gv SOLH B91 .... 181 H3
WALM/CURD B76 .... 78 D5
Wilford Rd HHTH/SAND B71 .. 71 H5
Wilkes Av WSLW WS2 .... 40 D3
Wilkes Cl BLOX/PEL WS3 ...... 17 G4
Wilkes Ct SEDG DY5 * 67 H4
Wilkes Rd CDSL WV8 .... 10 D4
Wilkes St HHTH/SAND B71 .... 72 A4
WLNHL WV13 .... 39 G4
Wilkin Rd BRWNH WS8 .... 8 D2
Wilkins Av BILS/COS WV14 ... 69 E1
Wilkinson Cl SCFLD/BOLD B73 . 77 F1
Wilkinson Cft WASH/WDE B8 . 111 C3
Wilkins Rd BILS/COS WV14 ... 53 H1
Wilkins Rd YDLY B25 .... 146 C1
Willaston Rd STETCH B33 ... 131 G3
Willclare Rd
LGN/SDN/BHAMAIR B26 .... 147 G3
Willcock Rd BKHL/PFLD WV2 . 52 C1
Willenhall La SMHTH WV12 ... 26 D3
Willenhall Rd BILS/COS WV14 . 54 B2
DARL/WED WS10 .... 38 B4
WOLV WV1 .... 38 B4
Willenhall St DARL/WED WS10 . 55 C1
Willerby Fold WOLV WV10 .... 13 E5
Willersey Rd MOS/BIL B13 .. 162 B2
Willes Rd WSNGN B18 .... 107 G3
Willett Rd HHTH/SAND B71 ... 72 A3
Willetts Dr HALE B63 ...... 137 F3
Willetts Rd NFLD/LBR B31 .. 175 E4
Willetts Wy CDYHTH B64 .... 121 F2
Willey Gv ERDE/BCHGN B24 ... 93 F4
William Booth La CBHAMNE B4 . 3 F2
William Cook Rd
WASH/WDE B8 .... 111 H4
William Edward St
BHTH/HG B12 .... 127 F5
William Green Rd
DARL/WED WS10 .... 56 C5
William Harper Rd
WLNHL WV13 .... 39 H4
William Henry St
VAUX/NECH B7 .... 109 G3
William Ker Rd TPTN/OCK DY4 . 86 A1
William Rd SMTHWKW B67 .... 123 H1
Williams Cl SMHTH WV12 ..... 26 A5
Williamson St BDMR/CCFT WV3 . 6 C7
William St BRLYHL DY5 ...... 119 F1
EDG B15 .... 126 C3
RUSH/SHEL WS4 .... 42 B2
WBROM B70 .... 86 C7
William St North LOZ/NWT B19 . 3 F1
William St West SMTHWK B66 . 106 D2
William Wiggin Av
BLOX/PEL WS3 .... 16 D5
Willingsworth Rd
DARL/WED WS10 .... 70 A3
Willingworth Cl BILS/COS WV14 . 53 E5
Willis Pearson Av
BILS/COS WV14 .... 69 F1
Willmore Gv HWK/WKHTH B38 . 176 D5
Willmore Rd
BFLD/HDSWWD B20 .... 90 D4
Willmott Cl MGN/WHC B75 .... 47 H1
Willmott Rd MGN/WHC B75 .... 47 H1
Willoughby Dr SOLH B91 ... 181 H4
Willoughby Gv SLYOAK B29 . 158 C2
Willow Av DARL/WED WS10 .... 55 C5
HRBN B17 .... 124 D3
WNSFLD WV11 .... 24 B1
Willow Bank BDMR/CCFT WV3 .. 34 C5
Willow Bank Rd DOR/KN B93 . 196 D2
Willow Cl CDYHTH B64 ...... 121 E3
HAG/WOL DY9 .... 152 B4
Willow Coppice
RIDG/WDGT B32 .... 157 C2
Willow Ct SMTHWK B66 ...... 105 H5
Willowdale Gra
DUNHL/THL/PER WV6 .... 22 F1
Willow Dr CDSL WV8 .... 10 C2
SHLY B90 .... 209 C3
Willow End HAG/WOL DY9 .... 136 B5
Willow Gdns
LDYWD/EDGR B16 .... 107 F3
WNSFLD WV11 .... 39 C1
Willow Hts CDYHTH B64 ..... 121 F3
Willowherb Cl DSYBK/YTR WS5 . 57 F4
Willowherb Wy SHLY B90 ... 208 D4
Willow Ms SLYOAK B29 ...... 158 B3
Willow Park Dr STRBR DY8 . 135 E3
Willow Ri BRLYHL DY5 ...... 119 E4
Willow Rd BDMR/CCFT WV3 .... 35 C5
BVILLE B30 .... 159 F4
DUDN DY1 .... 84 A3
GTB/HAM B43 .... 73 F3
SOLH B91 .... 180 A1
Willows Crs BHTH/HG B12 ... 143 H3
Willowside RUSH/SHEL WS4 .. 29 H4
Willows Rd BHTH/HG B12 .... 144 A3
RUSH/SHEL WS4 .... 29 H4
WSL WS1 .... 5 K5
The Willows ACGN B27 ...... 146 C3
DUDS DY2 .... 85 H5
HLYWD B47 .... 192 C4
WALM/CURD B76 .... 78 D4
WMBN WV5 .... 80 D2
Willow Wy
CHWD/FDBR/MGN B37 .... 132 C2
Wills Av HHTH/SAND B71 ..... 71 H4
Willsbridge Covert
ALE/KHTH/YWD B14 .... 177 H4
Wilson Dr HLGN/YWD B28 .... 175 H2
Wills St LOZ/NWT B19 ...... 108 C1
Wills Wy SMTHWK B66 .... 106 D1
Wilmcote Cl BHTH/HG B12 ... 144 A1
Wilmcote Dr MGN/WHC B75 .... 48 A4
Wilmcote Rd SOLH B91 ...... 165 E3
Wilmington Rd
RIDG/WDGT B32 .... 140 C1
Wilmore La HLYWD B47 .... 191 G5
Wilmote Gv STRBR DY8 .... 134 D1
Wilmot Av CSHL/WTROR B46 . 115 F3
Wilmot Dr ERDW/GRVHL B23 .. 76 B4
TPTN/OCK DY4 .... 85 H1

Wilmot Gdns DUDN DY1 ....84 A4
Wilnecote Gv
  PBAR/PBCH B42 ....90 C2
Wilner's Vw BLOX/PEL WS3........17 H2
Wilsford Dr
  ALE/KHTH/YWD B14...............177 H4
  RUSH/SHEL WS4 ....29 E2
Wilson Dr MGN/WHC B75 ....63 G3
  OLDBY B69 ....86 A3
Wilson Rd BILS/COS WV14 ....68 C4
  BRLYHL DY5 ....109 E1
  HRBN B17 ....124 D1
  LGLYGN/QTN B68 ....123 H4
  LOZ/NWT B19........................108 D1
Wilson St DOR/KN B93.............197 G2
Wilson St TPTN/OCK DY4 ....85 G2
Wilton Cl SEDG DY3 ....67 G4
Wilton Rd BFLD/HDSWWD B20....80 B5
  ERDW/GRVHL B23 ....92 D1
  SPARK B11............................144 D2
Wilton St LOZ/NWT B19 ....108 C1
Wiltshire Cl WSLW WS2 ....41 H1
Wiltshire Dr HALE B63................120 B5
Wiltshire Wy HHTH/SAND B71 ....71 C4
Wimbledon Dr STRBR DY8 ....135 H5
Wimborne Rd WOLVN WV10 ......134 C4
Wimbourne Rd
  LDYWD/EDGR B16 ....125 F1
  WALM/CURD B76 ....63 G4
Wimperis Wy GTB/HAM B43 ....59 G4
Wimpole Gv KGSTG B44 ....75 H4
Wimshurst Meadow
  WOLVN WV10 ....13 F3
Wincanton Cft CBROM B36 ....111 G1
Winceby Rd
  DUNHL/THL/PER WV6............34 D2
Winchcombe Cl DUDN DY1
  HIA/OLT B92 ....152 C5
Winchcombe Rd HIA/OLT B92 ...147 H5
Winchester
  BLKHTH/ROWR B65 ....104 C5
  HAG/WOL DY9 ....152 C3
Winchester Dr
  CHWD/FDBR/MGN B37 ....132 A2
  STRBR DY8 ....135 G4
Winchester Gdns
  NFLD/LBR B31.........................175 G2
Winchester Gv HDSW B21 * 107 E1
Winchester Ms ALDR WS9 ....44 B1
Winchester Ri DUDN DY1 ....84 A4
Winchester Rd
  BFLD/HDSWWD B20 ....90 D5
  HHTH/SAND B71 ....71 F3
  WOLVN WV10 ....12 C5
Winchfield Dr HRBN B17 ....124 B5
Wincote Dr
  DUNHL/THL/PER WV6............35 G1
Wincrest Wy BKDE/SHDE B34 ....113 E4
Windermere Dr
  FOAKS/STRLY B74 ....45 F2
  KGSWFD DY6 ....99 H3
Windermere Rd
  DUNHL/THL/PER WV6.............21 H2
  HDSW B21 ....89 C4
  MOS/BIL B13 ....161 H1
Windfall Ct ERDE/BCHGN B24....93 H2
Winding Ml North
  BRLYHL DY5 * 119 G5
Winding Ml South
  BRLYHL DY5 ....119 G5
Windlass Cft NFLD/LBR B31 ....175 F1
Windleaves Rd ERDE/BCHGN B24...113 C2
Windmill Av
  CSHL/WTROR B46 ....115 F2
  RBRY B45 ....173 G5
Windmill Bank WMBN WV5 ....65 E4
Windmill Cl NFLD/LBR B31 ....159 E5
Windmill Cottages
  PBAR/PBCH B42 * 90 A1
Windmill Crs BDMR/CCFT WV3 ....35 E4
  SMTHWK B66 ....107 E4
Windmill End DUDS DY2 ....103 E4
Windmill Cdft KGSWFD DY6 ....99 E1
Windmill Hl HALE B63.................118 D5
  NFLD/LBR B31 ....158 D5
Windmill La BDMR/CCFT WV3 ....35 E4
  DOR/KN B93 ....198 D2
  HOCK/TIA B94 ....199 E3
  SMTHWK B66 ....107 E4
Windmill Prec SMTHWK B66 ....106 D4
Windmill Rd SHLY B90 ....179 G3
Windmill St CBHAMW B1 ....126 D3
  DARL/WED WS10 ....55 H5
  DUDN DY1...............................84 A4
  SEDG DY3 ....83 F1
  WSL WS1 ....4 E6
Windmill Vw BILS/COS WV14 .....68 A4
Windridge Crs HIA/OLT B92........165 H2
Windrow
  DUNHL/THL/PER WV6............34 B1
Windrush Cl BLOX/PEL WS3 ....28 C1
Windrush Gv SLYOAK B29 ....160 A3
Windrush Rd HLYWD B47 ....192 D1
Windsor Av
  ETTPK/GDPK/PENN WV4 ....51 E2
  LGLYGN/QTN B68 ....123 E1
Windsor Cl
  BLKHTH/ROWR B65 ....104 A4
  HALE B63 ....138 B4
  NFLD/LBR B31 ....189 C2
  RBRY B45 ....174 A3
Windsor Crs DUDS DY2 ....102 D3
Windsor Dr ERDE/BCHGN B24 ....93 E1
  HIA/OLT B92 ....147 H5
Windsor Gdns BDMR/CCFT WV3...50 A1
  DSL WV8 ....10 B4
Windsor Ga SHHTH WV12 ....40 A1
Windsor Gv RUSH/SHEL WS4 .....18 D3
Winsor PI ERDW/GRVHL B23 ......92 D2
  VAUX/NECH B7 * 127 C1

SCFLD/BOLD B73 ....76 B2
STRBR DY8 ....134 C4
TPTN/OCK DY4 ....69 G3
WMBN WV5 ....64 D5
Windsor St BILS/COS WV14 ....53 G2
  VAUX/NECH B7 ....109 C5
  WSL WS1 ....57 E1
Windsor St South
  VAUX/NECH B7 ....109 G5
Windsor Ter
  LDYWD/EDGR B16 * 125 H3
Windsor St RIDG/WDGT B32 ......157 F3
Windsor Wy DARL/WED WS10 ....40 B5
Windsor Wy RUSH/SHEL WS4 .....29 F5
Winds Point HG DY9 ....152 C4
Windward Wy CBROM B36 ....113 H2
Windyridge Rd
  WALM/CURD B76 ....78 B5
Winford Av KGSWFD DY6...........100 A5
Wingate Cl HWK/WKHTH B38 ....176 D1
Wingate Rd WSLW WS2 ....40 C3
Wing Cl WSLW WS2 ....40 D1
Wingfield Cl
  CHWD/FDBR/MGN B37 ....131 H1
Wingfield Rd
  CSHL/WTROR B46 ....115 F4
  PBAR/PBCH B42 ....74 C4
Wingfoot Av WOLVN WV10 ....23 F2
Wingfoot Wy
  ERDE/BCHGN B24 ....93 G5
Winkle St WBROM B70 ....87 F2
Winnall Cl BILS/COS WV14 ....68 D1
Winnie Rd SLYOAK B29 ....159 G1
Winnington Rd
  WASH/WDE B8 ....111 G2
Winnipeg Rd
  HWK/WKHTH B38 ....177 E5
Winrush Cl SEDG DY3 ....83 F3
Winscar Cft SEDG DY3 ....83 G3
Winsford Cl HALE B63 ....138 C1
  WALM/CURD B76 ....63 E5
Winsham Gv HDSW B21 ....107 F1
Winslow Dr
  DUNHL/THL/PER WV6............36 A1
Winson Green Rd WSNGN B18 ...107 G4
Winson St WSNGN B18 ....107 G4
Winstanley Rd STETCH B33 ......129 H2
Winster Av DOR/KN B93 ....196 C4
Winster Gv KGSTG B44 ....74 D1
Winster Rd GTB/HAM B43 ....73 F4
  WOLVN WV10 ....38 B4
Winston Dr
  BFLD/HDSWWD B20 ....80 B5
  RMSLY B62 ....172 C1
Winston Rd SEDG DY3 ....80 C4
Winterbourne Cft
  ALE/KHTH/YWD B14...............177 H5
Winterbourne Rd SOLH B91.........181 F1
Winterley Gdns SEDG DY3 ....67 G5
Winterley La RUSH/SHEL WS4 ...29 E3
Winterton Rd KGSTG B44 ....60 C4
Winthorpe Dr SOLH B91 ....181 H3
Wintney Cl HRBN B17 ....124 C5
Winton Gv WALM/CURD B76 ....78 C5
Winwood Heath Rd
  RMSLY B62 ....172 A3
Winwood Rd
  BLKHTH/ROWR B65 ....122 C1
Winwoods Gv
  RIDG/WDGT B32 ....157 E2
Wiremill Cl KGSTG B44 ....75 E5
Wirral Rd NFLD/LBR B31 ....158 B4
Wiseacre Cft SHLY B90 ....179 C3
Wiseman Gv KGSTG B44 ....76 B2
Wisemeadow SHLY B90 ....179 C3
Wisemore WALM/CURD B76 ....4 D2
Wishaw Gv
  CHWD/FDBR/MGN B37 ....113 H4
Wishaw La WALM/CURD B76 ....79 C4
Wisley Wy RIDG/WDGT B32 ....141 F2
Wistaria Cl NFLD/LBR B31 ....158 C4
Wisteria Dr DYSBK/YTR WS5 .....58 C4
Wisteria Gv KGSTG B44 ....75 E1
Wistmans Cl DUDN DY1 ....83 F5
Wistwood Hayes
  WOLVN WV10 ....13 F3
Witham Cl WALM/CURD B76 ....78 C2
Witham Ct SOLH B91 * 182 A4
Withdean Cl SPARK B11 ....145 F2
Witherford Cl SLYOAK B29 ....159 E2
Witherford Cft SOLH B91 ....180 D3
Witherford Wy SLYOAK B29 ......159 E2
Withern Wy SEDG DY3 ....83 F3
Withers Rd CDSL WV8 ....10 D4
Withers Wy HHTH/SAND B71 ....71 H1
Withington Covert
  ALE/KHTH/YWD B14...............177 H4
Withy Hill Rd MGN/WHC B75 ....63 C1
Withymere La WMBN WV5 ....65 G5
Withymoor Rd DUDS DY2 ....89 F3
  STRBR DY8 ....118 C5
Withy Rd BILS/COS WV14 ....53 G5
Withywood Cl SHHTH WV12 ....25 H1
Witley Av HALE B63 ....138 A3
Witley Crs OLDBY B69 ....104 A2
Witley Farm Cl SOLH B91 ....182 A3
Witley Rd NFLD/LBR B31 ....176 B3
Witney Dr
  CHWD/FDBR/MGN B37 ....131 H2
Witton Bank RMSLY B62 ....139 H1
Witton La AST/WIT B6 ....91 F5
  HHTH/SAND B71 ....71 E3
Witton Lodge Rd
  ERDW/GRVHL B23 ....75 H4
Witton Rd AST/WIT B6 ....109 E1
  ETTPK/GDPK/PENN WV4 ....51 G2
  STRBR DY8 ....135 E3
Wixford Gv SHLY B90.................180 D5
Wobaston Rd CDSL WV8 ....11 F4
Woburn Av SHHTH WV12 ....25 H4

Woburn Crs GTB/HAM B43..........73 F2
Woburn Dr BRLYHL DY5.............118 D4
  RMSLY B62 ....121 G5
Woburn Gv ACGN B27.................135 H4
Wodehouse Cl WMBN WV5 ....80 C1
Wodehouse La SEDG DY3 ....66 A3
Woden Av WOLVN WV11 ....24 C4
Woden Cl WMBN WV5 ....64 C4
Woden Rd WNSFLD WV11 ....24 C4
Woden Rd WOLVN WV10 ....37 H1
Woden Rd East
  DARL/WED WS10 ....56 B3
Woden Rd North
  DARL/WED WS10 ....55 G3
Woden Rd South
  DARL/WED WS10 ....70 D2
Woden Rd West
  DARL/WED WS10 ....55 F4
Wolfsbane Dr RUSH/SHEL WS4 ...57 G5
Wolfson Dr HRBN B17 ....142 B3
Wollaston Ct STRBR DY8 ....134 C1
Wollaston Crs WNSFLD WV11 .....24 D4
Wollaston Rd KINVER DY7 ....117 C5
  STRBR DY8 ....118 A5
Wollerton Gv MGN/WHC B75 ......63 F2
Wollescote Rd HAG/WOL DY9 ...136 B4
Wollscote Dr SOLH B91 ....181 H4
Wolmer Rd WNSFLD WV11 ....14 D5
Wolseley Av ACGN B27 ....144 C4
Wolseley Bank WOLVN WV10 .....23 H5
Wolseley Cl CBROM B36 ....96 A5
  WOLVN WV10 ....23 H4
Wolseley Dr WASH/WDE B8 ....111 E2
Wolseley Ga WOLVN WV10 ....23 H5
Wolseley Rd BILS/COS WV14 ......53 F1
  WBROM B70 ....70 C5
Wolseley St BORD B9 ....127 H2
Wolston Cl SHLY B90..................163 F5
Wolverhampton Rd
  BLOX/PEL WS3 ....17 G4
  BLOX/PEL WS3 ....27 F1
  CDSL WV8 ....10 B4
  KGSWFD DY6 ....99 G1
  KINVER DY7 ....116 D5
  LGLYGN/QTN B68 ....123 E1
  SEDG DY3 ....52 B5
  WNSFLD WV11 ....14 D4
  WOLVN WV10 ....13 H4
  WSL WS1 ....41 E3
Wolverhampton Rd East
  ETTPK/GDPK/PENN WV4 ....52 C4
Wolverhampton Rd South
  RIDG/WDGT B32 ....132 B2
Wolverhampton Rd West
  WLNHL WV13 ....40 B3
Wolverhampton St
  BILS/COS WV14 ....53 G2
  DARL/WED WS10 ....54 D2
  DUDN DY1 ....84 B5
  WLNHL WV13 ....39 H4
  WSL WS1 ....4 C3
Wolverley Av
  ETTPK/GDPK/PENN WV4 ....50 D3
  STRBR DY8 ....134 C1
Wolverley Crs OLDBY B69 ....104 B4
Wolverley Rd HALE B63 * 138 B5
  HIA/OLT B92 ....148 B5
  RIDG/WDGT B32 ....157 F2
Wolverson Cl SHHTH WV12 ....40 A1
Wolverson Rd ALDR WS9 ....19 G5
Wolverton Rd
  CHWD/FDBR/MGN B37 ....132 B5
  DUDS DY2 ....85 E5
  RBRY B45 ....188 C2
Wombourne Cl SEDG DY3 ....67 E3
Wombourne Pk WMBN WV5 ....80 D2
Wombourne Rd SEDG DY3 ....80 D3
Wombrook Dr WMBN WV5 ....64 B5
Woodacre Rd
  ERDE/BCHGN B24 ....93 G2
Woodall Rd AST/WIT B6 ....91 F5
Woodall St BLOX/PEL WS3 ....27 G2
  CDYHTH B64 ....120 C3
Woodard Rd TPTN/OCK DY4 ....70 A4
Woodard Av SEDG DY3 ....83 E2
  WNSFLD WV11 ....24 C4
Wood Bank Rd
  BDMR/CCFT WV3 ....35 E5
Woodbank Rd SEDG DY3 ....67 E4
Woodberry Dr
  WALM/CURD B76 ....78 C1
Woodberry Wk ACGN B27 ....146 D4
Woodbine Av SMHTH B10 * 128 B4
Woodbine Cft
  LGN/SDN/BHAMAIR B26 ....147 G1
Woodbourne Rd
  SMTHWK B66 ....124 A2
Woodbridge Cl BLOX/PEL WS3 ...16 C4
  RUSH/SHEL WS4 ....29 F1
Woodbridge Rd MOS/BIL B13 ....144 B4
Woodbrooke Gv
  NFLD/LBR B31.........................158 D4
Woodbrooke Rd BVILLE B30 ......159 F3
Woodburn Rd SMTHWK B66 ......107 F2
Woodbury Cl BKDE/SHDE B34 ...112 C3
  BRLYHL DY5 ....119 F1
  RMSLY B62 ....122 D4
Woodbury Gv SOLH B91 ....181 H5
Woodbury Rd RMSLY B62 ....123 E4
Woodchester Rd DOR/KN B93 ....169 H1
Woodchurch Gra
  SCFLD/BOLD B73 ....76 D3
Wood Cl CSHL/WTROR B46 ....115 F2
Woodclose Rd
  CHWD/FDBR/MGN B37 ....131 H1
Woodcock Cl NFLD/LBR B31 ......174 C4
Woodcock La ACGN B27 ....146 D4
  NFLD/LBR B31 ....158 A2
Woodcock La North
  ACGN B27 ....146 D3
Woodcock St CBHAMNE B4 ....3 J2
Woodcombe Cl BRLYHL DY5 .....119 E1
Wood Common Gra
  BLOX/PEL WS3 ....17 G3
Woodcote Dr DOR/KN B93..........199 F4
  WASH/WDE B8 ....110 D4
Woodcote PI LOZ/NWT B19 * 108 C2

Woodcote Rd
  DUNHL/THL/PER WV6............35 G1
  ERDE/BCHGN B24 ....93 H1
Woodcote Wy
  FOAKS/STRLY B74 ....60 D2
  WSNGN B18 ....108 A5
Wood Ct BFLD/HDSWWD B20 .....90 A4
Wood Cft HLYWD B47 ....192 D2
Woodcroft Av
  BFLD/HDSWWD B20 ....89 G3
  TPTN/OCK DY4 ....84 C1
Woodcroft Cl BLOX/PEL WS3 ....118 B4
  CDYHTH B64 ....121 F4
Woodcross La BILS/COS WV14 ....67 H1
Woodcross St BILS/COS WV14 ....67 H1
Woodend BFLD/HDSWWD B20 ....73 G5
Wood End La ERDE/BCHGN B24...92 D3
Woodend Pl
  DUNHL/THL/PER WV6.............35 H1
Wood End Rd DSYBK/YTR WS5 ...43 F5
  ERDE/BCHGN B24 ....92 D5
  WNSFLD WV11 ....24 C4
Woodfall Av BVILLE B30 ....159 H5
Woodfield HAG/WOL DY9 ....184 B1
Woodfield Av BRLYHL DY5 ....100 D2
  CDYHTH B64 ....120 D4
  ETTPK/GDPK/PENN WV4 ....52 B3
  HAG/WOL DY9 ....136 D5
  OLDBY B69 ....105 E5
Woodfield Cl DSYBK/YTR WS5 ....58 C3
Woodfield Crs SPARK B11 ....144 A4
Woodfield Dr BHTH/HG B12 ....144 C1
Woodfield Hts
  DUNHL/THL/PER WV6.............35 H1
Woodfield La RMSLY B62 ....171 H5
Woodfield Rd
  ALE/KHTH/YWD B14...............161 F2
  BHTH/HG B12 ....144 C1
  SEDG DY3 ....83 E2
  SOLH B91 ....164 D4
Woodford Av CBROM B36 ....114 A2
Woodford Cl ALDR WS9 ....30 B3
Woodford Cl CROWN WV9 ....11 H5
Woodford Green Rd
  HLGN/YWD B28 ....163 E2
Woodford La WMBN WV5.............64 B3
Woodfort Rd GTB/HAM B43 ....73 C4
Woodgate Dr RIDG/WDGT B32 ...157 E1
Woodgate Gdns
  RIDG/WDGT B32 ....140 A5
Woodgate La
  RIDG/WDGT B32 ....140 A5
Woodgate Wy RIDG/WDGT B32 ...184 C1
Woodglade Cft
  HWK/WKHTH B38 ....176 C3
Woodgreen Cft
  LGLYGN/QTN B68 ....123 G5
Wood Green Rd
  DARL/WED WS10 ....55 H5
  WSNGN B18 ....107 F5
Woodhall Cl TPTN/OCK DY4 ....69 G3
Woodhall Cft HIA/OLT B92 ....147 H1
Woodhall Rd
  ETTPK/GDPK/PENN WV4 ....51 E4
Woodham Cl RBRY B45 ....173 G4
Woodhaven RUSH/SHEL WS4 .....29 F3
Wood Hayes Cft WOLVN WV10 ...14 A5
Wood Hayes Rd WNSFLD WV11 ...24 C1
Woodhill Cl WMBN WV5 ....64 D5
Wood Hill Dr WMBN WV5 ....80 C2
Woodhouse Fold
  WNSFLD WV11 ....24 D5
Woodhouse Orch
  HAG/WOL DY9 ....184 C1
Woodhouse Rd
  DUNHL/THL/PER WV6.............35 F2
  RIDG/WDGT B32 ....141 E1
Woodhouse Rd North
  DUNHL/THL/PER WV6.............35 F1
Woodhurst Rd MOS/BIL B13 ......144 C3
Wooding Crs TPTN/OCK DY4 ......70 A5
Woodington Rd
  MGN/WHC B75 ....63 C3
Woodland Av BRLYHL DY5 ....120 A3
  DUDN DY1 ....84 C3
  DUNHL/THL/PER WV6.............21 E5
  STRBR DY8 ....152 B5
Woodland Centre
  SHHTH WV12 ....26 C3
Woodland Ct HAG/WOL DY9 ......153 F1
  SHHTH WV12 ....26 C3
Woodland Cottages
  ETTPK/GDPK/PENN WV4 ....51 F4
Woodland Ct LICHS WS13 ....12 D1
Woodland Crs
  BDMR/CCFT WV3 ....50 D1
Woodland Dr SMTHWK B66 ....106 A2
  SPARK B11 ....145 E4
Woodland Gv GTB/HAM B43 ....58 C5
  SEDG DY3 ....82 D3
Woodland Ri CDYHTH B64 ....121 F4
  SCFLD/BOLD B73 ....76 D3
Woodland Rd BDMR/CCFT WV3 ...50 D1
  HDSW B21 ....107 E1
  NFLD/LBR B31 ....175 H2
  RMSLY B62 ....122 D4
Woodlands Av
  CSHL/WTROR B46 ....115 E4
  DSYBK/YTR WS5 ....58 C3
Woodlands Cottages
  ETTPK/GDPK/PENN WV4 ....51 F4
Woodlands Crs BLOX/PEL WS3 ...17 H2
Woodlands Farm Rd
  ERDE/BCHGN B24 ....94 B2
Woodlands La SHLY B90 ....180 B5
Woodlands Paddock
  BVILLE B30 ....159 G5
Woodlands Park Rd
  BVILLE B30 ....159 G5
Woodlands Rd RBRY B45 ....187 F1
  BILS/COS WV14 ....68 C3
  SPARK B11 ....145 E4
  WMBN WV5 ....64 B5
  WMBN WV5 ....80 C1
Woodlands St SMTHWK B66 ......107 E4
The Woodlands CDYHTH B64 .....121 G5
  MGN/WHC B75 ....63 G2
  STRBR DY8 ....135 G5

Woodlands Wy
  CHWD/FDBR/MGN B37 ....132 D3
Wood La ALDR WS9 ....31 G2
  BFLD/HDSWWD B20 ....90 B4
  BLOX/PEL WS3 ....17 H2
  BRGRVW B61 ....185 C5
  CHWD/FDBR/MGN B37 ....132 A4
  ERDE/BCHGN B24 ....45 E4
  HRBN B17 ....141 C1
  RIDG/WDGT B32 ....157 E1
  SHHTH WV12 ....26 C3
  WBROM B70 ....70 C5
  WOLVN WV10 ....12 D5
Wood Lane Cl SHHTH WV12 * 26 C3
Woodlawn Gv KGSWFD DY6 ....99 H4
Woodlea Dr ERDE/BCHGN B24 ...92 D4
  SOLH B91 ....164 B1
Wood Leasow
  RIDG/WDGT B32 ....140 D5
Woodleaves HLYWD B47 ....178 B5
Woodleigh Av HRBN B17 ....142 B3
Woodleigh Cl HALE B63 ....138 C2
Woodleigh Rd
  CSCFLD/WYGN B72 ....77 F2
The Woodleys
  ALE/KHTH/YWD B14...............178 D1
Woodloes Rd SHLY B90 ....194 B3
Woodman Cl DARL/WED WS10 ....56 B4
  HALE B63 ....159 E4
Woodman Gv MGN/WHC B75 ....48 A2
Woodman La HAG/WOL DY9 ......170 B1
Woodmeadow Rd BVILLE B30 ....177 E2
Woodnorton Dr MOS/BIL B13 ....144 A3
Woodnorton Rd
  BLKHTH/ROWR B65 ....122 D2
Woodpecker Gv CBROM B36 ......114 A2
Woodpecker Rd STETCH B33 .....112 B5
Woodperry Av SOLH B91 ....182 A4
Woodridge AST/WIT B6 ....91 E5
Woodridge Av
  RIDG/WDGT B32 ....140 B3
Woodridge Rd HALE B63 ....138 C2
Wood Rd DUNHL/THL/PER WV6...35 F2
  RIDG/WDGT B32 ....140 B3
  WMBN WV5 ....65 F4
Woodrough Dr MOS/BIL B13 .....144 D5
Woodrow Crs DOR/KN B93 ....197 E3
Woodruff Wy DSYBK/YTR WS5 ...57 G5
Woodrush Dr HLYWD B47 ....192 C2
Woods Bank Ter
  DARL/WED WS10 ....55 E3
Woods Crs BRLYHL DY5 ....120 A3
Woodsetton Cl DUDN DY1 ....68 B5
Woodshires Rd HIA/OLT B92 ......164 A3
Woodside
  CHWD/FDBR/MGN B37 ....113 G5
  FOAKS/STRLY B74 ....46 C3
Woodside Cl DSYBK/YTR WS5 ....58 B3
Woodside Cv DOR/KN B93 ....197 E4
Woodside Dr FOAKS/STRLY B74 ...32 A5
Woodside Gv CDSL WV8 ....10 D4
Woodside Rd DSYBK/YTR WS5 ...58 B3
  DUDS DY2 ....101 H3
Woodside Wy ALDR WS9 ....30 D5
  RIDG/WDGT B32 ....157 E2
  SHHTH WV12 ....26 C3
  SOLH B91 ....164 A5
Woods La BRLYHL DY5 ....119 F5
  CDYHTH B64 ....120 C4
Woodsome Gv
  ERDW/GRVHL B23 ....76 A4
Woodsorrel Rd DUDN DY1 ....83 H2
The Woods
  ALE/KHTH/YWD B14...............161 F1
Woodstile BKDE/SHDE B34 ....112 D3
Woodstock Cl DSYBK/YTR WS5 ...58 B3
  DUDN DY1 ....84 A5
  STRBR DY8 ....102 A1
Woodstock Crs DOR/KN B93 ......196 D5
Woodstock Dr
  FOAKS/STRLY B74 ....46 B1
  STRBR DY8 ....117 G2
Woodstock Rd HDSW B21 ....107 H1
  MOS/BIL B13 ....144 C3
  WOLV WV1 ....3 G3
Wood St DARL/WED WS10 ....55 H2
  DUDN DY1 ....101 H3
  ETTPK/GDPK/PENN WV4 ....51 H1
  HAG/WOL DY9 ....136 D2
  STRBR DY8 ....117 H5
  TPTN/OCK DY4 ....69 G5
  WLNHL WV13 ....39 G3
  WOLVN WV10 ....23 G5
Woodthorne Cl SEDG DY3 ....83 F4
Woodthorne Rd
  DUNHL/THL/PER WV6.............21 E4
Woodthorne Rd South
  DUNHL/THL/PER WV6.............21 E5
Woodthorpe Dr
  HAG/WOL DY9 ....136 B4
Woodthorpe Gdns
  ALE/KHTH/YWD B14...............161 E5
Woodthorpe Rd
  ALE/KHTH/YWD B14...............160 D5
Woodvale Dr HLGN/YWD B28 .....179 C1
Woodvale Rd HLGN/YWD B28 ....179 C1
  RIDG/WDGT B32 ....157 E1
Woodville Gdns SEDG DY3 ....67 H2
Woodville Rd
  ALE/KHTH/YWD B14...............161 F2
  HRBN B17 ....141 C1
Woodward PI HAG/WOL DY9 ......136 A3
Woodwards Cl WSLW WS2 ....41 F5
Woodwards PI WSLW WS2 ....41 F5
Woodwards Rd WSLW WS2 ....41 F5
Woodward St
  HHTH/SAND B71 ....87 H2
Woodway ERDE/BCHGN B24 ....94 B1
Woodwells Rd WASH/WDE B8 ....111 E4
Woolacombe Lodge Rd
  SLYOAK B29 ....142 A5

Woolmore Rd
 ERDW/GRVHL B23 .... 92 A2
Woolpack Cl
 BLKHTH/ROWR B65 .... 103 C5
Wooton Gv *KGSTG* B44 .... 76 B5
Wootton Gv *WNSFLD* WV11 .... 24 D5
Wootton Rd *BDMR/CCFT* WV3 .... 50 C1
 NFLD/LBR B31 .... 189 C1
Worcester Bar *CBHAMW* B1 * 2 C6
Worcester Cl *HAG/WOL* DY9 .... 152 C5
 MGN/WHC B75 .... 47 H2
Worcester Ct *BDMR/CCFT* WV3 ... 51 G2
Worcester Gn *HHTH/SAND* B71 ... 71 C4
Worcester Gv
 DUNHL/THL/PER WV6 .... 34 B1
Worcester La *HAG/WOL* DY9 .... 152 D2
 MGN/WHC B75 .... 47 H2
Worcester Ri *SLYOAK* B29 .... 160 B1
Worcester Rd *DUDS* DY2 .... 121 E1
 HAG/WOL DY9 .... 169 C1
 LGLYGN/QTN B68 .... 123 E4
 WLNHL WV13 .... 40 B3
Worcester St *BKHL/PFLD* WV2 .... 6 E6
 CBHAM B2 .... 3 C6
 STRBR DY8 .... 135 C3
Worcester Wk *CBHAM* B2 * 3 C6
Word Hl *HRBN* B17 .... 124 B5
Wordsworth Av
 ETTPK/GDPK/PENN WV4 .... 52 C4
Wordsworth Ct
 DUNHL/THL/PER WV6 .... 34 C1
Wordsworth Rd *BLOX/PEL* WS3 ... 28 A2
 SEDG DY3 .... 82 D1
 SHHTH WV12 .... 26 C3
 SMHTH B10 .... 128 B5
 WOLVN WV10 * 24 A2
Wordsworth St
 HHTH/SAND B71 .... 87 C1
Worfield Cl *RUSH/SHEL* WS4 .... 42 C1
Worfield Gdns
 BDMR/CCFT WV3 .... 51 F2
Works Rd
 LGN/SDN/BHAMAIR B26 .... 149 E4
World's End Av
 RIDG/WDGT B32 .... 140 D1
World's End La
 RIDG/WDGT B32 .... 140 D2
Worlds End Rd
 BFLD/HDSWWD B20 .... 90 A3
Worleys Wharf Av
 WASH/WDE B8 .... 92 A1
Worsey Dr *TPTN/OCK* DY4 .... 70 B5
Worthen Gv *NFLD/LBR* B31 .... 175 C5
The Worthings *BVILLE* B30 .... 160 B4
Worthy Down *WNSFLD* WV11 .... 25 F5
Wortley Av *WOLVN* WV10 * 23 C4
Worton Rd *HAG/WOL* DY9 .... 136 C5
Wragby Cl *COVEN* WV9 .... 12 B4
Wrekin Cl *HALE* B63 .... 154 C1
Wrekin Dr *BDMR/CCFT* WV3 ...... 36 A5
 HAG/WOL DY9 .... 136 B3
Wrekin Gv *SHHTH* WV12 .... 25 H1
Wrekin La
 DUNHL/THL/PER WV6 .... 21 E5
Wrekin Rd *KGSTG* B44 .... 75 F5
 SCFLD/BOLD B73 .... 77 E2

Wrekin Vw *BRWNH* WS8 .... 19 G2
Wrekin View Rd *SEDG* DY3 .... 67 E5
Wren Av *DUNHL/THL/PER* WV6 ... 34 B2
Wrenbury Dr *BILS/COS* WV14 ..... 54 C1
Wrens Av *KCSWFD* DY6 .... 100 C5
 TPTN/OCK DY4 .... 84 C1
Wrens Hill Rd *DUDN* DY1 .... 84 B1
Wrens Nest Cl *SHLY* B90 .... 194 A5
Wrens Nest Rd *DUDN* DY1 .... 84 A2
Wrens Park Av
 WALM/CURD B76 .... 78 A4
Wren St *DUDN* DY1 .... 68 B5
 DUDS DY2 .... 102 B4
Wrentham St *DIG/EDG* B5 .... 127 E4
Wretham Rd *LOZ/NWT* B19 .... 108 B3
Wrexham Av *WSLW* WS2 .... 40 D4
Wright Av *WNSFLD* WV11 .... 24 D5
Wrighton Cl *SHHTH* WV12 .... 26 A2
Wrighton Dr *BRLYHL* DY5 .... 83 E5
Wright Rd *WASH/WDE* B8 .... 110 C5
Wrights La *HAG/WOL* DY9 .... 136 D4
Wright St *BILS/COS* WV14 .... 54 A4
 HALE B63 .... 138 C3
 SMHTH B10 .... 128 B4
 WOLVN WV10 * 37 F1
Wrottesley Park Rd
 DUNHL/THL/PER WV6 .... 34 B1
Wrottesley Rd
 DUNHL/THL/PER WV6 .... 21 F5
 CTB/HAM B43 .... 73 F2
Wrottesley Rd West
 DUNHL/THL/PER WV6 .... 20 D4
Wrottesley St *DIG/EDG* B5 .... 3 G7
Wroxall Cl *BRLYHL* DY5 .... 118 D4
Wroxall Gv *MOS/BIL* B13 .... 161 C4
Wroxall Rd *SOLH* B91 .... 164 A4
Wroxham Gin *WLNHL* WV13 .... 39 F5
Wroxton Rd *YDLY* B25 .... 130 A4
Wulfruna Gdns
 BDMR/CCFT WV3 .... 36 B4
Wulfruna St *WOLV* WV1 .... 7 F3
Wulfrun Sq *WOLV* WV1 .... 7 G5
Wulfrun Wy *WOLV* WV1 .... 7 F5
Wyatt Cl *DIG/EDG* B5 .... 143 C2
Wyatt Rd *MGN/WHC* B75 .... 63 H2
Wychall Dr *WNSFLD* WV11 .... 13 E3
Wychall La *HWK/WKHTH* B38 .... 176 B3
Wychall Park Gv
 HWK/WKHTH B38 .... 176 B3
Wychall Rd *NFLD/LBR* B31 .... 175 H2
Wychbold Cl *SHHTH* WV12 .... 26 A1
Wychbold Ct *HAG/WOL* DY9 .... 153 E2
Wychbold Crs *STETCH* B33 .... 131 E1
Wychbury *WALM/CURD* B76 ...... 78 C2
Wychbury Ct *HALE* B63 .... 138 C4
Wychbury Dr *HAG/WOL* DY9 .... 153 E3
Wychbury Rd *BDMR/CCFT* WV3 ..50 C1
 BRLYHL DY5 .... 119 C4
 HAG/WOL DY9 .... 153 E2
 RIDG/WDGT B32 .... 157 E2
Wyche Av *ALE/KHTH/YWD* B14 ..177 F1
Wychelm Farm Rd
 ALE/KHTH/YWD B14 .... 178 C4
Wych Elm Rd *BRWNH* WS8 .... 18 D2
Wycherley Wy *CDYHTH* B64 .... 121 E4
Wychnor Gv *HHTH/SAND* B71 ... 72 A1
Wychwood Av
 DOR/KN B93 .... 183 F5

Wychwood Crs
 LGN/SDN/BHAMAIR B26 .... 147 G1
Wyckham Cl *HRBN* B17 .... 141 G3
Wyckham Rd *CBROM* B36 .... 113 H2
Wycome Rd *HLGN/YWD* B28 .... 162 D4
Wye Cliff Rd
 BFLD/HDSWWD B20 .... 108 B1
Wye Cl *DUNHL/THL/PER* WV6 ... 34 C1
 WALM/CURD B76 .... 78 A4
Wyegate Cl *CBROM* B36 .... 114 A1
Wyemanton Cl *CTB/HAM* B43 .. 73 E2
Wye Rd *BLOX/PEL* WS3 .... 28 A1
Wykeham Gv
 DUNHL/THL/PER WV6 .... 34 B2
Wyken Cl *DOR/KN* B93 .... 198 C1
Wyld Cl *HHTH/SAND* B71 .... 71 E3
Wylde Crs *BLKHTH/ROWR* B65 .. 104 A5
Wylde Green Rd
 CSCFLD/WYGN B72 .... 77 G2
Wymering Av *WNSFLD* WV11 .... 25 F5
Wynall La *HAG/WOL* DY9 .... 136 D4
Wynall La South *HAG/WOL* DY9.. 137 E4
Wynbrook Gv *SHLY* B90 .... 195 C2
Wynchcombe Av
 ETTPK/GDPK/PENN WV4 .... 50 D4
Wyndcliff Rd *BORD* B9 .... 128 B5
Wyndham Gdns *BVILLE* B30 ..... 176 C1
Wyndham Rd *LDYWD/EDGR* B16 125 H3
Wyndhurst Rd *STETCH* B33 ...... 112 A5
Wyndley Cl *FOAKS/STRLY* B74 .. 32 D4
Wyndley Dr *SCFLD/BOLD* B73 ... 62 B4
Wyndley Gv *CSCFLD/WYGN* B72 .. 77 G1
Wyndley La *SCFLD/BOLD* B73 ... 62 A4
Wyndmill Crs *HHTH/SAND* B71 .. 72 B2
Wynds Covert
 ALE/KHTH/YWD B14 .... 177 H3
Wyndshiels *CSHL/WTROR* B46 .. 115 C3
Wynds Point *NFLD/LBR* B31 ..... 158 D5
The Wynd *SEDG* DY3 .... 67 F2
Wynfield Gdns
 ALE/KHTH/YWD B14 .... 161 F5
Wynford Rd *ACGN* B27 .... 146 C2
Wyn-Griffith Dr *TPTN/OCK* DY4..85 C3
Wynne Crs
 ETTPK/GDPK/PENN WV4 .... 50 C5
Wynn Rd
 ETTPK/GDPK/PENN WV4 .... 51 F2
Wynn St *EDG* B15 .... 126 D4
Wynstead Covert
 ALE/KHTH/YWD B14 .... 177 G3
Wyre Cl *HHTH/SAND* B71 .... 71 F3
Wyre Cl *ALDR* WS9 .... 19 F5
Wyre Rd *STRBR* DY8 .... 118 A5
Wyrley Cl *BRWNH* WS8 .... 9 F1
 SHHTH WV12 .... 26 A3
Wyrley Rd *AST/WIT* B6 .... 91 C3
 MGN/WHC B75 .... 47 H4
 WNSFLD WV11 .... 25 C4
Wyrley St *WOLVN* WV10 .... 37 H1
Wyrley Wy *ERDW/GRVHL* B23 .... 75 C5
Wythall Green Wy *HLYWD* B47 .. 192 A5
Wythall Rd *HALE* B63 .... 138 C5
Wythwood Cl *HAG/WOL* DY9 ... 153 F1
Wythwood Gv *HLYWD* B47 .... 193 E2
 TPTN/OCK DY4 .... 69 C3
Wythwood Rd *HLYWD* B47 .... 192 D2
Wyton Av *LGLYGN/QTN* B68 .... 123 C2
Wyvern Cl *FOAKS/STRLY* B74 .... 62 B1

 LGLYGN/QTN B68 .... 105 F5
 SHHTH WV12 .... 25 C3
Wyvern Gv *SLYOAK* B29 .... 142 A5
Wyvern Rd *FOAKS/STRLY* B74 .. 62 B1
Wyvis Cl *BDMR/CCFT* WV3 .... 36 A3

Y

Yale Dr *WNSFLD* WV11 .... 25 E5
Yale Rd *WLNHL* WV13 .... 54 C1
Yardley Cl *LGLYGN/QTN* B68 .... 123 F3
Yardley Fields Rd *STETCH* B33.. 129 H2
Yardley Green Rd *BORD* B9 ...... 128 D3
Yardley Rd *ACGN* B27 .... 146 C5
Yardley St *DARL/WED* WS10 .... 55 E1
 HAG/WOL DY9 .... 136 A1
Yardley Wood Rd
 ALE/KHTH/YWD B14 .... 178 D1
 MOS/BIL B13 .... 161 H5
Yare Gv *WLNHL* WV13 .... 40 B4
Yarnborough Hl *STRBR* DY8 ..... 135 C5
Yarnbury Cl
 ALE/KHTH/YWD B14 .... 178 A4
Yarn Cl *HLYWD* B47 .... 192 C3
Yarner Cl *DUDN* DY1 .... 85 C5
Yarningale Rd *ALE/KHTH/YWD* B14 .. 160 C5
Yarningale Cl *SHLY* B90 .... 191 C1
Yarningale Rd *SCFLD/BOLD* B73 .. 180 D1
Yarningale Rd
 ALE/KHTH/YWD B14 .... 160 C5
Yarn La *SHLY* B90 .... 194 A2
Yarrow Cl *BLOX/PEL* WS3 .... 18 A2
 WNSFLD WV11 .... 25 F5
Yarrow Dr *HWK/WKHTH* B38 ... 176 D5
Yarwell Cl *WOLVN* WV10 .... 37 F1
Yateley Av *PBAR/PBCH* B42 ..... 74 A4
Yateley Crs *PBAR/PBCH* B42 ... 74 A4
Yateley Rd *EDG* B15 .... 125 C5
Yatesbury Av *CVALE* B35 .... 94 B3
Yates Cft *FOAKS/STRLY* B74 ..... 32 D4
Yates La *BLKHTH/ROWR* B65 .... 122 C2
Yeadon Gdns *BDMR/CCFT* WV3 .. 35 H5
Yeames Cl *CTB/HAM* B43 .... 58 D5
Yelverton Cl *BLOX/PEL* WS3 ...... 16 D3
Yelverton Dr *EDG* B15 .... 125 C5
Yeman Rd *LGLYGN/QTN* B68 .. 123 H1
Yemscroft Flats
 RUSH/SHEL WS4 * 28 C4
Yenton Gv *ERDE/BCHGN* B24 .... 77 G5
Yeomanry Cl *MGN/WHC* B75 ... 63 G2
Yeomans Wy *MGN/WHC* B75 ... 63 F2
Yerbury Gv *ERDW/GRVHL* B23 .. 91 G1
Yew Croft Av *HRBN* B17 .... 141 G1
Yewdale *HRBN* B17 .... 142 A3
Yewhurst Rd *SOLH* B91 .... 180 D1
Yew St *BDMR/CCFT* WV3 .... 6 B5
Yew Tree Av *HAG/WOL* DY9 .... 170 B5
Yew Tree Gdns *CDSL* WV8 .... 10 C3
Yew Tree Hills *DUDS* DY2 .... 120 C1
Yewtree La
 BLKHTH/ROWR B65 .... 121 H2
Yew Tree La *BILS/COS* WV14 ..... 68 D2
 DARL/WED WS10 .... 71 E1
 DUNHL/THL/PER WV6 .... 35 E1
 LGN/SDN/BHAMAIR B26 .... 130 A5
 RIDG/WDGT B32 .... 173 H2

 SOLH B91 165
Yew Tree Pl *RMSLY* B62 155
Yew Tree Ri *WALM/CURD* B76 63
Yewtree Rd *FOAKS/STRLY* B74 .. 44
 SCFLD/BOLD B73 62
Yew Tree Rd *AST/WIT* B6 91
 CBROM B36 113
 DSYBK/YTR WS5 57
 DUDS DY2 102
 EDG B15 126
 HALE B63 138
 MOS/BIL B13 143
 RUSH/SHEL WS4 28
 SMTHWK B67 106
Yew Tree Vls
 SCFLD/BOLD B73 * 77
Yockleton Rd *STETCH* B33 131
York Av *BDMR/CCFT* WV3 36
 WLNHL WV13 40
 WSLW WS2 41
Yorkbrooke Dr
 LGN/SDN/BHAMAIR B26 147
York Cl *BVILLE* B30 160
 TPTN/OCK DY4 84
York Crs *BDMR/CCFT* WV3 35
 BKDE/SHDE B34 113
 DARL/WED WS10 55
 STRBR DY8 117
Yorkdale Cl *SEDG* DY3 83
York Dr *CBROM* B36 111
Yorke Av *BRLYHL* DY5 118
York Gdns *BDMR/CCFT* WV3 36
Yorkies Cl
 CHWD/FDBR/MGN B37 131
Yorklea Cft
 CHWD/FDBR/MGN B37 131
Yorkminster Dr
 CHWD/FDBR/MGN B37 132
York Rd *ALE/KHTH/YWD* B14 161
 BDMR/CCFT WV3 35
 BLKHTH/ROWR B65 121
 DUDS DY2 121
 ERDW/GRVHL B23 92
 HDSW B21 107
 HLGN/YWD B28 162
 LDYWD/EDGR B16 125
 RUSH/SHEL WS4 29
York St *HRBN* B17 142
 WOLV WV1 7
Yorks Wood Dr
 CHWD/FDBR/MGN B37 113
York Ter *WSNGN* B18 108
Young St *WBROM* B70 87
Yoxall Gv *STETCH* B33 130
Yoxall Rd *SHLY* B90 180

Z

Zions Cl *CDYHTH* B64 121
Zion St *TPTN/OCK* DY4 69
Zoar St *BDMR/CCFT* WV3 6
 SEDG DY3 83
Zouche Cl *STRBR* DY8 118

The 3b Business Village
 HDSW B21 .... 107 F2
A1 Trading Estate
 SMTHWK B66 .... 106 C2
 SMTHWKW B67 .... 124 C3
Abberley Industrial Centre
 SMTHWK B66 .... 107 F4
Abbey CP School
 BLOX/PEL WS3 .... 16 A4
Abbey Infant School
 SMTHWKW B67 .... 124 A2
Abbey Junior School
 SMTHWKW B67 .... 124 A3
Abbey Tutorial College
 CBHAMNW B3 .... 2 E3
Abu Bakr Girls School *WSL* WS1 ... 4 B7
Ace Business Park
 STETCH B33 .... 131 E2
Acupoint Magneto Clinic
 SHHTH B10 .... 128 C5
Adderley Primary School
 WASH/WDE B8 .... 128 B1
Adderley Trading Estate
 WASH/WDE B8 .... 110 A5
Albert Bradbeer Infant School
 NFLD/LBR B31 .... 189 F1
Albert Bradbeer Junior School
 NFLD/LBR B31 .... 189 F1
Albert Pritchard Infant School
 DARL/WED WS10 .... 56 A3
Albion Business Park
 SMTHWK B66 .... 106 A1
Albion Industrial Estate
 WBROM B70 .... 87 E4
Albion Road Junior School
 HHTH/SAND B71 .... 106 C1
Albion Road Junior School
 WLNHL WV13 .... 39 H3
Alcott Hall Primary School
 CHWD/FDBR/MGN B37 .... 132 B3
Alderbrook School *SOLH* B91 ... 181 F3
Alder Coppice Primary School
 SEDG DY3 .... 67 E2
Aldersley High School
 CDSL WV8 .... 22 A1
Aldersley Leisure Village
 DUNHL/THL/PER WV6 .... 22 B4
Aldridge School *ALDR* WS9 .... 30 A5
Alexander Industrial Park
 BILS/COS WV14 .... 53 G4
Alexandra High School &
 Sixth Form Centre
 TPTN/OCK DY4 .... 69 H5
Alexandra Industrial Estate
 TPTN/OCK DY4 .... 69 F5

Alexandra Medical Centre
 HALE B63 .... 138 B2
Alexandra Theatre *DIG/EDG* B5 ... 3 F6
Al-Furqan Community College
 SPARK B11 .... 145 H3
Al Furqan Primary School
 SPARK B11 .... 145 H3
Al Hijjrah School *BORD* B9 .... 128 B2
Al-Hira School *BHTH/HG* B12 ... 144 B1
Al Huda Girls School
 WASH/WDE B8 .... 110 B4
Alison Nicholas Golf Academy
 PBAR/PBCH B42 .... 74 C3
Allens Croft Primary School
 ALE/KHTH/YWD B14 .... 160 B5
All Saints CE J & I School
 HHTH/SAND B71 .... 71 C5
All Saints Industrial Estate
 SMTHWK B18 .... 108 A4
Alma Industrial Estate
 DARL/WED WS10 .... 55 E2
Alston Primary School
 BORD B9 .... 129 E1
Alumrock Medical Centre
 WASH/WDE B8 .... 110 C5
Alumwell Community School
 WSLW WS2 .... 41 E4
Alumwell Infant School
 WSLW WS2 .... 41 E3
Alumwell Junior School
 WSLW WS2 .... 41 E3
Amblecote Primary School
 STRBR DY8 .... 118 B4
AMC Cinema
 LDYWD/EDGR B16 .... 126 A3
Amptrosik Trading Estate
 WMBN WV5 .... 80 B2
Anchor Brook Industrial Park
 ALDR WS9 .... 30 B4
Anderton Park Primary
 School
 BHTH/HG B12 .... 144 C3
Anglesey Primary School
 LOZ/NWT B19 .... 108 C2
Anglo African Industrial Park
 DUDS DY2 .... 86 C4
Anita Myatt Health Centre
 ETTPK/GDPK/PENN WV4 .... 50 D4
Annie Lennard Infant School
 SMTHWKW B67 .... 124 A1
Arcadian Shopping Centre
 DIG/EDG B5 .... 3 C7
Archbishop Grimshaw
 RC School
 CHWD/FDBR/MGN B37 .... 131 H1

Archbishop Ilsey Catholic
 Technology College &
 Sixth Form Centre
 ACGN B27 .... 146 C4
Arden Hotel & Leisure Club
 HIA/OLT B92 .... 149 F5
Arden Industrial Estate
 WASH/WDE B8 .... 111 F2
Arden Primary School
 SPARK B11 .... 145 G2
Arden School
 DOR/KN B93 .... 197 F3
Armoury Trading Estate
 SPARK B11 .... 145 F1
Arran Medical Centre
 CBROM B36 .... 114 A2
Arrow Industrial Estate
 SHHTH WV12 .... 25 H3
Arthur Terry School
 FOAKS/STRLY B74 .... 47 E3
Ashbourne Centre
 ERDW/GRVHL B23 .... 92 C3
Ashford Industrial Estate
 BKHL/PFLD WV2 .... 52 D1
Ashfurlong Health Centre
 MGN/WHC B75 .... 48 A5
Ashmore Park Clinic
 WNSFLD WV11 .... 25 C2
Ashmores Industrial Estate
 DUDN DY1 .... 84 D3
Ashtree Medical Centre
 BVILLE B30 .... 160 A4
Ashurst Park Primary School
 STRBR DY8 .... 117 H3
Aston Cross Business Park
 AST/WIT B6 .... 109 C3
Aston Expressway
 Industrial Estate
 AST/WIT B6 .... 109 E4
Aston Hall *AST/WIT* B6 .... 109 F1
Aston Health Centre
 AST/WIT B6 .... 91 E5
Aston Manor Cricket &
 Lucas Sports Club
 PBAR/PBCH B42 .... 90 D1
Aston Manor School
 AST/WIT B6 .... 109 F3
Aston Science Park
 VAUX/NECH B7 .... 3 K2
Aston Tower Primary School
 AST/WIT B6 .... 109 F2
Aston University
 CBHAMNE B4 .... 3 J1
Aston Villa FC (Villa Park)
 AST/WIT B6 .... 91 F5

Aston Wood Golf Club
 FOAKS/STRLY B74 .... 32 C4
Astoria Hotel
 LDYWD/EDGR B16 .... 125 F3
Atlas Trading Estate
 BILS/COS WV14 .... 69 F1
 SPARK B11 .... 145 F2
Attock Community Sports & CC
 MOS/BIL B13 .... 162 A1
Attwood Business Centre
 TPTN/OCK DY4 .... 136 D2
Autobase Industrial Estate
 TPTN/OCK DY4 .... 85 H3
Avery Dell Industrial Estate
 BVILLE B30 .... 159 H4
Axcess 10 Business Park
 DARL/WED WS10 .... 40 C5
Baggeridge Country Park
 SEDG DY3 .... 66 A5
Bagley Industrial Park
 DUDS DY2 .... 102 D5
Balliol Business Park
 COVEN WV9 .... 11 C4
Banners Gate Infant School
 SCFLD/BOLD B73 .... 60 D4
Banners Gate Junior School
 SCFLD/BOLD B73 .... 60 C4
Bantock House & Park
 BDMR/CCFT WV3 .... 36 B4
Barber Institute of Fine Arts
 EDG B15 .... 142 D3
Barford Primary School
 LDYWD/EDGR B16 .... 125 C1
Barnfield Trading Estate
 TPTN/OCK DY4 .... 69 E4
Baron Business Centre
 HAG/WOL DY9 .... 136 C2
Barons Court Industrial Estate
 ALDR WS9 .... 19 E5
Barons Court Trading Estate
 ALDR WS9 .... 19 E5
The Barr Beacon School
 ALDR WS9 .... 59 F3
Bartley Green FC
 RIDG/WDGT B32 .... 157 G1
Bartley Green Health Centre
 RIDG/WDGT B32 .... 157 F1
Bartley Green Technology
 College *RIDG/WDGT* B32 .... 157 G1
Barton Industrial Estate
 BILS/COS WV14 .... 54 A1
Baskerville Special School
 HRBN B17 .... 141 G1
Bath Walk Industrial Estate
 BHTH/HG B12 .... 144 A2

Baverstock GM School
 ALE/KHTH/YWD B14 178
Bayer Hall Clinic
 BILS/COS WV14 68
Beacon CP School
 SCFLD/BOLD B73 60
Beacon Hill Cemetery
 Beacon Hill Cemetery
 ETTPK/GDPK/PENN WV4 6
Beaconside Primary School
 RBRY B45 188
Beacon Trading Estate
 ALDR WS9 30
Bean Road Industrial Estate
 TPTN/OCK DY4 69
Bearwood Medical Centre
 SMTHWKW B67 106
Bearwood Primary School
 SMTHWK B66 106
Bearwood Shopping Centre
 SMTHWK B66 106
Beaufort Special School
 CBROM B36 111
Beaufcorm College
 ALE/KHTH/YWD B14 160
Beauty Bank Primary School
 STRBR DY8 99
Beechcole CP School
 WSLW WS2 27
Beeches Hospital
 WOLV WV1 6
Beeches Pool & Fitness Centre
 EDG B15 125
Belbroughton CE First School
 HAG/WOL DY9 196
Belfont Trading Estate
 RMSLY B62 121
Bell Barn Shopping Centre
 EDG B15 126
Belle Vue Medical Centre
 EDG B15 126
Belle Vue Primary School
 WSLW WS2 40
Bellfield J & I School
 NFLD/LBR B31 175
Bells Farm Primary School
 ALE/KHTH/YWD B14 177
The Bell Shopping Centre
 NFLD/LBR B31 175
Bennetts Well Primary School
 CHWD/FDBR/MGN B37 113
Benson Community School
 WSNGN B18 108
Benson Industrial Estate
 WSNGN B18 108

ntley Bridge Business Park WNSFLD WV11 ...... 24 C5
ntley Bridge Leisure Park WNSFLD WV11 ...... 38 B1
ntley Cemetery WLNHL WV13 ...... 40 B3
ntley Drive Primary School WLNHL WV13 ...... 41 F2
ntley Heath CE Primary School DOR/KN B93 ...... 196 D3
ntley Lane Industrial Park WSLW WS2 ...... 41 F2
ntley Mill Industrial Estate WSLW WS2 ...... 40 D3
ntley West Primary School WSLW WS2 ...... 40 D3
rrybrook Primary School WOLVN WV10 ...... 24 B1
scot Industrial Estate DARL/WED WS10 ...... 55 F5
st Western Premier Moor Hall Hotel & Spa MCN/WHC B75 ...... 47 H4
st Western The Fairlawns at Aldridge ALDR WS9 ...... 31 E4
st Western Westley Hotel ACGN B27 ...... 146 B4
wan Industrial Estate BRLYHL DY5 ...... 118 C2
verley Hotel RUSH/SHEL WS4 ...... 42 C1
ylls Acre Primary School BDMR/CCFT WV5 ...... 50 B1
kenhill Trading Estate CHWD/FDBR/MGN B37 ...... 149 H2
kford Road Industrial Estate AST/WIT B6 ...... 91 G5
brook CE Middle School CDSL WV8 ...... 10 D4
brook Medical Centre CDSL WV8 ...... 10 D4
esley Primary School MOS/BIL B13 ...... 162 A4
ston Cemetery BILS/COS WV14 ...... 53 G1
ston Central Industrial Estate BILS/COS WV14 ...... 54 A3
ston CE Primary School BKHL/PFLD WV2 ...... 53 F2
ston Health Centre BILS/COS WV14 ...... 53 H1
ston High School BILS/COS WV14 ...... 53 H1
ston Industrial Estate BILS/COS WV16 ...... 54 C4
agle Primary School BDMR/CCFT WV5 ...... 36 C5
ston Key Industrial Estate BILS/COS WV14 ...... 54 C3
ston Leisure Centre BILS/COS WV14 ...... 53 H2
ston Public Library & Art Gallery BILS/COS WV14 ...... 54 A2
ston Town FC BILS/COS WV14 ...... 54 B2
HWK/WKHTH B38 ...... 176 C5
ches First School CDSL WV8 ...... 21 F1
ches Green J & I School ERDE/BCHGN B24 ...... 93 F3
chfield Independent Girls School AST/WIT B6 ...... 109 E1
chfield Primary School AST/WIT B6 ...... 90 D5
chills CE Primary School WSLW WS2 ...... 4 B2
chills Health Centre WSLW WS2 ...... 4 A1
chley Industrial Estate OLDBY B69 ...... 104 C4
ch Road East Industrial Estate AST/WIT B6 ...... 91 H4
ningham Alexander Stadium PBAR/PBCH B42 ...... 74 C5
mingham Area Civil Service Sports Club HIA/OLT B92 ...... 149 G5
ningham Botanical Gardens & Glasshouses EDG B15 ...... 125 H5
mingham Business Centre WBROM B70 ...... 88 B4
mingham Business Park CHWD/FDBR/MGN B37 ...... 133 E4
mingham Christian Centre CBHAMNW B3 ...... 3 F4
mingham City College BORD B9 ...... 129 E1
mingham City FC (St Andrews Stadium) BORD B9 ...... 127 H3
mingham College of Food, Tourism & Creative Studies CBHAMNW B3 ...... 2 D4
mingham Community College CSCFLD/WYGN B72 ...... 62 C3
mingham Conservatoire (University of Central England) CBHAMNW B3 ...... 2 D5
2 Birmingham Crematorium PBAR/PBCH B42 ...... 90 C1
mingham Heartlands Hospital BORD B9 ...... 129 F2
mingham Hebrew Congregation CBHAMNW B1 ...... 2 E7
mingham International Airport LGN/SDN/BHAMAIR B26 ...... 149 G3
mingham Marriott Hotel EDG B15 ...... 126 B4
2 Birmingham & Midland Hospital for Woman SPARK B11 ...... 145 E4
2 Birmingham Mint WSNGN B18 ...... 2 B1
mingham Museum & Art Gallery CBHAMNW B3 ...... 2 E5
2 Birmingham Nuffield Hospital EDG B15 ...... 142 D2

Birmingham One Industrial Estate CBHAMW B16 ...... 2 B4
Birmingham Repertory Theatre CBHAMW B1 ...... 2 D5
Birmingham Wheels Adventure Park BORD B9 ...... 128 A2
Birmingham Womens Hospital HRBN B17 ...... 142 B2
Birmingham (Yardley) Crematorium YDLY B25 ...... 146 D2
Bishop Ashbury's Cottage GTB/HAM B43 ...... 72 D2
The Bishop Challoner RC School ALE/KHTH/YWD B14 ...... 161 E2
Bishop Milner RC Secondary School DUDN DY1 ...... 84 A3
Bishop Veseys Grammar School FOAKS/STRLY B74 ...... 62 C2
Bishop Walsh Catholic School WALM/CURD B76 ...... 77 H1
Bishop Wilson CE Primary School CHWD/FDBR/MGN B37 ...... 132 C1
Bi-Tec Industrial Park WOLV WV1 ...... 37 H4
Blackbrook Valley Industrial Estate DUDS DY2 ...... 102 A3
Blackbrook Valley Industrial Park BRLYHL DY5 ...... 102 A4
Black Country Living Museum DUDN DY1 ...... 84 D3
Blackheath Primary School BLKHTH/ROWR B65 ...... 121 H5
Blackheath Trading Estate BLKHTH/ROWR B65 ...... 122 C2
Black Lake Industrial Estate AST/WIT B6 ...... 71 E5
Blackwood School FOAKS/STRLY B74 ...... 45 E4
Blakedown CE First School KIDD DY10 ...... 168 C4
Blakeley Heath Primary School WMBN WV5 ...... 81 E1
Blakenall RC BLOX/PEL WS3 ...... 27 G3
Blakenall Heath Junior School BLOX/PEL WS3 ...... 27 G2
Blakenhale Infant School STETCH B33 ...... 130 D3
Blakenhale Junior School STETCH B33 ...... 130 D3
Blakenhall Industrial Estate BDMR/CCFT WV3 ...... 51 H1
Blakesley Hall YDLY B25 ...... 130 A3
Blakesley Hall Primary School STETCH B33 ...... 129 H3
Blanford Mere Primary School KGSWFD DY6 ...... 100 A2
Bleakhouse Clinic LGLYGN/QTN B68 ...... 123 C3
Bleakhouse Junior School LGLYGN/QTN B68 ...... 123 C3
Blossomfield Infant School SHLY B90 ...... 180 D2
Blowers Green Primary School DUDS DY2 ...... 102 B1
Bloxwich Business Park WSLW WS3 ...... 27 F3
Bloxwich CE Primary School BLOX/PEL WS3 ...... 27 F1
Bloxwich Golf Club BLOX/PEL WS3 ...... 16 D3
Bloxwich Hospital BLOX/PEL WS3 ...... 27 F2
Bloxwich Lane Industrial Estate WSLW WS2 ...... 41 E2
Bloxwich Leisure Centre WSLW WS2 ...... 27 G2
Blue Coat CE Comprehensive School WSL WS1 ...... 5 F5
Blue Coat CE Infant School WSL WS1 ...... 5 F6
Blue Coat CE Junior School WSL WS1 ...... 5 G5
The Blue Coat School HRBN B17 ...... 142 C1
Blythe Business Park SHLY B90 ...... 195 F5
Blythe Special School CSHL/WTROR B46 ...... 115 G5
BMI Priory Hospital DIG/EDG B5 ...... 143 F2
Boddis Industrial Park CDYHTH B64 ...... 121 G2
Boldmere Clinic SCFLD/BOLD B73 ...... 76 D2
Boldmere Golf Club SCFLD/BOLD B73 ...... 61 G5
Boldmere J & I School SCFLD/BOLD B73 ...... 76 D2
Boldmere St Michaels FC SCFLD/BOLD B73 ...... 76 D3
Bordesley Green Girls School WASH/WDE B8 ...... 128 C1
Bordesley Green Primary School BORD B9 ...... 129 E2
Bordesley Green Trading Estate WASH/WDE B8 ...... 128 B1
Borough Cemetery DUDS DY2 ...... 102 B1
Bosworth Wood Primary School CBROM B36 ...... 95 H5
Boulton Industrial Centre WSNGN B18 ...... 108 B4
The Boundary Hotel WSL WS1 ...... 5 H1
Boundary Industrial Estate WOLVN WV10 ...... 12 C2
Bournville Infant School BVILLE B30 ...... 159 G3
Bournville Junior School BVILLE B30 ...... 159 G3
Bournville College of Further Education SLYOAK B29 ...... 159 E3
Bournville School of Art & Craft BVILLE B30 ...... 159 G5
Bournville School & Sixth Form Centre NFLD/LBR B31 ...... 159 E4

Bowlplex LDYWD/EDGR B16 ...... 126 A3
Brackendale Shopping Centre SHHTH WV12 ...... 40 B1
Bradford Street Clinic WSL WS1 ...... 4 D5
Braidwood School for Deaf Children ERDW/GRVHL B23 ...... 75 H5
Bramford Primary School BILS/COS WV14 ...... 68 A5
Brandhall Clinic LGLYGN/QTN B68 ...... 123 F4
Brandhall Golf Club LGLYGN/QTN B68 ...... 123 E2
Brandhall Primary School LGLYGN/QTN B68 ...... 123 F3
Brandon Way Industrial Estate WBROM B70 ...... 86 D3
Brandwood End Cemetery ALE/KHTH/YWD B14 ...... 178 A1
Brasshouse Infant School SMTHWK B66 ...... 106 C2
Brasshouse Language Centre LDYWD/EDGR B16 ...... 2 B7
Brays Special School LGN/SDN/BHAMAIR B26 ...... 147 G1
Breener Industrial Estate BRLYHL DY5 ...... 118 D3
Brickhouse J & I School BLKHTH/ROWR B65 ...... 121 C1
Bridge Industrial Estate SOLH B91 ...... 165 E2
Bridge Special School GRVL/GRVHL B23 ...... 92 C2
Bridge Street Industrial Estate DARL/WED WS10 ...... 70 D2
The Bridge Trading Estate SMTHWK B66 ...... 106 D2
Brierley Hill Cemetery BRLYHL DY5 ...... 118 D2
The Brierley Hill Health Centre BRLYHL DY5 ...... 119 F1
Brierley Hill Primary School BRLYHL DY5 ...... 119 F2
The Brierley Trading Estate BRLYHL DY5 ...... 119 E1
Brierly Hill Leisure Centre BRLYHL DY5 ...... 119 G1
The Brier Special School BRLYHL DY5 ...... 119 G1
Brindley Place CBHAMW B1 ...... 2 C6
Brineton Industrial Estate WSLW WS2 ...... 4 A6
Bristnall Hall High School LGLYGN/QTN B68 ...... 123 H1
Broadcott Industrial Estate CDYHTH B64 ...... 121 G5
Broadfield House Glass Museum KGSWFD DY6 ...... 99 H4
Broadmeadow J & I School BVILLE B30 ...... 177 F3
Broadwak Retail Park WSL WS1 ...... 56 D2
Broadway Medical Centre WSL WS1 ...... 57 F2
Broadway Plaza LDYWD/EDGR B16 ...... 126 A3
Broadway School BFLD/HDSWWD B20 ...... 91 E4
Broadwell Industrial Park OLDBY B69 ...... 87 E5
Broadyn Trading Estate CDYHTH B64 ...... 121 G3
Brockmoor Industrial Park KGSWFD DY6 ...... 118 C1
Brockmoor Primary School BRLYHL DY5 ...... 119 E1
Bromford Road Industrial Estate OLDBY B69 ...... 87 E5
Bromley Hills Primary School KGSWFD DY6 ...... 100 B5
Bromley Primary School BRLYHL DY5 ...... 100 D4
Brookfields Primary School WSNGN B18 ...... 2 A1
Brooklands Hospital CHWD/FDBR/MGN B37 ...... 132 B4
The Brook Primary School STRBR DY8 ...... 118 B3
Brookside Industrial Estate DARL/WED WS10 ...... 56 B5
Brook Street Business Centre TPTN/OCK DY4 ...... 69 E5
Brookvale Primary School ERDW/GRVHL B23 ...... 91 H2
Brookvale Trading Estate AST/WIT B6 ...... 91 G3
Brownhills Business Park BRWNH WS8 ...... 9 F3
Brownhills Clinic BRWNH WS8 ...... 9 F5
Brownhills Comprehensive School BRWNH WS8 ...... 9 F3
Brownhills West JMI School BRWNH WS8 ...... 8 C2
Brownhills West Station BRWNH WS8 ...... 8 C1
Browning Street Industrial Estate LDYWD/EDGR B16 ...... 2 A6
Brownmead Primary School BKDE/SHDE B34 ...... 112 D5
Brunswick Park Trading Estate DARL/WED WS10 ...... 56 B4
Brymill Industrial Estate TPTN/OCK DY4 ...... 69 E3
BSA Business Park SPARK B11 ...... 145 F1
BT Tower CBHAMW B1 ...... 2 E5
Bullring Shopping Centre 3 H6
Bull Ring Trading Estate BHTH/HG B12 ...... 3 K7
Bull Street Trading Estate BRLYHL DY5 ...... 118 D3
Burman Infant School SHLY B90 ...... 180 A3
Burnt Tree Industrial Estate TPTN/OCK DY4 ...... 85 H4
Burnt Tree J & I School OLDBY B69 ...... 85 G4
Burton Industrial Estate CDYHTH B64 ...... 121 E4

Bushbury Baths WOLVN WV10 ...... 23 C1
Bushbury Cemetery WOLVN WV10 ...... 13 F5
Bushbury Health Centre WOLVN WV10 ...... 13 E5
Bushbury Hill J & I School WOLVN WV10 ...... 23 H1
Busill Jones JMI School BLOX/PEL WS3 ...... 26 D2
The Business Centre SPARK B11 ...... 145 H1
Butts JMI School RUSH/SHEL WS4 ...... 5 F1
Cadbury College HWK/WKHTH B38 ...... 176 D4
Cadbury World BVILLE B30 ...... 159 H3
Calderfields Golf Club & Academy RUSH/SHEL WS4 ...... 43 E5
Caldmore JMI School WSL WS1 ...... 4 E7
Caldmore Medical Centre WSL WS1 ...... 4 E7
Calthorpe Special School BHTH/HG B12 ...... 127 C4
Cambrian Wharf CBHAMW B1 ...... 2 C5
Cambridge Tutorial College SMHTH B10 ...... 128 B4
Campanile Hotel VAUX/NECH B7 ...... 109 F4
Camp Hill Old Edwardians RFC SHLY B90 ...... 180 B2
Canal Side Industrial Estate BRLYHL DY5 ...... 118 D3
Canal View Industrial Estate STRBR DY8 ...... 118 C3
Canning Wharf CBHAMNW B1 ...... 2 D4
Cannon Business Park BILS/COS WV14 ...... 68 C2
Canterbury Cross Primary School BFLD/HDSWWD B20 ...... 90 D4
Cape Hill Medical Centre SMTHWK B66 ...... 107 E5
Cape Primary School SMTHWK B66 ...... 107 E5
Cardinal Wiseman Catholic School KGSTG B44 ...... 75 F1
Carlton Business Centre VAUX/NECH B7 ...... 109 E4
Carlyle Business Park WBROM B70 ...... 86 D1
Carters Green Medical Centre WBROM B70 ...... 87 G2
Caslon Primary School HALE B63 ...... 137 F3
Castle Bromwich Business Park CVALE B35 ...... 94 B5
Castle Bromwich CC CBROM B36 ...... 95 G5
Castle Bromwich Hall Gardens CBROM B36 ...... 112 C1
Castle Bromwich Infant School CBROM B36 ...... 113 C1
Castle Bromwich Junior School CBROM B36 ...... 113 F2
Castlecroft JMI School BDMR/CCFT WV3 ...... 35 F4
Castle High School DUDN DY1 ...... 84 B4
The Castle Pool & Adventure Play Centre CVALE B35 ...... 95 E4
Castle Special School BLOX/PEL WS3 ...... 16 C5
Castle Vale Health Centre CVALE B35 ...... 94 B3
Castle Vale Industrial Estate WALM/CURD B76 ...... 94 C1
Castle Vale Shopping Centre CVALE B35 ...... 94 B3
Castle View Industrial Estate TPTN/OCK DY4 ...... 85 F3
Causeway Green Primary School LGLYGN/QTN B68 ...... 122 D5
C&C Site RMS/DY B62 ...... 172 A1
Cemetery of St Joseph VAUX/NECH B7 ...... 109 H2
Central Business Park STETCH B33 ...... 131 F3
Central Clinic DUDS DY2 ...... 84 D5
Central Hall CBHAMNE B4 ...... 3 H3
Central Industrial Estate BKHL/PFLD WV2 ...... 52 D1
Central Park Industrial Estate DUDS DY2 ...... 121 E1
Central Trading Estate KGSWFD DY6 ...... 82 B5
Centre Link Industrial Estate VAUX/NECH B7 ...... 109 H3
Century Industrial Estate KGSTG B44 ...... 60 A4
Chad Vale Primary School EDG B15 ...... 125 F5
Chamber of Commerce WSL WS1 ...... 5 G2
Chamber of Commerce & Industry BDMR/CCFT WV3 ...... 6 A3
Chancel Industrial Estate DARL/WED WS10 ...... 55 F3
KGSWFD DY6 ...... 81 H5
KGSWFD DY6 ...... 100 A1
WLNHL WV13 ...... 39 H3
WOLV WV1 ...... 37 H4
Chancel Way Industrial Estate AST/WIT B6 ...... 91 G3
Chandos Primary School DIG/EDG B5 ...... 127 C5
Chapel Fields Junior School HIA/OLT B92 ...... 147 F4
Chapel Street Industrial Estate DUDS DY2 ...... 102 D1
Charlemont Primary School HHTH/SAND B71 ...... 72 A3
Charles Street Industrial Estate TPTN/OCK DY4 ...... 86 C1
Charnwood Business Park BILS/COS WV14 ...... 53 G3

Charterfield Shopping Centre KGSWFD DY6 ...... 99 H1
Chase Watersports Centre BNTWD WS8 ...... 8 C1
Cheapside Industrial Estate BHTH/HG B12 ...... 127 F3
Chelmsley Wood Industrial Estate CHWD/FDBR/MGN B37 ...... 114 A4
Chelmsley Wood Shopping Centre CHWD/FDBR/MGN B37 ...... 132 B2
Chelsea Trading Estate AST/WIT B6 ...... 109 G3
Cherry Oak Special School SLYOAK B29 ...... 142 B5
Cherry Orchard Primary School BFLD/HDSWWD B20 ...... 90 A3
Cherry Trees Special School WMBN WV5 ...... 64 D5
Cherrywood Industrial Estate WASH/WDE B8 ...... 128 B1
Cheston Industrial Estate AST/WIT B6 ...... 109 H2
Cheswick Green Primary School SHLY B90 ...... 195 E3
Chilcote Primary School HLGN/YWD B28 ...... 179 H1
Chillington Works Industrial Estate WOLV WV1 ...... 37 H4
The Chiropody Surgery YDLY B25 ...... 129 H3
Chivenor Primary School CVALE B35 ...... 94 C4
Christ Church CE Infant School DUNHL/THL/PER WV6 ...... 36 D1
Christ Church CE Junior School DUNHL/THL/PER WV6 ...... 35 C1
Christ Church CE Primary School BLOX/PEL WS3 ...... 27 H3
OLDBY B69 ...... 105 E1
SPARK B11 ...... 127 H5
Christ Church Infant School DUNHL/THL/PER WV6 ...... 35 E2
Christ Church Primary School WSL WS1 ...... 68 D2
Christ the King RC Primary School KGSTG B44 ...... 75 F3
Chuckery Primary School WSL WS1 ...... 5 H4
Churchbridge Industrial Estate OLDBY B69 ...... 104 D3
Churchfield Industrial Estate DUDS DY2 ...... 102 C1
Churchill & Blakedown Golf Club KIDD DY10 ...... 168 A3
Churchill Precinct DUDN DY1 ...... 84 D5
Church Lane Health Centre STETCH B33 ...... 130 B1
Church Lane Industrial Estate HHTH/SAND B71 ...... 71 G5
Church of Ascension CE Primary School KGSWFD DY6 ...... 99 F1
Cineworld SOLH B91 ...... 182 A2
City College ACGN B27 ...... 146 C4
City College Birmingham BKDE/SHDE B34 ...... 113 F3
HDSW B21 ...... 108 A2
HRBN B17 ...... 142 B1
STETCH B33 ...... 130 D4
City Hospital WSNGN B18 ...... 107 H5
City of Wolverhampton College BKHL/PFLD WV2 ...... 7 G5
City Plaza Shopping Centre CBHAM B2 ...... 3 F5
City Road Primary School LDYWD/EDGR B16 ...... 125 F1
The City Technology College CHWD/FDBR/MGN B37 ...... 114 A5
City Trading Estate LDYWD/EDGR B16 ...... 125 H1
Claregate Primary School DUNHL/THL/PER WV6 ...... 22 B3
Clarkes Industrial Estate SCFLD/BOLD B73 ...... 77 E2
Clearwater Industrial Estate BKHL/PFLD WV2 ...... 52 D1
Clent Hills HAG/WOL DY9 ...... 154 A5
Clent Hills Country Park (NT) HAG/WOL DY9 ...... 171 E1
Clent Parochial First School HAG/WOL DY9 ...... 170 D3
Cleton Street Business Park TPTN/OCK DY4 ...... 85 H3
Clifton Infant School BHTH/HG B12 ...... 144 C2
Clifton Junior School BHTH/HG B12 ...... 144 C2
Clifton Road Industrial Estate BHTH/HG B12 ...... 144 B2
Clothier Street Primary School WLNHL WV13 ...... 39 G2
CMT Industrial Estate OLDBY B69 ...... 105 E1
Coalpool Clinic BLOX/PEL WS3 ...... 28 B4
Coal Pool Lane Cemetery BLOX/PEL WS3 ...... 42 B1
Cobham Business Centre WASH/WDE B8 ...... 128 B1
Cockshut Hill Technology College LGN/SDN/BHAMAIR B26 ...... 130 C4
Cocks Moors Woods Leisure Centre ALE/KHTH/YWD B14 ...... 178 B1
Codsall Cemetery CDSL WV8 ...... 10 B2
Codsall Clinic CDSL WV8 ...... 10 C4
Codsall Middle School CDSL WV8 ...... 10 C4
Cofton Medical Centre NFLD/LBR B31 ...... 189 G1
Cofton Primary School NFLD/LBR B31 ...... 189 G2
Coldland Colts FC SOLH B91 ...... 165 H4
Colebourne Primary School BKDE/SHDE B34 ...... 112 A4

Coleshill Cemetery
CSHL/WTROR B46 .... 115 G3
Coleshill CE Primary School
CSHL/WTROR B46 .... 115 F3
Coleshill Clinic
CSHL/WTROR B46 .... 115 G3
Coleshill Heath
Primary School
CHWD/FDBR/MGN B37 ......132 C4
Coleshill Hotel
CSHL/WTROR B46 .... 115 G3
Coleshill Industrial Estate
CSHL/WTROR B46 .... 97 F4
Coleshill Leisure Centre
CSHL/WTROR B46 .... 115 F3
Coleshill School
CSHL/WTROR B46 ....133 G1
Coleshill Town FC
CSHL/WTROR B46 ....133 G1
The College High School
KGSTG B44 .... 75 G5
College of Continuing
Education
WSL WS1 .... 57 E1
Colley Lane Health Clinic
HALE B63 .... 137 G1
Colley Lane Primary School
HALE B63 .... 137 F1
Collingwood Primary School
WOLVN WV10 .... 13 E5
Colmers Farm J & I School
RBRY B45 .... 174 B5
Colmers Farm Secondary
School *RBRY* B45 .... 174 B5
Colmore J & I School
ALE/KHTH/YWD B14 .... 160 D3
Colonial Industrial Centre
CDYHTH B64 .... 120 D5
Colton Hills School
ETTPK/GDPK/PENN WV4 ..... 51 H4
Comfort Inn
LDYWD/EDGR B16 .... 125 F3
Community High School
CDSL WV8 .... 10 C3
Community Leisure Centre
TPTN/OCK DY4 .... 68 D5
Coneygre Industrial Estate
TPTN/OCK DY4 .... 85 F4
Connect Business Park
WASH/WDE B8 .... 128 A2
Conway Primary School
SPARK B11 .... 144 D1
Cookley Wharf Industrial
Estate *BRLYHL* DY5 .... 118 C1
Cooper & Jordan CE J & I
School *ALDR* WS9 .... 30 C4
Copperfield House Hotel
SLYOAK B29 .... 143 E4
Coppice High Community
School *WNSFLD* WV11 .... 25 H2
Coppice Junior School
HIA/OLT B92 .... 165 G3
Coppice Primary School
HLYWD B47 .... 192 C2
MGN/WHC B75 .... 47 G4
Coppice Side Industrial Estate
BRWNH WS8 .... 8 D5
Copt Heath Golf Club
DOR/KN B93 .... 183 E5
Copthorne Hotel *BRLYHL* DY5 ..101 G5
CBHAMNW B3 .... 2 D5
Corbett Hospital *STRBR* DY8 ...118 C3
Corbett Industrial Estate
DUDS DY2 .... 102 C3
Corngreaves Hall Golf Club
CDYHTH B64 .... 121 F4
Corngreaves J & I School
CDYHTH B64 .... 120 D3
Corngreaves Trading Estate
CDYHTH B64 .... 120 D5
Cornwall Industrial Estate
SMTHWK B66 .... 107 E2
WASH/WDE B8 .... 110 A5
Cornwall Road Industrial
Estate *SMTHWK* B66 .... 107 E2
Corpus Christi RC Primary
School *STECH* B33 .... 129 H2
Corus Hotel Solihull *SHLY* B90 ..195 E1
Coseley Medical Centre
BILS/COS WV14 .... 68 C3
The Coseley School
BILS/COS WV14 .... 68 B2
Coseley Swimming Pool
BILS/COS WV14 .... 68 C3
Cotteridge Health Clinic
BVILLE B30 .... 160 A5
Cottesbrooke Infant School
ACGN B27 .... 146 D3
Cottesbrooke Junior School
ACGN B27 .... 146 C3
Cotwall End Primary School
SEDG DY3 .... 67 E4
County Bridge Primary School
WLNHL WV13 .... 40 C4
Courtfarm Primary School
ERDW/GRVHL B23 .... 76 C5
Crabtree Clinic
CHWD/FDBR/MGN B37 .... 131 H2
Cradley Cemetery *HALE* B63 ....120 C5
Cradley CE Primary School
HALE B63 .... 120 C5
Cradley Heath Community
Recreation Centre
DUDS DY2 .... 121 E2
Cradley High School
HALE B63 .... 137 F1
Cradley Town FC *HALE* B63 ...137 G3
Craig Croft Health Clinic
CHWD/FDBR/MGN B37 ...... 132 C2
Craig Croft Industrial Estate
CHWD/FDBR/MGN B37 ...... 132 C2
Cranmore Industrial Estate
SHLY B90 .... 181 E5
Cranmore Infant School
SOLH B91 .... 181 E4
Crescent Industrial Park
DUDS DY2 .... 102 B2
Crescent Theatre
LDYWD/EDGR B16 .... 2 B6

Crescent Works Industrial Park
DARL/WED WS10 .... 40 B4
Crestwood Park Primary
School *KGSWFD* DY6 .... 100 C4
The Crestwood Secondary
School *KGSWFD* DY6 .... 100 B4
Crocketts Lane Primary
School *SMTHWK* B66 .... 106 C4
Croft Foundry Industrial
Estate *WLNHL* WV13 .... 39 G3
Croft Industrial Estate
CHWD/FDBR/MGN B37 ...... 132 B2
Croft Street JMI School
WSLW WS2 .... 41 H1
Cromwell Primary School
VAUX/NECH B7 .... 109 G3
Cronehill Primary School
WBROM B70 .... 87 G2
Cronehills Health Centre
WBROM B70 .... 87 H3
Crossings Industrial Estate
BLOX/PEL WS3 .... 27 E2
Cross Quays Business Park
OLDBY B69 .... 86 A4
Cross Street Health Centre
DUDN DY1 .... 84 C5
Crossways Shopping Centre
WOLVN WV10 .... 38 A2
Crown Wharf Shopping Centre
WSLW WS2 .... 4 C2
Crown Wharf Shopping Centre
WSLW WS2 .... 41 G1
Crystal Leisure Centre
STRBR DY8 .... 135 F2
Culwell Industrial Park
WOLVN WV10 .... 7 J2
Culwell Trading Estate
WOLVN WV10 .... 37 H1
Dadsford Bridge Industrial
Estate *STRBR* DY8 .... 118 A2
Dame Elizabeth Cadbury
School *BVILLE* B30 .... 159 G3
Dame Ellen Pinsent School
HRBN B17 .... 124 D2
Damson Wood Infant School
HIA/OLT B92 .... 165 F3
Danescourt Crematorium &
Cemetery
DUNHL/THL/PER WV6 .... 21 F4
Danesmore Park Primary
School *WNSFLD* WV11 .... 25 F1
Darlaston Central Trading
Estate *DARL/WED* WS10 ..... 55 G1
Darlaston Clinic
DARL/WED WS10 .... 55 F2
Darlaston Community School
DARL/WED WS10 .... 54 D2
Darlaston FC *DARL/WED* WS10 ..55 F2
Darlaston Road Industrial
Estate *DARL/WED* WS10 ..... 55 F3
Dartmouth Golf Club
HHTH/SAND B71 .... 72 A5
Dartmouth High School
GTB/HAM B43 .... 58 B5
David Lloyd Birmingham
ACGN B27 .... 60 A5
Daw End School
RUSH/SHEL WS4 .... 28 D4
Dawley Brook Primary
School *KGSWFD* DY6 .... 99 G2
Dawley Trading Estate
KGSWFD DY6 .... 99 H1
Daylesford Infant School
HIA/OLT B92 .... 147 G4
Days Inn *SPARK* B11 .... 128 A5
Deanery CE Primary School
WALM/CURD B76 .... 78 B3
Deansfield High School
WOLV WV1 .... 38 C3
Deeley Industrial Estate
WSLW WS2 .... 27 F4
Deepdale Industrial Estate
DUDN DY1 .... 83 G3
The Dell Stadium *BRLYHL* DY5 ..100 D4
Delph Road Industrial Estate
BRLYHL DY5 .... 119 E3
Delph Road Industrial Park
BRLYHL DY5 .... 119 F3
Delta Trading Estate
BKHL/PFLD WV2 .... 37 H5
Delves J & I School
DYSBK/YTR WS5 .... 57 G3
Dental Health Centre
KGSTG B44 .... 75 F1
Dental Hospital
CBHAMNE B4 .... 3 G2
Department of Art (University
of Central England)
CBHAMNW B3 .... 2 E4
Devonshire J & I School
SMTHWK B67 .... 106 A4
Deykin Avenue J & I School
AST/WIT B6 .... 91 G4
D'Eyncourt Primary School
WOLVN WV10 .... 24 B3
Diana Princess of Wales
Hospital (for Children)
CBHAMNE B4 .... 3 G3
Dickens Heath Primary School
SHLY B90 .... 193 H2
Digbeth Coach Station
DIG/EDG B5 .... 3 J7
Dingle Primary School
KGSWFD DY6 .... 100 C5
Dock Lane Industrial Estate
DUDN DY1 .... 84 B5
Dock Meadow Drive
Industrial Estate
ETTPK/GDPK/PENN WV4 ..... 53 E4
Doranda Way Industrial Park
HHTH/SAND B71 .... 85 H1
Dormston Secondary School
SEDG DY3 .... 67 G3
Dormston Trading Estate
DUDN DY1 .... 83 H2
Dorothy Pattison Hospital
WSLW WS2 .... 41 F4
Dorothy Purcell Junior School
BILS/COS WV14 .... 54 D5
Dorridge CC *DOR/KN* B93 .....198 C2

Dorridge J & I School
DOR/KN B93 .... 197 E5
Dorrington Primary School
PBAR/PBCH B42 .... 74 A5
Doulton Trading Estate
BLKHTH/ROWR B65 .... 103 F5
Dovecote J & I School
CDSL WV8 .... 22 A1
The Dovecote Surgery
LGLYGN/QTN B68 .... 123 H1
Downing Close Health Clinic
DOR/KN B93 .... 197 E4
Dreamwell Industrial Estate
SPARK B11 .... 145 H1
Droicon Industrial Estate
BLKHTH/ROWR B65 .... 103 H5
Droicon Trading Estate
BLKHTH/ROWR B65 .... 103 H4
Druids Heath Golf Club
ALDR WS9 .... 30 C2
Duddeston Mill Trading Estate
WASH/WDE B8 .... 110 A5
Dudley Castle & Zoological
Gardens *DUDN* DY1 .... 84 D4
Dudley Central Trading Estate
DUDS DY2 .... 102 B1
Dudley College *BRLYHL* DY5 ...119 F3
DUDN DY1 .... 84 B5
Dudley College
(Mons Hill Campus)
DUDN DY1 .... 84 B2
Dudley Golf Club
BLKHTH/ROWR B65 .... 103 G3
Dudley Kingswinford RFC
KGSWFD DY6 .... 99 E2
Dudley Leisure Centre
DUDN DY1 .... 84 C5
Dudley Museum & Art Gallery
DUDN DY1 .... 84 C5
Dudley Town Hall
DUDN DY1 .... 84 C4
Dudley Water Sports Centre
DUDN DY1 .... 120 B1
Dudley Wood Primary School
DUDS DY2 .... 120 C2
Dunstall Hill Trading Estate
DUNHL/THL/PER WV6 .... 23 E2
Dunstall Hill Primary School
DUNHL/THL/PER WV6 .... 37 E1
Dunton Trading Estate
VAUX/NECH B7 .... 110 B2
Durberville Road Industrial
Estate *BKHL/PFLD* WV2 ...... 52 D1
Eagle Industrial Estate
DUDN DY1 .... 70 B4
Eagle Trading Estate
HALE B63 .... 138 C3
Earls High School *HALE* B63 ..138 D3
Eastbourne House School
ACGN B27 .... 146 C3
Eastfield Primary School
WOLV WV1 .... 37 H3
East Park J & I School
WOLV WV1 .... 38 B5
East Park Trading Estate
BKHL/PFLD WV2 .... 37 H5
Eaton Wood Medical Centre
ERDE/BCHGN B24 .... 93 H3
Ebrook Adult Training Centre
CSCFLD/WYGN B72 .... 62 D5
Eclipse Industrial Estate
TPTN/OCK DY4 .... 85 E1
Eclipse Trading Estate
TPTN/OCK DY4 .... 85 E1
Edgar Stammers Primary
School *BLOX/PEL* WS3 .... 28 B3
Edgbaston Golf Club *EDG* B15 ..143 F1
Edgbaston Health Clinic
EDG B15 .... 142 C2
SOLH B91 .... 164 B4
Edgbaston High School for Girls
& Preparatory Department
EDG B15 .... 125 H5
Edgbaston Shopping Centre
LDYWD/EDGR B16 .... 126 A4
Edgewood Road Clinic
RBRY B45 .... 188 B2
Edward Street Hospital
WBROM B70 .... 87 G3
Electra Park Industrial Estate
AST/WIT B6 .... 91 H5
Electric Cinema *DIG/EDG* B5 ....3 F6
The Elowes Hall School
SEDG DY3 .... 83 E1
Elmdon Trading Estate
CHWD/FDBR/MGN B37 ...... 149 G1
Elmore Green JMI School
BLOX/PEL WS3 .... 27 E1
Elms Farm Primary School
STECH B33 .... 131 E5
Elms Health Centre *HALE* B63 ..137 F1
Elm Terrace Clinic *OLDBY* B69 ..85 H5
Elston Hall Primary School
WOLVN WV10 .... 12 D5
Embassy Industrial Park
HAG/WOL DY9 .... 136 D2
Emmanuel Infant School
ERDW/GRVHL B23 .... 77 E3
Empire Industrial Park
ALDR WS9 .... 29 H2
English Martyrs RC Primary
School *SPARK* B11 .... 145 E3
Enterprise Trading Estate
BRLYHL DY5 .... 119 H1
Erdington Hall Primary School
ERDE/BCHGN B24 .... 92 D4
Erdington Industrial Park
ERDE/BCHGN B24 .... 94 B3
Erdington Medical Centre
ERDW/GRVHL B23 .... 92 C1
Erdington Pool & Turkish Suite
ERDW/GRVHL B23 .... 93 E2
Essington Light Industrial
Estate *WNSFLD* WV11 .... 14 D3
Ettingshall Primary School
BKHL/PFLD WV2 .... 53 F1
Euro Business Park *OLDBY* B69 ..86 C5
European Business Park
OLDBY B69 .... 104 C2
Eversfield Preparatory School
SOLH B91 .... 182 A1

Express by Holiday Inn
HLGN/YWD B28 .... 163 E4
Expressway Industrial Estate
AST/WIT B6 .... 109 E3
Eye Infirmary
BDMR/CCFT WV3 .... 6 B4
Fairfax School *MGN/WHC* B75 ..63 F3
Fairfield First School
BRGRVW B61 .... 185 H5
Fairfield Villa FC *BRGRVW* B61 ..185 H5
Fairhaven Primary School
STRBR DY8 .... 117 H1
Fairway Primary School
NFLD/LBR B31 .... 176 B3
Falcon Lodge Clinic
MGN/WHC B75 .... 63 G3
Fallings Heath Cemetery
DARL/WED WS10 .... 55 H3
Fallings Park Industrial Estate
WOLVN WV10 .... 23 H5
Fallings Park Primary School
WOLVN WV10 .... 24 A3
Fazeley Industrial Estate
DIG/EDG B5 .... 3 K5
Featherstone Primary School
ERDW/GRVHL B23 .... 92 C2
Feldon Lane Clinic *HALE* B63 ....119 C5
Fernbank Medical Centre
WASH/WDE B8 .... 111 E5
Ferndale Primary School
GTB/HAM B43 .... 73 G3
Field Road Cemetery
BLOX/PEL WS3 .... 27 G1
Field Road Industrial Estate
BLOX/PEL WS3 .... 27 G2
Firs Primary School
CBROM B36 .... 112 A1
Fir Tree Primary School
DSYBK/YTR WS5 .... 57 G4
Five Ways Shopping Centre
EDG B15 .... 126 B3
The Foot Clinic *CBHAMNW* B3 ....2 E4
Fordhouse Road Industrial
Estate *WOLVN* WV10 .... 23 E2
Fordhouses CC *WOLVN* WV10 ...12 D3
Forest Oak School *CBROM* B36 ..95 G5
Forge Trading Estate
RMSLY B62 .... 139 E2
Formans Trading Estate
SPARK B11 .... 145 F4
Fort Industrial Park *CVALE* B35 ..94 B5
The Fort Shopping Park
ERDE/BCHGN B24 .... 93 G5
Foundry Primary School
WSNGN B18 .... 107 F3
Fountain Court Hotel
LDYWD/EDGR B16 .... 125 E3
Four Dwellings High School
RIDG/WDGT B32 .... 140 B2
Four Dwellings Infant School
RIDG/WDGT B32 .... 140 B2
Four Oaks J & I School
FOAKS/STRLY B74 .... 46 C1
Four Oaks Medical Centre
MGN/WHC B75 .... 47 F5
Four Oaks Saints CC
FOAKS/STRLY B74 .... 32 C5
Four Seasons Art Gallery
ERDE/BCHGN B24 .... 93 E1
Fox & Goose Shopping Centre
WASH/WDE B8 .... 111 G3
The Fox Hollies Leisure Centre
HLGN/YWD B28 .... 163 E1
Fox Hollies Special School
ACGN B27 .... 163 E1
Foxmill Estate *SPARK* B11 ....145 F5
Foxyards Primary School
TPTN/OCK DY4 .... 84 C1
Frank F Harrison
Comprehensive School
SHHTH WV12 .... 26 D3
Frankley Community High
School *RBRY* B45 .... 173 H3
Frankley Health Centre
RBRY B45 .... 174 A4
Frankley Industrial Park
RBRY B45 .... 174 B4
Friar Park Clinic
DARL/WED WS10 .... 56 D5
Frogmill Junior School
RBRY B45 .... 174 B3
Gainsborough Trading Estate
STRBR DY8 .... 135 H3
Garretts Green Trading Estate
STECH B33 .... 131 E3
Gas Street Basin *CBHAMW* B1 ...2 C6
Gatehouse Trading Estate
BRWNH WS8 .... 9 G3
Gate Medical Centre
WASH/WDE B8 .... 110 B3
Gay Hill Golf Club *HLYWD* B47 ..178 C5
George Auden School
NFLD/LBR B31 .... 158 B5
George Betts Primary School
SMTHWK B66 .... 105 G2
George Dixon School &
Sixth Form *HRBN* B17 ...... 125 E2
George Fentham Endowed
Primary School
HIA/OLT B92 .... 167 G4
George Salter High School
WBROM B70 .... 87 E2
Gibbons Industrial Park
KGSWFD DY6 .... 100 C2
The Giffard RC Primary School
DUNHL/THL/PER WV6 .... 22 B5
Gig Mill Primary School
STRBR DY8 .... 135 E4
Gilbertstone Primary School
LGN/SDN/BHAMAIR B26 .... 146 D2
GK Davies Industrial Estate
HALE B63 .... 137 E1
Glebefields Health Centre
TPTN/OCK DY4 .... 69 G3
Glebe Fields Primary School
TPTN/OCK DY4 .... 69 G2
Glenmead J & I School
KGSTG B44 .... 74 D3
Glynne Primary School
KGSWFD DY6 .... 99 G5

Golden Hillock School
SPARK B11 .... 145 F1
Goldtel Industrial Estate
ETTPK/GDPK/PENN WV4 ..... 53 E3
Goldthorne Medical Centre
BKHL/PFLD WV2 .... 52 A2
Goldthorn Park Primary School
ETTPK/GDPK/PENN WV4 ..... 52 B3
Good Hope Hospital
MGN/WHC B75 .... 62 D2
Gornal Wood Cemetery
SEDG DY3 .... 83 G5
Gornal Wood Crematorium
SEDG DY3 .... 82 D5
Goscote Hospital
BLOX/PEL WS3 .... 28 B2
Goscote Industrial Estate
BLOX/PEL WS3 .... 28 A1
Gossey Lane J & I School
STECH B33 .... 131 E2
Gracechurch Shopping Centre
CSCFLD/WYGN B72 .... 62 B3
Grace Mary Primary School
OLDBY B69 .... 104 A3
Graiseley Primary School
BKHL/PFLD WV2 .... 37 E5
Granada Industrial Estate
OLDBY B69 .... 104 D3
Granby Business Park
STECH B33 .... 131 F3
Grand Theatre *WOLV* WV1 ......7 G4
The Grange Arts & Media
Centre *WSL* WS1 .... 42 D4
The Grange Playhouse
WSL WS1 .... 42 D4
The Grange School
HAG/WOL DY9 .... 136 B3
Gravel Hill Surgery
WMBN WV5 .... 65 F5
Gravelly Industrial Park
ERDE/BCHGN B24 .... 110 C1
Grazebrook Industrial Estate
DUDS DY2 .... 102 A3
Grazebrook Industrial Park
DUDS DY2 .... 102 B3
Great Barr Business Park
PBAR/PBCH B42 .... 90 A1
Great Barr Golf Club
GTB/HAM B43 .... 58 D4
Great Barr Hotel & Conference
Centre *GTB/HAM* B43 .... 72 D2
Great Bridge Industrial Estate
TPTN/OCK DY4 .... 70 A4
Great Bridge Primary School
TPTN/OCK DY4 .... 70 A5
Great Western Industrial
Estate *WSNGN* B18 .... 107 G3
Green Acres Primary School
BILS/COS WV14 .... 54 B2
Greenfield Primary School
RUSH/SHEL WS4 .... 29 E3
STRBR DY8 .... 135 F2
Greenfield Surgery
STRBR DY8 .... 135 F2
Greenholm J & I School
KGSTG B44 .... 75 E4
Green Lane Industrial Estate
BORD B9 .... 128 C3
Green Meadow Primary
School *SLYOAK* B29 .... 158 B3
Green Rock J & I School
BLOX/PEL WS3 .... 28 A4
Greet Primary School
SPARK B11 .... 145 F3
Greets Green Road Industrial
Estate *WBROM* B70 .... 86 D1
Gregston Industrial Estate
OLDBY B69 .... 105 F3
Grendon Primary School
ALE/KHTH/YWD B14 .... 178 C2
Grestone Primary School
BFLD/HDSWWD B20 .... 89 G2
Greswold Primary School
SOLH B91 .... 164 B2
Griffin Business Park
CHWD/FDBR/MGN B37 ...... 132 C2
Griffin Industrial Estate
BLKHTH/ROWR B65 .... 103 H2
Griffins Brook Medical Centre
SLYOAK B29 .... 159 H4
Grimstock Country House
Hotel *CSHL/WTROR* B46 ..... 97 H3
Grosvenor Shopping Centre
NFLD/LBR B31 .... 175 H1
Grove Medical Centre
BKHL/PFLD WV2 .... 37 H5
Grove Primary School
BKHL/PFLD WV2 .... 52 A2
Grove School *HDSW* B21 ...... 107 H3
Grove Vale Primary School
GTB/HAM B43 .... 73 G1
Guardian Angels RC Primary
School *BKDE/SHDE* B34 .... 113 H1
Guest Hospital *DUDN* DY1 ...... 85 E3
Gun Barrel Industrial Centre
CDYHTH B64 .... 138 A1
Guns Village Primary School
WBROM B70 .... 87 E2
Gunter Primary School
ERDE/BCHGN B24 .... 94 A3
Gupta Trading Estate
OLDBY B69 .... 86 B1
Guru Nanak Sikh Temple
BDMR/CCFT WV3 .... 6 A1
Guru Nanak Sikh Temple
SMTHWK B66 .... 106 A3
Guy Motors Industrial Park
WOLVN WV10 .... 12 B1
GWS Industrial Estate
DARL/WED WS10 .... 55 H5
Haden Hill Leisure Centre
CDYHTH B64 .... 121 G2
Hadley Stadium *SMTHWK* B66 ..106 A1
Hagley Cemetery
HAG/WOL DY9 .... 154 A1
Hagley Golf & Country Club
HAG/WOL DY9 .... 153 G4
Hagley Hall *HAG/WOL* DY9 ....153 H5
Hagley RC High School
STRBR DY8 .... 153 G4

Halas Industrial Estate
HALE B63 ....138 D2
Halcyon Gallery *CBHAM* B2 ......3 F6
Halesbury Special School
RMSLY B62 ....122 C4
Halesowen CC *HALE* B63 ....138 D5
Halesowen Cemetery
HALE B63 ....138 C3
Halesowen CE Primary
School *HALE* B63 ....138 C3
Halesowen College *HALE* B63 ....138 C2
Halesowen FC (The Grove
Recreation Ground)
HALE B63 ....138 C2
Halesowen Golf Club
RMSLY B62 ....139 F2
Halesowen Harriers FC
HALE B63 ....137 F2
Halesowen Health Centre
HALE B63 ....138 D4
Halesowen Industrial Park
RMSLY B62 ....138 D1
Halesowen Leisure Centre
HALE B63 ....138 D4
Hale Trading Estate
TPTN/OCK DY4 ....85 H1
Hallfield School *EDG* B15 ....126 A5
Hall Green Cemetery
BILS/COS WV14 ....69 E1
Hall Green J & I School
HHTH/SAND B71 ....71 G2
Hall Green Little Theatre
ACGN B27 ....146 A5
Hall Green Secondary School
HLGN/YWD B28 ....162 C2
Hall Green Stadium
HLGN/YWD B28 ....162 D1
Hallmoor Special School
STECH B33 ....130 D1
Hall of Memory *CBHAM* B1 ......2 D5
Hamd House School
SMHTH B10 ....128 C4
Ham Dingle Primary School
HAG/WOL DY9 ....136 A5
Hamilton Special School
HDSW B21 ....107 F1
Hams Hall International Freight
Terminal
CSHL/WTROR B46 ....97 G3
Hams Hall National
Distribution Park
CSHL/WTROR B46 ....97 H2
Hamstead Hall School
BFLD/HDSWWD B20 ....73 G5
Hamstead J & I School
GTB/HAM B43 ....73 F4
Handsworth Boys Grammar
School *HDSW* B21 ....107 C1
Handsworth Cemetery
HDSW B21 ....88 D4
Handsworth Golf Club
BFLD/HDSWWD B20 ....89 F2
Handsworth Leisure Centre
BFLD/HDSWWD B20 ....107 H1
Handsworth RFC
GTB/HAM B43 ....58 B4
Handsworth Wood Girls
School & Sixth Form Centre
BFLD/HDSWWD B20 ....88 A3
Harborne Church Farm Golf
Club *HRBN* B17 ....141 H3
Harborne Golf Club
RIDG/WDGT B32 ....141 G2
Harborne Hill School *EDG* B15 ..142 C1
Harborne Pool & Fitness
Centre *HRBN* B17 ....141 H2
Harborne Primary School
HRBN B17 ....142 A1
Harden Primary School
BLOX/PEL WS3 ....28 A3
Hargate Primary School
HHTH/SAND B71 ....87 G2
The Harper Bell School
BHTH/HG B12 ....127 G4
Harry Mitchell Leisure Centre
SMHWKW B67 ....106 B4
Harvey Road Health Centre
LGN/SDN/BHAMAIR B26 ..130 A5
Harvey Works Industrial
Estate *HALE* B63 ....138 B1
Harvills Hawthorn Primary
School *WBROM* B70 ....70 D4
Hasbury CE Primary School
HALE B63 ....138 B5
Haslucks Green Junior School
SHLY B90 ....180 A2
Hastingwood Industrial Park
ERDE/BCHGN B24 ....93 F5
Hatchford Brook Golf Club
LGN/SDN/BHAMAIR B26 ..148 C3
Hatchford Brook Primary
School *HIA/OLT* B92 ....148 A4
Hatchford CM Primary School
CHWD/FDBR/MGN B37 ....131 H2
Hateley Heath Primary School
HHTH/SAND B71 ....71 F4
Hatherton Lane Primary
School *WSLW* WS2 ....26 D4
Hawbush Primary School
BRLYHL DY5 ....118 D2
Hawkesley Church Primary
School *HWK/WKHTH* B38 ..190 C1
Hawkesley Health Centre
HWK/WKHTH B38 ....190 C1
Hawksmill Industrial Estate
SMHTH B10 ....128 A3
Hawthorne Primary School
KGSTG B44 ....75 G4
Hawthorns Business Centre
SMTHWK B66 ....106 D1
Hawthorns Health Centre
SMTHWK B66 ....106 D1
Haybridge High School &
Sixth Form
STRBR DY8 ....152 B4
Hayes Trading Estate
HAG/WOL DY9 ....137 E1
Hayes Trading Estate
HAG/WOL DY9 ....137 E1

Hayley Green Hospital
HALE B63 ....154 D2
Hayward Industrial Park
ALDR WS9 ....30 A3
Hazel Oak School *SHLY* B90 ..180 A3
Healthcare Clinic
CSCFLD/WYGN B72 ....77 F3
The Heartlands High School
VAUX/NECH B7 ....109 G5
Heath Clinic *SOLH* B91 ....165 F5
Heathfield Foundation Technology
College *CDYHTH* B64 ....121 F2
Heathfield Primary School
LOZ/NWT B19 ....108 C1
Heathlands Primary (NC)
School *BKDE/SHDE* B34 ....112 B2
Heath Lane Cemetery
WBROM B70 ....71 H4
Heath Lane Hospital
HHTH/SAND B71 ....71 H4
Heath Lodge Hotel
CHWD/FDBR/MGN B37 ....132 D4
Heath Mount Primary School
WOLVN WV10 ....24 A5
Heath Street Industrial Estate
SMTHWK B66 ....107 F4
Heath Town Leisure Centre
WOLVN WV10 ....38 A1
The High Arcal Secondary
School *SEDG* DY3 ....67 H5
Highclare St Paul's School
FOAKS/STRLY B74 ....62 B1
Highclare School
CSCFLD/WYGN B72 ....77 G2
Highclare the Abbey School
ERDW/GRVHL B23 ....93 E1
Highcroft Hospital
ERDW/GRVHL B23 ....92 B3
Highfield Primary School
WASH/WDE B8 ....110 C4
Highfields Primary School
BILS/COS WV14 ....68 C1
Highfields Primary School
BLKHTH/ROWR B65 ....122 A4
Highfields Industrial Estate
ETTPK/GDPK/PENN WV4 ..50 B3
Highgate Business Centre
BHTH/HG B12 ....144 D1
Highgate Medical Centre
BHTH/HG B12 ....127 F5
Highgate Primary School
DUDS DY1 ....101 H3
Highgate Retail Park
BHTH/HG B12 ....127 F5
Highgate Trading Estate
BHTH/HG B12 ....127 F5
Highgate United FC *SHLY* B90 ..193 G2
High Meadow Infant School
CSHL/WTROR B46 ....115 F1
Highters Heath J & I School
ALE/KHTH/YWD B14 ....178 D2
Hillary Primary School
WSLW WS2 ....56 C1
Hill Avenue Primary School
ETTPK/GDPK/PENN WV4 ..52 D5
Hillcrest Business Park
DUDS DY2 ....102 C2
Hillcrest Industrial Estate
CDYHTH B64 ....120 D4
Hillcrest School & Community
Centre *DUDS* DY2 ....102 B4
Hillcrest School & Sixth Form
Centre *RIDG/WDGT* B32 ....141 E4
Hillmeads Health Centre
HWK/WKHTH B38 ....177 E4
Hillstone Primary School
BKDE/SHDE B34 ....113 F4
Hill Top Industrial Estate
WBROM B70 ....70 D3
Hilltop Medical Centre
LGLYGN/QTN B68 ....123 G2
Hilltop Public Golf Course
WBROM B70 ....89 E2
Hilton Cross Business Park
WOLVN WV10 ....13 H1
Hilton Main Industrial Estate
WNSFLD WV11 ....14 A2
Hilton Trading Estate
ETTPK/GDPK/PENN WV4 ..52 D3
Himley Country Hotel
SEDG DY3 ....81 F3
Himley Hall Golf Centre
SEDG DY3 ....81 H2
Himley Hall & Park *SEDG* DY3 ..81 H2
Himley House Hotel *SEDG* DY3 ..80 C5
Himley Plantation
Nature Reserve *WMBN* WV5 ..81 E3
Hingley Industrial Park
DUDS DY2 ....120 C3
Hive Industrial Centre
WSNGN B18 ....108 A3
HM Prison *WSNGN* B18 ....107 G4
Hob Green Primary School
HAG/WOL DY9 ....136 C5
Hobmoor Primary School
YDLY B25 ....129 H4
Hobs Moat Medical Centre
HIA/OLT B92 ....147 G5
Hockley Brook Trading Estate
WSNGN B18 ....108 A2
Hockley Heath Pavilion
(Sports Centre)
HOCK/TIA B94 ....198 A5
Hockley Hill Industrial Estate
WSNGN B18 ....108 B4
Hodge Hill Girls School
CBROM B36 ....111 G2
Hodge Hill School
CBROM B36 ....111 G2
Holiday Inn *SOLH* B91 ....147 H4
Holliday Wharf *CBHAM* B1 ......2 D7
The Hollies Clinic
LGLYGN/QTN B68 ....105 F5
Hollies Industrial Park
BDMR/CCFT WV3 ....6 D7

Holloway Bank Trading Estate
BKHL/WED WS10 ....70 D2
Holly Bush Medical Centre
CDYHTH B64 ....123 H5
Hollyfield Primary School
MGN/WHC B75 ....63 F4
Holly Hall Clinic *DUDN* DY1 ....101 H2
Hollyhedge Primary School
HHTH/SAND B71 ....72 A3
Holly Hill Infant School
RBRY B45 ....173 H5
Holly Lane Cemetery
SMTHWKW B67 ....105 H4
Holly Lodge High School
SMTHWKW B67 ....105 H4
Holly Park Industrial Estate
ERDE/BCHGN B24 ....93 G4
Hollywood Primary School
ALE/KHTH/YWD B14 ....178 C4
Holte School *LOZ/NWT* B19 ....108 D2
Holt Farm Primary School
RMSLY B62 ....121 E4
Holy Child Sch *EDG* B15 ....143 F1
Holy Cross Catholic Primary
School *WALM/CURD* B76 ....63 G5
Holy Family RC Primary School
SMHTH B10 ....128 C5
Holyhead Primary School
DARL/WED WS10 ....55 F5
Holyhead School *HDSW* B21 ..107 F1
Holy Name RC Primary School
GTB/HAM B43 ....73 G2
Holy Rosary RC Primary School
WOLV WV1 ....38 A4
Holy Souls RC Primary School
ACGN B27 ....146 C4
Holy Trinity Catholic Primary
School *BILS/COS* WV14 ......54 A2
Holy Trinity CE Primary School
BFLD/HDSWWD B20 ....90 C4
BRWNH WS8 ....18 D1
WBROM B70 ....87 H5
Holy Trinity RC School
SMHTH B10 ....128 A4
Holywell Primary School
RBRY B45 ....187 F1
Horrell Road Health Centre
LGN/SDN/BHAMAIR B26 ..130 C5
Horse Shoe Associated FC
SHLY B90 ....193 H2
Hotel Clarine
LDYWD/EDGR B16 ....125 C3
Hotel du Vin & Bistro
CBHAM B1 ....3 F4
Hotel ibis *CBHAM* B1 ....126 D3
DIG/EDG B5 ....3 G7
SMHTH B10 ....127 H5
Howard Street Industrial
Estate *WBROM* B70 ....70 D4
Howley Grange Primary
School *RMSLY* B62 ....140 A2
HRS Business Park
STECH B33 ....130 D3
HRS Industrial Estate
STECH B33 ....131 E3
Hudson Industrial Estate
BKHL/PFLD WV2 ....52 D1
Hulbert Industrial Estate
DUDS DY2 ....102 B3
Huntingtree Industrial Estate
HALE B63 ....138 A3
Hurst Business Park
BRLYHL DY5 ....101 H5
Hurstgreen Primary School
RMSLY B62 ....122 C4
Hurst Hill Primary School
BILS/COS WV14 ....68 A3
Hydesville Tower School
WSL WS1 ....5 H2
IKEA store Wednesbury
DARL/WED WS10 ....56 A2
Ikon Gallery *CBHAM* B1 ....2 C6
IMAX Cinema *DIG/EDG* B5 ....3 K4
Imex Business Park
BKHL/PFLD WV2 ....52 A1
BORD B9 ....128 D2
SPARK B11 ....144 C5
STECH B33 ....111 H4
TPTN/OCK DY4 ....85 G3
Imex Industrial Estate
WSNGN B18 ....108 A5
Indian High Commission
WSNGN B18 ....2 C1
Industrial Kingston Estate
BORD B9 ....127 G3
Industrial Weston Estate
SPARK B11 ....145 G3
Infant Welfare Clinic
GTB/HAM B43 ....73 G5
Inkeeper's Hotel *DOR/KN* B93 ..197 H5
Innkeeper's Lodge
HIA/OLT B92 ....147 H3
KGSWFD DY6 ....99 G3
RIDG/WDGT B32 ....123 G5
The Innkeeper's Lodge Hotel
SCFLD/BOLD B73 ....62 A5
International Convention
Centre *CBHAM* B1 ....2 C5
International School &
Community College
STECH B33 ....131 F1
Izons Lane Industrial Estate
WBROM B70 ....86 D5
Jack o'Watton Business Park
CSHL/WTROR B46 ....96 D3
Jack o'Watton Industrial
Estate *CSHL/WTROR* B46 ..96 D3
James Bridge Cemetery
DARL/WED WS10 ....40 D5
James Watt Industrial Park
KGSTG B44 ....167 E3
Jamia Mosque
DUNHL/THL/PER WV6 ......6 A1
Jane Lane Special School
WSLW WS2 ....40 D2
Janet Shaw Clinic
CHWD/FDBR/MGN B37 ....132 A4
JAS Industrial Park
OLDBY B69 ....104 C5
Jerome Retail Park *WSL* WS1 ..4 C5

Jervoise J & I School
SLYOAK B29 ....158 C1
Jessons CE First & Middle
School *DUDN* DY1 ....84 A5
Jewellery Quarter *WSNGN* B18 ..2 C1
The Jewellery Quarter
Discovery Centre
WSNGN B18 ....108 B4
Jewish Cemetery *AST/WIT* B6 ..91 C1
JFK Memorial *CBHAM* B4 ....3 F3
John Black Day Hospital
CHWD/FDBR/MGN B37 ....132 B4
John Willmott School
WALM/CURD B76 ....63 F4
Joseph Chamberlain Sixth
Form College
BHTH/HG B12 ....127 F5
Joseph Leckie Comprehensive
School *WSL* WS1 ....57 E3
Joseph Turner Primary School
TPTN/OCK DY4 ....69 H4
Josiah Mason College
CVALE B35 ....94 D3
DUDN DY1 ....101 H1
KGSTG B44 ....74 D2
MOS/BIL B13 ....144 A5
Jubilee Business Park
HAC/WOL DY9 ....136 D2
Jubilee Park Primary School
TPTN/OCK DY4 ....69 H3
Junction 2 Industrial Estate
WSNGN B18 ....2 B1
Junction 6 Industrial Park
AST/WIT B6 ....91 H4
Junction Industrial Estate
SMTHWK B66 ....106 B2
Jurys Inn
CBHAMW B1 ....2 C6
Karis Medical Centre
LDYWD/EDGR B16 ....125 H3
Kates Hill Primary School
DUDS DY2 ....103 E1
Kelvin Way Trading Estate
WBROM B70 ....105 F1
Key Business Park
ERDE/BCHGN B24 ....93 H3
Key Hill Cemetery
WSNGN B18 ....2 B1
Keyway Retail Park
WLNHL WV13 ....38 D2
Keyway Retail Park
WLNHL WV13 ....39 H5
Khalsa Industrial Estate
SMTHWK B66 ....107 F5
Kineton Green Infant School
ACGN B27 ....163 H1
King Charles Primary School
WSLW WS2 ....40 D3
King David Primary School
MOS/BIL B13 ....144 B5
King Edwards Road (Boys)
EDG B15 ....143 E3
King Edwards VI Aston School
AST/WIT B6 ....109 F1
King Edwards VI Handsworth
School *HDSW* B21 ....108 A2
King Edward VI Camp Hill
School for Boys
ALE/KHTH/YWD B14 ....160 D3
King Edward VI Camp Hill
School for Girls
BVILLE B30 ....160 D2
King Edward VI College
STRBR DY8 ....135 G1
King Edward VI Five Ways
School *RIDG/WDGT* B32 ....157 G2
King Edward VI Girls High
School *EDG* B15 ....143 E3
Kingfisher Industrial Estate
WBROM B70 ....86 C2
Kingfisher Primary School
CBROM B36 ....114 A1
King George V Primary School
HHTH/SAND B71 ....88 A3
Kingsbury Business Park
ERDE/BCHGN B24 ....79 C5
Kingsbury School
ERDE/BCHGN B24 ....92 D4
Kings Business Park
GTB/HAM B43 ....59 H5
The Kings CE School
DUNHL/THL/PER WV6 ......21 F5
Kings Cinema *WBROM* B70 ....87 H3
Kings Heath Boys School
MOS/BIL B13 ....161 G4
Kings Heath CC
ALE/KHTH/YWD B14 ....161 G4
Kings Hill Business Park
DARL/WED WS10 ....55 G4
Kings Hill Clinic
DARL/WED WS10 ....55 G3
Kings Hill JMI School
DARL/WED WS10 ....55 G3
Kingshurst City Technology
College
CHWD/FDBR/MGN B37 ....132 B1
Kingshurst Clinic
CHWD/FDBR/MGN B37 ....114 A4
Kingshurst J & I School
CHWD/FDBR/MGN B37 ....114 A3
Kingsland Primary School
KGSTG B44 ....60 B4
Kings Norton Boys School
BVILLE B30 ....176 C1
Kings Norton Business Centre
BVILLE B30 ....176 D1
Kings Norton Girls School
BVILLE B30 ....176 D1
Kings Norton High School
HWK/WKHTH B38 ....176 D5
Kings Norton Primary School
BVILLE B30 ....177 D2
Kingsthorpe Community Primary
School *KGSTG* B44 ....75 H1
Kings Road Industrial Estate
YDLY B25 ....145 H1
Kingstanding Leisure Centre
KGSTG B44 ....75 H3
Kingstanding Special School
KGSTG B44 ....75 E2

Kingsthorne Primary School
KGSTG B44 ....75 G2
The Kingswinford Secondary
School *KGSWFD* DY6 ....99 H2
Kingswood School
SHLY B90 ....180 B3
Kitwell J & I School
RIDG/WDGT B32 ....157 E3
Klaxon Industrial Estate
SPARK B11 ....145 H3
Knowle CE Primary School
DOR/KN B93 ....197 G1
Knowle & Dorridge CC
DOR/KN B93 ....197 G4
Knowle FC *DOR/KN* B93 ....197 G1
Knowle Village CC
DOR/KN B93 ....197 G1
La Caverna Hotel
LGN/SDN/BHAMAIR B26 ..148 A3
Ladypool Primary School
SPARK B11 ....144 D1
Ladywood Arts & Leisure
Centre *LDYWD/EDGR* B16 ..126 A2
Ladywood Middleway Health
Centre *CBHAMW* B1 ....126 A1
Lakeside JMI School
WLNHL WV13 ....39 E2
Lakeside Medical Centre
DUNHL/THL/PER WV6 ......34 C1
Lakey Lane Primary School
HLGN/YWD B28 ....163 E2
Lanchester School *CBROM* B36 ..95 C5
Lane Green First School
CDSL WV8 ....10 D3
The Lane Medical Centre
BHTH/HG B12 ....144 D2
Lanesfield Primary School
ETTPK/GDPK/PENN WV4 ..53 E5
The Lanes Shopping Centre
SCFLD/BOLD B73 ....77 F4
Langley High School
LGLYGN/QTN B68 ....105 F5
Langley Primary School
HIA/OLT B92 ....163 H4
OLDBY B69 ....104 D4
Langley School *HIA/OLT* B92 ..163 H3
Langley Special School
MGN/WHC B75 ....63 G2
Langley Swimming Centre
LGLYGN/QTN B68 ....105 F5
Lansdowne Health Centre
WSNGN B18 ....107 H5
Lapal Primary School
RMSLY B62 ....139 H3
Lasercare Clinics *EDG* B15 ....126 B4
Laurie Pike Health Centre
AST/WIT B6 ....108 D1
Leamore Industrial Estate
WSLW WS2 ....27 E3
Leamore Primary School
BLOX/PEL WS3 ....27 G3
Lea Road Medical Practice
BDMR/CCFT WV3 ....36 C5
Leasowes Community College
RMSLY B62 ....139 C1
Leaverstock Industrial Estate
STECH B33 ....131 E3
Lee Bank Business Centre
CBHAMW B1 ....2 E7
Legg Brothers Industrial
Estate
ETTPK/GDPK/PENN WV4 ..52 D3
Leigh J & I (NC) School
WASH/WDE B8 ....110 C3
Leighswood Junior School
ALDR WS9 ....30 B3
Leighswood School *ALDR* WS9 ..30 B2
Lemar Industrial Estate
BVILLE B30 ....160 C1
Lennon Indoor Market
KGSTG B44 ....69 F5
Leona Industrial Estate
RMSLY B62 ....122 B3
Leviss Industrial Estate
STECH B33 ....111 H5
Lewisham Industrial Estate
SMTHWK B66 ....106 C2
Leyhill Health Centre
NFLD/LBR B31 ....158 A4
Ley Hill Primary School
NFLD/LBR B31 ....157 H5
Leys Industrial Estate
BRLYHL DY5 ....118 C1
Lickey Hills Country Park
RBRY B45 ....188 A4
Lickey Hills Golf Club
RBRY B45 ....188 A4
Lifford Trading Estate
BVILLE B30 ....177 E1
Light Hall School *SHLY* B90 ..180 B4
Light House Cinema
WOLV WV1 ....7 G3
Lightwoods Primary School
LGLYGN/QTN B68 ....123 H4
Linden Road Instruction
Swimming Pool
BVILLE B30 ....159 H3
Lindens Primary School
FOAKS/STRLY B74 ....60 B2
Lindley Lodge Industrial Estate
ALDR WS9 ....29 G4
Lindsworth North School
ERDW/GRVHL B23 ....77 E5
Lindsworth School
BVILLE B30 ....177 G2
Link One Industrial Park
TPTN/OCK DY4 ....70 C5
Linkwood Industrial Estate
STRBR DY8 ....135 F1
Lion Industrial Park *ALDR* WS9 ..30 A1
Little Aston CP School
FOAKS/STRLY B74 ....32 A4
Little Aston Golf Club
FOAKS/STRLY B74 ....45 H1
Little Bloxwich CE (V) School
BLOX/PEL WS3 ....17 F4
Little London JMI School
WLNHL WV13 ....39 G3
Locarno Primary School
TPTN/OCK DY4 ....69 F5

The Lock Museum
WLNHL WV13 ....39 F4
Lode Heath School *SOLH* B91 .. 165 E4
Lodge Farm Primary School
SHHTH WV12 ....40 C1
Lodge Forge Trading Estate
CDYHTH B64 ....120 C5
Lodge Hill Cemetery
SLYOAK B29 ....158 D1
Lodge Hill Crematorium
SLYOAK B29 ....141 H5
Lodge Primary School
WBROM B70 ....87 F3
Long Acre Trading Estate
VAUX/NECH B7 ....109 H2
Long Knowle Primary School
WNSFLD WV11 ....24 C2
Long Lane Medical Centre
RMSLY B62 ....122 B3
Long Lane Trading Estate
RMSLY B62 ....122 B3
Longmoor Special School
SCFLD/BOLD B73 ....60 D4
Longwill Special School
NFLD/LBR B31 ....158 C5
Lordswood Boys School
HRBN B17 ....124 C4
Lordswood Girls School
HRBN B17 ....124 D4
Lordswood Medical Practice
HRBN B17 ....141 H1
Lower Farm JMI School
BLOX/PEL WS3 ....17 E3
Lower Gornal Medical Centre
SEDG DY3 ....82 D4
Low Hill Medical Centre
WOLVN WV10 ....23 C3
Loxdale Industrial Estate
BILS/COS WV14 ....54 A4
Loxdale Primary School
BILS/COS WV14 ....54 B4
Lozells Primary School
LOZ/NWT B19 ....108 D2
Lugman Medical Centre
WSL WS1 ....56 D1
Lutley Primary School
HALE B63 ....154 D1
Lye Business Centre
BRLYHL DY5 ....119 H5
Lye CC *HAG/WOL* DY9 ....136 B2
Lye Town FC *HAG/WOL* DY9 ..... 136 B2
Lye Valley Industrial Estate
HAG/WOL DY9 ....136 D1
Lye & Wollescote Cemetery
HAG/WOL DY9 ....136 C3
Lyndon Green J & I School
LGN/SDN/BHAMAIR B26 .... 147 F1
Lyndon School *HIA/OLT* B92 .. 147 G4
Lyng Primary School
WBROM B70 ....87 G5
Macdonald Burlington Hotel
CBHAM B2 ....3 F5
Magreal Industrial Estate
LDYWD/EDGR B16 ....125 H1
Maidensbridge Primary School
KGSWFD DY6 ....81 F5
The Mailbox *CBHAMW* B1 ..... 2 E6
Mainstream Forty Seven
Industrial Park
VAUX/NECH B7 ....110 A4
Mainstream Industrial Park
VAUX/NECH B7 ....110 A5
Malmaison Hotel *CBHAMW* B1 .. 2 E7
Malt Mill Lane Trading Estate
RMSLY B62 ....122 B4
Mander Shopping Centre
WOLV WV1 ....7 F4
Manders Industrial Estate
WOLVN WV10 ....37 H2
Maney Hill Primary School
CSCFLD/WYGN B72 ....77 H1
The Manor General Hospital
WSLW WS2 ....41 G4
Manor High School (Foundation)
DARL/WED WS10 ....56 D5
Manor Industrial Estate
WSLW WS2 ....4 A4
Manor Park Primary School
AST/WIT B6 ....109 C1
Manor Primary School
BILS/COS WV14 ....68 D1
FOAKS/STRLY B74 ....45 G4
Manor Way Primary School
HALE B63 ....139 E4
Mansfield Green Primary School
AST/WIT B6 ....109 E1
Maple Business Park
VAUX/NECH B7 ....109 H3
Maple Leaf Industrial Estate
WSLW WS2 ....41 F2
Marlborough J & I School
SMHTH B10 ....128 C3
Marlow Estate
BLKHTH/ROWR B65 ....121 H3
Marshalls Industrial Estate
BKHL/PFLD WV2 ....52 A1
Marsh Hill Primary School
ERDW/GRVHL B23 ....91 H2
Marston Green Clinic
CHWD/FDBR/MGN B37 .... 132 A5
Marston Green Infant School
CHWD/FDBR/MGN B37 ..... 132 A5
Marston Green Junior School
CHWD/FDBR/MGN B37 .... 132 A5
Marston Road Industrial Estate
BKHL/PFLD WV2 ....52 A1
Mary Elliot Special School
WSLW WS2 ....42 A1
Maryvale Catholic Primary
School *KGSTG* B44 ....75 E1
Maryvale Institute *KGSTG* B44 .. 75 F1
Maternity Welfare Clinic
ETTPK/GDPK/PENN WV4 .... 50 D2
Matthew Boulton College of
Further & Higher Education
CBHAMW B4 ....3 J3
DIG/EDG B5 ....126 D4
Matthew Boulton Community
Primary School
HDSW B21 ....107 G2

Maybrook Industrial Estate
BRWNH WS8 ....19 F2
The Mayfair Centre *CBHAM* B2 .. 3 G6
Mayfield Preparatory School
WSL WS1 ....5 H6
Mayfield Special School
LOZ/NWT B19 ....108 C1
Maypole Health Centre
ALE/KHTH/YWD B14 ....178 B2
Meadow Green Primary School
HLYWD B47 ....192 C5
Meadows Primary School
NFLD/LBR B31 ....175 E3
Meadow View JMI School
GTB/HAM B43 ....59 H5
Meadwood Industrial Estate
BILS/COS WV14 ....54 A3
Media Centre *WOLV* WV1 ..... 7 G5
Meeting Lane Industrial
Estate *BRLYHL* DY5 ....118 D3
Megabowl *BRLYHL* DY5 ....119 F2
Menzies High School
HHTH/SAND B71 ....71 G3
Mere Green Combined School
MGN/WHC B75 ....47 F3
Merridale Cemetery
BDMR/CCFT WV3 ....6 A7
Merridale Primary School
BDMR/CCFT WV3 ....6 A6
Merry Hill Shopping Centre
BRLYHL DY5 ....119 H2
Merstone School
CHWD/FDBR/MGN B37 .... 132 A3
Mesty Croft Primary School
DARL/WED WS10 ....56 A5
Metalloys Industrial Estate
WALM/CURD B76 ....94 D1
Middlemore Business Park
ALDR WS9 ....29 C4
Middlemore Industrial Estate
HDSW B21 ....88 D5
SMTHWK B66 ....106 D1
Middleton Trading Estate
WOLVN WV10 ....39 E3
Middleway Industrial Estate
BHTH/HG B12 ....127 F5
Midland House Dawley
Trading Estate *KGSWFD* DY6 .. 99 H1
Midland Institute *CBHAMW* B3 .. 2 E4
Midlands Arts Centre Cinema
BHTH/HG B12 ....143 H3
Milking Bank Primary School
DUDN DY1 ....83 G4
Millard Industrial Estate
WBROM B70 ....87 E5
Millbank Industrial Estate
WOLVN WV10 ....23 F3
Millfield CP School *BRWNH* WS8 .. 9 C5
Millfield Special School
HHTH/SAND B71 ....71 H3
Mill Lodge Primary School
SHLY B90 ....179 C3
Minworth Industrial Park
WALM/CURD B76 ....78 D5
WALM/CURD B76 ....95 E1
Minworth J & I School
WALM/CURD B76 ....95 F1
Moat Farm J & I School
LGLYGN/QTN B68 ....123 G1
Mobarak Health Centre
BHTH/HG B12 ....144 A2
Monarch Industrial Estate
SPARK B11 ....146 A2
Monkspath Business Park
SHLY B90 ....181 E5
Monkspath Primary School
SHLY B90 ....195 H2
Monmer Close Industrial Estate
WLNHL WV13 ....39 H2
Monmore Business Park
BKHL/PFLD WV2 ....52 D1
Monmore Green Greyhound Stadium
BKHL/PFLD WV2 ....38 A5
Monmore Park Industrial Estate
BKHL/PFLD WV2 ....52 D1
Montgomery Primary School
SPARK B11 ....128 A5
Montgomery Street Business Centre
SPARK B11 ....145 E1
Monway Industrial Estate
DARL/WED WS10 ....55 F5
Monyhull Hospital *BVILLE* B30 .. 177 H2
The Moore Group Business
Centre *WSL* WS1 ....4 E7
Moor Green FC
HLGN/YWD B28 ....162 C3
Moor Green J & I School
MOS/BIL B13 ....160 C1
Moor Green Sports Centre
SLYOAK B29 ....143 G5
Moor Group Business Centre
WSL WS1 ....4 E7
Moor Hall Golf Club
MGN/WHC B75 ....47 H4
Moor Hall Primary School
MGN/WHC B75 ....47 H5
Moorlands Primary School
HHTH/SAND B71 ....71 F3
Moor Lane Trading Estate
AST/WIT B6 ....91 F2
Moor Street Industrial Estate
BRLYHL DY5 ....119 E2
Moreton Community School
WOLVN WV10 ....23 H1
Moseley CC *SHLY* B90 ....163 C5
Moseley CE Primary School
MOS/BIL B13 ....144 B5
Moseley Golf Club
ALE/KHTH/YWD B14 ....161 G2
Moseley Hall Hospital
MOS/BIL B13 ....144 A4
Moseley Old Hall (NT)
WOLVN WV10 ....13 G2
Moseley Park School &
Technology College
BILS/COS WV14 ....39 G5
Moseley School *MOS/BIL* B13 .. 145 E5
Mossley Clinic *BLOX/PEL* WS3 .. 26 D1
Mossley Primary School
BLOX/PEL WS3 ....16 B5

The Mount Hotel
DUNHL/THL/PER WV6 ....35 E3
Mount Pleasant Primary
School *BRLYHL* DY5 ....119 C3
Mount Street Business Centre
VAUX/NECH B7 ....110 A3
Mount Street Business Park
VAUX/NECH B7 ....110 B2
Moxley Industrial Centre
DARL/WED WS10 ....55 C5
Moxley Medical Centre
DARL/WED WS10 ....55 E2
Mucklow Hill Industrial Estate
RMSLY B62 ....139 E2
Mucklow Hill Trading Estate
RMSLY B62 ....139 E2
Municipal Art Gallery
WOLV WV1 ....7 F3
Munrow Sports Centre
EDG B15 ....142 D3
Nansen J & I School
WASH/WDE B8 ....110 D4
National Exhibition Centre
BHAMNEC B40 ....150 A2
National Indoor Arena
CBHAMW B1 ....2 B5
National Institute of
Conductive Education
MOS/BIL B13 ....143 H3
National Motorcycle Museum
HIA/OLT B92 ....150 C4
National Sea Life Centre
LDYWD/EDGR B16 ....2 B5
The Natural Health Centre
HWK/WKHTH B38 ....176 D3
Nature Park *WALM/CURD* B76 .. 94 C1
Neachells Lane Industrial
Estate *WNSFLD* WV11 ....38 D1
Nechells Primary School
VAUX/NECH B7 ....110 A1
Nelson Mandela Primary
School *BHTH/HG* B12 ....144 C2
Nelson Primary School
LDYWD/EDGR B16 ....2 A4
Neptune Industrial Estate
WLNHL WV13 ....39 H5
Netherbrook Primary School
DUDS DY2 ....120 D2
Netherton Business Park
DUDS DY2 ....120 D1
Netherton CC *DUDS* DY2 .... 102 B5
Netherton CE Primary School
DUDS DY2 ....102 B4
Network Park Industrial
Estate *VAUX/NECH* B7 ....110 A5
The New Art Gallery Walsall
WSLW WS2 ....4 C3
Newbridge Preparatory School
TETT/PER WV6 ....36 A1
New Cross Hospital
WNSFLD WV11 ....24 B5
New Cross Industrial Estate
WOLV WV1 ....38 A2
Newfield Park Primary School
HALE B63 ....138 C2
New Hall Hotel
WALM/CURD B76 ....78 A1
New Hall J & I School
MGN/WHC B75 ....63 H3
Newhampton Arts Centre
WOLV WV1 ....6 D2
New Invention Junior School
SHHTH WV12 ....26 A3
Newman College of Higher
Education *RIDC/WDGT* B32 .. 157 G2
Newshire Industrial Estate
SPARK B11 ....145 F1
Newton Industrial Estate
BORD B9 ....128 B2
Newtown Health Centre
LOZ/NWT B19 ....108 D5
Newtown Primary School
WBROM B70 ....86 B3
Newtown Shopping Centre
LOZ/NWT B19 ....109 E3
Ninestiles School
ACGN B27 ....163 F1
Nonsuch Primary School
RIDG/WDGT B32 ....140 D5
Norfolk House School
EDG B15 ....125 F4
Norman Green Sports Centre &
Athletics Track *SOLH* B91 .. 181 G2
Northbrook Health Centre
SHLY B90 ....163 G5
Northfield Manor Primary
School *SLYOAK* B29 ....158 D3
Northfield Pool & Fitness
Centre *NFLD/LBR* B31 .... 175 F2
Northfield Road Primary
School *DUDS* DY2 ....102 D4
Northcote Secondary School
WOLVN WV10 ....13 E4
Northmoor Industrial Estate
BRLYHL DY5 ....119 F1
Northside Business Centre
WSNGN B18 ....107 G4
North Solihull Sports Centre
& Track
CHWD/FDBR/MGN B37 .... 132 A1
North Street Industrial
Estate *BRLYHL* DY5 ....119 E2
North Worcestershire Golf
Club *NFLD/LBR* B31 ....174 D3
Novotel
CBHAMW B1 ....2 B6
LGN/SDN/BHAMAIR B26 .. 149 C3
WOLV WV1 ....7 H4
Oak Cottage Primary School
SOLH B91 ....164 A4
Oakdale Trading Estate
KGSWFD DY6 ....81 H5
KGSWFD DY6 ....100 A1
Oakeswell Health Centre
DARL/WED WS10 ....56 A5
Oakham Primary School
DUDS DY2 ....103 H2
Oak House *WBROM* B70 .... 87 F4
The Oak Industrial Park
KGSWFD DY6 ....82 A5

Oaklands Primary School
ACGN B27 ....146 C5
Oakleigh Trading Estate
BILS/COS WV14 ....68 B1
Oak Meadow Primary School
WNSFLD WV11 ....25 C3
The Oaks Primary School
ALE/KHTH/YWD B14 ....177 H5
Oak Street Industrial Estate
CDYHTH B64 ....120 D3
Oak Street Trading Estate
BRLYHL DY5 ....119 H3
Oakwood Special School
ALDR WS9 ....19 G4
Ocker Hill J & I School
TPTN/OCK DY4 ....70 A3
Odeon Cinema *CBHAM* B2 ..... 3 G6
CSCFLD/WYGN B72 ....62 B5
Ogley Hay Infant School
BRWNH WS8 ....9 F4
Oldbury Business Centre
LGLYGN/QTN B68 ....123 E2
Oldbury Green Retail Park
OLDBY B69 ....104 D1
Oldbury Health Centre
OLDBY B69 ....105 E1
Oldbury Leisure Centre
OLDBY B69 ....104 C3
Oldbury Road Industrial
Estate *SMTHWK* B66 ....105 H2
WBROM B70 ....86 D4
Oldbury United FC
BLKHTH/ROWR B65 ....122 C1
Old Bush Trading Estate
BRLYHL DY5 ....119 G1
Old Church CE Primary School
DARL/WED WS10 ....55 E2
Oldfield Trading Estate
CDYHTH B64 ....120 D4
Old Forge Trading Estate
HAG/WOL DY9 ....136 C1
Old Halesonians RFC
HAG/WOL DY9 ....153 H2
Old Hall Industrial Estate
BLOX/PEL WS3 ....27 G2
Oldhall Special School
WSLW WS2 ....26 C5
Old Hill CC *CDYHTH* B64 .... 121 F4
Old Hill Primary School
CDYHTH B64 ....121 F3
Oldknow Junior School
SMHTH B10 ....128 C5
Old Limberlost Sports Club
BFLD/HDSWWD B20 ....90 A3
Old Park Industrial Estate
DARL/WED WS10 ....55 C4
Old Park Primary School
DARL/WED WS10 ....55 C5
Old Park Special School
DUDN DY1 ....101 H1
Old Rep Theatre *DIG/EDG* B5 .. 3 F7
The Old Square Shopping
Centre *WSL* WS1 ....5 F3
Oldswinford CE Primary
School *STRBR* DY8 ....135 C4
Old Swinford Hospital School
STRBR DY8 ....135 C5
Olive Hill Primary School
RMSLY B62 ....122 B5
Olton Golf Club *SOLH* B91 .. 164 C3
One Stop Retail Park
PBAR/PBCH B42 ....90 D3
Open University *HRBN* B17 .. 142 B1
Oratory RC Primary School
LDYWD/EDGR B16 ....125 H2
Orchard Lane Clinic
HAG/WOL DY9 ....136 C3
The Orchard School
SMTHWK B66 ....106 A2
Orthodontists Surgery
EDG B15 ....146 A4
Osborne Primary School
ERDW/GRVHL B23 ....93 E1
Ounsdale High School
WMBN WV5 ....64 D4
Ounsdale Sports Centre
WMBN WV5 ....64 D4
Our Lady of Compassion RC
Primary School
HIA/OLT B92 ....163 H3
Our Lady of Fatima RC Primary
School *HRBN* B17 ....124 B5
Our Lady of Lourdes RC
Primary School
MOS/BIL B13 ....162 B5
Our Lady of the Wayside RC
Primary School *SHLY* B90 .. 180 C5
Our Lady & St Chad RC
Secondary School
WOLVN WV10 ....23 H2
Our Lady & St Kenelm RC
Primary School *HALE* B63 .. 138 C4
Our Lady & St Rose of Lima RC
Primary School
SLYOAK B29 ....158 D1
Our Ladys RC Primary School
STETCH B33 ....131 F2
The Oval Primary School
STETCH B33 ....130 B2
Owen Road Industrial Estate
WLNHL WV13 ....40 A4
Owen Road Trading Estate
WLNHL WV13 ....40 A4
Oxbarn Social & Sports Club
BDMR/CCFT WV3 ....51 F1
Oxford Street Industrial Park
BILS/COS WV14 ....54 B3
Oxley Park Golf Club
WOLVN WV10 ....23 E3
Paddys Wide Water Industrial
Estate *BRLYHL* DY5 ....101 E4
Paget Primary School
ERDE/BCHGN B24 ....92 C2
Palfrey Girls School *WSL* WS1 .. 4 D4
Palfrey Infant School
WSL WS1 ....56 D1
Palfrey Junior School
WSL WS1 ....56 D1

Pallasades Shopping Centre
CBHAM B2 ....3 F6
Palmers Cross Primary School
DUNHL/THL/PER WV6 ....21 H2
Paper Mill End Industrial Estate
KGSTG B44 ....74 D5
Parkbrook Industrial Centre
HAG/WOL DY9 ....136 D2
Park Clinic *ERDW/GRVHL* B23 .. 93 E1
Parkfield Clinic
BKHL/PFLD WV2 ....52 C3
Parkfield High School
ETTPK/GDPK/PENN WV4 .... 52 C5
Parkfield Primary School
ETTPK/GDPK/PENN WV4 .... 52 C5
WASH/WDE B8 ....128 C1
Park Hall Hotel & Conference
Centre
ETTPK/GDPK/PENN WV4 .... 52 A4
Park Hall Infant School
DSYBK/YTR WS5 ....58 A1
Park Hall Junior School
DSYBK/YTR WS5 ....58 A1
Park Hall School *CBROM* B36 .. 95 C5
Park Lane Industrial Estate
HHTH/SAND B71 ....88 C5
Park Lane Trading Estate
OLDBY B69 ....105 E2
WOLVN WV10 ....23 G1
Park Medical Centre
SMHTH B10 ....128 C5
Parkrose Industrial Estate
SMTHWK B66 ....106 D1
Parkside Industrial Estate
WOLV WV1 ....37 H4
Park Trading Estate
WSNGN B18 ....108 A3
Park View School
WASH/WDE B8 ....110 C4
Parkway Industrial Centre
VAUX/NECH B7 ....109 G5
Pavilions Shopping Centre
CBHAMW B4 ....3 H5
Pdh Industrial Estate
DARL/WED WS10 ....55 E4
WLNHL WV13 ....38 D2
Peartree Industrial Estate
DUDS DY2 ....102 A5
Pedmore CE Primary School
HAG/WOL DY9 ....152 D1
Pedmore Road Industrial
Estate *BRLYHL* DY5 ....101 H5
Pegasus Primary School
CVALE B35 ....94 C3
Pelsall Clinic *BLOX/PEL* WS3 .. 18 A3
Pelsall Village School
BLOX/PEL WS3 ....17 H1
Pendeford Business Park
COVEN WV9 ....11 H
Pendeford Health Centre
COVEN WV9 ....12 A
Pendeford High School
WOLVN WV10 ....12 A
Pendeford Mill Nature
Reserve *COVEN* WV9 ....11 C
Pendene Complimentary
Medical Centre *WOLV* WV1 .. 6 C
Penn Cemetery
ETTPK/GDPK/PENN WV4 .... 50 D
Pennfields Health Centre
BDMR/CCFT WV3 ....6 C
Penn Fields School
BDMR/CCFT WV3 ....51 F
Penn Golf Club
ETTPK/GDPK/PENN WV4 .... 66 C
Penn Hall Special School
ETTPK/GDPK/PENN WV4 .... 51 F
Penn Hospital
ETTPK/GDPK/PENN WV4 .... 51 F
Penn Industrial Estate
DUDS DY2 ....120 C
Penn Manor Medical Centre
ERDW/GRVHL B23 ....93 E1
Penn Road Retail Park
BKHL/PFLD WV2 ....36 E
Penns Primary School
CSCFLD/WYGN B72 ....77 E
Pens Meadow Special School
STRBR DY8 118
The Pensnett School of
Technology *BRLYHL* DY5 100
Pensnett Trading Estate
KGSWFD DY6 100
The Pensnett Trading Estate
KGSWFD DY6 100
Percy Business Park
OLDBY B69 104
Percy Shurmer Primary
School *DIG/EDG* B5 127
Perry Barr Greyhound
Stadium *PBAR/PBCH* B42 .... 9C
Perry Beeches J & I School
PBAR/PBCH B42 74
Perry Common Primary
School *ERDW/GRVHL* B23 9
Perryfields High School
RMSLY B62 123
Perryfields Primary School
RMSLY B62 123
Perry Hall Primary School
WNSFLD WV11 ....
Perry Street Industrial Estate
BILS/COS WV14 ....
Personal & Child Health
Centre *BVILLE* B30 ....
Perton Clinic
DUNHL/THL/PER WV6 3
Perton First School
DUNHL/THL/PER WV6 ....
Perton Middle School
DUNHL/THL/PER WV6 ....
Perton Park Golf Club
DUNHL/THL/PER WV6 ....
Peterbrook Primary School
SHLY B90 ....
Peters Hill Primary School
BRLYHL DY5 ....

Pheasey Clinic
CTB/HAM B43 ....59 G5
Pheasey Park Farm Primary
School *CTB/HAM* B43 ....59 G4
Phillips Street
Industrial Estate
AST/WIT B6 ....109 E3
Phoenix Business Park
VAUX/NECH B7 ....109 G3
Phoenix Industrial Estate
BILS/COS WV14 ....54 B4
Phoenix International
Industrial Estate
WBROM B70 ....86 D1
Phoenix Road Industrial
Estate *WLNHL* WV13 ....38 D2
Phoenix Works Industrial
Estate *DARL/WED* WS10 ....40 C5
Piccadilly Cinema
SPARK B11 ....144 D2
The Picture House
STRBR DY8 ....135 G3
WSNW/WDE B8 ....111 E4
Pines Special School
CBROM B36 ....112 B1
Pinfold Industrial Estate
BLOX/PEL WS3 ....27 G2
Pinfold Street Primary School
DARL/WED WS10 ....55 E3
Planetary Industrial Estate
WLNHL WV13 ....38 C1
Planet Ice Arena *DIG/EDG* B5 ....3 H7
Plantsbrook School
CSCFLD/WYGN B72 ....62 C4
Pleck Business Park *WSLW* WS2 ...4 A4
Pleck Industrial Estate
WSLW WS2 ....41 G5
Pool Hayes Comprehensive
School *SHHTH* WV12 ....25 H5
Pool Hayes Primary School
WNSFLD WV11 ....25 H4
Poplar Road Clinic
ALE/KHTH/YWD B14 ....161 F1
Poplar Trading Estate
AST/WIT B6 ....91 F1
Portersfield Industrial Estate
CDYHTH B64 ....120 C4
Portland Hotel
LDYWD/EDGR B16 ....125 E3
Portway Road Industrial
Estate *OLDBY* B69 ....104 C3
Powke Lane Industrial Estate
BLKHTH/ROWR B65 ....121 G2
Premier Business Centre
HAG/WOL DY9 ....136 D2
Premier Business Park
WSLW WS2 ....4 B5
Premier Lodge *MGN/WHC* B75 ...63 F1
Premier Partnership Industrial
Estate *KGSWFD* DY6 ....100 C5
Premier Trading Estate
VAUX/NECH B7 ....109 F4
Premier Travel Inn
AST/WIT B6 ....109 F4
BHAMNEC B40 ....133 F5
CBHAMNW B1 ....2 D6
CNCK/NC WS11 ....11 H4
EDG B15 ....2 B7
HAG/WOL DY9 ....153 H3
KGSWFD DY6 ....100 B2
OLDBY B69 ....104 B2
RBRY B45 ....178 B5
SHLY B90 ....180 B2
SHLY B90 ....195 F3
WBROM B70 ....86 D1
WOLVN WV10 ....12 D2
WSLW WS2 ....12 D2
Preston College *WLNHL* WV13 ....39 G4
Priestley Smith Special School
ERDW/GRVHL B23 ....75 H5
Primrose Hill Primary School
HWK/WKHTH B38 ....176 D5
Primrose Hill Trading Estate
DUDS DY2 ....102 D3
Primrose Lane Health Centre
WOLVN WV10 ....24 A2
Primrose Trading Estate
DUDS DY2 ....102 C5
Prince Albert Primary School
STETCH B33 ....130 D1
Princes End Industrial Park
BILS/COS WV14 ....69 E2
Princethorpe J & I School
SLYOAK B29 ....158 C2
Priory Clinic *DUDN* DY1 ....84 B3
Priory Courts *CBHAMNE* B4 ....3 G4
Priory Green Primary School
COVEN WV9 ....12 A5
Priory House Industrial Estate
WSNGN B18 ....108 B4
Priory Junior Mixed & Infants
School *BLOX/PEL* WS3 ....27 F3
Priory New Way Industrial
Estate *AST/WIT* B6 ....109 E4
Priory Primary School
DUDN DY1 ....84 B3
The Priory School
DARL/WED WS10 ....71 H1
Prospect Trading Estate
CBHAMW B1 ....2 C4
Providence Industrial Estate
HAG/WOL DY9 ....136 C1
The Pytchley Golf Club
WALM/CURD B76 ....78 A5
Pudcast Road Industrial Estate
WOLV WV1 ....37 H3
Quality Hotel *BDMR/CCFT* WV3 ...36 D5
WSLW WS2 ....40 D3
Quarry Bank Primary School
BRLYHL DY5 ....120 A3
Queen Alexandra College
HRBN B17 ....141 G1
Queen Elizabeth Hospital
EDG B15 ....142 C2
Queen Elizabeth Psychiatric
Hospital *EDG* B15 ....142 C3
Queen Marys Grammar School
WSL WS1 ....5 J6
Queen Marys High School
RUSH/SHEL WS4 ....5 G1

Queensbury Special School
ERDE/BCHGN B24 ....92 D3
Queens College *EDG* B15 ....142 D2
Queens Court Trading Estate
WBROM B70 ....86 D3
Queen Street Cemetery
WSLW WS2 ....4 A6
Queensway Trading Estate
DIG/EDG B5 ....3 J4
Queen Victoria Primary School
SEDG DY3 ....67 F3
Quinton Business Park
RIDG/WDGT B32 ....140 A2
Quinton Cemetery
RMSLY B62 ....122 D5
Quinton CE Primary School
RIDG/WDGT B32 ....140 A1

Racecourse Road Industrial
Estate
DUNHL/THL/PER WV6 ....22 C5
Raddleban J & I School
SLYOAK B29 ....159 H1
Radleys Primary School
RUSH/SHEL WS4 ....29 E3
Radway Industrial Estate
SHLY B90 ....195 E1
Rainbow Business Park
WLNHL WV13 ....39 H2
Rake Gate Infant School
WOLVN WV10 ....22 D1
Rake Gate Junior School
WOLVN WV10 ....22 D1
Raleigh Industrial Estate
HDSW B21 ....88 D5
Ramada Hotel *SOLH* B91 ....182 A2
WALM/CURD B76 ....78 A4
Rathvilly School
NFLD/LBR B31 ....175 H2
Rea Business Park
VAUX/NECH B7 ....109 H5
Reaside Clinic *RBRY* B45 ....174 H4
Reaside Junior School
RBRY B45 ....173 G4
Reddal Hill Primary School
CDYHTH B64 ....121 E3
Reddicap Trading Estate
MGN/WHC B75 ....62 D4
Red Hall Primary School
SEDG DY3 ....83 E3
Redhill J & I School *YDLY* B25 ...129 E5
Redhill Secondary School
STRBR DY8 ....135 H2
Red Hill Street Clinic
WOLV WV1 ....37 E1
The Red House Glass Cone
STRBR DY8 ....118 A2
Redhouse Industrial Estate
ALDR WS9 ....29 F4
Redhouse JMI School
ALDR WS9 ....29 G5
Rednal Hill J & I School
RBRY B45 ....188 B1
Red Rooster Industrial Estate
ALDR WS9 ....29 G4
Redwood Business Park
SMTHWK B66 ....105 G2
Reedswood Retail Park
WSLW WS2 ....41 F1
Reflex Industrial Park
WLNHL WV13 ....39 F2
Regents Park Primary School
SMHTH B10 ....128 A4
Regent Special School
OLDBY B69 ....85 G5
Regis Medical Centre
BLKHTH/ROWR B65 ....122 A3
Reliance Trading Estate
ETTPK/GDPK/PENN WV4 ....53 F3
Renaissance Solihull Hotel
SOLH B91 ....181 H1
Reynalds Cross School
SOLH B91 ....181 H3
The Ridge Primary School
STRBR DY8 ....134 C2
Ridgewood High School
STRBR DY8 ....134 C1
Ridpool Primary School
STETCH B33 ....130 D1
Riland Industrial Estate
MGN/WHC B75 ....62 C3
River Brook Medical Centre
BVILLE B30 ....160 B2
RMN Business Centre
HAG/WOL DY9 ....136 D2
Robert Clinic *BVILLE* B30 ....159 G5
Roberts Primary School
SEDG DY3 ....83 G2
Robin Hood Cemetery
SHLY B90 ....163 F5
Robin Hood Golf Club
HIA/OLT B92 ....163 G4
Robin Hood Primary School
HLGN/YWD B28 ....163 H4
Robins Business Park
TPTN/OCK DY4 ....70 C4
Rocky Lane Trading Estate
VAUX/NECH B7 ....109 G3
Rollingmill Business Park
WSLW WS2 ....4 A5
Romney House Industrial
Estate *DARL/WED* WS10 ....54 D1
Rood End Cemetery
LGLYGN/QTN B68 ....105 G2
Rood End Primary School
LGLYGN/QTN B68 ....105 G3
Rookery Primary School
HDSW B21 ....89 G5
Rosary RC Primary School
WASH/WDE B8 ....128 C1
Rosedale CE Infant School
SHHTH WV12 ....26 B5
Rosewood Special School
DUDN DY1 ....83 G5
Rosliston School
HLGN/YWD B28 ....163 E5
Rotton Park Medical Centre
LDYWD/EDGR B16 ....125 F1
Rotunda *CBHAM* B2 ....3 G1
Rough Hay Primary School
DARL/WED WS10 ....55 E1

Rough Wood Nature Reserve
SHHTH WV12 ....26 C4
Rounds Green Primary School
OLDBY B69 ....104 C1
Rovex Business Park
SPARK B11 ....145 H2
Rowley Hall Primary School
BLKHTH/ROWR B65 ....104 A5
Rowley Regis Cemetery &
Crematorium
BLKHTH/ROWR B65 ....121 G2
Rowley Regis College
BLKHTH/ROWR B65 ....121 H1
Rowley Regis Hospital
BLKHTH/ROWR B65 ....121 H1
Royal Birmingham Society of
Arts *CBHAMNW* B3 ....2 D2
Royal Brierley Trading Estate
BRLYHL DY5 ....119 E1
Royal Orthopaedic Hospital
NFLD/LBR B31 ....158 D5
Royal Theatre *CDYHTH* B64 ....120 D3
The Royal Wolverhampton
Junior School
BDMR/CCFT WV3 ....51 G1
The Royal Wolverhampton
School *BDMR/CCFT* WV3 ....51 H1
RSPB Sandwell Valley Nature
Reserve *GTB/HAM* B43 ....73 E5
Rubery Clinic *RBRY* B45 ....187 G1
Ruckleigh School *SOLH* B91 ......182 A1
Rufford Primary School
HAG/WOL DY9 ....136 A2
Rushall Community College
RUSH/SHEL WS4 ....28 D4
Rushall JM School & Education
Development Centre
BLOX/PEL WS3 ....28 C1
Russell Medical Centre
DARL/WED WS10 ....70 D1
Russells Hall Hospital
BRLYHL DY5 ....101 F2
Russells Hall Primary School
DUDN DY1 ....83 G5
Ryders Green Primary School
WBROM B70 ....87 E2
Ryders Hayes JMI School
BLOX/PEL WS3 ....18 A2
Sacred Heart RC Primary
School *BFLD/HDSWWD* B20 ....90 D5
TPTN/OCK DY4 ....85 F2
Saddlers Shopping Centre
WSL WS1 ....4 D4
Sai Medical Centre *WSLW* WS2 ....4 A3
St Albans CE Primary School
WNSFLD WV11 ....25 H2
St Albans CE School
BHTH/HG B12 ....127 F5
St Albans RC Primary School
ALE/KHTH/YWD B14 ....178 B1
St Alphege CE Infant School
SOLH B91 ....182 A2
St Alphege CE Junior School
SOLH B91 ....182 A3
St Ambrose Barlow RC
Primary School
HLGN/YWD B28 ....163 E4
St Andrews CE Infant School
DUNHL/THL/PER WV6 ....36 B1
St Andrews Industrial Estate
BORD B9 ....128 A2
St Andrews Primary School
BORD B9 ....127 H1
St Andrews RC Primary School
HIA/OLT B92 ....147 G5
St Annes CE Primary School
WLNHL WV13 ....39 H2
St Anne's RC JMI School
FOAKS/STRLY B74 ....45 E5
St Annes RC Primary School
BHTH/HG B12 ....127 G4
CHWD/FDBR/MGN B37 ....132 A2
St Anthonys RC Primary
School
CHWD/FDBR/MGN B37 ....114 A4
WOLVN WV10 ....12 D4
St Augustines Catholic Primary
School *HDSW* B21 ....89 F4
St Augustines Primary School
SOLH B91 ....181 G3
St Barnabas CE Primary School
ERDE/BCHGN B24 ....93 F3
St Bartholomews CE Primary
School
ETTPK/GDPK/PENN WV4 ....51 E5
St Benedict Biscop CE Primary
School *WMBN* WV5 ....65 E4
St Benedicts Infant School
SMHTH B10 ....128 D5
St Bernadettes RC JMI School
BRWNH WS8 ....9 F4
St Bernadettes RC Primary
School *SMHTH* B10 ....129 F4
St Bernards RC Primary School
MOS/BIL B13 ....162 A1
St Brigids CE Primary School
NFLD/LBR B31 ....175 F2
St Catherine of Siena RC
School *EDG* B15 ....2 E7
St Chads Catholic Primary
School
LOZ/NWT B19 ....109 E4
St Chads RC Cathedral
CBHAMNE B4 ....3 F2
St Chads RC Primary School
LOZ/NWT B19 ....108 D4
SEDG DY3 ....67 F4
St Christophers RC Primary
School *CDSL* WV8 ....10 C5
St Clares Primary School
BFLD/HDSWWD B20 ....90 B5
St Clements CE Primary
School *VAUX/NECH* B7 ....109 H2
St Columbas RC Primary
School *RBRY* B45 ....188 D1
St Cuthberts RC Primary
School *WASH/WDE* B8 ....111 G5
St Dunstans RC
Primary School
ALE/KHTH/YWD B14 ....161 E2

St Edmund Campion RC
School *ERDW/GRVHL* B23 ....77 F5
St Edmunds Catholic School
BDMR/CCFT WV3 ....35 H2
St Edmunds RC Primary
School *WSNGN* B18 ....108 A5
St Edwards RC Primary
School *CSHL/WTROR* B46 ....115 G4
St Edwards RC Primary
School *CSHL/WTROR* B46 ....133 G1
SLYOAK B29 ....160 B1
St Francis of Assisi RC School
ALDR WS9 ....30 C5
St Francis RC Primary School
LOZ/NWT B19 ....108 B3
RUSH/SHEL WS4 ....29 E1
St Francis Xavier RC Primary
School *OLDBY* B69 ....105 E1
St George & St Teresa RC
Primary School
BDN B93 ....197 G4
St Georges CE Primary School
LDYWD/EDGR B16 ....125 H3
St Georges School Edgbaston
EDG B15 ....126 B4
St Georges Sixth Form & CE
Primary School
LOZ/NWT B19 ....108 D4
St Gerards Orthopaedic
Hospital
CSHL/WTROR B46 ....115 G4
St Gerards RC Primary School
CVALE B35 ....94 D2
St Giles CE Primary School
WLNHL WV13 ....39 H3
St Gregorys RC Primary School
SMTHWK B66 ....124 B2
St Huberts RC Primary School
LGLYGN/QTN B68 ....123 C3
St James CE Junior School
SHLY B90 ....180 B3
St James CE Primary School
HDSW B21 ....89 F5
OLDBY B69 ....104 B4
STRBR DY8 ....117 H5
St James Medical Centre
HDSW B21 ....107 F1
St James Primary School
BRWNH WS8 ....9 F4
RBRY B45 ....188 A1
St John Bosco RC Primary
School *HHTH/SAND* B71 ....71 F4
St John Fishers RC Primary
School *NFLD/LBR* B31 ....189 H1
St John & St Monica RC
Primary School
MOS/BIL B13 ....144 A3
St Johns CE JMI School
ALDR WS9 ....19 F4
St Johns CE Primary School
DARL/WED WS10 ....70 D1
LDYWD/EDGR B16 ....126 A2
SEDG DY3 ....80 C4
SPARK B11 ....145 E4
WNSFLD WV11 ....15 E3
St Johns Retail Park
BKHL/PFLD WV2 ....7 F6
St John the Baptist RC
School *CBROM* B36 ....114 A2
St John Wall RC School
HDSW B21 ....89 F4
St Josephs Catholic Primary
School *DARL/WED* WS10 ....55 E1
FOAKS/STRLY B74 ....62 C1
STRBR DY8 ....135 F5
St Josephs RC Primary School
BVILLE B30 ....159 G5
DUDS DY2 ....85 E5
VAUX/NECH B7 ....109 H3
St Judes CE Primary School
DUNHL/THL/PER WV6 ....36 B2
St Kenelms CE First School
RMSLY B62 ....172 C1
St LaurenCE CE J & I School
NFLD/LBR B31 ....175 H1
St Lukes CE Aided Primary
School *BKHL/PFLD* WV2 ....51 H1
St Margaret Mary RC Primary
School *ERDW/GRVHL* B23 ....76 A5
St Margarets CE Primary
School *CTB/HAM* B43 ....58 C4
HIA/OLT B92 ....147 F5
St Margarets Hospital
DYSBK/YTR WS5 ....43 G5
St Marks CE Primary School
BRLYHL DY5 ....101 E2
St Marks RC Primary School
PBAR/PBCH B42 ....73 H4
St Martin de Porres RC
Primary School
MOS/BIL B13 ....144 C4
St Martins CE Primary School
BILS/COS WV14 ....69 G1
TPTN/OCK DY4 ....85 H1
St Martins Industrial Estate
OLDBY B69 ....105 E3
St Martins Market *DIG/EDG* B5 ....3 H7
St Martins School *SOLH* B91 .....182 A2
St Mary & Johns RC Primary
School *BKHL/PFLD* WV2 ....37 F5
St Mary Magdalene CE Primary
School *HHTH/SAND* B71 ....71 H5
St Mary of the Angels RC JMI
School *ALDR* WS9 ....30 B5
St Mary's Abbey (Remains)
RMSLY B62 ....139 F5
St Mary & St Ann RC Primary
School *ERDW/GRVHL* B23 ....92 C3
St Mary & St Margarets CE
Primary School
CBROM B36 ....112 D1
St Marys RC Primary
School *BFLD/HDSWWD* B20 ....90 B4
KGSWFD DY6 ....99 H2
SLYOAK B29 ....159 F1

St Marys RC Primary School
BRLYHL DY5 ....119 G3
DARL/WED WS10 ....55 H4
HRBN B17 ....141 G2
WOLVN WV10 ....24 A3
St Marys the Mount RC School
WSL WS1 ....5 H7
St Matthews CE Primary School
SMTHWK B66 ....106 D4
VAUX/NECH B7 ....109 G5
St Michaels CE High School
BLKHTH/ROWR B65 ....104 B4
St Michaels CE Primary School
BLOX/PEL WS3 ....17 G5
DUNHL/THL/PER WV6 ....22 A5
HDSW B21 ....108 A2
RIDG/WDGT B32 ....157 G2
St Michaels RC Primary School
BDMR/CCFT WV3 ....50 D1
St Nicholas CE VC First School
CDSL WV8 ....10 B3
St Nicholas RC JMI School
SCFLD/BOLD B73 ....76 D1
St Patricks Catholic Primary
School
CHWD/FDBR/MGN B37 ....132 C2
WSLW WS2 ....4 C1
St Patricks RC Primary School
WNSFLD WV11 ....24 C5
WSNGN B18 ....107 H5
St Pauls CE (A) Primary School
COVEN WV9 ....12 A5
St Pauls CE Primary School
TPTN/OCK DY4 ....69 F5
St Pauls RC Primary School
HWK/WKHTH B38 ....177 F4
St Pauls School *BHTH/HG* B12 ..144 C2
St Pauls School for Girls
LDYWD/EDGR B16 ....125 G3
St Peter & Paul RC Primary
School *ERDE/BCHGN* B24 ....93 G3
St Peters CE Junior School
HRBN B17 ....142 A3
St Peters C JMI School
BLOX/PEL WS3 ....16 D5
St Peters Collegiate Secondary
School *BDMR/CCFT* WV3 ....36 A2
St Peters RC Primary School
RIDG/WDGT B32 ....157 G1
St Peters RC School *SOLH* B91 ..181 H3
St Philips Cathedral
CBHAMNW B3 ....3 F4
St Philips RC Primary School
SMTHWK B66 ....106 D3
St Philips RC Sixth Form
College *LDYWD/EDGR* B16 ....125 H4
St Saviours CE Primary School
WASH/WDE B8 ....110 B4
St Stephens CE Primary
School *WOLVN* WV10 ....37 G1
St Teresas RC Primary School
BFLD/HDSWWD B20 ....90 A4
ETTPK/GDPK/PENN WV4 ....52 C3
St Thomas Aquinas RC
School *BFLD/HDSWWD* B20 .....176 B2
St Thomas CE Primary School
EDG B15 ....126 D4
WNSFLD WV11 ....15 E3
St Thomas Community
Network *DUDS* DY2 ....85 E3
St Thomas More Catholic
School *WLNHL* WV13 ....39 H5
St Thomas More RC Primary
School
LGN/SDN/BHAMAIR B26 ....147 H2
St Thomas of Canterbury RC
JMI School *BLOX/PEL* WS3 ....28 B4
St Vincents RC Primary
School *VAUX/NECH* B7 ....127 H1
St Wilfrids RC Primary School
CBROM B36 ....112 B1
Salafi Independent School
SMHTH B10 ....128 B4
Salford Trading Estate
AST/WIT B6 ....110 A1
Salisbury Place Industrial
Estate *BDMR/CCFT* WV3 ....6 C6
Salisbury Primary School
DARL/WED WS10 ....55 G1
Saltbrook Trading Estate
HALE B63 ....120 A5
Saltley Business Park
WASH/WDE B8 ....110 B3
Saltley Health Centre
WASH/WDE B8 ....110 C4
Saltley Industrial Centre
WASH/WDE B8 ....128 A1
Saltley Leisure Centre
WASH/WDE B8 ....129 E1
Saltley School *WASH/WDE* B8 ...129 E1
Saltley Trading Estate
WASH/WDE B8 ....110 A4
Salvation Army *CBHAMNE* B4 ......3 F2
Sandown First School
DUNHL/THL/PER WV6 ....34 D1
Sandwell Borough FC
OLDBY B69 ....104 C2
Sandwell Business
Development Centre
OLDBY B69 ....105 G2
Sandwell Business Park
SMTHWK B66 ....105 G1
Sandwell Business &
Technology Centre
LGLYGN/QTN B68 ....122 D2
Sandwell College
LGLYGN/QTN B68 ....123 E1
SMTHWK B66 ....106 C4
WBROM B70 ....87 G3
Sandwell District General
Hospital
HHTH/SAND B71 ....87 H1
Sandwell Health Authority
Clinic *CDYHTH* B64 ....121 E3
Sandwell Park Golf Club
HHTH/SAND B71 ....88 B4
Sandwell Park Industrial
Estate *HHTH/SAND* B71 ....88 B5
Sandwell Valley
HHTH/SAND B71 ....72 C5

Sandyhill Industrial Estate
 HLGN/YWD B28 .... 180 A1
Sapcote Business Centre
 SMHTH B10 .... 145 G1
Sapcote Industrial Estate
 CDYHTH B64 .... 121 F1
Sapcote Trading Centre
 AST/WIT B6 .... 91 G3
 CDYHTH B64 .... 121 F1
 SMHTH B10 .... 145 G1
Sarehole Mill *MOS/BIL* B13 ...... 162 B2
Sarephed Medical Centre
 SMTHWKW B67 .... 106 C4
Sargent Turner Trading
 Estate *HAG/WOL* DY9 .... 136 D1
Satellite Industrial Park
 WNSFLD WV11 .... 38 C1
School of Jewellery (University
 of Central England)
 CBHAMW B1 .... 2 C2
Scott Arms Shopping Centre
 GTB/HAM B43 .... 73 C2
Sears Retail Park *SHLY* B90 .... 180 C4
Sedgley Golf Centre *SEDG* DY3 .. 66 D5
Selly Manor Museum
 BVILLE B30 .... 159 H3
Selly Oak Health Centre
 SLYOAK B29 .... 159 G1
Selly Oak Hospital
 SLYOAK B29 .... 159 H1
Selly Oak Industrial Estate
 SLYOAK B29 .... 159 G1
Selly Oak School *SLYOAK* B29 .. 159 G2
Selly Park Technology College
 for Girls *SLYOAK* B29 .... 160 B1
Seth Somes Track *RMSLY* B62 .. 139 E5
Severne Primary School
 ACGN B27 .... 163 G2
Shaftmoor Industrial Estate
 HLGN/YWD B28 .... 145 H5
Sharmans Cross Junior School
 SOLH B91 .... 181 E1
Shaw Hill Primary School
 WASH/WDE B8 .... 110 C5
Shaw Park Business Village
 WOLVN WV10 .... 23 F4
Sheldon CC *YDLY* B25 .... 129 H4
Sheldon Country Park
 LGN/SDN/BHAMAIR B26 ...... 148 C1
Sheldon Heath Community
 School
 LGN/SDN/BHAMAIR B26 ...... 131 E4
Shelfield Clinic
 RUSH/SHEL WS4 .... 29 E2
Shelfield Sports & Community
 College *RUSH/SHEL* WS4 .... 18 C5
Shell Corner Trading Estate
 RMSLY B62 .... 122 B4
Shelter Waterside
 Industrial Estate
 ETTPK/GDPK/PENN WV4 .... 53 C3
Shenley Court School
 SLYOAK B29 .... 158 B3
Shenley Lane Community
 Association Sports Centre
 SLYOAK B29 .... 158 C4
Shenstone Trading Estate
 HALE B63 .... 139 C3
Sherborne Wharf
 LDYWD/EDGR B16 .... 2 A6
Shireland Hall Primary School
 SMTHWK B66 .... 125 E1
Shireland Language College
 SMTHWK B66 .... 124 C1
Shire Oak School *BRWNH* WS8 .. 19 G2
Shirestone Primary School
 STETCH B33 .... 131 F2
Shirley Clinic *SHLY* B90 .... 180 B2
Shirley Heath Junior School
 SHLY B90 .... 180 C4
Shirley Park Sports Club &
 Golf Club *SHLY* B90 .... 195 G4
Shirley Road Health Clinic
 ACGN B27 .... 163 F1
Short Heath Clinic
 SHHTH WV12 .... 26 B4
Short Heath Primary School
 ERDW/GRVHL B23 .... 76 B5
Shorth Heath Junior School
 SHHTH WV12 .... 26 B5
Showcase Cinema *DUDN* DY1 .. 85 E3
 WSLW WS2 .... 40 D4
Showcase Cinema
 ERDE/BCHGN B24 .... 93 H4
Showell Road Industrial
 Estate *WOLVN* WV10 .... 23 F4
The Shrubbery School
 WALM/CURD B76 .... 78 B4
Silhill FC *SOLH* B91 .... 181 E1
Silver End Business Park
 BRLYHL DY5 .... 118 D4
Silver End Industrial Estate
 BRLYHL DY5 .... 118 D3
Sladefield Infant School
 WASH/WDE B8 .... 111 E4
Slade Primary School
 ERDW/GRVHL B23 .... 92 B4
Sledmere Primary School
 DUDS DY2 .... 102 D3
Small Heath Business Park
 SMHTH B10 .... 128 D5
Small Heath Lower School
 SMHTH B10 .... 128 B5
Small Heath Trading Estate
 SPARK B11 .... 145 F1
Smestow Bridge Industrial
 Estate *WMBN* WV5 .... 64 A5
Smestow Secondary School
 BDMR/CCFT WV3 .... 35 F4
Smethwick Medical Centre
 SMTHWKW B67 .... 106 C3
Smethwick Swimming Centre
 SMTHWKW B67 .... 124 B2
Smith's Wood School
 CBROM B36 .... 114 A3
Sneyd Community School
 BLOX/PEL WS3 .... 16 A5
Snow Hill Clinic *BKHL/PFLD* WV2 .. 7 G5
Soho Health Centre
 HDSW B21 .... 107 H2

Soho House *WSNGN* B18 .... 108 A2
Solihull College *SOLH* B91 .... 181 G2
Solihull Hospital *SOLH* B91 .... 182 B1
Solihull Ice Rink *HIA/OLT* B92 .. 147 H4
Solihull Retail Park *SHLY* B90 .. 180 C4
Solihull School *SOLH* B91 ...... 182 B1
Solihull Sixth Form College
 SOLH B91 .... 182 B3
Somerville Primary School
 SMHTH B10 .... 128 B4
South Birmingham College
 BHTH/HG B12 .... 3 K7
 HLGN/YWD B28 .... 162 C2
Southside Business Centre
 BHTH/HG B12 .... 144 C2
South Staffordshire Golf Club
 DUNHL/THL/PER WV6 .... 21 G4
Sovereign Trading Estate
 STRBR DY8 .... 135 E2
Sparkbrook Health Centre
 SPARK B11 .... 127 H5
Sparkhill Pool & Fitness
 Centre *SPARK* B11 .... 145 E3
Spartan Industrial Centre
 WBROM B70 .... 70 C5
Speedwell Trading Estate
 SPARK B11 .... 146 A1
Spines Clinic *WMBN* WV5 .... 64 D5
Spinners End Industrial
 Estate *CDYHTH* B64 .... 120 D3
Spon Lane Industrial Estate
 SMTHWK B66 .... 105 H1
Spon Lane Trading Estate
 WBROM B70 .... 87 G4
Springdale J & I School
 ETTPK/GDPK/PENN WV4 .... 50 C3
Springfield Industrial Estate
 OLDBY B69 .... 105 F2
Springfield Infant School
 MOS/BIL B13 .... 145 F5
Springfield Junior School
 BLKHTH/ROWR B65 .... 103 C5
Springfield Primary School
 BLKHTH/ROWR B65 .... 103 C5
Spring Hill Industrial Estate
 WSNGN B18 .... 108 A5
Spring Lane Industrial Estate
 SHHTH WV12 .... 40 A1
Spring Road Industrial Estate
 ETTPK/GDPK/PENN WV4 .... 53 E4
Springvale Business Park
 BILS/COS WV14 .... 53 F4
Springvale Industrial Park
 BILS/COS WV14 .... 53 F4
Spring Vale Primary School
 ETTPK/GDPK/PENN WV4 .... 52 C4
Stafford Road Sports Club
 BLOX/PEL WS5 .... 16 D5
Stag Industrial Estate
 BILS/COS WV14 .... 54 C4
Stambermill Industrial Estate
 HAG/WOL DY9 .... 136 A1
Stanhope Road Clinic
 SMTHWKW B67 .... 124 B1
Stanville Primary School
 LGN/SDN/BHAMAIR B26 ...... 147 H1
Starbank Primary School
 SMHTH B10 .... 129 F4
Start Point Trading Estate
 SPARK B11 .... 145 F3
Station Road Industrial
 Estate *BLKHTH/ROWR* B65 .... 122 B2
 CSHL/WTROR B46 .... 115 F1
Stechford Cascades
 STETCH B33 .... 130 A1
Stechford Health Centre
 STETCH B33 .... 130 A2
Stechford Primary School
 STETCH B33 .... 129 H2
Stechford Retail Park
 STETCH B33 .... 112 A5
Stechford Trading Estate
 STETCH B33 .... 112 A5
Steetley Industrial Estate
 BILS/COS WV14 .... 68 C4
Stephens Industrial Estate
 SPARK B11 .... 145 H5
Stevens Dental Health Centre
 STRBR DY8 .... 135 F3
Stirchley Primary School
 BVILLE B30 .... 160 A4
Stirchley Trading Estate
 BVILLE B30 .... 160 B3
Stock Exchange *CBHAMNW* B3 .... 2 E4
Stockland Clinic
 ERDW/GRVHL B23 .... 92 B2
Stockland Green Health Centre
 ERDW/GRVHL B23 .... 92 B2
Stockland Green School
 ERDW/GRVHL B23 .... 92 A2
Stone Cross Clinic
 HHTH/SAND B71 .... 72 A2
Stourbridge CC *STRBR* DY8 .... 118 B5
Stourbridge Cemetery
 STRBR DY8 .... 134 D3
Stourbridge Clinic *STRBR* DY8 .. 135 H3
Stourbridge Crematorium
 STRBR DY8 .... 134 D3
Stourbridge FC *STRBR* DY8 .... 135 F1
Stourbridge Golf Club
 STRBR DY8 .... 152 C1
Stourbridge Industrial Estate
 STRBR DY8 .... 135 G1
Stourbridge RFC *KINVER* DY7 .. 134 B1
Stourvale Industrial Estate
 HAG/WOL DY9 .... 136 D1
Stourvale Trading Estate
 HALE B63 .... 137 H1
Stowheath Industrial Estate &
 New Enterprise Centre
 BKHL/PFLD WV2 .... 38 A5
Stow Heath J & I School
 WLNHL WV13 .... 38 D4
Stowlawn Primary School
 WOLV WV1 .... 38 B3
Straits Primary School
 SEDG DY3 .... 82 D1

Stratford Road School Clinic
 SPARK B11 .... 145 F5
Strawberry Lane Industrial
 Estate *WLNHL* WV13 .... 38 C2
The Streetley School
 FOAKS/STRLY B74 .... 60 B2
Streetly Cemetery
 ALDR WS9 .... 44 D3
Streetly Clinic
 FOAKS/STRLY B74 .... 45 E5
Streetly Crematorium
 ALDR WS9 .... 44 D3
Streetly Hockey & CC
 FOAKS/STRLY B74 .... 45 G4
Streetly Methodist Recreation
 Centre *FOAKS/STRLY* B74 .... 45 F5
Streetsbrook Infant School
 SHLY B90 .... 180 C1
Stuart Bathurst RC High School
 DARL/WED WS10 .... 56 B3
Stuart Crystal *STRBR* DY8 ...... 118 A3
Summerfield Hospital
 WSNGN B18 .... 107 H5
Summerfield Primary School
 WSNGN B18 .... 107 G5
Summer Hill Industrial Park
 CBHAMW B1 .... 2 A3
The Summerhill Secondary
 School *KGSWFD* DY6 .... 99 F4
Sundridge Primary School
 KGSTG B44 .... 60 A4
Sunfield School
 HAG/WOL DY9 .... 170 C1
Sunrise Business Park
 STRBR DY8 .... 118 A5
Sunshine Infant School
 BLOX/PEL WS3 .... 27 G2
Sutton Arts Theatre
 CSCFLD/WYGN B72 .... 62 C4
Sutton Coldfield College
 ERDE/BCHGN B24 .... 93 E2
 ERDW/GRVHL B23 .... 92 A2
 FOAKS/STRLY B74 .... 62 C2
 KGSTG B44 .... 75 E4
 MGN/WHC B75 .... 47 H2
 WALM/WDE B8 .... 110 D2
Sutton Coldfield Crematorium
 MGN/WHC B75 .... 48 C3
Sutton Coldfield Girls School
 SCFLD/BOLD B73 .... 62 B5
Sutton Coldfield Golf Club
 FOAKS/STRLY B74 .... 45 H4
Sutton Coldfield Hospital
 SCFLD/BOLD B73 .... 62 B4
Sutton Coldfield Town FC
 CSCFLD/WYGN B72 .... 62 C5
Sutton Coldfield Town Hall
 SCFLD/BOLD B73 .... 62 C4
Sutton Coldfield Cemetery
 MGN/WHC B75 .... 62 D2
The Sutton Special School
 DUDN DY1 .... 101 H1
Sutton Town Sports Club
 CSCFLD/WYGN B72 .... 62 C4
Sutton United FC
 MGN/WHC B75 .... 63 E3
The Swallows Industrial Estate
 SHLY B90 .... 194 D1
Swallows Rise Business Park
 BRLYHL DY5 .... 119 C1
Swan Lane Industrial Estate
 WBROM B70 .... 87 E1
Swan Medical Centre
 YDLY B25 .... 129 H5
Swanpool Medical Centre
 TPTN/OCK DY4 .... 69 G3
Swanshurst Girls School
 MOS/BIL B13 .... 161 G3
Sycamore Green Primary
 School *DUDN* DY1 .... 83 H1
Sycamore House Medical
 Centre *WSL* WS1 .... 5 J7
Sycamore Industrial &
 Trading Estate
 HDSW B21 .... 107 F2
Symphony Hall *CBHAMW* B1 ...... 2 C5
Talbots Lane Trading Estate
 BRLYHL DY5 .... 119 G3
Tamar Medical Centre
 DUNHL/THL/PER WV6 .... 34 C1
Tamebridge Industrial Estate
 PBAR/PBCH B42 .... 91 E2
Tame Road Industrial Estate
 AST/WIT B6 .... 91 H5
Tame Valley Primary School
 CBROM B36 .... 111 H1
Tandon Medical Centre
 SEDG DY3 .... 83 G1
Tansey Green Trading Estate
 BRLYHL DY5 .... 100 D1
Telsen Industrial Centre
 AST/WIT B6 .... 109 F3
Temple Meadow Primary
 School *CDYHTH* B64 .... 121 F3
Tenterfields Primary School
 HALE B63 .... 139 E3
Tettenhall College
 DUNHL/THL/PER WV6 .... 35 H1
Tettenhall Wood Special School
 DUNHL/THL/PER WV6 .... 35 F2
Thameside Primary School
 DARL/WED WS10 .... 71 C1
Thinktank at Millennium Point
 CBHAMNE B4 .... 3 K4
Thistle Hotel *CBHAMNE* B4 .... 3 F5
 ERDE/BCHGN B24 .... 125 G3
Thornleigh Trading Estate
 DUDS DY2 .... 102 A2
Thorns Community College
 BRLYHL DY5 .... 119 F4
Thorns Primary School
 BRLYHL DY5 .... 119 G5
Thornton Junior School
 WASH/WDE B8 .... 111 H4
Three Crowns Special School
 DYSBK/YTR WS5 .... 43 H4
Tidbury Green Primary School
 SHLY B90 .... 193 G4
Tile Cross Trading Estate
 STETCH B33 .... 131 F3

Timberley Primary School
 BKDE/SHDE B34 .... 113 F3
Timbertree Primary School
 CDYHTH B64 .... 121 E5
Tindal Primary School
 BHTH/HG B12 .... 144 B2
Tipper Trading Estate
 HALE B63 .... 137 E2
Tipton Green Junior School
 TPTN/OCK DY4 .... 85 F2
Tipton Sports Academy
 TPTN/OCK DY4 .... 69 H2
Tiverton J & I School
 SLYOAK B29 .... 142 D5
Tiverton Road Pool & Fitness
 Centre *SLYOAK* B29 .... 159 H1
Tividale Business Park
 TPTN/OCK DY4 .... 85 H3
Tividale Comprehensive School
 OLDBY B69 .... 86 A5
Tividale FC *OLDBY* B69 .... 85 H5
Tividale Hall Primary School
 OLDBY B69 .... 85 G5
Tividale Medical Centre
 OLDBY B69 .... 104 B1
Tividale Primary School
 OLDBY B69 .... 85 H4
Tollgate Shopping Precinct
 SMTHWKW B67 .... 106 B3
Topcliffe Primary School
 CVALE B35 .... 94 C3
Touchwood Shopping Centre
 SOLH B91 .... 182 A1
Tower Hill Health Centre
 PBAR/PBCH B42 .... 74 A5
Tower Works Industrial Estate
 BDMR/CCFT WV3 .... 6 A6
Town Gate Retail Park
 DUDN DY1 .... 85 F4
Town Junior School
 CSCFLD/WYGN B72 .... 62 C4
Town Wharf Business Park
 WSLW WS2 .... 4 B3
T P Riley Community School
 BLOX/PEL WS3 .... 17 E5
Tractor Spares Industrial
 Estate *WLNHL* WV13 .... 38 D3
Trading Estate Parkview
 HWK/WKHTH B38 .... 176 D2
Travelodge *BRLYHL* DY5 .... 101 G5
 EDG B15 .... 2 C7
 LGN/SDN/BHAMAIR B26 ...... 147 E1
 OLDBY B69 .... 104 B2
 RIDG/WDGT B32 .... 156 D3
 SCFLD/BOLD B73 .... 76 D1
Trescott Primary School
 NFLD/LBR B31 .... 174 D2
Trevor Street Industrial Estate
 VAUX/NECH B7 .... 110 A3
Trident Retail Park
 BORD B9 .... 127 G2
Trident Shopping Centre
 DUDN DY1 .... 84 C5
Trinity Business Park
 HIA/OLT D92 .... 149 H4
Trinity CE Primary School
 WOLVN WV10 .... 37 H1
Tromans Industrial Estate
 DUDS DY2 .... 120 D1
Truck Stop Business Park
 SPARK B11 .... 146 B1
Tudor Grange School
 SOLH B91 .... 181 G3
Tudor Grange Sports Centre &
 Pool *SOLH* B91 .... 181 H2
Tudor Industrial Estate
 SPARK B11 .... 146 B2
Turves Green Boys School
 NFLD/LBR B31 .... 175 G5
Turves Green Girls School
 NFLD/LBR B31 .... 175 G4
Turves Green Primary School
 NFLD/LBR B31 .... 175 G4
Twickenham Primary School
 KGSTG B44 .... 76 A2
Two Woods Industrial Estate
 BRLYHL DY5 .... 119 G3
Two Woods Trading Estate
 BRLYHL DY5 .... 119 H3
Tyburn Industrial Estate
 ERDE/BCHGN B24 .... 93 H4
Tyseley Industrial Estate
 SPARK B11 .... 145 G2
Tyseley Locomotive Works
 Visitor Centre *SPARK* B11 .... 145 H2
UCI Cinema *BRLYHL* DY5 .... 119 C2
 SHLY B90 .... 195 E1
Uffculme Clinic *MOS/BIL* B13 .. 143 H5
Uffculme Special School
 MOS/BIL B13 .... 161 E1
Ulverley Primary School
 HIA/OLT D92 .... 164 D2
Union Business Park
 WSLW WS2 .... 4 C4
Unisant Trading Estate
 CDYHTH B64 .... 121 F2
University of Birmingham
 CBHAMNE B4 .... 3 J2
 EDC B15 .... 142 D4
University of Central England
 CBHAMNE B4 .... 3 J2
 CBHAMNW B3 .... 2 E5
 EDG B15 .... 126 A4
 PBAR/PBCH B42 .... 90 D3
University of Central England
 (Institute of Art & Design)
 CBHAMNE B4 .... 3 J1
University of Central England
 (Technology Innovation Centre)
 CBHAMNE B4 .... 3 K3
University of Wolverhampton
 BDMR/CCFT WV3 .... 35 H5
 WOLVN WV10 .... 23 E4
 WOLVN WV10 .... 38 B1
 WSL WS1 .... 57 G1
 WSLW WS2 .... 41 G4
University of Wolverhampton
 (North Site) *WOLV* WV1 .... 7 F2
University of Wolverhampton
 (South Site) *WOLV* WV1 .... 7 F3

Uplands Cemetery
 SMTHWKW B67 .... 124↓
Uplands Junior School
 BDMR/CCFT WV3 .... 35↓
Uplands Manor Primary School
 SMTHWKW B67 .... 124↓
Upper School & Sixth Form
 SMHTH B10 .... 128↓
Usam Trading Estate
 WOLVN WV10 .... 12↓
Valley Infant School
 HIA/OLT B92 .... 149↓
Valley Park Campus
 DUNHL/THL/PER WV6 .... 22↓
Vaughan Trading Estate
 TPTN/OCK DY4 ....
Vauxhall Trading Estate
 VAUX/NECH B7 .... 109↓
Vector Industrial Park
 HHTH/SAND B71 .... 71↓
Venkat Medical Centre
 OLDBY B69 .... 13↓
Vernon Trading Estate
 RMSLY B62 ....
Victoria Health Centre
 SMTHWK B66 .... 106↓
Victoria Infant School
 TPTN/OCK DY4 .... 85↓
Victoria Park Primary School
 SMTHWK B66 .... 106↓
Victoria Trading Estate
 NFLD/LBR B31 .... 158↓
Villiers Primary School
 BILS/COS WV14 ....
Villiers Trading Estate
 BKHL/PFLD WV2 .... 52↓
Visit Centre *WSNGN* B18 .... 107↓
Vival Health & Leisure Club
 SOLH B91 ....
Vulcan House Industrial
 Estate *SOLH* B91 .... 165↓
Vulcan Industrial Estate
 WSLW WS2 .... 27↓
Wake Green FC *SHLY* B90 ...... 179↓
Wallbrook Primary School
 BILS/COS WV14 .... 69↓
The Wallows Industrial Estate
 BRLYHL DY5 .... 101↓
Walmley CC *WALM/CURD* B76 .. 78↓
Walmley Golf Club
 CSCFLD/WYGN B72 .... 77↓
Walmley Infant School
 WALM/CURD B76 .... 77↓
Walsall Business Park
 ALDR WS9 .... 30↓
 ALDR WS9 .... 43↓
Walsall CC *WSL* WS1 ....
Walsall College WSLW WS2 .... 4↓
Walsall College of Arts &
 Technology *WSLW* WS2 ....
Walsall FC (Bescot Stadium)
 WSL WS1 .... 56↓
Walsall Gala Baths *WSL* WS1 .. 4↓
Walsall Golf Club *WSL* WS1 ..... 57↓
Walsall Leather Museum
 WSLW WS2 ....
Walsall Museum & Library
 WSL WS1 ....
Walsall RFC *WSL* WS1 .... 57↓
Walsall Wood Cemetery
 ALDR WS9 .... 19↓
Walsall Wood Primary School
 ALDR WS9 .... 19↓
Ward End Medical Centre
 WASH/WDE B8 .... 111↓
Ward End Primary School
 WASH/WDE B8 .... 111↓
Warley High School
 LGLYGN/QTN B68 .... 121↓
Warley Infant School
 LGLYGN/QTN B68 .... 104↓
Warley Woods Golf Club
 SMTHWKW B67 ....
Warner Village Star City
 VAUX/NECH B7 .... 110↓
Warren Farm Primary School
 KGSTG B44 ....
Warstones Primary School
 ETTPK/GDPK/PENN WV4 .... 51↓
Wartell Bank Industrial Estate
 KGSWFD DY6 ....
Warwick Road Trading Estate
 SPARK B11 .... 145↓
Warwickshire CCC (Edgbaston)
 EDG B15 .... 2↓
Waseley Hills Country Park
 BRGRVW B61 .... 17↓
Waseley Hills High School
 RBRY B45 .... 18↓
Washington Street Industrial
 Estate *DUDS* DY2 ....
Washwood Heath Technology
 College *WASH/WDE* B8 .... 111↓
Waterfall Lane Trading Estate
 CDYHTH B64 ....
Waterfront Business Park
 BRLYHL DY5 .... 119↓
Waterloo Industrial Estate
 CHWD/FDBR/MGN B37 .... 115↓
Watermill Primary School
 WNSFLD WV11 .... 25↓
Water Orton CC
 CSHL/WTROR B46 .... 97↓
Water Orton Industrial Estate
 CSHL/WTROR B46 ....
Waterside Industrial Estate
 BKHL/PFLD WV2 .... 5↓
 BLKHTH/ROWR B65 .... 104↓
Watery Lane Industrial Estate
 WLNHL WV13 .... 3↓
Watling Street Business Park
 CNCK/NC WS11 ....
Watling Street JMI School
 BRWNH WS8 ....
Wattville Primary School
 SMTHWK B66 ....
Wattville Road Industrial
 Estate *SMTHWK* B66 .... 10↓
Waverley Campus
 SMHTH B10 .... 12↓

Webnor Industrial Estate
BKHL/PFLD WV2 .... 53 E2
Wednesbury CC
DARL/WED WS10 .... 56 A4
Wednesbury Chiropody Surgery
DARL/WED WS10 .... 55 H5
Wednesbury Leisure Centre
DARL/WED WS10 .... 55 G5
Wednesbury Medical Centre
DARL/WED WS10 .... 70 C1
Wednesbury Oak Primary
School *TPTN/OCK* DY4 .... 69 F2
Wednesbury Rugby Club
DARL/WED WS10 .... 70 D2
Wednesbury Trading Estate
DARL/WED WS10 .... 55 G4
Wednesfield FC
WNSFLD WV11 .... 24 C4
Wednesfield High School
WNSFLD WV11 .... 25 E5
Wednesfield Village Primary
School *WNSFLD* WV11 .... 24 D5
Wednesfield Way Industrial
Estate *WNSFLD* WV11 .... 38 D1
Welford Primary School
BFLD/HDSWWD B20 .... 108 B1
Wellington Industrial Estate
BILS/COS WV14 .... 68 C4
Welsh House Farm Primary
School *RIDG/WDGT* B32 ...... 141 F3
Welsh RFC *HIA/OLT* B92 .... 149 C5
Weoley Castle Health Centre
SLYOAK B29 .... 158 C1
Weoley Golf Club
DUNHL/THL/PER WV6 .... 21 E3
Wergs Golf Club
BDMR/CCFT WV3 .... 35 H4
Westacre Infant School
BORD B9 .... 128 A2
West Bromwich Albion FC
(The Hawthorns)
HHTH/SAND B71 .... 88 C5
West Bromwich Dartmouth CC
HHTH/SAND B71 .... 88 B5
Westcroft Special School &
Sports College
WOLVN WV10 .... 13 H5
West Cross Shopping Centre
SMTHWK B66 .... 105 H2
Western Business Park
RMSLY B62 .... 121 H5
WSNGN B18 .... 107 G3
Westfield Primary School
WMBN WV5 .... 65 E4
Westgate Trading Estate
ALDR WS9 .... 29 G4
West Heath Hospital
HWK/WKHTH B38 .... 176 A5
West House School
EDG B15 .... 126 C4
The Westmead Hotel
ALVE B48 .... 189 H4
West Midlands Hospital
HALE B63 .... 137 H2
Westminster Industrial Estate
DUDS DY2 .... 120 D2
Westminster Primary School
BFLD/HDSWWD B20 .... 90 C5

Westminster School
TPTN/OCK DY4 .... 69 G5
West Park Hospital *WOLV* WV1 .... 6 C3
West Park Primary School
WOLV WV1 .... 6 C1
Westwood Business Park
AST/WIT B6 .... 91 H4
Wharton Street Industrial
Estate *VAUX/NECH* B7 .... 110 B1
Wheelers Lane Technology
College *MOS/BIL* B13 .... 161 F3
Wheeler Street Shopping
Centre *LOZ/NWT* B19 .... 108 C3
Whetstone Field Primary
School *ALDR* WS9 .... 44 B1
Whitecrest Primary School
GTB/HAM B43 .... 74 A1
Whitehall Industrial Park
TPTN/OCK DY4 .... 86 C1
Whitehall Infant School
WSL WS1 .... 57 F1
Whitehall Junior School
WSL WS1 .... 57 F1
Whitehall Clinic
OLDBY B69 .... 104 B4
Whitehouse Common
Primary School
MGN/WHC B75 .... 62 D1
Whitesmore School
CHWD/FDBR/MGN B37 .... 131 H3
Whitgreave J & I School
WOLVN WV10 .... 23 G2
Whitmore Medical Centre
WOLV WV1 .... 6 E1
Whitmore Reans Health Centre
DUNHL/THL/PER WV6 .... 36 C1
Whitworth Industrial Park
BORD B9 .... 128 A2
Wholesale Markets
DIG/EDG B5 .... 3 H7
Widney Junior School
SOLH B91 .... 181 F4
Widney Manor Cemetery
DOR/KN B93 .... 196 C2
Widney Manor Golf Club
SHLY B90 .... 196 A1
Wightwick Hall Special School
DUNHL/THL/PER WV6 .... 34 C3
Wightwick Manor (NT)
DUNHL/THL/PER WV6 .... 34 D4
Wilkes Green J & I School
HDSW B21 .... 89 G5
Wilkinson Primary School
BILS/COS WV14 .... 54 B5
Willenhall Industrial Estate
WLNHL WV13 .... 40 A2
Willenhall Lane Industrial
Estate *BLOX/PEL* WS3 .... 27 E2
Willenhall Lawn Cemetery
SHHTH WV12 .... 26 C5
Willenhall Leisure Centre
WLNHL WV13 .... 39 H4
Willenhall School Sports
College *SHHTH* WV12 .... 26 C5
Willenhall Town FC
WLNHL WV13 .... 39 F2
Willenhall Trading Estate
WLNHL WV13 .... 39 F4

William Cowper Primary
School
LOZ/NWT B19 .... 109 E3
William Hanke Industrial
Estate
BRLYHL DY5 .... 119 G3
Willingsworth High School
TPTN/OCK DY4 .... 69 H1
Wilson Stuart Special School
ERDW/GRVHL B23 .... 76 A5
Windmill Hill (Look out)
RBRY B45 .... 173 E5
Windmill Works Industrial Park
DUDS DY2 .... 102 B2
Windsor High School
HALE B63 .... 138 B3
Windsor Industrial Estate
VAUX/NECH B7 .... 109 G4
Windward Way Industrial
Estate
CBROM B36 .... 113 H1
Windy Arbor Primary School
CHWD/FDBR/MGN B37 .... 132 D1
Winster Grove Industrial
Centre *KGSTG* B44 .... 74 D1
Winster Grove Industrial
Estate *KGSTG* B44 .... 75 E1
Wishaw Golf Course
WALM/CURD B76 .... 79 F1
Withymoor Primary School
BRLYHL DY5 .... 119 F3
Withy Road Industrial Estate
BILS/COS WV14 .... 53 G5
Witton Industrial Estate
AST/WIT B6 .... 91 G4
Witton Park Industrial Estate
AST/WIT B6 .... 91 G5
Woden Primary School
WOLVN WV10 .... 37 G1
Wodensborough Community
Technology College
DARL/WED WS10 .... 71 F1
Wodensfield Primary School
WNSFLD WV11 .... 24 B4
Wollescote Business Park
HAG/WOL DY9 .... 136 D2
Wollescote Primary School
HAG/WOL DY9 .... 136 D3
Wolverhampton Business Park
WOLVN WV10 .... 12 D2
Wolverhampton CC
DUNHL/THL/PER WV6 .... 21 G4
Wolverhampton Central Baths
WOLV WV1 .... 6 D3
Wolverhampton College
WOLV WV1 .... 53 F1
Wolverhampton Girls High
School
DUNHL/THL/PER WV6 .... 36 B2
Wolverhampton Grammar
School *BDMR/CCFT* WV3 ...... 36 B3
Wolverhampton Healthcare
WOLVN WV10 .... 38 B1
The Wolverhampton Nuffield
Hospital
DUNHL/THL/PER WV6 .... 35 G2
Wolverhampton Racecourse
DUNHL/THL/PER WV6 .... 22 C4

Wolverhampton Wanderers FC
(Molineux Stadium)
WOLV WV1 .... 6 E1
Wombourne Cricket Tennis &
Bowling Club *WMBN* WV5 .... 65 E4
Wombrook Business Centre
WMBN WV5 .... 64 C4
Wombrook Industrial Estate
WMBN WV5 .... 64 C5
Woodbourne Priory Hospital
HRBN B17 .... 125 E3
Woodcock Hill Primary
School
NFLD/LBR B31 .... 158 A3
Woodcock Sports Centre
CBHAMNE B4 .... 3 J2
Woodcross Clinic
BILS/COS WV14 .... 68 A1
Wood End Primary School
WNSFLD WV11 .... 24 C3
Woodfield J & I School
ETTPK/GDPK/PENN WV4 ..... 51 F2
Woodgate Business Park
RIDG/WDGT B32 .... 140 B5
Woodgate Primary School
RIDG/WDGT B32 .... 157 F1
Woodgate Valley
RIDG/WDGT B32 .... 140 C3
Woodgate Valley Health
Centre *RIDG/WDGT* B32 ..... 140 C5
Wood Green High School
College of Sport
DARL/WED WS10 .... 56 B3
Wood Green Junior School
DARL/WED WS10 .... 55 H4
Woodhouse J & I School
RIDG/WDGT B32 .... 141 E1
Woodlands Cemetery
CBROM B36 .... 114 C4
Woodlands Hotel *HRBN* B17 ... 124 D3
Woodlands Infant School
SHLY B90 .... 180 B5
Woodlands Primary School
SHHTH WV12 .... 26 B4
The Woodrush High School
HLYWD B47 .... 192 C2
Woodrush Rugby Club
HWK/WKHTH B38 .... 191 F4
The Woodsbank Industrial
Estate *DARL/WED* WS10 ...... 55 F4
The Woodsbank Trading
Estate *DARL/WED* WS10 ...... 55 F4
The Woodsetton Special
School *SEDG* DY3 .... 67 H4
Woodside Industrial Estate
DUDS DY2 .... 101 H4
Woodstock Girls School
MOS/BIL B13 .... 144 C3
Woodthorne Primary School
DUNHL/THL/PER WV6 .... 35 E1
Woodthorpe Primary School
ALE/KHTH/YWD B14 .... 161 E5
Woodview Primary School
EDG B15 .... 126 C4
Wordsley Green Health
Centre *STRBR* DY8 .... 117 H2
Wordsley Green Shopping
Centre *STRBR* DY8 .... 117 H2

Wordsley Hospital
STRBR DY8 .... 118 A1
Works Trading Estate
SMTHWK B66 .... 106 C2
Worlds End J & I School
RIDG/WDGT B32 .... 140 D2
The Worsley School
KGSWFD DY6 .... 118 B1
Wren's Nest National Nature
Reserve *DUDN* DY1 .... 84 B2
Wrens Nest Primary School
DUDN DY1 .... 84 A2
Wrottesley Hall
CDSL WV8 .... 20 A2
Wulfrun Shopping Centre
WOLV WV1 .... 7 F5
Wulfrun Trading Estate
WOLV WV1 .... 23 E5
Wychall Farm Primary School
NFLD/LBR B31 .... 176 A3
Wylde Green Primary School
SCFLD/BOLD B73 .... 77 F4
Wyndcliffe Primary School
BORD B9 .... 128 B3
Wyndley Leisure Centre
FOAKS/STRLY B74 .... 62 A3
Wyndley Swimming Baths
SCFLD/BOLD B73 .... 62 A4
Wynford Industrial Trading
Estate *ACGN* B27 .... 146 C2
Wynford Road Industrial
Estate *ACGN* B27 .... 146 C2
Wythall Cemetery
HLYWD B47 .... 192 A5
Wythall Health Centre
HLYWD B47 .... 192 C1
Yardley Cemetery
YDLY B25 .... 146 D2
Yardley Green Health Centre
SMHTH B10 .... 128 D3
Yardley Green Medical Centre
SMHTH B10 .... 128 A4
Yardley Medical Centre
YDLY B25 .... 129 F5
Yardleys School
SPARK B11 .... 145 G4
Yardleys Secondary School
SPARK B11 .... 145 H3
Yardley Wood Health Centre
MOS/BIL B13 .... 162 A5
Yardley Wood Primary School
ALE/KHTH/YWD B14 .... 179 F1
Yarnfield Primary School
SPARK B11 .... 146 A4
Yenton Junior School
ERDE/BCHGN B24 .... 77 F5
Yew Tree Community
Junior School
AST/WIT B6 .... 91 G5
Yew Tree Primary School
DSYBK/YTR WS5 .... 57 H4
SOLH B91 .... 165 G5
York Mead Primary School
HLGN/YWD B28 .... 145 G5
Yorks Wood Primary School
CHWD/FDBR/MGN B37 .... 113 H4
Zip Theatre
WOLV WV1 .... 6 D1

Acknowledgements

Schools address data provided by Education Direct

Petrol station information supplied by Johnsons

Garden centre information provided by:

Garden Centre Association   Britains best garden centres

Wyevale Garden Centres

The statement on the front cover of this atlas is sourced, selected and quoted
from a reader comment and feedback form received in 2004

Street by Street QUESTIONNAIRE

Dear Atlas User

Your comments, opinions and recommendations are very important to us. So please help us to improve our street atlases by taking a few minutes to complete this simple questionnaire.

You do not need a stamp (unless posted outside the UK). If you do not want to remove this page from your street atlas, then photocopy it or write your answers on a plain sheet of paper.

Send to: Marketing Assistant, AA Publishing, 14th Floor Fanum House, Freepost SCE 4598, Basingstoke RG21 4GY

ABOUT THE ATLAS...

Please state which city / town / county you bought:

Where did you buy the atlas? (City, Town, County)

For what purpose? (please tick all applicable)

To use in your local area ☐   **To use on business or at work** ☐

Visiting a strange place ☐   **In the car** ☐   **On foot** ☐

Other (please state)

Have you ever used any street atlases other than AA Street by Street?

Yes ☐   No ☐

If so, which ones?

Is there any aspect of our street atlases that could be improved?
(Please continue on a separate sheet if necessary)

continued overleaf

Please list the features you found most useful:

_____
_____

Please list the features you found least useful:

_____
_____
_____

LOCAL KNOWLEDGE...

Local knowledge is invaluable. Whilst every attempt has been made to make the information contained in this atlas as accurate as possible, should you notice any inaccuracies, please detail them below (if necessary, use a blank piece of paper) or e-mail us at *streetbystreet@theAA.com*

_____
_____
_____

ABOUT YOU...

Name (Mr/Mrs/Ms) _____

Address _____

                                  Postcode _____

Daytime tel no _____

E-mail address _____

Which age group are you in?

Under 25 ☐   **25-34** ☐   **35-44** ☐   **45-54** ☐   **55-64** ☐   **65+** ☐

Are you an AA member?   **YES** ☐   **NO** ☐

Do you have Internet access?   **YES** ☐   **NO** ☐

Thank you for taking the time to complete this questionnaire. Please send it to us as soon as possible, and remember, you do not need a stamp (unless posted outside the UK).

We may use information we hold about you to, telephone or email you about other products and services offered by the AA, we do NOT disclose this information to third parties.

Please tick here if you do not wish to hear about products and services from the AA. ☐

ML33y